Looking at Children

An Introduction to Child Development

Looking at Children

An Introduction to Child Development

David F. Bjorklund
Florida Atlantic University

Barbara R. Bjorklund
Florida Atlantic University

Brooks/Cole Publishing Company
Pacific Grove, California

Brooks/Cole Publishing Company
A Division of Wadsworth, Inc.
© 1992 by Wadsworth, Inc., Belmont, California 94002.

Printed in the United States of America
10   9   8   7   6   5   4   3   2   1

Library of Congress Cataloging-in-Publication Data

Bjorklund, David F.
    Looking at children : an introduction to child development /
  David F. Bjorklund, Barbara R. Bjorklund.
       p.   cm.
    Includes bibliographical references and index.
    ISBN 0-534-13704-0
    1. Child development.   I. Bjorklund, Barbara R.   II. Title.
  HQ767.9.B55   1992
305.23'1—dc20   91-38905
                                              CIP

Sponsoring Editor: *Vicki Knight*
Marketing Representative: *Bob Podstepny*
Editorial Assistant: *Heather L. Graeve*
Production Editor: *Penelope Sky*
Production Assistants: *Fiorella Ljunggren and Kay Mikel*
Manuscript Editor: *Margaret C. Tropp*
Permissions Editor: *Mary Kay Hancharick*
Interior and Cover Design: *Katherine Minerva*
Cover Photo: *Barbara Bjorklund / Child Development
Association, Inc.*
Art Coordinator: *Lisa Torri*
Interior Illustration: *Precision Graphics*
Photo Editor: *Ruth Minerva*
Photo Researcher: *Gail Meese*
Typesetting: *Weimer Typesetting Company, Inc.*
Printing and Binding: *R. R. Donnelley & Sons Company*

Credits continue on page 545.

To our parents

Beverly and Hank Bjorklund
Mary and Paul Ridgdill

Who gave us our nature
and are still giving us our nurture

About the Authors

David Bjorklund is a professor of psychology at Florida Atlantic University, where he has taught courses in child development for the past 16 years. He has published widely in the field of cognitive development, particularly in the area of children's memory. He is the author of *Children's Thinking: Developmental Function and Individual Differences* (Brooks/Cole) and *Children's Strategies: Contemporary Views of Cognitive Development* (Erlbaum). He is a member of the editorial board of the *Journal of Experimental Child Psychology.*

Barbara Bjorklund has taught child development at a variety of universities and community colleges, and has done research in cognitive and social development at Florida Atlantic University and the Mailman Center for Child Development at the University of Miami. She has written popular articles for *Parents Magazine, Baby Times,* and *South Florida Parenting,* and has appeared on the NBC Today Show as a child development expert. She serves as coordinator of the Children's Rights Campaign for South Florida Amnesty International. She is also a professional photographer who specializes in photographs of children, several of which appear in this book.

From 1987 to 1990, David and Barbara Bjorklund wrote a monthly column for *Parents Magazine,* and are authors of *The Parents Book of Discipline* (Ballentine, 1990). They continue to write about child development for magazines and newspapers and to collaborate on child development research. The Bjorklunds live in Fort Lauderdale, and have four children and four grandchildren.

Preface

We believe that child development is the most important course students will take in college. The information they gain helps in the lifelong quest for self-knowledge, increases students' effectiveness in their professional interactions with children, makes them enlightened taxpayers and thoughtful voters on issues affecting children, and enriches their personal relationships with children. We also believe that information on a subject as important as child development should be firmly rooted in science and theory.

We are very particular about textbooks when we teach child development courses. Most books fall into one of two categories. Either the authors teach research and theory, neglecting the practical applications of the subject, or they teach practical applications without a serious evaluation of research and theory. Our solution was to use research-based books and add practical applications in lectures. Now we have brought these two components together in one text.

Authors' Perspective

Between us we have more years of graduate studies and research experience than we care to admit, and almost as many years of teaching and parenting. It is difficult to achieve a balanced view of both sides of some issues, so we have let our own perspective shine through. We believe, for example, in scientific explanations of evolution and in biological mechanisms for early development of attachment and language. We are against academic lessons for infants (and fetuses), for early sex education, and for a disciplined family lifestyle. We don't think TV is intrinsically bad, we think divorce may be better for children than living with a dysfunctional marriage, and we think that homosexuality is often determined before birth. Our interpretation of current respected scientific research influenced our selection of material. Viewpoints that have historical merit are presented as history.

We believe that the human child comes in one basic model and that it has remained essentially the same for 100,000 years. The difference between the long-ago cave baby and today's high-tech child are cultural, not innate. We thus include both research that is universal in its application and that which focuses on cultural differences. Although we are proud that developmental psychology is a "made in America" science, we also know that important research is being conducted throughout the world. We have visited research centers in Europe and met with developmentalists from Canada, South America, and Japan. Our annual conferences are multinational. We have included research from all parts of the globe.

Our personal preference is also reflected in the topical organization of this book. We firmly believe that the study of development cannot be chopped into age levels and still retain its integrity. Development is by nature continuous; by dividing it topically we can appreciate changes as they occur. A myth of child development publishing seems to be that topical books are only for advanced courses; chronological books are for introductory courses. We intend to lay that myth to rest.

Our students are anywhere from 18 to 65, and many are already working in day-care centers, hospitals, or social service agencies. Many are parents (and grandparents), and although they may not be familiar with the scientific framework of child development, they know a lot. We have often learned as much from our students as they have learned from us, and we maintain an adult-to-adult tone throughout the book.

Organization

The book consists of four main sections. Part One, "Introduction to Child Development," includes Chapter 1, in which we introduce central concepts and look at the history of childhood and the state of children in the world today; and Chapter 2, in which

we discuss the role of theory in child development, research methods and ethics, and how science about children is communicated among scientists and to the public.

Part Two, "The Beginnings of Development," includes Chapter 3, on genetics; Chapter 4, on prenatal development, birth, and the neonate; and Chapter 5, on physical growth. These are all important topics that students often find challenging; we thus communicate complicated ideas in interesting, straightforward ways. Development is based in biology, and students can best appreciate other aspects of the subject when they understand the processes that underlie growth and change.

Part Three, "Cognitive Development," consists of six chapters. How children think and how their thought processes change with age have become a primary focus for psychologists and educators. A central tenet of this book, as of the field as a whole, is that a child's behavior can be accurately assessed only if we understand how the child makes sense of the world. This is true both for such intellectual behaviors as school work and such social behaviors as imitating one's parents. In Chapter 6 we examine perception and attention. We devote Chapter 7 to Jean Piaget's theory of cognitive development. In Chapter 8 we look at learning, thinking, and remembering, with topics ranging from conditioning in infancy and infantile amnesia to the development of memory strategies and metacognition. In Chapter 9 we review research on language development, including how parents influence children's language, the development of communication skills, and the relation between language and thought. In Chapter 10 we discuss individual differences in intelligence, examining intelligence measurement, environmental factors that influence intelligence, the stability of intelligence over time, and the evolution of human intelligence. In Chapter 11 we consider the role of culture, particularly schooling, in children's intellectual development.

In Part Four, "Becoming a Social Being," are six chapters. In Chapter 12, on attachment, we look at the mother–infant bond, the factors that influence the quality of attachment, and the consequences of attachment for later life. In Chapter 13 we look at families, in terms of parenting styles, child abuse, the effects of divorce on children, and day care. Chapter 14 is about children's peer interactions and friendships, social status, prosocial behavior, and aggression, including a look at schoolyard bullies and their victims. Chapter 15 starts with how the concept of self develops; then we examine empathy in children, their social perspective, and their moral development. In Chapter 16, on gender, we consider the biological, social, environmental, and cognitive factors that influence a child's developing sense of gender. We also show that cultural assumptions about sex differences in behavior and thought may be stereotypical, exaggerated, or simply wrong, although some are based in reality. We conclude in Chapter 17 with the development of sexuality, an important issue that is often slighted in child development textbooks. We examine what little research there is on the subject, look at what children know about where babies come from, and establish the origins of sexual orientation.

Pedagogical Features

Chapter structure Each chapter begins with an outline and a story that reflects the topic under discussion. At the end of each chapter is a list of key terms and concepts, organized by topic. Many of these terms are boldfaced at their first appearance in the text and defined in the glossary at the end of the book.

Selection of topics In addition to such basic topics as physical growth, Piagetian theory, and the role of peer and family in child development, there are chapters on subjects that are not usually covered, including "Culture, Schooling, and Cognition" (Chapter 11), and "The Development of Sexuality" (Chapter 17).

State of the Art sections At the end of each chapter we feature a contemporary real-world topic. For example, Chapter 4, "Prenatal Development, Birth, and the Neonate," concludes with a description of the new technologies for fighting infertility; in Chapter 8, "Learning, Thinking, and Remembering," we discuss children as eyewitnesses in court; and in Chapter 12, "Attachment," we address the issue of families in crisis. In other State of the Art sections we apply developmental principles to examinations of illiteracy, day care, schoolyard bullies, and the absence of black role models for inner city boys.

Boxes We have highlighted contributions by professionals who use the principles of child development in their work with children. A clinical child psychologist explains how theory affects her therapy for an encopretic child. A school psychologist discusses attention problems in the classroom, a sex education coordinator talks about how understanding children's thinking helps in his job, and an educator describes the symptoms and treatment of anorexia nervosa.

Day-to-day details about doing research are also presented in boxed sections. Students will appreciate what is actually involved in research instead of simply learning the types of designs and analyses. For example, we follow one of our own research projects, step by step, for four years, from proposal to publication, including funding, working with local school boards and human subjects committees, and revisions. In another box we examine the nuts and bolts of a longitudinal study that has been going on in Munich for ten years. And a Rumanian scientist describes conducting a research project despite political revolution and a shortage of funds.

To demonstrate the practical application of the text material, we have boxed our adaptations of popular articles we published elsewhere. They provide humor, advice, and a look at children, development, education, and parenthood from a perspective that is not found in other textbooks.

We include a variety of interviews that make the book enjoyable and realistic. For instance, in our discussion of Piagetian stages we talk to children who explain how they judge people's ages. In a section on memory strategies, children of different ages tell how they go about remembering an important phone number. When looking at children's social groups, we asked children who they liked to play with, and why. To convey parents' discomfort at discussing sex with children, we included college students' recollections of what their parents told them about the origin of babies. A letter from a young father to his newborn daughter captures the effect a baby has on a new parent.

Acknowledgments

We began this book with the guidance and encouragement of Phil Curson of Brooks/Cole Publishing Company; the expertise of managing editor Vicki Knight helped us complete it. We express our gratitude to them, to our production editor Penelope Sky, our photography editor Ruth Minerva, our designer Katherine Minerva, and everyone else at Brooks/Cole who made the job of textbook author a joy.

Books have a way of becoming part of their authors' lives, and when the authors are married to each other the book joins the family. We are grateful to our family: they lived with this book for four years; they found themselves in stories and examples and photos; they labored with us before the deadlines and celebrated with us afterwards. We especially acknowledge three of our grandchildren, Brittany Zeman, Jeffrey Arciola, and Benjamin Zeman. They were born while we worked on this project and their development made the subject come alive before our very eyes once again.

Part of this book was written at the Max Planck Institute for Psychological Research in Munich, and we express our gratitude to Dr. Franz Weinert and Dr. Wolfgang Schneider for their gracious hospitality. Other portions were written at the University of North Carolina at Chapel Hill; we are grateful to Dr. Peter Ornstein and the developmental psychology division for the office space, library services, and lively discussions.

We would like to thank the following conscientious professional reviewers for their many helpful comments: Ruth L. Ault, Davidson College; Patricia F. Chappell, Austin Peay State University; Louella Jean Fong, Western Kentucky University; Catherine Hackett-Renner, Christian Brothers University; Kevin R. Hughes, Western Kentucky University; Janina M. Jolley, Clarion University; Seth Kalichman, Loyola University; Kenneth D. Kallio, State University of New York, Geneseo; Jacqueline Muir-Broaddus, Southwestern University; Andrew F. Newcomb, University of Richmond; Betsy L. Nichols, Tompkins Cortland Community College; David Page, Nazareth College; Pamela T. Reid, City University of New York; Ann Southerland, Pensacola Junior College; and R. Gene Wiggins, Alabama Agricultural and Mechanical University.

Finally, we thank our colleagues, friends, and students who took the time to read drafts of the manuscript and to provide constructive criticism: Elizabeth Ashley; William Cassel; Clay Cavedo; Thomas Coyle; Lee Ellis; Jane Gaultney; Brandi Green; Tamar Hale; Adele Hamilton; Katherine Harnishfeger; Jacqueline Heyliger; B. J. Liberty; John Money, David Perry, and Glenna Zeman.

David F. Bjorklund
Barbara R. Bjorklund

Brief Contents

test 1

Test 2

test 3

final + all of above.

Contents

Part Four   Becoming a
Social Being   311

12 *Attachment:*
The First Relationship   312

13 *Family Relations   336*

Looking at Children

An Introduction to Child Development

Introduction to Child Development

Concepts and History of Child Development

The ancient Greek historian Herodotus wrote in the fifth century B.C. of an Egyptian pharaoh who wished to discover what the first language was, and thus which race of people was the oldest in the world. To do this, he directed that two newborn infants be removed from their parents and given to a shepherd, who was to raise the children in an isolated cottage and never utter a word to them. Their first words, reasoned the pharaoh, would be from the first language ever spoken on earth. One day, the shepherd reported that the children spoke their first word, "becos." Upon confirming this, the pharaoh acknowledged that the Phrygians and not the Egyptians were the original inhabitants of the world. The proof was that *becos* is the Phrygian word for bread.

We don't know whether this ancient tale is fact or fiction. Nevertheless, it suggests that questions uniquely concerned with child development have a very long history. It also indicates that some people from bygone eras at least thought about conducting experiments to test these questions, even though the experiments themselves may have been ethically abhorrent and based on simplistic and obviously incorrect theories.

For us, as for many people throughout history, questions of development are fascinating. One reason for this widespread interest is that *everyone* knows *something* about human development, and, whether we are conscious of it or not, we each have implicit theories of how children progress from helpless infants to independent adults. The theories we hold are important to us because the way we think about development influences our attitudes and behaviors toward children, which in turn affect children themselves. Our influence is most pronounced when we deal with children directly—as parents, teachers, or counselors, for instance. But as members of a democratic society, we indirectly influence children by our stand on issues such as education, day care, and prenatal health care. The wisest decisions are based on solid knowledge of child development.

Thus, the goal of this book is to help students develop a keen appreciation of children and their development. A scientific approach need not be dry and lifeless, but can enhance our sense of wonder, producing a deeper, richer understanding of the miracle of development.

Development: A Definition and Some Central Issues

The process of development is a call to order. From two elementary cells, the egg and sperm, a multicellular organism grows. Cells divide and differentiate, producing bone, muscle, gut, and brain. The process is not random or chaotic, but highly organized. After birth, development continues to be orderly. From a mass of sensations and experiences, from consumption of foods ranging from mother's milk to sushi, mind and body develop in a predictable fashion.

Development as Change in Structure and Function

Development as change over time   At its simplest, **development** refers to predictable change in structure or function over time.[1] But all changes in form or behavior cannot be considered developmental. For example, development can be contrasted with learning, which can also be defined as a change over time. But learning usually occurs over brief periods, whereas development typically occurs over longer periods. Moreover, learning is a direct function of specific experience, and because every individual has unique experiences, different people will have different learning histories. Development is rooted in biology, so its general course is known for all biologically normal members of a species in all but the most atypical of environments.

Despite this predictability, individual differences do exist among children at any age. These early variations affect how children make sense of their environment and how others perceive and respond to them, making the eventual outcome a function of many interacting factors.

Structure, function, and development   Before delving into the specifics of child development, we must first define the two key concepts in our definition of development: **structure** and **function.** Structure refers to some substrate of the organism. Usually when we refer to structure we mean something

[1]*Development* refers to changes over the life span—from conception to death. The focus of this book is child development, beginning during the prenatal period and continuing through adolescence. Despite our emphasis, development should not be thought of as something that ends at 18, but rather as a lifelong process.

Development through childhood is orderly and predictable, not random and chaotic.

concrete, such as muscle, neural tissue, or body parts. However, in a more general way, structure can also describe mental knowledge. For example, an infant's knowledge of its mother changes as a result of repeated experiences with her. Similarly, a child's understanding of certain words or concepts changes with experience. A 2-year-old may believe that all four-legged animals are called "doggies," including daddy when he gets down on the floor on his hands and knees. With experience, a child's knowledge of dogs, and animals in general, changes. "Structure" can be applied to the underlying meaning of words, concepts, and social relations.

Function, on the other hand, refers to action related to a structure. Thus, the firing of a neuron, the flexing of a muscle, and the bringing to consciousness of an idea are all examples of function. These are all activities inherent in the structures themselves. Function also refers to actions external to the structures. These include events that can best be described as "experience."

Development is usually thought of in terms of **bidirectionality of structure and function.** What this means is that structure and function interact to produce a particular pattern of development. Children are limited to functions (behaviors) that are within the capability of their structures. For example, children cannot run if they do not have the muscle structure necessary for running; they cannot solve the problem 7 + 5 = ? if they do not have the mental structures required for addition. But the activity of the structure can result in self-generated changes. Thus, when children exercise their muscles or their mental knowledge, changes in the structure itself can occur, which in turn can lead to changes in function.

Let us provide an example from biology of the bidirectional nature of structure and function. Chick embryos show spontaneous movement before their muscle and skeletal development is complete. When embryonic chicks are given a drug to paralyze them temporarily for as little as one or two days, deformations of the joints of the legs and toes develop (Drachman & Coulombre, 1962). In other words, spontaneous activity (function) of the limbs is necessary for proper development of the skeleton (structure).

The bidirectionality of structure and function is important in human development as well: children are active participants in and important contributors to their own development. Thus, we need to look

Children join the world prepared to take an active part in their own development.

beyond environment or genetic makeup for the causes of development, and examine the behavior of children themselves in dynamic interaction with their surroundings.

For social and cognitive development, the bidirectionality of structure and function is perhaps best understood in terms of the **transactional model,** which assumes that the child is an active force in his or her own development. In terms of behavioral development, children's biological constitutions influence how they perceive the environment and how others in the environment respond to them. As a child develops, the environment is as much changed by the child as the child is by the environment (Bell, 1979). We will discuss the transactional model in more detail later in this chapter.

Issues in Child Development

Although developmental psychology is concerned with changes throughout the lifespan, from conception to death, we focus in this book on development throughout childhood. Child-developmental psychologists are a varied lot and are interested in a wide range of topics, from changes in neural brain structures during prenatal development to physical aggression in the schoolyard. But developmental psychologists all deal, at some level, with several basic, related issues: How stable is behavior over a period of time, and can a behavior pattern, once established, be easily changed? Does development proceed in discrete stages, or is change over time gradual? What are the roles of nature (biology, genetics) and nurture (environment, learning) in development? These issues are implicit throughout this book.

The stability and plasticity of human behavior

Given that a particular behavioral pattern has been established, to what extent will it remain constant over time? Will a precocious infant become a bright 3-year-old and later a talented adult? Will an abused child recover from maltreatment to become a well-adjusted and productive member of society? Will a "difficult" infant become a "difficult" child and adult, or are such periods merely transitory stages? Once patterns have been established, can they be modified by later experience? In short, is human behavior characterized by **stability** or **plasticity**?

For the better part of this century, it was believed that individual differences in intelligence were relatively stable over time and not likely to be strongly modified by subsequent environments. Many scientists believed that early life experience played a critical and nonreversible role in establishing certain aspects of social and intellectual behavior. Jerome Kagan (1976) referred to this view as the "tape recorder model" of development: every experience was "taped" for posterity, and it was impossible to rewrite or erase something once it had been recorded. The evidence for this view came from studies of children reared in nonstimulating institutions (Skeels & Dye, 1939; Spitz, 1945). Infants who received little in the way of social or physical stimulation showed signs of mental and motor retardation as early as 3 or 4 months of age. These deleterious effects intensified as children remained institutionalized, and were maintained long after children left the orphanages (Dennis, 1973; Goldfarb, 1947). However, research in the 1960s and 1970s, using both children and animals as subjects, showed that the harmful effects of early experience were not always permanent—that, under some conditions, drastic reversals in behavior could be realized (Kagan & Klein, 1973; Skeels, 1966; Suomi & Harlow, 1972; see Chapter 10).

It is apparent today that development is more plastic than we once thought. We realize that, although early experience is important in influencing development, later experience plays a role as well. We are also aware that some behaviors are more easily modified than others. One of the chores of the developmentalist is to determine which aspects of development can be modified through experience and which are likely to remain constant despite changes in the environment. As should be apparent by now, there is no single answer to all developmental questions, and the important issue of the stability and plasticity of development is a complicated one.

The concept of stage in child development

When speaking of children, we often refer to stages. The "terrible twos" are notorious, and we may describe a 4-year-old who insists on wearing a snorkel, diving mask, and fins everywhere (including on tricycle rides around the neighborhood) as being "in a

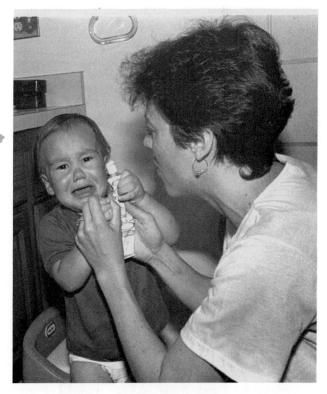

"Stage" is more than an abstract concept in any household that includes a 2-year-old.

stage." In everyday parlance, we use the term **stage** to refer to a period of time in which children display a certain type of behavior. Stages are transitory; children eventually grow out of one, often into another.

Developmental psychologists think of stages in a similar way: children in one stage are characterized by behavior that is qualitatively different from behavior of children in earlier or later stages. This idea is best reflected in intellectual, or cognitive, theories. For example, according to Jean Piaget, children during infancy understand the world in relation to their physical action on objects. This is qualitatively different from the intelligence of the 2- or 3-year-old, who can understand the world in terms of symbols, such as language. However, very young children lack the mental tools of logic, so their understanding of the world is different from that of an older child or adult. The point in stage theories is that behavior or thought at any one stage is of a different type than the behavior or thought at another stage. The 4-year-old is not just a smaller version of the 12-year-old, but rather is a qualitatively different being who understands the world in a different way than the older child. Stage theorists hold that changes from one stage to another are discrete, reflecting **discontinuity of development.** This means that the change from one style of behaving or thinking to another is relatively abrupt. Figure 1.1a illustrates the steplike nature of developmental change postulated by stage theorists.

A contrasting belief is that developmental changes are mainly quantitative in nature. That is, as children get older the types of things they do aren't very different, but they are able to do things more skillfully. In cognitive development, for example, it is possible that as children age they are able to hold more things in memory, know the meaning of more words, and process information faster (Bjorklund, 1989). All of these are quantitative, or countable, changes. Such quantitative changes are said to be **continuous** in nature, with development occurring gradually. Figure 1.1b illustrates the smooth nature of developmental change postulated by nonstage theorists.

Whether development is essentially discontinuous and qualitative (stagelike) or continuous and quantitative (nonstagelike) has been the subject of much debate. The issue is important because it concerns the underlying mechanisms of development.

Nature/nurture. Perhaps the central issue of all psychology, historically, has been that of nature/nurture. To what extent is behavior—personality, psychopathology, thought, or patterns of development—a function of one's biological constitution or of one's social and physical environment?

The obvious answer, of course, is that nature and nurture interact to produce a particular developmental pattern. The real question is *how* nature and nurture interact. The current transactional view, mentioned previously, holds that a child's biological constitution will influence how that child experiences the environment. For example, a highly active 2-year-old, by refusing to remain confined in a play-

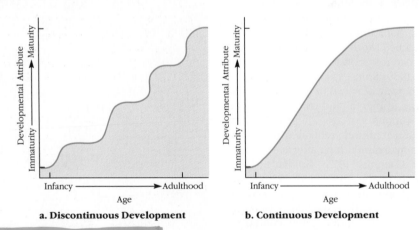

a. **Discontinuous Development**   b. **Continuous Development**

Figure 1.1 Stage, or discontinuity, theorists propose that development proceeds in a steplike fashion (a), with qualitative changes from one stage to the next occurring abruptly. Nonstage, or continuity, theorists propose that development proceeds in a continuous fashion (b), with quantitative changes occurring gradually over time.

Children who don't like being confined are often given more opportunity to explore than more placid children.

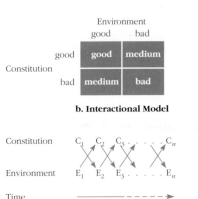

Figure 1.2 Main-effect, interactional, and transactional models of development.
Source: From "Early Influences on Development: Fact or Fancy," by A. Sameroff, *Merrill-Palmer Quarterly,* 1975, *21*(4), 267–294. Copyright © 1975 by Wayne State University Press. Reprinted by permission.

pen, may have a greater number of experiences outside the playpen than a less active child. Similarly, a child who processes language easily may be more apt to take advantage of available reading material than a child whose genetically based talents lie in other areas, such as the ability to comprehend spatial relations. Environment is thus very important from this perspective; but it is one's biology that influences which environments are most apt to be experienced and how those experiences will be interpreted.

The Transactional Model as an Alternative to the Nature/Nurture Issue

The transactional model provides an alternative way to view the nature/nurture issue. In this view, developmental outcomes are not simply the result of good or bad biology, or good or bad environments. Rather, development is seen as *the continuous and bidirectional interchange between an active organism, with a unique biological constitution, and a changing environment*.

Arnold Sameroff (1975) contrasted the transactional model of development with main-effect models and one type of interactional model (see Figure 1.2). Main-effect models (a) assume that a child's developmental outcome is determined only by biology or environment. A popular alternative is a version of an interactional model (b), which assumes that good biology can moderate the effects of poor environment, and vice versa. Neither type of model, claimed Sameroff, properly captures the na-

ture of development. In contrast, the transactional model views development as resulting from a different type of interaction between biology and environment, seeing development as a more complicated and dynamic system. It views the child as continuously interacting with the environment and being changed as a result of this transaction (as the environment is similarly changed). From this perspective, it is inappropriate to ask how much of development is contributed by nature and how much by nurture. The more appropriate question is: how do nature and nurture *transact* to produce a particular pattern of development?

Describing the "big picture" Although the transactional model of development may appear to describe well the development of any single child, how can such a model be applied to children in general? Although each individual child is unique, there are enough commonalities among children's constitutions and environments that general developmental patterns can be predicted. For example, Sameroff and Chandler (1975) proposed that (a) some caregiving environments are more likely than others to produce intellectually and socially competent children and (b) children who experience birth-related trauma are especially susceptible to nonsupportive caretaking. Thus, the negative consequences of early biological impairment are exaggerated in nonsupportive environments. That is, they proposed a transaction between infants' biological constitutions and their environments. Supportive environments were defined as those in which the parents were reasonably educated, had steady incomes, and experienced minimal amounts of family stress (middle socioeconomic status, or middle SES). Nonsupportive, or high-risk, environments were defined as those in which parents had little formal education, low income, and substantial stress (low socioeconomic status, or low SES).

Support for the transactional model   Sameroff and Chandler tested their model by examining the outcomes for children experiencing anoxia (lack of oxygen) at birth as a function of their socioeconomic level. Although differences in developmental level between normal and biologically impaired infants are obvious at birth in both lower- and middle-SES groups, these differences are diminished and often eliminated by age 6 or 7 in middle-SES homes. In lower-SES homes, however, the differences persist or increase with age. Sameroff and Chandler speculated that distressed infants—characterized by more aversive cries, slower attainment of social-developmental milestones such as smiling and vocalizing, and a generally sickly appearance—receive different types of treatment in different environments. In reasonably affluent and well-educated families, these distressed children are likely to receive additional attention and stimulation, speeding their recovery. In deprived, stressed, and poorly educated families, these same infant characteristics result in a pattern of reduced attention, which helps perpetuate their cognitive and social deficits. Thus, there is a transaction between family and child: the particular characteristics of the child interact with the particular characteristics of the family, yielding distinct patterns of development.

In an experimental test of the transactional model, Philip Sanford Zeskind and Craig Ramey

(1978, 1981) investigated the effects of different caretaking environments as a function of infants' biological status at birth. In their study, infants from poor, rural environments who had been classified as "high risk" for mental retardation were assigned to one of two caregiving environments. Infants in one group received medical care and nutritional supplements and participated in an educationally oriented day-care program beginning at approximately 3 months of age (experimental group). Infants in a control group received the medical care and nutritional supplements but did not participate in the day-care program. Within each group, approximately half the infants were classified as fetally malnourished at birth and the rest as biologically normal (see Table 1.1). Fetally malnourished infants are typically characterized by aversive cries, lethargy, and delayed development.

At 3 months of age, fetally malnourished infants in both the experimental and control groups were developmentally delayed relative to the normal infants (that is, those who had not been fetally malnourished). However, when children were administered IQ tests at 24 and 36 months, the picture changed dramatically. First, children in the experimental group had higher IQs than children in the control group, demonstrating the overall effectiveness of the educational program on intelligence in high-risk children. Second, IQ patterns differed between the fetally malnourished and normal infants as a function of which group they were in. For the experimental children, there was no difference in IQ between those classified as fetally malnourished at birth and those classified as normal; both showed IQs comparable to the population average. In the

Table 1.1   Mean IQ scores at 36 months for fetally malnourished and biologically normal children as a function of participation in educational day care

	Biologically Normal	Fetally Malnourished
Experimental (Day-Care) Group	98.1	96.4
Control Group	84.7	70.6

Source: Adapted from "Sequelae of Fetal Malnutrition: A Longitudinal, Transactional, and Synergistic Approach," by P. S. Zeskind and C. T. Ramey, *Child Development*, 1981, *48*, 1314–1321. Copyright © The Society for Research in Child Development, Inc. Reprinted by permission.

control group, however, IQ differences between the fetally malnourished and normal infants were substantial. Both groups of children had significantly lower IQs than children in the experimental group, but the effect was especially large for the fetally malnourished infants. IQ scores at 36 months for the four groups of children in this experiment are shown in Table 1.1. In general, the developmental pattern observed in this experiment is similar to that found by Sameroff and Chandler (1975) for anoxic babies: the effects of a nonsupportive environment (the control group) were especially harmful for biologically distressed children.

Zeskind and Ramey also measured degree of mother-child interaction in the home. They found no difference in the amount of maternal attention received by fetally malnourished and normal infants in the experimental group. However, by 24 months, fetally malnourished infants in the control group received less attention from their mothers than did normal control children. They proposed that the increased responsivity of fetally malnourished infants receiving the educational day care resulted in increased attention from their mothers and a generally positive developmental outcome. In contrast, the continued withdrawn and sickly behavior of the fetally malnourished infants in the control group resulted in less maternal attention, exaggerating the injurious effects of the initial biological impairment.

The transactional approach to development does not belong to any one theorist or to any one area of developmental psychology. There is no single theory that best represents the transactional approach to development, and some theorists place greater emphasis on the role of the child (or of the environment) than others. But the general view that development proceeds as the result of a continuous, bidirectional interchange between an active child, with his or her own biologically determined characteristics and a changing environment, is one that is shared by most contemporary developmentalists and one that we shall assume throughout this book.

History of Developmental Psychology

A New Science

Although interest in child development is not new, developmental psychology is a relative newcomer to the field of science. However, it is also one of the most "user-friendly" of the sciences. Whereas few people are personally concerned with the latest findings in astrophysics or polymer chemistry, new trends in developmental psychology are met with widespread interest and become popular topics not only in research labs and university classes, but also in popular magazines and on TV talk shows.

It is difficult to separate the beginnings of developmental psychology from the beginnings of other fields of psychology. The late 1800s was a fertile time for science, in both Europe and North America. Out of that era came experimental psychology and developmental psychology, not as parent and child, but more as siblings.

Wilhelm Wundt, the father of experimental psychology, developed the field of psychophysics—the study of how the human senses are affected by the physical world. Early experimental psychology clearly showed the mark of his thinking, as human subjects were trained to report sensations they experienced in response to various visual, auditory, and other types of stimuli. Wundt had little scientific use for untrained subjects, and even less for children, whom he viewed as incomplete adults. He took issue with colleagues who felt that adult minds could be understood only through the study of children's minds. "The exact opposite is the case," Wundt argued (Cairns, 1983). Needless to say, child-developmental psychologists do not agree with this view. Their scientific roots are in biology (Cairns, 1983), and they perceive the development of a living thing to be equally as important as its adult functioning—if not more so.

Important Figures in Early Developmental Psychology

Wilhelm Preyer (1841–1897) Preyer was a German biologist who became interested in the development of embryos in various species, including humans. He believed that, of all species, humans are least mature at birth and that important developmental steps continue throughout childhood. This view is reflected in the titles of his two major works, *The Special Physiology of the Embryo* and *The Mind of the Child*.

Preyer introduced rigorous scientific methods to the study of children, including objectivity, reliability, experimental control of laboratory conditions, and interobserver agreement. Some of Preyer's findings were wrong (for example, that newborns lack the ability to hear), but many were right (for example, that experience affects the structural development of the brain). More important, he brought the rigors of biology to the study of human development and showed that our species could be investigated alongside other animals without any loss of our special status as humans.

Alfred Binet (1857–1911)   Binet had a less than illustrious background before coming to developmental psychology, having dropped out of both law

Alfred Binet, the French psychologist who refined experimental methodology and made developmental psychology a valid and mature science.

school and medical school. Although Wundt and his colleagues were in their heyday at Leipzig, Binet, a Frenchman, did not study their work because he could not read German. Instead, he studied with neurologist Jean Martin Charcot and later did research with Charcot and Charles Ferre on hypnotism and electromagnetic influences on hypnotic states. Their methodology was controversial, their findings unreplicable, and just when it seemed that Binet had struck out for the third time, he became interested in the work of Balbiani, an embryologist who worked in the same hospital as Charcot and Ferre. In Balbiani's lab, Binet learned about the new concepts of evolution, genetics, and development. He also learned sound experimental methods. After receiving his doctorate in natural sciences, he became director of the physiological psychology lab at the Sorbonne (Wolf, 1973); he also married Balbiani's daughter (Cairns, 1983).

During the next 17 years, until his death, Binet wrote an average of several books and a dozen journal articles each year, on subjects such as children's memory, experimental methodology, children's perception, and invertebrate neurology. Binet's work was important because its approach was from outside the mainstream of experimental psychology. He criticized Wundt's methods as artificial, arguing that reducing human behavior to rigidly controlled laboratory conditions resulted in eliminating factors that might be important to the behavior being studied, especially with children. He also criticized American psychologists such as Hall, who seemed to define the value of an experiment by the number of subjects used rather than the results (Cairns, 1983).

Binet's work was not above criticism itself, some of it well deserved. But he was "learning a trade for which there were no masters" (Cairns, 1983, p. 48). He devised research designs to fit the problem instead of fitting the problem to the design at hand. He studied the development of intelligence by close investigation of individuals well known to him (his daughters) and also by looking at large groups (Paris schoolchildren). His work ranged from short-lived findings on the psychic life of lower animals to the enduring test of intelligence, the Stanford-Binet, that is still in use today.

G. Stanley Hall (1844–1924)   Hall was the first American Ph.D. in psychology, the founder of the first major psychology journal in North America

G. Stanley Hall, the American psychologist who inspired, organized, and motivated leaders of the child study movement.

(*American Journal of Psychology,* begun in 1887), founder of the first English-language child psychology journal (*Pedagogical Seminary,* begun in 1891), and the first president of the American Psychological Association. He was also a minister, philosopher, textbook writer, and college president. As Robert Cairns (1983) explains, "Hall did not change careers, he cumulated them" (p. 51).

Hall first studied philosophy and theology (Hilgard, 1987). After receiving his doctorate in psychology from Harvard, he went to Germany to study with Wundt. There he learned the questionnaire method used to evaluate groups of children so that teachers would know what knowledge they already had and where to begin instruction, depending on the composition of the class. For example, rural children as a group might be found to know more about nature than urban children as a group; thus, a school official with both urban and rural schools to administer would know to start instruction about nature at a more basic level in the urban schools (Ross, 1972).

Hall returned to the United States and began using the questionnaire method in the Boston schools. He then went to Baltimore and established an experimental psychology lab at Johns Hopkins University, where many early leaders in the field were trained. Later, Hall was asked to serve as the first president of Clark University in Worcester, Massachusetts, where he spent the second half of his career.

At Clark University, Hall, like others at that time, became interested in evolution and development. He established a school of developmental study and trained students such as Arnold Gesell and Lewis Terman, who would become leaders of the next generation of developmental psychology.

Hall believed that children develop according to a master plan and that parents and teachers should refrain from instructing children, to allow their natural development to unfold. He believed that the development of children (ontogeny) parallels the evolutionary development of our species (phylogeny): "ontogeny recapitulates phylogeny." This theory was the basis of much early developmental research, and, although the theory proved false (Gould, 1977), the research provided the foundation for today's developmental psychology.

Hall's contributions to developmental psychology were more as an innovator and inspirator than a researcher or theoretician. He introduced scientific methods to child study, insisted on practical applications of scientific inquiry, and organized influential groups that made valuable contributions to developmental psychology. Cairns (1983) describes Hall's role as that of a "catalyst": the influence he had on those around him was more important than his own research and theories.

James Mark Baldwin (1861–1934) Baldwin studied with Wundt in Leipzig before receiving his Ph.D. in philosophy from Princeton. An ardent evolutionist, Baldwin used his training in experimental psychology to observe his own children's development and to relate it to the development of the human species.

Although Baldwin's career in developmental psychology lasted only 16 years, he had a strong influence on the field. His first two books on cognitive development were immediately successful, and he was elected fourth president of the American Psychological Association. He founded the first psychology laboratory in Canada, was one of the founders

James Mark Baldwin, the American psychologist who stressed Darwinian evolution and defined the course for the next generation of developmental psychologists.

and first editors of the journal *Psychological Review,* and also wrote articles on biology and the history of psychology. In 1903 he accepted a professorship at Johns Hopkins University, where six years later his career was cut short because of a sex scandal (see Broughton & Freeman-Moir, 1982). He became an expatriate, living the rest of his life in Mexico and France. Although he remained active in academia, helping establish the National University of Mexico and later serving as a professor in Paris, his career in American psychology had ended (Hilgard, 1987).

In spite of giving so few years to developmental psychology, Baldwin was influential in defining the framework within which the developmental process can best be studied. He believed that developmental psychology should progress along the lines of Darwinian evolution and should include the development of human consciousness and social order.

Baldwin's work in developmental psychology involved little experimentation or practical demon-

stration of his ideas, but his writings served to point the way for others, notably Jean Piaget (see Chapter 7). Ironically, as Cairns (1983) points out, Baldwin's ideas first influenced biologists and sociologists; developmental psychology later borrowed them back.

Sigmund Freud (1856–1939) Freud was trained as a medical doctor in Vienna and did early research in neurobiology. One of his major areas of interest was the development of the fetal brain, both in humans and in other species. He went to Paris and studied neurology with Maurice Charcot, three years before Binet. Both Freud and Binet were interested in the relationship between physical symptoms and

Sigmund Freud, the Austrian physician and founder of psychoanalysis who theorized that childhood experiences affected adult functioning.

mental states, especially hysterical symptoms that had no physical cause and disappeared under hypnosis. Freud returned to Vienna to set up a practice in neurology. He found that hypnosis was not necessary for probing the unconscious mind—that patients readily revealed their darkest secrets during free association and in recounting their dreams (Hilgard, 1987).

Freud's experiences while treating patients' physical symptoms with mental techniques revealed information about the workings of the mind, especially its development. Although Freud's approach was based on a medical model—finding a cure for a disorder—his theory was based on showing how things develop correctly so that practitioners could pinpoint the time during development when things began to go wrong.

Freud's major contribution to psychology in general was the discovery of the unconscious part of the mind. His contribution to developmental psychology in particular was the idea that the unconscious was formed during early childhood and that adult mental disorders could be caused by events that had happened many years before and were long forgotten by the conscious mind. Although this gave new importance to childhood, it also gave new reasons for parents to worry about their child-rearing methods. Freud's psychosexual theory of development will be discussed in Chapter 17.

John B. Watson (1878–1958)   Watson, known as the father of behaviorism, had an effect on all branches of psychology, including developmental psychology. Behaviorists believe that the environment is the major factor in explaining the behavior of an organism—that the majority of our behavior is learned. From 1913, when Watson announced his theory, until the 1960s, American psychology was strongly influenced by the behaviorist point of view.

Watson began college at 16, skipped the bachelor's degree, and received his master's degree at 21. He wanted to study with Baldwin at Princeton, but didn't meet the entrance requirements of "reading Latin and Greek," so he studied psychology and neurology at the University of Chicago, receiving his Ph.D. at 25.

Baldwin was at Johns Hopkins in 1908, and he offered Watson a job as full professor. Watson accepted and, for the next 12 years, with time out to

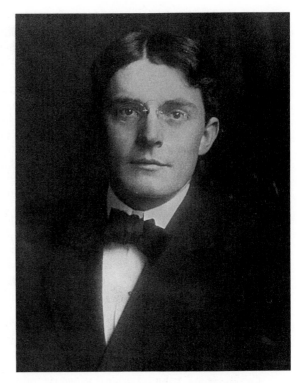

John B. Watson, the American psychologist who founded behaviorism and later taught parents to use its principles in childrearing.

serve in World War I, he did the experimental work and scientific writing that established behaviorism as the prominent theory of the first half of the 20th century.

Watson's work with children began when he returned to work after the war, but there is disagreement about his reasons. In his own writing, Watson (1926) claims that he studied children to find the learning history of adults. However, a more pragmatic version of the story comes from Ernest Hilgard (1987), who contends that Watson returned from the war to find his labs moved to a building with no facilities for animals, so he began working with children "as the next best material available"—not such an abrupt change when one considers that Watson drew little distinction between "man and brute."

Regardless of his impetus, Watson's fame as a developmentalist is based on two experiments showing the role of conditioning in the development of emotions. In the first (Watson & Morgan, 1917), he showed that infants come equipped with only three innate emotions—fear, rage, and love—evidence that other emotions are acquired later in infancy and during childhood. The second experiment (Watson & Raynor, 1920) showed how such learning could take place. Watson conditioned a young boy named Albert to be afraid of a white rat by sounding a loud gong each time the boy was shown the rat. Albert's innate fear of the loud sound quickly became associated with the rat. After the experimental trials, the child showed fear to the rat alone, a conditioned or learned response to a previously neutral stimulus.

Watson's years as an academic researcher came to an abrupt end in 1920 when he was dismissed from Johns Hopkins as the result of an "unfortunate domestic incident" (Hilgard, 1987). After leaving Hopkins, he wrote his controversial child-rearing manual *Psychological Care of Infant and Child* (1928), which achieved considerable popularity among parents. Watson advocated an emotional detachment between mothers and children, warning that too much love would make the child a social invalid, overly dependent on the approval of others (Hilgard, 1987). He discouraged parents from picking up crying babies because it would reinforce them for crying and condition them to cry more readily the next time they wanted to be held. To Watson, emotions were handicaps, maternal instincts were nonexistent, and science could provide better parenting than tradition (Cairns, 1983). In other words, parents need to use their heads instead of their hearts.

Throughout the 1930s, Watson repeated these themes in popular magazine articles and lectures. His ideas became the keystone of modern, scientific child rearing and held sway for several decades, until they were overshadowed by cognitive psychology. Watson ended his working years as vice-president of an advertising agency.

The pioneers of developmental psychology were a motley crew. They came from France, Austria, Germany, and the United States. They were trained in philosophy, theology, biology, and medicine. Many stumbled into their calling after several wrong turns and chose their professions for reasons that were not always clearcut. For example, Freud opened a

clinical practice because he realized that professorships were scarce in Austria, especially for Jews, and he needed to make a decent living before his fiancee's father would consent to their marriage. Watson got his first taste of science when, as a student at Fordham, he took a part-time job assisting in the chemistry lab. Later, as a graduate student at the University of Chicago, Watson's ideas took on a new twist when his part-time janitorial work involved tending the rats in the neurology laboratory.

We like to put our intellectual forebears on pedestals, revering them for their genius and their insight. The truth is that, despite their ultimate contributions, many of our ancestors in child development were not fully appreciated by their contemporaries; many fell into the field when other, more desirable opportunities were closed to them; and some developed reputations as the Gary Harts and Jimmy Swaggarts of their day. Yet they began a discipline that would flourish throughout the 20th century, setting the foundation of a science that has important things to say about the nature of humans and about the rearing and educating of children.

Developmental Psychology Goes Public

Child study movement   Of all the early researchers in developmental psychology, G. Stanley Hall is the most contradictory. His theories were wrong, his research was haphazard, and he bent his findings to support his beliefs rather than basing his beliefs on his findings. Although he began the developmental psychology program at Clark University, where many illustrious developmental psychologists studied, none acknowledged him as their teacher or inspiration (Cairns, 1983). And yet, of all the figures in the early years of developmental psychology, he was the most directly responsible for bringing this science out of its ivory tower and making it accessible to the public through the **child study movement.**

Hall believed that the findings of developmental psychology should be applied to children in an immediate, practical way. To this end, he formed the Child Study Section of the National Education Association, bringing developmental psychology directly to American teachers. To reach parents, he supported the formation of regional child study associations during the 1880s and 1890s. By the turn of the

Cora Bussey Hillis, the Iowa farm wife who promoted the idea that science could improve the lives of children.

century, these associations had spread across the United States and were working together as a powerful advocate for children (Ross, 1972).

Child research centers began in the Midwest, where parents were comfortable with the role of agricultural science in their everyday lives. An Iowa mother and farm wife, Cora Bussey Hillis, who had seen several of her children die in infancy, felt that parents needed more knowledge about children's health and development. She pushed for a child research center using the slogan "If research can help us raise corn and hogs, why not children?" The results were the Child Welfare Research Station at the State University of Iowa and, shortly afterward, the Merrill-Palmer Institute in Detroit. These two research centers became the models for many others that were formed across the United States and Canada during the 1920s and 1930s (Sears, 1975). The facility at the State University of Iowa still trains

students in developmental psychology, and the Merrill-Palmer Institute still sponsors developmental psychology research and publishes its journal, the *Merrill-Palmer Quarterly*. Nor has Cora Bussey Hillis been forgotten; every two years, when the Society for Research in Child Development meets, an informal gathering of researchers hold a banquet in her honor.

World War I World War I gave momentum to the child study movement in several ways. First, it created the need to evaluate, both physically and mentally, large groups of young men from many backgrounds and all parts of the country. The military commissioned psychologists to devise tests that would make these evaluations reliably and quickly (Sears, 1975), thus initiating the first large-scale program of intelligence testing.

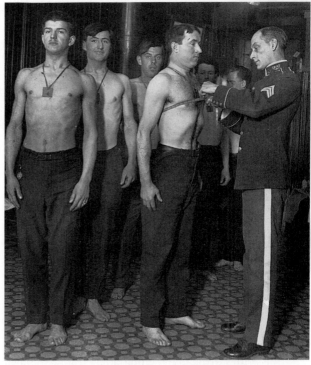

World War I required the evaluation of young men in great numbers, which led to group intelligence testing and increased interest in human development.

Second, when the country's young men were evaluated, it was found that more than half suffered from one or more problems rooted in childhood. Although these problems were not new, their extent was surprising. It was impossible during wartime to ignore the medical, dental, and intellectual deficits of America's young (Sears, 1975).

A third influence of World War I was more indirect. After winning the war, Americans were feeling prosperous, positive, and extremely proscience. If military and industrial problems could be solved through the natural sciences, such as chemistry and physics, then why couldn't we solve our domestic problems by means of the social sciences, such as psychology and sociology (Smuts, 1985)?

After World War I, the U.S. government set up the National Academy of Sciences to coordinate scientific research being done in government facilities, private industry, and university research institutes. By 1924, the academy included a committee on child study. Today, the National Academy of Sciences Committee on Child Study has become the independent, self-supporting **Society for Research in Child Development (SRCD),** with more than 4,000 members, including most active developmental psychologists (Smuts, 1985). They meet as a national group in odd-numbered years, hold smaller regional meetings in even-numbered years, and publish the journal *Child Development.*

In 1919, President Woodrow Wilson convened the second White House Conference on Children (the first had been called by Theodore Roosevelt in 1909) and proclaimed 1919 the Year of the Child (Sears, 1975). The White House Conference on Children continued to be convened every ten years until the 1980s, when it was canceled by President Ronald Reagan (Kozol, 1988).

A vast amount of postwar money was channeled into developmental research, mostly from private funds. Merrill-Palmer expanded its institute in Detroit, the Fels soap company funded the institute of child study that still bears its name, and the Commonwealth Fund financed a longitudinal study at Berkeley headed by Lewis Terman. John D. Rockefeller outdid them all by setting up the Laura Spelman Rockefeller Memorial Fund, an endowment of $74 million used to start major child study research centers at the University of California at Berkeley, the University of Minnesota, Columbia University, and Yale University, to establish smaller centers at other

Laura Spelman Rockefeller, in whose memory $74 million was endowed in the 1930s to establish major child study centers across the United States.

universities, and to pay for expansion of various existing facilities (Smuts, 1985). Today these institutions remain centers for research in child development, and the longitudinal studies serve as a valuable source of data for contemporary researchers (see Chapter 2).

In 1931, following developmental psychology's first decade of rapid growth, Carl Murchison edited the first *Handbook of Child Psychology*. It contained 22 chapters on different topics, written by 22 noted developmentalists (Sears, 1975). Five more handbooks followed, in 1933 (edited by Murchison), 1946 and 1954 (edited by Leonard Carmichael), and 1970 and 1983 (edited by Paul H. Mussen). The 1983 *Handbook* contained 47 chapters, more than twice the number in the 1931 book. The changing array of topics included in these handbooks provides a good indication of the "development" of developmental psychology (see Table 1.2).

Table 1.2 Changes in topics in child psychology handbooks during 52 years

Chapter Topics	Murchison 1931	Murchison 1933	Carmichael 1946	Carmichael 1954	Mussen 1970	Mussen 1983
Psychoanalysis	X	—	—	—	—	—
Dreams	X	—	—	—	—	—
Drawing	X	—	—	—	—	—
Eidetic imagery	X	X	—	—	—	—
Motor development	X	X	—	—	—	—
Organic drive theory	X	X	—	—	—	—
Gifted children	X	X	X	X	—	—
Learning	X	X	X	X	X	X
Language	X	X	X	X	X	X
Cross-culture	X	X	X	X	X	X
Moral development/behavior	X	X	X	X	X	X
Research methods	X	X	X	X	—	X
Sex-typing/sex differences	—	X	X	X	X	X
Cognitive processes	X	X	—	—	X	X
Aggression	—	—	—	—	X	X
Behavioral genetics	—	—	—	—	X	X
Ethology	—	—	—	—	X	X
Sensory and perceptual development	—	—	—	—	X	X
Physiological and neurological development	—	—	—	—	X	X
Infant cognition and perception	—	—	—	—	X	X
History	—	—	—	—	X	X

World War II World War II had a disruptive influence on developmental psychology as most young men were called into military service—including developmental psychologists. Although their academic backgrounds made them valuable as administrative and psychological personnel, the field of developmental psychology suffered from a loss of researchers and funding. By the end of the war, the SRCD journal, *Child Development,* was three years behind its publication schedule (Sears, 1975).

The postwar period, however, brought renewed optimism about family life and the value of science. Government funding increased, so that institutions no longer had to rely on private foundations. Finally, the postwar baby boom, with its soaring U.S. birthrate, led to increased interest and need for child-rearing information, education, and developmental studies.

The years since World War II have brought a rapid increase in child-development research, and the number of journals devoted primarily or exclusively to this field has skyrocketed. The past three decades have also brought changes in theoretical focus. Behaviorism, with its emphasis on a passive child and an active environment, is no longer a major force in developmental psychology, although its influence is still felt. Today, as we have described, developmental psychologists are more apt to view the child as taking an active role in his or her own development.

State of the Art
Toward a More Global View of Childhood

A Brief History of Changes in Adults' Perceptions of Children

The role children play in the lives of adults has changed drastically since the early days of recorded history. In fact, children's lives have not always been as valued as they are now. Archaeological research has shown that as far back as 7000 B.C., children were killed as religious sacrifices and sometimes buried in walls of buildings to "strengthen" the structures. In many societies, infant girls were killed to provide higher ratios of males in the population. Up until the fourth century A.D., parents routinely (and legally) killed their newborns if they were not perfectly healthy at birth, if there were too many children in the family, if the child was female, or if the child was illegitimate. In 374 A.D., the Romans outlawed infanticide. For the next thousand years or more, parents simply abandoned their unwanted infants to die outside the city gates. Children were also sold as slaves and used as collateral for loans (de Mause, 1974).

In the 1600s, child abandonment was outlawed in most parts of Europe, and foundling homes were established to provide for the basic needs of unwanted children. When Vincent de Paul established the first foundling home in Paris, the response was so great that the home was filled within the first week and laws had to be written against transporting infants into the city from surrounding areas. A century later, 25% of the infants born in Paris became foundlings. Vincent de Paul was later canonized by the Catholic church, and today in most U.S. cities, St. Vincent de Paul societies run shelters, soup kitchens, and thrift shops to "alleviate the suffering of the poor" (Katz, 1986).

In 1749, London physician William Cadogan published an essay claiming the "Preservation of Children" as a matter of concern for "Men of Sense." Criticizing the child-rearing practices of mothers and nursemaids who had been trained by grandparents and unenlightened physicians of the past, Cadogan extolled the advances made in the field of medicine and then gave his advice on child rearing, much of which is consistent with today's practices: infants should not be swaddled and tightly bound by too much clothing; they should not be fed rich food immediately after birth; they should be breastfed by their own mothers at home and not sent away to a wet nurse for the first few years (Kessen, 1965). Although his tone and premise were condescending to women, his essay was evidence that adults in some circles were beginning to take the well-being of children seriously.

Some writers believe that adults practiced emotional detachment from their infants, often not even

Although the industrial revolution meant long hours and hard work for many children, it also increased their economic value to family and society.

naming them until they were older, in order to prepare themselves for the high probability of the child's death (Sommerville, 1972). Health conditions improved during the 1700s, and by 1800 an infant born in London had a better than 50% chance of living to celebrate his or her fifth birthday (Kessen, 1965). As the likelihood of survival improved, so did the quality of children's lives.

Economics played a part in advancing adults' perceptions of children, as children became more valuable as farm laborers or factory workers. The industrial revolution made use of children's unskilled labor, and many children in the 18th and 19th centuries spent long hours working in factories, mills, and mines (Sommerville, 1972).

The beginning of this century has been called the high point of childhood in Western culture. Great works of literature were centered on children, including *Alice's Adventures in Wonderland* by Lewis Carroll and James Barrie's *Peter Pan,* and great composers wrote music for children's amusement, including Robert Schumann's *Kinderscenen* and Felix Mendelssohn's *Kinderstucke.* This era of idealizing childhood had little to do with the real needs of children; the ideal of innocence and goodness personified was hard for children to live up to (Sommerville, 1972). Still, it did lead to kinder perceptions of children by the adults in their lives, and it stirred an interest in the scientific study of child development.

The 1990s and Children Are Not All Living Happily Ever After

These historical developments and positive trends might seem to suggest that all children are now living happily ever after. A glance at any recent newspaper tells us otherwise.

In southern Asia, more than 2 million children have been born into slavery or sold into servitude to pay their families' debts (Tarrant, 1989). In Brazil, more than 457 children and adolescents were killed in 1989 by police—either on duty or in "death squads"—in an effort to clean up the streets (Amnesty International, 1990). According to U.N. estimates, some 200,000 children under the age of 15 are bearing arms worldwide (Stanley, 1990). On this planet each day, 40,000 children die from preventable causes. More than 7 million children in the world today are refugees (Amnesty International, 1990).

These Cambodian boys are among the currently estimated 200,000 children under 15 who serve in armed military forces around the world.

Box 1.1

United Nations Convention on the Rights of the Child (unofficial summary)

Children have the right to life, to survival, and to maximum development.

Children have the right to a name and a nationality.

Children have the right to know, to maintain contact with, and to be cared for by both parents.

Children have the right to leave or enter any country in order to maintain contact with their parents.

Children have the right to express an opinion in matters affecting the child, and to have that opinion heard.

Children have freedom of thought, conscience, and religion.

Children have freedom of association and peaceful assembly.

The State shall provide children with legal protection of their privacy, family, home, and correspondence.

The State shall recognize that both parents have responsibility for the upbringing of a child and shall assist parents in this responsibility and provide childcare for working parents who need it.

The State shall protect children from physical and mental injury or abuse, neglect, and exploitation by adults.

Children who have been deprived of families have the right to special protection and alternative care.

Children who are refugees have the right to protection and assistance, including help in locating missing family members.

Children who are disabled have the right to special care and training to help achieve self-reliance and a full and active life in society.

Children have the right to the highest attainable standard of health care and access to medical services. The state should work to diminish child and infant mortality, combat disease and malnutrition, ensure health care for expectant mothers, provide access to health education, develop preventive health care, and abolish harmful traditional practices.

Children have the right to an adequate standard of living. The State should assist parents who cannot meet this responsibility and should try to recover maintenance for the child from responsible persons both within the State and abroad.

Children have the right to education. The State should provide free and compulsory primary education and ensure equal access to secondary and higher education. The State should also ensure that school discipline reflects the child's human dignity.

Children have the right to enjoy their own culture, to practice their own religion, and to use their own language.

Children have the right to leisure, play, and participation in cultural and artistic activities.

The State shall protect children from economic exploitation and from engaging in work that threatens their health, education, and development.

The State shall protect children from illegal narcotic and psychotropic drugs, and from their production and distribution.

The State shall protect children from sexual exploitation, including prostitution and pornography.

The State shall protect children from being sold, abducted, or trafficked.

The State shall protect children from torture or any other cruel, inhuman, or degrading punishment, including capital punishment or life imprisonment for offenses committed under the age of 18. Children who have been legally detained have the right to be treated with dignity and respect, to be separated from adult offenders, to maintain contact with family members, and to have prompt access to legal assistance.

The State shall protect children from taking direct part in wartime hostilities before the age of 15, and from being recruited into the armed forces before the age of 15.

The State shall make these rights known to both adults and children.

Source: Adapted from "UN Convention on the Rights of the Child: Unofficial Summary of Articles," by S. Hart, *American Psychologist,* 1991, *46*(1), 50–52. Copyright 1991 by the American Psychological Association. Reprinted by permission.

Children should be protected from economic exploitation and enjoy their right to leisure, play, and the arts of their culture.

Closer to home, the Coalition for the Homeless estimates that 3 to 4 million Americans are homeless, most of them in families, with another 10 million "at high risk for homelessness"—that is, paying more than half their income for housing (Kozol, 1988). According to the Centers for Disease Control, more than 500,000 American preschoolers suffer from malnutrition and are at risk for permanent mental retardation (Brown & Pizer, 1987). One million U.S. teenagers cannot read at a third-grade level (Kozol, 1985).

One ray of hope for the world's children is the United Nations Convention on the Rights of the Child (U.N. General Assembly, 1989), which was ratified by 69 of 71 member nations at the World Summit for Children in September 1990 (the United States being one of the two nations that did not sign). This convention, summarized in Box 1.1, has the status of a legally binding treaty for the nations that ratified it and is considered by many to signal the beginning of the most important time in history for children's rights (Hart, 1991).

The Human Child: One Basic Model

Children have inhabited our planet for more than 100,000 years. Some estimate that 48 billion children have been born since the dawn of history (Berger, 1983). Although we humans have made giant strides of progress in improving our lives, the fact remains that the basic-issue child has changed little during our tenure on this planet. Other than improvements in health and nutrition, there is little difference between a baby born thousands of years ago in a cave and one born last week in a high-tech hospital birthing suite. Our great advances over thousands of years have been in changing the environments that infants are born into, not the infants themselves.

This is an important point, and one that is missed by many professionals responsible for children's well-being. For example, a common way of thinking among some primary educators today is that the 1990 model first-grade brain is more advanced than the 1960 model, and that children today can learn concepts in first grade that would have been second- or third-grade concepts a generation ago. On the surface, it makes sense. We humans have learned a lot in the past 30 years. But it's the *information* that has changed, not the learning equipment. It's advanced software, not hardware.

Infants born into slavery, oppression, poverty, and ignorance are not different-model infants from those whose pictures adorn our desks in fancy frames. And though we are not in a position to solve the problems of all the children in the world, we can at least acknowledge their equal value and regret their lost potential.

The point is not to condemn the adults in those children's lives any more than we should condemn the adults throughout history who have held views of children as less important and less valuable than we consider them today. The point is for those of us who know different to expand our enlightened sights past our own nurseries and classrooms and laboratories to include all the children of our planet.

Summary

Development refers to change in structure or function over relatively long periods of time. Unlike learning, developmental changes are relatively predictable and characterize all normal members of the species. Structure refers to some substrate of the organism, including muscle and nerve tissues, but also mental knowledge. Function refers to action related to the structure, and can be internal (emanating from the structure) or external (outside the structure, or experience). The relationship between structure and function is bidirectional: structure and function interact with each other to produce a particular pattern of behavior.

Issues relating to the stability and plasticity of behavior have also been a focal point for developmental theory and research, with evidence accumulating that although early experiences are important in influencing behavior, later experiences play an important role as well. The question of how stagelike human development is centers around the issue of whether age-related changes are discontinuous and abrupt, reflecting qualitative changes, or continuous and gradual, reflecting quantitative changes. Perhaps the most prominent issue in developmental psychology is that of nature/nurture—the extent to which patterns of development are a function of biology versus experience. The field has shifted its opinion over the century on this issue, with the current perspective emphasizing the transaction of biological and environmental factors. The transactional model of development represents a general frame of reference in which to view development rather than a well-defined theory. This approach emphasizes the bidirectional relationship between children and their environments.

Child-developmental psychologists are interested in describing changes in children's behavior over time and understanding the mechanisms underlying those changes. Developmental psychology had its origins in biology and was not an outgrowth of experimental psychology, which viewed children only as incomplete adults. Key figures in early developmental/child psychology include Wilhelm Preyer, a biologist studying embryological development; Alfred Binet, the originator of the IQ test; G. Stanley Hall, the first American-trained Ph.D. in psychology; James Mark Baldwin, an intellectual predecessor to Piaget; Sigmund Freud, the founder of psychoanalysis; and James B. Watson, the father of behaviorism. The child study movement was spurred by G. Stanley Hall and by lay people in the Midwest such as Cora Bussey Hillis, who helped establish the Child Welfare Research Station at the State University of Iowa. World War I gave momentum to the child study movement as a result of large-scale testing, the discovery that many men suffered from problems rooted in childhood, and the prosperity that followed the war. The Society for Research in Child Development (SRCD), an international organization, had its beginnings in the concern for children that followed World War I. Research in child development was slowed during World War II but skyrocketed thereafter. Although the theories that guide research today are often different from those popular earlier in the century, the influence of earlier research and theory is still felt.

Adults' perceptions of children have changed dramatically over the centuries, resulting in differences in how children are treated. Even in the 1990s, however, millions of children are born into slavery, oppression, poverty, and ignorance.

Key Terms and Concepts

development
> structure
> function
> bidirectional relationship

transactional model

stability

plasticity

stage
> quantitative versus qualitative differences
> continuity versus discontinuity of
>> development

nature/nurture

child study movement

Society for Research in Child Development (SRCD)

United Nations Convention on the Rights of the
> Child

The Scientific Study of Children

Two first-year graduate students in developmental psychology had devised an idea for a research project. They set up a situation in which mothers and toddlers would come into a toy-filled room and their social interactions would be observed over a 15-minute period. The graduate students developed a coding scheme that described most of the social behaviors that could occur between a mother and her young child. After spending the better part of a semester watching and recording mother-toddler interactions, they had a total of 18 mother-toddler pairs (and 2 father-toddler pairs) and data for 42 separate categories of behavior. Being new at scientific research, they sought the advice of the resident methodologist/statistician, a fourth-year graduate student who specialized in the design and analysis of psychological studies.

"What you have here," he said, "is what we call a Polynesian Island Study. It's as if you measured everything you could possibly think of about the handful of natives on a small Polynesian island. You have more measures than subjects, you don't have a central question, and you don't have a way of organizing your measures to make any statement about your results. Your idea may have been very interesting, but the way you've collected the data, I can't help you make any sense out of what you've got."

Being a scientist means doing research, and doing research means formulating hypotheses and developing techniques to test them. This is where methodology comes in. What most people are really interested in are the results or interpretations of a study; but coherent results and interpretations can be achieved only when the study was designed properly. How we design our studies determines how (or whether) we can analyze the results and what sense we can make of them. A study may produce provocative findings, but depending on how the study was conducted, the results may be of very limited application. This in itself is not necessarily bad, but it is essential that the consumers of this information—other scientists, students, or the public—understand what the limitations of the study are so that they can make responsible judgments about its findings.

In this chapter we explore the scientific study of child development. We discuss first what it means to be a science, giving examples from the field of child development. We next explore the basic research methods of developmental psychology and look at two ways of examining change over time. We then discuss some of the problems of doing research with children, the ethics of this research, and how research gets published. We conclude with a look at how scientific research is communicated to the public and how one can evaluate it when it appears in newspapers, magazines, and popular books.

The Science of Developmental Psychology

What is science? How does a scientific explanation differ from a nonscientific one? The science of developmental psychology describes development and behavior; it also explains the causes of development and patterns of behavior. What makes this scientific is that the descriptions are based on objective and reliable observations, and the explanations are based on a possible chain of physical or psychological causes.

Describing Behavior

Objectivity To be described scientifically, a behavior must be *objective;* that is, it must be clearly observable, irrespective of the observer's emotion, prior expectation, or personal belief. This is sometimes more easily said than done. Much of what is of interest to psychologists cannot be observed and measured directly. How strong is the attachment of an infant to its mother? How is information stored in memory? Can infants recognize familiar faces? It is one thing to measure how many inches a baby crawls in a 3-minute period; it is quite another to measure unobservable events.

What psychologists who are interested in these phenomena do is find some evidence from children's observable behavior that will provide them with clues to the underlying concepts they are interested in. Thus, for example, psychologists interested in mother-infant attachment may look at how many seconds it takes an infant to be soothed by its mother following a brief separation; psychologists interested in the organization of children's memory may examine how many items they remember from a list of familiar words compared to how many items they remember from a list of unfamiliar words; and psychologists interested in infants' recognition of faces may examine the number of seconds babies spend looking at a picture of a face they have seen frequently versus one they have never seen before. In each case, some overt and measurable action of a child is used as an indication of some covert behavior. The measure may or may not be the most appropriate, but it is objective, permitting others to examine the same behavior. Other scientists can then argue whether the particular measure chosen is the best one for studying the behavior of interest.

Reliability   Making a behavior objective is only the first step in scientific description; its measurement must also be reliable. **Reliability** comes in two types. The first is **interobserver reliability:** the same behavior seen by one observer is also seen by a second observer. This requires that the behavior in question be carefully defined ahead of time. For ex-

Is this aggression or not? Researchers must define their terms carefully when studying children's behavior.

ample, if two observers are sent to a school playground to observe aggression in children, they must first know what constitutes aggression. Clearly a right cross to the nose is an aggressive act, but what about the friendly shove, the headlock during a playground wrestling match, or the verbal taunt that starts a scuffle? Even when definitions are agreed upon, will different people record the behaviors similarly? To ensure interobserver reliability, most investigations require at least two independent observers to record the target behavior. If they generally agree with one another—say, 90% of the time—the data are considered reliable and worthy of further analysis. If not, it's back to the drawing board.

The second type of reliability is **replicability.** If we observe some behavior in our laboratory, will another scientist be able to replicate it—observe the same thing under the same conditions in his or her laboratory? Or, even more basic, if we observe some behavior in our lab this week, will we find the same thing if we repeat our observations three weeks from now? The goal of science is to obtain some broad truths that will hold regardless of who is doing the observing and when. Phenomena that can be found only in one person's laboratory, or only once, are curiosities, not scientific data. They may have resulted from unrecognized quirks in the lab procedures, a special sample of children selected as subjects, or simply chance. Good scientists and good scientific procedures sometimes produce unreplicable findings. However, when research is reported in the scientific literature, the methods used to obtain the findings are included, and the replicability of the research can then be assessed. Thus, even after a scientific project has been completed and the results published, judgments of scientific merit must wait, for only if a finding is replicable can it be judged an important step in science.

Scientific Explanations

Science does more than describe behavior; it also attempts to explain it. After an experiment has been designed, performed, and the results calculated, those results need to be explained in natural cause-and-effect terms. Thus, concluding that a child behaves in a certain way because of experiences in a previous life does *not* qualify as a scientific explanation. Even if the child's behavior is described in objective terms, is reliably recorded and replicable, this explanation of the behavior goes beyond the natural world and is not within the realm of science.

Does this mean that we can only explain behavior in terms of what we already know scientifically—that we cannot discover new patterns of cause and effect that go beyond our current understanding? Not at all. What it does mean is that we should be pragmatic, sticking close to simple and conventional explanations whenever we can. To suggest a complex, extraordinary explanation of some behavior requires that all simple and conventional explanations be considered first and judged inadequate. The more unusual the explanation for a behavior, the more evidence is required for its acceptance. Science moves ahead on new explanations, but the old explanations must first be proved inadequate before being replaced.

The Role of Theory in Child Development

Most explanations in science take the form of theories. A **theory** organizes facts and provides the framework for understanding behavior. According to Paul Cozby, Patricia Worden, and Daniel Kee (1989), theories make "the world more comprehensible by providing a few abstract concepts around which we can organize and explain a variety of behaviors" (pp. 15–16).

Theories are important not only for organizing facts, but also for directing research. The theories we hold help determine the types of questions we ask. For example, if we believe that development occurs in stages, the research questions we ask will be different than if we believe that development is continuous. Without theories, facts are merely isolated bits of information. Theories permit us to explain known phenomenon and, even more important, make predictions.

An important feature of any scientific theory is that it can be disproved. A theory is not a statement about the world that relies solely on opinion or faith; rather, it is a statement about known facts that can be potentially disproved by new facts. If a theory is found to be incorrect because of new discoveries, these findings do not contradict the previous facts,

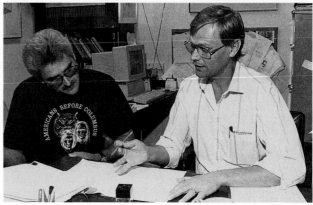

For every ten minutes a researcher spends with a child gathering data, several hours are spent in the office, planning, analyzing, and writing.

only how they are explained. For example, the theory that birth defects are caused by experiences of the mother (such as being frightened by an elephant) has been replaced by the theory that birth defects are caused by genetic abnormalities or external agents the fetus is exposed to (such as drugs ingested by the mother). The fact of the birth defect remains.

Theories are like noses: everybody has one. This is especially true of scientists. There have been several major theoretical approaches to the study of children, with hundreds of variations on these major theories. Some approaches, such as behaviorism, dominate research for decades and then are replaced by newer views of development. Others

Although some theories generate vigorous debate, it is fact and not simply opinion that determines the longevity of any theory. *Source:* Reprinted by permission: Tribune Media Services.

equally venerable, such as Piaget's theory of cognitive development (see Chapter 7), continue to influence contemporary research but have gone through substantial modification in the process.

Most of the research presented in this book has been motivated by theory. Rather than reviewing the major theoretical approaches to development here, we will discuss theory throughout the book, in the context of the behavior the theory explains. Almost all good research is based on theory. Understanding the theory behind the data can often provide a clearer interpretation of the facts.

Research Methods of Developmental Psychology

Many of the research methods used and the research problems encountered by child developmentalists are the same as those in other areas of psychology.

However, because developmental psychologists study change over relatively long periods of time, some methods are unique to this field. And because the subjects we study are infants and children, some research problems arise that are not usually encountered by psychologists who study college sophomores or laboratory rats.

Methods of Empirical Research

The term *research* in psychology typically refers to the empirical study of some topic, research that involves the collection of data—whether observations of children in a natural setting, children's responses to problems in a laboratory task, students' scores on an achievement or IQ test, or the ratings given by teachers on some dimension of personality. These data are then analyzed, often using statistics, to find out something about the nature of children's behavior or development. Besides collecting and analyzing data, scientists may also review and interpret earlier research and theory or construct a theory independent of new data. These endeavors are also in the realm of science, but they are not empirical research.

Correlational studies In **correlational studies,** the relationship between two or more factors of interest is assessed. After the data have been collected, a statistical test, called a correlation (represented by r), is performed, and the magnitude of the correlation is assessed to determine if the relationship is greater than would be expected by chance. Correlations can range from -1.0 to $+1.0$, with zero reflecting a lack of any systematic relationship between two factors. A zero correlation, for example, would be expected between shoe size and IQ: the size of one's foot should not be related to one's general intellectual ability. A positive correlation would be expected between height and weight (in fact, it's about 0.65): the taller a person is, the heavier one is apt to be. A negative correlation would be expected between a student's grade point average and the number of errors made on a midterm exam: better students (as reflected by GPA) are likely to make fewer errors on tests than less proficient students.

The idea of correlation can be represented visually by scatterplots, as shown in Figure 2.1 (page 34). In Figure 2.1a, the relationship between a score on a test (factor Y) and the number of hours people studied for that test (factor X) is presented as a perfect positive relationship ($r = +1.0$).[1] In this example, each point on the graph corresponds to a certain number of hours studied and a certain score

[1]When reporting positive correlations, such as $r = +1.0$, the plus sign is usually omitted. Thus, a correlation of 1.0 reflects a perfect *positive* relationship.

on the test. As can be seen, people who studied very little received the lowest grades, people who studied a lot received the highest grades, and people who studied some intermediate amount received intermediate grades. Figure 2.1b shows a perfect negative correlation ($r = -1.0$) between amount of prenatal care and frequency of birth defects. The more prenatal care women receive, the lower the incidence of birth defects.

In real life, of course, we rarely find perfect relationships. Figures 2.1c and 2.1d show more moderate correlations (of about $+.65$ and $-.80$,

Box 2.1

The Encopretic Child

**Hilda Besner, clinical psychologist
Fort Lauderdale, Florida**

In the clinical field it is very important to have a strong theoretical framework within which to operate. This gives the clinician a clear understanding and reference point in helping the client with the presenting problems.

For example, Amanda, an 8-year-old girl, was brought to therapy by her mother. The presenting problem was that Amanda was continuously constipated, going to the bathroom only once every two to three weeks during the past eight months. The parents were continually arguing with Amanda and restricting her. They felt they had tried every alternative—ignoring, bribing, pleading, screaming, punishing—but nothing seemed to work. Much of the family discussion and interactions centered on Amanda's toilet behavior. Their physician said that there was nothing physically wrong with Amanda and suggested that they see a psychologist. At the initial appointment the parents were beside themselves with anxiety and eager to solve the problem.

In order for the psychologist to work with Amanda, it was necessary to understand that success-

respectively). Figure 2.1e shows what a scatterplot would look like if there were no relationship between two factors ($r = 0.0$). In this case, knowing the value of one factor (shoe size) would not help at all in predicting the second factor (IQ).

Correlational studies are used frequently in developmental research. For example, if one were interested in the relationship between children's viewing filmed aggression and engaging in aggressive behavior, one would first need to identify measures of aggression in film and of aggressive behavior. The next step would be to see if changes in one measure (viewing filmed aggression) are associated with changes in the other measure (aggressive behavior). This is what Joseph Dominick and Bradley Greenberg (1972) did in their study of 434 fourth-, fifth-, and sixth-grade boys. They assessed the amount of violent television the children watched and then related it to their approval of violence and their willingness to use violence themselves. They reported that high exposure to violence on TV was associated with greater approval of violence and a greater willingness to use violence.

ful toilet training generally occurs during the second to third year of life. In analytical theory, this is the anal phase of development, when children recognize that they can gain some independence and mastery over their bodies and their environment. It is also the time when parents begin to reward and punish their children in an attempt to control some of their children's actions.

Usually a child's lack of success in bladder or bowel performance is met with unacceptance by the parent. For many children this is the first clash with their mother, and many childhood disturbances may have their origin during this phase. Once children learn to control their bladder or bowel movements, they utilize this as an effective means of gaining control over the parent. The more the adult tries to exert control over the child, the more the child may continue to exhibit difficulties with bladder or bowel performance.

This theoretical background made it easy to begin exploring the dynamics of the relationship between Amanda and her parents. Amanda had been toilet trained at an early age, when her usual behavior was to use the toilet once every two to three days. Amanda's mother had been remarried six months earlier to a man whom Amanda did not like. Prior to this marriage, her mother's life had revolved primarily around Amanda. Amanda thought her mother's marriage would give her a father, but her stepfather did not spend much time with her, and she felt ignored and rejected. Amanda had tried to express some of these feelings to her mother, but she felt that her mother did not want to hear what she had to say. Therefore, Amanda began to withdraw and became angrier and more resentful.

Therapy focused on helping Amanda feel that she could exert some control over her environment, trying to improve the relationship between Amanda and her mother, increasing positive interactions between Amanda and her stepfather, establishing some experiences in which Amanda felt successful, and removing the household focus from Amanda's toilet behavior. Within a matter of six weeks, Amanda began experiencing more regular bowel movements. Without a good understanding of the developmental process of encopresis, it might have taken much longer to achieve positive results in therapy.

Reprinted by permission.

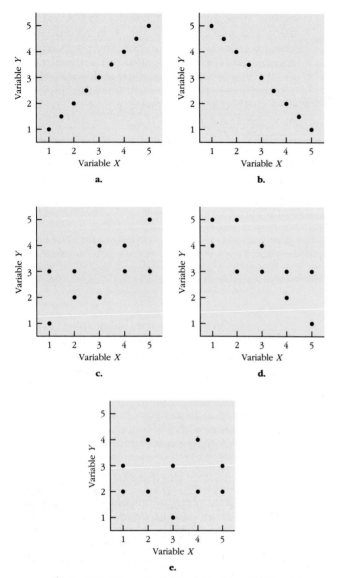

Figure 2.1 Examples of scatterplots of different degrees of relationship between two factors, X and Y. Perfect relationships are shown in a. (positive, $r = 1.0$) and b. (negative, $r = -1.0$). More realistic relationships are shown in c. ($r = .65$) and d. ($r = -.80$). Figure e. shows no relationship between the two factors ($r = 0.0$).

Given this finding, it would be tempting to conclude that watching violent television *causes* chil-

dren to be aggressive (or at least to have aggressive attitudes). However, the correlational nature of this study precludes such an interpretation. When all we have is a correlation, we only have information about a relationship; we do not know which factor caused which. In this example, although the interpretation that watching aggressive television leads to aggressive behavior makes intuitive sense, it is also possible (and some would argue more likely) that children who are aggressive tend to select violent television programs. Does aggressive TV cause kids to be aggressive, or do aggressive children watch more aggressive TV? This issue cannot be resolved through correlational methods, which can only establish a relationship between the two factors.

Experimental studies **Experimental studies** involve the manipulation of one or more factors and observation of how these manipulations change the behavior under investigation. To investigate the relationship between viewing violent television and behaving aggressively, for example, we could manipulate the TV viewing of children and assess the consequences. This is what Lynette Friedrich and Aletha Stein (1973) did with a sample of preschool children. After recording the level of aggressive behavior during school hours for three weeks, they divided the children into three groups. Each group viewed one of three types of television shows during the first half-hour of the school day: aggressive programs (such as "Batman" and "Superman"), prosocial programs ("Mister Rogers' Neighborhood"), and neutral programs (such as Disney nature films). Aggressive behavior during school was assessed again during the four-week period when children watched the programs and the two-week period afterward.

Friedrich and Stein reported that viewing aggressive television did result in increased aggressive behavior, *but only for those children who were high in aggression to begin with.* The experimental manipulation of TV viewing permitted Friedrich and Stein to state that watching aggressive programs *caused* aggressive behavior. However, their careful measurement of aggression prior to classroom TV viewing allowed them to determine exactly which children were most influenced by the aggressive content of the programs.

Although the example provided here is of an experiment conducted in children's natural environment, most experiments are conducted in laboratory settings. Children are tested under conditions in which the researcher can control extraneous factors that may influence a child's behavior. Labs need not be small rooms with white walls located in the corner of a university building. Laboratory studies can be conducted anywhere a researcher has control over what experiences the child has at that time. Much of child-developmental laboratory work, in fact, is carried out in small rooms in schools or day-care centers.

Case studies and diaries   A **case study** is a detailed description of an individual made by an expert observer. Usually, the details of the history or reactions of a particular person are recorded by a clinical psychologist and serve as the raw data for building a theory. Sigmund Freud's entire theory of psychosexual development was based on case studies of his patients—most of them adults recalling childhood experiences.

Some data can be collected ethically only by the case-study method. For example, there are several case studies that document the behavior and development of children raised in highly unusual early environments (Curtiss, 1977; Kuluchova, 1976). Perhaps the most famous is that of a boy thought to be raised in the wild, first published in 1806 by Jean-Marc Itard (1962). Itard recorded the behavior and development of the Wild Boy of Averyon, providing interesting and important data about the child's adjustment to human society after an early life of deprivation. Studies such as this could not be duplicated in a laboratory. The number of children involved is so small, and their experiences so different from one another, no group study could be done.

Another form of case study is the diary. The field of child development began with parents' systematic observations of their own children's development (C. Darwin, 1877; Preyer, 1882/1888–1889). Much can be learned from such careful, up-close observation, and a great deal of the influential work of the Swiss psychologist Jean Piaget (1952) was based on the careful observation and recording of the development of his three children over their first two years of life. Diaries can also be kept by parents at the request of researchers for specific behaviors. For example, Daniel Ashmead and Marion Perlmutter (1980) asked mothers to keep careful records of their toddlers' memory-related behavior. From these records, Ashmead and Perlmutter were able to document some remarkable memory abilities in very young children that had previously gone unnoticed.

Case studies and diaries are very useful for collecting information that would be difficult to get at otherwise, but there are limits to what one can learn from this approach. How do we know that what we observe for one or two children holds true for children in general? Also, how reliable are the observations? The investigator has only one person's interpretation of the events—sometimes that of a proud parent. Would another observer see the same thing? Despite these problems, the case-study method has produced important data for developmental psychologists, and these findings can serve as the basis for more systematic studies of child development and behavior.

Naturalistic studies   Diaries can be thought of as one form of **naturalistic studies,** in which the researcher attempts to intervene as little as possible, observing what goes on in a natural environment. Naturalistic studies are the favorite tool of ethologists, who study the behavior of animals in their natural habitats. Such work is important in child development as well. For example, Roger Barker (1965) provided detailed descriptions of school-age

Child development research does not always take place in the laboratory.

children as they went about their daily routines, believing that we must begin with an understanding of how children interact in their natural environments before proceeding further.

Although it seems obvious that understanding children's behavior in their natural settings is important, naturalistic approaches to the study of child development have not been widely used, at least not in North America. One reason has been the perceived necessity of making child development a "real" science, implying laboratory testing with rigorous experimental controls (McCall, 1977). Commenting on this bias, Urie Bronfenbrenner stated in 1977 that much of developmental psychology is the "science of behavior of children in strange situations with strange adults for the briefest possible period of time" (p. 513). Now that child developmentalists have proved to most of the scientific community that they are indeed scientists, it is time, urged Robert McCall (1977), to get back to naturalistic observation.

This can be done, and is now being done, without compromising the rigors of experimental design. For example, the experiment cited previously on the effect of television aggression on children's behavior (Friedrich & Stein, 1973) included observation in a naturalistic setting. Correlational studies can also be done in a naturalistic setting. Laura Berk (1986) observed first- and third-grade children during daily math periods and related their behavior during these times (particularly the incidence of talking to themselves) to their school performance. Berk reported interesting relationships among age, the nature of the problems, and children's performance on math tests that would have been difficult to assess in a laboratory situation.

Clinical interviews **Clinical interviews** are conversations in which the examiner probes a child's knowledge about certain topics. Unlike naturalistic studies, which attempt to be as unobtrusive as possible, the clinical interview requires an intense relationship between examiner and child. Jean Piaget used this technique extensively in his studies of children's cognitions, questioning his own children and others. Here, for example, is an excerpt of an interview with a child concerning the common belief that young children have that the moon follows

Jean Piaget used the clinical interview method in his research on children's thinking.

them when they are walking (from Piaget, 1969, p. 218):

Interviewer: What does the moon do when you are out walking?
Child: It follows us.
Interviewer: Why?
Child: Its rays follow us.
Interviewer: Does it move?
Child: It moves, it follows us . . .
Interviewer: Has it ever happened to you that it couldn't follow you?
Child: Sometimes when one runs.
Interviewer: Why?
Child: One's going too fast.
Interviewer: Why does it follow us?
Child: To see where we are going . . .
Interviewer: When there are lots of people in town what does it do?
Child: It follows someone . . . Several people . . .

With its rays. [The moon] stays still and its rays follow us.

Such interviews can provide insights into the thoughts of children. However, there are many problems associated with the clinical method. Unlike most experimental or correlational studies, in which each child receives the same set of instructions, children in a clinical interview will each have a different experience, making it difficult to generalize the findings. Also, it would be relatively easy for an interviewer to bias a child's responses or to get off the track. Piaget, acknowledging the difficulty of doing clinical interviews, stated that to become a skilled interviewer required daily practice for a year (Flavell, 1963).

Longitudinal and Cross-Sectional Designs

By definition, developmental psychology is concerned with change over time. Perhaps the most obvious way to assess developmental change is to follow a person or group of people over an extended period of time, documenting the changes as they age. This approach is used in **longitudinal studies.** An alternative approach is to look for differences among people of different ages. Thus, for example, instead of testing the same children at ages 4, 6, 8, and 10 (the longitudinal approach), one can examine four different groups of children at each of these four ages and note the differences in their behavior. This approach is used in **cross-sectional studies.**

Each method has its inherent strong and weak points. Longitudinal designs represent a true developmental approach, in that they record change over time within the same person. This cannot be said for cross-sectional studies. Although a group of 6-year-olds may show greater social skills than a group of 4-year-olds, for example, one does not know, using a cross-sectional design, whether the 6-year-olds with the most social skills were also the most socially skilled at age 4. We know that social skills improve with age, but we don't know the pattern of change within individual children. Without that knowledge, we are limited in what we can say about the mechanisms of developmental change. Thus, the major strength of the longitudinal method—its ability to

assess change within individuals over time—represents the major weakness of the cross-sectional approach.

The major weakness of the longitudinal method is that it is expensive and time-consuming. The difficulties and advantages of the longitudinal approach are discussed in Box 2.2 (page 38) by a German psychologist involved in a longitudinal study of children's intellectual development.

Not surprisingly, most research that finds its way into child-development journals is cross-sectional in nature. However, major longitudinal studies, following people from birth to adulthood, have been conducted, and the data from these studies are valuable. Studies begun in the late 1920s—one at the Fels Institute in Yellow Springs, Ohio, and another at the University of California at Berkeley—continue to be the source of important data about development. Some of the important topics investigated with data from these longitudinal databases have been age-related changes in intelligence (Bayley, 1949; Honzik, Macfarlane, & Allen, 1948; McCall, Appelbaum, & Hogarty, 1973), patterns of infant cognition (McCall, Eichorn, & Hogarty, 1977), personality (Kagan & Moss, 1962), and the effects of parenting style on later behavior (Kagan & Moss, 1962).

Longitudinal work is necessary to assess the stability of individual differences, as well as the continuity versus discontinuity of development. One way researchers have found to assess change within individual children over time in a relatively economical way is through smaller-scale longitudinal studies. For example, researchers at the University of Minnesota are following a group of children from infancy through early childhood, assessing the long-term consequences of early mother-infant attachment (Arend, Gove, & Sroufe, 1979; Egeland, Jacobvitz, & Sroufe, 1988; Matas, Arend, & Sroufe, 1978). And researchers at the Max Planck Institute for Psychological Research in Munich, Germany, are in the middle of an extensive longitudinal study of children's cognitive abilities that is planned to cover a ten-year span (Weinert & Schneider, 1987). Concentrating on a narrow range of issues, as the Minnesota group is doing, or studying children extensively for several years rather than decades, as the Munich group is doing, enables researchers to gather important developmental information in a way that is more efficient than larger-scale longitudinal projects but more informative than the economical cross-sectional approach.

Problems Doing Research with Children

Finding children   For all their delightfulness, children can cause problems for researchers. Diffi-

Box 2.2

Life with a Longitudinal Study

Wolfgang Schneider
Max Planck Institute for Psychological Research,
Munich, Germany, and the University of
Würzburg, Würzburg, Germany
During the past two decades, there have been many complaints that most developmental studies cannot be considered truly developmental because they focus on developmental *differences* among various age groups and ignore developmental *changes* within individuals over time. Accordingly, the major criticism is that cross-sectional designs, used in more

than 90% of developmental studies done today, cannot replace longitudinal studies.

Given these frequent complaints, it seems surprising that there are still not many longitudinal studies around. I will concentrate first on selected practical problems of longitudinal studies and then on potential benefits of longitudinal studies with young children.

Practical Difficulties

The first obstacle that comes to mind when practical aspects of longitudinal studies are considered is cost. There is no doubt that long-term, comprehensive longitudinal studies are expensive. Staff has to be trained, tasks have to be carefully developed and pretested, and samples of children must be recruited. Regarding the sample problem, longitudinal researchers depend on the compliance of their subjects over a long period of time. For example, as they try to keep the dropout rate as low as possible, they have to invest additional time and money whenever a subject moves to another city and must be tested there. In order to keep the children and their parents interested in the study, it is often necessary to send birthday cards or small presents every year.

An example of the unexpected practical problems we experienced in our Munich longitudinal study may be instructive. At the beginning, when the children were about 4 years old, our team of investigators traveled around the area, testing the children in their kindergarten classrooms (there is no distinction between preschool and kindergarten in Germany). Our experimenters had extreme difficulties with a group of five children from a specific kindergarten who were not willing to interact with the investigators because the weather was nice and they preferred playing outside in the sandbox. In a typi-

culties arise in simply finding children to use as research subjects. Laboratory rats can be ordered by telephone and delivered UPS for $7.56 apiece, and

college sophomores are typically willing to perform in experiments in exchange for course credit or money. Although children will gladly comply with

---

cal cross-sectional study, it is relatively easy to find a substitute if your target child does not comply. This is not true for longitudinal studies. In this particular case, our experimenters had to visit the kindergarten four times until they found the kids ready to participate (they managed to catch a rainy day). Needless to say, a lot of time and travel money were wasted because of such problems.

Two other practical difficulties concern the problem of publishing your results in a timely fashion and the timeliness of long-term longitudinal enterprises. It usually takes several years before the first longitudinal results are ready for publication, and this can cause problems for young scientists in the publish-or-perish world of academia. By the time the results are available, publishing them may be difficult because the topic of investigation may be out of fashion. In sum, there seem to be several practical obstacles that deter researchers from undertaking longitudinal studies.

Major Advantages of Longitudinal Studies

One of the most obvious advantages of longitudinal studies is that one is able to focus on changes occurring over time within the same person or within a group of people. Insight into the continuity or discontinuity of growth functions can be obtained only via longitudinal studies. In addition, the longitudinal approach can be very helpful in terms of the extent to which individual differences between children at one age are stable over time. That is, is a child who is highest on a measure at age 5 highest on the same measure at age 8? An example drawn from our own longitudinal study with young children may illustrate the case.

When we assessed memory performance, we found overall low group stabilities (test/retest cor-

relations) for the interval between 4 and 6 years ($r = .35$). Analyses of individual stabilities revealed a subgroup of children who contributed considerably to the overall low stability, showing low performance at the first measurement point and improving significantly from time point 1 to time point 2. Excluding these 20 children from the analysis led to a considerable increase in stability over time for the sample of about 200 children ($r = .65$). A closer look at the results for the extremely instable children revealed that they had low scores on most measures obtained at time 1. The fact that we had included numerous measures of intellectual and social competencies helped in solving the puzzle. We found that our instable children were also extremely shy: they had difficulty interacting with unfamiliar experimenters.

It appears, then, that the instability over time of these children's memory data cannot be simply reduced to a statistical regression-towards-the-mean effect but has to be linked to specific personality characteristics that offer a substantive explanation for the phenomenon. Undoubtedly, it would have been very difficult, if not impossible, to identify these children in a cross-sectional memory experiment. At the same time, it seems obvious that factors such as shyness can considerably influence young children's performance in cross-sectional experiments with unfamiliar experimenters. Our longitudinal finding suggests that more attention has to be devoted to this point in future studies with young children.

Reprinted by permission.

the requests of a researcher, the problem is finding a large source of willing subjects.

When dealing with children between the ages of about 5 and 18 years, the best source is the schools. Often, research projects must be approved by school boards, principals, teachers, and always, children's parents. Once approval has been obtained, the next problem is finding a place to conduct the study. Schools often provide small rooms suitable for testing, but much improvisation may be required to make the testing environment appropriate to the specific project. Because researchers are guests of the schools, they must comply with school schedules. This often means suspension of testing during certain hours of the day and limited access to the testing rooms, not to mention the problems of fire drills, Valentine's Day parties, and field trips. Principals, teachers, and parents are reluctant to have children miss too much class instruction for the sake of an experiment, meaning that most studies must be designed to be run as quickly as possible.

Working with preschoolers today presents similar opportunities and problems. Twenty years ago, more young children stayed at home, and there were few large groups of preschool children available for testing. Increasingly, however, "preschool" children spend a significant portion of their early years in some institutional setting, be it a day-care center or educational nursery school.

Work with newborns is often done in hospitals shortly after delivery, making the newborn, like the college sophomore, a captive audience. Once babies leave the hospital, however, finding them as research subjects can be difficult. Many scientists conduct research in the babies' homes. Others transport babies and mothers to their labs, or bring the labs to them

College psychology classes are a plentiful source of adult research subjects. Finding children is usually more difficult.

Development can be studied in two basic ways. In the longitudinal design (small photos), the same child is tested over a period of many years. In the cross-sectional design (large photo), children of different ages are tested a single time.

(using mobile trailers and renovated recreational vehicles). Still other research is done at day-care centers.

The problem of subject loss   Once a suitable sample of children has been found, the next step is getting them to cooperate. In any study, a few children will be unable or unwilling to complete the testing. Are those children who complete testing different in any way from those who do not? For example, in a study by Steven Friedman (1972), newborn infants demonstrated memory for a visual pattern over a brief interval. However, of 90 infants who began the study, 50 were excluded for reasons such as crying or falling asleep. Of the remaining 40 babies, memory was indicated in 29. What do these results say about the memory abilities of newborns? As Friedman noted, that depends on the characteristics of the 50 babies who never completed the task. If they are different from those infants who completed testing, it can affect the results of the experiment.

There are many reasons why infants and children may not complete a research project. Are children who complete testing different from children who

Box 2.3

Ethical Standards for Research with Children

The principles listed below were published in the Winter 1990 SRCD Newsletter and are a revision of the standards last included in the 1987 Directory.

Principle 1. *Non-harmful procedures:* The investigator should use no research operation that may harm the child either physically or psychologically. The investigator is also obligated at all times to use the least stressful research operation whenever possible. . . . When the investigator is in doubt about the possible harmful effects of the research operations, consultation should be sought from others. . . .

Principle 2. *Informed Consent:* Before seeking consent or assent from the child, the investigator should inform the child of all features of the research that may affect his or her willingness to participate and should answer the child's questions in terms appropriate to the child's comprehension. The investigator should respect the child's freedom to choose to participate in the research or not by giving the child the opportunity to give or not give assent to participation as well as to choose to discontinue participation at any time. . . . Investigators working with infants should take special effort to explain the research procedures to the parents and be especially sensitive to any indicators of discomfort in the infant. . . .

Principle 3. *Parental consent:* The informed consent of parents, legal guardians or those who act in loco parentis (e.g., teachers, superintendents of institutions) similarly should be obtained, preferably in writing. Informed consent requires that parents or other responsible adults be informed of all the features of the research that may affect their willingness to allow the child to participate. This information should include the profession and institution affiliation of the investigator. Not only should the right of the responsible adults to refuse consent be respected, but they should be informed that they may refuse to participate without incurring any penalty to them or to the child.

Principle 4. *Additional consent:* The informed consent of any persons, such as school teachers for example, whose interaction with the child is the subject of the study should also be obtained. . . .

Principle 5. *Incentives:* Incentives to participate in a research project must be fair and must not unduly exceed the range of incentives that the child normally experiences. . . .

Principle 6. *Deception:* Although full disclosure of information during the procedure of obtaining consent is the ethical ideal, a particular study may necessitate withholding certain information or deception. Whenever withholding information or deception is judged to be essential to the conduct of the study, the investigator should satisfy research colleagues that such judgment is correct. . . .

do not? Investigators have shown that in some cases, this appears to be true, with cooperative children showing different patterns of performance than less cooperative children (Bathurst & Gottfried, 1987). This means that developmental psychologists must keep in mind the children who do *not* complete their projects as well as those who do.

The Publication Process

Once a scientist has an idea, that idea must be translated into an experimental design, subjects found, and data collected and analyzed. Once the results

are in, they must be written in an appropriate form and then submitted to a journal for publication.[2] There are dozens of journals that publish research in child development. Several of the leading journals

[2]It is typically to journal articles that the phrase "publish or perish" refers. For university-based scientists, publishing best-selling books or popular magazine articles rarely counts for much in one's academic standing. When a developmental psychologist is hired to do research, the journal article is the finished product: it is the way his or her work becomes a part of the science. Unpublished research makes no contribution to the advancement of science. Thus, "publish or perish" applies not only to a person's career, but also to science itself.

Principle 7. *Anonymity:* To gain access to institutional records, the investigator should obtain permission from responsible authorities in charge of records. Anonymity of the information should be preserved and no information used other than that for which permission was obtained. . . .

Principle 8. *Mutual responsibilities:* From the beginning of each research investigation, there should be clear agreement between the investigator and the parents, guardians or those who act in loco parentis, and the child, when appropriate, that defines the responsibilities of each. The investigator has the obligation to honor all promises and commitments of the agreement.

Principle 9. *Jeopardy:* When, in the course of research, information comes to the investigator's attention that may jeopardize the child's well-being, the investigator has a responsibility to discuss the information with the parents or guardians and with those expert in the field in order that they may arrange the necessary assistance for the child.

Principle 10. *Unforeseen consequences:* When research procedures result in undesirable consequences for the participant that were previously unforeseen, the investigator should immediately employ appropriate measures to correct these consequences, and should redesign the procedures if they are to be included in subsequent studies.

Principle 11. *Confidentiality:* The investigator should keep in confidence all information obtained about research participants. The participants' identity should be concealed in written and verbal reports of the results, as well as in informal discussion with students and colleagues. . . .

Principle 12. *Informing participants:* Immediately after the data are collected, the investigator should clarify for the research participant any misconceptions that may have arisen. . . .

Principle 13. *Reporting results:* Because the investigator's words may carry unintended weight with parents and children, caution should be exercised in reporting results, making evaluative statements, or giving advice.

Principle 14. *Implications of findings:* Investigators should be mindful of the social, political and human implications of their research and should be especially careful in the presentation of findings from the research. This principle, however, in no way denies investigators the right to pursue any area of research or the right to observe proper standards of scientific reporting.

Source: As followed by members of the Society for Research in Child Development. Adapted from Winter 1990 *SRCD Newsletter.* Reprinted by permission.

publish mainly empirical research articles on a wide range of topics in child development. These include *Child Development,* published by the Society for Research in Child Development (SRCD), *Developmental Psychology,* published by the American Psychological Association (APA), and the *Journal of Experimental Child Psychology.* Many journals are more specialized, dealing·only with certain topics in development or child behavior (such as *Cognitive Development, Journal of Educational Psychology,* and *Journal of Child Language*) or with certain periods of development (such as *Infant Behavior and Development, Journal of Early Adolescence,* and *Ad-*

olescence). Others publish reviews of research and theoretical statements (such as *Developmental Review* and *Human Development*). Depending on the topic and findings, one (and only one) journal is selected, and the review process is begun.

The next step is the often long process of **peer review,** in which other professionals evaluate the merit of the research and make recommendations to the journal editor concerning whether or not the work should be published. Merely because someone has a Ph.D. does not mean that his or her research will automatically be published by a reputable scientific journal. In the major journals of the field,

Box 2.4

Diary of a Research Project

December 1981: We submit a research proposal concerning developmental differences in children's memory first to the Institutional Review Board at Florida Atlantic University, which determines that human subjects are not at risk, and then to the National Science Foundation and the Spencer Foundation.

June 1982: The Spencer Foundation approves the project and provides funds to support a research associate to conduct the studies.

June 1982–August 1982: We conduct several preliminary (or pilot) experiments and, based on the results, plan two new experiments. We write to the Palm Beach and Broward County, Florida, school boards, explaining our planned research, then follow up with phone calls to appropriate individuals.

September–December 1982: The school boards grant us permission to conduct research in the schools. We contact school principals, make appointments, explain the research plan, and request permission to work with students in their schools. Three of the four schools contacted approve our project; the fourth is overcrowded and has no place for us to work.

We prepare letters explaining the project, along with permission forms that parents must sign and

return if their children are to participate in the study. We meet with teachers, explain the nature of our project, and request that they pass out letters to the students. Approximately 70% of the children eventually return permission forms.

We begin research simultaneously on two experiments. One research associate, one graduate assistant, and one undergraduate assistant visit the schools daily and interview children one at a time. After testing 12 first-graders, 6 third-graders, and 6 fifth-graders, we examine our results and make some modifications in our procedures. Data collection continues with the modified procedures throughout the month of December.

January–June 1983: Data are tabulated and analyzed. The results are generally as we expected, although not exactly. We design a third experiment to provide a better test for our hypotheses.

August 1983: We contact principals (at different schools) and obtain permission to conduct research at their schools. We send permission letters, meet with teachers, and once letters are returned, begin testing.

September 1983–January 1984: We collect and analyze the new data, then write up the results of all three experiments in a single paper, which we sub-

only 10% to 30% of manuscripts submitted are eventually accepted for publication. In other words, between 70% and 90% of the research papers submitted to these journals are rejected. Although this does not ensure that only the best work ever gets published, it does mean that each piece of research gets a careful and critical look before it is published in an academic journal. Box 2.4 presents the chronology of one of our own research projects. Although not all research reports that are eventually published go through such an arduous process, most researchers would find this sequence of events familiar.

State of the Art
Being a Wise Consumer of Scientific Information

Completing an introductory course in child development should provide students with a good basic understanding of our science. It should also enable students to understand and evaluate information encountered in more advanced developmental courses, in the professional literature of related fields, and in the popular media—newspapers, magazines, and television. This last category has become a major source of scientific information, and those

mit to *Developmental Psychology* to be considered for publication.

April 16, 1984: The manuscript has been read by three anonymous reviewers. Reviewer A found some problems with our presentation, but believes the paper should be accepted for publication pending revision. Reviewer B believes the first two experiments are flawed and weak, but the third experiment is strong. Reviewer C thinks there are some problems in our interpretations. The editor tells us we can revise the manuscript and resubmit it if we believe we can adequately address the reviewers' concerns.

April–May 1984: We read the reviewers' comments carefully. We decide, reluctantly, to eliminate the first two experiments, realizing that they are detracting from the significance of the third experiment. We expand our rationale for certain manipulations, justifying why we chose to use certain procedures and why we interpreted the results as we did. The paper is revised and resubmitted to *Developmental Psychology* on May 25, 1984.

July 19, 1984: Two of the original reviewers have reread the manuscript, and their comments are returned to us. The editor writes, "In essence, both consultants agree you did an excellent job on the revision. However, they also judge that another revi-

sion is necessary . . . It seems quite clear that if you can successfully address the concerns raised by the consultants they will recommend 'accept,' if you can't they will recommend 'reject.' "

July–August 1984: We conduct two new analyses and also make some smaller changes suggested by the reviewers. We choose not to make some modifications that the reviewers suggested and explain our justification for these decisions in a letter to the editor. We submit the second revision on August 14, 1984.

September 17, 1984: The two original reviewers have reread the manuscript, and the editor writes, "Both consultants now judge that the manuscript should be accepted . . . and I am pleased to accept it for publication in *Developmental Psychology.*"

November 1985: The article is published in the November issue of *Developmental Psychology,* approximately four years after our original proposal and nearly two years after initial submission to *Developmental Psychology.*

Source: David F. Bjorklund and Barbara R. Bjorklund (1985). Organization versus item effects of an elaborated knowledge based on children's memory. *Developmental Psychology, 21,* 1120–1131.

who predict future trends say that it will remain so during the next decade (Naisbitt & Aburdene, 1990).

The publication of scientific news in the popular media reflects the trend of the 1970s and 1980s toward self-reliance. Instead of relying on experts, people began applying the "do-it-yourself" principle, using everything from home pregnancy tests to divorce kits. A society that can do desktop publishing and fix its own plumbing, the thinking goes, can certainly make its own decisions about scientific research.

Another reason scientific findings are released through the popular media is that the professional media are slow. A research project that has been completed, analyzed, reviewed, and accepted by a journal often has to wait six months to a year to reach the journal's subscribers. Textbooks take from six months to a year after the final draft is complete to get to the campus bookstores. In comparison, a newspaper article or TV spot can be released to the public in one or two days, and magazine articles can be out in a matter of weeks. Also, we must admit, science from the popular media is easier to understand than science from the journals; researchers are selected for their research skills, not necessarily their writing skills. As long as the information is written in standard English, research journals focus more on the content than the readability.

Faster dissemination of information in a more easily understood form is a valid reason, we believe, for publishing developmental science in the popular media. We applaud the personal involvement Americans have in their families' well-being, and we too are frustrated by the long publication delays of conventional science channels. In fact, if it weren't for the popular media, this textbook would not be as up to date as it is in several chapters—most notably, Chapter 3 on genetics.

However, there are a few aspects of developmental science in the popular media that we believe to be unfortunate and misleading. One of these problems is that developmental science is often not assigned to science writers, but to lifestyle writers who also cover fashion news and charity balls. It is difficult to summarize findings of developmental research properly if you don't have a science background.

According to Dr. Robert McCall, Director of the University of Pittsburgh Office of Child Development and Professor of Psychology, writers and editors invest more time and are more concerned with accuracy in articles about the "hard" sciences, such as physics and astronomy, and sometimes have the attitude that small mistakes in interpreting a "soft" science like psychology are of little consequence.

I argue, however, that just the opposite is true. People may be interested in the Great Red Spot of Jupiter, but the accuracy of new information about it does not cause them to change any part of their lives. Not so with scientific information about child development. People are interested in the topic and it relates *directly* to their lives. If anything, science reporting about child development should be more carefully done than science reporting for the "hard sciences." (R. B. McCall, personal communication, 1991)

We do not mean to imply that you can't trust anything you read, only that the research findings reported in the popular press must be carefully evaluated, using some of the information presented in this chapter. On what data are the reporter and scientist basing their conclusions? How was the study done? Were there proper control groups? Have the results of the study gone through the peer review process and been published in a journal? Although this process is one of the reasons it takes so long to get scientific information to the public, it is a safeguard that the work is reputable. This doesn't mean that journal articles are "absolute truth," but it does assure the public that the complete research article has been evaluated by a group of scientists and deemed worthy of publication. This is not necessarily so when a scientist publishes a book or presents research results at a conference or professional meeting. Popular books and conference papers rarely go through the same rigorous review process a journal article does.

What can be done to evaluate media coverage of developmental research? When the report is based on a journal article, the answer is simple: get a copy of the scientific journal in which it appeared. If the story in the popular media cites the journal, go to the library and make a copy of the article. If the library doesn't have that journal, get it through interlibrary loan. If the popular media article only gives the researcher's name, look him or her up in *Psychological Abstracts* or *Child Development Abstracts*. See what other research articles by that person have been published, and get the author's address. A letter to the scientist, or even a phone call, may get you the information you want.

We as a society have become highly dependent on science and technology. This is true not only for VCRs, CD players, and personal computers, but also for scientific information about children. As scientists, we are pleased that important information about development, education, and child rearing has a solid research base and that the public takes this research seriously. But science isn't easy, even when it deals with small, adorable children. One must be a knowledgeable consumer in order to get the most out of what developmental psychology has to offer, and that means understanding how science is done and how it is reported.

Summary

The scientific study of behavior requires the objective and reliable observation of children's behavior. Reliability refers to (a) interobserver reliability and (b) replicability. Scientific explanations are based on natural cause and effect, without the intervention of magical agents.

A theory is a form of explanation that organizes specific facts. Theories make predictions, generate research, and are modified or rejected as demanded by data.

In correlational studies, the relationship between two factors is assessed. Correlational research cannot make statements about cause and effect, only about how two factors vary with respect to each other. In experimental studies, the researcher manipulates one or more factors and assesses the effects on behavior. This permits the researcher to make some statement about cause and effect. Case studies and diaries are used by clinicians and other researchers and involve a detailed description of a single individual. They can be useful for generating hypotheses and examining conditions that it would be unethical to examine experimentally. Naturalistic studies evaluate children in their natural habitats. Clinical interviews (or the clinical method) involve an intense relationship between an examiner and a child. The clinical method, used extensively by the

Swiss psychologist Jean Piaget, can provide a researcher with insights into children's thinking.

Two techniques for studying change over time are the longitudinal method and the cross-sectional method. In longitudinal research, the same children are tested over an extended period of time, whereas in cross-sectional research different children are tested at each age of interest. Longitudinal designs permit the researcher to make statements about change within an individual, although they are costly in time and effort. Cross-sectional designs do not lend themselves to making statements about change within an individual, but are economical to run.

Finding children as research subjects and getting them to cooperate entail complications not faced by psychologists who study college students or laboratory animals. Doing research with children presents ethical considerations that are somewhat different from those faced by researchers doing research with animals or adults, and most child developmentalists follow the ethical standard of the Society for Research in Child Development. Once research has been completed, it is usually submitted to a professional journal where it undergoes the process of peer review.

Research on child development is often written about in the popular media by nonscience writers. A knowledge of methodology can help one evaluate and benefit from the results of scientific research.

Key Terms and Concepts

objectivity
reliability
    interobserver reliability
    replicability
theory
empirical research
    correlational studies
    experimental studies
    case studies and diaries
    naturalistic studies
    clinical interviews
longitudinal method
cross-sectional method
ethical standards
peer review

Two

The Beginnings of Development

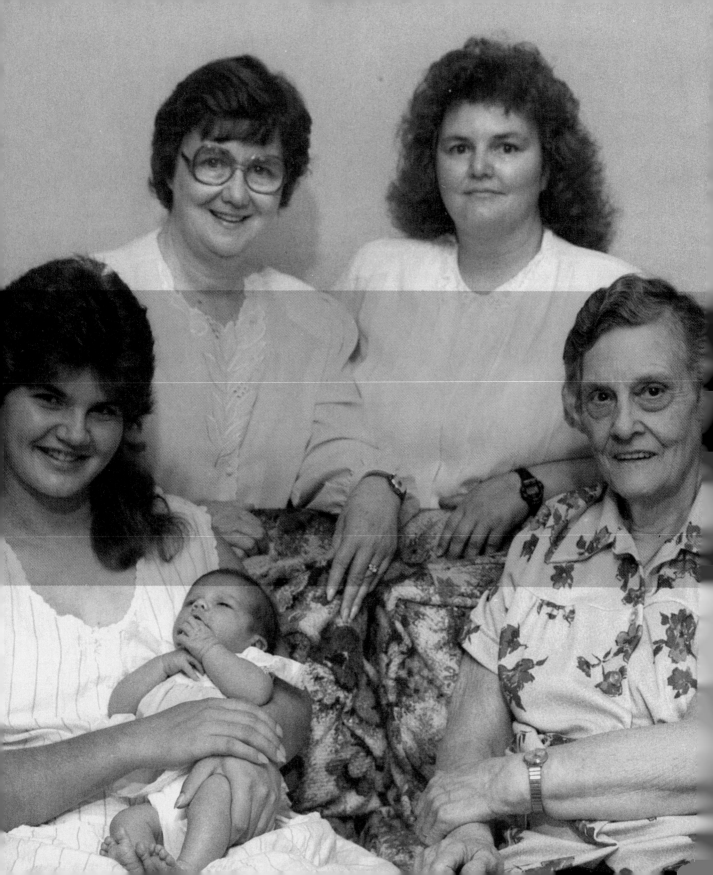

Genetics:
The Basis
of Development

The scene is a tidy house on a fall day in Holland, Michigan. Mildred van Dyke, a jovial woman of generous size, is welcoming people to her home. This is to be a three-day marathon of relatives visiting from various corners of the state. The smell of coffee comes from the tidy kitchen, and the World Series game is on the TV set in the family room. To the casual observer, it would seem like a typical family reunion, but a closer look shows an important difference.

As the relatives enjoy coffee and catching up on family news, one after another disappears into the basement for a half-hour or so and then returns to the activity upstairs. This gathering is not just a family reunion; it is one of Roger Kurlan's "Dracula parties." Kurlan is a neurologist who is collecting blood samples from members of families affected with Tourette's syndrome. Mildred van Dyke (not her real name) has a form of the disease, and so does her 12-year-old son.

Mildred's form of Tourette's syndrome involves repeated involuntary movements known as tics: she touches her cheek repeatedly as she talks and plucks at the front of her sweater. She is also a compulsive housekeeper, changing all the family bedsheets each morning and rearranging the clothes in the closets precisely each day. Mildred's son has a more obvious form of the disorder, which includes head-bobbing, lurching, jerking, and making belching sounds.

When Mildred's symptoms appeared in early adulthood, she believed that she was "going crazy." She went to several doctors, but none could make a diagnosis. When her son developed similar symptoms, she said, it almost broke her heart. By that time, enough information was available to diagnose the disorder as Tourette's syndrome. Now, Mildred says, if her son has to have it, she is glad she does, too, because not many unaffected parents could understand the condition.

Although Tourette's syndrome was identified a century ago, these tics and noises were not considered enough of a "condition" to study scientifically until recently. And when neurologists such as Roger Kurlan began studying them, little was known about their hereditary transmission. Now, because of research done with a half-dozen large families such as the van Dykes, patterns of genetic transmission for Tourette's syndrome are beginning to show up, and it is hoped that the blood samples and medical his-

tories of the family members will hold the key to understanding this chronic disorder.

The scientific study of inheritance is not just white lab coats, computers, and test tubes, Lois Wingerson (1990) reminds us as she describes the van Dyke "reunion" in her book, *Mapping Our Genes*. "These studies begin as they must with ordinary people" (p. 76).

The Study of Human Inheritance

Early Understandings

Although the term **gene** was not coined until 1909, humans have long been aware of heredity and have used its principles for more than 10,000 years to improve the quality of domesticated plants and animals. The early understanding of heredity was simple: "Like produces like" (Lush, 1951). The seedlings of tall wheat plants would be tall, and the pups of gentle dogs would be gentle. Of course there were exceptions, but this general rule of heredity worked for practical purposes and remained in effect for centuries.

There was not a tremendous amount of progress made in the study of heredity until the 17th and 18th centuries, when philosophers and scientists in Europe began pondering the place of humans in nature. One English family contributed more than its fair share to our understanding of genetics: Erasmus Darwin and his two grandsons, Charles Darwin and Sir Francis Galton. Erasmus Darwin promoted the idea that the traits of different species are "improved" by nature. According to the senior Darwin's thinking, farmers hadn't "invented" selective breeding, they had simply "discovered" a natural mechanism and directed it to their own purposes. Further study of this mechanism was taken up by the younger members of the family.

Charles Darwin Charles Darwin advanced this viewpoint with his work as a naturalist aboard a Royal Navy survey ship exploring the southern coast of South America. He was impressed, for example, with the variety of traits found in different species of finches. Each type had a different-shaped beak, which corresponded to the type of food available in its natural habitat. Darwin believed that the various species were descended from a common ancestor, and as they spread from island to island, they slowly evolved physical structures appropriate to the conditions present in their new surroundings.

This way of thinking was not new at the time. A group of scientists known as "natural theologists" had been collecting samples of species from all over the world. Their purpose was to show the wondrous design of nature—the Grand Design—and to argue that it could only be the product of God. In fact, it was for this purpose that Charles Darwin, trained as a theologian, had been hired to accompany the navy survey ship and gather samples on the voyage.

Darwin, however, hesitated to make his findings public as "natural theology." He had extended his ideas beyond the simple description of the great varieties found in nature. He had begun to believe that all species evolved one from another and, furthermore, that scientists could find the mechanism of this natural evolution without simply attributing it to "the Grand Designer."

Charles Darwin finally published his book *On the Origin of Species* in 1859. It had an immediate impact on the scientific community and is considered by many today to be one of the most important books ever written. The crux of the theory is that many more members of a species are born in each generation than will survive. They all have different combinations of inherited traits; that is, there is substantial variation among members of a species. Conditions in the environment for that particular generation cause some members of the species to survive and reproduce, while others do not—a process that Darwin referred to as "natural selection" (Mayr, 1982). The inherited traits of the survivors will be passed on to the next generation of that species, whereas the traits of the nonsurvivors will not. Through this mechanism, over the course of many generations, the predominant traits of a species will change.

Sir Francis Galton Another grandson of Erasmus Darwin, and first cousin to Charles Darwin, was Francis Galton. He was already well known as a geographer, explorer, and inventor when *On the Origin of Species* was published. After reading it, he wrote to Charles Darwin to thank him "in the same way converts from barbarism" thank a missionary for freeing them from their old superstitions and giving them freedom of thought. Galton's words of praise were not empty ones. He turned his immense curiosity and energy to a lifetime study of the inheritance of human mental abilities (Pearson, 1924).

Within five years, Galton had published two magazine articles on inherited human talents and characteristics and had started a book on hereditary genius. The major thrust of his work was that some families have a greater number of talented and accomplished individuals than would be expected by chance.

To fully appreciate Galton's pioneering spirit, one must consider his accomplishments in the context of his time. He gathered enormous amounts of data in an era when standard measurements did not exist. To measure such diverse human abilities as taste, smell, hearing, judgment of the vertical, discrimination of weight, and memory span, he devised tests, equipment, and controlled procedures. To arrange his data into meaningful statistics, he invented the concepts of the mean, correlations, and percentiles. And to measure vast numbers of people, he set up a booth at the 1884/85 International Health Exhibit in London, where more than 9,000 individuals paid for the privilege of being subjects in his research. He repeated his tests again at the Chicago World's Fair in 1893 (Hilgard, 1987). Galton later offered cash prizes for "careful and complete" family records he could examine for evidence of inherited characteristics (Plomin, DeFries, & McClearn, 1990).

How good were Galton's data, gathered with these innovated, unproven methods? Today's researchers tell us that his data were highly reliable and, a century later, still provide the only information available on some types of sibling resemblance (Johnson, McClearn, Yuen, Nagoshi, Ahern, & Cole, 1985). Galton also pioneered the use of twins and adopted individuals to assess the role of nature versus nurture in behavior. As with several other prominent figures in the history of developmental psychology, Galton's methods were probably more important than his findings. However, Galton is considered by many to be the father of behavioral genetics, a field closely related to developmental psychology.

Exceptions to the rule of heredity When the subject of heredity progressed from the farmyards into the laboratory, the general rule "Like produces like" was found lacking. A corollary became apparent: "Like does not always produce like" (Lush, 1951). Although farmers were unconcerned with the exceptions to the rule, scientists were not. They wanted to know more. How does this happen? Is there a pattern? One late-19th-century idea was that of blending: the traits of parents were averaged in their offspring. Tall father and short mother would have children of average height; black sheep and white sheep would have gray offspring. If blending occurred, however, why weren't all members of a species "average" after a few generations? Why and how did some traits show up in a generation of offspring when neither parent displayed that trait?

Gregor Mendel   The key to solving these dilemmas was found in the research of a Moravian monk, Gregor Mendel—although his work was not discovered by the scientific community for some 40 years. Mendel's work was a masterpiece of methodical research and carefully formulated conclusions. Working in the garden of his monastery in what is now Czechoslovakia, Mendel spent years growing pea plants and recording the traits that appeared in successive generations. In 1865 (six years after Darwin's *On the Origin of Species* and the same year as Galton's *Hereditary Genius*), Mendel presented a research report to the National Science Society of Brunn, Moravia, detailing his findings. Society members were so impressed that they published a written report of his work in their journal the next year. Surprisingly, few took notice of the article, including Darwin and Galton. In fact, there is evidence that Charles Darwin had an unopened letter from Mendel in his files as he wrote some of his later papers (Allen, 1975).

Mendel's findings were the basis for two laws. The first was the **law of segregation,** which states that for each inherited trait there are two elements of heredity. These elements segregate during reproduction so that an offspring receives either one element or the other, never some blend of both. Thus, according to this law inherited traits are passed down in segregated, unblended form from generation to generation. True varieties remain, and the blending of traits to produce "universal averageness" does not happen. The second was the **law of independent assortment,** which states that when two traits of a parent are considered (such as height of plant and color of flower), each trait is inherited independently. In other words, according to this second law inheritance of one trait does not affect inheritance of another.

Mendel's first paper was followed by a second four years later, in 1870. After that, Mendel became involved in dealing with the tax problems of the monastery and died in 1884 without resuming his research. It was not until 1900 that three biologists, working independently, made discoveries similar to Mendel's. While looking at records of past research, they discovered Mendel's articles, and being true gentlemen and scholars, they gave him credit in their research papers. Within two years Sir Archibald Garrod had applied Mendel's principles to humans, and within a decade he had identified several disorders that were transmitted according to Mendelian genetics (albinism and several metabolic disorders) (Pierce, 1990). The rest, as they say, is history. Mendel is now generally considered to be the father of genetics, and his laws of segregation and independent assortment, with some exceptions, remain at the foundation of today's scientific knowledge (Plomin, DeFries, & McClearn, 1990).

Today's Science of Heredity

Although knowledge of genetics has progressed dramatically since the early 1900s, the fundamentals of Mendelian inheritance have formed the basis of the science of human heredity, which is widely used today in research and in genetic counseling.

Genotypes and phenotypes   Basically, our inherited traits are determined by pairs of genes. Most inherited human traits are determined by more than one pair of genes, but in order to simplify explanation, we will consider hair color (red versus nonred), which may be determined by one gene pair. Although each person has two genes for hair color, only one color will be expressed. The two genes a person has for a trait are that person's **genotype,** and the actual expression of the trait is his or her **phenotype.** For example, an individual may have two red genes for hair color, two nonred genes, or one of each, constituting his or her genotype for hair color. The phenotype may be either red or nonred. (See Figure 3.1.)

Dominant and recessive traits   It is easy to predict that individuals with the genotype red/red will have the phenotype red and that individuals with the genotype nonred/nonred will express the phenotype

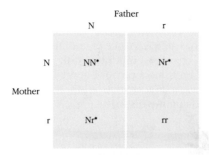

Father

N   r

	N	r
N	NN•	Nr•
r	Nr•	rr

Mother

N = Dominant gene for nonred hair
r = Recessive gene for red hair
• = Nonred hair in the phenotype

Figure 3.1 Genotype versus phenotype for red/nonred hair. Both mother and father have nonred hair (phenotype) but carry the recessive gene for red hair. They can expect three-fourths of their offspring to have nonred hair and only one-fourth (those with two recessive genes, rr) to have red hair.

nonred. But what happens when the genotype is mixed—when one gene is for red and one is for nonred? The answer is that one member of the genotype will be **dominant** and the other **recessive,** and the dominant trait will be expressed in the phenotype. In the case of hair color, nonred is the dominant trait. When an individual has the genotype red/nonred, the nonred gene will dominate the red gene, and the phenotype will be nonred. In general, the only way a recessive trait such as red hair can be expressed in the phenotype is if a person has two recessive genes.

Genes and development   What determines an individual's genotype? Where does this pair of genes come from? The answer is that, generally speaking, one gene of each pair comes from the person's biological mother and the other from his or her biological father. The complete genetic makeup of an individual is set at conception and is present in the nucleus of each cell in his or her body (with the exception of the ova cells in females and the sperm cells in males).

Some genes determine fetal development and others are expressed throughout the lifespan. Through research on patterns of human inheritance, scientists have found that genes influence our physical appearance and well-being (hair, eye, and skin color; height and weight; patterns of maturation and aging; and susceptibility to certain diseases), as well as our personalities, intelligence, and talents (see Bouchard, Lykken, McGue, Segal, & Tellegen, 1990; Plomin, 1989).

The area of inheritance that has been most widely researched is the genetic transmission of certain disorders within families, with the goal of giving family members information about their chances of passing on this disorder to their children. We will examine two such disorders and how they are transmitted.

Tay Sachs disease and inheritance of recessive traits
Tay Sachs disease was discovered in 1887 by an American physician named Bernard Sachs. Infants with Tay Sachs disease appear normal at birth but fail to develop muscle control or intellectual ability. After the first year, they lose any developmental progress they have made, become blind and deaf, are unable to eat, and die before the age of 3. Sachs found that this disorder had been described by English physician Warren Tay a few years previously, and he acknowledged this by naming the disorder Tay Sachs disease.

Like red hair, Tay Sachs disease is transmitted genetically from parent to child by a single gene (see Figure 3.2). The gene can be either Tay Sachs or non-Tay Sachs. Because the non-Tay Sachs gene is dominant, only the genotype of two Tay Sachs genes will result in the Tay Sachs phenotype.

It should be apparent that in order for children to express a recessive trait (whether red hair or Tay Sachs disease), they must receive *two* genes for that trait. This means that both parents must have those genes in their genotypes, and both must pass them along to their children. When the trait is a harmless one such as red hair, the chances are greater that the trait will be passed on—first because it occurs more frequently in the population, and second because it is possible for one or both parents to have both genes for that trait (for example, red/red) and still be healthy. Traits such as Tay Sachs disease occur less frequently in the population, and no adults have two Tay Sachs genes in their genotype because such individuals will not survive beyond infancy.

Environmental factors also play a part in Tay Sachs disease. First, most people who carry a gene for Tay Sachs disease come from a certain part of the world (Eastern Europe) and belong to a certain religion (Ashkenazi Judaism) that encourages its members to marry within the group. The result is a greater number of Tay Sachs carriers living in the same area and marrying other Tay Sachs carriers than would be expected if individuals in the world population were paired by chance. One in 30 members of this group is a carrier for Tay Sachs, and one in 3600 Ashkenazi infants was born with this disorder before widespread genetic testing began in 1977.

Most of the debilitating inherited disorders are transmitted in this way by *recessive* genes, making it unlikely that they will be passed on to the next generation in great numbers. If neither parent or only one parent carries the gene, none of the children will be afflicted. If both parents carry the gene, a child has a 25% chance of not inheriting either gene; a 50% chance of inheriting only one recessive gene, thus becoming a carrier but not having the disorder; and only a 25% chance of inheriting both genes and expressing the disorder.

Traits that follow recessive pattern of inheritance
   Albinism: lack of skin pigment
   Alopecia: general loss of body hair
   Baldness: pattern baldness (head only) in females
   Blindness: some types
   Blood type: RH positive

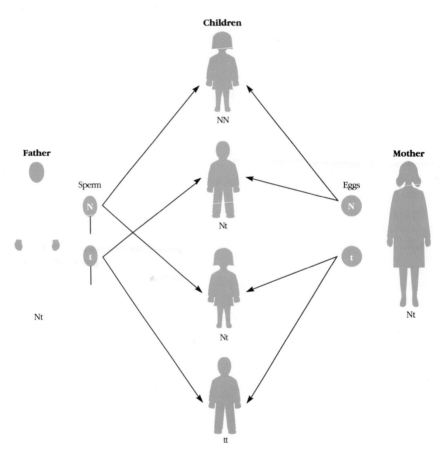

Figure 3.2 Genetic transmission of Tay Sachs disease, a recessive trait. N = dominant, non-Tay Sachs gene; t = recessive, Tay Sachs gene. People with Nt do not have Tay Sachs but are carriers for the disease. Only people with two recessive genes (tt) are afflicted with the disease.

Cretinism: some types caused by lack of thyroid enzymes

Cystic fibrosis: metabolism disorder of mucous producing glands

Deafness: some types that are present at birth (40–60%)

Dwarfism: some types

Galactosemia: lack of enzyme to digest milk

Hurler's syndrome: fatal enzyme deficiency

Meckel's syndrome: multiple birth defects

PKU: lack enzyme to neutralize digestion waste in blood

Sickle-cell anemia: defect in blood hemoglobin

Tay Sachs disease: fatal inability to develop muscle control or intellectual ability

Thalassemia major: various defects in blood hemoglobin

Wilson's disease: inability to metabolize copper

Few debilitating disorders are transmitted on dominant genes because any individual who has the gene present in his or her genotype will have the disorder and will usually not live to pass it on to the next generation. A notable exception to this rule—a dominant trait that is extremely debilitating and yet has continued to be transmitted to new generations—is **Huntington's disease.**

Huntington's disease and inheritance of dominant traits Huntington's disease, first identified by George Huntington in 1872, causes devastating neurological deterioration. It usually appears in middle age with personality changes, followed by movement disorders, mental deterioration, and death. Because it does not usually appear until an individual is well into childbearing age, the gene can be transmitted to the next generation before parents are aware that they have the disorder themselves.

Because the Huntington's disease gene is dominant, an individual who has the gene in the genotype will exhibit the disorder (see Figure 3.3). Furthermore, only one parent with the gene is necessary for transmitting the disorder to the next generation. When one parent has the Huntington's disease gene, each child has a 50% chance of inheriting that gene and developing the disease in adulthood.

By studying the pedigrees of families with Huntington's disease, one could fairly easily predict which family members had the 50–50 chance of expressing the disorder in middle adulthood. The difficult part was for that person to decide whether to take the chance of having children who might also be afflicted. Tests are now available to determine if an individual has the Huntington's gene, and counseling is given both before and after the tests. It is hoped that new techniques will soon lead to an intervention in the disease process.

Traits that follow dominant pattern of inheritance

Alzheimer's disease: early onset, some families

Asthma: some families

Baldness: male pattern (head only)

Blindness: some types

Blood type: RH negative

Breast cancer: almost all male forms, some female forms (about 10% of all breast cancers)

Brittle bone disease: defect in collagen production

Colon and rectal cancer: predisposition for

Color blindness (blue/green): defect in blue pigment receptors

Deafness: 20–30% of deafness present at birth

Dwarfism: some types

Dysplastic nevi: large number and variety of moles, may lead to severe form of skin cancer, melanoma

Finger abnormalities: extra digits, abnormally short, webbed

Hemophilia: one type known as von Willibrand's disease

Huntington's disease: adult-onset neurological deterioration

Marfan's syndrome: defect in connective tissue

Neurofibromatosis: multiple tumors along nerves

Polygenic Inheritance

Mendelian genetics describes well how genes interact to produce a particular outcome. They describe how a single set of genes affects the phenotype, such as hair color and some inherited diseases. Most physical and psychological characteristics, however, are *not* under the influence of a single pair of genes. Rather, our intelligence, personalities, and even our height and weight are influenced by many different genes. This type of influence, or **polygenic inheritance,** is the rule rather than the exception.

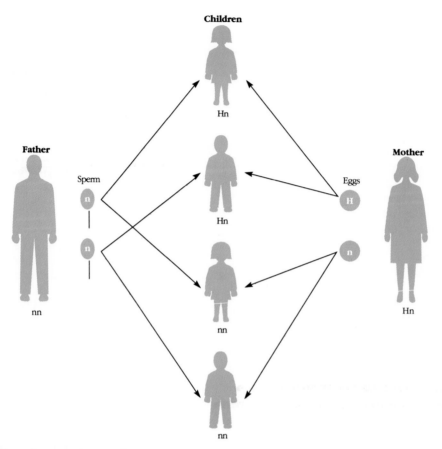

Figure 3.3 Genetic transmission of Huntington's disease, a dominant trait. H = dominant gene for Huntington's; n = recessive, non-Huntington's gene. Because the gene for Huntington's disease is dominant, only one gene (Hn) is necessary for a person to be afflicted with the disease.

Traits that are inherited but pattern is yet unknown

Alcoholism (type 1): begins well into adulthood and involves periods of drinking interspersed with periods of abstinence (males and females). Genetic predisposition plus environmental influences seem to be involved.

Alcoholism (type 2): begins in adolescence and involves aggression, arrests, and antisocial behavior (males). Genetics seems to play a bigger part, with male children of type 2 alcoholics being 9 times more likely than other males to be type 2 alcoholics themselves.

Allergies

Alzheimer's disease: most cases of early onset

Anorexia nervosa and bulimia: may be linked with inheritance of depression

Congenital heart defects

Coronary artery disease

Depression: bipolar and unipolar

Diabetes: juvenile onset and maturity onset. Both tend to run in families, but as separate diseases.

Down syndrome (translocation)

Dyslexia

Epilepsy

Eye color

Glaucoma

Hair color

Height
High blood pressure
Left-handedness
Nearsightedness
Neural tube defects: spina bifida, anencephaly
Obesity
Premature death from natural causes, especially
    infection
Psoriasis
Rheumatoid arthritis
Schizophrenia

Sleepwalking
Stuttering
Twins: fraternal

Having an appreciation of Mendelian genetics helps us understand how many debilitating diseases are acquired and has given biologists insights into the complexities of inheritance. But there is no single gene for intelligence or personality or athletic excellence; these complex traits are multiply determined, with environment also playing a crucial role.

Box 3.1

Why Are Genetic Diseases So Common?

Genetic diseases such as Tay Sachs lead to an early death. Infants unfortunate enough to inherit two recessive genes for Tay Sachs do not grow up to reproduce, and it has only been in this century, with the help of modern medicine, that children afflicted with diseases such as sickle-cell anemia or thalassemia are likely to live to adulthood. The question that many people have asked themselves is "Why haven't these death-dealing genes disappeared?" Evolution is supposed to favor characteristics that enhance the chances of a species' surviving. Obviously, genes that lead to early death don't do much for the survival of the individual who possesses the genes, and they don't get passed on by that person to the next generation. Why, then, do they persist?

One possibility is that they arise anew in every generation through mutations. However, we know the inheritance pattern of most genetic diseases: they run in families. They rarely happen "out of the blue," as would be expected if they were the result of random mutations. Also, known mutations are relatively rare and could not account for the high frequency with which genetic diseases occur.

A more likely possibility is that there is some survival advantage associated with having these disease-causing genes, either for the person with the disease

or for people who are carriers for the disease. That is, having the gene for the disease may convey some benefit that offsets its harmful effects.

There is one genetic disease for which there is good evidence that this is so: *sickle-cell anemia*. Sickle-cell anemia, like Tay Sachs, occurs only when a person has two recessive genes for the disease. The disease interferes with the transport of oxygen in the blood. The red blood cells, normally disk-shaped, are distorted and shaped like a sickle, or half-moon. This is most apt to occur upon exposure to low levels of oxygen. Because of their shape, the sickle cells tend to pile up and block small blood vessels, resulting in pain and destruction of tissue (Pierce, 1990).

Sickle-cell anemia is found primarily among people of central African descent. Among American blacks, about one in 625 children is born with the sickle-cell trait. It has been estimated that nearly 10% of American blacks carry the sickle-cell gene (that is, have one recessive sickle-cell gene and one dominant normal gene) (Pierce, 1990). In some parts of Africa, the frequency of carriers is as high as 40% (Diamond, 1989).

Although having two recessive sickle-cell genes
(Continued)

Current Research Tools for Studying Human Inheritance

Human inheritance can be approached from a variety of perspectives, and one does not necessarily need a Ph.D. in biochemistry to develop an understanding of human heredity. In fact, much of what is important about inheritance for the layperson and behavioral scientist alike can be understood by looking at patterns of characteristics among families. For some types of analyses, complicated statistics are necessary; for others, they are not. In all cases, patterns of human inheritance tell us important things about genetic transmission. How these patterns are passed on from one generation to the next is the job of the biochemist, but discerning the pattern falls within the scope of modern psychology.

Family Pedigree Charts

Charts using standardized symbols to show biological relationships within a family and incidence of inherited traits date back to Galton's time and are still used today (see Figure 3.4). These **family**

Box 3.1 (Continued)

means having the disease, and in the past the probability of an early death, having just one recessive gene provides some benefit. People with a *single* sickle-cell gene have a significant advantage over people who have *no* sickle-cell gene where malaria is common: because their red blood cells are poor at supporting the growth of the malaria parasite, they are less likely to die of the disease. Carriers in these areas are thus more likely to live to reproduce than noncarriers, keeping the gene in the gene pool. The benefit is not to those who have the disease, but to those who are carriers (Pierce, 1990).

There has been speculation that other genetic diseases may afford some advantages to carriers, keeping the recessive genes from becoming extinct (Diamond, 1989). For example, being a carrier for thalassemia—a blood disease that occurs predominantly in people of Mediterranean, Africa, and Asian descent—may also provide some protection against malaria. Having a single recessive gene for Tay Sachs disease may have helped fight against tuberculosis, a leading killer centuries ago, especially in the urban ghettos where many European Jews (the main target of Tay Sachs) were confined. The gene for cystic fibrosis—the most common recessive genetic disease among whites—may protect carriers against bacterial infections that cause diarrhea, a major childhood killer in the past (and in parts of the underdeveloped world today).

It is also possible that a person afflicted with a genetic disease may reap some advantage from his or her recessive genes. One advantage may be to increase the likelihood of ever being born. For example, parents who are carriers for a form of diabetes (that is, one normal gene and one that predisposes the person toward diabetes) should be equally likely to have children who carry the normal gene as they are to have children who carry the diabetes gene. Of infants actually born to such parents, however, up to 72% have the diabetes gene, rather than the 50% that would be expected (Diamond, 1989). This suggests that having the diabetes gene provides some protection against miscarriage. In a sense, the cost of being born was paid by having a gene that predisposes one to diabetes.

Genetic diseases, particularly those that strike children, seem cruelly unfair. Some of these diseases may reflect a grim "deal" evolution has made with us. The genes responsible for these calamities may have helped our ancestors or our current relatives survive; or they may have made it possible for us to be born at all.

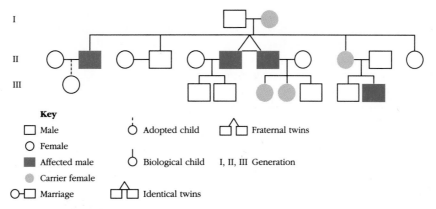

Figure 3.4 Example of a family pedigree chart: transmission of red/green color blindness in three generations.

pedigree charts have become increasingly important as more and more disorders are found to follow inherited patterns.

Central Registries for Inherited Diseases

Another approach to the study and early detection of inherited disorders is having a central registry in which information is collected about the families of individuals who have a particular disorder. Once the pattern of inheritance is ascertained, family members who appear at risk for the disorder can begin early detection procedures and hopefully prevent occurrence of the disorder.

One central registry has recently been instituted by the Gilda Radner Ovarian Cancer Foundation. Actor Gene Wilder, husband of the late comedienne, sponsors a drive to collect information about patients with ovarian cancer in hopes of identifying young women whose inheritance puts them at risk for the disorder, as Gilda's did, and warning them to have early examinations and early treatment, as she did not. Other central registries for inherited disorders include the National High Risk Registry at the Strang Breast Cancer Institute, New York City, and the National Familial Brain Tumor Registry at Johns Hopkins Oncology Center in Baltimore.

The Twin Study Method

Begun by Galton in the 19th century, the **twin study method** is still used to determine the degree of inheritance involved in various disorders. By investigating the similarity of occurrence of a disorder in people of different degrees of genetic similarity, we can get a measure of the degree to which a certain trait is inherited.

The least related people within a population are two individuals chosen at random from a large sample—"two strangers who pass on the street." Next in line would be distantly related individuals such as cousins, then more closely related individuals such as parent/child and siblings, and finally identical twins (who share the same genetic inheritance). To determine the extent to which a trait is inherited, various statistics can be applied to measurements taken of pairs of people with different degrees of relatedness. One frequently used statistic is a **concordance rate,** which is found by examining pairs of people in different categories of relatedness when one member of the pair has the trait. The concordance rate is the percentage of second members of the pair who also have the trait. When identical twins have significantly higher concordance rates than less-related pairs, it is an indication that the trait is influenced more by inheritance than by environment.

Another frequently used statistic for determining the inheritedness of a trait is the correlation (see Chapter 2). In this application, individual measurements are taken of pairs of people in two or more groups who differ in degree of relatedness. For example, for the trait of height, the correlation between identical twins is about .90 (1.0 is perfect). This means that if you know the height of one twin, you can predict very accurately the height of the second twin. The correlation between nonidentical

Identical twins (left) share the complete genetic inheritance, whereas fraternal twins (right) share only half. The effects of this difference become more apparent with age.

twins for height is about .50. This means you can predict reasonably well the height of one twin by knowing the height of the other, but not nearly so well as you can for identical twins. The correlations for height between randomly selected, unrelated people is 0. Height is a good example of a trait that is substantially influenced by heredity, and this is reflected in the pattern of correlations obtained between people of different degrees of relatedness.

Of course, identical twins have more in common than their genetic makeup; they also share almost

identical environments. However, fraternal twins make a good control group for concordance studies as well as correlational studies. They share the same environment, as identical twins do, but not the same genes. Most of the studies that set out to investigate the contribution of inheritance to a particular trait partially control for environmental differences by comparing concordance rates or correlations of identical twins with those of fraternal twins.

In the United States, the National Academy of Sciences maintains a database of information on about

16,000 male twins born between 1917 and 1927 who served in the armed services during World War II and the Korean War (Hrubec & Neel, 1978). Other large data banks are available in Finland, Sweden, and Norway. These registries have been used to investigate inherited patterns of many disorders and are available to researchers today.

The ideal way to examine the role of genetics versus environment is to have a comparison group of individuals with the same genetic makeup but different environments—in other words, identical twins who were adopted at birth by two different sets of parents and raised without contact with each other. Unlikely as this sounds, a small group (several hundred) of these individuals has been used in U.S. research projects in Minnesota (Bouchard, 1984; Bouchard, Lykken, McGue, Segal, & Tellegen, 1990), in Sweden (Pederson, Friberg, Floderus-Myrhed, McClearn, & Plomin, 1984), and in Finland (Langinvainio, Koskenvuo, Kaprio, & Sistonen, 1984). The findings of these and other studies with respect to the inheritance of certain behavioral characteristics will be discussed later in this chapter.

Adoption Studies

Another way to investigate the role of inheritance versus environment is through **adoption studies,** which compare similarity of biological mother/child pairs with similarity of adoptive mother/child pairs. Mothers share similar environments with their children, regardless of biological relatedness, but they share similar genes only with their biological children, not their adopted children. When concordance rates or correlations for biologically related pairs are higher than for pairs related by adoption, the trait is considered to be more a result of heredity; when the rates are similar, the trait may be more a result of environment.

A valuable source for this type of study is found in countries such as Denmark and Sweden, which keep detailed records on many aspects of the lives of their citizens, including identification of the biological parents of adopted children. Through these records, researchers have been able to show that some disorders, such as alcoholism and schizophrenia, follow patterns of biological relatedness more than they follow patterns of environmental relatedness. Thus, the biological child of an alcoholic parent has a greater chance of suffering from alcoholism than does the biological child of a nonalcoholic individual—regardless of whether the child grows up in an alcoholic family or a nonalcoholic family (Bohman, Cloninger, Sigvardsson, & von Knorring, 1987). The same pattern has been found for obesity (see Pierce, 1990): adopted children are more similar in their weight tendencies to their biological parents than to their adoptive parents.

The Concept of Heritability

Heritability refers to the extent to which differences in any trait within a population can be attributed to inheritance. Heritability is expressed as a statistic that ranges from 0 (none of the difference in a trait is attributed to inheritance) to 1.0 (100% of the difference in a trait is attributed to inheritance). It is not necessary for our purposes to explain how the statistic is computed, merely that it reflects the proportion of variance (difference) in an observed trait that is due to genetic variability.

Heritability is a population statistic, in that it describes average differences among people within a population. It does not tell us "how much" of any one person's intelligence or height or personality characteristics can be attributed to genetic factors (that is, "how much" of one's height is inherited). Rather, it tells us only what percentage of the difference in a trait within a specific population can be attributed to inheritance, on average. This is not always an easy concept to grasp, but it is a very important one.

For purposes of illustration, assume that individual differences in height are due to two factors and two factors only: inheritance and diet. On the mythical island Louie-Louie, every person receives 100% of his or her nutritional needs (no one receives more). The average height of men on Louie-Louie is 6 feet. If you were to meet two men from this island, one 6 feet 1 inch tall and the other 5 feet 11 inches tall, 100% of the 2-inch difference in their height would be attributed to inheritance. Heritability would be 1.0. The reason is that the environments (in this case, diets) are homogeneous, or perfectly identical. No differences in environments exist; therefore, any difference in height between people must be attributed to inheritance.

What would happen if a famine hit the island, changing the diet of the people and thus the average height from 6 feet to, say, 5 feet 10 inches? If the change were uniform (for example, everyone received 75% of his or her nutritional needs), the heritability would still be 1.0. Although the environment has changed drastically, it has changed equally for everyone. Thus, because the environments remain homogeneous, 100% of the difference in height between people can still be attributed to inheritance.

If the effects of the famine were not uniform, however, the picture would change. If some people still received 100% of their nutritional needs, others 75%, and still others only 50%, when you met two men from Louie-Louie who differed by 2 inches in height you would know that, on average, some proportion of this difference must be attributed to differences in diet. That is, heritability has changed to something less than 1.0—say, .60. The more heterogeneous, or different, the environments are, the lower heritability will be. Heritability is thus relative, varying with the environmental conditions in which people within the population live.

If heritability for height were .60, this would *not*

Box 3.2

Doing Research in Rumania on the Inheritance of Depression

Dr. Maria Grigoroiu-Serbanescu
Institute of Neurology and Psychiatry,
Bucharest, Rumania

In 1985 we were surprised by American scientific reports of high rates of overall psychopathology and affective disorders (especially major depression) among children of affectively ill parents and children of normal parents. We decided to perform a ten-year follow-up study of high risk types in our own population, keeping in mind the well-known assumption in population genetics that different populations may have different rates of disorder and risk.

For the first stage of the study we selected 65 families in which one parent was a manic-depressive (bipolar or BP) patient. These families included 104 proband children aged 10–17. We matched a control sample of 104 children with the probands according to sex, age, and socio-cultural background, but these children came from families in which both parents were psychiatrically normal. (Published data in the *Journal of Affective Disorders, 16,* 1989, 167–179, reported on only 47 BP families with 72 children and 61 control families with 72 children.) A second sample of proband children consisted of 96 offspring aged 10–17 of endogenous unipolar depressive (UP) parents and 96 control children of normal parents.

Methods

A problem in past studies has been that "normal" families may be hiding mental illness. For the two control groups, we asked the employers and social service workers of two large businesses, a school, and a hospital to suggest names of long-term employees who were not known to suffer from mental disorders and who matched a proband family in profession, education, and age and sex of their children. (We used employers and social service workers because they have access to employees' hospitalization and sick leave records.) After the recommended persons agreed to participate in the study, our research staff interviewed them and their spouses, eliminating as subjects those in whom psychiatric diagnoses were nevertheless made.

In order to get comparable results we used American diagnostic criteria and American psychiatric interviews along with investigative tools we developed, including personality inventories and scales to measure disorders, psychosocial functioning, parental attitudes, and familial atmosphere.

Our approach differed from previous high risk studies of affective disorders in that we investigated

mean that 60% of one's height was inherited—that if a person is 5 feet tall, 3 of those feet are inherited and 2 feet are due to diet. It means that, on average, 60% of the differences in height between people are due to inheritance.

The concept of heritability is the same regardless of whether one is studying height, intelligence, temperament, political affiliation, or any other physical or psychological characteristic. One difference, however, between physical attributes such as height and psychological attributes such as intelligence or personality is that of measurement. When one ex-

presses height in terms of inches or meters, one is relatively confident that the measure accurately reflects the underlying concept. There is less confidence with many psychological concepts.

All about Chromosomes

Chromosomes and Human Inheritance

Long before the beginning of this century, scientists had agreed that the basic unit of living things was the cell, and technology was developed to improve

both parents (when available) of proband and control offspring. In our psychiatric and psychological investigation of the children, we used multiple sources of information: both parents, other close relatives, teachers' reports, and the child's own testimony. A psychiatrist who was unaware of the mental status of the parents made the final diagnoses of the children.

Findings

Psychic disorders reached significantly higher rates in children of BP and UP parents than in children of normal parents. Our global rates of psychopathology, which ranged from 61% to 48% in proband children, were comparable with American rates. But the rates of depressive disorders were much lower in our proband and control samples (10%–12% in the proband groups and 2%–5% in the control groups).

The best predictors of a child's psychopathological status were the severity of the illness in the affectively ill parent and age at onset; the psychopathologic status of the other parent; the presence of the psychopathology in the relatives of both parents; a violent familial atmosphere; and low economic status. The psychopathologic risk was increased for the children if anxious symptoms ac-

companied depressive episodes of the unipolar depressive parent, and if the affected parent was the mother.

Challenges

One general problem in doing family studies is that it is difficult to persuade both normal and psychiatrically disturbed families to participate. In Rumania (as elsewhere) there is a social stigma attached to being "mad." Some parents are afraid to learn that their children might be at risk for psychic disorders, and when their fears are confirmed they develop guilty feelings toward their children and spouses. It is also difficult to find truly normal families for the control groups, because likely candidates often turn out to be hiding psychiatric and psychological disorders.

Finally, a family longitudinal study is expensive, and funding for research in our country was poor during the Ceausescu regime. Our study has therefore been supported largely by the members of the research team, who have paid for transportation to the subjects' homes, their investigative tools and technical research devices, and for the necessary literature.

microscopes and staining techniques to study the cell and its components more closely. It was found that each cell nucleus contained a collection of rod-shaped bodies and that the number of bodies, or **chromosomes,** was constant in all cells of an individual organism. Different species had different numbers of chromosomes, and all members of the same species had the same number of chromosomes. Scientists soon decided that these chromosomes played an important part in heredity.

During the 1930s the chromosomes of fruit flies were carefully detailed, but for some reason human chromosomes were not a topic of interest. Until the 1950s, in fact, students were taught that humans had 48 chromosomes instead of 46 (Tijo & Levan, 1956).

The 46 human chromosomes (see Figure 3.5) come in 23 pairs and contain vast amounts of genetic material. The information contained in those genes directs our prenatal development from a single-celled zygote to a fully developed infant, directs our postnatal development from infancy through adulthood, and plays an important role in determining our appearance, personality, and behavior.

The process of mitosis When we begin life at conception, we have only 46 chromosomes, total. As we develop into a multicelled embryo, our chromo-somes duplicate and divide within the nucleus of each of those cells, giving us a complete set of 46 chromosomes in each cell of our developing bodies. This process of cell division for growth and development is called **mitosis**.

During mitosis, chromosomes duplicate themselves exactly. Each new cell has a set of chromosomes that are perfect copies of the original. Deviation does not occur under normal conditions. Many cells go through this duplication process daily, whereas others seldom do (nerve cells, liver cells). Cancer cells divide much more rapidly than healthy cells.

The process of meiosis Another type of cell division, called **meiosis,** occurs when germ cells (ova in females and sperm in males) are being formed, and plays a central role in heredity. During meiosis, chromosomes duplicate themselves and the cell divides; but instead of stopping there as in mitosis, the cells divide again. This time, however, the chromosomes do not duplicate themselves. The result is four cells with 23 single chromosomes each (see Figure 3.6).

Meiosis takes place in different locations in males than in females, and also at different times of devel-

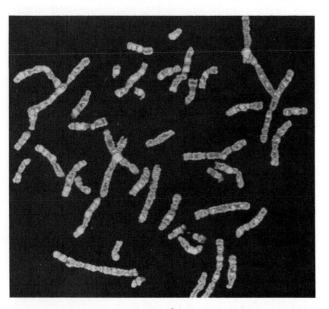
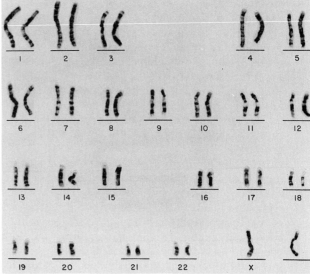

Figure 3.5 Chromosomes are studied by taking a photograph of a microscope display of stained nuclei and then cutting out the chromosomes and arranging them in pairs, numbered 1 to 23, according to size and shape.

Meiosis

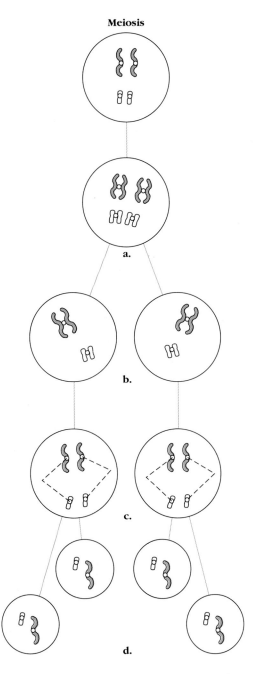

Figure 3.6 During meiosis the chromosomes in the germ cell duplicate (a) and the cell divides (b), as in mitosis. The cells then divide a second time (c). However, the chromosomes don't duplicate themselves during this second division. The result is four cells with 23 single chromosomes each (d).

opment. A lifetime supply of ova is formed in the ovaries of females while they are still fetuses; at sexual maturity, only slight finishing touches are necessary each month for an ovum to "ripen" and be released for possible fertilization. Sperm, on the other hand, are formed in the testes of sexually mature males, and this process takes place on an "as needed" basis. When conception takes place, and the 23 chromosomes from the father's sperm and the 23 chromosomes from the mother's ovum join to produce a single-celled zygote containing 46 chromosomes, the sperm is one to five days old, whereas the egg is the mother's age plus a few months. This is one reason that mother's age is a bigger factor in birth defects than father's age: ova are older and have been exposed to more environmental agents than sperm.

Guarantees of inherited variability   The process of meiosis gives two guarantees for inherited variability. The key element for heredity is that none of these sets of 23 chromosomes is the same as the set the individual received from either parent. During the second division (Figure 3.6c), the chromosomes shuffle themselves, and although each germ cell ends up with one from each pair, maternal and paternal members of each chromosome pair are selected at random. With 23 pairs, the possible combinations from random selection number 8 million. This number represents the vast variety of chromosome arrangements each individual can pass on to his or her offspring, and gives an indication of why siblings are always different even though they are products of the same parents.

Another key element for heredity is the process of **crossing-over,** which takes place during meiosis before the first cell division (Figure 3.6a). As chromosomes duplicate themselves, but before they completely divide, they exchange pieces of genetic material (see Figure 3.7). Not only do we give our children a potpourri of chromosome selection from our mothers and fathers, but also a patchwork arrangement of genetic material within each chromosome itself.

Two types of chromosomes   The 23 human chromosome pairs are grouped into two major classifications: **autosomes** (or body chromosomes) and **sex chromosomes** (see Figure 3.5). Autosomes are pairs 1 through 22. Each autosome is the same size and shape as its matching partner.

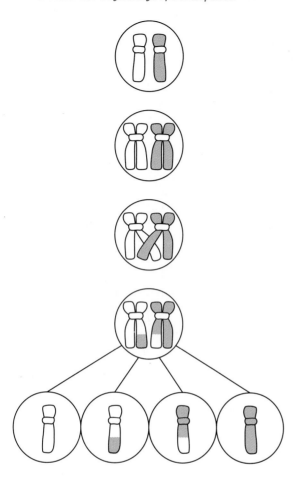

Figure 3.7 Crossing-over: the mutual exchange of material between chromosome pairs. This process takes place during meiosis, when ova or sperm are being formed.

The two sex chromosomes—the 23rd pair—determine an individual's genetic sex and carry the genes for sex-specific structures and functions. In females, the two sex chromosomes are the same size and are called XX. In males, one is large and identical to the female sex chromosome, X; the other is about one-fifth the size of the first and is called Y.

Because all males have XY sex chromosomes and all females have XX sex chromosomes, it is easy to see how parents determine their offspring's gender. The child receives one member of each chromosome pair from each parent. Because the mother has only X chromosomes, that is what she contributes to

any child she bears. The father, on the other hand, can give a child an X or a Y. If he gives the child an X, it will be added to the mother's X and the child will be female (XX). If the father gives a Y, it will be added to the mother's X and the child will be male (XY) (see Figure 3.8).

Color blindness and sex-linked inheritance   Earlier in this chapter, when we discussed inheritance of recessive and dominant characteristics, we stated that a recessive trait is expressed in the phenotype only if a person has two genes for that trait. There is at least one common exception to this rule, and it relates to genes carried on the 23rd chromosomes.

There are some genetically determined characteristics that appear more frequently in males than in females. These range from serious disorders such as Duchenne muscular dystrophy and some forms of hemophilia to relatively benign conditions such as red/green color blindness. Each of these characteristics, as well as others listed below, is passed on through the sex chromosomes.

Recall that in the 22 autosomal pairs, both chromosomes are alike. If there is a point on chromosome 6 that codes for hair color, for instance, there will be a corresponding point on its partner that codes for the same trait. This is not necessarily so for the sex chromosomes. In males, the X member of the pair is about five times larger than the Y. The smaller Y chromosome carries less genetic informa-

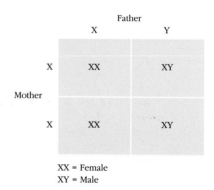

Figure 3.8 The sex of a fetus is determined by which chromosome it gets from its father. If the fetus receives an X chromosome, a female develops; if the fetus receives a Y chromosome, a male develops. The mother provides the fetus with one of her two X chromosomes.

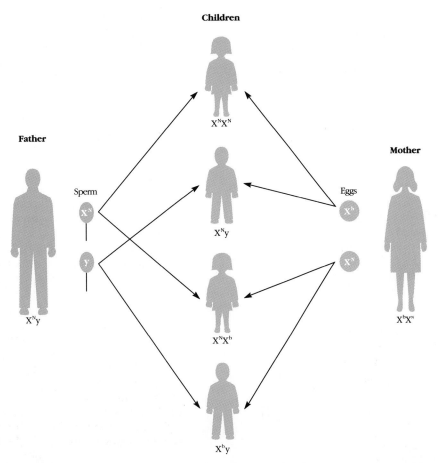

Children

Father

Mother

Sperm

Eggs

X^N

X^b

$X^N X^N$

$X^N y$

X^N

$X^N X^b$

$X^b X^N$

$X^N y$

$X^b y$

Figure 3.9 Genetic transmission of color blindness, a sex-linked (X-linked) trait. Because the gene for color vision (and color blindness) is carried on the X chromosome only, males (XY) get their only gene for color vision from their mothers.

tion than the larger X chromosome. Traits that are transmitted through the sex chromosomes reflect **sex-linked inheritance.**

As with autosome genes, sex-linked genes may be dominant or recessive. If a trait is recessive—as Duchenne muscular dystrophy, hemophilia, and color blindness are—then females, having two Xs, will not express the trait if only one gene for the disorder is present. What is unusual about sex-linked inheritance is that males *will* express the trait if only one recessive gene is present on the X, because they have no corresponding dominant gene on the Y chromosome to be expressed instead. This means that recessive sex-linked characteristics are

passed along from mothers to their sons. The only way a daughter can express the recessive trait is if she receives the recessive gene on both of her X chromosomes. The typical inheritance pattern of color blindness, from carrier mother's to color-blind sons, is shown in Figure 3.9.

Although sex-linked characteristics are almost always associated with genes on the larger X chromosome (**X-linked inheritance**), a few genes are found only on the smaller Y chromosome (**Y-linked inheritance**). The most significant of these is the **testis determining factor gene,** which somehow instructs the body to build testes, early in the prenatal period (Pierce, 1990). The testes then produce male hormones, which stimulate the development of other male characteristics.

Traits that follow a sex-linked heredity pattern

Color blindness (red/green): defects in red and green receptors

Deafness: 2% of cases present at birth

Dwarfism: some types

G6PD (glucose 6 phosphate dehydrogenase deficiency): defect of blood components that causes harmful reactions to certain medicines and foods (aspirin, phenacetin, fava beans)

Hemophilia: classic type and hemophilia B (Christmas disease)

Hunter syndrome: enzyme deficiency that causes neural destruction

Lesch-Nyhan syndrome: fatal enzyme deficiency

Muscular dystrophy (Duchenne): missing protein important to muscle function

Chromosome Abnormalities

We can learn much about chromosome function by studying chromosome dysfunctions. During the process of meiosis, accidents sometimes happen. Parts of a chromosome can break off and become attached to another chromosome, producing germ cells with missing pieces or germ cells with extra pieces. Other times, something goes wrong with chromosome duplication, resulting in germ cells with only 22 chromosomes, or 24. We don't know how often this happens during meiosis because many of these defective germ cells fail to join with others in conception, and we don't know how many otherwise normal babies may have unknown chromosome abnormalities that have little effect on their health and behavior. Of the zygotes that are formed, however, about half have chromosome abnormalities; most of these result in spontaneous abortions

An extra chromosome on the 21st pair gives 47 chromosomes to Down syndrome children, who have similar physical features and varying degrees of mental retardation.

(miscarriages). At birth, one in every 200 babies has an obvious chromosome abnormality (Boué, 1977). Of those, about half have abnormalities of the autosomes, and half have abnormalities of the single pair of sex chromosomes (Plomin et al., 1990).

Abnormalities of the autosomes: **Down syndrome**
Probably the most familiar chromosome abnormality is **Down syndrome.** Once called "mongolism," it is now known by the name of its discoverer, John Langdon Down, who was superintendent of an institution for mentally retarded children in Surrey, England, in the 1860s. Down noticed that about 10% of his patients were very similar in appearance, although they were not related. He carefully described the traits these children had in common: a broad, flat face, thick tongue, small nose, and oriental-like eyes resulting from epicantral folds of the eyelids. In 1959, a chromosome abnormality was discovered in Down syndrome individuals—the first abnormality found in the autosomes. Instead of having 46 chromosomes, individuals with Down syndrome had 47, the extra one being a third member of the 21st pair, giving the disorder its technical name, *trisomy 21,* or third body on the 21st pair. Since 1959, several other types of Down syndrome have been found, also involving the 21st pair, but trisomy 21 is responsible for about 95% of Down syndrome cases.

The incidence of Down syndrome births increases with the age of the mother. Once a woman reaches 35 years of age, the chances of her giving birth to a Down syndrome child increase substantially. Apparently, the older the egg, the greater the chances are that it has been exposed to environmental agents resulting in chromosomal abnormalities. Recent evidence has shown, however, that in about 25% of cases the source of the abnormal 21st chromosome is the father (Magenis & Chamberlin, 1981).

Because of the known relationship between maternal age and Down syndrome, many pregnant women age 35 and over have amniocentesis—a prenatal diagnostic test that can detect chromosomal abnormalities in the fetus (see Chapter 4). A woman can thus know in about the 20th week of pregnancy if she is carrying a Down syndrome child and can use this information in her decision whether to have an abortion. As a result of prenatal testing, the incidence of Down syndrome births has decreased, dropping from 1 in 600 twenty years ago to 1 in 1000 today (Plomin et al., 1990).

For other abnormalities of the body chromosomes, see Table 3.1.

Abnormalities of the sex chromosomes: **Turner syndrome**   This disorder was first identified in 1938 by Henry Turner, a physician and hormone specialist, who had seen seven female patients with similar traits that he believed were caused by hormone deficiencies. The women, all in their late teens or early

Table 3.1 Abnormalities of the autosomes (body chromosomes)

Anomaly	Type and Location	Incidence per Live Births	Symptoms
Edward's syndrome	Trisomy 18	1:5000	Multiple congenital problems, early death
D-trisomy syndrome (Patau syndrome)	Trisomy 13	1:6000	Multiple congenital problems, early death
Cri du chat	Missing part of short arm of chromosome 4 or 5	1:10,000	High-pitched cry, early death
Down syndrome	Trisomy 21	1:1000	Mental retardation, poor muscle tone, distinctive facial features, heart anomalies
Prader-Willi syndrome	Missing part of chromosome 15	1:10,000 to 25,000	Poor muscle tone and color, small hands and feet, obesity at 2 or 3 years of age
Wolf-Hirschhorn syndrome	Missing part of chromosome 4		Severe mental and growth retardation, facial anomalies, seizures, early death
3q+ syndrome	Extra piece of chromosome 3		Severe mental and growth retardation, head and chest deformities, early death

Table 3.2 Abnormalities of the sex chromosomes

Anomaly	Type and Location	Incidence per Live Births	Symptoms
Turner syndrome	XO	1:2500	Some physical signs, hormone deficiencies, specific spatial deficits
Females with extra X chromosome(s)	XXX XXXX XXXXX	1:1000	For XXX, some retardation; for others, unknown
Klinefelter's syndrome, males with extra X chromosome(s)	XXY XXXY XXXXY XXYY	2:2000	For XXY, sexual development problems, tall, some retardation; for others, unknown
Males with extra Y chromosome(s)	XYY XYYY XYYYY	1:1000	Tall, some retardation
Fragile X syndrome	Fragile site on X chromosome	1:2000	Mental retardation, enlarged testicles, large head and ears

20s, had not matured sexually. They had extra connecting tissue on the neck, a low hairline on the back of the head, and deformed elbows. Turner published his findings and this cluster of symptoms became known as **Turner syndrome.**

In 1959, improved equipment and techniques showed that Turner syndrome females lacked a second X chromosome. Turner syndrome is thus designated as XO, meaning that one X chromosome is present and one is absent, leaving affected women with only 45 chromosomes.

Because the first women diagnosed with Turner syndrome were those whose symptoms were extreme enough to require medical help, it was considered a serious debilitating disorder. Today, by screening healthy members of the population, researchers have found that the vast majority of Turner syndrome cases are less severe and respond well to hormone replacement treatment. However, by studying the traits found in Turner syndrome women, such as poor spatial ability and directional sense, researchers have gained information about what role the second X chromosome plays in the development of normal females (Berch & Bender, 1990).

Turner syndrome occurs in one of every 2500 live births. It is not connected to mother's age, nor does it run in families. Of conceptions resulting in XO

fetuses, 98% are spontaneously aborted (Plomin, et al., 1990).

For other examples of abnormalities of the sex chromosomes, see Table 3.2.

Molecular Genetics

During the first half of the 20th century, geneticists worked on a variety of organisms to demonstrate the functions of genes in inheritance. Although they had gathered quite a lot of knowledge about the effects of genes and the appearance of chromosomes, they still had little evidence of exactly what genes were and exactly how they worked.

In 1953, American postdoctoral student James Watson and English graduate student Francis Crick, working together at Cambridge University, reviewed all the evidence available about the nature of genes and pooled their scientific knowledge and intuition to propose a model for the role of deoxyribonucleic acid (**DNA**) in heredity. Their model was confirmed through subsequent research, and the field of *molecular genetics* was born—with these two students, Watson and Crick, as the proud fathers (Judson, 1979).

The science of molecular genetics studies the chemical basis of heredity. Although its complexity makes it difficult for anyone but a molecular geneticist to understand, some knowledge about its workings can serve to demystify the process of genetic inheritance. Genes do not work by some sort of magic; they work through chemical processes, as do other human functions such as digestion and respiration. And genes do not directly determine our behavior, but are subject to effects of the environment. Finally, genes are not unchangeable; in fact they are becoming subject to control by science.

All about DNA

Each chromosome is made up of one strand of DNA. The sets of DNA molecules are the same within each cell of an individual, and no two individuals have the same sets of DNA molecules (except identical twins).

DNA is made up of chains of nucleotide pairs, coiled up around itself within the chromosome "like a mass of barbed wire" (Pierce, 1990). Our 46 chromosomes contain 3 billion nucleotide pairs (Plomin, DeFries, & McClearn, 1990). The nucleotides of DNA come in four types: adenine, thymine, guanine, and cytosine (abbreviated A, T, G, and C, respectively). Although the sequence of these elements is not rule-bound, the combination of pairs follows this order: A always pairs with T, and G always pairs with C (see Figure 3.10).

Protein production Three base (nucleotide) pairs, depending on their order, code for production of an amino acid. Twenty amino acids combine in different assortments and amounts to form the thousands of proteins that make up a living organism. A gene is simply a segment of base pairs that code for a particular protein. Depending on the protein, a gene can be represented by as few as three base pairs or as many as a thousand, with the average gene being made up of several hundred base pairs. It is estimated that humans have 50,000 to 100,000 genes (McKusick, 1986).

From smallest to largest, then, bases form pairs that make long chains of DNA. Three pairs make an amino acid, and a number of amino acids make a protein. The unit of nucleotide pairs that make a certain protein is called a gene. For example, one of the important types of proteins our genes make is enzymes, which serve as catalysts for many of our body processes. They speed up processes and enable processes to occur that otherwise might not. The presence of enzymes and their timing are critical to our development and day-to-day functioning. Genes, then, direct the production of proteins, which in turn affect our development, our health, and our behavior through normal biological pathways. Important, yes; magical, no.

Mutations Sometimes in the course of cell division, accidents occur, either in mitosis (formation of body cells) or in meiosis (formation of sex cells). Two such **mutations,** involving entire chromosomes, have already been discussed: Down syndrome and Turner syndrome. However, most mutations involve one or more genes—a defect in the DNA duplication process. If the mutation occurs during meiosis, the result is an egg or sperm that carries inaccurate genetic information. If this germ cell is involved in conception, and results in a live birth, the mutation (genetic misinformation) will be part of the new individual's genetic makeup and be present in each of his or her body cells. In addition, this faulty DNA can be passed on to the offspring of this individual via the DNA in his or her germ cells.

An example of meiotic mutation is a type of he-

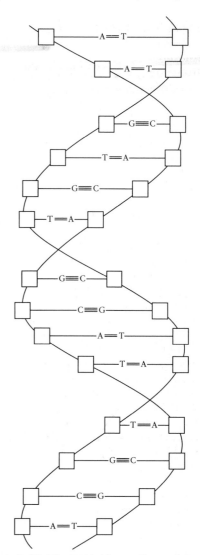

Figure 3.10 The DNA (deoxyribonucleic acid) molecule is composed of pairs of nucleotide bases twisted into a spiral.

reditary dwarfism. Although this disorder is inherited following the pattern of dominant autosomal traits, it can also occur spontaneously in a family with no history of dwarfism. This happens when a segment of DNA involved in bone growth is coded incorrectly during formation of germ cells in the dwarfed individual's parents. This genetic accident, or mutation, introduces dwarfism into the family pedigree where it will be passed down following the pattern of dominant traits.

Another type of mutation occurs in the body cells after conception has taken place. If mutation occurs early during the prenatal period, the result can be a **genetic mosaic**—an individual having normal genes in some cells and mutated genes in others (Plomin et al., 1990). One type of Down syndrome involves an individual with some cells containing the normal number of chromosomes (46), and others showing the trisomy pattern (47).

A second type of body-cell mutation occurs after birth, often in late adulthood, resulting in cancer. Normal genes altered through mutation instruct their cells to produce proteins that promote rapid, aggressive growth. Some cancer cells seem to arise from random genetic accidents; others are the result of factors in the environment, such as chemicals that alter the DNA code. These chemicals, called carcinogens, include cigarette smoke, X-rays, radiation from the sun, and some viruses.

A combination of germ-cell and body-cell mutations can also cause cancer. Mutations of germ cells can result in an individual who is predisposed for cancer. When carcinogens are present in the environment, such individuals are more likely to suffer mutation of the body-cell DNA that results in cancer. This is how some common forms of cancer, such as breast cancer and colorectal cancer, occur more frequently in some families, but are still "caused" by mutations of the body-cell genes later in life (see Pierce, 1990).

Mutations should not be considered as only negative events, although most are harmful. Some mutations of the germ cells provide useful variations in a species and are passed on for generations, becoming a part of the species' genetic endowment. In fact, contemporary evolutionary theory "views mutation as the ultimate source of the genetic variability on which natural selection depends" (Plomin et al., 1990, p. 92).

Research Tools for Molecular Genetics

Genetic dissection   One technique being used to investigate the role of particular groups of genes is to cause a mutation in simple organisms, look for behavioral changes, and then search for the genes responsible for the changes (Plomin et al., 1990). Organisms such as bacteria and paramecia are used in this research because of their limited repertoire of behavior. Using this technique, known as genetic dissection, specific segments of DNA have been found in bacteria that are responsible for sensing certain types of nutrients, for moving clockwise or counterclockwise, and for duration of movement (Parkinson, 1977).

Recombinant DNA   Techniques have been developed that allow scientists to "snip out" pieces of DNA and transplant them into simple organisms, usually bacteria. This technique, **recombinant DNA** (also called gene cloning or genetic engineering), is considered by some to be the most powerful experimental tool in all of science (Pierce, 1990).

Once a segment of DNA has been identified as a code for a certain protein, that protein can be "manufactured" by inserting the DNA into bacteria, creating a one-celled organism that is now programmed to produce that protein. As the new form of bacteria divide and reproduce, so does the transplanted DNA, and soon millions of bacteria clones are producing the protein. This method has been used commercially since 1976, when Genentech, the first biotechnology company, was formed. Now more than 400 such companies are in business using recombinant DNA techniques to create new products in fields such as pharmaceuticals, agriculture, and waste management (Pierce, 1990).

The process is also used to manufacture larger supplies of organic substances, such as insulin, whose supply used to depend on animal sources, and human growth hormone, which earlier was supplied only from human cadavers. Safer vaccines are being manufactured by recombinant DNA processes because it is possible to isolate the proteins that provide immunity instead of including unnecessary substances that might lead to harmful reactions.

Genetic linkage   Although Mendel's law of segregation says that traits are inherited separately, this is not always the case. Sometimes traits are linked, and this **genetic linkage** provides the basis for some of the most exciting research being done today.

Genes that are located close to each other on a chromosome are more apt to be inherited together than genes that are located farther apart. The reason for this is crossing-over: when chromosome chunks are exchanged, the genes close together on one

Box 3.3

Tracking Genetic Diseases

Studies have been done linking Freidrich's ataxia (a degenerative neurological disease that appears in mid-adulthood) with a segment of DNA named MCT112 that has been located on the 9th chromosome. Although Freidrich's ataxia was identified in 1863, it was not known to be an inherited disorder for several reasons. One was the difficulty in diagnosing it apart from other, similar neurological disorders. Another was the high infant mortality rates in past times, making it difficult to see family patterns. However, in Louisiana, when three out of six children of Betty LeBlanc were diagnosed with the disease in the early 1980s, she began gathering information about her family and her husband's family as far back as she could research. Working with geneticists, she was determined to beat this disease.

Interestingly, Betty and her husband were Cajuns, a close-knit group of people who left France in the 1600s for Nova Scotia, and then emigrated to Louisiana in the 1700s. They had retained their Catholic religion, and many marriage and birth records were available through the church. After researching her genealogy, this woman gathered together as many living relatives as she could find and convinced them to donate blood for investigation of their DNA. For the next few years, several teams of geneticists studied the DNA samples, and one group found that the family members affected by Freidrich's ataxia also had a segment of chromosome 9 with a unique sequence of DNA. This segment had been found a few years earlier and named MCT112, but nothing else was known about it. In all likelihood, MCT112 did not contain the gene for Freidrich's ataxia, but because it "traveled" along with the disorder, it was considered to be located very close to the disease gene (Wingerson, 1990).

This evidence is enough for prenatal screening. Using amniocentesis or chorionic villus sampling (described in Chapter 4), parents in a family like the LeBlancs can find out if the fetus being carried has the MCT112 marker and, hence, the disease. However, for many couples abortion is not an option, so they now wait for research that will find the gene itself and a treatment or cure for the disease.

Geneticists in the past decade have studied other family groups to find genetic linkage to other diseases. In Pennsylvania, large kinship groups from the Old Country Amish have been studied to find information about the inheritance of bipolar depression. In Ghana, a family was traced back nine generations to 1670, establishing a pattern for sickle-cell anemia. A Dutch kinship group in Michigan has been studied for clues to Tourette's syndrome, a neurological disorder that causes uncontrollable shrugs, blinks, twitches, and vocalizations (sometimes spoken obscenities). And a kinship group near Lake Maracaibo in Venezuela has been a valuable source of information and blood samples in research on Huntington's disease (Wingerson, 1990).

To date the research has been successful in most areas. Sickle-cell disease research now can screen adults to identify carriers. Members of families with a history of Huntington's disease can now be tested to determine if they carry the dominant gene and will develop the disease in mid-adulthood. Early research on the Amish and bipolar depression found linkage on chromosome 11, but subsequent studies have failed to confirm it (Wingerson, 1990).

The special populations being used for linkage research do not necessarily have more genetic disorders than other people in the world, but for religious and cultural reasons they have lived in relative isolation and married within their group for many generations. They are usually easy to interview and test because they live in small geographic areas and also because they stay in contact. If the group is a religious one, church records are plentiful, showing marriages, births, and deaths. In the case of the Mormons (Church of the Latter-day Saints), researching and recording family pedigrees is part of their religious teachings. An added attraction of groups such as the Mormons and the Amish is that religious rules forbid them to smoke or to use alcohol and caffeine, practices that can increase the environmental risks to one's health. Because many kinship groups do not keep in touch with one another, do not keep records, and do not live in the same area, linkage research would be much more difficult in those families.

chromosome are more likely to travel together to a second chromosome. Thus, if you know that a certain disease is inherited in a kinship group (several related families) and you find a chromosome marker that is always present in the diseased individuals (but not in normal family members), you know that the gene for the disorder is located close to the marker on the same chromosome. In this way, genetic linkage helps provide clues to pinpointing the location of specific genes.

Genetic mapping Molecular geneticists are currently working on an ambitious project to map the human genome, seeking to identify the sequence of all 3 billion base pairs of human DNA. During the first year of this **genetic mapping** project, a team of researchers sequenced 5000 base pairs. In 1977, a new technique was introduced that enabled one individual to sequence 15,000 base pairs in the same amount of time. New equipment that attaches different fluorescent dyes to each of the four bases and then "reads" the bases automatically can now sequence 15,000 base pairs in two days. It is expected that the complete sequence of DNA for one of the smaller chromosomes will be completed by 1992 and that the entire human genome may be sequenced by the year 2000 (Plomin et al., 1990).

To further appreciate the progress predicted by Robert Plomin and his associates (1990), consider that simply printing the sequence of base pairs for a single person's 46 chromosomes would require the equivalent of 13 volumes of the *Encyclopedia Britannica* (McKusick, 1986). Then the task remains to discover the function of the genes in that sequence.

State of the Art
Is Biology Destiny?

We are what our genes make us. There is no doubt that the genes we receive from our parents dictate our development. In actuality, of course, there are no genes for arms, legs, eyes, and ears. Rather, genes code for amino acids, which in turn combine to form proteins—the basic building blocks of life. Most of us can easily accept the idea of genetic influence on our physical development, but balk at thinking that

our behavior and personalities are also governed to a significant extent by our genes. The field of research that studies genetic effects on behavior and complex psychological characteristics such as intelligence and personality is referred to as **behavioral genetics.** The argument against a genetic influence on behavior goes something like this: "If we are what our genes determine us to be, then there is little hope of modifying the human spirit or human behavior through environmental intervention. If genes affect not only blood type and eye color but also behavior, personality, and intelligence, biology truly is destiny."

Yet biology rarely dictates anything in an absolute way. All genetic effects are moderated by environmental ones. Even the genes for eye color must be expressed in a developing embryo, which is exposed to uncountable environmental factors as a result of its own development. The fact that genes influence behavior does not mean that environment plays only an inconsequential role. In fact, recalling our discussion of the transactional model of development in Chapter 1, it should be clear that stating a straightforward genetic (or environmental) "cause" for a particular behavioral outcome is inappropriate. What we must ask ourselves is how genetic factors transact with environmental factors to produce a given outcome.

The view that genetic causes do not necessarily mean destiny is expressed by Richard Dawkins, a sociobiologist who firmly believes that our social behavior (such as altruism) is greatly influenced by genetics:

People seem to have little difficulty in appreciating the modifiability of "environmental" effects on human development. If a child has had bad teaching in mathematics, it is accepted that the resulting deficiency can be remedied by extra good teaching the following year. But any suggestion that the child's mathematical deficiency might have a genetic origin is likely to be greeted with something approaching despair: if it is in the genes, "it is written," it is "determined" and nothing can be done about it. This is pernicious rubbish on an almost astrological scale. Genetic causes and environmental causes are in principle no different from each other. Some influences of both types may be hard to reverse; others may be easy to reverse. Some may be usually hard to reverse but easy if the right agent is applied. The important point is that there is no general reason for expecting genetic influences to be any more reversible than environmental ones. (Dawkins, 1982, p. 13)

Thus, even a scientist whom others consider to be an extremist with respect to the role of genetics on behavior does not believe that genes are destiny. To deny the significant role of genetics in behavior is to place one's head in the sand; but to proclaim that genetics determines our personalities, intellects, and behavior is to seriously misinterpret reality.

Genetic Effects on Behavior

There is a growing literature today demonstrating significant genetic effects on many complex psychological factors (see Bouchard et al., 1990; Plomin, 1989; Plomin, DeFries, & McClearn, 1990). To phrase it another way, socially important factors such as intelligence, personality, and psychopathology are highly heritable. Table 3.3 presents the correlations for monozygotic and dizygotic twins and heritability estimates (expressed in percentage terms) for several psychological characteristics. Table 3.4 presents the concordance rate for first-degree relatives (siblings or parent/child) and monozygotic twins for several psychological disorders.

Based on twin and adoption studies, about 50% of the differences in IQ among people can be attributed to genetics, although some researchers put the estimate as high as 70% (Bouchard et al., 1990). Similar estimates of heritability (that is, about 50%) have been found for more specific measures of cognitive ability, such as vocabulary, spelling, reading disability, and speed of processing (see Plomin, 1989). Personality characteristics, such as being extroverted or shy, show somewhat lower, but still substantial, heritability (Bouchard, 1985; Buss & Plomin, 1984; McCartney, Harris, & Bernieri, 1990).

Various forms of psychopathology have also shown to be highly heritable. For example, the concordance rate of identical twins for schizophrenia is about 40% compared to about 7% for nonidentical twins (Plomin, 1989). Delinquent and criminal behavior also seems influenced by genetics: the concordance rate of identical twins is greater than that of nonidentical twins for delinquent behavior, and adoption studies show that the biological children of criminals are more prone to criminality than the children of noncriminals (see Wilson & Herrnstein,

Table 3.3 Correlations among identical and nonidentical twins and estimated heritability for a variety of psychological traits

Trait	Correlation for Nonidentical Twins	Correlation for Identical Twins	Estimated Heritability
IQ	0.60	0.85	40–60%
Personality	0.30	0.50	40%
Delinquent behavior	0.70	0.85	30%
Occupational status	0.20	0.40	40%
Specific cognitive abilities	0.50	0.70	30–50%
Criminal behavior	0.30	0.70	80%
Vocational interest	0.25	0.50	50%
Academic performance	0.50	0.75	50%
Creativity	0.50	0.60	20%

Source: Based on data from *Behavioral Genetics, A Primer,* Second Edition, by R. Plomin, J. C. DeFries, and G. E. McClearn. Copyright © 1990 by W. H. Freeman and Co. Reprinted by permission.

Table 3.4 Concordance rate for several psychological disorders for first-degree relatives (siblings, parent/child) and identical twins

Trait	Risk for First-Degree Relatives	Risk for Identical Twins
Schizophrenia	10%	40%
Major depressive disorder	10%	65%
Anorexia nervosa	unknown	55%
Bipolar depression	5%	unknown
Tourette's syndrome	10%	50%
Attention deficit disorder	30%	unknown

Based on data presented in Plomin, DeFries, and McClearn (1990).

1985). Recent studies have also found significant genetic influences for some unlikely behaviors and attitudes, including religious beliefs (Waller, Kojetin, Bouchard, Lykken, & Tellegen, 1990), holding "traditional" attitudes (Tellegen, Lykken, Bouchard, Wilcox, Segal, & Rich, 1988), and the amount of time young children spend watching television (Plomin, Corley, DeFries, & Fulker, 1990).

What these results indicate is that there is a substantial effect of genetics on a wide range of psychological characteristics. But how does one account for the high heritability of religiosity or TV viewing? There are certainly no genes for how much television one watches. Likewise, remember that there are no genes for IQ, extroversion, vocabulary, or even height; genes code for amino acids, not for specific behaviors or traits. When we find a genetic effect on children's television viewing, it means that "some unspecified genetic differences among children indirectly affect the extent to which children watch television" (Plomin, Corley, DeFries, & Fulker, 1990, p. 371). It does not mean that evolution has somehow planted genes in humans for sitting in front of a box and watching moving visual images (eating potato chips or not).

Behavioral genetics has shown not only how important genetics is in complex psychological phenomena, but also how important environment is. For example, Robert Plomin (1989) points out that while the 40% concordance rate of schizophrenia for identical twins shows a substantial influence of heredity in this serious psychopathology, it also demonstrates the significance of environment: in 60% of cases, only one twin will become schizophrenic, despite their identical genetic makeup. Additional evidence for the role of environment in genetic characteristics is that children with the same chromosome abnormalities display widely different deficits (Netley, 1986). Also, children with sex-chromosome abnormalities from stable families show fewer abnormal traits and less abnormal development than do those from less stable families (Bender, Linden, & Robinson, in press). Thus, the new findings and interpretations of behavioral genetics have not diminished the role that environment plays in development. They have, however, changed how we look at that role.

How Do Genes Influence Behavior?

There is much mystery yet in how genes affect behavior. A currently popular interpretation of genetic effects on behavior holds that genes have an indirect, though powerful, effect on behavior by influencing the types of environments people choose. One's genes determine to a large extent the type of stimulation and experiences one prefers, and people seek out environments that match their genetic preferences (Bouchard et al., 1990; Scarr & McCartney, 1983). With age, children become increasingly independent of their parents' influence and freer to select their own environments in which to experience life. This accounts for the fact that siblings become *less* alike the longer they live together (Plomin

& Daniels, 1987; McCartney et al., 1990), a somewhat counterintuitive finding. As children grow up, they search for their own niche in the world. Such a view suggests that environment plays a critical role in shaping the personalities and intellects of children, much as proposed by the behaviorists of years gone by. What is different about today's proposal is that genes determine which experiences a child will have. In the words of Sandra Scarr and Kathleen McCartney (1983), "genes drive experience." From this perspective, it is clear that the issue is not nature versus nurture; nor is it appropriate to ask "how much" nature versus "how much" nurture. Rather, following Thomas Bouchard and his colleagues (1990), the correct formula seems to be "nature via nurture." Such a perspective acknowledges the important role that genetics plays in every aspect of our being, but it also acknowledges the equally significant role of environment and the possibility of intervention even for highly heritable traits.

Summary

The understanding of inheritance was advanced in the 19th century by Charles Darwin, the author of modern evolutionary theory, and Sir Francis Galton, who was the first to study scientifically the inheritance of human intelligence. Gregor Mendel is credited as being the father of genetics with his discovery of the laws of segregation and independent assortment.

Modern genetics makes a distinction between one's genotype (the genes one inherits) and phenotype (one's observed characteristics) and between dominant and recessive traits. There are a number of techniques for studying human inheritance, including family pedigree charts, central registries for inherited diseases, twin studies, and adoption studies, all of which can be used to determine the heritability of a given trait.

Chromosomes contain thousands of genes. During the process of meiosis, they divide and separate to form sperm cells in males and ova in females. Humans have 23 chromosome pairs—22 autosomal pairs and the single pair of sex chromosomes (XX in females and XY in males). Gender of a child is determined by the male, who provides either an X (eventual female) or Y (eventual male) chromosome to an offspring, whereas the female always provides an X. Most sex-linked characteristics are passed along from mothers to sons because there is no gene on the Y chromosome to counteract the effect of a single recessive gene on the X chromosome (X-linked inheritance). About half of all chromosome abnormalities are related to the autosomes (as in Down syndrome) and half to the sex chromosomes (as in Turner syndrome).

Genes are made of deoxyribonucleic acid (DNA). DNA codes for the production of amino acids, which, in combination with one another, form proteins. Mutations are defects in the duplication of DNA and are one source of genetic variation. The role of DNA in development is being investigated through techniques such as genetic dissection, recombinant DNA, genetic linkage, and genetic mapping.

Behavioral genetics refers to the study of the genetic basis of behavior and psychological characteristics, such as intelligence and personality. Twin and adoption studies have shown that intelligence, personality, and psychopathology are highly heritable. According to contemporary theory, one's genes determine the types of environment a person will experience, with environment then playing a major role in shaping psychological characteristics.

Key Terms and Concepts

variation
natural selection
law of segregation
law of independent assortment
genotype
phenotype
dominant
recessive
Tay Sachs disease
Huntington's disease
polygenic inheritance
family pedigree charts
central registries
twin studies
> concordance rate
adoption studies
heritability
chromosomes
> mitosis
> meiosis
> crossing-over
> autosomes
> sex chromosomes (X, Y)
> sex-linked inheritance
>> X-linked
>> Y-linked
> Down syndrome
>> trisomy 21
> Turner syndrome
molecular genetics
> DNA (deoxyribonucleic acid)
> mutations
>> genetic mosaic
> genetic dissection
> recombinant DNA
> genetic linkage
> genetic mapping
> behavioral genetics

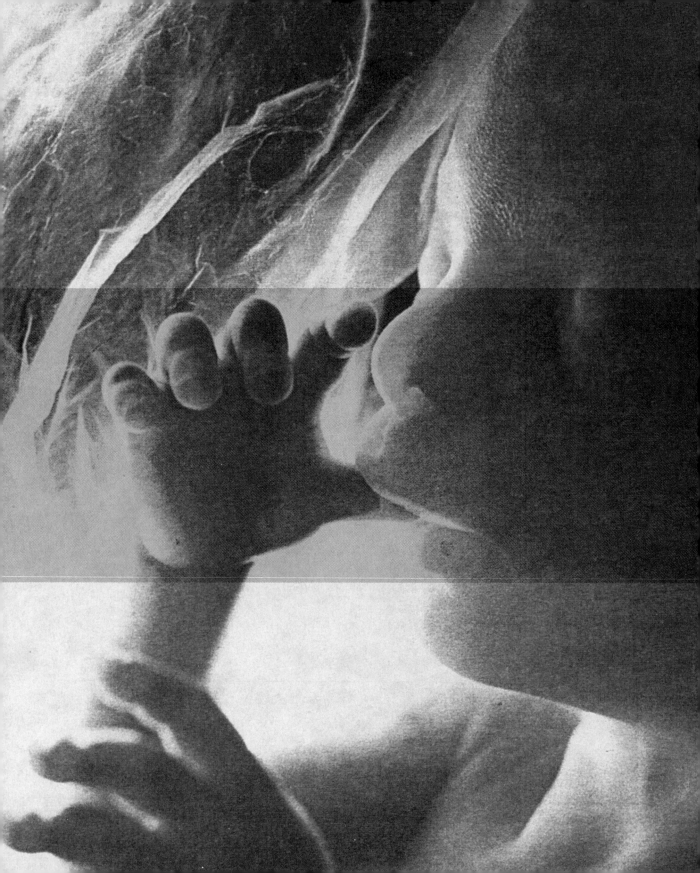

In the Beginning: Prenatal Development, Birth, and the Neonate

Agnes and Becky were discussing their pregnancies over coffee one afternoon—not an unusual scene. However, these two women happened to be grandmother and granddaughter; they had given birth in the same community two generations apart. Their experiences, they discovered, were quite different.

Agnes, an attractive woman in her early 70s, talked about her morning sickness. "I spent the first month of my pregnancy in bed, so sick that I couldn't keep anything down. It made me angry, too, because everybody said it was 'all in my head,' as though I was looking for sympathy or something. Now I read that it's real and that there's something you can take for it."

"Not me," interrupted her granddaughter, Becky, dressed in jeans and a T-shirt. "I couldn't take anything for any reason. My doctor said not even to take aspirin unless I was on death's doorstep." She looked over to check on her baby, sleeping in his stroller.

"Aspirin?" said Agnes. "Now what on earth could an aspirin tablet do to you?"

"Well, the doctor said that aspirin makes it difficult for blood to clot, and in the baby it might cause problems," answered Becky. "Even Mom didn't take any medicine when she was pregnant with me."

"Yes," said Agnes, "but she smoked. I remember that, and I didn't like it one bit. Now the experts say that it's dangerous—bad enough to be written on the sides of cigarette packs. Their big bugaboo back then was gaining weight. I think the doctor let your mother gain about 15 pounds with you."

Becky laughed, "I gained twice that with Michael and never heard a word of warning."

Agnes said, "Well, I could gain all I wanted, but I wasn't allowed to drive during the last three months, or exercise much. And they didn't like pregnant women to swim at all. Now they have exercise videos for pregnant women and water ballet classes at the pool!"

"One thing I think you and Mom missed out on is natural childbirth," said Becky. "Tom and I went to class and practiced breathing exercises at home. I think we could have delivered the baby ourselves before we were through with training films. And you didn't have Dad and Grandpa with you in the delivery room. That was so important for Tom."

"Well, Grandpa didn't even like to come into the hospital with me!" said Agnes. "He would check me in and practically leave the car running outside. Then he would go wake up his mother and she would cook him breakfast and pamper him until the doctor called and told him it was a girl or a boy. Then he would go home, shower, get dressed up, and come to visit with flowers and chocolates."

"You mean he wasn't even there when the baby was born?" asked Becky. "Didn't you feel awful?"

"Actually, Becky, *I* wasn't even there when the baby was born. I had a wonderful doctor who would put us out cold when the labor got too hard and we woke up in the hospital room several hours later when the baby was ready to nurse," explained Agnes.

"Wonderful?" asked her granddaughter. "Didn't you worry about the effect on the baby?"

"Not really," said Agnes. "We pretty much trusted our doctors to do the right thing back then."

"Such differences," said Agnes, looking down at the sleeping child in the stroller. "I wonder what things will be like when Michael has children."

Becky laughed, "You mean when his wife has children, don't you, Grandma?"

"Not necessarily," said the older woman, with a sparkle in her eye.

In this chapter we examine the beginnings of development, from conception through birth and into the first month of life. The important social and emotional relationship between parents and children will be discussed separately in Chapter 12, "Attachment."

Prenatal Development

Conception

Almost everyone knows where babies come from, but the actual process of conception is a complicated one with many mysteries still to be solved. Each month, beginning some time after menarche and ending with menopause, a woman releases an ovum from one of her ovaries. Typically, the two ovaries take turns, and all the ova that a woman will ever have are present in her ovaries at birth. But these ova are not ready for fertilization until years later when they are released and find their way down the

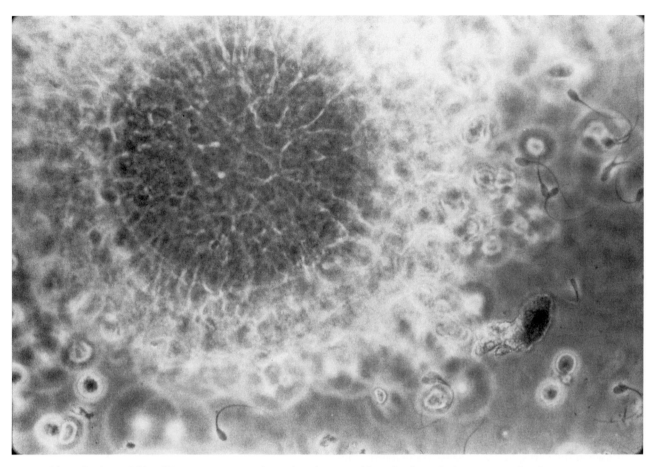

Although about 250 million sperm are released, only several hundred reach the ovum and only one can impregnate it.

fallopian tubes, where conception occurs (see Figure 4.1).

In contrast to the one egg that the female releases each month, the male releases 250 million sperm in each ejaculation. Of these, most will die and never reach the fallopian tubes, and of the several hundred or so that do make it to the ovum, only one can impregnate it. Each sperm consists of a bulbous head and long slender tail. The tail is in continuous motion, propelling the sperm into the uterus and up the fallopian tube to the ovum. The ovum itself is the size of a pinpoint, just barely visible to the naked eye, whereas sperm are microscopic.

Conception can occur only during the brief period when the ovum is in the fallopian tube. The ovum can survive for about 24 hours, making it seem that the window of opportunity for pregnancy is narrow indeed. The sperm, however, can survive in the uterus and fallopian tubes for as long as 85 hours, "waiting" for an ovum to be released (Reinisch, 1990). This means there is about a three- or four-day period (three days before ovulation and one day after) during which intercourse is most apt to lead to pregnancy. If the ovum is not impregnated by a sperm, it dies and the hormone system of the woman continues its regular cycle, with menstruation following about two weeks after ovulation.

This three- or four-day fertile period can be difficult to calculate. Some women have irregular menstrual cycles, making it hard to know exactly when

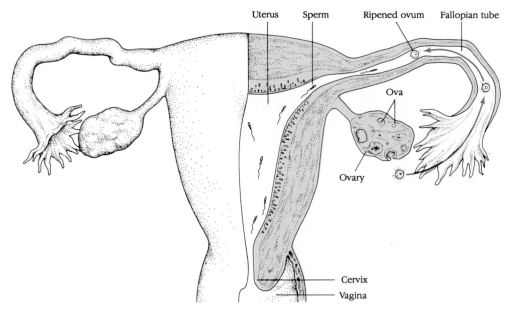

Figure 4.1 Female reproductive system. An ovum is released from the ovary and travels down the fallopian tube to the uterus. If conception is to occur, it will happen in the fallopian tube.

ovulation will occur. And although sperm survive in the uterus and fallopian tubes for only three or four days, they can become trapped in the folds of the cervix (see Figure 4.1) and remain viable for up to eight days. During the middle of a woman's reproductive cycle, the mucus of the cervix changes, allowing trapped sperm to swim into the uterus. This corresponds roughly with the beginning of ovulation, increasing the chances that conception will occur (Reinisch, 1990).

Although the concern here is with conception, many couples throughout the world find it difficult to conceive. "Infertility" is the inability to conceive after a year or more of regular sexual relations without contraception (Sher & Marriage, 1988). By this definition, approximately 9% of the population in the United States is infertile at any given time during the childbearing years. This figure rises to about 15% if it includes women who are unable to carry a pregnancy to live birth (Menning, 1988). The reasons for the current infertility rate are many and are just as likely to be found in the male as in the female. They include a rise in venereal diseases; the fact that many women in industrialized countries are delaying pregnancy and child rearing until later in life;

the use of such recreational drugs as marijuana and cocaine, which affect the structure of the sperm and egg; and side effects of using contraceptives such as the pill and IUDs. Approximately 90% of the causes of infertility are physical, not psychological, and it is curable in about half of those cases (Menning, 1988).

Sex Ratios

Because half of a man's sperm carry an X chromosome and half carry a Y chromosome, the probability of having a female baby (two Xs—one from the mother and one from the father) should be identical to that of having a male baby (mother's X plus Y from father). In actuality, however, there are about 106 boys born for every 100 girls. When spontaneous abortions (miscarriages) are considered, the estimates for males and females *conceived* range from 116 to 160 boys for every 100 girls (Volpe, 1971).

The lopsided sex ratio of males to females is related to the differences between X-carrying and Y-carrying sperm. The Y-carrying sperm (potential boys) are smaller and faster swimmers than the X-carrying sperm (potential girls). Because they are faster, more Y-carrying sperm than X-carrying sperm will reach the ovum, and by the law of averages, more males will be conceived than females. But Y-carrying sperm are less resistant to the acidity of the female reproductive tract than are X-carrying sperm, making it more likely that the slower X-carrying sperm will survive. To make matters more complicated, the reproductive tract becomes less acidic (more alkaline) closer to the time of ovulation, again affording an advantage to the Y-carrying sperm.

When fertilization occurs, the prenatal period officially begins. The time between conception and birth is generally divided into three subperiods: the periods of the **zygote,** the **embryo,** and the **fetus.**

The Period of the Zygote ~ 2 weeks.

With conception, a biologically unique individual is begun. The 23 chromosomes of the ovum and the 23 chromosomes of the sperm merge to form a nucleus consisting of 46 chromosomes, the full human complement. The period of the zygote lasts up to two weeks, beginning with conception and ending with implantation in the uterine wall.

Once a sperm has impregnated an ovum, a chemical barrier is set up, preventing entrance of any additional sperm. If a second sperm should enter the egg, the resulting embryo will not survive. (Twins are *not* the result of two sperm impregnating the same ovum.) The zygote then begins a process of growth, with cells duplicating by mitosis. Sometimes, during these early cell divisions, the cells separate into two unique clusters, and each cluster continues to grow independently. This is how identical (or maternal) twins are produced. Because they develop from a single fertilized ovum, or zygote, they are technically known as monozygotic twins. The resulting individuals are genetically identical, although they may experience different conditions in the uterus. Nonidentical (or fraternal) twins result when a woman produces two viable ova in a month, and each is fertilized. Technically known as dizygotic twins, they are as similar to each other genetically as any other two siblings. Fraternal twins may be both boys, both girls, or one of each. It is even possible for fraternal twins to have different fathers—one supermarket tabloid story that has some scientific basis. Some women produce two ova every month, making it likely that each pregnancy they have will result in fraternal twins. Producing nonidentical (but not identical) twins runs in the mother's family, although the exact pattern of inheritance is not yet known.

Cell division is slow and even for the first several days, and by the fourth day after conception the zygote consists of 60 to 90 cells. From this point, cells begin to divide at different rates and into different structures, forming a hollow sphere called the **blastocyst.** After about one week, the blastocyst enters the uterus and begins to burrow into the soft, spongy tissue of the uterine wall. The blastocyst secretes special enzymes that break down cells of the uterine wall. It ruptures small blood vessels in the uterus and begins receiving nutrients directly from the mother. During this time, cells appear that will become the **umbilical cord** (which connects the embryo to the placenta), the **amniotic** and **chorionic sacs** (membranes that encase and protect the baby), and the **yolk sac** (which produces blood cells until the embryo's liver, spleen, and bone marrow can produce them.) With implantation, the **placenta** begins to form. This will serve as the transport system between the mother and her baby. In the placenta, the mother's blood flows around capillaries from the embryo, and it is here that nutrients (including oxygen) are passed from mother to baby and waste products are passed in the other direction. The blood of the mother and embryo do not mix, but other substances can exchange through the placenta's semipermeable membrane. Which substances can and cannot cross this barrier has been the focus of much research aimed at protecting the fetus from harmful agents.

The Period of the Embryo – 6 weeks.

The implantation of the blastocyst into the uterine wall marks the end of the period of the zygote and the beginning to the period of the embryo. Between 25% and 35% of blastocysts will implant successfully, resulting in pregnancy (Sher & Marriage, 1988).

The entire embryonic period lasts a mere six weeks, but the changes that occur in this brief time are dramatic. At implantation, the blastocyst is merely a small clump of cells shaped much like a rubber ball with one side pushed in. By the end of this period, most major organs have formed and are functioning to some extent.

Development is most rapid for the nervous system, but a heart is beating and blood is circulating as early as the fourth week after conception (L. K. Moore, 1977). By the end of the first month, the embryo is only one-fourth of an inch long, and most of that length is its head. The embryo also has a tail and gill arches—vestiges of our evolutionary past that will have disappeared by birth.

During the second month, facial features begin to develop. The ears, nose, mouth, and external portions of the eyes are apparent, making it clear by the seventh week that the embryo is human. Arms, legs, and toes are formed, the circulatory system is working, and digestive and respiratory systems are fully formed but not yet functioning (Barclay, 1985). By the eighth week, the kidneys are functioning and excreting urine. The embryo is now capable of movement, although it is jerky and not coordinated, with the whole body or large segments of the body reacting in a general way to stimulation (Hoffer, 1981). Finer muscle control and voluntary movement must wait until the next period of development.

The oversized head of the embryo during these early weeks reflects a pattern of development that will characterize the child throughout its growth: development proceeds from head to foot. This head-downward developmental trend, referred to as

cephalocaudal development, characterizes both prenatal and postnatal growth (see Figure 4.2). Cephalocaudal development characterizes all mammals, but is especially prominent in humans, whose large brain (relative to body size) needs to develop early (and continue to develop for a long period of time) in order to promote survival.

The Period of the Fetus - till birth

The skeleton of the embryo consists of cartilage. About the end of the eighth week, cartilage begins to be replaced by true bone (L. K. Moore, 1977), marking the beginning of the fetal period. During the embryonic period, all organ systems were formed, though not perfected. The time from now through birth—the longest period of prenatal development—is devoted to perfecting the organs, changing proportions, and growth.

By the 12th week of life, the genitals have become apparent, and the sex of the child can be determined. Primitive lungs begin to expand and contract, apparently in practice for later breathing. Around the 16th to 18th week, an important event occurs for the mother, although it is an inconsequential one for the fetus. It is at this time that the mother first feels the baby move. This is referred to as **quickening,** and in the past it has been used as an

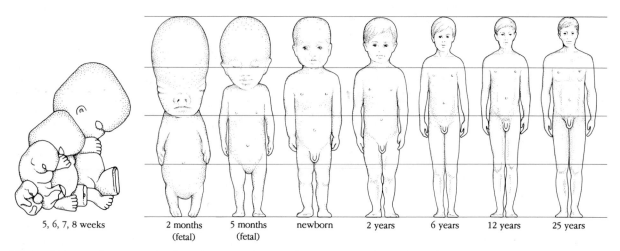

5, 6, 7, 8 weeks   2 months (fetal)   5 months (fetal)   newborn   2 years   6 years   12 years   25 years

Figure 4.2 Age changes in body proportions from embryonic stage through adulthood. Note how the head becomes proportionally smaller relative to the body with age.

indication that the baby is a living being. In fact, the first signs of movement are late in the embryonic period, but these early movements are not noticed by the mother because the embryo is so small (Barclay, 1985).

During the last eight weeks or so before birth, development consists mainly of growth; no new structures develop during this time. Although a full-term gestation period is considered to be 38 weeks, infants have a reasonable chance of living, in a highly protective environment, if they are born as early as the 26th or 27th week. An infant born much earlier than this would not be likely to live because of the immaturity of its respiratory system. The lungs are able to exchange limited amounts of gases beginning between the 26th and 29th weeks, and if the infant weighs more than 1000 grams, it has a fair chance of survival (Barclay, 1985).

Environmental Effects on Prenatal Development

The unborn child spends about 38 weeks in the protective environment of its mother's womb. But it is an environment nonetheless, and we can reasonably talk about environmental effects and experiences of the embryo and fetus. Most discussion of these environmental effects concerns factors that hinder or interfere with normal growth and development. Maternal malnutrition has received considerable attention, as have the effects of **teratogens,** which are defined as any agents external to the embryo/fetus that interfere with development. Among known teratogens for human development are alcohol, tobacco, narcotic drugs, some nonnarcotic drugs, radiation, and diseases in the mother. It was once believed that the placenta served as an efficient filter, blocking out all agents in the mother that did not belong in the fetus and letting only "the good stuff" through. We know now that this is not the case and that any substance that circulates in the mother's blood can potentially enter the baby's system.

Before discussing these harmful influences, we should mention that the effect of external agents on a fetus depends on timing. The same agent may have a serious effect on development at one time but little or no effect at another. Generally, the most serious effects for development occur during the embryonic period, when all major organ systems are being formed. This is the time when pregnant women

should be most careful about ingesting anything that may prove harmful to the developing baby. Unfortunately, it is also a time when many women are unaware that they are pregnant. Anything that interferes with how genetic instructions are carried out at this time can affect the organization of an entire organ system. There are different critical periods for the formation of different organ systems.

Maternal nutrition It was believed well into this century that a poorly nourished pregnant woman was hurting only herself—that the baby she was carrying would take what nutrients it needed from the mother (Barclay, 1985). By the 1940s it was obvious that this was not the case. Animal studies had clearly shown that malnourished mothers produced a higher proportion of deformed and abnormally small offspring (Osofsky, 1975). Similar studies with humans are more difficult to do, of course, but studies relating pregnant women's diets to the outcomes of their pregnancies showed clearly that women with poor diets had smaller and less healthy babies.

Unless a woman is severely malnourished, there will be no adverse effects on her infant if the malnourishment occurs during the embryonic period. Although this is the most rapid period of development, the embryo is small and requires relatively little in the way of nutrition from the mother. The effects of maternal malnutrition become greater later in pregnancy, with poor nutrition affecting especially the growth of the brain (see Storfer, 1990).

Smoking Although smoking is becoming less popular in the United States, about 30% of American women continue to smoke, and it is still very popular among both sexes in Europe and Asia. The health hazards to smokers are well known, and the hazards to their unborn children are also becoming well publicized, as reflected in the warnings on packs of cigarettes sold in the United States. It is now well documented that women who smoke during pregnancy have smaller babies, a higher incidence of spontaneous abortions, and infants with a slower rate of postnatal growth, relative to women who do not smoke (Barclay, 1985; Witter & King, 1980).

The detrimental effects of smoking are related to the gases carried in cigarette smoke, including nicotine, carbon monoxide, and cyanide compounds. These gases pass through the placenta to the fetus

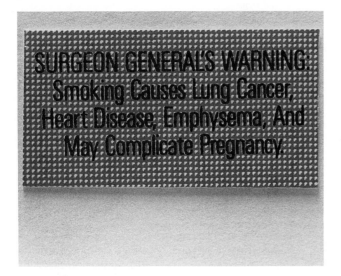

Pregnant women are warned that smoking can be dangerous to unborn children.

and prevent the absorption of oxygen. The high levels of carbon monoxide in cigarette smoke are particularly deleterious to proper growth (Burear, Shapcott, Berthiames, Monette, Blouin, Blanchard, & Begin, 1983).

Alcohol   It is only recently that the effects of alcohol as a teratogen have become well known (Jones & Smith, 1973). Alcohol passes through the placenta to the fetus and is distributed throughout its body and into the surrounding amnionic fluid, where it remains for twice as long as it does in the mother's body. The fetus can swallow this alcohol-polluted fluid, meaning that alcohol can affect the fetus longer than it does the mother (Brien, Loomis, Tranmer, & McGrath, 1983).

Babies born to women who consume large amounts of alcohol during pregnancy are at risk for a cluster of abnormalities that has been termed **fetal alcohol syndrome (FAS).** Many FAS infants are born with facial abnormalities, such as small eyelid openings, elongated midface, flattened profile, and underdeveloped jaws. There is frequently brain damage, including microcephaly, in which the forebrain (and thus the head) is very small and the child is severely retarded. Many FAS children show behav-ioral problems, such as hyperactivity, irritability, and poor physical coordination. The extent of the serious abnormalities shown by FAS infants is related to the amount and duration of alcohol consumption during pregnancy: the more a woman drinks and the longer she drinks, the higher is the risk of FAS (Hanson, Jones, & Smith, 1976).

Does this mean that it's safe to drink only occasionally, or only late in pregnancy? Unfortunately, there are no guidelines for safe drinking in pregnancy. For example, a recent study of 5-year-olds' motor performance has shown an effect of moderate alcohol consumption by mothers during pregnancy (Barr, Streissguth, Darby, & Sampson, 1990). Helen Barr and her colleagues reported a relationship between amount of alcohol consumed during pregnancy and children's errors and response speed on a test of fine motor behavior, as well as an effect on children's balance. The effects were most dramatic when alcohol was consumed before women knew they were pregnant. These results suggest that no level of exposure is absolutely safe. Thus, the best advice, given by most obstetricians today and by the United States Surgeon General (Surgeon General's Advisory on Alcohol and Pregnancy, 1981), is to use little or no alcohol at any time during pregnancy.

FAS is a major problem in the United States, and a leading cause of mental retardation, with approximately 5000 FAS infants born every year. (Dorfman, 1989).

Narcotic drugs   Babies born of women addicted to heroin are at risk for a variety of problems, including low birth weight, physical deformities, respiratory problems, and stillbirth. Between 70% and 90% of babies born to heroin-addicted mothers experience some symptoms of withdrawal shortly after birth (Householder, Hatcher, Burns, & Chasnoff, 1982). These infants remain irritable and restless over the first four to six months of life and are less responsive to visual and tactile stimulation, causing their caregivers to report frustration in dealing with them (Householder et al., 1982). Even though these physical characteristics usually disappear before the end of the first year, they can set up a pattern of interaction between children and their caregivers that is not conducive to healthy development (Zeskind & Ramey, 1978). Fewer complications are reported when pregnant women take methadone (a legal, "safe" alternative to heroin), although the infants still experience withdrawal symptoms (Householder et al., 1982).

Until recently, heroin was the major narcotic drug known to adversely affect prenatal development. Although the damaging effects of cocaine and marijuana were known from animal studies, there was little conclusive evidence about these drugs' effects on humans. However, with the increasing use of crack cocaine in urban areas throughout the United States, more and more infants are being born with serious birth defects that are attributed to their mother's chronic drug use. According to some estimates, as many as 1 in 10 babies born at urban hospitals shows signs of being prenatally exposed to cocaine (March of Dimes Birth Defects Foundation, 1989a).

There is no single profile of an infant born to a crack cocaine mother. Some appear healthy, whereas others show a wide range of physical and behavioral abnormalities (U.S. House of Representatives, Ways and Means Committee, Subcommittee on Human Resources, 1990). Some are highly excitable and jittery; others are sluggish and depressed; some are both.

The crack cocaine epidemic has all but crippled many urban hospitals around the country. Many crack babies are abandoned by their mothers and are unable to establish attachments with adults. As they grow up, the evidence suggests, they develop language more slowly and are particularly distractible. We must be careful, however, in attributing all the abnormalities observed in crack babies solely to crack cocaine. Most mothers addicted to crack cocaine are multiple drug users, many are undernourished, some have sexually transmitted diseases, and most receive little or no prenatal care. Each of these factors can affect a developing fetus (U.S. House of Representatives, Ways and Means Committee, Subcommittee on Human Resources, 1990). Crack cocaine may be the primary cause of the many disabilities seen in these infants, but they have experienced multiple assaults on their systems before ever being born, and crack cocaine is only one.

Nonnarcotic drugs   It is not only illicit drugs that have been linked to prenatal deformities; a number of prescription and over-the-counter drugs have also been associated with abnormalities. The most infa-

mous case involved thalidomide, a drug widely used in Europe, Canada, and Japan between 1957 and 1962 as a mild remedy for pain and sleeplessness. It was also used to alleviate the nausea often associated with the early stages of pregnancy. When an epidemic of birth defects swept these parts of the world, it was found that thalidomide caused deformities of the limbs. Sometimes arms and legs were entirely missing; in other cases, rudimentary hands or feet emanated directly from the shoulders or hips (Lenz & Knapp, 1962). The drug was withdrawn from the market in December of 1961. The effects of thalidomide depended on when during pregnancy it was taken. Women who took the drug early in pregnancy, between the third and seventh weeks, had babies with deformed limbs. The drug apparently interfered with the genetic instructions responsible for forming arms and legs, fingers and toes, but had no noticeable effects on the development of other systems. In fact, despite the extent of the abnormalities in some children, there are generally no effects on intelligence (Taussig, 1962), and many "thalidomide babies," now in their 30s, have grown up to be productive adults.

One other prescription drug that made headlines a decade or so ago was **diethylstilbestrol (DES).** A synthetic form of estrogen, DES was prescribed for women to prevent miscarriages, and no ill side effects on the fetus were observed. However, 15 to 20 years later, a higher incidence of a rare vaginal cancer was found in women whose mothers had taken DES during pregnancy. It was then discovered that DES causes abnormal development of the vaginal cells during prenatal development. Although a majority of DES daughters show abnormal vaginal cell growth (Johnson, Driscoll, Hertig, Cole, & Nickerson, 1979), only a small proportion—less than one-tenth of one percent—ever develop cancer (Orenberg, 1981). There also appears to be a higher incidence of genital abnormalities among men whose mothers took DES (Stillman, 1982), and both males and females exposed to DES have higher rates of infertility (Sher & Marriage, 1988). These findings indicate that a harmful agent taken during pregnancy may have delayed consequences for the child that are not revealed until adulthood.

Pharmaceutical companies and government agencies routinely test the effects of new drugs on pregnant animals, but for all practical purposes, it is wisest for a pregnant woman to take as few drugs as possible and to take none without consulting her doctor.

Radiation   High doses of radiation can produce severe damage to a developing embryo/fetus, including microcephaly (abnormally small brain), physical deformities, and spontaneous abortions. It is unusual for pregnant women to receive high dosages of radiation, the exception being medical treatment for cancer. But a "natural experiment" occurred in Hiroshima and Nagasaki, Japan, at the end of World War II, when pregnant women, far enough from the epicenter of the atomic blasts to survive, later gave birth. Physical deformities, such as microcephaly, occurred only if the women were in their first 18 weeks of pregnancy—again demonstrating the role of timing in the effect of a teratogen (Miller, 1979).

The low levels of radiation exposure associated with dental X-rays should not be enough to cause any damage, but, as with alcohol, there are no guidelines to determine what is safe. Therefore, pregnant women should postpone X-rays until after pregnancy if possible, or wear a lead apron if X-rays must be administered (Barclay, 1985).

Maternal disease   The placenta also permits the passage of some microorganisms that cause disease. For instance, the relatively mild disease rubella (German measles), if contracted by the mother during the first two months of pregnancy, can result in blindness, deafness, and other deformities (Gregg, 1942). Chicken pox can result in defects of fetal muscles and bones if the mother contracts the disease during the first trimester (March of Dimes Birth Defects Foundation, 1989b). However, if the mother contracts rubella or chicken pox after the third month of pregnancy, the chances of any associated birth defects are minimal.

Other infectious diseases have been associated with an increased incidence of spontaneous abortion, premature birth, and/or birth defects, including mumps, rubeola (red measles), malaria, syphilis, herpes, and toxoplasmosis (Cohen, 1984). Toxoplasmosis is transmitted by contact with an infected cat or by soil contaminated by cat feces. Although the disease is rarely serious for the mother, it can cause brain and eye damage in the unborn child (White & Sever, 1967).

Perhaps the most common infectious disease that is passed along to a developing fetus is cytomegalovirus, a form of herpes that affects the salivary glands. It can also be transmitted to the infant during birth, as can its close relative, herpes simplex 2, the most common sexually transmitted disease in the United States. The herpes virus can cause a range of deformities and even death. Because the virus is most easily passed on to the child during vaginal birth, women who have the disease are advised to have Caesarean section deliveries (Visintine, Nahmais, & Josey, 1978).

Recently, the AIDS epidemic has spread to children by way of their mothers. AIDS (acquired immune deficiency syndrome) is typically transmitted sexually, by the exchange of blood products, or by sharing contaminated needles (intravenous drug users). But pregnant women who have AIDS are likely to pass the disease on to their children at or before birth. Studies in the United States and also in Africa, where the disease is more common in the heterosexual population, report that about 50% of babies born to mothers with AIDS will have the disease themselves at birth, and that 95% of these infected infants will die within their first three years (Seabrook, 1987). Many infected infants do not show symptoms immediately after birth, however, suggesting that the actual infection rate may be even higher. It is not certain whether the AIDS virus infects the infant prenatally or at birth, when the umbilical cord separates from the placenta, permitting exchange of blood between mother and infant.

More recent research has shown that not all newborns testing positive for antibodies to the HIV virus, which causes AIDS, actually have the disease. In 40% to 80% of infants with the HIV antibodies, the positive testing reflects a passive transfer to the infant of antibodies from the mother, and not the virus itself. The HIV antibodies will be lost by these infants six to nine months after birth. Unfortunately, it is difficult to distinguish which infants have only their mothers' HIV antibodies and which have the virus themselves (Florida Medical Association, 1989).

As of November 1988, there were 1230 confirmed cases of pediatric AIDS in the United States. It is estimated that by the end of 1991 there will be 3000 such cases, with another 10,000 children testing positive for the HIV virus (APA Task Force on Pediatric AIDS, 1989).

Prenatal Diagnostic Testing

A major advance in medicine over the past few decades has been the ability to evaluate the health of a fetus that is still in the womb. Today, several methods of prenatal diagnostic testing enable obstetricians to get a clear picture of the developing fetus.

Ultrasound   **Ultrasound,** or sonography, has become a safe and readily available diagnostic tool found in many obstetricians' offices. It uses variations in high-frequency sounds—sonar—to produce a visual image of the fetus, much as ships use sonar to detect submarines. The mother's abdomen is scanned by a hand-held device that emits high-frequency sounds. The sounds bounce off the fetus, and a computer translates the resulting pattern into a picture on a monitor. Ultrasound is truly a noninvasive technique: there are no needles, drugs, pain, or X-rays, and both parents and physician can see the results of the test immediately. In fact, many

ultrasound technicians take Polaroid pictures for early entries in the baby book. Ultrasound can be used to confirm pregnancy, estimate the size and developmental age of the fetus, determine that the infant is alive by detecting the faint fetal heartbeat, and detect multiple births.

Alpha-fetoprotein testing (AFP)   Another low-risk diagnostic tool is **alpha-fetoprotein (AFP) testing.** In this technique, a sample of blood is drawn from the mother around the 16th week of pregnancy, and it is analyzed for the presence of alpha-fetoprotein. If found, the fetus may have a neural-tube defect such as spina bifida (in which there is an abnormal opening in the spinal column) or anencephaly, in which the brain does not develop properly, resulting in profound retardation. If the first test is positive, a second test is performed. AFP testing is not an accurate procedure: perhaps 20% of neural-tube defects are missed, and even if two consecutive tests are positive, there is still only a 4% to 10%

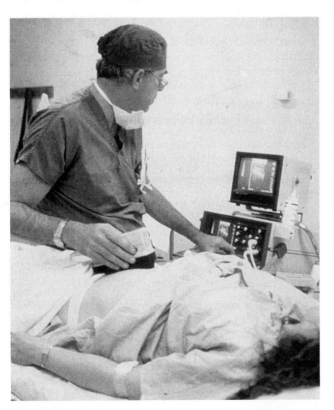

Sound waves bounce off the fetus and project a moving image on the monitor.

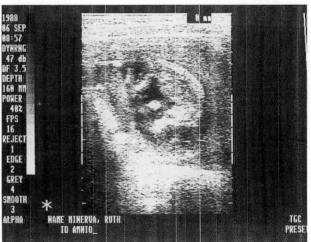

Ultrasound is a noninvasive technique that is commonly used to evaluate fetal development.

chance that the fetus actually has a neural-tube defect (Cherry, 1987). Because of this, a more definitive test will usually be done if there are two positive AFP testings, the most common test being amniocentesis.

Amniocentesis   **Amniocentesis** is the most commonly used prenatal screening technique for diagnosing chromosome abnormalities. In this procedure, a thin needle is passed through the skin of the pregnant woman's abdomen and, guided by ultrasound, into the amnionic sac. The amnionic sac contains the fetus and the amnionic fluid in which it floats. A small portion of the fluid is then withdrawn. In the fluid are skin cells from the fetus. These cells are placed in a lab culture, where they multiply, and are then analyzed for chromosome abnormalities. The amnionic fluid can also be analyzed for signs of spinal fluid (evidence for spina bifida) and for chemicals that signal an incompatibility between the blood of the mother and the blood of the fetus (Rh incompatibility). Complications resulting in fetal injury or miscarriage are relatively rare, occurring in about one in every 600 cases (Cherry, 1987). Amniocentesis can be done some time after the 16th week of pregnancy, with test results available two to three weeks later.

Chorionic villous sampling   One of the limitations of amniocentesis is that it cannot be done prior to the 16th week of pregnancy and requires additional weeks for the cells to be cultured and analyzed for chromosome abnormalities. A technique that can be used during the first trimester is **chorionic villous sampling** (CVS). Using ultrasound as a guide, a small tube is passed through the cervix into the uterus as early as the 9th to 12th week of pregnancy. Small pieces of tissue from a portion of the placenta called the chorion are drawn into the tube. The tissue collected from the chorion can be tested within one to two days. The advantages of CVS over amniocentesis seem obvious, but it is a relatively new technique and does not have the safe track record that amniocentesis has. There is evidence that the spontaneous abortion rate for women who have CVS is 1 to 3 percent (Cherry, 1987). Although the risk is slight, it is still substantially greater than with amniocentesis, and the technique is not yet recommended for women in low-risk groups. However, it looks as though this will soon become the standard prenatal diagnostic test.

Fetal monitoring and fetoscopy   Other recent advancements in prenatal diagnosis include **fetal monitoring,** in which the physiological characteristics (such as heartrate) of the fetus are monitored, and **fetoscopy,** which involves passing a viewing instrument through the abdomen into the amniotic sac. Fetoscopy is still in the experimental stage and has considerable risk associated with it. However, it has been used successfully for fetal surgery—operating on a fetus while still in the uterus. Fetal monitoring is used routinely in many medical centers, giving the medical staff information concerning the status of the fetus during labor and delivery.

Birth

Without complications, childbirth (see Figure 4.3) occurs about 270 days after the onset of the mother's last menstrual period. The process is described in three stages. The first is **labor,** which lasts about 12 hours and begins with small, periodic twinges as the cervix begins to open (dilate) and the birth canal softens (effaces). Labor intensifies into harder, more frequent contractions as the infant's head is pushed lower and lower, until it begins to emerge from the cervix. At this point, the second stage begins, known as **delivery.** Normal delivery is relatively quick, seldom lasting more than an hour and often only a few minutes. The infant's head passes down the birth canal, and little assistance is needed except to lift the infant out and cut the umbilical cord. The third stage, **afterbirth,** follows delivery and lasts about 15 minutes. This stage involves expulsion of the placenta as it separates from the wall of the uterus along with other membranes still in the uterus. Once the placenta is detached, the uterus contracts where the placenta separated to stop the bleeding.

Caesarean Section Delivery

Not all births occur according to plan, and in nearly 25% of deliveries in the United States it is deemed necessary to remove the baby through a surgical incision in the abdomen. This is called a **Caesarean section,** or **C-section,** because, according to legend, Julius Caesar was delivered in this fashion.

C-sections are used in cases of difficult labor, in which a vaginal birth would be highly risky for

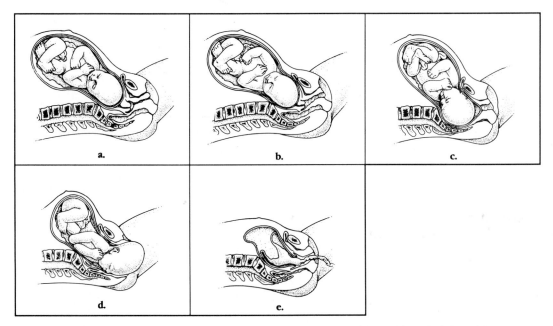

Figure 4.3 The birth process: (a) baby in uterus before the onset of labor; (b) early labor; (c) cervix completely dilated and baby ready for birth; (d) the baby's head begins to emerge; (e) afterbirth.

either the infant or the mother. Some of the common conditions making C-sections necessary are: breech birth, with babies having their feet or buttocks pointed toward the cervix; the baby's head is too large in relation to the mother's pelvic structure; the placenta is implanted over the cervical opening; contractions of the uterus are not strong enough to push out the baby.

With past C-section techniques, it was difficult for a woman to have a vaginal delivery once she had had a C-section—hence the old adage, "once a Caesarean, always a Caesarean." However, new techniques have made it possible for a C-section mother to have a normal, vaginal birth with subsequent children. A relatively new, hybrid variety of delivery is the VBAC—vaginal birth after Caesarean.

Childbirth through the Ages

The process of birth for humans has undergone many changes in our history. These changes tend to mirror society's changing attitudes toward the family in general, and women and children in particular.

The earliest recorded accounts of childbirth, dating back to the second century A.D., attest to its being presided over by women. The mother-to-be was usually assisted by other women—family members and friends, who were there for moral support, and older women who were valued for their experience both in bearing children and in assisting others. These childbirth experts became known as midwives and were the main source of childbirth assistance until the 1900s, when doctors took over the business of delivering babies. Other changes over time have involved maternal nutrition, complications of childbirth, disease and infection, and the use of anesthesia.

Health of the mother   Difficulties in childbirth, historically, often resulted from malnutrition of the mother during her own childhood, causing small stature and bone deformities. Pelvic openings that were too small or twisted caused long, difficult labors and sometimes the death of both mother and infant, simply because there was no room for the baby to pass through the pelvic opening.

Since the early 1900s, when the cause of rickets was discovered and children's nutrition improved, birth complications due to bone structure are no longer common in middle-class Western women.

When structural problems do occur, they can be detected early and safe Caesarean deliveries performed.

Normal complications of childbirth   Even when mother and infant are both healthy, complications happen. In about 5% of births, the infant is not in the normal head-down position, but is head-up (breech) or sideways (transverse). Although most breech births are ultimately delivered normally after prolonged labor, infants in other positions have to be repositioned, or some other intervention is needed. In the past, assistance in such cases included version (the manual turning of the infant inside the uterus) and embryotomy (crushing the infant's head and removing the dead infant with a hooked instrument). Today, Caesarean deliveries are used when the baby cannot be repositioned easily.

Another normal complication is hemorrhaging after the placenta is expelled. Without drugs to stop the bleeding from the veins and arteries in the uterus, women could bleed to death, even after a successful delivery.

Eclampsia, also known as toxemia, was once a common complication of first pregnancies. Preceded by sediment in the urine and swollen wrists and ankles, this condition of late pregnancy would lead to convulsions and sometimes death. No treatment was known, and many women believed it was just another unavoidable risk of pregnancy. Eclampsia has since been connected with hypertension and is controllable as blood pressure is monitored throughout the course of pregnancy.

Disease and infection   A major source of infection was the use of instruments by physicians and midwives working at the hospital or in the home. Tissue torn and bruised by forceps or hands inserted into the uterus to turn the infant is more susceptible to infection. It has been estimated that this use of instruments was responsible for about 33% of maternal infections in one hospital in 1904—decades before antibiotics were developed (Shorter, 1982).

A second major source of infection was the unwashed examining hand. Birth attendants of both genders felt compelled to routinely examine the prospective mother's cervix to see "how things were doing," even though this procedure was more to satisfy their own curiosity (and that of the awaiting family) than for any reason relevant to the birth itself. Since antiseptic procedures were not widely known until 1867, centuries of childbirth-related infections originated in this way.

A third major source of infection was a septic environment: bacteria in the home or hospital—in the air, on clothing, or on bathroom or bedroom surfaces—invaded the mother after childbirth.

Between 1870 and 1939, the rate of death from infection among new mothers declined dramatically in North America, in both home and hospital births. At the same time, the new industrial economy freed parents somewhat from producing large numbers of children. Birth control became more reliable and acceptable, and birth itself was not necessarily viewed as a life-threatening trauma. Children became a pleasure, and parents were able to concentrate on other aspects of childbirth than sheer physical survival.

The use of anesthesia   Anesthesia had been used for childbirth since 1847, when ether and chloroform were discovered. As childbirth became safer and other issues moved to the fore, new pain relievers were found. Twilight sleep, introduced in Freiberg, Germany, in 1902, soon became available to physicians throughout Europe and North America. This mixture of morphine and scopolomine allowed women to drift through labor in a semiconscious state. The effect of this "improvement" on childbirth practices was to move birth from the home to the hospital and to give priority to medical staff—physicians and nurses—rather than midwives, at least in middle- and upper-class urban areas.

Over the next 30 years, twilight sleep was replaced by a whole pharmacy of drugs used during childbirth, not only during the delivery (second) stage of birth but also during the labor (first) stage. Because the mother was often unconscious, more medical intervention and use of instruments was needed to deliver the child. Childbirth was no longer *assisted* by others; it was *performed* by others, much like an appendectomy.

The downfall of anesthetized childbirth was the discovery of its harmful effect on the child. Investigating the impact of different factors on the developing fetus, scientists began to discover the effects of drugs given to the mother. Shortly after physicians had adjusted their obstetrical procedures to fit anesthetized childbirth, a new movement began.

The year 1944 marked the American publication of Grantly Dick-Read's book, *Childbirth without Fear: The Principles and Practices of Natural Child-*

birth. Dick-Read, a British obstetrician, believed that women had been subjected to a fear of childbirth from childhood and that this deep-seated fear caused muscular tension which, in turn, made labor painful. His solution was to educate women (and society in general) to see childbirth as a joyous and satisfying event. Dick-Read also made popular the myth that primitive women who gave birth "naturally" had no fear of childbirth and, as a result, experienced no pain (Sandelowski, 1984).

What resulted was a combination of natural and medically assisted childbirth procedures—an Americanization of natural childbirth. Women still had their babies in hospitals without family members present. The labor rooms were stark, clinical, and furnished with hospital beds. Laboring women were usually grouped together in one room. An IV dripping saline was inserted in the woman's arm as standard procedure, just in case she needed anesthesia. Even though no use of instruments was planned, surgical preparation, including enemas and shaving of the pubic area, was also routine. Assistance during labor was provided by floor nurses, who would come and go with their appointed shifts. The result of this was that no one person stayed with the mother-to-be during the entire period. And to top it off, not many of these fearless women found childbirth to be painless. In a 1949 study of 400 women, only 2% reported experiencing no pain (Goodrich, 1950).

What emerged from this chaos was the current attitude toward childbirth assistance. Midwives and home birthing were rediscovered as alternatives to hospital births. In contrast to earlier times, however, childbirth had become a safer process regardless of where it occurred or who assisted.

The 1980s brought new economic factors into the arena of childbirth. Hospitals overbuilt, and medical costs soared. To keep obstetrical patients using their facilities, hospitals created birthing centers. There couples can attend prenatal classes on childbirth preparation, and older siblings can tour the facility before the baby comes. Labor and delivery take place in a cozy bedroom setting, attended by the father and any other people the mother wants. Once the baby is delivered, it is immediately handed to the wide-awake mother and father and remains in the room with the mother until she is stabilized and moved to a conventional room. There the options continue, with the mother deciding between rooming-in (keeping the baby in her room), nursery

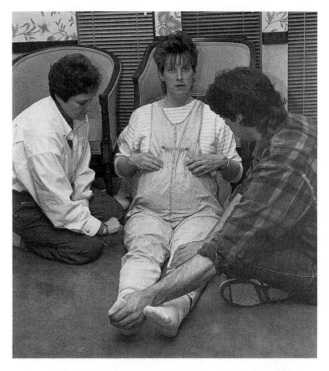

Many of today's parents-to-be take a team approach to childbirth preparation.

care, or any combination of the two. Many hospital birthing centers offer additional "perks" for couples who choose them, including champagne dinners for the new parents, family parties for all the relatives, and "birth day" parties so other children in the family can greet the new baby.

The Baby at Birth

Newborn babies, it is said, look like little old men—all bald and wrinkled. Their heads are often misshapen as a result of being squeezed through the birth canal. Fortunately, the bones of their skulls are flexible, and their heads will shortly settle into a more pleasing shape. Likewise, their faces may be distorted and may even have suffered bruises—both conditions that change within days of birth.

Of far greater significance than the newborn's appearance is its health. The transition from life in the uterus to life in the outside world is a dramatic one. For the first time, the infant must breathe for itself rather than receiving oxygen through the placenta. It must adjust from a cozy world of 98.6 degrees to

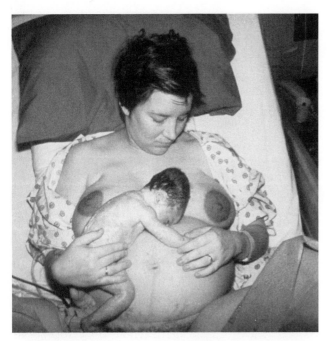

Mother and infant share a quiet moment between the end of one stage in their relationship and the beginning of another.

Table 4.1 The Apgar test

Sign	Score		
	0	1	2
Heart rate	No heart beat	Under 100 beats per minute	100 to 140 beats per minute
Breathing (respiratory effort)	No breathing	Irregular, shallow breathing	Strong breathing and crying
Reflex irritability	No response	Weak reflexive response	Strong reflexive response (sneezing, coughing, grimacing)
Muscle tone	Limp	Weak flexion of arms and legs	Strong flexion of arms and legs
Color	Blue body and extremities	Body pink, extremities blue	Completely pink

Source: Adapted from Apgar, 1953.

one that is in all likelihood much cooler (mid-70s for most hospital births). Soon it must obtain nourishment from eating, rather than receiving it passively through the umbilical cord. These changes are substantial indeed. Birth unquestionably represents a major discontinuity, with many physiological systems changing drastically and abruptly. Understandably, not all infants make the transition easily.

Infants who do not adjust immediately to the external world need special medical attention. Delivery room personnel quickly assess the newborn's survival chances using the standardized **Apgar test.** Named for Dr. Virginia Apgar (1953), the test is used to evaluate a baby's biological fitness by assigning a score of 0, 1, or 2 for each of five areas: heart rate, breathing (or respiration), reflex irritability, muscle tone, and color (see Table 4.1). The Apgar is given at one minute and again at five minutes after birth. A score of 7 or higher means the baby is in good health (10 is perfect). Scores between 4 and 6 indicate that the infant may require special help establishing breathing or other vital signs; a score of 3 or

lower reflects serious danger and calls for emergency intervention.

Transition to Parenthood

With the birth of their first child, a man and a woman become parents; they go from being a couple to being a family. For most couples, the introduction of a baby produces a dramatic change in lifestyle. Many young women are anxious about becoming mothers and self-critical throughout the transition to parenthood. For most women, a new infant does cause problems, but positive feelings about their babies show a steady increase over time. In contrast, positive feelings about their husbands tend to peak in the months prior to birth and are at their lowest in the months immediately after the baby is born (Fleming, Ruble, Flett, & Van Wagner, 1990).

The Neonate

It was once believed that **neonates** (infants from birth through the first month of life) made no sense

Box 4.1

Becoming a Parent

Dr. Gabriele Gloger-Tippelt,
Psychology Department at the University
of Heidelberg, Germany

If you ask women or men in their midlife years to list events that have brought the most profound changes in their lives, they will name the birth of their first (and following) child among the top-ranking life events. Yet, because of the widespread acceptance of contraceptive methods and changing values, we observe a broad variation in the timing and circumstances of becoming a parent. The life plans of many women in modern societies include prolonged education, job experience, a satisfying partnership, and enjoyment of common leisure activities with this partner before they actively plan for parenthood. Some women/couples postpone parenthood until their 30s or 40s, hoping that prenatal diagnostics will minimize the risks of a late pregnancy. Single-parent families have become more common. A very different pattern develops for the teenage mother, whose maternity is sometimes unplanned but gradually accepted.

The timing of parenthood has implications for the course of adult lives. Personal and social conditions preceding the first pregnancy determine the ability of young adults to cope with pregnancy, birth, and the needs of a very dependent baby. Such conditions include the quality of the partnership, level of education, economic security, amount of birth preparation, and social support. As the biological alterations during this phase of life are well known, we have to focus more on the psychological and social aspects of the transition to parenthood. For the woman, these include a major transformation of her body image and identity. Also, both partners are undergoing shifts in social categorization: they may perceive themselves as being no longer in their youth, but becoming mature persons; as being no longer a loving couple, but a "mother" and a "father." Moreover, the first birth brings radical changes in the daily routine and division of labor, moving the couple in the direction of more traditional, sex-typed roles: the woman caring for the child and the home, the man continuing his career and providing the family income. Not surprisingly, women in particular report that they are less satisfied in their marriage during the first months after birth. Becoming a parent is not a single event, but rather a chain of events with successive new tasks that give new mothers and fathers a chance gradually to develop a sense of competence in the parental role. As a result, despite the many strains and stresses during the early phase of family formation, most couples emphasize the enriching and gratifying experience of having children.

Reprinted by permission.

of their world and responded randomly to events surrounding them. Clearly the motor, perceptual, and cognitive abilities of the neonate are quite limited, but they do exist. Babies come into the world "preorganized," in that they respond to certain stimulation in a specified way and are prepared to perceive and learn some forms of information more readily than others.

Box 4.2

A Birthday Letter from Dad

June 30, 1988

Dear Brittany,

The first eight weeks of your life have been filled with conflicting emotions for me—overwhelming joy at your arrival and intense frustration at trying to learn to be a father. With all the books we've read and the class we took, I still don't know the "right" answers.

Your birth was spectacular! Mom and I had taken a childbirth preparation class when you were still four months from arrival, which really helped us know what to expect and stay calm. Mom went into labor and we went to the hospital twice, and they sent us home each time when she didn't progress after a few hours. The third time, the doctor gave her Pitocin and the labor started for real. I stayed with her all morning and all afternoon except when the doctor sent me out for lunch, and then I set a hospital record for gobbling it down so I could get back.

By dinner the contractions had almost stopped again. The doctor said that things weren't going right and that he would have to do a Caesarean. I have never felt anything like that before, and I don't think I ever will again. Things are like that with your first child. The doctor gave us a few minutes alone, and we prayed for your healthy delivery. The difficult part was that we had spent nine months hoping and praying that everything would be perfect. We knew that complications happen, but we thought that if we did everything right before you were born, it wouldn't happen to us. But there was no time to dwell on it. Mom went into the operating room and the doctor told me to get ready, so I scrubbed and put on a gown and hat.

Entering the operating room made me apprehensive for the first time that day, but Mom was strong enough for both of us. Nobody has that reserve of inner strength like your Mom. She was awake throughout the surgery and I sat by her, held her hand, and talked to her. The surgery only lasted about 30 minutes, but it seemed like 30 days in some ways and like 30 seconds in others. The result was you! They asked me what your name was going to be, and I couldn't speak. There you were, breathing air for the first time. I was in shock.

Mom recovered in record time; Dad recovered several weeks later. You are still amazing. Your personality is already showing as you struggle to get into a more comfortable position or to get a better view of things. You are intensely curious, determined to do things, and always calm in difficult situations. Your Aunt Debbie said that she would have a dozen kids if they could all be like you. Mom and I think that God sent you first as an incentive for us to have more brothers and sisters for you.

I don't know what the future holds for us. I try to think of the big girl who will be able to read this someday, and I wonder who will be helping you with the words. I wonder if there is something important to say that I have left out. Life is a lot like that—you only get one chance, and all you can do is your best. I guess all parents have successes and failures, and as much as I would like it to be untrue, I'm sure I will fail you sometimes. I truly hope not.

You have become the second person in the world that I love unconditionally. The greatest hope I can have is that we will stay close to each other and that in your life you will find happiness.

Love, Dad

Reprinted by permission.

Reflexes

Newborn babies can move their heads, arms, and legs, and sometimes they seem to do nothing but squirm, almost randomly, particularly when they are distressed. But there is much more to a neonate's motor abilities than just these squirmings. Newborns come into the world with a set of motor reflexes (simple responses to simple stimuli); some of the more important and better studied of these are described in Table 4.2.

Some neonatal reflexes have obvious survival value. For example, infants will turn their heads away from an object that obstructs breathing. The survival value for such a reflex is obvious, as is the reflex for sucking. An infant who had to learn to suck would have a very difficult time obtaining nutrition, and thus would not be likely to live. Related to nursing is the rooting reflex, whereby infants turn their heads in the direction of stimulation when they are stroked on the cheek or corner of the mouth. The palmar grasp, in which infants spontaneously grasp an object (such as a finger) placed in the hand, was probably of more practical value to our distant ancestors for clinging to tree branches or the hair on their mother's back.

Most neonatal reflexes gradually disappear over the first six months or so, as infants become increasingly able to direct their own actions intentionally. It appears, however, that many infant reflexes, in addition to helping babies survive during the early months of life, also serve as the basis for the motor programs involved in voluntary control. For example, the walking reflex is displayed when neonates are held upright with their feet touching a flat surface: they will lift one foot after another, as if walking. It is many months, of course, before infants can truly walk, but classic research by Philip Zelazo and his colleagues (Zelazo, Zelazo, & Kolb, 1972) demonstrated that this neonatal reflex may be related to the intentional movements infants use later in walking. Although the reflex typically disappears in the second month, they showed that babies who exercised the reflex (that is, babies stimulated to use the walking reflex daily from the second through the eighth week of life), developed more regular walking movements compared to a control group of infants who did not get the chance to exercise their walking reflex. Moreover, those in the exercise group walked on their own more than one month earlier than did control infants.

Table 4.2 Neonatal reflexes

Reflex	Eliciting Stimulus	Response	Approximate Course of Development
Moro	Loud sound, loss of support, sudden movement	Extension of forearms and fingers followed by return to chest	Disappears within 3 months
Palmar	Pressure against palm	Grasping	Disappears within 4–6 months
Plantar	Pressure to balls of feet	Flexion of toes (toe grasping)	Disappears within 10 months
Walking	Upright position and feet touching level surface	Walking movements	Disappears within 2 months
Righting of head and body	Head or leg turning	Trunk or head movement in the same direction	Disappears within 1 year
Withdrawal	Painful stimulus	Limb withdrawal	Permanent
Rooting	Stimulation around mouth region	Head movement toward stimulus	Disappears within 4–6 months
Sucking	Object inserted into mouth	Sucking	Disappears within 4–6 months
Crawling	Prone position and pressure applied alternately to soles of feet	Crawling pattern	Disappears within 4 months
Swimming	Placed in water with head supported	Swimming movements	Disappears within 5 months
Climbing	Held in horizontal position	Climbing movements	Disappears within 6 months

Why does the reflex typically disappear? Esther Thelen (1983) proposed that as infants gain weight during their early months, they no longer have the muscle strength to lift their heavy legs. Thelen and her co-workers demonstrated this, in part, by showing that infants' stepping movements increase when their legs are submerged in water (Thelen, Fisher, & Ridley-Johnson, 1984). As infants gain in strength, the reflex returns near the end of the first year to aid them in learning to walk. Thelen suggested that the exercise given babies in the Zelazo experiment served to build their leg muscles, thus giving them the increased strength necessary to use the reflex and permitting them to stand and walk at an earlier age (Thelen, 1983).

Box 4.3

Sudden Infant Death Syndrome (SIDS)

Perhaps 8000 American infants each year go to sleep one night and never wake up. They die from what has been termed **Sudden Infant Death Syndrome (SIDS),** or crib death. These babies suffocate in their sleep, often with few signs beforehand of any medical problem. SIDS is most apt to occur in infants between 1 and 6 months of age, in the winter, in nonwhite and poor families, and in preterm infants (Lewak, Zebal, & Friedman, 1984). It is the number-one killer of infants after the critical first few days of life.

The exact cause of SIDS is not known. Although most parents of infants who die of SIDS have no clue that their babies were at risk, there is some indication that these infants were biologically vulnerable from birth. An examination of Apgar scores for babies who died of SIDS indicates that many showed respiratory abnormalities and poor muscle tone (Lipsitt, Sturner, & Burke, 1979). Yet other researchers have failed to find differences in birth characteristics between infants who die of SIDS and those who do not (Waggener, Southall, & Scott, 1990).

Several hypotheses have been generated to explain SIDS. Louis Lipsitt (1979, 1982) has proposed that SIDS victims may be unable to clear their respiratory passages reflexively of mucus or saliva. These infants also fail to learn voluntary ways of clearing their respiratory passages, making them especially susceptible to choking.

Another theory that has received considerable attention is that SIDS is a form of apnea—brief periods of sleep when breathing stops. Apnea occurs in all infants, but most babies automatically begin breathing again after a few seconds. Infants who succumb to SIDS, however, fail to resume breathing and thus suffocate. Although the apnea theory of SIDS makes intuitive sense, the data supporting the theory are meager (see Culbertson, Krous, & Bendell, 1988), and some researchers have argued that behavioral factors, such as temperamental and behavioral differences between infants, should be more seriously considered for predicting and preventing SIDS (Lipsitt, 1990).

For infants who are at risk for SIDS (for example, infants born prematurely and those who have had a sibling die of SIDS), special electronic monitoring devices have been developed. Babies are attached to the monitors, and whenever breathing stops an alarm sounds, alerting parents to pick up their babies and pat them rapidly on the back. Typically, this is enough to restart their breathing. Not surprisingly, parents who are on a life-and-death watch with their infants show signs of stress. The equipment is not perfect, and there are many false alarms. The monitoring equipment does save lives, however. Yet thousands of infants still die of SIDS each year, making it clear that monitoring devices alone are not enough. We need to be able to predict more accurately which infants are likely to succumb to SIDS and the reasons for their vulnerability so that new interventions can be developed.

Basic Perceptual and Cognitive Abilities of the Neonate

The first great American psychologist, William James (1890), described the world of the young infant as "one great blooming buzzing confusion." This view of young infants as passive nonperceivers was held by many psychologists and physicians well into the 1950s and 1960s and continues to be held by many despite evidence to the contrary.

In the past 30 years, we have learned enough about the perceptual and cognitive abilities of infants to know that James's view was wrong. Although newborns' skills in these areas are greatly limited, they do exist. They can also learn, adjusting their behavior to conditions in their environment, and they develop preferences for certain sensations in the first week of life. There is also some controversial evidence that they are able to imitate adult facial gestures.

Skin and body-orientation senses   The sense of touch actually consists of several different senses. There are separate receptors for pressure, pain, and temperature, all of which are functioning in the neonate. Newborns are especially sensitive to slight changes in temperature and are very receptive to being touched. This sensitivity to touch is apparent during the early fetal period (Carmichael, 1970), and several studies have demonstrated more rapid development in groups of premature infants receiving tactile stimulation (Scarr-Salapatek & Williams, 1973; Solkoff, Yaffe, Weintraub, & Blase, 1969; White & LaBarba, 1976). For example, in a study by Jerry White and Richard LaBarba (1976), premature infants were assigned to one of two groups. Babies in the control group received standard nursery care. Babies in the experimental group received the same care, but were also stroked for four 15-minute periods each day for their first ten days. Experimental infants drank significantly more formula and gained significantly more weight over the course of this brief treatment than did control infants. Changes in weight (expressed in grams) over the first ten days of life for the experimental and control infants are shown in Figure 4.4. The fact that the only difference between the two groups was the tactile stimulation they received indicates that such stimulation is not

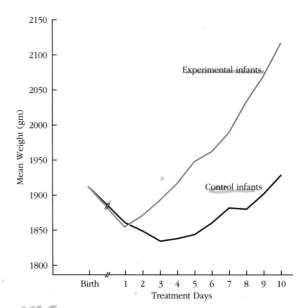

Figure 4.4 Average weight gain of premature infants given extra handling and those given standard nursery care. *Source:* From "The Effects of Tactile and Kinesthetic Stimulation on Neonatal Development in the Preterm Infant," by J. L. White and R. C. LaBarba, *Developmental Psychobiology,* 1976, *9,* 569–577. Copyright © 1976 by John Wiley & Sons, Inc. Reprinted by permission.

only perceived by premature infants, but fosters physical development.

Of the skin senses, pain is likely the least developed, although, as any parent will tell you, the sense does function early in life. Infant boys experiencing circumcision, done without benefit of anesthesia, will wail, demonstrating dramatically that their pain receptors are working. However, these boys are soon able to nurse, to interact with their mothers, and to sleep, suggesting that their pain perception is not as keen as that of an older child (Gunnar, Malone, Vance, & Fisch, 1985). One possible reason for neonates' seeming insensitivity to pain is that, during birth, the body produces natural opiates that block pain receptors.

An awareness of the position of one's body in space (vestibular sense) is also well developed at birth. Newborns display a startle response, extending their forearms and later returning them to their chest (the Moro reflex) to a sudden movement or loss of support. Also, as all grandmothers know, one of the most effective techniques for soothing fussy babies involves regular alterations of their body position, usually accompanied by tactile stimulation (Korner & Thoman, 1972). That is, babies can be comforted by being rocked and hugged.

Chemical senses   The chemical senses of gustation (taste) and olfaction (smell) are reasonably well developed at birth. Newborns show different facial expressions, tongue movements, and physiological responses for each of the four basic tastes of sweet, sour, salty, and bitter, and show a preference for sweet substances (Cowart, 1981; Rosenstein & Oster, 1988; Steiner, 1979).

Babies can also discriminate among a wide variety of odors early in life (Steiner, 1979) and develop preferences for certain odors within the first week. For example, in a study by Aidan Macfarlane (1975), 6-day-old nursing babies were able to discriminate their mothers' odor from that of other women. Mothers wore breast pads in their bras between nursings. Two breast pads were placed on either side of an infant's head—one pad from the mother and the other from another woman. Although there were no differences in infants' behaviors in this situation at 2 days of age, by day 6, babies turned to their own mother's pad more often than to another woman's. That is, not only can babies discriminate odors, they quickly learn to make associations with odors and to modify their behavior accordingly.

In more recent work using a procedure similar to that of Macfarlane, researchers reported that bottle-fed 2-week-old infants preferred the breast odor of a lactating female over that of a nonlactating female (Makin & Porter, 1989).

Hearing   Auditory perception is well developed in the newborn. Infants appear to be more sensitive to high-frequency than to low-frequency tones (Trehub, Schneider, & Endman, 1980), and this may explain their preference for female over male voices. As with olfaction, infants less than 1 week old have been shown to recognize their mothers on the basis of sound. Anthony DeCasper and William Fifer (1980) measured the rate at which 1- to 3-day-old infants sucked on a pacifier and then conditioned

babies to alter their sucking rate (faster for half the babies and slower for the other half) to the tape-recorded voices of their mothers or an unfamiliar woman. DeCasper and Fifer reported that these young infants varied their sucking rate to hear their mothers' voices, indicating that not only could they discriminate the mother's voice from another woman's, but they had acquired a distinct preference for the mother's voice in a matter of days.

There is some evidence that neonates' preference for their mothers' voices may be acquired in utero. In a study by Anthony DeCasper and Melanie Spence (1986), pregnant women read aloud one of three passages twice a day during the last six weeks of their pregnancy. Shortly after birth, the neonates were tested for which passages, if any, they preferred, as reflected in their patterns of nonnutritive sucking. First, the researchers determined a baseline sucking rate for each baby—that is, how rapidly the infant sucked on a nipple when no passage was being played. They then placed earphones over the baby's ears and played either the passage read during pregnancy or a new one. For some infants, the familiar passage was played whenever they increased their sucking rate, and the novel passage was played whenever their sucking rate declined; for other infants, the pattern was reversed. DeCasper and Spence reported that infants were more apt to alter their sucking rate to hear the familiar passage than to hear the new passage. Furthermore, the reinforcing value of the story was independent of who recited it—the infant's mother or another woman. These results present unambiguous evidence of prenatal conditioning to auditory patterns. Not only were the newborns' auditory systems working well, but they had learned to discern the auditory characteristics of these often-repeated stories.

Vision   Because of the absence of light in utero, vision does not function prenatally. Newborns can perceive light, as demonstrated by the pupillary reflex (constriction of the pupil to bright light and dilation of the pupil to low levels of illumination), and apparently see the world in color (Adams, Maurer, & Davis, 1986). However, **accommodation,** or focusing of the lens, is relatively poor at birth. Early research indicated that infants are born with a fixed lens, so that only stimuli approximately 20 centimeters away (about 8 inches) are in focus (Haynes, White, & Held, 1965). More recent work by Martin

Banks (1980) indicates that, under favorable stimulus conditions, accommodation is adultlike by as early as 2 months of age, with many younger infants displaying good accommodative ability.

Newborns will visually track a moving object, but their eyes will not necessarily be moving together in harmony. Convergence refers to both eyes looking at the same object, an ability apparently not possessed by newborns (Wickelgren, 1967). Convergence and coordination (both eyes following a moving stimulus in a coordinated fashion) improve over the first months of life and are adultlike by 6 months (Aslin & Jackson, 1979). Studies attempting to determine the visual acuity of infants—their ability to see clearly—have yielded varied results, depending on the technique used. Estimates of newborn acuity range from 20/400 to 20/600 (adult normal is 20/20), making neonates legally blind (and disqualifying them for a driver's license). Acuity improves over the next several months and, by some estimates, reaches adult levels by 6 months (see Walk, 1981).

Despite their limited visual abilities, there is evidence that newborns can see objects—that is, they can discriminate between two visual patterns. Several techniques are used to determine whether infants can tell the difference between two patterns, but the simplest is based on visual preferences. In this technique, introduced by Robert Fantz (1958), researchers show two patterns (either together or one at a time), and the amount of time the infant spends looking at each pattern is noted. If babies look longer at one pattern than another, we conclude that they can discriminate between the two patterns and prefer one to the other. The apparatus used by Fantz in his early studies of infant perception is shown in Figure 4.5. Using this and other techniques, research has shown that infants in the first days of life can discriminate between visual stimuli if they are sufficiently discrepant (Fantz, 1961; Friedman, 1972). And what do babies like to look at? Generally, they prefer to look at moving stimuli with high contrast.

Newborns have an impressive array of perceptual capabilities. They can see, hear, taste, and smell; they can make subtle discriminations among stimuli and have innate preferences for some. Their perception is not as acute as that of the toddler or even the 5-month-old, but their world is not merely a "blooming buzzing confusion."

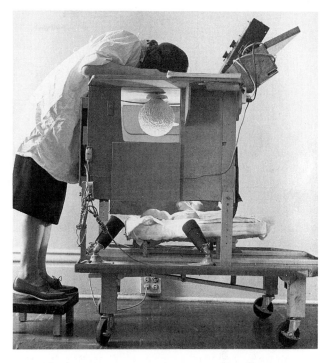

Figure 4.5 Apparatus used to assess infants' visual preferences (from Fantz, 1962).

Learning Can newborns learn? As we have seen in our discussion of perception, the answer is yes. In the experiment by Macfarlane (1975), infants less than a week old learned to discriminate between their mothers' odor and that of other women, and the experiment by DeCasper and Spence (1986) showed that some learning of basic auditory patterns occurs even prenatally.

Newborns can learn some things easily; they will modify their behavior in order to receive some type of reward. The trick, of course, is to find a behavior that infants can control themselves and to find something that infants find rewarding. Behaviors that newborns can control include sucking rate, head turning, and kicking, all of which have been used in learning experiments. Reinforcements have included milk, human voices, and music (Lipsitt, 1982). In one experiment, for example, newborns would suck on a pacifier in order to hear music as opposed to nonrhythmic noise (Butterfield & Siperstein, 1972), demonstrating both an ability to learn and an innate preference for patterned (nonrandom) sound.

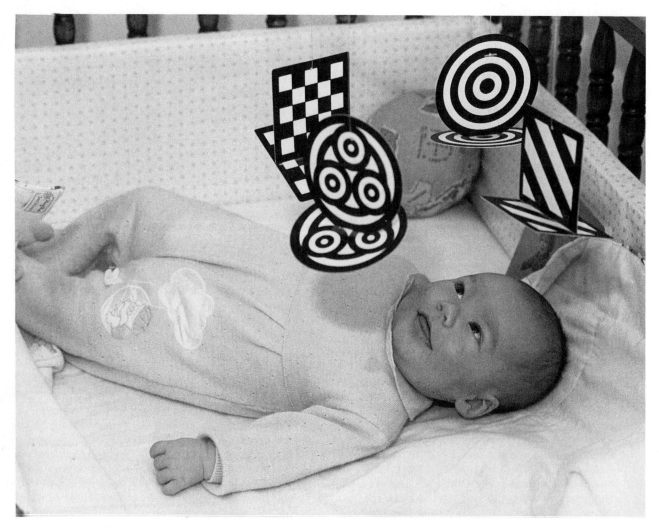

An infant enjoys a crib mobile, a "moving stimulus with high contrast."

The evidence for learning in infants during the first weeks of life is impressive. Infants are limited in the things they can do to show us that they are learning, but babies in the first month are clearly acquiring important information about the sights, sounds, tastes, and smells in their environments and adjusting their behavior, to the extent that they can, accordingly. For example, during the first month infants make adjustments to nursing (Piaget, 1952), and the subtle modifications infants make to their mothers can be viewed as a form of learning.

Neonatal imitation   A hallmark of human intelligence is the ability to learn from observation. Imitation—the ability to reproduce some behavior as a result of watching—is viewed by Albert Bandura and others as the primary way new information is acquired. Given the importance of imitation as a cognitive skill, it is little wonder that a report by Andrew Meltzoff and M. Keith Moore (1977) of imitation of facial expressions by 6- to 21-day-old babies caused quite a stir. **Neonatal imitation** is illustrated in Figure 4.6 by infants' responses to modeled facial ges-

Prenatal Development

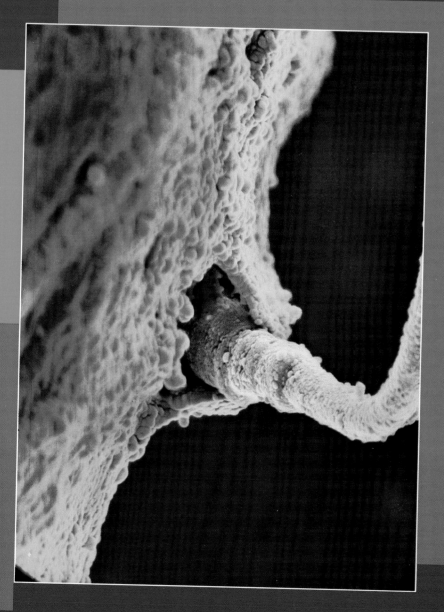

Although a quarter-billion sperm may start the journey to the egg, only one will burrow its way in.

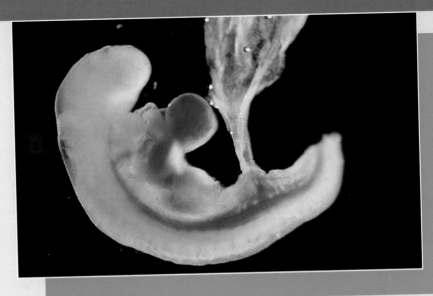

At one month after conception a primitive heart is beating and blood is circulating through the embryo.

The embryo receives nourishment from the placenta through the umbilical cord.

By twelve
weeks the
hands and feet
are well
formed.

Early
growth is
fastest in
the head
region.

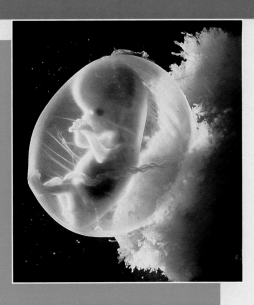

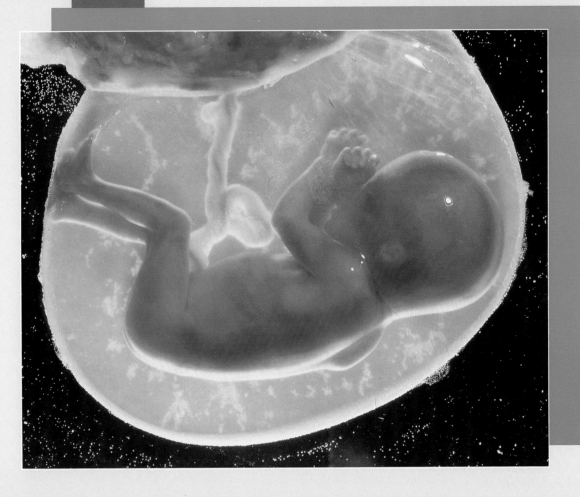

During the last three
months the fetus gains in
size and weight as organ
systems are perfected.

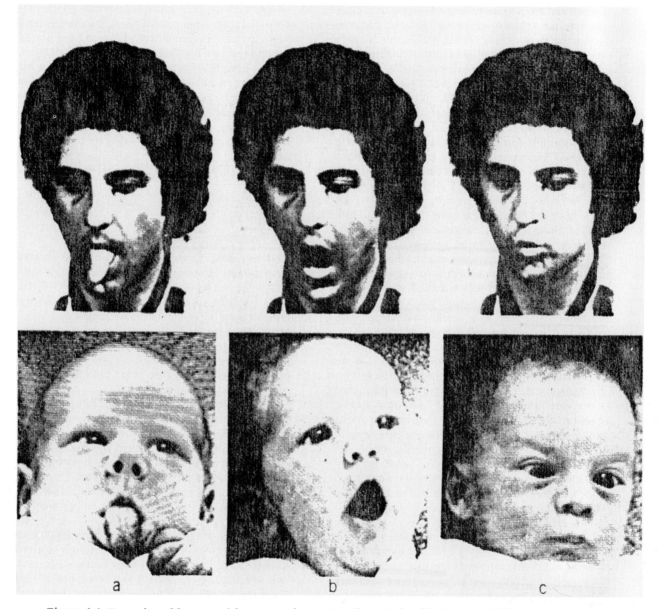

Figure 4.6 Examples of faces used for neonatal imitation (from Meltzoff & Moore, 1977).

tures. The number of tongue protrusions and mouth openings that infants made in response to an adult model were counted from video recordings of the sessions and contrasted with the number of each gesture made during baseline periods (that is, when no gestures were modeled). Meltzoff and Moore reported that infants made significantly more tongue protrusions to the tongue model than to the open-mouth model or during baseline. Similar patterns of results were found for mouth opening.

Meltzoff and Moore interpreted these results as clear evidence for selective imitation of facial gestures during the first month of life. Other researchers have also reported imitation of tongue protrusion in infants during the first month (Abravanel & Sigafoos, 1984; Heimann, 1989), and several have reported imitation in newborns (Field, Woodson, Greenberg, & Cohen, 1982; Meltzoff & Moore, 1983; Reissland, 1988; Vinter, 1986).

The effect is somewhat elusive, however, and a number of experimenters have failed to replicate early imitation using procedures similar to those used by Meltzoff and Moore (Hayes & Watson, 1981; Kaitz, Meschulach-Sarfaty, Auerbach, & Eidelman, 1988; Koepke, Hamm, Legerstee, & Russell, 1983; Lewis & Sullivan, 1985; McKenzie & Over, 1983). Moreover, imitation of facial gestures actually declines over the first year of life. For the most-studied facial gesture of tongue protrusion, every investigator who has examined infants of different ages reports a peak in imitation sometime during the first two months followed by a decline within weeks to chance values (Abravanel & Sigafoos, 1984; Fontaine, 1984; Gardner & Gardner, 1970; S. W. Jacobson, 1979). This is indeed perplexing, in that we have what appears to be a sophisticated cognitive phenomenon that actually decreases in frequency over a very brief period of time. Moreover, Sandra Jacobson (1979) has shown that tongue protrusions can also be elicited by a variety of tonguelike stimuli, such as a pen moved toward the infant's face.

These findings have suggested to some that neonatal imitation is not true imitation and is not related to the imitation seen later in infancy. Jacobson proposed that tongue protrusions may be functional in early nursing. Another possibility was proposed by David Bjorklund (1987a), who suggested that the apparent imitation by young infants may play a role in early social development. The matching of adult facial gestures by the infant may help to maintain social interaction between the two, with these reflexes declining when infants are able to intentionally direct their gaze and control their head and mouth movements to social stimulation, sometime between the second and fourth months of life. Tentative support for this position has recently been provided by Mikael Heimann (1989), who found a relationship between imitation in newborns and mother-infant social interactions at 3 months of age.

Although there is still much debate concerning the nature of neonatal imitation, recent research suggests that it is qualitatively different from the imitation found in later infancy (Anisfeld, 1991; Bjorklund, 1987a; Heimann, 1989). What we see in the newborn may facilitate its attachment to its mother or aid in nursing, making it an important ability. But it does not appear to be the basis for later imitation—the important cognitive skill that develops over infancy and childhood—despite their surface similarities.

State of the Art
In Vitro Fertilization and Beyond

Modern biological and medical science has devoted vast amounts of research time and money to investigating the secrets of reproduction. Much of that effort has been focused on ways to prevent conception. Modern contraceptives have allowed us, in effect, to separate sex from reproduction. Widespread contraceptive use has made 20th-century life less complicated, and is also helping stem a worldwide population explosion that, some believe, threatens our very existence on this planet.

Greater knowledge about the biology of reproduction has been used not only to prevent pregnancy but also to enhance the fertility of couples who have difficulty conceiving. Until recently, there has only been one way to conceive a child: egg and sperm uniting as a result of sexual intercourse. Now technology has changed all that, giving many infertile couples the opportunity to be parents.

A majority of cases of infertility, perhaps 70% to 85%, can be treated successfully through conventional techniques. This still leaves a substantial number of couples—perhaps 500,000 people in the United States—facing infertility each year. For them, the new technologies—specifically, in vitro fertilization (IVF)—offer their best chance of becoming biological parents (Sher & Marriage, 1988).

In Vitro Fertilization (IVF)

In vitro fertilization (IVF) refers to fertilization of the egg by the sperm outside of the woman's body. More specifically, fertilization takes place in a "test tube," or other suitable laboratory container, where the resulting embryo is nurtured for a few days until it is returned to the mother's body. The first successful human IVF was achieved in England by Drs. Robert Edwards and Patrick Steptoe and resulted in the birth of Louise Brown on July 24, 1978. The first American IVF baby was born in 1981.

In vitro fertilization is a costly, time-consuming, and emotionally draining experience. The cost for a single cycle (month) can be as high as $8000, and the success rate per attempt is only between 10% and 25% (Menning, 1988).

The procedure involves the use of conventional fertility drugs to stimulate ovulation. Once the eggs are ripe, they are retrieved from the ovaries in a surgical procedure called a laparoscopy. The woman is anesthetized, and a small incision is made near the navel. Using a telescopelike instrument equipped with a high-intensity light source and lenses, the surgeon locates the eggs and then, using another instrument, sucks them out. Although the number of eggs retrieved will vary, six to eight per retrieval attempt is common (Sher & Marriage, 1988).

The eggs are then mixed with the husband's sperm (usually obtained fresh by masturbation). The man's sperm is prepared by separating it from the semen and washing it in a special liquid that simulates the chemical action that occurs naturally in a woman's body. A high concentration of sperm

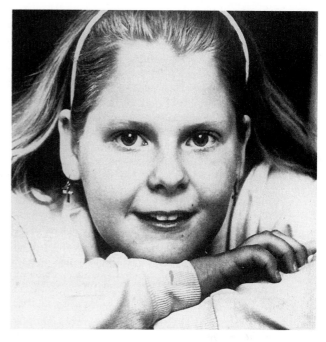

Louise Brown, now a teenager, was the first child to be conceived through IVF. Today, more than 20,000 children around the world are products of this procedure.

is then obtained and several drops, containing about 50,000 sperm, are added to each egg in a petri dish.

According to Geoffrey Sher and Virginia Marriage (1988), in about 70% to 80% of cases, the inseminated egg will become fertilized. Within 24 to 48 hours, the egg develops a coating that must be carefully removed before implantation (a process that occurs naturally in the fallopian tubes). At this time, the embryologist can determine whether insemination was successful or not. Those eggs that did become fertilized are now ready for implantation.

It is typically the case that several embryos are available for implantation; if so, the couple must decide how many to implant. The likelihood that an IVF embryo will implant successfully is no greater than 8% to 10% (about 25% to 35% of embryos implant in natural conception). Because of this low implantation rate, several embryos are usually transplanted, increasing the chance of multiple births. What to do with the remaining embryos is up to the

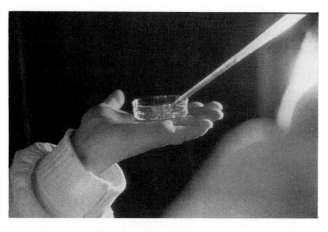

Science and technology have made parenthood a reality for many infertile couples.

couple. They may be destroyed, or frozen for possible implantation in the future. Implantation itself is usually done about 48 to 72 hours after egg retrieval. The physician places a catheter loaded with embryos through the woman's cervix and into her uterus, where the embryos are ejected. If implantation occurs, the woman may be given hormonal treatment to support pregnancy (Sher & Marriage, 1988).

A total of 20,000 IVF procedures were performed in the United States in 1988 (Sher & Marriage, 1988). Worldwide, IVF has produced about 20,000 births since its introduction in 1978 (Elmer-Dewitt, 1990).

Alternatives and Additions to IVF

Gamete intrafallopian transfer **(GIFT)** The **gamete intrafallopian transfer** procedure, known by the acronym **GIFT,** was developed by Dr. Richard Asch in 1984. In GIFT, the woman is given fertility drugs and eggs are retrieved, as in the IVF procedure. The physician then introduces both the retrieved eggs and sperm directly into the fallopian tubes (through a laparoscopy procedure). Thus, fertilization occurs not in a petri dish, but in the woman's body. According to Sher and Marriage (1988), the pregnancy rate with this procedure is about 20% to 25%, which is comparable to the rates for IVF. Others place the success rate of GIFT considerably higher, however, in some cases as high as 50% (Elmer-Dewitt, 1990; Silber, 1991).

A variant of GIFT is a new procedure called **zygote intrafallopian transfer (ZIFT),** in which fertilization occurs in a petri dish but the zygotes (fertilized eggs) are implanted into the fallopian tubes (Sher & Marriage, 1988). Proponents of both GIFT and ZIFT argue that these procedures permit the embryo to reach the uterus via the natural route, increasing the chances of implantation.

Embryo freezing As mentioned previously, when many embryos are produced, one option available to couples is **embryo freezing** for later implantation. The optimal phase for freezing an embryo is when it has divided into eight cells. The embryo is placed in a plastic straw in liquid nitrogen and apparently can be kept indefinitely, although the longest recorded freezing of an embryo that was successfully implanted is 28 months (Elson, 1989). The first human born of a frozen embryo occurred

in 1984 in Australia (Menning, 1988). As of 1989, more than 4000 embryos were in cold storage in the United States (Elson, 1989).

There have been some legal disputes over who owns frozen embryos. For example, in Tennessee, frozen embryos were at the center of a divorce dispute between Mary and Junior Davis. The wife wanted the couple's frozen embryos kept in storage in case she wished to use them or donate them in the future; her husband wanted them destroyed. In May 1990, the court ruled in favor of the wife, who later stated that she would donate the embryos to an infertility clinic so that they could be used by a childless couple. Junior Davis has appealed the decision, saying "There is just no way I am going to donate them. I feel that's my right. If there were a child from them, then I would be a parent to it. And I don't want a child out there to be mine if I can't be a parent to it" ("New Turn," 1990). In another case, a couple who moved from New Jersey to California asked that their frozen embryos be transferred from the Norfolk, Virginia, clinic that had extracted the eggs and stored the embryos to a Los Angeles infertility clinic. The director of the Norfolk clinic refused, sending the matter to court. Another court battle ensued when the frozen embryos of a wealthy Los Angeles couple were left parentless when the two died in a plane crash. Do the embryos inherit their parents' wealth? Who gets custody of the embryos? There are no easy answers, and decisions in any one case usually do not affect cases in other states or countries.

Embryo transfer For women who have healthy uteruses but who cannot produce their own eggs, **embryo transfer** is a possibility. This involves finding another woman to donate an egg. First, the menstrual cycles of the two women are synchronized within a day or two of each other with the aid of drugs. Then the donor woman receives fertility drugs to increase the number of eggs she produces, and the eggs are retrieved and fertilized with the sperm of the infertile woman's husband, all following the standard IVF procedures. The only difference is that the woman providing the egg and the woman implanted with the embryos are not the same (Menning, 1988).

A new twist in embryo transfer came with the announcement by Mark Sauer and his associates

(Sauer, Paulson, & Lobo, 1990) that they had impregnated six postmenopausal women using eggs donated by younger women and fertilized with sperm from the older women's husbands. Four of the women gave birth to healthy children, one miscarried, and one child was stillborn—an outcome that Sauer and associates state is similar to what one would expect for younger women. This new technology, allowing women in their late 40s and 50s (and theoretically even later) to carry a pregnancy to term, may have significant implications for a generation of couples who have postponed starting a family. It may also have implications for the generation to follow, who will be teenagers when their parents are ready for retirement.

A variant on embryo transfer occurs when a woman can produce eggs but has no uterus or the eggs will not implant successfully in her uterus. In this case, the egg and sperm from a couple can be fertilized using standard IVF procedures but implanted in the uterus of another woman. In this case, the pregnant woman is genetically unrelated to the child she is carrying, and is referred to as a **gestational surrogate.**

Since 1987, about 80 infants have been born to gestational surrogates, most of them in the United States (Tifft, 1990). Recently, one case made national headlines when the gestational surrogate changed her mind after the baby was born, stating that she had bonded with the infant and wanted to keep the child for herself. The California judge in the case sided with the genetic parents over the gestational surrogate, stating that the gestational surrogate was a "genetic stranger" to the child and, therefore, had no legal right to claim parenthood. The gestational mother has appealed the case (Tifft, 1990).

Surrogate motherhood   One alternative to IVF that involves little in the way of modern technology is **surrogate motherhood,** sometimes referred to as "rent-a-womb." Variants of this technique are ancient, with one well-known case cited in the Book of Genesis:

> Now Sarah, Abraham's wife, bore him no children. She had an Egyptian maid whose name was Hagar. And Sarah said to Abraham, "Behold how the Lord has prevented me from bearing children. Go in to my maid; it may be

that I shall obtain children by her." (Genesis 16:1–3)

In today's practices, surrogate motherhood usually involves an infertile couple finding a woman willing to become pregnant with the husband's sperm (through artificial insemination) and to relinquish all rights to the baby at birth. In the United States, a small business has grown up around surrogate motherhood. Businesses solicit potential surrogates and match them with infertile couples; they may also arrange medical services for the pregnant woman, as well as legal and counseling services. The total fee for these services may be between $25,000 and $50,000, with the surrogate usually receiving about $10,000. This fee is paid to the surrogate for her services, not for the baby, because in most states it is illegal to buy a baby (Menning, 1988).

The potential complications of surrogate motherhood should be obvious. What if the pregnant woman decides she wants to keep the baby? What if,

"Let me get this straight. One bouquet goes to the mother who donated the egg. A second goes to the mother who housed the egg for insemination. A third goes to the mother who hosted the embryo and gave birth to the child. A fourth goes to the mother who raised it and a fifth goes to the mother with legal custody."

Box 4.4

The GIFT of Triplets

There is a deep pain associated with infertility. David and Yovonda had been trying unsuccessfully to have children for three years. Yovonda recalls, "Seeing new mothers with babies who kiddingly complained about wishing the child was of the opposite sex was very disturbing. We attended a meeting of RESOLVE [a nonprofit support group for infertile couples and associated professionals], and there was so much hostility from many of the people there. They were desperate and trying to place the blame for their inability to have children on their physicians. We understood their hostility and grief but didn't share it, and we never returned."

What they did was investigate a gamete intrafallopian transfer (GIFT) program. Because Yovonda's fallopian tubes were healthy, she was an ideal candidate for the program. After retrieving several ripe eggs from Yovonda's ovaries, doctors implanted them, along with sperm from David, into her fallopian tubes. Within two weeks, they found out that Yovonda was pregnant.

They knew that the chance of multiple births with GIFT was high (about 1 in 10), so they were not surprised to learn that Yovonda was carrying triplets. "We tried to have children for three years," David said, "and now we're having three at once—one for each year."

Multiple pregnancy meant prolonged bed rest for Yovonda, beginning in the 17th week of pregnancy. She needed to consume 3000 calories a day, and the bed rest ensured that the triplets were getting the calories they needed to develop. In her 26th week, she was hospitalized and began receiving drugs to foster the lung development of her triplets and to prolong the pregnancy. In her 31st week of pregnancy, Yovonda delivered three healthy babies: Elyse Hope (3 pounds 12 ounces), Kathleen Anne (4 pounds 8 ounces), and David Michael (3 pounds 13 ounces).

Although they were described as healthy premature babies, because of their low birth weights each spent time in the neonatal intensive care unit, and they spent their first five weeks in the hospital. David and Yovonda visited daily. They held them, changed them, brought dirty clothes home to wash and new clothes back to the hospital to dress their triplets in. "It was important to feel necessary," said Yovonda, "to feel that you're doing things that all mothers do to take care of their babies."

When they finally brought the triplets home, Yovonda and David learned how challenging taking care of three babies can be. They received support from a national organization, The Triplet Connection, which sent a monthly newsletter and put them in touch with other parents of triplets in their area. They found that talking with other parents of triplets, getting their advice and encouragement, was very helpful in preparing them for some of the joys and challenges that lay ahead as the triplets grew. They also received help from their neighbors and the women's group at their church. At least two people were needed to feed the triplets, and when David or Yovonda was not home, one of the neighbors or churchwomen would come over for 20 minutes or so to help out.

They found that living with triplets required scheduling. At first, they tried feeding them separately at 20-minute intervals, but this just didn't work out, and they now feed them all at once. Beginning at about 8 months, they were able to lay the three of them in their infant seats and prop up a bottle for each. For solid food, Yovonda and David seat them in a circle, giving each a spoonful of food before going on to the next. For the most part, the triplets have learned to take turns, but things don't always run smoothly. "There are no absolute rules," David says. "Sometimes you just have to attend to the one who is screaming the loudest. At first it was David Michael, then a few months later Kathleen, so they take turns at that, too. But generally, we stick with the turn taking, and they seem to have adjusted to it quite well—so far, anyway."

Yovonda and David tell about their GIFT triplets, Elyse, Kathleen, and David.

David and Yovonda make an active attempt to treat each child equally—to give each one an equal amount of attention, including what they call "private time," when each triplet has Mom or Dad to him- or herself. They recognize the individuality of each child and that each requires special concentration. At the end of a day, they often take inventory of who received the most care, and if anyone seems to have been shortchanged that day, David or Yovonda tries to spend a little extra time with that child.

Yovonda and David are amazing parents. They see their babies as a blessing from God and the GIFT program. Multiple births are a frequent consequence of programs such as GIFT, and it takes special parents, like David and Yovonda, plus support from friends and family, to raise three children at once.

after the baby is born and given to the parents, the surrogate mother wants visitation rights? These possibilities became reality in one much-publicized case in New Jersey, known as the Baby M case. William and Elizabeth Stern, the would-be parents, found themselves in court with Mary Beth Whitehead, the surrogate mother, over the custody of Baby M. Although Mary Beth Whitehead had signed an agreement to give up the baby, she changed her mind. In a 1988 ruling, the court sided with the natural father, William Stern, stating that they believed that the Sterns could provide a better environment for the child.

The controversy stemming from the Baby M case and the gestational-surrogate case mentioned earlier have not gone unnoticed. A National Coalition Against Surrogacy has lobbied to ban surrogacy of all types. As of this writing, 13 states have laws banning commercial surrogacy. Surrogacy of all types has also been outlawed in Germany.

What's in the Future?

In the decade or so that IVF has been practiced, it has gone from being a medical oddity with diabolical, Orwellian overtones (test-tube babies, artificial wombs) to quiet respectability. Yet the new technologies, seen as godsends by many childless couples, are still viewed with caution or even moral indignity by others. IVF and similar technologies are not sanctioned by the Catholic church and some conservative Protestant church groups, and no government money is available to researchers working in this area (Menning, 1988). Furthermore, few insurance companies cover medical costs for these procedures. As we've seen, there are some complex legal and ethical issues involved in the new treatment of infertility, particularly surrogate motherhood and embryo transfer when the woman carrying the child is not the one who donated the egg. There are other important issues, too, including the rights of embryos. Once conceived in a petri dish, who decides their fate?

Despite the controversies, most Americans favor basic IVF and related procedures and believe that infertile couples who want a child should have access to the techniques that can help them (Bonnickson, 1989). The new technologies, however, must be administered ethically, with further advances (particularly in the area of genetic engineering) made

cautiously. And, according to Andrea Bonnickson (1989), both the public and the policymakers believe that procreation should be a private matter, with legislators staying out of the business of passing laws about reproduction. There seems to be a reservoir of public trust in the goodness of science and a belief that technology should be permitted to bring pregnancy and happiness when nature cannot.

Summary

Conception occurs when sperm and ovum join in the fallopian tube. Prenatal development is divided into three periods. The period of the zygote begins with conception in the fallopian tube and ends with implantation in the wall of the uterus. During the period of the embryo, all the major organ systems are formed, though not perfected, with development proceeding head downward (cephalocaudal development). The period of the fetus begins at about 8 weeks and continues until birth, with the fetus perfecting its organs and gaining in size and weight.

Maternal malnutrition can result in smaller and lighter babies and can affect parent-child interaction after birth. Teratogens—external agents that adversely affect the developing embryo/fetus—are apt to have the most severe effect during the embryonic period. Some common teratogens include maternal smoking; maternal alcohol consumption, which can lead to fetal alcohol syndrome, or FAS; narcotic drugs, such as heroin and cocaine; nonnarcotic drugs, such as thalidomide and DES; radiation; and maternal diseases.

Prenatal diagnostic testing may include ultrasound, alpha-fetoprotein (AFP) testing, amniocentesis, chorionic villous sampling, fetal monitoring, and fetoscopy. Perceptual abilities develop before birth, with research indicating that auditory conditioning is possible in utero.

Childbirth occurs in three stages: labor, which lasts about 12 hours and intensifies as the infant's head is pushed toward the cervix; delivery, which often lasts only a few minutes and rarely more than an hour; and afterbirth, which lasts for about 15 minutes after delivery and involves expulsion of the placenta. When birth complications occur, a Caesarean section (C-section) is often required, with the infant being removed through a surgical incision in the mother's abdomen.

Childbirth practices have gone through substantial changes over the centuries, with women and families taking more control of childbirth and having a broader range of options.

Neonates possess a number of reflexes, some of which have obvious survival value, such as rooting and sucking. By 1 week of age, babies can discriminate their mothers from other women by smell and the sound of their voices, and can see well enough to tell the difference between visual patterns. Newborns can learn. There is also evidence of neonatal imitation of facial gestures, although this behavior decreases over the first two months, and some researchers believe that it has a role in nursing or early interaction and is not true imitation.

Infertility is relatively common in the United States, and in vitro fertilization (IVF) and related technologies (such as GIFT, ZIFT, embryo freezing, and embryo transfer) have revolutionized its treatment. The new technologies raise legal and ethical concerns, however, as does surrogate motherhood.

Key Terms and Concepts

conception
    ovum
    ovaries
    fallopian tube
    sperm
    uterus
    cervix
    infertility
    zygote
blastocyte
umbilical cord

amnionic sac
chorionic sac
yolk sac
placenta
embryo
cephalocaudal development
fetus
quickening
maternal malnutrition
teratogens
fetal alcohol syndrome (FAS)
thalidomide
DES (diethylstilbestrol)
prenatal diagnostic testing
    ultrasound
    alpha-fetoprotein (AFP) testing
    amniocentesis
    chorionic villous sampling
    fetal monitoring
    fetoscopy
labor
delivery
afterbirth
Caesarean section (C-section)
Apgar test
neonate
reflexes
sudden infant death syndrome (SIDS)
accommodation (of lens)
convergence
coordination
acuity
visual preferences
neonatal imitation
in vitro fertilization (IVF)
gamete intrafallopian transfer (GIFT)
zygote intrafallopian transfer (ZIFT)
embryo freezing
embryo transfer
    gestational surrogate
    surrogate motherhood

The Course
of Physical
Growth

When our daughter, Debbie, was in fourth grade, she came home one day with an unusual story. She had been standing in line at the pencil sharpener when the girl in front of her confided in a whisper, "I hope *they* don't pop out while we're up here." When Debbie asked what "they" were, her classmate replied, "You know" and pointed to her chest. Later, at recess, Deb's friend explained that she had recently asked her mother when she would have breasts. Her mother laughed and said, "Don't worry about it, they'll just 'pop out' someday." Instead of laying her daughter's worries to rest, her mother's answer had only added to her anxiety. Pop out? When? Where? Would it happen at school when she was waiting for the pencil sharpener? Debbie told her she didn't think it would happen that way, but she would ask her parents to be sure.

After hearing the story, we were touched by the young girl's misunderstanding. Her mother's intentions were good; she just missed the boat on her choice of words. We explained to Debbie that physical maturation was much slower than that, and that when adults talk about a child's "shooting up like a beanpole" or "growing up overnight," they are exaggerating. Breasts develop slowly, and girls don't have to worry about any sudden growth spurts embarrassing them in public. Deb talked to her friend, and as far as we know, everyone lived happily ever after.

In the study of child development, physical growth often takes a back seat to other types of development—cognitive, social, and emotional. As the memory of that worried fourth-grader reminds us, however, physical development involves more than just predictable changes in a child's size and shape. Those changes affect the way adults view children and the way children view themselves. Physical changes underlie all aspects of a child's being and, in some cases, can have profound effects on school performance, relationships with family members, choice of after-school activities, and choice of friends. Biological changes underlie psychological development; there is no psychology without biology (John Money, personal communication, 1990).

Physical growth involves not only increased size but changes in proportions, and not only external but internal changes. Some of the most notable changes for our purposes are those in the brain, which controls physical functions as well as intellec-

tual, social, and emotional responses, and in the endocrine system, which, by the hormonal messages it sends throughout the body, affects our physical appearance and is primarily responsible for the abrupt changes that occur in adolescence.

Changes in Size and Proportion

Growth Curves

All parts of the body do not grow at the same rate. Figure 5.1 shows growth curves for various organ systems. The "general" curve shows the pattern for height: a sharp increase during infancy, slow growth during middle childhood, and a growth spurt during the teen years into early adulthood. The brain and head, in contrast, grow rapidly over the first four or five years, continuing the rapid growth of the prenatal period. The reproductive system (including

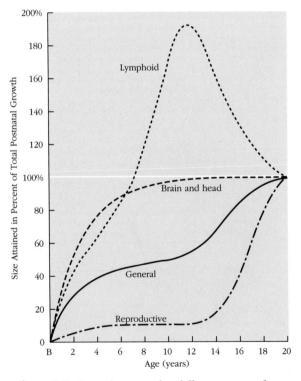

Figure 5.1 Growth curves for different parts of the body. *Source:* Scammon, 1930.

both internal and external genitals) seems to lie dormant until the start of puberty, when it matures quickly over a very brief period. And the lymphoid system, which includes the thymus and lymph glands, seems to go into overdrive during middle childhood, only to shift into neutral at puberty.

Growth curves for height are shown in Figure 5.2. Boys are slightly larger than girls at birth and maintain their size advantage until girls' adolescent growth spurt, which begins, on average, two years before boys'. Boys continue to grow slowly during those two years, then gain height even more rapidly than girls during their own growth spurt.

In general, girls reach maturity sooner than boys. Girls attain 50% of their adult height sooner than boys (1.75 years versus 2 years), enter puberty earlier, and stop growing sooner. This difference in rate of growth (that is, how *fast* one grows, as opposed

to how big one becomes) is apparent even during the prenatal period. The skeleton of girls is three weeks more advanced than that of boys midway through the fetal period, and girls have a four- to six-week advantage in skeletal development at birth. By the beginning of puberty, this advantage is a full two years. Girls also develop permanent teeth (but not baby, or milk, teeth) earlier than boys, and are also physiologically more mature in other organ systems at birth, which may account in part for their higher survival rate in the early months (Tanner, 1978).

Skeletal Development

Changes in height are closely related to the growth of bones. Because there is so much variability among adults in height, using height as a measure of a child's physical maturation can be very misleading. Bones do reach an adult level independent of size, however, making a child's degree of skeletal development (or skeletal age) a good indicator of level of maturation (Tanner, 1978).

The skeleton of the embryo is initially formed of cartilage, which is gradually replaced by bone tissue (see Chapter 4). This process of **ossification,** which begins prenatally, is not complete until early adulthood.

The fastest growing bones during the first two years are those of the skull, which reaches 90% of its adult size by age 5. To enable the infant's head to change shape during birth, the bones of the skull are separated by six gaps, known as "soft spots" or **fontanels,** which are filled with fibrous tissue. The largest gap—the anterior fontanel on the top of the head—is slightly more than an inch across and can be felt easily. This gap closes by a child's second birthday, but all gaps in the skull are not totally closed until puberty.

Sexual Differentiation

Size, motor skills, and mental abilities change substantially over the first two years, but from the second year through the elementary school years, growth is a gradual affair. All this changes at **puberty,** which is defined as "the period at which the testes, prostate gland and seminal vesicle, or the uterus and vagina, suddenly enlarge" (Tanner, 1978, p. 60).

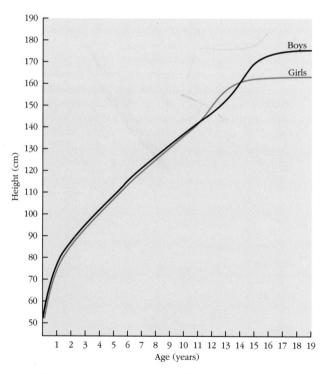

Figure 5.2 Growth curves (height) for boys and girls. *Source:* Reprinted by permission of the publishers from *Fetus into Man: Physical Growth from Conception to Maturity,* by J. M. Tanner, Cambridge, Mass.: Harvard University Press, copyright © 1978 by J. M. Tanner.

Many physical changes occur during puberty, including the spurt in height discussed earlier. During puberty, boys' chests and shoulders grow as cartilage cells in those areas respond to male sex hormone. In girls, hips widen in response to female sex hormone. Other skeletal changes involve the facial bones, particularly in boys: the brow ridges grow, making the forehead more prominent, and both jaws grow forward (Tanner, 1978).

Associated with skeletal differences between the sexes are differences in fat and muscle. Fat constitutes slightly more than 30% of body weight for the average young adult female and slightly less than 20% for the average young adult male. Muscle takes an opposite developmental course, with boys developing more muscle (and strength) during their adolescent growth spurt than girls. Girls also develop muscle during their growth spurt, however, and because their growth spurt starts two years earlier than boys', there is a period of about two years (between 10 and 12 years) during which girls are actually more muscular (and stronger) than boys (Tanner, 1978).

Another set of changes involves enlargement and adult functioning of the reproductive organs. Related changes also occur in secondary sexual characteristics, including the development of facial hair in boys and breasts in girls. The age sequence of events at puberty are shown separately for boys and girls in Figure 5.3.

Changes for boys   For boys, the first sign of puberty is usually enlargement of the testes, accompanied by changes in color and texture of the scrotum. This is followed by the appearance of pubic hair and enlargement of the penis. (In Figure 5.3, development of pubic hair is rated on a scale from 2 to 5, with 2 representing the earliest stage of growth and 5 the adult status.) As is obvious to anyone who has gone through puberty, there is substantial variability in the onset and completion of adolescent growth. For example, acceleration of penis growth typically begins at about 12.5 years and is complete by about 14.5 years; but this development may begin as early as 10.5 years or as late as 14.5 years and still be within the normal range (Tanner, 1978).

The development of facial hair begins above the lips and typically does not occur until about 14 years of age. Growth of body hair begins gradually and usually continues for some time after puberty. Boys' voices also change during this time, becoming deeper. As the vocal chords lengthen, producing the lower tone, the adolescent's voice sometimes "breaks." This occurs relatively late in puberty, although not all boys experience "voice breaking."

These external changes reflect a more significant underlying change: the development of reproductive capability. Puberty is nature's transition from developing child to reproductive adult. In boys, the prostate gland and seminal vesicles enlarge during puberty. The prostate gland makes most of the sem-

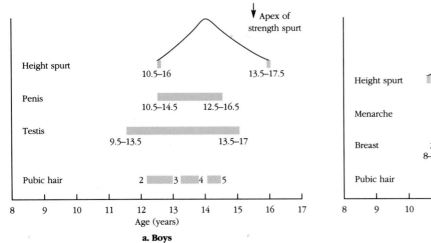

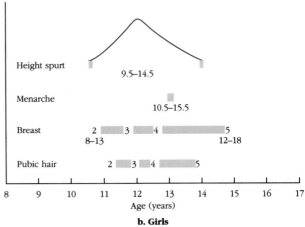

a. Boys

b. Girls

Figure 5.3 Sequence of events at puberty. *Source:* Adapted from "Variation in the Pattern of Pubertal Changes in Boys," by W. A. Marshall and J. M. Tanner, *Archives of Diseases in Childhood,* 1970, *45,* 13–23. Reprinted by permission of the British Medical Association.

inal fluid; the seminal vesicles add a substance that aids in sperm mobility, thus increasing the likelihood that conception will occur. Although the neural paths underlying orgasm are present from infancy, there is no true ejaculation until puberty. The first spontaneous ejaculation typically occurs about a year after penis growth begins, often during sleep (nocturnal emissions) and often accompanied by erotic dreams ("wet dreams"). Initially, the seminal fluid contains fewer viable sperm than in early adulthood, resulting in a period of lower fertility (Tanner, 1978). This lower fertility, however, is a matter of degree, and not a reliable method of birth control; boys *can* become fathers early in puberty.

Changes for girls   Girls show the same variability in growth patterns as do boys, but girls usually enter puberty earlier (see Figure 5.3). Breast development typically begins at about age 11 in North American and European girls, but the normal range extends from 9 to 13 years of age. Pubic hair usually appears after breast development begins, but the two events are relatively independent (Tanner, 1978).

Perhaps the clearest sign of "womanhood" throughout the world is the first menstrual period, called **menarche.** This occurs relatively late in puberty, usually between the ages of 12.8 and 13.2 years for girls of European descent. Again, there is substantial variability, with 95% of all girls having their first menstrual period between the ages of 11 and 15 years.

Although menarche represents mature development of the uterus, it does not necessarily reflect full reproductive capability. As with boys, there is a period of between 1 and 1.5 years when fertility is low. Often menstrual periods are irregular over the first year or so, and a ripe egg is not produced. However, this does not happen in all girls (Tanner, 1978), and girls *can* become pregnant during the year following menarche.

Factors Influencing Growth

A person's eventual height, weight, and strength, as well as the timing of growth, depend upon genetic inheritance, nutrition, and exercise. Genes set limits on stature: height, as well as the timing of puberty, is more similar for identical twins than fraternal twins (Bouchard et al., 1990). Genes, as we have seen, exert their influence by manufacturing proteins that affect the functioning of biological systems—in this

Chronological age tells only part of the story of physical development. Two children with birthdays only weeks apart can show differences in physical growth and maturation.

case, the series of glands known as the **endocrine system.**

Hormones and growth   Glands produce **hormones** that are released into the blood system. Hormones can be viewed as chemical messengers sent through the bloodstream with instructions from one part of the body to another. Certain cells, however, are sensitive to certain hormones, making the hormonal communication system a very specific one.

Dozens of hormones are produced in different glands throughout the body. Central control of hormone production is governed by a brain structure called the hypothalamus, which triggers the release of hormones by the **pituitary gland,** located nearby. Acting as a master gland, the pituitary releases hormones that influence growth directly and also indirectly, by causing other glands to release hormones that affect growth. As a hormone circulates through the body, certain cells detect its concentration; when it reaches a certain level, the pituitary sends out another signal that reduces or stops its production. Thus, the endocrine system functions by way of a feedback loop, much like a thermostat: hormones are produced, their levels monitored, and production reduced or stopped when target levels have been achieved.

Human growth hormone is produced directly by the pituitary, stimulating the duplication of most body cells. Children who do not produce a sufficient amount will grow slowly, retaining normal proportions but attaining an adult height of only four feet or so. This condition can be diagnosed and is treated with supplemental doses of human growth hormone. Unlike many other hormones, however, this one is species specific. Until recently, it could be obtained only from human corpses, making it difficult and costly to produce. Human growth hormone can now be produced in the laboratory using recombinant DNA procedures, making it more readily available and affordable for children who need it.

The pituitary gland influences the gonads (testes and ovaries), the thyroid, and the adrenals. The ovaries produce **estrogen** and **progesterone,** and the testes produce **testosterone** (a form of **androgen**), hormones that promote sexual maturation and activate portions of the brain that control sexual arousal. The thyroid gland, located in the neck, begins early in the fetal period to produce **thyroxine,** a hormone that influences brain development. Children with a thyroxine deficiency at birth can become mentally retarded unless treated immediately; thy-

Box 5.1

Steroids and Adolescent Athletes

Anabolic steroids are synthetic androgens that have been used by athletes for more than two decades to build body mass and muscle tissue, and thus increase strength. Although they can be obtained legally for medical purposes, athletes generally obtain them illegally through contacts made at commercial gyms. As with any illegal drug, it is difficult to estimate how widely used they are. Recent evidence makes it clear, however, that they are no longer restricted to professional and college athletes but are also used with increasing frequency in high schools. In one recent survey, it was estimated that between 250,000 and 500,000 adolescents (mostly males) in the United States are currently using anabolic steroids. Many of the self-reported steroid users in this survey (47.1%) reported that their main reason for using the drugs was to "improve athletic performance"; another 26.7% reported using steroids simply to improve their appearance (Yesalis, 1990).

So what's the harm in improving one's bulk and strength through drug use? Repeated steroid use has been associated with damage to the liver, heart, and reproductive system. When used by children, steroids may accelerate pubertal growth and limit eventual adult height (Langston, 1990). Equally damaging can be the psychological side effects—notably, increased irritability and aggressiveness. Prolonged use of steroids has also been associated with increased incidence of psychopathology. In one study of 41 athletes who reported using steroids, 5 (12.2%) met the clinical criteria for psychotic symptoms, and 9 (22%) showed manic-depressive disorders (Katz & Pope, 1988).

The potential danger of steroid use is obvious. Prolonged use of these drugs can have serious physical and psychological effects, including increased aggressiveness that can be turned against family, friends, or unsuspecting bystanders. There is also some evidence that the effects may be exaggerated when steroid use begins early in adolescence, making the easy availability of these drugs a potential time bomb for thousands of young people.

roxine deficiencies later in childhood result in slow body and skeleton growth, but no brain damage. The **adrenal glands,** located on top of the kidneys, produce adrenalin and also androgens. In boys, these androgens join with testosterone to facilitate physical growth (including muscle bulk) and the development and maintenance of secondary sexual characteristics. In girls, androgens are believed to be responsible for the adolescent growth spurt and the growth of pubic hair.

Historical trends in growth Although the biological basis of physical growth is unquestioned, environmental factors such as nutrition also affect rate of maturation and eventual size. Not only can environmental factors influence the growth of a single child, but large-scale environmental changes can affect growth trends of entire nations over time.

Because of improved nutrition and disease control, the average height of children and their rate of maturation in industrialized societies has increased steadily over the past century. Figure 5.4 presents Swedish data on the average height of boys and girls measured in 1883, 1938, and 1968. Similar patterns have been documented in nearly all European countries, as well as the United States and Canada (Tanner, 1978). Figure 5.5 presents the average age of

menarche over a 100-year span in several European countries, showing a gradual but steady decline over time.

Environmental factors influencing growth Children living in an environment of constant stress secrete reduced amounts of human growth hormone; when the stress is removed, hormone production increases and normal growth resumes. J. M. Tanner (1978) cites several interesting examples of the effects of stress on children. In one case, children living in an orphanage under the direction of a particularly sadistic schoolteacher showed reduced growth despite adequate food. Other case studies have shown that when children who have stopped growing are removed from a chronically stressful home environment and placed in a supportive foster home, they quickly catch up with their peers in height. The change in height for such children is similar to that of children who are deficient in human growth hormone and are given replacement therapy.

The main environmental influence on growth, however, is nutrition. Without question, malnutrition delays growth. Although this is easily demonstrated in laboratory studies with animals, there is enough real-world evidence on a large scale to make it clear

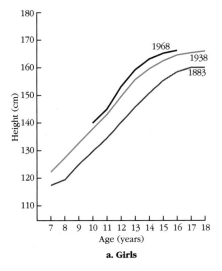

a. Girls

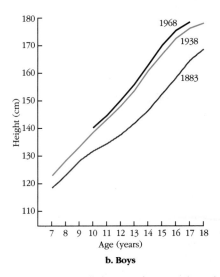

b. Boys

Figure 5.4 Historical trends in growth of Swedish girls and boys. *Source:* From "The Secular Trend in Physical Growth in Sweden," by B. O. Ljung, A. Bergsten–Brucefors and G. Lindgren, *Annals of Human Biology,* 1974, *1,* 245–256. Reprinted by permission of Taylor and Francis, Ltd.

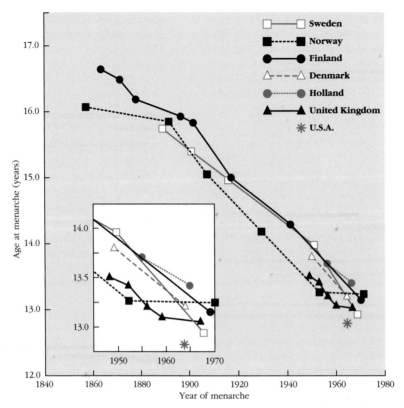

Figure 5.5 Historical trends in age at menarche, 1870–1970. *Source:* Reprinted by permission of the publishers from *Fetus into Man: Physical Growth from Conception to Maturity,* by J. M. Tanner, Cambridge, Mass.: Harvard University Press, copyright © 1978 by J. M. Tanner.

that children who do not get enough to eat grow more slowly; if malnourishment is prolonged, these children will have smaller stature as adults than those who eat well. This is clearly demonstrated in the growth patterns of children who experienced famine or substantially reduced nutrition during World War II (see Tanner, 1978). The effects of malnutrition on growth are apt to be most severe for children under 5 years of age, particularly when accompanied by infection or disease. The effects of malnutrition on intelligence have also been observed (Winick, 1976). Poor nutrition leads to reduced activity—less exploration, less play, and less social interaction—which "may be a more potent cause of delay in intellectual and emotional development than any nutritional effect on the nervous system" (Tanner, 1978, p. 129). It is worth noting that children subjected to brief periods of starvation typically recover; although their growth is slowed, they retain the ability to catch up when good nutrition is resumed.

Although malnutrition is a serious problem worldwide, including in the United States and Canada, overnutrition leading to **obesity** is also of concern in most technological societies. Obesity is defined as a body weight at least 20% higher than normal for a person's height, age, sex, and stature. Between the late 1960s and early 1980s, the obesity rate increased 54% for American children between 6 and 11 years of age and 39% for teenagers (Gortmaker, 1988).

Obese children often grow up to be obese adults. Heredity plays a significant role in how people gain and maintain weight: adopted children are more similar in weight to their biological parents than their adoptive parents (Plomin, DeFries, & Mc-

Clearn, 1990). But environmental factors also play a role in obesity. Food has social as well as physical importance. Some parents use food as a reward for their children's behavior and feed infants at the first indication of emotional distress (Birch, 1981). Not surprisingly, some children (and adults) search for food at the first sign of emotion—be it joy, sadness, or boredom. Some mothers expect their children to eat large amounts of food, and their children comply to please them. Under these conditions, food consumption becomes a substitute for parental attention and affection (M. T. Erickson, 1987).

Being overweight is related to a number of serious physical problems, including high blood pressure, heart disease, and diabetes, but it has equally serious psychological consequences for children. Many overweight preschoolers are very dependent upon their mothers and fail to develop comfortable relationships with peers. Entering school can be a traumatic experience, in part because of a lack of social skills. Obese children are rarely happy children; they tend to be withdrawn and dependent, have low self-esteem, and be less popular than their slimmer agemates (M. T. Erickson, 1987).

Overweight children not only eat more than normal weight children, but also exercise less. There has been speculation that the increase in obesity among children over the past 20 years has been caused by the increase in television viewing (Gortmaker, 1988). Although blaming TV for the problems of American children seems to have become a national pastime, the evidence linking TV viewing with obesity is compelling. The amount of television children watch predicts later obesity better than any other single factor, other than a history of being overweight (Kolata, 1986). Simply put, children who are watching television are not outside playing. The importance of physical fitness for children and what parents can do about it are discussed briefly in Box 5.2.

American children rank low in physical fitness and high in risk for heart disease. Some experts blame television.

Box 5.2

Physically Fit Families

Parents today are very health conscious. They watch their diets and exercise regularly, trying to maintain (or regain) their youthful fitness. But that ideal of firmness and flexibility adults work so hard to obtain may not be a reality for their children. While parents' concern about fitness is at an all-time high, children's fitness is the pits.

To put it simply, American schoolchildren today are, as a group, physically unfit. Their poor strength and endurance is reflected by lower and lower scores on the President's Fitness Challenge Test, where almost half of them fail to do one chin-up or run a mile in less than ten minutes. Their poor eating habits are shown by an obesity rate that is half again as high as last generation's. And the health implications for their future are made clear in the findings that 40% of American children already show one or more of the three danger signs for heart disease—high blood pressure, high cholesterol, or obesity.

What is to blame? The most-cited source is television viewing, which occupies children's minds and bodies for an average of 25 hours each week. Another culprit is the school curriculum that tries to remedy decreasing academic skills by increasing classroom time at the expense of physical education. More blame can go to the fast-paced lifestyle of modern times, which has made regular family meals together nearly obsolete and gives children much of the responsibility for selecting their own diets—even though they lack any notion of nutritional values. The list goes on and on, but the bottom line is a familiar one: parents are the major influence in their children's lives and have the prime responsibility for their health and well-being.

What can parents do? For one thing, they can start thinking of physical fitness as a family concern, not just a painful necessity for middle-aged adults. Parents who are involved in exercise and wise eating programs are already serving as good role models for their children. It should be easy to encourage the kids to join in. School-age children are eager to

Finding time for shared outdoor activities is the first step toward family fitness.

set foot in the grown-up world and share interests with their parents.

Doctors recommend aerobic exercise at least three times a week for adults, and that's a good recommendation for children, too. Some of the best forms of aerobic exercise are walking, swimming, and bicycling—activities well-suited for family togetherness.

One of the most difficult things parents can do to improve their family's physical fitness is to cut down on their television viewing. Busy days lead to collapse at night, and many parents feel that at least family members are watching television *together*. This is true, but some small changes can be made even in the most dedicated video family, such as choosing one 30-minute time slot each evening to get out of the house for a walk. Another idea is having an exercise bike in the TV room for family members to take turns riding while they watch TV.

The surprise families find as they take a difficult first step toward fitness is that the second step is easier. Replacing one TV show with a walk each evening helps reduce the families' evening exhaustion and clears the mental cobwebs, paving the way to other creative ideas for active family fun.

Adapted from D. F. Bjorklund and B. R. Bjorklund (June, 1989). Physically fit families. *Parents Magazine*, Vol. 64, No. 6.

Box 5.3

Anorexia Nervosa

Dr. Felicia F. Romeo
Florida Atlantic University
Author of Understanding Anorexia Nervosa
(1986), Charles C Thomas Publishers,
Springfield, IL.

Anorexia nervosa is a serious eating disorder that affects mainly adolescent girls and young adult women (only about 5%–10% of victims are males). As many as 1 in 200 females between 12 and 18 years of age—the high-risk group—may develop anorexia nervosa. Anorexia nervosa results from a combination of factors—cultural, physical, and psychological—that impinge upon an emotionally vulnerable girl.

Our society places great emphasis upon thinness as the ideal for females. Fashion models, actresses, and celebrities are thin, and they represent feminine standards for beauty and glamour. Consequently, many females are perpetually on diets in an effort to attain this cultural ideal. Adolescents are particularly vulnerable to social and cultural pressures; at the same time, they are experiencing pubertal developmental changes that appear to add body weight, including growth in the breast and hip areas. Many adolescents diet, but some take it to life-threatening extremes.

The essential features of anorexia nervosa are an intense fear of becoming obese, a decrease in body weight or failure to develop body weight consistent with age and maturity, and refusal to maintain body weight at a minimal normal weight for age and height. Although some anorexics are overweight prior to the onset of dieting, many are at normal weight levels. However, they still receive encouragement from parents and friends to continue their dieting.

The anorexic begins by reducing her intake of carbohydrates. She also begins an exercise regime—generally solitary activities, such as running and sit-ups. As the disorder progresses and family members become concerned about her weight loss, the anorexic stubbornly refuses to discontinue dieting. She has lost her ability to appraise her body image and size realistically, declaring that she is "too fat" even when she is 25% below her normal weight. This body-image distortion is a reinforcer for dieting, thus perpetuating a self-destructive cycle. Eventually, the anorexic, skeletal in appearance, requires emergency medical assistance for starvation and malnutrition.

Anorexia nervosa calls for a comprehensive treatment strategy that includes physicians, psychologists or psychiatrists, dietitians, and social workers. Without massive intervention, the prognosis is not encouraging. Only about one-third to one-half of victims recover completely; tragically, approximately 5% of victims die of starvation and related complications.

Reprinted by permission.

Psychological Consequences of Physical Growth

Adults tend to use level of physical development as a general cue to a child's age, and to react accordingly. Thus, children who are big for their age sometimes get treated by adults—even their parents—as if they were older. This can cause problems if age-appropriate behavior (of, say, a 4-year-old) clashes with inappropriate expectations (because the child looks 5 or 6).

The dramatic physical changes of adolescence, combined with the self-consciousness typical of this age, make adolescents feel awkward about changes in their body proportions and acutely aware of comparisons between their own development and that of their peers. Adolescents' reactions to physical changes will depend to some extent on their expectations; menstruation in girls and nocturnal emissions in boys can be frightening if they have not been prepared for them. But even if changes are anticipated and not alarming, they can have important consequences for social development.

Because girls generally begin puberty before boys, a girl who develops early may be two years more advanced than other girls her age and four years ahead of the boys in her peer group. There is some evidence that early-maturing girls are not as popular or poised as late-maturing girls (H. E. Jones, 1971), although these effects are apparently short-lived, disappearing when the other girls catch up in physical development (Faust, 1960).

The effects of early versus late maturation are even greater for boys. Research has consistently shown that early-maturing boys have a social advantage over late-maturing boys (Duke, Carlsmith, Jennings, Martin, Dornbusch, Gross, & Siegel-Gorelick, 1982; M. C. Jones, 1965; Jones & Bayley, 1950). Unlike their female counterparts, early-maturing boys are not overly conspicuous, because many girls have already begun their adolescent growth spurt. Because of their greater height and strength, early-maturing boys are more likely to excel in sports, which play an important role in the social world of adolescent boys. At the same time, their burst into

Physical growth and maturation affect sports performance, which in turn affects social status.

"manhood" serves as a social signal, to themselves and others, that they are more responsible and have interests different from those of their less mature peers. As a result, early-maturing boys are more self-assured and sociable and have higher achievement aspirations (Duke et al., 1982).

Differences between early- and late-maturing boys apparently persist long after the late maturers have caught up. Mary Cover Jones (1965) followed early- and late-maturing boys into adulthood and reported that the early maturers continued to score higher on tests of self-assurance and leadership. The late maturers had some advantages of their own, however: they were more flexible in their thinking and showed greater overall insight into their behavior. Jones suggested that the late maturers learned adaptability and perceptiveness as a result of being slow to develop in a social environment that valued size and strength.

Development of the Brain

The human brain is arguably the most marvelous invention in the universe. Unlike the brain of any other species, ours provides us with self-awareness and a behavioral flexibility that allows us to create culture and adapt to a limitless diversity of environments.

The human brain is not equipped from birth to deal with the many complexities of life; it must develop. This development is characterized by periods of rapid growth followed by periods of slower change. Moreover, development is not always a matter of growth, but sometimes of loss—the systematic death of brain tissue.

As with all other biological systems, the brain is functioning at birth; in respect to size, it is far ahead of most other organs. By 6 months, the brain weighs 50% of what it will in adulthood; at 2 years, about 75%; at 5 years, 90%; and at 10 years, 95% (Tanner, 1978). In contrast, total body weight is about 20% of adult weight at 2 years, and only 50% at 10 years (see Figure 5.1).

Neuronal Development

The brain, and the nervous system in general, is a communication system. Electrical and chemical signals are transmitted from one specialized cell to an-

other, and the result, in humans, is a living, thinking being. These specialized cells are called **neurons,** or nerve cells. Estimates of the number of neurons in the mature human brain vary from 10 billion to more than 100 billion. Each neuron is connected to hundreds, and in many cases thousands, of other neurons via **synapses**—small spaces between neurons though which messages are passed. The result is many trillion connections among neurons, making the brain an extremely complex organ indeed.

The main part of the neuron is the cell body, which contains the nucleus (see Figure 5.6). Extending from the cell body is the **axon,** a long fiber that carries messages away from the cell body to other cells. Other, more numerous fibers, called **dendrites,** receive messages from other cells and transfer them to the cell body. Unlike most other cells in the body, neurons are not compressed together, but are separated by synapses. Electrical messages flowing down the axon of one cell cause the release of certain chemicals into the synapse. These chemicals move across the space between the cells and are "read" at the dendrites of the adjacent cell, which convert the message back to an electrical signal and pass it on to their cell body. Conditions present at the synapse (amount of chemicals available, presence of drugs) affect the transmission of messages to and from the brain.

Proliferation, migration, and differentiation of neurons Neurons go through at least three stages of development (Nowakowski, 1987; Spreen, Tupper, Risser, Tuokko, & Edgell, 1984). The first stage, referred to as **proliferation,** is the process of cell division by mitosis. Proliferation occurs early in development, during the prenatal period.

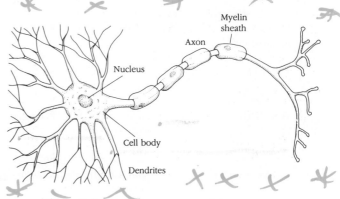

Figure 5.6 Primary structures of the neuron

The second stage is **migration,** when cells, once produced, move to what will be their permanent position in the brain. There they collect together with other cells to form the major parts of the brain. Not all cells migrate at the same time, but most cells have arrived at their final position by 20 weeks after conception (Spreen et al., 1984).

The third stage in neuronal development is **differentiation.** Once at their final destination, neurons become bigger, produce more dendrites, and extend their axons farther and farther away from the cell body. It is during this stage that synapses are created. When an axon meets an appropriate dendrite from another neuron, a synapse is formed.

This process of synapse formation is rapid during the prenatal period and continues to be rapid through the early months of life. But then a complementary process begins: **selective cell death.** Many more neurons and synapses are produced than are actually needed. What determines whether synapses will be formed and maintained and whether neurons will live or die? William Greenough, James Black, and Christopher Wallace (1987) proposed that the nervous system of animals (including humans) is prepared by evolution to "expect" certain types of stimulation—for example, a lighted three-dimensional world consisting of moving objects. Early experience of viewing such a world is sufficient for the visual nervous system to develop, resulting in normal vision. Those neurons and connections that receive the species-expected experience live and become organized with other activated neurons; those that don't receive such activation die. Thus, the infant comes into the world "prewired" to develop certain abilities, but the actual development of those abilities is substantially influenced by experience. What is hard-wired seems to be a susceptibility to certain environmental experiences, not the circuitry for detailed behaviors themselves.

Myelinization Once neurons have proliferated, migrated, differentiated, and formed synapses, there still remains an important developmental step: **myelinization. Myelin** is a fatty substance that surrounds the axons of neurons and promotes faster transmission of electrical signals.

The process of myelinization is a gradual one, beginning during the prenatal months and continuing into adolescence and beyond. Figure 5.7 shows

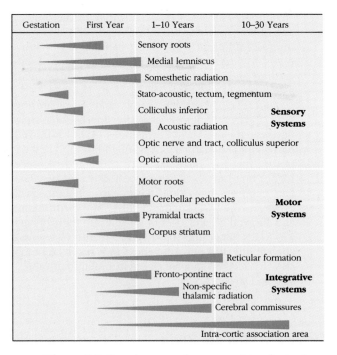

Figure 5.7 Developmental pattern of myelinization for different areas of the human brain. *Source:* From "The Myelenogenetic Cycles of Regional Maturation of the Brain," by P. I. Yakovlev and A. R. Lecours. In A. Minkowski (ed.), *Regional Development of the Brain in Early Life.* Copyright © 1967 Blackwell Scientific Publications, Ltd. Reprinted by permission.

the schedule of myelinization for various parts of the human brain. The thin line on the left denotes when myelinization for that brain structure begins; the thicker line on the right indicates when it has reached adult levels. Note that myelinization of the sensory systems begins prenatally and that most sensory structures are completely myelinated within the first year. This corresponds to the well-developed sensory abilities of human newborns and the adult-like sensory capacities they possess long before they can speak. Myelinization of the motor areas follows close behind; most of these brain structures are completely myelinated before the second year. Again, this corresponds to the development of motor abilities in young children, most of whom are walking well before their second birthday. Integrative systems correspond to the higher brain areas involved in complex cognition. Myelinization of these areas proceeds more slowly, continuing well into childhood and adolescence, and is correlated with the development of more complex mental processes, such as language, that are under the control of these regions of the brain (Bjorklund & Harnishfeger, 1990; Lacours, 1975).

Development of the Cerebral Cortex

At the broadest level of conceptualization, the brain can be divided into three major parts: the **hindbrain,** which contains the cerebellum, critical in motor coordination and maintaining balance; the **midbrain,** the top of the brain stem, which serves as a relay system between various parts of the brain; and the **forebrain,** which contains the **cerebral cortex** and is responsible for higher sensory, motor, and intellectual functioning. The forebrain is a more recent evolutionary invention and is more fully developed in humans than in any other species (with the possible exception of dolphins). The cerebral

cortex has many different areas, each with different functions (see Figure 5.8).

Organization of the cerebral cortex The cerebral cortex is a convoluted series of lobes surrounding the rest of the brain. The cerebral cortex consists of two approximately equal halves, or hemispheres, connected by a thick mass of nerves called the **corpus callosum.** The cerebral cortex can be further divided into regions, or areas. Primary areas include the various sensory regions, which receive information directly from the senses, and motor regions, which send instructions directly to muscles. Secondary areas are those that integrate information and have many connections with other areas of the brain. Known as the association (or "thought") regions, they are responsible for our more complex mental functioning.

Different regions of the brain develop at different rates, with myelinization of the associative areas lagging far behind myelinization in the sensory and motor areas. Other signs of cerebral development include density of neurons (that is, the number of

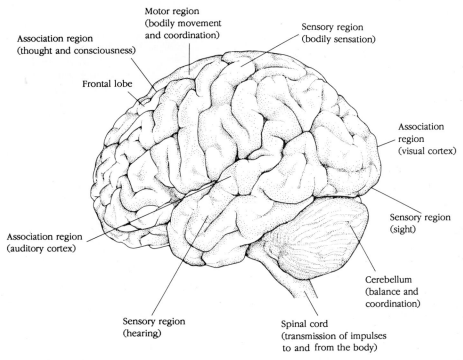

Figure 5.8 Lateral view of the left side of the human brain

neurons per cubic centimeter), size of neurons, and length of axons and dendrites (Tanner, 1978).

Cerebral lateralization   The two **hemispheres** of the brain are not completely identical, and researchers have hypothesized that certain mental skills or abilities are limited to (or better developed in) one hemisphere than the other. Evidence of this **cerebral lateralization** comes from studies of brain-damaged people and individuals whose right and left hemispheres have been surgically disconnected. These studies suggest that in right-handed people, the left hemisphere is specialized for processing language and other analytic, logical, or temporal information, whereas the right hemisphere is best suited for processing nonverbal, spatial, and visual information (Corballis & Beale, 1983; Gazzaniga, 1985; Springer & Deutsch, 1985). It is overly simplistic to propose that any particular type of information processing is limited to one side of the brain or the other; in neurologically intact people, both hemispheres are involved in most if not all cognitive tasks. (Remember that one hemisphere knows what the other is doing because they are connected by the corpus callosum.) Nevertheless, it has been clearly documented that the two hemispheres do process information differently and that the left hemisphere (in right-handed people and some left-handers as well) is primarily responsible for the production and comprehension of language. What has long interested developmental psychologists is when such lateralization comes about and its relation to language development.

One test for lateralization is the dichotic listening task, in which different audio signals are presented simultaneously to a person's left and right ears, and the person is asked periodically to make decisions about information coming into one or the other. (Sensory information from the right side of the body is processed in the left hemisphere, which also directs motor activity on the right side; similarly, the right brain receives information from and directs movement on the left side of the body.) Evidence of lateralization is demonstrated when people show a right-ear advantage—that is, they show faster or more accurate performance when information is presented directly to the left hemisphere. Variants of this task have been used with children as young as 2 years of age (Hiscock & Kinsbourne, 1980), and the results consistently reveal a right-ear advantage for children (Witelson, 1987). Other research has

shown that 1- to 4-month-old infants change their sucking rate more to changes in language sounds presented to the right ear than to the same sounds presented to the left ear (Entus, 1977). Even newborns seem to be biased to process language with the left side of their brains. In research that measured the electrical reaction of newborns' brains to various sounds, the left hemisphere responded more to language sounds than did the right, whereas music and other nonlanguage sounds produced greater reactions from the right hemisphere (Molfese & Molfese, 1980, 1985).

These results indicate that lateralization is a characteristic of the infant (even newborn) brain. Left-brain biases are found for motor behavior as well as language, with infants and young children showing a right-side bias for head turning, visually directed hand reaching, and manipulation of objects (Witelson, 1987). This does not necessarily preclude further changes in lateralization. For example, although young children show a preference for the left or right hand (Annett, 1970; Ramsay & Weber, 1986),

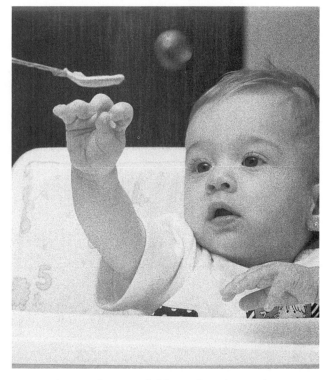

Infants and young children often show a distinct preference for using the right hand.

these preferences become stronger over childhood (Coren, Porac, & Duncan, 1981; Merola & Lieder-man, 1985). Such evidence does not necessarily imply that lateralization increases with age, but it does suggest, at least, that with age and experience, children become increasingly reliant on one hemisphere over the other to perform certain tasks (Witelson, 1987).

Plasticity of the Brain

Plasticity, discussed in Chapter 1, refers to the ability to change. With respect to the nervous system, to what extent can new neurons be produced, new synapses be formed, and different parts of the brain take over a function intended for another part? Given certain experiences at certain times during life, what are the potential outcomes for a single neuron, bundle of neurons, or larger brain structure?

Neuronal Plasticity

Concerning the production of new neurons, there is no plasticity. Newborns come into the world with more neurons than they will ever need. From birth on, there is a loss of neurons—rapid over the first year and more gradual thereafter. Virtually no new neurons are formed after birth.

The picture is different for the formation of new synapses. Although it was believed not too many years ago that synapse production was limited to infancy, more recent research indicates that new synaptic connections can be formed throughout life (see Greenough et al., 1987). What causes new synapses to form? The answer is experience.

In studies dating back to 1949, researchers have raised groups of laboratory animals (mostly rats and mice) in enriched environments—animals raised together in cages filled with platforms, toys, and mazes—and compared their brain development and learning ability to those raised in unadorned individual cages (Diamond, Rosenzweig, Bennett, Lindner, & Lyon, 1972; Hebb, 1949; Hymovitch, 1952; Turner & Greenough, 1985). These experiments have shown that rats and mice raised in enriched environments are superior at a wide range of complex tasks, such as maze learning. The differences in learning ability are of a general nature, and the most likely explanation seems to be that "the groups differ

in the amount of stored knowledge upon which they can draw in novel situations" (Greenough et al., 1987, p. 547). Concerning changes found in their brains, enriched animals have heavier and thicker cerebral cortexes, larger neurons with more dendrites, and more synaptic connections. In one study, enriched rats had 20%–25% more synapses per neuron in their visual cortexes than did rats raised in individual cages (Turner & Greenough, 1985). Moreover, these effects are not limited to infant animals; older animals also derive behavioral and brain benefits from living in a stimulating environment (Greenough, McDonald, Parnisari, & Camel, 1986).

Synaptic plasticity is greatest in infancy. With age and experience, neurons and synapses already formed begin to die, thus rendering certain connections impossible. Although the plasticity to form new synapses decreases with age, we do retain a substantial neural plasticity throughout life (Lerner, 1984). What changes is the degree to which experience can change the brain and the intensity of the experience needed to produce change.

Recovery of Function from Brain Damage

Perhaps the best evidence of the plasticity of the nervous system comes from case studies of people who have experienced brain damage and exhibit deficits in physical or mental functioning. These studies document the process of readjustment and the effect of age.

Since the 19th century, numerous reports have indicated that children who experience brain damage to the language areas of the left hemisphere before they are able to speak are able to attain more advanced levels of language than older children or adults who experience similar brain damage (Annett, 1973; Woods & Carey, 1979). Likewise, left-hemisphere brain injury in children who can already talk may produce a temporary loss of language ability, but in many cases language is recovered and the child talks again at a near-normal level. Studies conducted on adults have not found that same degree of recovery (see Witelson, 1985). Full recovery of language is rare, however, even in young children, indicating that the human brain is not completely plastic even early in life (Witelson, 1987).

When brain damage affects more general cognitive functioning, rather than a specific cognitive ability such as language, the results are different (Witelson, 1987). Evidence reviewed by Bryan Kolb

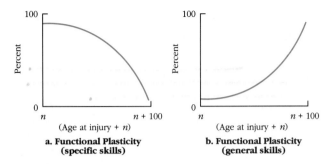

a. **Functional Plasticity (specific skills)**

b. **Functional Plasticity (general skills)**

Figure 5.9 Theoretical relationship between age at brain damage and recovery of function: specific skills versus more general skills. *Source:* Adapted from "Neurobiological Aspects of Language in Children," by S. F. Witelson, *Child Development,* 1987, *58,* 653–688. Copyright © The Society for Research in Child Development, Inc. Reprinted by permission.

and Ian Whishaw (1990), from both animal and human research, demonstrates that younger children and animals show more permanent deficits than older children and animals after brain damage to areas that control general processes, such as IQ, brain size, and some species-typical behaviors. In one study, for example, brain damage before the age of 1 resulted in lower IQs for children than similar brain damage that occurred after a child's first birthday (Riva & Cazzaniga, 1986); another study reported greater reductions in IQ for children who suffered brain damage before the age of 5 than for those who suffered similar injury after 5 (Kornhuber, Bechinger, Jung, & Sauer, 1985). In research with rats, Kolb and Whishaw (1981) reported that brain lesions inflicted shortly after birth resulted in a smaller adult brain than did similar lesions inflicted on adult animals.

In general, whereas brain damage affecting a specific skill, such as language, can be better compensated for when it occurs earlier in life, the reverse appears to be true for brain damage that affects more general intellectual abilities. In some cases, early insults affect how large portions of a system will develop, much like the effects of teratogens during the embryonic period; in other cases, early brain insults can be compensated for by a pliable system that can still make adjustments to unexpected changes. The relationship between age at injury and degree of plasticity for specific and general skills is illustrated in Figure 5.9.

Motor Development

As children's bones and muscles grow, they become more willing and able to move their bodies. Children progress from sitting to standing to walking to running, all in a relatively brief period of time. By early childhood, children can not only run well, but climb trees, keep their balance while walking along a curb, and swing hand-to-hand on a set of monkey bars. At the same time that such gross motor behaviors are developing, children are also perfecting their fine motor capabilities, especially control and coordination of the hands and fingers. The newborn's reflexive grasp becomes refined so that by the end of the first year children can pick up Cheerios with their fingers and guide them quickly and accurately to their mouths. It is not until years later, however, that they develop the fine motor coordination necessary for precise writing, and even

The reflexive grasp of the newborn develops over time into increasingly fine motor skills.

longer before they can type proficiently or dash off a quick signature at the bottom of a check.

Motor development proceeds on its regular course because it is determined largely by maturation of the brain. Yet events in the outside world also influence motor development, and a child's motor abilities, in turn, affect cognitive and social aspects of development. The 12-month-old who can walk (or run) is treated differently than the 12-month-old who is still crawling. Older children who have the coordination to excel in sports and games find themselves in different social situations than less well coordinated children. In short, changes in motor development have greater consequences for children than simply giving them an increased ability to move about.

Gross Motor Development

Babies are born with well-developed reflexes such as grasping and sucking, but for the most part, when they are put somewhere, that's where they'll stay until someone moves them. This immobile period doesn't last long, however. By 4 or 6 months, many infants are able to move from place to place by lying on their stomachs and pulling themselves along with their arms. This is not a very efficient form of locomotion, and few infants who move in this way travel far, but within several months, most infants are on their hands and knees, crawling to where they want to go. Not all infants crawl. Some "scoot," propelling themselves in a sitting position, others roll, and still others "ambulate" on hands and feet, with their knees or elbows off the floor. Whatever the early locomotive style, it is soon followed by upright walking, which brings new freedom to the toddler.

Children's abilities to run, jump, balance, throw, and catch, along with their general coordination, improve regularly over the preschool years. Table 5.1 presents a list of motor activities and the range of ages at which they are usually accomplished.

Fine Motor Development

Fine motor movements are those using individual body parts to control small objects. Although some people are quite proficient at picking up objects with their toes, fine motor control in humans is typically expressed in terms of manual skills. Infants come into the world with a reflexive grasp. Over the course of the first year, this grasp becomes less re-

Infants often show individual differences in crawling styles.

flexive and more under an infant's intentional control. However, the key to fine motor control is getting the hands to move in coordination with incoming visual information, or eye–hand coordination.

During the first months of life, infants will follow a moving object with their eyes and may thrust a hand out and attempt to grab it, but such attempts are rarely successful. At the same time, infants "discover" their hands and will spend much time staring at them or looking back and forth between their hands and some object (Williams, 1983). Infants are able to inspect objects visually before they are able to pick them up; cephalocaudal development means that the muscles controlling their eye movements develop ahead of the muscles controlling their fingers and hands. However, the rudiments of **visually guided reaching** can be seen in the first few months of life. Three-month-olds can reach for and grasp an object if it is presented on the same side as the reaching hand, and 6-month-olds are able to reach for objects presented in front of them or on the opposite side from the reaching hand. Thus, at about the time most infants can sit unaided, they are able to visually direct their hands to reach objects in front of them or to either side. This enables them to grasp a second object if one hand is already busy and to begin to explore objects with two hands (Provine & Westerman, 1979). Eye-hand coordination continues to improve, but before the end of the first year infants have acquired the basics of this important skill that they will use continually throughout their lives (Williams, 1983).

Fine motor skills must develop beyond simple visually guided reaching if a child is to become a

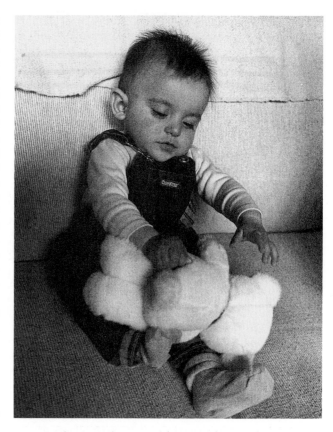

By the time they are able to sit alone, infants can direct their hands to reach objects in front of them.

Table 5.1 Denver developmental norms for selected behaviors

Behavior	Percent of Population Passing by Age			
	25%	50%	75%	95%
Prone, lifts head				.7 mo.
Prone, head up 90 degrees	1.3 mo.	2.2 mo.	2.6 mo.	3.2 mo.
Sits, head steady	1.5 mo.	2.9 mo.	3.6 mo.	4.2 mo.
Rolls over	2.3 mo.	2.8 mo.	3.8 mo.	4.7 mo.
Sits without support	4.8 mo.	5.5 mo.	6.5 mo.	7.8 mo.
Stands holding on	5.0 mo.	5.8 mo.	8.5 mo.	10.0 mo.
Gets to sitting position	6.1 mo.	7.6 mo.	9.3 mo.	10.0 mo.
Walks holding furniture	7.3 mo.	9.2 mo.	10.2 mo.	12.7 mo.
Walks well	11.3 mo.	12.1 mo.	13.5 mo.	14.3 mo.
Walks up steps	14.0 mo.	17.0 mo.	21.0 mo.	22.0 mo.
Jumps in place	20.5 mo.	22.3 mo.	2.5 yr.	3.0 yr.
Balances on one foot for 5 seconds	2.6 yr.	3.2 yr.	3.9 yr.	4.3 yr.
Heel-to-toe walk	3.3 yr.	3.6 yr.	4.2 yr.	5.0 yr.
Catches bounced ball	3.5 yr.	3.9 yr.	4.9 yr.	5.5 yr.

Source: Adapted from "The Denver Developmental Screening Test," by W. K. Frankenberg and J. B. Dodds, *Journal of Pediatrics,* 1976, *71,* 181–191. Reprinted by permission.

proficient member of society. In some cultures, the motor abilities involved in weaving, carving, sculpting, or creating stone tools are valuable skills that children must master on the way to adulthood. In technological societies such as ours, the fine motor skills involved in drawing or writing are critical to adult functioning. These skills were studied extensively by Florence Goodenough (1926). Table 5.2 presents the ages and stages of children's abilities for copying a design. The earliest stages reflect unstructured and apparently nongoal-directed movements. Gradually over the preschool years, children's copying becomes goal-directed, as they begin to pay attention to the stimulus and attempt to re-create what they see. However, even by age 5, children's copying skills are not complete. Similarly, in the early school years, children's writing is typically limited to learning how to form letters and

The motor skills children need to master for adulthood differ from culture to culture.

Table 5.2 Goodenough's stages of design copying

Stage	Age	Description
I	1 yr.	Scribbling. Motor actions unrelated to any goal and undirected by visual schema.
II	2 yrs.	Scribbling. Spontaneous production but child now is visually responsive to the scribbles and gives them post hoc meaning.
III	2½ yrs.	Child's preponderant response to any request to copy and/or draw is to scribble with inclusion of closed loops and parts of loops.
IV	3 yrs.	Copying. The child begins to pay attention to characteristics of visual model presented to her or him to be copied.
	4 yrs.	Copying. The child begins to make differential drawings that involve *angular* as well as smooth contours.
	5 yrs.	Copying. There is a definite organization of drawing in relationship to the visually presented model, but copying is still being refined.

Source: Goodenough, 1926.

copying words written by adults. The amount of physical effort young school-age children exert in simply copying prevents them from using writing as a serious form of verbal expression until early adolescence. Children are not free to become skilled writers until the physical act of writing can be accomplished effortlessly (Kroll, 1981).

State of the Art
The Advantages of Slow Growth

Students of development often find physical growth less exciting than, say, the development of intelligence, language, aggression, and emotions. Yet human growth is a dynamic and exciting subject—dynamic because physical growth involves the complex interaction of biological and environmental factors, and exciting because it is the unique character of our physical development that is responsible for the many features we associate with being human. It is our species' particular rate of growth that differentiates us from other mammals and affords us the time to develop a nervous system that gives us our unmatched intelligence and behavioral flexibility.

Human development is slow in two ways. In the obvious way, it takes us many years to reach adulthood; we spend a greater proportion of our lives in childhood than any other mammal. For example, among primates, sexual maturity is achieved in lemurs at approximately 2 years, in macaque monkeys at 4, in chimpanzees at 8, and in humans at approximately 15 years (Poirier & Smith, 1974).

Development is also slow in a less obvious way that is related to evolution. Many of the adult characteristics of humans are actually embryonic or neonatal characteristics of our distant ancestors. Using the chimpanzee as a model for what our distant ancestors may have been like, we find many features in *adult* humans that resemble those of *infant* chimps.[1] Chimps "outgrow" these features; humans

---

[1]We must emphasize that humans did *not* evolve from chimpanzees or gorillas. Humans, chimpanzees, and gorillas shared a common ancestor between 5 and 10 million years ago, and each species has evolved from that point. Chimpanzees and gorillas are our close genetic cousins, and differences among the species can be used to assess the different paths that evolution has taken over this time span.

don't. The tendency toward slow development and retention of infantile characteristics of an evolutionary ancestor has been termed **neoteny** (de Beer, 1958; Gould, 1977).

The Slowing of Development in Evolutionary Time

The neotenous nature of humans is perhaps most easily seen with respect to facial features. At birth, the faces of a human infant and an infant chimpanzee are remarkably similar. The proportions of the chimp's face change drastically with age, however: prominent brow ridges develop, and the jaws (both upper and lower) jut out. The facial proportions of humans change in the same directions, but not nearly as much (with men showing more "apelike" changes than women).

Many other neotenous features have had a significant impact on the development of our species. For example, the angle at which our spines connect with our skulls is such that we can stand and walk upright on two legs, a technique known as bipedality. This opening in the skull is at a different place in adult chimpanzees and gorillas, and their typical form of locomotion involves using the knuckles of their hands as well as their feet to scramble over the ground. Although adult humans and chimps differ anatomically in this respect, embryonic chimps and humans do not: the orientation of this opening in chimpanzees during the prenatal period is the same as in humans. In chimpanzees, the orientation shifts in development, whereas in humans, the embryonic orientation is retained—an adaptation that resulted in our ability to walk upright, the first major step in the development of homo sapiens (Eccles, 1989).

Although bipedality is central to our definition of human, perhaps the most outstanding human trait is intelligence. In this area, we have clearly developed beyond our evolutionary ancestors rather than having our development retarded to some earlier embryonic or infantile state. But even in intellectual evolution, neoteny plays a role. Because we are so dependent upon learning for survival, our brains must be larger in proportion to our bodies than other species'. This is achieved, in part, by continuing the rapid rate of prenatal brain growth into postnatal life.

Growing Up Slowly

The need to learn   The cave baby born 100,000 years ago and the 1990s model differ little in biology. But whereas the cave baby would have lived the wheel-less, plow-less life of a primitive member of our species, the 1990s baby will grow up to send computer mail around the world and fly in supersonic jets. The different lifestyles and thinking styles are the results of culture. Once agriculture was developed and the wheel invented, these technological advances became available to future generations through cultural transmission, allowing the next generation to contribute its own inventions. Whereas other species advance through the genes of their members, passing on the biological traits best suited to their environment, we advance by teaching the new generation all the knowledge our generation has received plus the current generation's contributions to that body of knowledge. In fact, the power and speed of cultural evolution has caused some to propose that, for humans, biological evolution by natural selection has ended (Dixon, 1981; Eccles, 1989). But cultural transmission requires a long childhood—a cultural apprenticeship.

The brain necessary for learning all that the culture has to offer must be relatively large. However, because the birth canals of human females are limited in size, much of our brain development must take place after birth. This means that human infants are born "prematurely," in the sense that our brains are not nearly as close to the final product as other primates'. The longer time necessary for the brain to develop also gives us more time to learn.

Learning in the young of many species is done through play. Research has shown that play is important in many primates for developing motor abilities, practicing and mastering social skills, and experimenting with survival skills in safe surroundings (Bruner, 1972; Dolhinow & Bishop, 1970). The same can be said about humans and other species that depend on behavioral flexibility (Oppenheim, 1981). In fact, some theorists believe that play is an important way we develop our intelligence (Dansky, 1980; Piaget, 1962). Although many animals play, only humans show the curiosity and need for novelty throughout the life span that result in continual learning and behavioral flexibility (Lorenz, 1971; Rheingold, 1985).

Chimps and gorillas are similar to humans in many ways, but they reach adulthood sooner and lose their curiosity and need for play as they grow older.

Slow growth and plasticity   It is our slow brain growth, continuing into adulthood, that provides us with the flexibility to make many changes within our lifetimes (Gould, 1977; Lerner, 1984). Although synaptic formation does continue into adulthood, brain plasticity is gradually reduced over time (Jacobson, 1969; McCall, 1981), making drastic changes in behavior or cognition more difficult with increasing age and maturity. Children have shown impressive

reversibility of the effects of an intellectually damaging environment when conditions in their lives change for the better during their second and third years (Clark & Hanisee, 1982; Skeels, 1966). Children's slow brain development protects them from the long-term consequences of an early harmful environment by giving them the opportunity to override these negative effects with positive ones in later years.

Some believe that slow growth is also the key to our future as a species. Robert Ornstein, a psychologist specializing in human consciousness, and Paul Erlich, a biologist specializing in issues of human population control, point out in their 1989 book, *New World, New Mind,* that the world in which humans evolved thousands of years ago was very different from the world of today. We evolved to respond quickly to immediate threats (a tiger approaching from the right, a man with a rock from the left) and to do things that would increase the number of offspring in the next generation. As a result, Ornstein and Erlich argue, modern humans are not well adapted for modern life, with its more subtle dangers such as overpopulation, ozone depletion, the greenhouse effect, and contaminated oceans. Humans, who respond best to short-term and obvious problems, must learn to respond to long-term and more subtle problems or prepare to live in a vastly different world than the one we inhabit now.

The key to changing our behavior in spite of our evolutionary past is to take advantage of the plasticity of human intelligence afforded by slow development. We, as a species, are capable of changing our way of viewing the world, but it is easier to develop this new perspective in our children than it is to re-educate adults. According to Ornstein and Erlich, through early education, children can learn to alter their species-typical behavior and so preserve life on this planet as we know it.

The Ornstein and Erlich proposal is a provocative one, and certainly one that deserves careful consideration, given what is at stake. For our purposes, their proposal demonstrates the creative power that slow growth affords our species. Our particular pattern of physical growth has not only played a key role in the evolution of homo sapiens, but may also play a key role in our continued survival.

Summary

Different organ systems grow at different rates, with the head and brain growing most rapidly early in life and the reproductive system taking the longest to reach maturity. In general, growth curves show that girls have more mature organ systems at birth, begin their adolescent growth spurt earlier, and grow up faster than boys. Ossification, the process whereby bone tissue replaces cartilage, begins early in the fetal period. Because the head grows rapidly early in life, the bones of the head are separated by fibrous-filled gaps called fontanels.

Puberty is defined as the period at which the testes, prostate gland, and seminal vesicles, or the uterus and vagina, suddenly enlarge. Puberty usually begins earlier in girls than in boys. Other changes include, for boys, adolescent growth spurt, presence of pubic and facial hair, enlargement of the penis, and deeper voices; and for girls, adolescent growth spurt, presence of pubic hair, breast development, and beginning of the menstrual period (menarche).

The endocrine system produces hormones that greatly influence growth. The hypothalamus signals the pituitary gland, which in turn releases human growth hormone, influencing growth directly, and also sends messages to other endocrine glands. The ovaries and testes produce estrogens and testosterone (related to androgens), respectively, which play an important role in growth at puberty. The thyroid gland produces thyroxine, which influences growth primarily during the prenatal period. The adrenal glands also produce androgens.

Children are growing taller sooner and are reaching sexual maturity at an earlier age than in generations past, effects that can be attributed to better nutrition and disease control. Stress can affect growth, but the most important single environmental influence on growth is nutrition. Malnourished children grow more slowly, although they retain the capacity for normal growth when good nutrition is resumed. Obesity in children is associated with a host of physical and psychological problems, and is increasing in the United States and in other parts of the world.

The nervous system consists of neurons, or nerve cells, which transport chemical and electrical signals. Neurons go through at least three stages of development: proliferation, migration, and differentiation. It is during this last stage that synapses are formed. Synapse formation is rapid during prenatal development and early infancy. A complementary process of selective cell death also occurs, with many neurons dying. All the neurons an individual will ever have are produced by early infancy, although recent evidence indicates that synapse formation occurs throughout life. Myelin is a fatty substance that surrounds axons, promoting faster transmission of electrical signals. Different areas of the brain begin and end the process of myelinization at different times; the degree of myelinization is related to levels of sensory, motor, and intellectual development.

The brain can be divided into three major parts: the hindbrain, the midbrain, and the forebrain. The forebrain contains the cerebral cortex, which is responsible for higher sensory, motor, and intellectual functions. The cerebral cortex is divided into two hemispheres, connected by the corpus callosum. Recent evidence suggests that lateralization—the specialization of the two hemispheres—is present to some degree in young infants.

Neuronal plasticity has been demonstrated most clearly in studies with animals, comparing those reared in deprived versus enriched environments. The plasticity needed to form new synapses declines with age, but does not disappear. Examination of the recovery of function after brain damage shows that in the case of specific abilities such as language, plasticity is greater the earlier the damage occurs; for more general functions such as intelligence, the opposite is true.

Both gross motor and fine motor skills develop with age. Fine motor development involves improved eye-hand coordination, beginning with the development of visually guided reaching in the first few months of life.

The rate of growth in humans is slow, relative to other species. Not only is much time required to reach sexual maturity, but humans retain many embryonic or neonatal characteristics of our evolutionary ancestors—a phenomenon known as neoteny. Many neotenous factors have had a significant impact on the evolution of homo sapiens, including maintaining the rapid embryonic rate of brain growth into the postnatal months. This long period of growth provides more time to learn the many complexities of human culture and greater plasticity of the brain early in life.

Key Terms and Concepts

growth curves
ossification
    fontanels
puberty
    menarche
endocrine system
    hormones
    hypothalamus
    pituitary gland
        human growth hormone
        gonads
        estrogen
        progesterone
        testosterone
        androgen
    thyroid gland
        thyroxine
    adrenal glands
malnutrition
obesity
anorexia nervosa

neurons
    synapses
    axon
    dendrites
    proliferation
    migration
    differentiation
    selective cell death
myelinization
    myelin
hindbrain
midbrain
forebrain
cerebral cortex
    hemispheres
    corpus callosum
    primary areas
        sensory regions
        motor regions
    secondary areas
        association regions
cerebral lateralization
    dichotic listening task
gross motor development
fine motor development
    eye-hand coordination
    visually guided reaching
neoteny

Three

Cognitive Development

6

Perception and Attention

A young music teacher and her artist husband were expecting their first baby. They had decided to raise their child in an atmosphere of culture and beauty, planning to expose the new baby early on to fine music and art. They hung their favorite paintings in the nursery and bought an FM radio so the child could hear selections from the classics on their favorite radio station.

However, their son was born prematurely and spent his first month in the neonatal intensive care unit (NICU) while the new parents traveled two and three times a day to participate in his sensory stimulation therapy. They rocked him, talked to him, and brought brightly colored pictures and toys to decorate his cubicle. When it was time to take him home, the NICU director cautioned them that he might not be able to sleep well in a dark, quiet room. She suggested leaving on a night-light and a radio in the nursery.

The new family came home together and found that the NICU director had been right. The baby slept fitfully for a few hours, but was wide awake and crying by midnight. The mother turned on the new radio and found that her favorite classical music station was not on the air that time of night; neither was her second favorite, semiclassical station. In fact, the only music they could tune in at that time was a country and western station from the next town. To her surprise, the music calmed the baby immediately, and he was soon sound asleep for the night.

From then on, the music teacher and her artist husband fell asleep to the twang of Waylon Jennings and Loretta Lynn piped into their bedroom through the nursery monitor. And they soon decided it sounded better than Beethoven because it was accompanied by the gentle rhythmic breathing of their son sleeping in the next room—home and healthy.

Perception is the basis of all cognition, and, as the story above illustrates, it is functioning from the earliest days of life. Before we can retrieve a thought, compare two stimuli, or create an image, we must have access to raw data from the external world. As we have seen, the perceptual system is functioning at birth but improves gradually and continually over infancy, giving children access to the basic information they need for more complicated cognitions. In this chapter, we will look more closely at the development of perception and attention.

Perception, Attention, and Memory in Infancy

Visual Perception

In Chapter 4, we described the visual preference technique developed by Robert Fantz to determine if infants can discriminate between two visual stimuli (see also Casey & Richards, 1988). Not only can infants see shortly after birth, but there are certain things they like to look at more than others. Because infants have no visual experience before birth, it is difficult to explain their early capabilities or preferences in terms of prenatal experience; it seems that some things are just innately more attractive to babies than others.

The development of visual preferences What babies like to look at depends on a variety of physical stimulus characteristics: movement, contour or contrast, complexity, symmetry, and curvature.

Other things being equal, babies will look more at a moving stimulus than at a stationary one (Haith, 1966). Infants are also attracted to areas of high contrast, as reflected by the outline, or contour, of an object. In a pioneering study, Philip Salapatek and William Kessen (1966) assessed the visual scanning of newborns. Infants less than 1 week old were placed in a modified looking chamber facing a white triangle painted on a black background. Their eye movements were recorded both when the triangle was present and when the triangle was not. The scanning patterns of newborns when the triangle was present (see Figure 6.1) reveal that infants' visual fixations were centered around the three angles of the triangles, the areas of highest contrast.

Infants' preference for contour increases with age (Brennan, Ames, & Moore, 1966). Because stimuli with more contour are also more complex, this means that older infants prefer to look at more complex stimuli than younger infants (Greenberg & O'Donnell, 1972; Karmel & Maisel, 1975). There is also evidence that infants as young as 4 months more easily process stimuli with vertical symmetry—that is, stimuli that are similar on the left and right sides (such as faces)—than nonsymmetrical stimuli (Bornstein, Ferdinandsen, & Gross, 1981; Humphrey, Humphrey, Muir, & Dodwell, 1986).

Some of Fantz's original work demonstrated that infants prefer curved stimuli, such as a bullseye, to linear (straight-line) stimuli of comparable contour

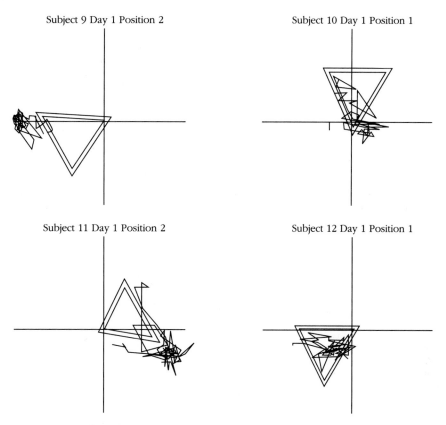

Subject 9 Day 1 Position 2

Subject 10 Day 1 Position 1

Subject 11 Day 1 Position 2

Subject 12 Day 1 Position 1

Figure 6.1 Scanning patterns of newborns. *Source:* From "Visual Scanning of Triangles by the Human Newborn," by P. Salapatek and W. Kessen, *Journal of Experimental Child Psychology,* 1966, *3,* 155–167. Reprinted by permission of Academic Press, Inc.

(Fantz, 1958). Holly Ruff and Herbert Birch (1974) similarly observed a preference for curvilinear stimuli in 3- and 4-month-old infants, but also found a preference for concentric stimuli, even if composed of straight lines (see Figure 6.2). This preference for curvature has been observed even in newborns (Fantz & Miranda, 1975). The bias toward curvature and concentricity may help explain young infants' preference for the human face.

Preferences for physical characteristics such as movement, contour, complexity, symmetry, and curvature continue to affect the attention of people throughout life. However, beginning sometime around 2 to 4 months, the psychological characteristics of a stimulus also begin to influence what will be attended to. By psychological, we refer to an ob-

ject's meaning rather than its appearance. As infants have experiences with different stimuli, meaning becomes attached to them. Stimuli that are slightly novel particularly influence infants' attention.

Jerome Kagan (1971) proposed that, beginning around 2 months, infants form **schemas** and that it is the similarity a stimulus has to previously formed schemas that determines attention. A schema is not an exact copy of a stimulus, but "a representation of an event that preserves the temporal and spatial arrangement of its distinctive elements without necessarily being isomorphic with the event" (Kagan, 1971, p. 6). Kagan proposed the **discrepancy principle** to explain infants' attention to novel stimuli. According to Kagan, infants are most attentive to stimuli that are slightly different from other stimuli

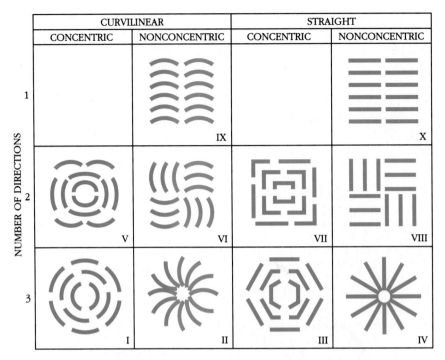

Figure 6.2 Stimuli used to assess infants' preferences for curvature and concentricity. *Source:* From "Infant Visual Fixation: The Effect of Concentricity, Curvilinearity, and Number of Directions," by H. A. Ruff and H. G. Birch, *Journal of Experimental Child Psychology,* 1974, *17,* 460–473. Copyright © 1974 by Academic Press. Reprinted by permission.

the infant has had previous experience with. A stimulus that differs only slightly from a baby's schema (for example, a bearded face when the infant is familiar with nonbearded faces) is apt to attract and maintain attention, whereas a highly familiar stimulus (a nonbearded face) or a highly discrepant one (a bearded face with its features scrambled) is apt to receive less attention. Subsequent research has provided support for Kagan's contention (McCall & Kennedy, 1980; McCall, Kennedy, & Appelbaum, 1977).

Depth perception An area of infant visual perception that has received considerable attention over the years is depth perception. At what age, and under what conditions, can infants perceive depth? One reason for the interest in the development of depth cues is their importance in early locomotion. Many parents have tales of their 8-month-old infants'

crawling off the side of the bed, sometimes to be caught by watchful parents and sometimes not. What cues must infants perceive in order to understand edges of beds and drop-offs on stairs? When do they develop? Can adults do anything to teach this important ability?

An apparatus designed to test these questions is the **visual cliff** (Gibson & Walk, 1960; Walk & Gibson, 1961), which usually consists of a glass-topped table with a solid leaf in its center. On one side of the leaf the infant sees a checkerboard pattern that is situated directly under the glass; this is referred to as the "shallow" side. On the other side, the checkerboard pattern is several feet below the glass; this is referred to as the "deep" side (see Figure 6.3). In a typical experiment, infants who can crawl (usually beginning around 7 or 8 months) are placed on the center leaf of the table, and their mothers call to

Figure 6.3 An infant on a visual cliff.

recent research by Joseph Campos, Bennett Bertenthal, and their colleagues (Bertenthal, Campos, & Barrett, 1984; Campos, Hiatt, Ramsey, Henderson, & Svejda, 1978) found that the tendency to show fear on the visual cliff was related to the amount of previous locomotor experience. Infants with more crawling and scooting experience were more apt to show fear than their less experienced peers, suggesting that this experience is important for depth perception.

In an interesting study of depth perception, the locomotive experience of one group of infants who did not crawl yet was "enriched" by letting them get around in walkers (a seat attached to a frame on wheels that permits infants to propel themselves by pushing on the floor with their feet). Unlike their noncrawling agemates who did not use walkers, the walker babies showed fear of height (reflected by heart-rate acceleration when placed on the deep side of a visual cliff), indicating that the experience in the walkers accelerated the development of depth perception (Bertenthal et al., 1984).

Self-produced movement and the development of vision The study by Bertenthal et al. (1984) suggests that there is something about self-propelled movement that facilitates perception—that perceptual systems do not develop in isolation, but in coordination with motor systems. In a study designed to examine the connection between locomotive experience and spatial (visual) memory, Rosanne Kermoian and Joseph Campos (1988) divided 8½-month-old infants into three groups: (a) prelocomotive (not yet crawling); (b) prelocomotive but with walker experience; and (c) locomotive (crawling). The infants were then tested with a series of tasks in which they had to retrieve an object hidden under a cloth. Infants with locomotive experience, whether by crawling or in a walker, showed more advanced performance on the object retrieval task than did the noncrawlers. Moreover, there were no differences in performance between the crawlers and the walkers, suggesting that it is the locomotor experience and not maturation that is responsible for the advanced spatial memory.

Perhaps the best-known research dealing with the role of self-propelled movement in perception is that of Richard Held and Allen Hein (1963). In this

them from one side of the cliff and then the other. The critical question is: will infants perceive the visual cues on the deep side and stay put, fussing and afraid to crawl to their mothers, or will they fail to perceive the depth cues and crawl happily across? Infants who show distress and refuse to crawl across the deep side (but who crawl agreeably across the shallow side) are said to have depth perception.

In general, early findings of Richard Walk and Eleanor Gibson indicated that babies rarely crawled to their mothers across the deep side. These findings suggest that once infants can crawl they display fear, and that little learning is necessary. However, more

classic study, kittens were raised in a darkened room and had visual experience only during training and testing. Pairs of kittens were used, one given normal visual-motor experience and the other given visual experience without associated motor experience. To do this, a special training apparatus was developed (see Figure 6.4). One kitten was harnessed to walk around the brightly decorated track (active kitten), whereas the other, confined to a gondola, received identical visual experiences without the associated motor feedback (passive kitten). Thus, both kittens had the same visual experience, and both had motor experience in their darkened room, but only the active kitten had visual experience contingent with movement. After training, both kittens were tested

on the visual cliff. Passive kittens showed no preference for one side over the other, indicating a lack of depth perception. By contrast, the active kittens consistently chose the shallow side, indicating that they could perceive depth.

The findings of Held and Hein (1963) with kittens and of Bertenthal, Campos, and their colleagues with children, make it clear that visual perception does not develop simply as a result of maturation or visual experience, but in conjunction with contingent motor experience. This research points to the importance of studying the development of the whole child and not just looking at one system in isolation from others.

Box 6.1

Is Beauty Only in the Eye of the Beholder?

One surprising visual preference recently found in young infants is for *attractive* female faces (Langlois, Roggman, Casey, Ritter, Rieser-Danner, & Jenkins, 1987). Judith Langlois and her colleagues asked college men and women to judge the attractiveness of adult Caucasian women from photographs. From these ratings, eight attractive and eight unattractive faces were selected, although the distribution of attractiveness was relatively normal (that is, there were no extremely attractive or unattractive faces). The photographs were selected so that all women had neutral expressions, medium to dark hair, and no glasses. In one part of the study, the researchers showed 2- to 3-month-old and 6- to 8-month-old infants pairs of faces varying in attractiveness (one attractive and one unattractive face) and measured their looking time. Both younger and older infants spent significantly more time looking at the attractive faces than at the unattractive faces, with approximately two-thirds of the infants showing a preference for the more attractive faces. Furthermore, the preference for more attractive faces was unrelated to how attractive an infant's mother was judged to be. In later research by Langlois and her colleagues, 12-month-old infants interacted with a

stranger who wore a professionally constructed attractive or unattractive mask. The babies played more with the stranger wearing the attractive than the unattractive mask. In a second study, 12-month-old infants spent more time playing with an attractive doll than an unattractive one (Langlois, Roggman, & Rieser-Danner, 1990).

One possible explanation for these findings is that attractive faces may have more of the physical stimulus characteristics that attract infant attention; that is, attractive faces may be more curvilinear, concentric, and vertically symmetrical than unattractive faces. Another possibility is that infants may be born with a schema, or abstract representation, of a human face, and attractive faces match that schema better than do unattractive ones. Recent evidence indicates that attractive faces are those that reflect the average of a range of facial features (for example, average nose length, average distance between the eyes)—that attractive faces are, in essence, average faces (Langlois & Roggman, 1990). Regardless of the reason, these data indicate that what was once believed to be a learned preference (attractiveness) may have its basis in biology.

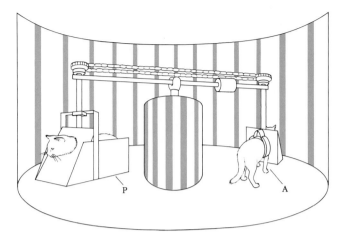

Figure 6.4 Apparatus used to study the effects of locomotor experience on visual perception (P = passive kitten, A = active kitten) (adapted from Held & Hein, 1963).

Auditory Perception

As we noted in Chapter 4, infants can hear at birth and within a matter of days can develop a preference for their mother's voice (DeCasper & Fifer, 1980). There is also evidence that infants can hear before birth, and that some auditory conditioning may be occurring at this time (DeCasper & Spence, 1986).

Speech perception   One particularly interesting aspect of infant auditory perception is the extent to which it is tuned in to language. By 1 month of age, infants are able to tell the difference between two basic language sounds, such as "pah" and "bah" (Eimas, Siqueland, Jusczyk, & Vigorito, 1971). They seem to synchronize their movements to speech sounds (Condon & Sander, 1974), and they seem to be most attentive to speech that is spoken in the exaggerated, highly intonated speech that adults often use when talking to babies (Stern, Spieker, & MacKain, 1982). More will be said of infants' abilities to process speech in our discussion of language development in Chapter 9.

Music perception   Although humans are especially prepared biologically to process language, we also seem to be well prepared to process music. Infants "sing" as well as babble, and there is some evidence that young infants are able to imitate the pitch, volume, melodic contour, and rhythm of their mothers'

songs (see Gardner, 1983). Moreover, specific types of brain damage affect musical abilities, suggesting that the ability to perceive and produce music is rooted in biology (Gardner, 1983).

There is recent evidence that infants can distinguish regular or natural musical patterns from irregular or unnatural ones. In one experiment (Krumhansl & Jusczyk, 1990), 4½- and 6-month-old infants listened to segments of Mozart minuets. Some of the segments had pauses inserted at the end of each musical phrase (natural), whereas other segments had pauses inserted in the middle of phrases (unnatural). Infants learned to control which music they heard—natural or unnatural—by turning their heads in the direction of the speaker playing the music they preferred. Overall, infants spent more time listening to the natural than to the unnatural versions, with 20 of 24 4½-month-olds and 22 of 24 6-month-olds showing this pattern. Given the infants' lack of musical experience, these results sug-

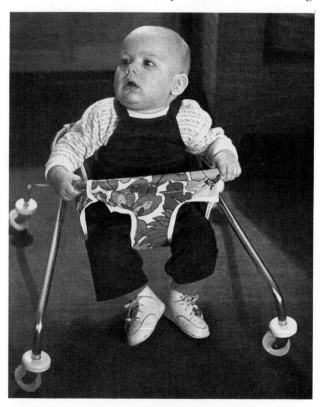

Infants who are allowed to get around on their own often show advanced perceptual abilities.

gest that music appreciation may not require a college class, but is a basic characteristic of the human nervous system.

Attention in Infancy: Habituation/Dishabituation

In studying perceptual development, researchers use the pattern of an infant's attention to a set of stimuli as an indication of whether that infant can discriminate between the two patterns. A more explicit test of infant attention is found in the habituation/dishabituation paradigm. **Habituation** refers to the decrease in responding that occurs as a result of repeated stimulation. For example, driving to school the first day of class, you might notice an unusually shaped tree on one corner of the campus. After a few weeks, you don't really notice it anymore: you have habituated to the stimulus of the tree. But if someone decorated it for the holidays, tied a yellow ribbon around it, or chopped it down, the change would surely catch your attention. In this case, your renewed attention would be considered **dishabituation.**

Habituation/dishabituation can be applied to infant perception. The amount of time babies look at visual stimuli is comparable to the student's interest in the campus tree: the longer infants are exposed to a visual stimulus, the less time they spend looking at it. Habituation is said to occur when an infant's looking time is significantly less than it was initially (often when visual fixation to the stimulus is 50% of what it was on the early trials). At that point, a new stimulus is presented, comparable to the campus tree with the added bow. If level of attention (that is, looking time) increases relative to what it was immediately before, dishabituation has occurred. Habituation and subsequent dishabituation have been reported for infants less than 2 days of age (Friedman, 1972; Slater, Earle, Morison, & Rose, 1985). A typical habituation/dishabituation curve is shown in Figure 6.5.

What does such a pattern mean? First, it demonstrates that infants can discriminate between the two stimuli. Babies may not have a preference for one over the other, but the fact that they respond to the new stimulus with increased attention means that they can tell the difference between the two. In fact, this paradigm is very useful in determining infant discrimination abilities when using stimuli for which infants may not have a decided preference, such as

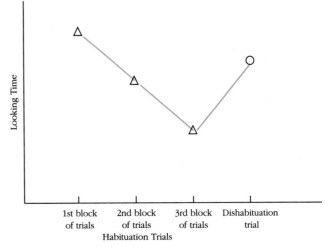

△ Looking time for familiarized stimulus presented during habituation trials
○ Looking time for novel stimulus presented following habituation

Figure 6.5 Typical results of a habituation/dishabituation experiment involving infant visual attention.

being able to tell the difference between blue and green (Bornstein, Kessen, & Weiskopf, 1976).

Second, habituation/dishabituation shows memory. Infants are discriminating between one stimulus that is physically present and another that is present only in memory. In a related procedure, infants are familiarized with a stimulus and later shown two stimuli—one familiar and one novel. As in the habituation/dishabituation paradigm, increased responding to the novel stimulus is interpreted as evidence of memory for the familiar (Fagan, 1973, 1974). Using these procedures, memory for visual stimuli has been found in newborns (Friedman, 1972), although other researchers have not always found evidence of memory in samples of very young infants (Cohen & Gelber, 1975). Friedman's results indicate that memory is within the capability of many human newborns, although the possibility exists that many infants do not possess such memory until several weeks after birth.

One important use of the habituation/dishabituation procedure has been as a tool for determining infants' use of mental categories. When we form categories, we are able to treat perceptually different objects as if they were the same *kind* of thing. Uncle Joe, Aunt Mary, Mommy, Daddy, and the stranger on the street are all unique individuals, but at one level they're all the same—they're all people. Our ability to categorize allows us to reduce an enormous amount of diverse information to manageable units. A 6-month-old given a new stuffed animal, rattle, or bottle can identify each object and act toward it accordingly, even though he or she has never seen that object before. Because each object is similar to something the child already knows, the objects can be categorized and dealt with easily. The process of categorization is central to human cognition and has its origins in infancy.

How can the basic habituation/dishabituation paradigm be used to assess infants' categories? One way is by varying the stimuli that are presented during the habituation trials, as Leslie Cohen and Mark Strauss (1979) did with 30-week-old infants. In their study, Cohen and Strauss habituated infants to a picture of a face of a single individual (Sally), as well as habituating other infants to several different individuals (Sally, Mary, Barbara, and Joan). In both the single- and multiple-face cases, the amount of responding declined with repeated exposure (that is, habituation). In the single-face case, infants were habituated to a specific stimulus (Sally); in the multiple-face case, they were habituated to a *category* of stimuli (women's faces). After habituation had occurred, a new female face was presented (Elizabeth). Infants who were habituated to only Sally showed dishabituation, seeing Elizabeth as a novel stimulus and increasing their attention to her picture. However, infants who were habituated to Sally, Mary, Barbara, and Joan responded to Elizabeth with continued habituation, treating her as just another example of a woman's face and nothing new. That is, even though they had never seen Elizabeth's face before, they categorized her as familiar and directed relatively little attention to it.

Cohen and Strauss interpreted their findings as evidence that 30-week-old infants can abstract "appropriate conceptual categories regarding the human face" (p. 422). By continuing to habituate to the new stimulus, infants are in effect telling us that, although the face is perceptually different from anything they've seen before, it is similar in general form to what they already know. They are telling us that they have acquired a category, or concept, for female faces.

Research over the past 15 years has shown that infants 6 to 7 months of age can organize objects into perceptual categories during relatively brief experimental sessions (Cohen & Strauss, 1979; Cornell, 1974; Fagan, 1976). Such categorization is less frequently observed for younger infants, although categorization has been reported in 3- and 4-month-olds for "simpler" categories, such as classifying objects according to their shape (Caron, Caron, & Carlson, 1979; Schwartz & Day, 1979), on the basis of a single common feature (Younger & Cohen, 1983) or in terms of color (Bornstein, Kessen, & Weiskopf, 1976).

These data do not mean that younger infants are unable to form more-complex perceptual categories based on everyday experiences. They mean that, in the first six months of life, the categorization process is not well developed in infants, although they do seem to be well prepared to form some simple types of visual categories.

The habituation/dishabituation paradigm has also been used to examine infants' categorization of real-world concepts. For example, research by Kenneth Roberts and his colleagues (Roberts, 1988; Roberts & Horowitz, 1986) showed that 9-month-old infants formed categories of concepts such as "birds" when they were habituated to highly typical members of a category (for example, pictures of *sparrow, robin, bluejay*), but not when less typical items were used (for example, pictures of *turkey, ostrich, chicken*). Like young children, infants are more apt to identify or form a category when provided with typical, as opposed to atypical, category exemplars (Anglin, 1977). The findings of these and other experiments are enlightening, suggesting that the limited categorization process of infants is qualitatively similar to that of older children and adults.

Perception during Childhood

Perceptual development is not complete at the end of infancy. Although a 2-year-old's visual and auditory systems are very well developed, children are increasingly required to make more precise discriminations among stimuli.

Interpreting Ambiguous Stimuli

Many things in the world are not what they appear to be, at least not on first inspection. Figure 6.6 pre-

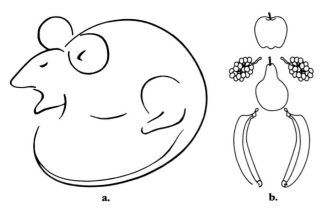

a.   **b.**

***Figure* 6.6** Examples of ambiguous figures.
Source: (a) From "The Role of Frequency in
Developing Perceptual Set," by B. R. Bugelski and
D. A. Alampay, *Canadian Journal of Psychology,*
1961, *15,* 205–208. Reprinted by permission.
(b) From *The Child's Reality: Three Developmental
Theories,* by D. Elkind. Copyright © 1978 by
Lawrence Erlbaum Associates, Inc.
Reprinted by permission.

sents two examples of **ambiguous figures.** The
first (a) can be seen as a rat or a man's face; the
second (b) can be seen as a collection of fruit or a
person. When presented with figures such as these,
3- and 4-year-old children typically see only one
thing or the other. They will report the rat but, if
asked, deny seeing the man, or vice versa. By 7 or 8
years of age, most children are able to see both possibilities in the same figure, though not simultaneously. By 10 or 11 years of age, children report
seeing both interpretations at the same time (Elkind,
1978).

Learning Distinctive Features

Eleanor Gibson (1969) proposed a theory of *perceptual learning* whereby children come to discover
distinctive features of stimuli in their environment.
That is, with experience, children learn which characteristics of an object differentiate it from another.
Perceptual learning is seldom explicitly taught to
children, but through normal interaction with their
environment, children learn which features are important for making discriminations; as might be expected, children from different environments and
cultures learn slightly different things.

Of particular importance for children in technological societies is learning the distinctive features
of letters. Our alphabet consists of letters that are
not always easy to distinguish from one another. For
example, 5-year-olds, even with preschool and "Sesame Street" experience, often confuse letters such
as *m* and *w,* and *b, d,* and *h* (Chall, 1983). Research
by Gibson and her colleagues, using abstract stimuli
similar to our alphabetic letters, found that 4- and
5-year-olds had more difficulty distinguishing between them than did 6- to 8-year-olds (Gibson, Gibson, Pick, & Osser, 1962). From this and related
research (see Gibson, 1969; Gibson & Levin, 1975),
it is clear that children's abilities to make some of
the perceptual discriminations necessary for reading
are not available to many preschoolers. Given this,
it is understandable why reading should not be part
of the regular preschool curriculum.

The very term perceptual learning implies that
how a person perceives the world varies as a function of his or her experience. The effects of experience on perception can be seen most readily when
comparing people who have grown up in vastly different cultures. Research has demonstrated, for example, that how people interpret three dimensions
in two-dimensional pictures, drawings, or photographs varies as a function of education and cultural
experience (Hudson, 1960). Even young children in
Western cultures use pictorial cues to infer three-
dimensions in photographs, whereas adults from
some non-Western cultures rarely provide three-
dimensional responses in interpreting drawings.

The effects of experience on perception are
nicely illustrated in Colin Turnbull's (1961) account
of an African Pygmy's first trip out of the forest and
his first encounter with a herd of buffalo crossing a
wide plain in the distance:

> [When Kenge] saw the buffalo, still grazing la-
> zily several miles away, far down below . . . he
> said "What insects are those?" At first I hardly
> understood; then I realized that in the forest
> the range of vision is so limited that there is
> no great need to make an automatic allowance
> for distance when judging size. . . . When I told
> Kenge that the insects were buffalo, he roared
> with laughter and told me not to tell such stu-
> pid lies. . . . As we got closer, the "insects" must
> have seemed to get bigger and bigger. Kenge
> . . . kept his face glued to the window, which

nothing would make him lower. . . . I was never able to discover just what he thought was happening—whether he thought that the insects were changing into buffalo, or that they were miniature buffalo growing rapidly as we approached. His only comment was that they were not real buffalo, and he was not going to get out of the car until we left the park. (pp. 252-253)

Field Dependence/Field Independence (FD/FI)

The concept of **field dependence/field independence (FD/FI)** has its origins in adult perception. Herman Witkin and his associates (Witkin, Dyk, Faterson, Goodenough, & Karp, 1962; Witkin, Lewis, Hertzman, Machover, Meissner, & Wapner, 1954) showed that some people had a difficult time perceiving component parts of a visual field separately from the whole. Witkin referred to such people as field dependent. Others were able to analyze the perceptual field into its discrete parts; Witkin referred to these people as field independent. One task that assesses the FD/FI dimension involves asking a person to find a figure embedded in a larger picture, known as the **Embedded Figures Test.** Field-independent people discover the hidden object much more quickly than do field-dependent people. The perception of field-dependent people is influenced by the entire perceptual field, making it difficult for them to analyze any specific component within the field; field-independent people are less affected by the global characteristics of a display and find it easier to discover the individual parts that make up the whole.

Developmental change and stability of FD/FI Researchers have found a general developmental trend toward increasing field independence: older children and adults take less time to identify objects in the Embedded Figures Test than do younger children (Witkin, Goodenough, & Karp, 1967). Longitudinal results from a sample of males, followed from age 10 to 24 years, showed a steady change toward field independence from 10 to 17 years; performance stabilized at this point, showing no further improvement or change when subjects were tested at 24 years of age. Although people became more field independent with age, individual differences in FD/FI were relatively stable over time, with field-dependent children becoming field-dependent adults (Witkin et al., 1967).

Implications of FD/FI for children's intellectual performance Numerous studies have compared the cognitive and intellectual abilities of field-dependent and field-independent children. With few exceptions, field-independent children perform at higher levels than do field-dependent children. This has been demonstrated for a variety of tasks over a broad age range. In one study (Okonji, Ogbolu, & Olagbaiye, 1975), children between the ages of 7 and 10 years were given a version of Piaget and Inhelder's (1967) three-mountain problem, in which children are asked to describe the view "seen" by a doll placed at various positions around a model of three mountains. Children's performance on this perspective-taking problem was strongly related to scores on the Children's Embedded Figures Test (average correlation = .90). Piaget and Inhelder suggested that the three-mountain problem involves the active restructuring of one's perspective, something that field-dependent children would have trouble doing, given their difficulty in separating parts from the whole. Similarly, field-dependent children have fared less well than field-independent children on a variety of other tasks involving scientific reasoning (Case, 1974; Kalyan-Masih, 1985; Linn, 1978).

Attention

When we tell children to "pay attention," we mean that we want them to concentrate on the task at hand and not let their minds wander to other things. Attention is used similarly in the psychological literature. Psychologists who study attention are interested in how and why people attend to some objects and events in the environment and not to others.

Factors That Attract and Maintain Attention

Earlier in this chapter, we saw how various physical and psychological factors were responsible for attracting and maintaining infants' attention, including motion, high contrast, and moderate novelty. Some of the same physical and psychological features are also important in catching and keeping the attention of older children and adults.

One important aspect of the world for today's children is television, and researchers have investigated some of the features of television that attract and maintain their attention (Alwitt, Anderson, Lorch, & Levin, 1980; Anderson, Alwitt, Lorch, & Levin, 1979). In one study, researchers observed preschoolers as they watched children's television shows such as "Sesame Street." They watched for changes in the children's attention during the shows and noted what was happening on the screen during those behavior changes (Alwitt et al., 1980). Among their results, they found that a change from one segment to another caused children who were not attending to the show to do so; but it also caused children who were viewing the show to stop doing so. Other changes, such as zooming in on a scene, resulted in children's looking away from the screen. Also interesting was the effect of commer-

"Why this poor mark in 'Listening Comprehension'? . . . Billy? Why this poor mark in . . ." *Source:* Reprinted with special permission of King Features Syndicate, Inc.

cials. The onset of a commercial was associated with *increased* attention from the children. But their attention to commercials was not maintained unless the commercial was specifically geared toward children.

Selective Attention

Selective attention refers to the ability to concentrate only on chosen stimuli and not to be distracted by other "noise" in the environment. In general, selective-attention abilities increase with age, with young children giving a disproportionate amount of attention to information irrelevant to the task at hand and not enough attention to important information (Lane & Pearson, 1982).

Young children's difficulties in keeping their minds on a single task is familiar to anyone who has had much dealing with them. Conversations with 5-year-olds rarely stay on a single topic; this is especially true of talkative children. For example, we asked 5-year-old Nicholas about his new baby brother, Jeffrey. He responded briefly and then quickly announced that he had a friend in school named Jeffrey. And speaking of school, his class had

"I MUST BE GROWIN' UP. I'M STARTIN' TO LIKE THE SHOWS BETTER THAN THE COMMERCIALS."

Children are often as attentive to television commercials as they are to the TV programs. *Source:* DENNIS THE MENACE® used by permission of Hank Ketcham and © by North America Syndicate.

Young children spend a lot of time and mental effort attending to irrelevant information instead of concentrating on the task at hand.

gone on a field trip that day to a bakery to see how bread was made. We asked a question about the field trip, but before he had completed that answer, Nicholas noticed a cat crossing the street and commented on that; then he asked if we knew that his dog was not house-trained yet. Before we could answer, he was describing the bread-baking process in response to our earlier question. Conversations with Nicholas can be very interesting, but it's hard to keep his attention focused on a single topic for very long. He is typical of children his age, being easily distracted both by external stimuli and by his own thoughts (see Harnishfeger & Bjorklund, 1992). In fact, his own comment sums it up very well: "Oops, I interrupted myself."

Selective attention in children has been extensively studied using tests of **incidental learning.** In a typical experiment, children are shown pairs of pictures like those in Figure 6.7. One member of each pair (the animal, for example) is designated as central, and children are told to remember it for later on; the other is designated as incidental, and children are told they can ignore it (Hagen, 1972; Hagen & Stanovich, 1977; Maccoby & Hagen, 1965). Following stimulus presentation, children are asked to recall the central stimuli; as would be expected, the older they are, the more they recall. Then, children are asked to recall the incidental stimuli—the ones they were supposed to ignore. Older children still remember more, but age differences are much smaller for incidental recall; in fact, after about age 11, the amount of incidental information remembered actually decreases (Hagen & Stanovich, 1977). This means that when instructed to remember one set of items and ignore another, younger children have more difficulty with *both* instructions (Schiff & Knopf, 1985). Teachers and parents need to recognize the possibility that young children's seeming

Figure 6.7 Stimulus materials used in central/incidental memory tasks. *Source:* From "Strategies for Remembering," by J. W. Hagen. In S. Farnham-Diggory (ed.), *Information Processing in Children.* Copyright © 1972 by Academic Press. Reprinted by permission.

inability to learn prescribed lessons may come about because they are filling their minds with incidental learning.

Attentional Strategies

When children must inspect something or make comparisons among objects, how do they allocate their attention? Do children attend to some parts of a display more than others? Do they compare two objects carefully before declaring them the same or different? Are there age differences in what they do? Stated another way, what attentional strategies do

children use when they must examine a stimulus or set of stimuli?

The classic work on developmental differences in children's attentional strategies is that of Elaine Vurpillot (1968). She showed children pictures of pairs of houses (see Figure 6.8) and asked them to tell whether the windows in the two houses were the same or different. While they were making their decisions, their eye movements were recorded by a camera concealed behind the picture. It was found that preschool children rarely looked at all the windows before making a judgment. For example, when there were 12 windows in the two houses, 4- and

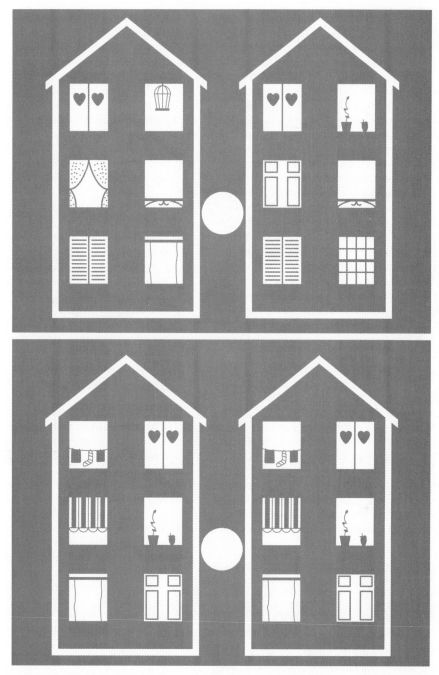

Figure 6.8 Children's eye movements are recorded as they determine whether the houses in each pair are the same or different. *Source:* From "The Development of Scanning Strategies and Their Relations to Visual Differentiation," by E. Vurpillot, *Journal of Experimental Child Psychology,* 1968, *6,* 632–650. Copyright © 1968 by Academic Press. Reprinted by permission.

5-year-olds, on average, made a decision after looking at only 7 of the 12 windows. Children aged 6 to 8 years old looked at between 10 and 12 windows, on average. Not surprisingly, the older children, who used a better strategy, were more often correct in their judgments than the less strategic preschoolers.

In more recent work, Patricia Miller and her colleagues have investigated the development of attentional strategies using a selective-attention task (Miller, 1990; Miller & Weiss, 1981). Children were shown a series of boxes with doors on top, arranged into two rows of six. On half of the doors were pictures of cages, meaning that those boxes contained pictures of animals; on the remaining doors were pictures of houses, meaning that those boxes contained pictures of household objects (see Figure 6.9). Children were told to find and remember the locations of all of one group of objects—either the animals or the household objects. They were also told that they could open any doors they wished during a study period. Researchers were thus able to observe children's attentional strategies by looking at the doors they chose to open during the study period.

The most efficient strategy, of course, is to open only those doors that have a drawing of the relevant category. In a series of experiments, Miller and her colleagues found a developmental sequence in attentional strategies (DeMarie-Dreblow & Miller, 1988; Miller, Haynes, DeMarie-Dreblow, & Woody-Ramsey, 1986; Woody-Ramsey & Miller, 1988). In a first stage, preschoolers showed no selective strategy, usually opening all the doors on the top first and then the doors on the bottom, regardless of what pictures were on the doors. In a second stage, children used the selective strategy, but only par-

tially; they still opened many irrelevant doors. In a third stage, children used the strategy—that is, they opened mainly relevant doors—but it did not help them remember the items' locations. Referring to this as a **utilization deficiency,** Miller (1990) proposed that although these children had the sophistication to use the strategy, its execution was so mentally effortful that they were not able to benefit from its use in terms of memory performance. Only in the fourth stage, usually late in the preschool years, were children able to use the attentional strategy and also benefit from its use.

Conceptual Tempo: Reflection/Impulsivity

Related to the idea of attentional strategies is **conceptual tempo,** which refers to how quickly a person makes decisions on complex tasks. People who make quick decisions about complex problems, making many errors in the process, have been labeled **impulsives.** At the other extreme are people who methodically evaluate all potential options, venturing a response only after giving considerable thought to a problem and usually arriving at correct solutions; such people have been labeled **reflectives.** Conceptual tempo is typically measured by means of perceptual matching tasks, in which subjects are presented with a stimulus and must find its exact match from a set of several similar stimuli.

The task most frequently used to measure reflection/impulsivity is the **Matching Familiar Figures Test (MFFT)** (Kagan, Rosman, Day, Albert, & Philips, 1964). Children are shown a single standard picture and are told that one of the six pictures on the lower page is exactly like the standard (see Figure 6.10). Their job is to find the matching picture. If a first response is incorrect, children are told so, and are asked to "find the picture on the bottom page that is exactly like the picture on the top page."

Based on the average time it takes to make first responses on all items and the total number of errors made, children are divided into four groups (see Figure 6.11). Children who are slow to respond and who make few errors are classified as reflectives; children who respond quickly and who make many matching errors are classified as impulsives. Approximately two-thirds of all children tested fall into the reflective or impulsive classifications. The remaining one-third are classified as fast-accurates (quick to respond, few errors) or slow-inaccurates

Figure 6.9 Apparatus used in studies of children's attentional strategies by Patricia Miller and her colleagues (courtesy of Patricia Miller).

Figure 6.10 Examples from the Matching Familiar Figures Test (courtesy of Jerome Kagan).

(slow to respond, many errors). Although these two groups of children have not been totally ignored by researchers (Ault, Crawford, & Jeffrey, 1972; Block, Block, & Harrington, 1974), most studies have concentrated on the characteristics of reflective and impulsive children.

The development of reflection/impulsivity Children become less impulsive with age. Neil Salkind and C. Frederick Nelson (1980) tabulated MFFT data for more than 2800 children, ranging in age from 5 to 12 years. (The data had been collected by more than 90 individual researchers over a decade's time.) Average MFFT error and latency scores over this age period are presented graphically in Figure 6.12. For boys and girls alike, errors show a steady decline until age 10, when performance stabilizes. Similarly, children respond more slowly over the 5- to 10-year-old period, but become somewhat faster at ages 11 and 12.

Consequences of an impulsive conceptual tempo Impulsive conceptual tempo has been associated with poor performance on a variety of cognitive tasks (Borkowski, Peck, Reid, & Kurtz, 1983; Butter, Kennedy, & Shoemaker-Kelly, 1982; Egeland, 1974; Erickson & Otto, 1973; Kagan, 1965; Kurtz & Borkowski, 1987). For this reason, many researchers have suggested that impulsive children can and should be taught to be more reflective in their approach to problems. A variety of procedures have been developed to train impulsive children to become more reflective. The most successful modification studies have been those that draw impulsive children's attention to stimulus details and require them to examine all possibilities before making a

	MFFT Errors	
	Below Median	Above Median
Below Median	Fast-Accurates	Impulsives
Above Median	Reflectives	Slow-Inaccurates

MFFT Latencies

Figure 6.11 Classification of children on the MFFT.

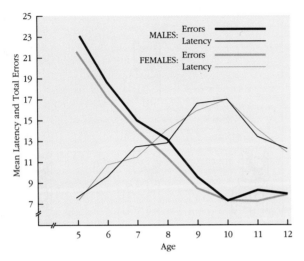

Figure 6.12 Total errors and average latency to first response on MFFT for males and females by age. *Source:* From "A Note on the Developmental Nature of Reflection-Impulsivity," by N. J. Salkind and C. F. Nelson, *Developmental Psychology,* 1980, *16,* 237–238. Copyright 1980 by the American Psychological Association. Reprinted by permission.

decision (Butter, 1979; Egeland, 1974; Meichenbaum & Goodman, 1971; Zelniker, Jeffrey, Ault, & Parsons, 1972). In general, impulsive children can be trained to use a reflective strategy, although the durability of such training is questionable.

It would seem obvious that reflective and impulsive children use different strategies on problem-solving tasks. Impulsive children's quick response times and high error rates imply that they don't evaluate all the alternatives, whereas the slow and generally correct performance of reflectives implies that they use a more thorough and exhaustive strategy in solving problems. This interpretation has been supported in several studies. For example, Ruth Ault and her colleagues (Ault, Crawford, & Jeffrey, 1972) examined the eye movements of 9-year-old children as they solved problems on the MFFT. Children classified as reflectives and fast-accurates made more systematic comparisons between the single standard and the six alternatives than did impulsive or slow-inaccurate children. In general, research using a variety of methodologies has shown that reflectives are better able to use effective problem-solving strategies than are impulsives (Cameron, 1984; Haskins &

McKinney, 1976; Mitchell & Ault, 1979; but see Zelniker & Jeffrey, 1976, for a somewhat different approach).

Attention-Deficit Hyperactivity Disorder

Although the normal development of children's attentional abilities has been studied extensively, when most people think of children and attention, they think of problems. School psychologists are kept busy by referrals of children whose parents or teachers describe them as hyperactive, inattentive, and impulsive. The American Psychiatric Association's Diagnostic and Statistical Manual (DSM III-R, 1987) describes **attention-deficit hyperactivity disorder (ADHD)** as "developmentally inappropriate degrees of inattention, impulsiveness, and hyperactivity" (p. 50). Estimates of the frequency of ADHD vary, but as currently defined, it is a common disorder, occurring in approximately 3 out of every 100 children, the vast majority of them boys (DSM III-R, 1987).

Children with ADHD typically have a difficult time sitting still. They are easily distracted and cannot sustain attention in school-related tasks or in play, often switching from one uncompleted project to another. They find it difficult to wait their turn in games or other group situations, often talking excessively and blurting out answers in class. It is easy to see why such behavior patterns would be disruptive to a classroom, causing teachers and classmates to become frustrated and impatient. Although the excessive motor activity of such children is obviously a source of problems, researchers are finding that cognitive limitations also play an important role in the ADHD syndrome (Meents, 1989).

There have been many hypotheses about the origins of ADHD, some environmental and others biological. Although there seems to be no single cause of ADHD, the evidence to date strongly suggests that, in most cases, it is due to chemical imbalances in the brain and is genetically based (Nichamin & Windell, 1984). In an extensive review of research on the disorder, Samuel Nichamin and James Windell (1984) concluded that it is not caused by "faulty diet, preservatives in food, visual disorders, schizophrenia, childhood head injuries, inadequately trained teachers, air pollution, or poor parenting" (p. 3), all of which have been proposed in the past.

Although it is questionable whether ADHD can be cured, it can be treated and controlled. In most schools, some behavioral therapy and/or special educational programming is attempted with ADHD children. One such therapy involves teaching children self-monitoring techniques. Children are first taught to discriminate appropriate from inappropriate attending behaviors and then to systematically observe their own behavior to determine whether or not they are being appropriately attentive (Kazdin, 1984).

⟶ TIME OUTS

⟶ TOKEN ECONOMICS

Although self-monitoring and other cognitive/behavioral therapies often produce improvements in attending, the most successful treatment programs usually include medication (Douglas, Barr, O'Neill, & Britton, 1986). Somewhat surprisingly, the preferred medication is typically a stimulant, which has been found to reduce hyperactivity and improve attention and school performance. There are, of course, potential side effects with medication, and much controversy exists concerning how and when ADHD children should be treated. Moreover, there

Box 6.2

Treating Children with Attention-Deficit Hyperactivity Disorder

Daniel D. Curtiss
School Psychologist
Seminole County, Florida

Students who cannot pay attention are a major problem in the classroom. Often, a teacher laments, "Johnny just can't pay attention." Not only do his grades suffer, but Johnny may be sent to the principal for discipline if his behavior disturbs other students. Poor grades and trips to the office can erode Johnny's confidence and self-esteem.

Many people must work together to help solve Johnny's attention problem. For example, the school

psychologist may observe him in the classroom while the teacher completes a rating scale. With these documents in hand, Johnny's parents may be advised to take him to a pediatrician to rule out medical conditions such as allergies that can cause or exacerbate inattentiveness. Based on the examination, the doctor may diagnose Johnny's condition as attention-deficit hyperactivity disorder and may prescribe stimulant medication such as Ritalin or Cylert to increase his attention span. Such medical intervention is often successful, but undesirable physical and psychological side effects make the use of stimulant therapy controversial. Therefore, an accurate diagnosis is essential, and any student placed on medication should also receive counseling to deal with issues of self-esteem.

Other types of behavioral intervention, such as relaxation training and self-monitoring, can be used to increase attention span, but these interventions require extra time and specialized training that most school personnel do not possess. The result is often overreliance on stimulant drug therapy to control attention deficits. Although attention problems are common, they are difficult to solve unless parents, teachers, and other trained specialists work together.

Reprinted by permission.

is debate concerning the diagnosis of ADHD (Meents, 1989). David Bohline (1985) has suggested that, in many cases, ADHD may be a symptom of other disorders and not a unique disorder itself. For example, the inattention of some high-activity children may be secondary to their more central problem of conduct disorder (Draeger, Prior, & Sanson, 1986).

The controversy concerning how to classify and deal with children who have attentional problems is an old one, and we expect that the years ahead will bring more modifications in their diagnosis and treatment. Regardless of how they are defined, however, attentional problems are real, and they represent a significant challenge to many parents and school personnel.

State of the Art
The Competent Infant

Babies have come a long way in a very brief period of time. The professional literature on the psychological capacities of infants just 30 or 40 years ago presented a picture of beings who were completely helpless and unable to make any sense of the stimulation that surrounded them. Behavior during the first two months of life was believed to be limited to reflexes; babies, for all practical purposes, were thought to see nothing, hear nothing, and know nothing.

This picture changed dramatically beginning in the 1960s, and research on infant perception and cognition continues in high gear today. In 1973, Joseph Stone, Harrietta Smith, and Lois Murphy collected 202 scientific papers in a single volume intended to capture the thrust of infancy research at that time. The title of their book, *The Competent Infant,* was meant to reflect the view that "from his earliest days, every infant is an active, perceiving, learning, and information-organizing individual" (p. 4). Research since then has only reinforced the view that babies, from the very beginning, are active participants in their own development.

The newfound competence of infants is due, of course, to a change in research approaches, not a change in the nature of infants. Unfortunately, some

people have misused these findings to support the view that infants today can learn advanced cognitive skills and are limited only by their parents' abilities to teach them—that given the right teaching methods, all things are possible. They believe that by starting education in the cradle, they can advance preschool children ahead of their peers intellectually, and that this edge will continue throughout a child's school years. Of course, this is a total misreading of the natural abilities and limitations of infants.

One example of how scientific research should *not* be carried over into the home nursery involves the work of Anthony DeCasper and Melanie Spence (1986), who reported convincing evidence that fetuses can perceive language and can learn something of its characteristics before birth. What they learn, however, are general patterns of sounds—the rhythm of language and the pitch of voices—*not* the content of speech. Although this may seem obvious,

Formal teaching sessions are not the best way for parents to enrich their child's early years.

there is at least one product available commercially that includes a horn-shaped object to be placed on a pregnant woman's abdomen to amplify a speaker's voice for the benefit of the fetus. The advertised purpose of this contraption is to provide the unborn child with language experiences (perhaps instilling an early appreciation of Shakespeare, Gore Vidal, or Dr. Seuss). There is absolutely no evidence that such early experience will have any effect on the unborn child's later intelligence, and every reason to believe that it will have none.

Another research project that is frequently extrapolated to faulty conclusions is one conducted by Burton White, Richard Held, and their colleagues (White & Held, 1966). In this study, infants reared in orphanages were handled more often and given more visual experiences than would otherwise have been the case; the result was faster development of

visual ability than in other orphanage-reared infants. This and other research clearly showed that infants can see during their earliest weeks and that they develop faster if they are not deprived of normal visual-tactile experience. But the extra experiences provided were comparable to what the average home-reared child already receives. There is no reason to believe that the more visual experiences children have, the more they will benefit. Yet a number of books on the market, and an even greater number of products, urge parents to bombard their newborns with everything from math flash cards to prints of Renaissance paintings.

The head guru of the baby-stimulation movement is Glenn Doman. His 1984 book, *How to Multiply Your Baby's Intelligence,* outlines the philosophy practiced at the Institute for the Achievement of Human Potential. Doman makes many of the points

Household items are often the best developmental toys for babies; most important is an involved parent.

contemporary infant researchers make: that babies and children are not just miniature adults, that they are active learners with intense curiosity. Some of his more extreme pronouncements about infants, however, go far beyond the research:

> It is easier to teach a one-year-old to read than it is to teach a seven-year-old.
> It is easier to teach a one-year-old math than it is to teach a seven-year-old.
> It is easier to teach a one-year-old *any* set of *facts* than it is to teach a seven-year-old.
> You can teach a baby anything that you can present in an *honest* and *factual* way. (p. 59)

No scientific research has ever suggested that any of these statements is true; a great deal of research strongly suggests that they are not.

Parents, day-care workers, and people shopping for baby gifts should beware. There is a big difference between products that *interest* an infant and products that *educate*. Crib mobiles with high contrast, movement, and curvilinearity are examples of products whose design is based on a proper interpretation of the relevant research. So are brightly colored bumper pads for cribs, mittens and socks with faces on them, and toys that play soft music. (One friend of ours bought a clear plastic pouch that attached to the bars of her baby's crib. In the water-filled pouch was a goldfish. The baby enjoyed looking at the fish swimming in the small container; we don't know how the fish felt about it.) Used to supplement interaction with parents and the stimulation of ordinary household activity, such products help provide an enriched environment in which the competent infant can develop according to his or her own plan.

Summary

Infants from birth display visual preferences for certain characteristics of stimuli, including movement, contrast (contour), vertical symmetry, curvilinearity, concentricity, and facial attractiveness. Beginning sometime between 2 and 4 months, infants' attention is also influenced by psychological features such as the novelty of a stimulus. Research using the visual cliff demonstrates that crawling infants will not crawl onto the deep side, and that their reluctance to do so is related to the amount of crawling experience. Other research has also shown the importance of self-propelled movement in the development of visual perception.

Young infants can discriminate among language sounds and categorize them much as adults do. They also appear to be biologically prepared to perceive music.

Habituation refers to the decrease in responding after repeated presentation of a stimulus; dishabituation refers to the increase in responding when a new stimulus is presented, and it is evidence of memory. The habituation/dishabituation paradigm has been used to assess infants' categories, with research showing that infants form real-world concepts much as older children do.

Age-related differences are evident in how children interpret ambiguous figures. Children learn the distinctive features of stimuli, with many 4- and 5-year-olds having difficulty distinguishing between letters such as *m* and *w*. One's experience influences perception, with the most dramatic differences being found between people of different cultures. Field dependence/field independence (FD/FI) refers to individual differences in how people abstract visual information, with children becoming more field independent with age. Field-independent children perform better than field-dependent children on a host of cognitive tasks.

Many of the factors that attract and maintain visual attention in infancy continue to influence attention in older children. Researchers have also investigated factors in television programming that attract and maintain children's attention.

Selective attention has been studied using central/incidental memory tasks. Older children are better able to ignore the incidental information than are younger children. Developmental differences in attentional strategies have also been found, with young children being less systematic than older children in their visual inspection of objects.

Conceptual tempo refers to individual differences in the speed with which people respond to complex problems. Reflectives respond slowly and make few errors; impulsives respond quickly and make many errors. Reflective children show superior performance on a variety of academic-type tasks, relative to impulsive children, and show more efficient problem-solving strategies. Children become increasingly reflective with age.

Children (mostly boys) with attention-deficit hyperactivity disorder (ADHD) show developmentally inappropriate degrees of inattention, coupled with impulsiveness and hyperactivity. ADHD children have difficulty performing school-related tasks and also display behavior problems. A relatively common phenomenon, ADHD is often treated with medication along with behavioral or cognitive therapy.

Infants are substantially more competent than we believed them to be 30 years ago, and their perceptual and cognitive abilities can be facilitated by specific experiences. However, their intellectual abilities are still limited, and there is no scientific evidence that intense educational enrichment during infancy will have long-term benefits.

Key Terms and Concepts

visual preference
    contrast
    contour
    vertical symmetry
    curvature
    concentricity
    schemas
    discrepancy principle
depth perception
    visual cliff
habituation/dishabituation
ambiguous figures
distinctive features
    perceptual learning
field dependence/field independence (FD/FI)
    Embedded Figures Test
selective attention
    incidental learning
    attentional strategies
    utilization deficiency
conceptual tempo
    impulsives
    reflectives
    reflection/impulsivity
    Matching Familiar Figures Test (MFFT)
attention-deficit hyperactivity disorder (ADHD)

Piaget's Theory

7

Five-year-old Heidi was watching her father prepare lunch. After spreading peanut butter and jam on one slice of bread and topping it with another, Dad cut the sandwich in two and then cut the halves into quarters. Seeing her sandwich cut into four pieces brought an immediate frown to Heidi's face. "Oh, Daddy," she sighed, "I only wanted you to cut it in *two* pieces. I'm not hungry enough to eat four!"

To us it may seem obvious that the amount of sandwich is the same regardless of whether it is cut into two pieces or four pieces or 40 pieces. But that's not the way it appears to young children, who sometimes draw erroneous (and humorous) conclusions about how the world works. Taking such pronouncements by young children seriously, Swiss psychologist Jean Piaget (1896–1980) formulated a theory to explain how thinking changes in quality over the course of development—a theory that has had unparalleled influence in child psychology.

Assumptions and Principles of Piaget's Theory

Piaget's formal education was in biology, and his theory of cognitive development has a strong biological flavor to it. He viewed intelligence as the way we as a species adapt to our environments. He also had a keen interest in philosophy, particularly epistemology—the study of knowledge. Thus, Piaget formulated a new approach to studying intellectual development that he called "genetic epistemology"—the study of the origins of knowledge using scientific methods. Basic assumptions of his theory (Piaget, 1967, 1983; Piaget & Inhelder, 1969) include the concepts of intrinsic activity, organization, and adaptation.

Intrinsic Activity

A fundamental assumption of Piaget's theory is that of **intrinsic activity.** Babies are born ready to make contact with their environment. They are not passive creatures, waiting to be stimulated by external forces before they respond, but are themselves the prime movers and shakers of their world. They actively seek stimulation, initiating action on objects and people who come in contact with them. Although children of any age can be enticed to learn some tasks by way of rewards, such external reinforcement is not necessary for development and learning

to occur. The motivation to learn and to develop is within the child. In short, Piaget believed that children play the central role in their own development—a view that minimizes the role of parents and teachers.

Children make sense of their surroundings by actively interpreting their experiences. Knowledge is not simply acquired; it is constructed, based on an interaction between the child at a particular age and his or her environment. As a result, children of different ages hold very different beliefs about the world. A 5-month-old believes that a bottle that falls out of sight under the crib ceases to exist; 4-year-olds believe that the sun follows them as they walk; 6-year-olds believe that they have more lemonade when it is served in a tall, skinny glass than in a short, stout one. From an adult perspective, this is all faulty reasoning. To Piaget, however, it demonstrated the constructive nature of cognition: reality is not absolute, but a construction based on one's past experiences and current mental abilities.

Functional Invariants

Piaget used the term **functional invariants** to describe processes that characterize all biological systems (including intelligence) and operate throughout the life span. Piaget proposed two functional invariants, both borrowed from biology: **organization** and **adaptation.**

Organization Organization refers to the fact that every intellectual operation is related to all other acts of intelligence—that intellectual abilities are coordinated with one another. Organization thus implies a tendency to integrate mental abilities into higher-order systems, or **structures.** A structure, or *scheme,* is some enduring knowledge base by means of which children interpret their world. It is these structures that are intrinsically active and that construct reality. For Piaget, cognitive development is the development of structures.

Adaptation: assimilation and accommodation Piaget's second functional invariant, adaptation, refers to the fact that the child (or, more properly, the child's structures) must adjust to environmental demands. This simple concept has two complementary components: **assimilation** and **accommodation.**

Assimilation refers to the incorporation of new information into already-existing schemes. This

Children construct reality based on what they know and their current cognitive structures. *Source:* Reprinted with special permission of North America Syndicate, Inc.

should not be viewed as the passive registration of new information, however. Assimilation is an active process, with the child sometimes distorting information to fit existing cognitive schemes. For example, after being read "Jack and the Beanstalk" the night before, 22-month-old Kristin greeted her parents in the morning with "Fee, Fi, Fo, Fum. I smell bacon and eggs." The line in the story, "I smell the blood of an Englishman," made no sense to Kristin, so she distorted what she remembered in order to assimilate it into her current world knowledge.

The complement of assimilation is accommodation—changing a structure in order to incorporate new information. When children are confronted with something they cannot quite understand, they can modify their structures to make use of this new information. For example, a 2-year-old given a magnet for the first time would have difficulty understanding it if she treated it as she did any other small metal object; she would have to alter her underlying structures in order to take advantage of its special properties. In other words, she can incorporate the special properties of magnets into her behavioral repertoire only if she changes the way she thinks. This, according to Piaget, involves accommodation.

Other forms of assimilation and accommodation can be found in early infancy. Take grasping, for example. Babies will reflexively grasp objects placed in the palms of their hands. This grasping scheme can be applied to a variety of objects that fit easily into the infant's hand. So, grasping the handle of a rattle, daddy's finger, or the railing of the crib all involve (primarily) assimilation. The infant is incorporating information to a pre-existing scheme. If this same infant were to be presented with a small, round ball, some alterations in hand movements would be required in order to apply the grasping scheme to this new object; that is, to "know" this new object, the infant would have to make small modifications in his or her hand movements. These modifications constitute (primarily) accommodation, permitting the infant to incorporate new data by slightly changing current schemes.

For another example of assimilation and accommodation, consider the 2-year-old who calls all men "Daddy." This child is using the verbal label she acquired for her father to refer to all adult males (assimilation). Now she must learn to restrict her use of the term "Daddy" to her father and find new terms for other men (accommodation), lest she cause embarrassment to her mother. Similarly, many college students reading this chapter will need to alter their way of thinking about children and development in order to make sense of Piagetian theory. Piaget is not easily assimilated, and, typically, much accommodation is required before his theory is understood and appreciated.

Piaget used the concepts of assimilation and accommodation to explain how thought develops. According to his theory, children strive to maintain a balance, or equilibrium, in their cognitive structures. When faced with information that does not fit their current thinking, they experience a state of disequilibrium, which is intrinsically unpleasant. To reestablish balance, they alter their cognitive structures, using accommodation, to incorporate new information. Accommodation occurs, however, only when the discrepancy between new information and the child's present thinking is small; if it is too great, the child will either ignore the information or distort it. Piaget referred to this process of changing structures to maintain a cognitive balance as **equilibration.**

For example, 6-year-olds presented with an algebra problem do not remain in a state of disequilibrium for long. They quickly realize they have no idea what these combinations of numbers and letters mean and go on to something else. In contrast, a 12-year-old may recognize the algebra problem as "math" and apply basic arithmetic knowledge to arrive at an answer ("Let's see, X is the 24th letter of the alphabet, so $2X$ must equal 48 . . ."). The answer will be wrong, but the problem will be distorted enough for the child to make some sense of the task. A slightly older child with slightly more mature knowledge may be able to think of X as an abstract "something," and calculate that if two Xs are 6, then one X must be 3, thus performing the accommodation necessary to solve the problem.

Stages of Development

The cornerstone of Piaget's theory is the idea of stages (see Chapter 1), with functioning at one stage being qualitatively different from functioning at other stages. Thus, children at any given stage have a unique way of viewing the world that is consistent with the rules they have derived so far and consistent with the reasoning of other children their age.

Piaget insisted that stages cannot be skipped. He believed that every structure in the psychology of intelligence is based on earlier structures, making it necessary for children to master the accomplishments of one stage before advancing to the next. Children may go through stages at different rates, and development may be arrested at a certain stage for some individuals, but the order in which children go through the stages is unalterable.

Table 7.1 Piaget's four stages of cognitive development

Period	Approximate Age	Major Characteristics
Sensorimotor	Birth–2 years	Intelligence is limited to the infants' own actions on the environment. Cognition progresses from the exercise of reflexes to the beginning of symbolic representation.
Preoperations	2–7 years	Intelligence is symbolic; use of language and imagery enables children to represent and compare objects mentally. Thought is intuitive rather than logical, and egocentric.
Concrete operations	7–11 years	Intelligence is symbolic and logical, and less egocentric, but still limited to concrete phenomena and past experience.
Formal operations	11 years onward	Children are able to generate and test hypotheses, introspect about their own thought processes, and think abstractly.

Piaget divided cognitive development into four major stages, or periods: sensorimotor, preoperations, concrete operations, and formal operations (see Table 7.1).

The Sensorimotor Period

The first stage, which extends from birth to about 2 years, is known as the **sensorimotor period.** Mental functioning changes more drastically during these two years than during any other period in development. First, there is a progression from a solely action-based to a symbol-based intelligence—that is, from cognition based on overt actions (sensorimotor) to one based on internal representations. Second, there is a related change in personal perspective—from an undifferentiated world with no notion of a separate self to one in which self and other are clearly distinguished. Piaget (1952, 1954, 1962) described these monumental changes as occurring in six substages (see Table 7.2).

Stages of the sensorimotor period At the earliest stage, that of **basic reflexes** (birth to 1 month), infants know the world only in terms of inherited action patterns, or reflexes. Piaget used the term *reflex*

broadly to include not only behaviors such as sucking and grasping, but also behaviors such as eye movements, orientation to sound, and vocalizations. Basically, infants during this first stage apply their reflexes to objects. If an object, such as a nipple, fits a reflex, such as sucking, the infant applies the reflex to the object and assimilates the object to an existing scheme—in other words, the baby nurses.

In stage 2, **primary circular reactions** (1 to 4 months), infants extend their reflexes to acquire new patterns of behavior that were not part of the basic biological package with which the child was born. For example, there is no basic reflex for thumb sucking. However, there are inherited patterns for moving one's arms and hands and for sucking. When, as a result of chance, babies find their fists or thumbs in their mouths, sucking ensues. Because sucking is intrinsically pleasing, the infant attempts to re-create the pleasurable experience. Much trial and error follows, but the result is an infant who can suck its thumb at will. Although this may not seem an impressive act of intelligence, it is an example of infants' learning to control some aspect of their behavior.

Infants' control of their world expands during the third stage, **secondary circular reactions** (4 to 8 months), as they learn to control not only their own bodies, but events in the external world. For example, when our daughter Heidi was about 4 months old, she was lying in a playpen with a "crib gym" strung over it—a complex mobile with parts that spin when they are struck. While flailing her arms and legs, she hit the mobile, causing it to spin. She happened to be looking at the mobile, and its movement caught her attention. She immediately stopped moving and stared intently at the object over her head. When it ceased moving, she began to shake her arms and legs, to squirm, and finally, to cry. Again she hit the mobile, and again she froze and quieted, staring straight ahead at the wonderful event she had caused.

As in the earlier stage, there is no intention beforehand to make interesting things happen. Infants don't start out intending to suck their thumbs, drop toys out of their cribs, or make mobiles spin. But in the process of doing what they can do, they discover interesting events and then attempt to re-create those events.

Our daughter, being in the stage of secondary circular reactions, did not approach this task in a logical and systematic fashion. She had no clear no-

Table 7.2 Substages of the sensorimotor period

Stage	Approximate Age	Major Characteristics
1. Basic reflexes	Birth–1 month	Cognition limited to inherited reflex patterns
2. Primary circular reactions	1–4 months	First acquired adaptations; extension of basic reflexes
3. Secondary circular reactions	4–8 months	Beginning of control of objects and events external to infant
4. Coordination of secondary circular reactions	8–12 months	Coordination of two previously acquired schemes to achieve a goal (goal-directed behavior)
5. Tertiary circular reactions	12–18 months	Discovery of new means through active experimentation, trial and error
6. Mental combinations	18–24 months	First signs of symbolic functioning (language and imagery)

tion of cause and effect. She had made the mobile move, but she did not know whether it was the movement of her legs, the turn of her head, or her vocalizations that made the difference. However, through a process of trial and error, she narrowed the options and eventually acquired control over the situation.

This is an important step in intellectual development. In this stage, babies begin to realize that they have some control over their world. Although the initial event occurs accidentally, once under their control, the action is theirs to use whenever and wherever they please. Not only could Heidi spin the mobile in her playpen; she could apply this new behavior to other objects in other locations. She could switch hands or adjust the strength of her stroke to produce slightly different outcomes. She had begun to master her world by acting intentionally on objects around her.

Next in development, infants learn to coordinate several of these accidental behavior patterns to achieve a goal. Piaget labeled this fourth stage **coordination of secondary circular reactions** (8 to 12 months). Suppose, for example, that a toy is set in front of a baby and an obstacle placed between the baby and the toy. At 6 or 7 months, babies are unable to get the desired toy, even though they are perfectly capable of moving the obstacle. Somewhere around 8 months, however, babies develop the ability to use one behavior (pushing an obstacle) in the service of another (retrieving a toy). This achievement of *goal-directed behavior* is a major advance in the development of intelligence.

Cognition takes a turn again beginning at about 12 months. Now, for the first time, infants invent slightly new behaviors to achieve their goals. They no longer have to wait until chance provides them with an interesting event; they can make interesting things happen themselves. Piaget called this fifth stage **tertiary circular reactions** (12 to 18 months).

Infants in this stage continue the process begun months earlier. They want to know what makes things tick and, more important, how *they* can make things tick. They are explorers and adventurers. "Is it possible to unravel the toilet paper and get it all into the toilet bowl without tearing the paper? How can I get onto the kitchen counter? Isn't it interesting how the music becomes so much louder when I turn this knob?" Adults are often perplexed as to why 15-

When 12- to 18-month-olds discover that *they* can make interesting things happen, they have reached the tertiary circular reactions stage.

month-olds find dog food and kitty litter so fascinating, why they are so interested in electric outlets and wastebaskets, and why they insist upon climbing out of their high chairs and manipulating and mouthing everything in reach.

Each of these interesting behaviors (often more interesting when seen in other people's children) reflects a developing cognitive system. Children are discovering as much about their world as they can and are learning more about the control they have over their environment. They learn that their action is independent of their parents and that they do not have to comply if they don't want to. They also learn the consequences of this defiance, as they must, and they modify their behavior accordingly—most of the time.

Although children at this stage are wonderful problem solvers, their intelligence is still limited to actions on objects. Babies know things by acting upon them; they cannot make mental comparisons or represent objects and events symbolically. So, for example, if a 15-month-old wants to see if her brother's tricycle fits under the coffee table, she needs to attempt to put it there physically. Even though the tricycle is a foot taller than the table, she cannot simply examine the two objects and discern that one is too big to fit under the other. She can learn this only by doing it. Her intelligence is one of action, not of thought.

It is not long, however, before infancy is left behind and a totally new way of understanding the world develops. Somewhere between the latter part of the second year and the beginning of the third, children become symbol users. They are able to make mental comparisons between objects, to retrieve memories from the past, and to anticipate the future. They no longer depend on their own direct actions to understand things; they can know the world through language and other symbols. This final stage of the sensorimotor period, **invention of new means through mental combinations** (18 to 24 months), is a transition between the action-oriented world of the infant and the symbol-oriented world of the child.

This change may not seem rapid, but in a matter of months the child is transformed into a very differ-

ent thinker. By 3 years, there is no doubt that the intelligence shown by children is uniquely human. Cognitively speaking, a 3-year-old child is much more like a 30-year-old adult than a 3-month-old infant. It is this change, more than anything else, that differentiates us from all other species. It is each individual's personal discovery of fire, and it forever changes how we understand ourselves and our world.

Object permanence   If a tree falls in the forest and no one is there to witness it, is there any noise? This old philosophical question would be answered very easily by young infants; according to their thinking, there cannot be a noise unless they are there to

Out of sight is not really out of mind for infants who have a good understanding of object permanence.

perceive it. Not only is there no noise, there is no tree and no forest. For infants, out of sight is literally out of mind.

According to Piaget, infants under 4 months have no concept of **object permanence**—no notion that objects have an existence in time and space independent of their own perceptions of or actions on those objects (Piaget, 1954). Thus, for example, 2- or 3-month-olds will follow their mother with their eyes, but when mother leaves their visual field, they will continue to gaze at the point where she disappeared and not anticipate her reappearance somewhere else. Obviously, object permanence is a cognitive skill necessary for normal intellectual functioning in all human cultures.

The first semblance of object permanence appears at around 4 months of age (secondary circular reactions). Now infants will attempt to retrieve objects that disappear, but only if the object is still partially visible. For example, babies will retrieve a toy that has been partially covered by a cloth, apparently realizing that the entire toy exists under the cloth even though they can see only a portion of it. They will not search, however, for a toy that is completely hidden, even if the hiding occurred right before their eyes.

Beginning at about 8 months, infants are able to retrieve a completely hidden object. To do this, infants must be able to use one behavior (removing an obstacle) in the service of another (retrieving a desired object). Object permanence is not yet complete, however, for if an object is hidden in one location and then moved to a second location, all while the child watches, the infant will search the first location and often act quite surprised not to find the object there.

At about 12 months, infants can solve the problem of consecutive hiding places. However, they still cannot solve what Piaget called "invisible displacements," in which an object is hidden in one container, then hidden under another container out of the child's direct vision. For example, Piaget (1954) related how his daughter Jacqueline at 18 months was perplexed when her father placed a potato in a box, put the box under a rug, and then brought out the empty box for her inspection, all while she watched. Jacqueline would look in the box and stare at the rug, but never search under it, de-

spite having watched her father hide the potato and seeing a lump in the rug as evidence that something must be under there. In order to solve invisible-displacement problems, children must be able to keep objects present in their minds, something that is not achieved until the last sensorimotor stage, beginning at around 18 months.

The sequence of object permanence described by Piaget has been replicated by other researchers (Kramer, Hill, & Cohen, 1975; Uzgiris & Hunt, 1975). More controversial, however, are the cognitive abilities that underlie object permanence. According to Piaget, failure to solve object-permanence tasks reflects an incomplete concept of objects: infants do not understand that objects are permanent in time and space. Other researchers have questioned this interpretation, providing evidence that infants have greater competence than Piaget proposed (see Baillargeon, 1987; Willatts, 1990). Some have suggested that a sense of object permanence is innate (Baillargeon, 1987; Spelke, 1985); others have suggested that failure to solve some object-permanence tasks is a function of other cognitive factors, notably memory (Bower, 1982; Diamond, 1985). At the least, infants must have some memory of an object before they can show evidence of object permanence.

Preoperational Thought

The transition from the action-based cognition of the sensorimotor period to the symbol-based thinking of the **preoperational period** is seen most obviously in the child's use of language. Beginning around 18 months, children start stringing words together into sentences. Piaget was firm in his belief that we use language because we think symbolically, and not vice versa—that language is a by-product of our ability to use symbols, not its cause. (Some theorists have taken the opposite view—that language use is the cause of our symbolic abilities.) Other examples of symbol use in young children are drawing, imagery, and symbolic play (for example, pretending a shoe is a telephone or feeding imaginary cereal to a doll). Each of these forms of cognition is available to most 2-year-olds, although how they use these symbols will improve dramatically over the next dozen years or so.

During the preoperational period, children's thinking, though symbolic, is not logical. For example, if a red stick is taller than a blue stick and a blue stick is taller than a green stick, then logically the red stick must be taller than the green one. This, however, is not an inescapable conclusion to 4- or 5-year-olds, who base their conclusions on what *seems* to be, regardless of what, by logic, must be. For example, if water is poured from a tall, skinny glass into a short, fat glass, the preoperational child is likely to say that the amount of water has changed. There seems to be less water in the short, fat glass because the height of the water is lower. If the truth be known, most adults would admit that there seems to be more water in the tall glass than in the short one, but because logic tells us that the amount is the same, our intellectual system overrides our gut-level impression. But for preoperational children, appearance is stronger than logic; they find no contradiction in stating that the amount of liquid changes when poured from one container to another. This is the intuitive nature of thought characteristic of the preoperational period.

Perceptual centration Preoperational children's emphasis on appearance led Piaget to propose the concept of perceptual **centration**—that their perception is centered on the most obvious dimension

Symbolic play is evident as a young toddler pretends to talk on the phone in a makeshift car.

Fantasy play reflects children's ability to use symbols. *Source:* CALVIN & HOBBES Copyright 1988 Universal Press Syndicate. Reprinted with permission. All rights reserved.

of a situation and that they attend to and make judgments based solely upon that dimension. In the water-level problem, for example, their attention is centered only on the difference in height of the water lines; according to Piaget, they are unable to consider the two dimensions of height and width simultaneously. Evidence for this comes from studies in which 4-year-olds were asked to pour water from a short, stout glass into a taller, narrower one. A screen placed in front of the second glass kept them from seeing how high the water rose (see Bruner, 1966). When asked if there was the same amount of water in the two glasses, most answered yes: since all they did was change containers, logically the amounts were the same. However, when the screen was removed and children saw the discrepancy in water level, most of them quickly changed their minds. When the evidence was right before their eyes, it overrode their budding logical system; preoperational children could not ignore what seemed to be less water in the shorter glass.

Evidence of young children's perceptual centration can also be found in their everyday thinking. For example, Piaget (1969) noted that preoperational children often use people's height as a means of estimating their age (see Boxes 7.1 and 7.2).

Egocentricity   **Egocentricity** is the tendency to interpret objects and events only from one's own perspective—the inability to put oneself in someone else's shoes, as it were. Egocentricity is usually thought of as a characteristic of preoperational children, associated with their tendency toward centration. They are less egocentric than the sensorimotor child, but more self-centered in cognitive perspective than the concrete operational children. According to Piaget, this egocentric perspective permeates the lives of young children, influencing their perceptions, language, and social interactions (see Box 7.3).

Much research on egocentricity has concentrated on young children's abilities to take the visual

Box 7.1

How Tall Is Old?

I (DFB) was working with a group of kindergarten children, trying to finish my master's thesis. At the end of one schoolday, a mother in her mid-20s asked if I was the man who was working with the children. When I said I was, she commented that I was much younger than she had pictured me. I was 23 at the time, looked 18, and was accustomed to "baby face" remarks.

"I asked my son about you," she said, "and he didn't have much to say. 'Is he young or old?' I asked, and he said 'Old.' 'Is he old like Mommy?' I asked, and he said you were much older. I then asked him if you were old like his teacher, and he said you were *much* older than his teacher."

Her son's kindergarten teacher was a woman in her mid- to late-50s and looked it. However, there was one difference between his teacher and me that was in my favor: his teacher was barely 5 feet tall, whereas I am slightly over 6 feet. Although he probably could have judged the age difference between his teacher and me on the basis of facial features, had he been motivated and taken the time, he went with what was, for him, the most obvious difference between us—our height. Taller is older.

Interpreting age as a function of height is something that young children do frequently. And, for their purposes, it usually suffices. First-graders are generally taller than kindergarteners, second-graders are generally taller than first-graders, and so on. Adults are bigger than everyone, and age differences among adults are rarely a concern for 5-year-olds.

perspective of others, beginning with Piaget and Barbel Inhelder's (1967) classic three-mountain problem. In this series of experiments, children were seated in front of a three-dimensional display of three mountains that differed in size, color, and form. A doll was moved to different locations around the display, and children were asked to select from a set of pictures the one that showed the doll's view. Piaget and Inhelder reported that most children under the age of 8 were unable to determine how the doll viewed the scene, but instead gave egocentric responses, choosing pictures that represented their own view of the mountains. That is, children stated that the doll saw what *they* saw. Other researchers have criticized Piaget and Inhelder's three-mountain task as overly difficult, and more

Box 7.2

How Children Judge People's Age

The difference in perception between a 5-year-old and an 8-year-old—that is, the extent to which they focus on a single dimension—can be seen in the following interviews:

Nicholas, age 5¹/₂

> *Interviewer:* "If a grown-up came into your classroom and asked you to guess how old he was, how do you think you would do it? What sort of things would you look at?"
> *Nicholas:* "I don't know. I'd measure. I'd measure by how high he is."
> *Interviewer:* "What if he was big?"
> *Nicholas:* "He'd be old, like 15 or 100."
> *Interviewer:* "OK. What if a new kid came to your school? How could you tell how old he was? What sort of things would you look at?"
> *Nicholas:* "His fingers."
> *Interviewer:* "His fingers? How could you tell by his fingers?"
> *Nicholas:* "I'd see how many fingers he held up."
> *Interviewer:* "Oh. What if he didn't hold up any fingers. How could you tell how old he was just by looking at him?"
> *Nicholas:* "I don't know. How big he is. If he was big, he'd be old, like Russell. If he was like me, he'd be 5. If he was little, he'd be 4. Or maybe 3. If he was a baby, he'd be real tiny."

Kristina, age 8¹/₂

> *Interviewer:* "If a grown-up came into your classroom and asked you to guess how old he was, how do you think you would do it? What sort of things would you look at?"
> *Kristina:* "I would usually look at his hair. If he has a lot of hair or is bald. And if his legs are hairy, and whether he had hair coming out his nose. And his skin and stuff. If he would be old, his hair would be gray and his skin would be wrinkled."
> *Interviewer:* "OK. What if a new kid came to your school? How could you tell how old he was? What sort of things would you look at?"
> *Kristina:* "Usually, if they're tall like me or if they're like Marci's size, they'd be like 8. If they were smaller, they'd be like 7 or 6."
> *Interviewer:* "So if they're taller they're older?"
> *Kristina:* "Yes."
> *Interviewer:* "Can you do the same thing with adults? Use how tall they are to tell how old they are?"
> *Kristina:* "No. With the height you can't really tell with a grown-up. And also kids don't have gray hair and wrinkled skin."

recent research has shown that children will make nonegocentric responses when provided with less complicated visual displays (Borke, 1975; Gzesh & Surber, 1985).

Box 7.3

First-Graders Are Never the Oldest

I was in the first grade at the time. We were at recess when a fellow student began to inquire about my family. "Do you have any brothers or sisters?" Glenn asked.

"Yah, I got three brothers," I said. "Who's the oldest?" he asked. "I am," I told him.

Glenn gave me a look of mild disgust. "You are not," he said. "You can't be. You're only in the first grade!"

Glenn was bigger than I was, so I didn't let the argument get too far out of hand, but I was displeased and confused that anyone should question my assertion that I was the eldest of four brothers.

As I was soon to find out, Glenn also had a brother. His brother, however, was a big brother—a third-grader—and as far as Glenn was concerned, all first-graders, if they had siblings at all, had to have older siblings. I assume that Glenn's brother had made the difference in their status clear to him, and that being a first-grader was considered about as low as one could go. The notion that a first-grader could have the status of older brother was simply not believable: it violated too substantially his knowledge of how the world worked.

This egocentric view of the world is easy to spot in young children. A kindergarten child will tell her parents a story about what happened to Billy at school and leave out much of the relevant information. *Everyone* knows about Billy. Surely that must include Mom and Dad.

A telephone conversation with a 4-year-old can be interesting, but in the absence of face-to-face visual cues, much important information is often lost. For example, the voice on the other end of the phone asks "What are you wearing today, Kelly?" and in response Kelly says "This," while looking down and pointing at her dress.

Allen, the son of a high school math instructor, asks another 7-year-old "What does your daddy teach?"— assuming that everyone's daddy must teach something. He knows there are other jobs in the world; in fact, *he's* going to be a fireman when he grows up. Nonetheless, daddies teach.

Even young children are not consistently egocentric, however. At 5, my daughter Heidi still frequently demonstrated the classic egocentric attitude described by Piaget. For example, one evening in her bath she placed her head under the running water and excitedly called me in to hear the new sound. "Listen to this, Daddy," she said as she lowered her head under the faucet again while I watched. In a different context, however, this same child showed a keen ability to take the perspective of another. One evening, sometime before the bath episode, she and I were beginning a prebedtime card game and

I was exhorting her to hurry because, I said, the game is more fun when you play it fast. Her response to that was quick. "No sir, Daddy," she said. "You only want to go fast so we can finish and you can put me to bed!" I had been caught. This child, who thought I could hear the rushing water when *her* head was under the faucet, in this instance, saw my perspective quite clearly.

In general, each of us sees the world from a slightly different perspective, but with age and experience our perspectives expand, becoming less personal and more cultural. Our world and the world of the young child are not exactly the same, even though we may reside in the same house and live through the same events. We should not be surprised that in telling the story of an afternoon together in the park, the child comes up with a different account of things than her father does. This is not necessarily due to the young child's poor memory; she may be remembering things very well. She just didn't see or experience the same things that her father did standing beside her. They saw and felt different things at the same place and time. This isn't a scene from "The Twilight Zone," just the normal differences in thinking and perspective between children and adults.

Adapted from D. F. Bjorklund (August 1986). Look at Me! *Parents Magazine*, Vol. 61, No. 8.

Concrete Operational Thought

By about the age of 7, children are no longer so easily taken in by appearances. Their perception is said to be decentered. The ability to separate oneself from the obvious aspects of a perceptual array and make decisions based on the entire perceptual field is defined as **decentration.** They are now entering the **concrete operational period.**

Perhaps the most critical difference between the preoperational child and the concrete operational child is that the older child is able to think following rules of logic. The most important logical rule underlying mental operations is **reversibility.** In arithmetic, for example, subtraction is the inverse, or reversal, of addition. If 5 plus 2 equals 7, then 7 minus 2 must equal 5. Understanding this rule is critical for children to learn arithmetic, and children who do not appreciate the logical necessity of reversibility in arithmetic will be doing little more than rote memorization. Reversibility, more generally, is the logical idea that for any operation there exists another operation that compensates for the effects of the first. For example, if water is poured from a short, fat glass into a tall, thin one, the increased height of the water is compensated for by a decrease in the width of the column.

Classification   One of the changes that, according to Piaget, differentiates the thinking of preoperational and concrete operational children is the ability to classify objects. Although concrete operational children can group objects according to a single dimension (for example, all red objects in one pile, all blue objects in another), they cannot group objects according to a multiple classification scheme (see Figure 7.1). As with perceptual centration and egocentricity, it is not until concrete operations that children can deal with multiple features of objects and events.

A concept often used in studying children's classification ability is **class inclusion.** Logically, a class of items must always be smaller than a more general, or inclusive, class in which it is contained; for example, the number of cocker spaniels (a class) must be smaller than the number of dogs (an inclusive class). In a typical class-inclusion problem (Inhelder & Piaget, 1964), children are given several examples from two subordinate categories of a single superordinate category (for example, seven pictures of dogs

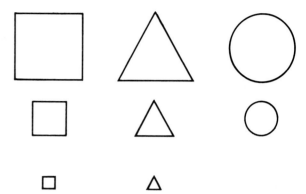

Figure 7.1 Multiple classification problem: Children must choose an object that completes the pattern.

and three pictures of cats—all animals). They are then asked whether there are more dogs or more animals. Although preschool children can give correct answers about two subordinate sets (for example, dogs versus cats), correct responses about a subordinate set and a superordinate set (for example, dogs versus animals) are more difficult and are not found reliably until late childhood or early adolescence (see Winer, 1980).

There has been much debate among psychologists concerning how children go about solving class-inclusion problems. One interesting study found that children of different ages approached the problems differently (McCabe, Siegel, Spence, & Wilkinson, 1982). Standard class-inclusion problems were given to 3- to 8-year-old children. The 3- and 4-year-olds could make little sense of the task and responded randomly, which gave them correct answers about 50% of the time. Many of the 7- and 8-year-olds, in contrast, understood the problem and applied a rule that led to consistently correct answers. The 5- and 6-year-olds also had a rule and applied it consistently; the problem was, the rule was wrong (pick the larger of the two subordinate sets). As a result, the rule produced consistently incorrect answers, giving these children lower scores than the 3- and 4-year-olds. A little knowledge *can* be a dangerous thing.

Piaget believed that operational thinking could not be developed through training, but only through children's interaction over time with their environment. However, there is evidence that children much younger than hypothesized by Piaget can solve class-inclusion problems as a result of training or when the task is modified. Children as young as 3 and 4 have been trained to solve class-inclusion problems correctly and to generalize that training to similar problems (Brainerd, 1974; Siegel, McCabe, Brand, & Mathews, 1978; Waxman & Gelman, 1986). Other researchers have modified considerably the class-inclusion task and report that preschoolers, without specific training, illustrate an understanding of class inclusion (Markman & Seibert, 1976; C. L. Smith, 1979; Steinberg & Anderson, 1975).

Conservation   For Piaget (1965a), the hallmark of concrete operations is **conservation**—understanding that an entity remains the same despite changes in its form. A classic example of a conservation task is the water-level problem discussed earlier (see Figure 7.2). Do children realize that the amount of water remains the same after pouring it into a different container, even though there seems to be more (or less) than there was originally? The concept of conservation applies to any substance that can be measured and has been studied with respect to dimensions of length, number, mass, weight, area, and volume.

Outside of the laboratory, conservation is something children are seldom taught. The idea of con-

"Is there the same amount of water in the two glasses, or does one have more?"

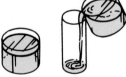

Water is poured from one of the original glasses to a taller, thinner glass.

"Is there the same amount of water in the two glasses now, or does one have more? Why?"

Figure 7.2 Conservation-of-liquid problem.

servation develops gradually, and once they have acquired it, most children assume they have always thought that way. Ask most 7-year-old conservers if ever in their lives they thought the glass with the higher water level had more water, and they will answer no—often giving you a funny look to think an adult would ask such a question.

With respect to conservation, as with other aspects of his theory, Piaget believed that he was assessing children's competencies—their fundamental abilities. If this were the case, it should not be possible to train children to conserve unless they are in a transition stage, almost ready to learn to conserve on their own. However, a number of researchers, using a variety of techniques, have demonstrated that nonconservers as young as 4 can be trained to conserve (Brainerd & Allen, 1971; Gelman, 1969). The magnitude of these training effects is greater for older than for younger children (Brainerd, 1977a), and few studies have produced convincing evidence that 3-year-olds can be trained to conserve (Field, 1987). In her review of the literature, Dorothy Field (1987) concluded that 76% of all studies had successfully trained preschool children in conservation; a smaller percentage of studies demonstrated generalization to other materials and transfer over delayed periods (one week or longer).

Despite the impressive training and transfer effects shown by a variety of researchers using a diversity of techniques, these training effects have so far been confined to the laboratory. Will 4-year-old children taught to conserve in the lab believe that they have the same amount of sandwich regardless of whether their dad cuts it into two pieces or four? Future research must investigate how well conservation training holds up beyond the laboratory, in children's lives at home and at school.

Closely related to conservation is the concept of identity (Piaget, 1968). Whereas conservation refers to quantity, identity refers to qualitative characteristics of type or kind. Early research by Rita De Vries (1969) demonstrated that young children frequently confuse changes in the appearance of an animal or person with changes in identity. For example, 3-year-olds generally believed that placing a dog mask on a cat changed the species of the animal, that boys wearing girls' clothes became girls (at least temporarily), and that people wearing masks changed their identities (see Box 7.4). School-age children no longer experience this type of confusion.

Box 7.4

Who Are You This Halloween?

Melanie was about 3 years old. Her father, whom she loved very much, was a professional clown. One afternoon Melanie had the treat of going to work with her dad. In the dressing room she watched with great interest as her father put on his clown outfit, then sat in front of the mirror and began applying his makeup. But before he could finish putting on his clown face, something unexplainable happened to Melanie. The fascinated little girl suddenly became terrified and ran screaming from the room to find her mother. She had, without warning, become frightened of the man in the clown suit and wanted no part of him.

Melanie clearly displayed a lack of what we call *constancy of personal identity:* she failed to realize that a person remains the same despite changes in appearance. Confusing her own father with an unfamiliar clown resulted in fear. Such reactions to changes in personal appearance are not uncommon in preschoolers.

Halloween is a time when parents often observe this phenomenon. It is not unusual for 2-, 3-, or even 4-year-olds to be all excited about wearing a Halloween costume, only to get upset when the mask is placed over their face. Granted, some children (as well as some adults) just don't like their faces covered. However, many children show distress only after seeing their image in the mirror. Wearing Darth Vader's cape and carrying his light saber are one thing, but they're not putting on the mask!

Similarly, children frequently become anxious when their parents dress up for a costume party. One 3-year-old was fascinated by her father's Big Bird outfit. She was very fond of both her daddy and Big Bird, and watched intently as her father got ready for the party. But things went too far when her dad placed the bird head over his own. "Take it off," she yelled. "You're not Big Bird. Take it off!" Whether she was upset about "losing" her father or about seeing a Sesame Street character come to life is not certain, but her father's transformation from Daddy to Big Bird was genuinely distressing.

By school age, most children realize that they will keep their own identity even if they pretend to be someone else.

Transformations of this type are not always upsetting to children; some kids like the change. This is evidenced by the number of broken limbs and skinned knees in children who don Superman Underoos, tie a cape around their necks, and proceed to jump from elevated objects believing they can fly. These children believe that when they are dressed as superheroes they actually possess some of their special powers. In addition to having problems with the constancy of personal identity, these children are confusing fantasy with reality—something that young children are wont to do. They are not stupid kids; preschoolers in general are easily confused about how changes in one's appearance affect one's identity. These young supermen and superwomen are just a little more adventurous than their agemates.

The Development of Formal Operations

Formal operations advance the logical rules acquired during the concrete operational period to the point that children can think about objects, ideas, events, and relations independent of their prior experience (Inhelder & Piaget, 1958). As one Piagetian scholar put it, "Concrete operations consist of thought thinking about the environment, but formal operations consist of thought thinking about itself" (Brainerd, 1978, p. 215). Formal operational thinkers are able to introspect about their own cognitions and produce new knowledge merely by reflecting on what they already know. They are also able to solve complex problems and to reason inductively, going from specific observations to broad generalizations, much as a scientist does when conducting experiments.

The hallmark of the formal operational period, however, is the ability to think hypothetically—or, as Piaget put it, **hypothetico-deductive reasoning.** Possibilities are more important than what is real.

Box 7.5

Santa Claus, the Easter Bunny, and the Tooth Fairy

We talk about the school years as marking the beginning of many new thinking abilities, but those years also mark the end of others, such as the belief in Santa Claus, the Easter Bunny, and the Tooth Fairy.

Parents are valued guides in children's early learning, but they sometimes reserve the right to perpetuate a few illusions for as long as possible. Despite their best efforts, however, children usually discover the truth on their own.

By 7 years or so, children see the distinction between fantasy and reality more clearly. They realize, for example, that climatic conditions at the North Pole would make running a toy industry difficult and that flying reindeer seriously violate things they have learned in school about wildlife. And their older schoolmates, proud of their newly acquired knowledge, sometimes go out of their way to tell younger children that Santa Claus does not exist—that one's mom and dad really buy the presents and place them under the tree.

Cindy Scheibe and John Condry (1987) of Cornell University conducted a study concerning children's belief in Santa Claus and other fantasy characters. They reported that sometime between their seventh and eighth birthdays, most children begin to have serious doubts about the Santa Claus story, although some hang onto the belief until age 10 or beyond. Eventually, most children realize that too much about Santa Claus just doesn't make sense, and this is usually supported by strong hints from their friends. Children's mental development progresses to the point where most have to suspend reality too much to truly believe the Santa Claus story.

Interestingly, Scheibe and Condry found that parents often underestimate their children's belief in Santa Claus, thinking that children know or suspect the truth to a greater extent than they actually do. Another interesting finding was that once children discover the truth about Santa Claus, it does not necessarily mean that they abandon their beliefs in other fantasy characters such as the Tooth Fairy. Apparently, middle-years children can be sophisticated enough to realize that Santa Claus is only make-believe, but still think that the money under their pillow for a lost tooth comes from the elusive Tooth Fairy.

Given the confusion middle-years children must experience over Santa Claus and other fantasy creatures, should parents continue to promote these myths? Based on interviews with older children, Professor Condry sees no harm in parents' promoting Santa Claus. Older children see it as a benevolent fib and express no resentment toward their parents for pushing the Santa Claus myth.

A month before our daughter Heidi's eighth Christmas she confided to us in a whisper that she "knew about Santa Claus"—an older playmate had told her. "Then why are you whispering?" we asked. "I don't want Nicky to find out," she said, "he's only 5."

Such thinking is critical for most forms of mathematics beyond arithmetic. If $2X + 5 = 15$, what does X equal? The problem does not deal with concrete entities such as apples or oranges, only with numbers and letters. Mathematics in general is based on hypotheses and not on reality. Let Y be 22, or 7, or -12, or 45 degrees, or the cosine of angle *ABC.* Once provided with a premise, formal operational thinkers can go on to solve a problem. They don't ask "Is Y really 22?" The problem is arbitrary and hypothetical; it can only be answered if approached abstractly, using a symbol system that does not require concrete reference points.

Another characteristic of formal operational thought is **inductive reasoning**—going from specific observations to broad generalizations. This is the type of thinking that characterizes scientists, who generate hypotheses and then test them systematically in experiments.

To assess scientific reasoning, Inhelder and Piaget (1958) used a series of tasks, including the following pendulum problem: Children are given a rod,

Some children cling to their belief in Santa long after their agemates begin to have doubts.

Yes, Virginia (and Nicky), there *is* a Santa Claus and a Tooth Fairy and an Easter Bunny for everyone, whether you believe in them yourself or, like Heidi, want to help keep the magic alive for younger ones in the family.

Adapted from D. F. Bjorklund and B. R. Bjorklund. (December 1989). Santa Claus, the Easter Bunny, and the Tooth Fairy. *Parents Magazine,* Vol. 64, No. 12.

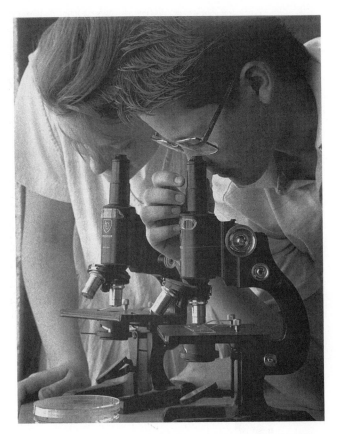

Young people are first able to reason scientifically during the formal operations stage.

strings of various lengths, and objects of varying weights. They are shown how to make a pendulum by attaching a string to the rod and a weight to the string. After seeing how the pendulum operates, children are asked to determine the factors responsible for the speed at which the pendulum swings. In addition to the length of the string and the weight of the object, children are told that they may vary the height from which they swing the object and the force of the push they give the object to start it swinging.

How can the scientific method be used to solve this problem? There are four possible factors to consider (string length, weight of object, height of release, and force of push), with several possible levels for each factor (for example, three lengths of string, four different weights). The first step is to generate a hypothesis. It doesn't matter if the hy-

pothesis is correct or not, so long as it is testable and yields noncontradictory conclusions. This initial step is within the ability of concrete operational children. The next step is to test this hypothesis. The trick is to vary a single factor while holding the others constant. For example, a child may examine the rate of oscillation using the 100-gram weight and short string with high release and easy push, then high release and hard push, then low release and easy push, then low release and hard push. The same routine can then be followed using different string lengths, and then different weights, until the child has tested systematically all of the various combinations. Table 7.3 presents the 16 possible combinations and their outcomes for a pendulum problem involving these four factors with only two levels for each factor (long versus short string, heavy versus light weight, low versus high release, easy versus hard push).

Concrete operational children often get off to a good start on this problem, but rarely arrive at the correct answer. Their observations are generally accurate (which is not the case for preoperational children), but they usually fail to isolate relevant variables and will arrive at a conclusion before exhaustively testing their hypotheses. For example, children may observe that the pendulum swings fast with a short string and a heavy weight and conclude

***Table* 7.3** Pendulum problem: possible combinations and outcomes

Weight of Object	Height of Drop	Force of Push	Length of String	
			Short	**Long**
Light	Low	Easy	Fast	Slow
		Hard	Fast	Slow
	High	Easy	Fast	Slow
		Hard	Fast	Slow
Heavy	Low	Easy	Fast	Slow
		Hard	Fast	Slow
	High	Easy	Fast	Slow
		Hard	Fast	Slow

that both string length and weight are jointly responsible for rate of oscillation. According to Inhelder and Piaget (1958), it is not until formal operations that children can test their hypotheses correctly, and, as scientists, arrive at the only possible, logical solution.

As with other aspects of Piaget's theory, there has been controversy concerning whether concrete operational children are capable of solving problems requiring scientific reasoning. In fact, researchers have been able to train young children to solve many formal operational problems (Siegler, Robinson, Liebert, & Liebert, 1973; Stone & Day, 1978). In general, research indicates that young children have better formal operational abilities than Inhelder and Piaget originally suggested, but they display these competencies only under limited conditions.

In other situations, however, research has shown that Piaget overestimated the tendency of adolescents and adults to use scientific-type reasoning. For example, Deanna Kuhn and her associates (Kuhn, Langer, Kohlberg, & Haan, 1977), using 265 adolescent and adult participants in a longitudinal study, administered a battery of formal operational tasks adapted from Inhelder and Piaget, including tests of scientific reasoning. Based on these tests, only about 30% of the adults were classified as having completely achieved formal operations. Most adults were classified as transitional between concrete and formal operations, and 15% demonstrated no formal operational abilities at all.

In another study, Noel Capon and Deanna Kuhn (1979) investigated adults' use of formal operational abilities in a practical task. They interviewed 50 women in a supermarket and asked them to judge which of two sizes of the same product was the better buy. For example, one task involved two bottles of garlic powder: the smaller bottle contained 1.25 ounces (35 grams) and sold for 41 cents; the larger bottle contained 2.37 ounces (67 grams) and sold for 77 cents. The women were given pencil and paper, told to use them if they wished, and asked to justify their choices. The most direct way to arrive at the correct answer is to compute the price per unit weight for each product and compare the two. This involves reasoning about proportions, which Inhelder and Piaget (1958) said was a scheme characteristic of formal operations. In fact, fewer than 30% of the women used a proportional reasoning strategy; at least 50% used a strategy that yielded, at best,

The ability to judge proportions is a formal operational skill that is necessary to comparison shopping.

inconclusive evidence and was just as likely to be wrong as right. For instance, some women used a subtraction strategy, saying, for example, "With the bigger one you get 32 more grams for 36 more cents," concluding that the bigger one was the better buy. Others merely relied on past experience, making statements such as "The big one must be cheaper," without providing any justification for the statement. In sum, formal operational reasoning was not observed for a majority of women on an everyday task. This does not mean that these adults would fail to display formal reasoning under some other conditions, but it does suggest that formal operations may not be characteristic of adult thought in general.

One other characteristic of adolescent thought that has attracted research attention is its peculiar form of egocentricity. Although egocentricity is usually associated with the preoperational period, adolescents, too, display their own brand of egocentric thought, believing, for example, that other people are as concerned with them as they are with themselves. This self-consciousness is coupled with teen-

Teenagers often believe that everyone is looking at them.

agers' increased awareness of the thoughts of others. David Elkind (1967; Elkind & Bower, 1979) said that adolescents feel as if they were constantly "on stage" or playing to an imaginary audience. A related concept is that of the *personal fable,* a term Elkind used to refer to the adolescents' belief that they are unique and invulnerable, a belief often reflected in reckless behavior and the belief that bad things happen only to other people.

Children's Humor

Piaget's theory has had an unprecedented influence on developmental psychology. Modifications of his stage theory have been applied to a wide range of child-development topics, including children's arithmetic (see Chapter 8), communication (Chapter 9), social role taking (Chapter 15), moral reasoning (Chapter 15), gender identification (Chapter 16), and knowledge of sexuality (Chapter 17). Another topic to which the theory has been applied is the

development of humor. Most child-development researchers investigating this area have emphasized the role that thinking abilities play in humor, with Piaget's theory serving as the model for explaining age changes in what children of different ages find funny.

Humor begins in infancy and early childhood. Like adults, infants and toddlers get great pleasure from the lighter side of life, but the things that make children smile and laugh change with age. The same event that causes uproarious laughter in a 3-year-old (for example, Daddy saying "hold your horses") will be understood by an 8-year-old in an entirely different way. The 3-year-old takes Dad literally and envisions herself holding the tails of several wild horses—a funny image indeed, especially if she is a city kid. The 8-year-old understands the statement as a figure of speech—a metaphor for "slow down." And the 2-year-old hasn't the foggiest idea what Dad is talking about, making the statement neither funny nor informative. Humor, then, is in the mind of the beholder, and because children's minds change so dramatically over their first dozen years, so does their sense of humor.

Most developmental researchers believe that humor depends on the child's ability to notice incongruity—a discrepancy between what is expected and what is experienced (McGhee, 1979; Pien & Rothbart, 1980; Shultz & Robillard, 1980). Because children know the world differently at different ages, their ideas of "what is expected" change. As a result, what is incongruous, and thus funny, to a young child will be considered really dumb by an older sibling. For example, the 2-year-old, who thinks the height of comedy is calling the family dog a "kitty," will probably not be joined in laughter by a 10-year-old sibling who has discovered "knock-knock" jokes —and vice versa.

Humor and Mental Effort

According to Paul McGhee (1974, 1976), incongruity is most apt to be seen as funny when the discrepancy is not too large and not too small. In other words, there is an inverted-U relationship between the magnitude of incongruity and the humor seen in a situation (see Figure 7.3). McGhee proposed that children (and adults, for that matter) gain the greatest satisfaction in resolving incongruities of some moderate degree of difficulty. Creating or compre-

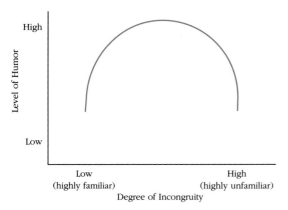

Figure 7.3 Relationship between incongruity and humor.

hending humor is seen as an intellectual challenge, rewarded by "pleasure in mastery." The funniest jokes, for both adults and children, are those that take a little mental effort to figure out. Too easy and they're boring; too difficult and they're not worth the effort.

McGhee (1976) tested this theory by comparing children's appreciation of jokes with their level of cognitive development. In one experiment, he tested children in grades 1, 2, and 5. Within the first and second grades, half the children were classified as conservers on Piagetian conservation tasks, and half as nonconservers. All the fifth graders were conservers. Subjects were read jokes requiring a knowledge of conservation for their appreciation—for example:

> Mr. Jones went into a restaurant and ordered a whole pizza for dinner. When the waiter asked if he wanted it cut into six or eight pieces, Mr. Jones said, "Oh, you'd better make it six! I could never eat eight!"

After reading each joke, the experimenter asked the child to rate how funny it was, using a 5-point scale. The children who found the jokes funniest were the first- and second-grade conservers. Nonconservers at those ages found nothing to laugh about; they would have asked for six slices also (or eight if they were really hungry). In contrast, fifth-graders found the joke trivial, taking little in the way of mental effort. Only for the young conservers is the joke funny. These children have only recently mastered conservation, and the challenge of such a

joke is in a moderate range of difficulty for them—neither too discrepant nor too obvious, but just right.

Humor and Cognitive Development

McGhee proposed four stages of humor development, beginning sometime late in the second year, when the capacity for fantasy and make-believe develops. In stage 1, children substitute one object for another in a playful game of pretending. For example, Piaget (1962) observed his daughter Jacqueline at 15 months clutching a cloth that vaguely resembled her pillow. She held it in her hand, sucked her thumb, and lay down closing her eyes. But while she was pretending to sleep, she was laughing hard. To this toddler, substituting the cloth for her pillow was funny.

Children's first verbal jokes occur in stage 2, which follows closely on the heels of stage 1. The simplest of these jokes involves calling something by its wrong name. A 2-year-old finds great mirth in calling the family cat a "cow," in labeling a hamburger "macaroni and cheese," or in pointing to an eye and calling it a nose. Such humor may not seem very sophisticated, but it requires greater abstraction than the object-dependent humor of stage 1. Children no longer need a physical prop to make a joke; playing with words is enough.

What is humorous to a stage 3 child is often a function of how absurd something looks. Recall that preschool children attend to the way things *seem* to them, rather than to less apparent, logical aspects of a stimulus. This overreliance on appearance affects children's humor. A picture of an elephant sitting in a tree is funny to a 3-year-old, and so is a picture of a fish swimming inside a car filled with water. These pictures are funny to 3-year-olds not because they defy logic, but just because they are unusual. The incongruity is visual, not logical. This extends to things that sound funny, too. Preschool kids make up series of nonsensical words, such as "potty, dotty, motty, cotty," or "daddy, faddy, baddy, saddy." There is no need to consider deeper meaning—they just seem funny.

Beginning around 6 or 7 years of age, children's humor changes dramatically and starts to resemble the humor of adults. According to McGhee, it is the ability to understand double meanings of words and sentences that is the hallmark of stage 4 and much of adult humor. A sentence with a serious (and obvious) meaning taken one way, can be funny if viewed differently. A favorite of some 6-year-olds we know involves a woman mailing three socks to her son who is away at college. Why did she mail three socks? Because he wrote and said he'd "grown another foot." Appreciation of the joke requires an understanding of the double meaning of "grown another foot." Most 7-year-olds have the ability to represent two meanings of a single word or phrase simultaneously, and from this time on, humor takes a distinctly adult form—although most adults are still apt to groan at jokes that have an 8-year-old rolling on the floor with laughter.

Thomas Shultz and his colleagues have studied extensively how children's appreciation of jokes and riddles develops over the school years (Shultz, 1972; Shultz & Horibe, 1974; Shultz & Pilon, 1973). In Shultz's experiments, children were told jokes and asked to rate how funny they were, using a 5-point scale. Children were later asked to explain the jokes or if they could have a second meaning. The extent to which children smiled or laughed at the jokes was also measured.

Shultz and his colleagues found that children of different ages could appreciate different types of jokes. Most jokes depend on a person's being able

Children's enjoyment of different jokes and riddles at different ages is the focus of serious developmental research.

to detect some ambiguity—to realize there is a double meaning, one serious and the other humorous. What is ambiguous varies, however, with the youngest children being able to appreciate only the simplest ambiguities. With age, children are increasingly able to "catch" the double meaning of more subtle jokes. The simplest type of ambiguity involves single words that sound alike:

Waiter, what's this?
That's *bean* soup, ma'am.
I'm not interested in what it's *been,* I'm asking what it is now!

This joke centers around the different meanings of similar-sounding words, "bean" and "been." Many knock-knock jokes also rely on this type of ambiguity for their humor:

Knock, knock.
Who's there?
Lettuce.
Lettuce who?
Let us out, it's cold in here!

Most children appreciate jokes involving this kind of ambiguity by 6 or 7 years.

Following close behind are jokes based on the dual meaning of a single word:

Order! Order in the court!
Ham and cheese on rye, Your Honor.

Here the humor doesn't derive from a confusion of two different words but revolves around two different meanings of the same word. Another joke of this type popular with 7- and 8-year-olds is:

How do you keep an elephant from charging?
Take away its credit card.

Most of the verbal jokes and riddles of elementary school children are based on these two types of ambiguity. More complex jokes involve ambiguities not of a single word but of the entire structure of a sentence:

I saw a man-eating shark in the aquarium.
That's nothing. I saw a man eating herring in the restaurant.

or

I would like to buy a pair of alligator shoes.
Certainly. What size does your alligator wear?

In these two jokes, the humor hinges not on the interpretation of a single word but upon how the whole sentence is interpreted. Appreciation of these more complex ambiguities is not usually attained until 11 or 12 years of age. However, young children may still laugh at these jokes if they are accompanied by a picture. The scene of a salesman fitting shoes on an alligator is funny even to 3-year-olds. It doesn't matter that they don't understand the two meanings of the sentence; one funny picture is worth two verbal ambiguities to a preschooler anytime.

Research has clearly demonstrated that children's understanding and appreciation of humor vary as a function of their level of cognitive development. Other factors also affect humor, of course. Some topics are more apt to be the source of humor than others (aggression, sex), and humor plays an important role in greasing the gears of social interaction. Yet the core of humor is cognitive. Simple, visual jokes can be comprehended by 3-year-olds, but as the basis of jokes becomes more abstract and less dependent upon visual cues, it becomes increasingly difficult for children to identify and resolve the ambiguity. Children's abilities to represent events, both real and unreal, and to view multiple meanings of a single situation determine what they find funny.

State of the Art
Piaget's Theory Today

What does Piaget's theory, initially formulated more than 60 years ago, tell us about development today? There is no doubt that Piaget continues to influence contemporary developmentalists. Developmental researchers cite his work more frequently than anyone else's. But much of the interest Piaget has generated has been in the form of criticism rather than praise. Does his theory paint an accurate picture of cognitive development, or is it ready to be relegated to the historical archives?

Obviously, we would not commit an entire chapter to this theory if we did not think it had substantial merit. But 20-some years of intense investigation (some would say 20 years of Piaget-bashing) have shown that Piaget's theory is not the final word. By modern standards, Piaget was wrong in many of the details of development—calling into question, for some, the logic of his entire theory.

For example, Piaget believed that development occurs spontaneously as children interact with their environment and that it cannot be hastened by specific, short-term instruction. Yet numerous investigators have demonstrated that children *can* be taught to perform at more advanced levels than they do spontaneously. Preoperational children can be trained to behave like concrete operational children (Bryant & Trabasso, 1971; Gelman, 1969), and concrete operational children can be trained to behave like formal operational children (Siegler et al., 1973; Stone & Day, 1978). Also, Piaget's notion of structures imply substantial homogeneity, or evenness, of cognitive functioning: a child's cognitions should be pretty much the same for all tasks he or she attempts. Yet other researchers have shown that evenness of cognitive functioning is often the exception rather than the rule (Fischer, 1980).

Despite evidence to the contrary, however, Piaget's description of development still captures much of the richness and uniqueness of children's thinking. Most preschool children *do* have a relatively egocentric perspective on the world, and their attention *is* centered on the obvious physical characteristics of stimuli. Most concrete operational children cannot provide rich introspections about their own thought processes, they don't think hypothetically, and they rarely approach problems in a scientific way. Under certain circumstances, children can be trained or biased to think in a more advanced way, but such training is usually limited and rarely transforms the child into a totally different type of thinker. In other words, Piaget's description of intellectual development has "ecological validity," in that it depicts well the day-to-day functioning of most children.

In essence, the question boils down to: "How stagelike is cognitive development?" (Flavell, 1982). Piaget proposed that it is highly stagelike; many contemporary psychologists deny that it is stagelike at all. Several theorists have tried to salvage the concept of developmental stages for some abilities, while admitting that other aspects of development don't follow the pattern.

Two currently popular neo-Piagetian theories are those of Robbie Case (1985) and Kurt Fischer (1980). Both of these theorists postulate stages similar to Piaget's, describing how children represent information; both believe that infants, children, and adolescents have qualitatively different ways of understanding the world. Yet Case and Fischer propose that some aspects of cognitive development are not stagelike, but develop with quantitative changes in information-processing abilities. Moreover, Fischer in particular stresses that children's cognitive abilities are never homogeneous, or even, at any one time—a clear violation of Piaget's theory. At any given time, says Fischer, a child's highest level of cognitive ability is limited by maturational factors, but children function at their highest, or optimal, level only on a small set of tasks—those for which they have received consistent environmental support. They perform at lower levels on tasks with which they are less familiar or involving skills they have not been encouraged by their environments to develop. In other words, Case and Fischer, unlike Piaget, believe that much of cognitive development is quantitative in nature and that unevenness should be seen as the rule, not the exception. Like Piaget, they believe that cognitive development is stagelike—just not as stagelike as Piaget thought it was.

The book is not closed on the nature of cognitive development. It is clear that much of development is stagelike, as Piaget said it was; however, there are other aspects of development that do not correspond to Piagetian sequences. Both types of development are important for understanding the child and the nature of cognitive growth, and both can be found in everyday examples of children's cognitions. To a large extent, what one finds depends upon where one looks.

Summary

Jean Piaget was the most influential developmental psychologist of all time. Trained as a biologist, he proposed a theory of the development of knowledge that he termed genetic epistemology. Key assumptions of the theory are that children are intrinsically active and that cognition is constructed by the child.

Piaget proposed two functional invariants, processes that are constant throughout life: organization and adaptation. Organization refers to the tendency to integrate mental abilities into higher-order systems, or structures. Adaptation refers to the tendency to adjust one's structures to environmental demands. Adaptation has two complementary components: assimilation, which occurs when children modify something in the environment to fit their current structures, and accommodation, which occurs when children change their structures to incorporate new information. Piaget's mechanism for cognitive change is his equilibration model, which incorporates the ideas of assimilation and accommodation to explain development.

Piaget divided development into four major periods: sensorimotor, preoperational, concrete operational, and formal operational. Cognition during the sensorimotor period is limited to children's perceptions and actions on objects and develops through a series of six stages. Object permanence—the knowledge that an object continues to exist even though it is out of one's immediate perception—develops gradually over the sensorimotor period.

Children's thinking in the last three periods is similar in that thought is based on mental representations. Preoperational thought, based on symbols, is not logical but intuitive in nature. Preoperational children are apt to center their perception on the most salient aspect of a visual field; they are also egocentric, in that they have difficulty seeing things from another person's perspective. Differences in thinking between preoperational and concrete operational children are apparent on classification and conservation tasks. Formal operations involve an ability to think hypothetically and inductively (like a scientist).

Children's humor develops as a function of their level of cognitive development. Humor is based on incongruity, and incongruity is most likely to be perceived when the discrepancy is of some intermediate magnitude.

Piaget's work has stimulated substantial research over the past 60-plus years. Many aspects of his theory have met with serious challenges. Yet Piaget's theory does capture much of the richness of children's thinking and describes reasonably well the way most children behave most of the time. More contemporary neo-Piagetian theories retain many of the stagelike qualities of Piaget's theory while incorporating new evidence about the nature of cognitive development.

Key Terms and Concepts

genetic epistemology
intrinsic activity
    constructive nature of cognition
functional invariants
    organization
        structures (schemes)
    adaptation
        assimilation
        accommodation
    equilibration
sensorimotor period
    basic reflexes
    primary circular reactions
    secondary circular reactions
    coordination of secondary circular reactions
        goal-directed behavior
    tertiary circular reactions

inventions of new means through mental
    combinations
object permanence
    invisible displacements
preoperational period
    intuitive nature of thought
    perceptual centration/decentration
    egocentricity
concrete operational period
    reversibility
    multiple classification
    class inclusion
    conservation
        identity
formal operations
    hypothetico-deductive reasoning
    inductive reasoning
incongruity

Learning, Thinking, and Remembering

No one can remember what 4-year-old Jason did to get his father so upset, but whatever it was, his father wanted no more of it.

"Jason, I want you to go over to that corner and just *think* about all this for a while," his father yelled.

Instead of following his father's orders, Jason stood where he was, not defiantly, but with a confused look and quivering lips, as if he were trying to say something but was afraid to.

"What's the matter now?" his father asked, his irritation still showing.

"But, Daddy," Jason said, "I don't know *how* to think."

Obviously, 4-year-old Jason did know how to think; he just didn't know that he did. The term *thinking* has a fairly specific meaning for most people. People "think" when they need to solve a difficult problem; something that can be done easily and automatically is said to be done "without thinking." Perception and attention, discussed in the previous chapter, involve important cognitive abilities, but recognizing a face or attending to a stimulus is not what people generally mean by "thinking." In this chapter, we focus on those activities that come to mind for most people when they think about "thinking": learning, problem-solving strategies, memory development, number and arithmetic concepts, and metacognition (what children know about their own thinking).

Children learn some fears through classical conditioning.

Learning

Classical and Operant Conditioning

Thinking and remembering imply learning—the acquisition of new knowledge through experience. In the early part of this century, the primary theoretical approach to learning was **behaviorism,** which held that behavior and development are shaped by environmental influences. Two principal types of learning were described: classical conditioning and operant conditioning.

In **classical conditioning,** discovered experimentally by Russian scientist Ivan Pavlov, a previously neutral stimulus is paired with another stimulus that elicits some response. For example, a particular tone might be paired with a puff of air to the eye. The tone is initially neutral in that it elicits no response from a person. The puff of air to the eye, however, does elicit a response—an eyeblink. After repeated pairings of the tone with the puff of air, eventually the tone will produce an eyeblink, even without the puff of air. In this example, the puff of air is referred to as the *unconditioned stimulus* and the tone as the *conditioned stimulus*. As you may recall from our discussion of John Watson in Chapter 1, emotional responses seem to be learned through classical conditioning. When a child associates a previously neutral stimulus with a stimulus that already elicits some response (a white rat paired with a loud gong, in Watson's famous experiment), eventually the new stimulus will elicit the emotion.

The other basic form of learning is **operant conditioning,** or learning through reward and punishment. In operant conditioning, some behavior of the child is reinforced, or rewarded, causing a change in the probability of that behavior in the future. For example, children who receive a reward (candy, money, praise) for good behavior can be expected to continue to show good behavior in the future. Patterns of reinforcement—that is, the distribution or frequency of rewards received for particular behaviors—can greatly affect learning (Reynolds, 1968); aversive stimuli (mild shocks for rats, spankings or a reprimand for children) can also affect behavior.

Learning in infancy   From our discussion of perception in Chapter 4, it is clear that learning begins at birth, or even before. Research has shown that infants less than a week old can learn to discriminate between the odor of their mothers and other women (Macfarlane, 1975) and that some learning of basic auditory patterns occurs prenatally (De-Casper & Spence, 1986).

Operant conditioning of newborns is relatively easy: they will modify their behavior in order to receive some type of reward. The trick, of course, is to find a behavior that infants can control themselves and something that infants find rewarding. Behaviors that newborns can control include sucking, head turning, and kicking, all of which have been used in operant-conditioning experiments. Reinforcements have included milk, human voices, and music (Lipsitt, 1982). For example, in one experiment, newborns would suck on a pacifier in order to hear music as opposed to nonrhythmic noise (Butterfield & Siperstein, 1972), demonstrating both an ability to learn and an innate preference for patterned sound.

Classical conditioning also seems to be within the capability of newborns (Fitzgerald & Brackbill, 1976), although it is limited to a few biologically prepared reflexes, such as sucking and blinking. However, the length of time between the neutral stimulus and the unconditioned stimulus must be shorter in young infants than in older children for conditioning to occur (Little, Lipsitt, & Rovee-Collier, 1984; Lintz, Fitzgerald, & Brackbill, 1967). Presum-ably, young infants cannot process information as efficiently and require more time to make the connection between the conditioned and unconditioned stimuli before learning takes place.

Behavior modification   Principles of classical and (especially) operant conditioning are used frequently by parents and teachers to control children's behavior and establish discipline. In fact, **behavior modification**—the use of operant conditioning principles to change behavior—is the basis of many parenting programs and popular books aimed at instructing parents in how to manage their children. Yet, although the principles of conditioning are as valid today as they were 50 years ago, contemporary researchers believe that operant and classical conditioning alone are not adequate to account for most of the learning that children do. One complaint about behavior-modification techniques is that children who are rewarded for desired behaviors often resort to earlier behaviors once the rewards are removed. That is, although behavior-modification techniques clearly work in controlling a child's current actions, they are less successful in shaping future behavior when rewards are no longer provided. In fact, children who are induced to comply by rewards (or punishments) may lose their intrinsic motivation for the behavior in question and be *less* likely to engage in it on their own (Lepper, Greene, & Nisbett, 1973). (A specific example of this, as it relates to helping others, will be discussed in Chapter 15.)

Learning by Observation

The primary limitation of operant and classical conditioning in explaining how children learn is that children (and adults) learn much about their world simply by watching. We do not need to be explicitly reinforced to learn something new. We can simply watch a model, retain the observed behavior, and be able to reproduce it at some later time. Not only can we learn overt behaviors from observing models; we can also learn attitudes and standards of judgment (Bandura, 1989a).

Recognizing the importance of learning by observation, a group of psychologists in the 1930s and 1940s developed a new theoretical approach known as "social learning theory" (Miller & Dollard, 1941;

Dollard, Doob, Miller, Mowrer, & Sears, 1939). According to this theory, imitation is the primary learning mechanism for most social behaviors. Social learning theory was later championed by Albert Bandura and his colleagues (Bandura & Walters, 1963), who initially proposed that children learn through observation by experiencing vicarious reinforcement; that is, they feel good (or bad) watching someone else get reinforced and modify their behavior accordingly. Over nearly three decades, Bandura's theory has become less behavioral and more cognitive until, in its latest version, he has renamed it **social cognitive theory** (Bandura, 1986, 1989a). It is now the dominant approach to studying children's social development.

Social cognitive theory   Bandura has proposed five capabilities that contribute to children's learning about their social world and their place in it, each of which develops *symbolization, forethought, self-regulation, self-reflection,* and *vicarious learning.* Symbolization is the ability to think about our social behavior in words and images. Forethought is the ability to anticipate the consequences of our actions and the actions of others. Self-regulation involves adopting standards of acceptable behavior for ourselves—aspirations, or hoped-for levels of accomplishment, as well as social and moral standards. A capacity for self-reflection allows people to analyze their thoughts and actions.

The final capability, vicarious learning, is the cornerstone of social cognitive theory. In contrast to earlier versions of social learning theory, children need not receive reinforcement for their modeling efforts nor even attempt to reproduce modeled behavior for learning to occur. They can watch a model and represent mentally what the model did; this mental symbol can then serve to guide their subsequent behavior, even if they never actually imitate what they observed. Bandura refers to this process as "observational learning."

Unlike earlier social learning theory, social cognitive theory proposes that children play an active role in interacting with their environment. As Piaget did, Bandura believes that children have as much effect on their environment as their environment has on them; he refers to this interaction as **reciprocal determinism.** Bandura (1989a) proposes that there are complex interactions among children's thoughts, feelings, and behaviors, as well

as between these and the external environment. How children feel or think about something affects their behavior; likewise, their behavior in certain situations influences their thought. We all try to make sense of our behavior, and we often change our thinking and beliefs to bring them into line with our actions (Gazzaniga, 1985). Children's behavior also influences how other people perceive and act toward them, which, in turn, affects their thinking and behavior. Thus, Bandura proposes a process of causation that gives serious attention to the internal states of children (their thoughts and emotions), their observable behaviors, and the perceptions and actions of others. Using the terminology adopted earlier in this book, Bandura's reciprocal determinism is clearly a transactional approach.

Observational learning   Bandura (1989a) has proposed four subprocesses that govern **observational learning:** *attentional processes, retention processes, production processes,* and *motivational processes* (see Figure 8.1). Information must be attended to, coded in memory, stored, retrieved, and the behavior performed at the appropriate time. Each of these factors changes with age, and a failure in any one area (retention, for example) rules out successful observational learning.

Children can learn from observation without ever actually producing the behavior. For instance, John Money and Anke Ehrhardt (1972) proposed that both boys and girls learn appropriate male and female sex roles, but typically imitate only the same-sex behavior. Learning the opposite-sex role is important in development because it informs a child what behaviors should complement his or hers. But although opposite-sex roles are learned, they are coded negatively and not imitated, whereas same-sex roles are coded positively and incorporated into a child's behavior.

Although imitation is not necessary for observational learning to occur, it is nonetheless an important component in observational learning and child development. Imitation is the clearest indication that children have learned through watching and the primary means by which children acquire new behaviors.

The development of imitation   Imitation begins early in infancy and changes in character with the

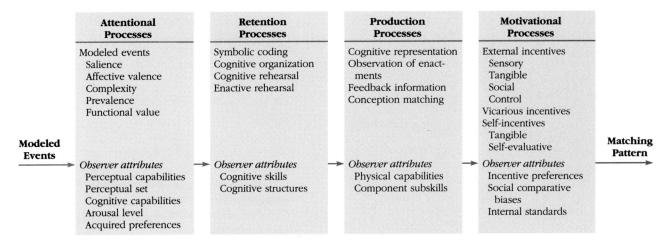

Attentional Processes	Retention Processes	Production Processes	Motivational Processes
Modeled events Salience Affective valence Complexity Prevalence Functional value	Symbolic coding Cognitive organization Cognitive rehearsal Enactive rehearsal	Cognitive representation Observation of enactments Feedback information Conception matching	External incentives Sensory Tangible Social Control Vicarious incentives Self-incentives Tangible Self-evaluative
Observer attributes Perceptual capabilities Perceptual set Cognitive capabilities Arousal level Acquired preferences	*Observer attributes* Cognitive skills Cognitive structures	*Observer attributes* Physical capabilities Component subskills	*Observer attributes* Incentive preferences Social comparative biases Internal standards

Modeled Events → ... → **Matching Pattern**

Figure 8.1 Subprocesses governing observational learning. *Source:* From "Social Cognitive Theory," by A. Bandura. In R. Vasta (ed.), *Annals of Child Development,* Vol. 6. Copyright © 1989 by JAI Press, Inc. Reprinted by permission.

advent of language and other symbolic tools late in the second year of life. Bandura's account of observational learning begins with children's ability to symbolically code events and actions they have seen, store them in memory, and imitate them at some later time. This is what Piaget (1962) referred to as "deferred imitation." Such imitative abilities, though apparently present to a limited extent early in the second year (Meltzoff, 1988), begin in earnest between 18 and 24 months of age (Piaget, 1962).

Children need to interact with adults of both genders to learn about their future roles in society.

Imitation during childhood has important implications for development. On the one hand, imitation serves as a means for children to acquire new behaviors, important in mastering their intellectual and physical worlds. Children may learn to walk, run, and throw simply by exercising their innately endowed abilities, but they learn to use a fork, to slide into second base, and to tap-dance largely through imitation. On the other hand, imitation also serves an important role in social development. It functions as a method of communication between children and their parents, and generally serves to sustain social interactions (Abramovitch & Grusec, 1978; Grusec & Abramovitch, 1982). There is an abundance of research showing that many socially important phenomena are acquired through observation without direct instruction (see Perry & Bussey, 1984; Shaffer, 1988).

Following Bandura's theory, after children have attended to a model and formed a mental representation of the behavior, they must convert that representation to action. Yet children observe some things that they do not have the motor ability to reproduce. For example, although 5-year-olds may watch and mentally practice the behaviors involved in driving a car, because of their short arms and legs (among other things), they are physically unable to produce those behaviors. Despite such obvious shortcomings, young children frequently overestimate their imitative abilities; they have watched a behavior being performed and believe that "seeing is knowing." (More than one parent has been shocked to see his or her young child behind the wheel of a moving car.) In a study in which mothers recorded the imitative attempts of their preschoolers, children overestimated their imitative abilities 55.5% of the time—stating that they were capable of imitating a behavior when they were not; cases of underestimation were rare, occurring in only 4.7% of the observations (Bjorklund, Gaultney, & Green, 1992). Young children have great confidence in their own abilities. To improve observational learning, however, children must learn to monitor their actions, compare them to the symbolic representations of

Preschoolers tend to greatly overestimate their ability to imitate older children and adults.

what they have observed, and correct mismatches. As these production processes improve with age, the difference between what children know and what they can produce declines (Bandura, 1989a).

Television as a Model for Learning

Children learn not only from watching other people, but also from watching film, videos, and television. There can be no question that television is an important socializing agent in today's society. American children between 3 and 14 years of age watch more than three hours of television per day, with the amount of TV decreasing some over adolescence into young adulthood (see Liebert & Sprafkin, 1988).

As a means of mass communication, television and its related technologies are the most important inventions of the 20th century. Events happening in remote corners of the globe can be broadcast live into our living rooms. Through television, we can learn of the habits, customs, and problems of people in other parts of the country or the world. Television can serve as a great education tool, bringing knowledge in an easily understood visual form that doesn't require reading skills. But does it? What do children learn from watching TV?

TV *and education*   Many programs on public and commercial TV are aimed at educating children. Perhaps the best known and most successful of these is "Sesame Street," which has the goal of fostering cognitive skills in preschool children.

"Sesame Street" has been a staple of children's television for more than 20 years and is seen in more than 40 countries worldwide (Liebert & Sprafkin, 1988). Its intended audience was children from disadvantaged homes, with the goal of minimizing the gap in cognitive performance between advantaged and less advantaged preschool children. Its popularity has been enormous among children of all socioeconomic groups, and it is now viewed regularly by nearly 6 million American preschoolers.

Early studies that evaluated the effects of "Sesame Street" were impressive. During the first season of "Sesame Street," Samuel Ball and Gerry Ann Bogatz (1970) assessed preschool children's basic cognitive skills (including knowledge of letters, numbers, and geometric forms) prior to watching the program. Some children were then encouraged to watch "Sesame Street," whereas others were not. Ball and

Bogatz then divided children into four groups, based on the amount of time they had watched the program, and retested them. It was clear that watching "Sesame Street" had had the desired effect: the amount of cognitive gain children showed was directly related to how much they had watched the show (see Figure 8.2).

A recent study has investigated the effect of watching "Sesame Street" on children's vocabulary development (Rice, Huston, Truglio, & Wright, 1990).

Box 8.1

I Watch, Therefore I Know

The first-grade class was getting fidgety. There were a few minutes left before the bell rang, so the teacher decided to fill the time with some entertainment. "Can anyone sing a song for us?" she asked, and several children gave renditions of their favorite tunes. "Can anyone dance?" she asked. Young David felt that this was his time to shine. "I can tap-dance!" he answered. He walked to the front of the room and proceeded to shuffle his feet, trying his best to imitate the dancers he had seen on TV. Well, the result was entertainment, but strictly comedy. His classmates roared with laughter, and even his teacher was unable to hide her amusement. Fortunately, the bell rang soon and the children lined up to go home, so David's stint in the spotlight was short-lived.

Looking back on that experience years later, an older and wiser David doesn't remember feeling particularly embarrassed, only surprised. He had seen dancers many times on TV and in the movies; as far as he was concerned, he was ready to dance. He couldn't understand what had gone wrong. Discouraged, he put aside his plans to be a star and became just another developmental psychologist.

David's experience as a first-grader is a common one. Most young children believe they are capable of doing many complex activities that their parents realize take more maturity, practice, and talent than they have at their tender years. And, in many cases, when children attempt these activities, they are not aware that they have missed the mark.

A good example of this mismatched thinking is the toddler who spreads a mixture of scouring powder and water all over the bathroom floor and proudly announces "All clean!" Although his par-

ents' initial reaction may be shock, a moment of thought should tell them that he truly believes his statement. After all, he has seen his elders clean the bathroom, he knows where the scouring powder is, and he even knows you need to add water. What he doesn't understand is that *doing* takes more than just *knowing*. And to further complicate things, he doesn't understand that his finished product is different from the sparkling clean bathroom Mommy and Daddy produce.

Children are the Monday morning quarterbacks of the world. Just as the TV fan *knows* how the football game should be played, children *know* how to play musical instruments, cook complex meals, and sail windsurfers—if only their parents would give them the chance. What these children haven't learned yet is that there is a distinction between knowing about something and actually being able to do it. They don't understand the difference between identifying a set of actions ("Look, that's tap-dancing!") and producing those actions themselves (shuffle, stumble, shuffle).

What these observations imply is that young children are often not in touch with what they know. They may be able to recognize a skilled behavior and understand what actions constitute that behavior. However, they are not cognizant of their own abilities, and, when they try to imitate, are often unaware that their attempt was unsuccessful. These skills do improve with age, but preschool children's optimism about their own abilities is often refreshing—even if they require careful watching to make sure they don't jump behind the wheel of the family car and decide they know how to drive.

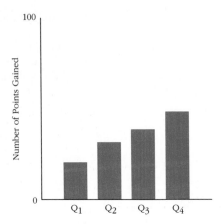

Figure 8.2 Relationship between time spent watching "Sesame Street" and improvement in cognitive skills. Children were divided into four groups, or quartiles, with children in Q_1 watching the least and children in Q_4 watching the most. *Source:* Adapted from *The First Year of Sesame Street: An Evaluation,* by S. Ball and G. Bogatz. Copyright © 1970 Educational Testing Services. Reprinted by permission.

Children ages 3 to 5 and 5 to 7 were observed for two years, and changes in their vocabulary were related to their TV viewing habits. It was found that "Sesame Street" had a positive effect on the vocabulary development of 3- to 5-year-old children, with lesser benefits for children older than 5. Other types of children's programs, such as cartoons, had no influence on the vocabulary of children of any age. These findings indicate that the program format of "Sesame Street" is well suited for preschool children's vocabulary development.

The "Sesame Street" generation   Television has been an everyday part of family life for the past 35 years. Many social critics blame television for the downslide in American children's school performance. Even "Sesame Street" has been criticized for shortening children's attention spans and making classroom learning seem boring by comparison to its rapid-fire visual format (Cook, Appelton, Conner, Shaffer, Tabkin, & Weber, 1975). It is widely believed that children's comprehension of television is fragmented and passive, promoting a passive attitude to

thinking in general (Lesser, 1977; Singer, 1980). A number of authors have suggested that the more television children watch, the poorer their school performance is. However, Daniel Anderson and Patricia Collins (1988), in reviewing the research evidence on the relationship between TV viewing and academic performance, found little evidence to support this assertion. They concluded that the impact of television is very small, particularly when children's IQs are considered, and that even for children most affected by television (those in low ability groups), the effects are small and sometimes nonexistent. They conclude that "the most likely effects on schooling come directly from the central content of television programming most watched by children" (p. 70) and believe that television can have a major impact on what children know (that is, their knowledge base).

TV *and advertising*   Although most of us may believe that the purpose of television is to entertain and inform, the essential purpose of commercial TV is to sell advertising. Advertisers pay for shows in the hope that millions of people will watch the program and, as a result, buy their products. As adults, we are aware of the purpose of commercials and, hopefully, can evaluate the merit of the products being sold. But how do children perceive commercials, and how do commercials influence children as consumers?

Even preschoolers can generally tell the difference between the "program" and the "commercial" (Levin, Petros, & Petrella, 1982). Younger children are more apt than older children to believe that commercials always tell the truth, but a majority of 5-year-olds do not believe that commercials are always truthful (Ward, Reale, & Levinson, 1972).

A number of studies have demonstrated that watching commercial television does influence children as consumers (see Liebert & Sprafkin, 1988). In one interesting study, Joann Galst and Mary Alice White (1976) followed women and their 4-year-old children during a trip to the supermarket, recording purchase-influencing attempts—the number of times children attempted to influence a purchase. They reported that children made an average of 15 purchase-influencing attempts during a 30-minute shopping trip (one purchase-influencing attempt every 2 minutes). Although many of the items children requested were things their mothers usually bought (for example, pasta, detergent), 36% were items that can best be described as junk food (for example, candy, sugared cereal, potato chips). On average, mothers bought 45% of the things their children requested. Relating children's supermarket behavior to their TV viewing, these researchers found that children who watched more commercial television made a significantly greater number of purchase-influencing attempts. This study clearly demonstrates that young children do have an influ-

Box 8.2

Family Television Viewing: Toward a Clearer Picture

Television bashing seems to have become a favorite child-rearing topic lately. While we have always urged parents not to let television viewing interfere with other important aspects of family life, we think a few words in its defense are in order.

Television Gives Children Firsthand Knowledge of a Larger World

Parents who do not allow their children to watch television are doing them a disservice. Because of it, our children's understanding of the world around them is light-years ahead of pre-TV generations. Thanks to television, our children have firsthand knowledge of the four corners of the world, they have seen and listened to major world leaders and experts in every field, and they have attended "live" historical events such as presidential inaugurations, congressional sessions, and space shuttle launches.

Not only does television aid our children's understanding of places and events, it also expands their social and cultural worlds. With television, a child on a farm can see how people live in urban areas, and an only child can get a taste of what it is like to live in a large family. When children learn about diversity, it helps them develop a deeper understanding of others and of themselves.

Television Does Not Cause Poor School Performance

Many people blame television for their children's poor grades and study habits. Although it is true that many children spend too much time watching TV, it is not realistic to think that they would fill those hours otherwise with school-related, intellectual activities. Several decades of research has failed to show that television viewing takes the place of learning activities. Instead, studies show that if children were not watching TV, they would be attending movies, listening to the radio, reading comic books, or playing organized sports. Parents need to do more than simply turn off the TV set if they want their children's school performance to improve. They have to take responsibility for filling the void with enriching activities.

Television Is a Stress Reducer

Television viewing often serves an important role as a stress reducer. We know of bright, talented children who routinely flop in front of the TV after school and half-watch, half-sleep for an hour or so every afternoon before getting on with their after-school music lessons, sports practices, and homework. This can be very upsetting to parents, especially if they have planned some interesting after-school activity or haven't seen their child in a few days. Parents need to reflect a few moments on their own schedules and how they feel when they come home from a hard day and want to unwind with a warm bath or cold drink. As long as their children seem happy and relaxed once they unwind, and the programs they watch are not inappropriate for their age, understanding parents will probably decide to back off and not add to the stress by nagging.

In the final analysis, television is like any other form of technology: its value depends on how it is used. Though there is no pride in having children who are couch potatoes, wise and thoughtful parents can use TV as a useful child-rearing tool.

Adapted from D. F. Bjorklund and B. R. Bjorklund. (November 1989). Kids and TV. *Parents Magazine*, Vol. 64, No. 11.

Some studies have focused on how TV commercials influence children's requests in the supermarket.

ence on what is bought at the supermarket and that commercial television does affect children as consumers.

Strategies

Much of cognition is automatic, in that it is done without a person's awareness. We are not conscious of the mental gymnastics that must be done to read the words on this page or identify the noise outside the window as the barking of our neighbor's St. Bernard. But much of what we consider "thinking" does have a significant conscious and intentional component to it. We actively try to remember a phone number, figure out which can of deodorant is the best buy, or solve the problem of how to store our jumbled spices on the kitchen shelves.

Most contemporary theories of cognition assume that we have a limited capacity for thinking—a finite amount of mental resources. We can only think about one thing at a time, and many of our mental operations are effortful, in that they consume a portion of these resources, leaving less behind for other aspects of thinking (Atkinson & Shiffrin, 1971; Hasher & Zacks, 1979; Shiffrin & Schneider, 1977). But the effort is usually well worth the mental cost

because using a deliberate process, or strategy, typically results in better thinking. **Strategies** are generally defined as goal-directed mental operations, used to facilitate task performance, that are deliberately implemented and potentially available to consciousness (Harnishfeger & Bjorklund, 1990). According to some theorists, age differences in strategy use—more than any other single factor—are responsible for age differences in thinking (see Bjorklund, 1990).

Even infants seem to show some signs of strategic, goal-directed behavior, as they search for missing toys or try to make their way around obstacles (Willatts, 1990). But the strategies of the infant and young child are ineffective compared to the strategies of older children and adults. In fact, a popular view in cognitive development during the 1960s and 1970s was that young children did not use strategies, at least not of their own accord. Research from a variety of perspectives demonstrated substantial changes in strategy use between 5 and 7 years of age (see Gholson, 1980; Gholson & Danziger, 1975; Kendler & Kendler, 1962), with preschool children seen as approaching memory and problem-solving tasks without a conscious plan of attack and without using any of the mental techniques that older children used, such as rehearsal. Most of these nonstrategic children could be easily trained to use simple strategies, and this resulted in improvements in their performance. This observation led John Flavell (1970) to describe young children as having a **production deficiency**—the ability to use a strategy but failure to produce one spontaneously. In contrast, children who showed a **mediation deficiency** (Reese, 1962) could not use a strategy even if it was demonstrated to them. (For a review of the history of research on strategy development, see Harnishfeger & Bjorklund, 1990.)

Today it is recognized that even young children use strategies, although the strategies of the young child may differ considerably from those used by older children (see Bjorklund, 1990; Wellman,

1988). Patricia Miller (1990) has identified a third "deficiency," which she calls a **utilization deficiency,** meaning that children are able to use a strategy but the strategy doesn't help them much. For example, in a study by Lynn Baker-Ward, Peter Ornstein, and Debra Holden (1984), 4-year-olds used the same strategy as 6-year-olds on a memory task, which was to organize pictures according to category (for example, putting pictures of animals in one pile and pictures of tools in another). However, the 4-year-olds didn't improve their memories as a result of using the strategy; only the 6-year-olds who used the strategy showed any benefit.

One explanation for utilization deficiencies involves the effortful nature of strategies. Strategies

Box 8.3

Children Tell Us about Their Strategies

Question: When you have to learn something for school, like spelling words, a part in a play, or things for a social studies test, what are some of the things you do to help you learn and remember?

"I think."—*Nicholas, age 5*

"Think. I remember it in my brain. I put it in the back of my brain and when I have to remember it, I bring it back to the front of my brain."—*Scott, age 6*

"We had to learn how to count money and it was very difficult. I told my mom and dad to get out some change, and they helped me count it. Then they gave me kind of like tests to see how much I learned before I had to do it at school."—*Lynsey, age 7*

"I try not to think about anything else except what I'm reading. For spelling, I keep reading things over and over and over again. I look at the words and see what places they are in and then I remember them. When we have a play, usually I highlight the parts I need to learn, then I read them a lot."—*Tracy, age 9*

"For spelling, I practice some of the hard words."—*Rhondine, age 9*

"Mom and Dad ask me the [spelling] words, and if I get them wrong, I write them 10 times. We do it again, and I write the wrong ones 20 times. That goes on until 50, then we go by 5s"—*Harris, age 10*

Question: If your friend tells you his new phone number when you're at school on the playground, and you have no pencil so you can't write it down, how would you remember it so that you could call him that night?

"I'd think hard. Then I'd ask him again."—*Bennet, age 5*

"Think inside my mind."—*Brian, age 6*

"I'd ride home with him [his friend] and ask him to say it over and over so I could write it down when I got home."—*Michael, age 6*

"I'd try real hard to remember it. I'd remember the first couple of numbers and hope the rest comes back to me."—*Katie, age 7*

"I'd keep saying it over and over."—*Sammie, age 8*

"I'd think of a beat to their phone number—like a rap song."—*Nichole, age 8*

"I'd remember it somehow—just automatically."—*Adam, age 8*

"I'd ask their dad's name and go home and look it up in the telephone directory."—*Maggie, age 9*

"I'd get a friend to memorize half of it."—*Ricky, age 9*

use up a child's limited mental resources, and young children use their resources less efficiently than older children. That is, strategies have a cost in terms of mental effort, and young children exert so much mental effort carrying out the strategy that they do not have enough left to perform other aspects of the task effectively, such as remembering (Bjorklund & Harnishfeger, 1987; Guttentag, 1984; Kee & Davies, 1988).

Researchers have proposed that developmental differences in the efficiency of processing are due to both maturation and experience (Bjorklund & Harnishfeger, 1990; Case, 1985; Dempster, 1985). With age, children process information faster (Kail, 1988), and faster processing translates into more efficient processing. Speed and efficiency of processing can also be aided by experience. Children who have more experience with a particular task or have more knowledge about a particular subject will process related information faster than less experienced children. Thus, for example, a young child who knows a great deal about baseball will be better able to deal with cognitive problems involving baseball knowledge than an older child who knows less about the sport. The effective use of strategies, then, is closely related to how quickly and efficiently children are able to process information.

The development of strategies is central to information-processing approaches to cognitive development. Children's use of strategies is related to how quickly they can process information and the amount and nature of the knowledge they possess, among other factors. In the sections that follow, it will become increasingly clear how much strategies contribute to differences in cognitive development, and how factors such as efficiency of processing and a child's knowledge base influence children's strategic approaches to problems.

Memory

A 10-month-old finds her bottle that seconds earlier was hidden behind a pillow on the couch; a 16-month-old sees a yardstick, stands against the kitchen door where "grow marks" from months past have been made, and places the yardstick above his head; a second-grader recites the names of her classmates to her mother while preparing Valentine's Day cards; a high school sophomore reviews the major battles of the Civil War while studying for an exam. Each of these acts has a common component: memory. Each young person retrieves previously stored information—the location of a bottle, the sequence of a family routine, a class roster, or the content of a history lecture—to achieve a specific goal.

Memory plays a central role in thinking. We believe that it is safe to say that no complex cognitive task, and few simple ones, can be executed without involving memory. However, the act of remembering is also influenced by simpler cognitive operations, such as directing one's attention and storing information efficiently. Thus, memory represents a central stage around which both simple and complex processes revolve.

The Development of Memory in Children

Recognition versus recall Recognition is the simplest form of remembering. When we recognize something, we realize that what we are experiencing now is the same as something we have experienced before. This is the type of memory that young babies show when they display dishabituation, responding differently to a new picture after seeing the same one over and over (see Chapter 6). Recognition requires relatively little mental effort. A stimulus, such as a song heard on the radio, either matches something one has heard before—or it doesn't.

A more demanding form of remembering is recall. Unlike recognition, where a stimulus is presented and the person must simply state whether it has been experienced previously or not, recall involves the active retrieval of information. Who was the third president of the United States? How many chromosomes does a normal human have? Who are all the cousins on your father's side of the family? What are you supposed to buy at the grocery store for the big party this weekend? The retrieval question, or cue, can help a person focus on the right information. If you were cued, for example, by being reminded of the names of your father's brothers and sisters or that the big weekend party was to be a barbecue, you might have an easier time remembering the desired information.

Recognition memory is usually easier than recall memory, with **cued recall** falling somewhere between recognition and **free recall** (recall without specific prompts). A similar picture emerges when we look at development. Children's recognition memory is relatively good, and age differences are often quite small (Brown & Scott, 1971; Daehler & Bukatko, 1977). When recall is required, however, age differences are larger. In general, the ability to recall information increases with age, and as they get older children require fewer prompts to produce successful memory performance (Bjorklund & Muir, 1988; Schneider & Pressley, 1989).

The distinction between cued recall and free recall in young children can be appreciated when one attempts to get information from a young child. A question such as "How was school today?" is apt to bring a response of "Fine." More detailed information may be forthcoming, however, if more specific questions are asked. For example, a 5-year-old boy who had spent the afternoon with his grandparents seeing his first play, *The Little Shop of Horrors,* was asked by his mother, "Well, how was your afternoon?" The child replied "OK." The mother persisted, "Well, did you have a good time?" The child said "Yeah." However, when prompted by his grandmother—"Tell your mother about Audrey II, the plant"—he provided copious details, telling how the plant ate some of the main characters, talked, sang, and how it took three people underneath it to make it move. The child had a wealth of information, but it could only be accessed when specific cues were provided. (For experimental confirmation of this, see Kobasigawa, 1974.)

Recall memory in infancy   Recognition memory in infants has been demonstrated using the habituation/dishabituation paradigm (see Chapter 6). The presence of recall memory in infants is much more controversial. Because infants can't use words, recall is more difficult to test.

One technique that taps recall memory in young infants was developed by Carolyn Rovee-Collier and her colleagues (Rovee-Collier & Fagen, 1981). In their procedure, a ribbon is tied to an infant's ankle and connected to a mobile in clear view over the crib. Infants quickly learn that when they kick their feet the mobile moves, and they soon kick repeatedly to make this happen. Later, Rovee-Collier and her colleagues placed these infants in the same situation to see if they could recall the actions necessary

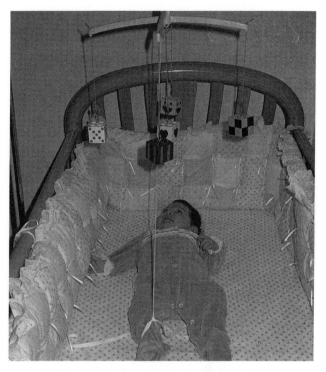

Researchers have used procedures such as this to demonstrate recall memory in infants as young as two weeks.

to make the mobile move. They found that 3-month-olds showed recall for a period of up to eight days after the initial training experience (Sullivan, Rovee-Collier, & Tynes, 1979), and that 6-month-old infants could recall the appropriate actions for up to three weeks under some conditions (Hill, Borovsky, & Rovee-Collier, 1988). They also found that infants as young as 8 weeks old showed recall for two weeks under optimal conditions (Vander Linde, Morrongiello, & Rovee-Collier, 1985).

Another research method that recently has been used to evaluate infant recall is that of search. Infants are shown objects, and then those objects are moved or hidden. The researchers then watch the infants as they search for the "lost" objects. This form of recall not only can be assessed experimentally in the laboratory but can also be observed in everyday life. For example, Daniel Ashmead and Marion Perlmutter (1980) asked parents to keep a diary of their infants' memory activities in the home. Nearly one-

Children show recall memory when they search for a lost object.

fourth of all activities reported by parents involved memory for the location of an object or person. An impressive example of recall via search in an 11-month-old infant is reflected in the following observation:

> Louise had been playing with a small doll bottle. She let it go on the floor and it rolled partially under the refrigerator. She went in her room and was playing for 15 to 20 minutes when she found her doll and went back to where she had left her bottle, picked it up, and went back to her room. (p. 8)

Recall from infancy and early childhood   We received a letter from a woman not too long ago who was worried because her 10-year-old son could remember very little from his preschool days. She said that she and her husband had always tried to be good parents but thought that her son's inability to remember things from early childhood was an indication that either they hadn't done a very good job after all, or they had done a truly terrible job and her son was repressing this painful period of his life. We wrote back to the woman, assuring her that her son's inability to remember events much before his

fourth birthday is quite normal, and that just because her child can't remember his experiences from this age doesn't mean that they didn't have an effect on him. Being unable to recall childhood events is not an indication that those events were unimportant to the individual.

The longer the delay between experiencing an event and recalling it, the less likely we are to remember it correctly, if at all; this is best illustrated by our general inability to remember events from infancy and early childhood (Cowan & Davidson, 1984; Sheingold & Tenney, 1982). In fact, when we do have memories of such long ago events, they are often not accurate—or not ours (see Box 8.4).

This inability to remember events from infancy and early childhood has been labeled **infantile amnesia.** There have been a number of hypotheses concerning why our recall of events from the early years of our life is so poor, including Freud's idea that the events of infancy are so painful that we actively repress them (see Spear, 1984; White & Pillemer, 1979). The most reasonable hypothesis, we believe, is that information is represented differently by very young children than it is by older children and adults. This perspective is consistent with the views of stage theorists such as Piaget, who contended that the *nature* of representation changes over childhood. The minds that reside in our heads *now* interpret information differently than did the minds that experienced the world when we were infants and toddlers. Recalling events today that were coded years ago in terms of physical action or pure sensation is an impossible task because today's mind uses symbol-based information processing. And even if we were able to retrieve a memory encoded in infancy, we would probably not be able to understand it.

Memory span   Most theories of memory make a distinction between short-term and long-term stores. The long-term store is our repository of memories. Presumably, it can hold an infinite amount of information for an infinite amount of time, although forgetting does occur. The short-term store, on the other hand, can only hold a limited amount of information (in adults, 7 ± 2 items) for a matter of seconds. The short-term store has also been referred to as primary memory, working memory, and the contents of consciousness. It is in the short-term store that information is consciously evaluated. The short-term store is where we live, cognitively speaking.

One issue that has concerned developmental psychologists is age differences in the capacity of the short-term store. Can older children hold more information in consciousness at any one time than younger children? Early research found what appeared to be substantial and regular age differences, based on memory-span tasks. *Memory span* refers to the number of items one can recall perfectly after only a brief exposure (for example, hearing one item per second). Memory span for digits (digit span) is commonly used on tests of intelligence and shows very regular developmental changes. Figure

Box 8.4

Memories from Infancy

I have one vivid memory from my infancy. We were living at my grandparents' house, and I had the croup (I think it's called bronchitis today). My crib was covered by a sheet, but I remember looking past the bars into the living room. I can hear the whir of the vaporizer, feel the constriction in my chest, and smell the Vicks Vaporub. To this day the smell of Vicks makes my chest tighten. I can claim no other memories until close to my third birthday, and they are not as real for me as this memory is.

Some years back, I related this memory to my mother. "David," she said, "you were such a healthy baby. You never had the croup. That was your brother, Dick. You were almost three years old then."

The fact that my earliest memory is of an event that never happened doesn't make it any less real for me. The feelings it invokes are intense, and knowing that they didn't happen, at least not to me, does not lessen their impact. It's still *my* infant memory. It's just that the infant was my younger brother, and I was only an observer.

Few of us have memories from our infancy, and for those of us who do, most can be explained as mine was. It's not a memory *of* infancy but a memory *about* infancy. In my case, it wasn't even a memory about *my* infancy, but rather about my brother's.

Maybe we can't unlock these infant memories under normal circumstances, but what about under special conditions, such as hypnosis? Many people under hypnotic spells claim accurate recollections of events that happened in infancy and before. I know people who claim vivid memories as a fetus, and we've all read about people who, under hypnosis, regress to earlier lives. Does recall under this special state prove that infant memories are really there, but just not available to our conscious minds? In all likelihood, no. Hypnosis is a state of extreme suggestibility, and, under the direction of a competent hypnotist, people often retrieve more detailed information than they would otherwise. However, recent research indicates that we invent as much when we remember the past under hypnosis as we do normally. For example, Jane Dywan and Kenneth Bowers of the University of Wa-terloo have shown that hypnotized people recall more false memories as well as true memories than do non-hypnotized people. We may be able to retrieve memories from infancy under hypnosis, and they may seem very real and often emotionally intense. However, there is no good evidence that these memories are any more real than my recollection of having the croup.

Recalling events from the past, even the recent past, is not easily done, at least not when we try to be precise. Some of our best memories may never have happened to us, at least not the way we remember them. Nonetheless, these memories are important. What we recall of our childhood colors our perceptions of that time and influences how we interpret the present and anticipate the future. However, many of these memories are reconstructions of what *should* have happened rather than what actually occurred, or are influenced by what happened months or years after the "remembered" event.

Adapted from D. F. Bjorklund. (June 1986). What Children Remember. *Parents Magazine*. Vol. 61, No. 6.

Few of us, even school-age children, remember further back than age three. *Source:* CALVIN & HOBBES. Copyright 1989 Universal Press Syndicate. Reprinted with permission. All rights reserved.

8.3 shows the highly predictable growth of digit-span ability from age 2 years through adulthood.

Despite these impressive and robust findings, more recent research has seriously questioned the idea that the capacity of the short-term store increases with age. For example, in one often-cited study, a group of graduate students at the University of Pittsburgh were given two simple memory tests. On one, they were read a series of numbers quickly (about one per second) and asked to recall them immediately in exact order. On a second test, they were shown briefly chess pieces on a chess board (again, about one chess piece per second), then given the pieces and asked to place them at their previous positions on the board. Their performance on these tasks was compared to that of a group of 10-year-olds. But, in all fairness, these were not typical 10-year-olds; they were all chess experts—winners of local tournaments or members of chess clubs. When memory for the chess positions was tested, the children outperformed the adults. This finding was probably not surprising, given the expert status of the children. But the critical question was: how would they do when remembering the numbers? Does being a chess expert cause one's memory capabilities to improve overall, or was the children's remarkable performance limited to what they knew best? The results support the latter interpretation. The adults, despite being outdone by the children when memory for chess positions was tested, were superior to the children when the test stimuli were numbers. The results of this experi-

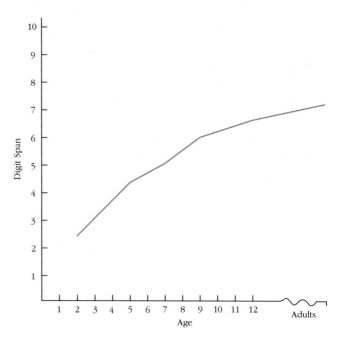

Figure 8.3 Children's digit span shows regular increases with age. *Source:* From "Memory Span: Sources of Individual and Development Differences," by F. N. Dempster, *Psychological Bulletin,* 1981, *89,* 63–100. Copyright 1981 by the American Psychological Association. Reprinted by permission.

School children can have longer memory spans than adults, depending on the information they are asked to remember.

ment, conducted by Michelene Chi (1978), can be seen in Figure 8.4.

What results such as these indicate is that children's short-term memory is not fixed but flexible. Under certain conditions, they can remember things as well as adults; in other situations, however, they act like kids. What this suggests is that the capacity of children's and adults' short-term stores is comparable; adults just make better use of it than do children (usually).

The Development of Memory Strategies

Psychologists have hypothesized that the well-established age differences in free recall, cited previously, can be accounted for by age-related differences in the use of **memory strategies,** or **mnemonics.** In fact, many researchers consider the development of memory to be synonymous with the development of memory strategies (Howe & O'Sullivan, 1990). Two of the most-investigated

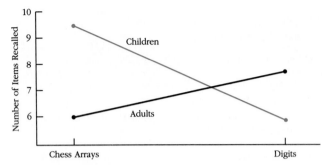

Figure 8.4 Average memory span for digits and chess arrays by chess-expert children and college-educated adults. *Source:* Adapted from "Knowledge Structure and Memory Development," by M. T. H. Chi. In R. Siegler (ed.), *Children's Thinking: What Develops?* Copyright © 1978 by Lawrence Erlbaum Associates, Inc. Reprinted by permission.

memory strategies in developmental psychology are **rehearsal,** in which a child repeats the target information, and **organization,** in which the child clusters together items into categories, themes, or other units.

Rehearsal In most studies of rehearsal, children are given sets of words or pictures to remember and then given the opportunity to practice or rehearse. Early studies found that older children rehearsed more than younger children and that, within an age group, how much children rehearsed was related to how much they remembered (Flavell, Beach, & Chinsky, 1966). Such findings led John Flavell and his colleagues to conclude that rehearsal is a powerful mnemonic that increases with age and that frequency of rehearsal (the absolute number of times one rehearses a word) determines level of memory performance (Flavell, 1970; Flavell et al., 1966).

Later research by Peter Ornstein, Mary Naus, and their colleagues (Ornstein & Naus, 1978; Ornstein, Naus, & Liberty, 1975; Ornstein, Naus, & Stone, 1977) questioned Flavell's frequency interpretation. In one study (Ornstein et al., 1975), they used an overt rehearsal procedure with children in grades 3, 6, and 8. In this procedure, children are presented a series of words to recall, with several seconds between the presentation of successive words. During this interval, children are told that they must repeat

out loud the most recently presented word at least once and, if they wish, they may practice any other words they like. Thus, rehearsal is made obligatory (they *must* rehearse each word at least once), and the experimenters are able to determine exactly what the children are doing.

Using this procedure, Ornstein and his colleagues found no differences in the frequency of rehearsal across the three grade levels, although recall still improved with age, a perplexing finding given the interpretation of the earlier study by Flavell et al. What they did find, however, were differences in the quality or style of rehearsal. Typical rehearsal techniques of a third-grade versus an eighth-grade child are shown in Table 8.1. Although the number of words rehearsed is similar for the two children, the style of rehearsing is very different. The younger child used a passive rehearsal style, repeating only the most recent word and possibly one other. In contrast, the older child used an active, or cumulative rehearsal style, repeating the most recent word and then rehearsing it together with previous words. From these and other data, Ornstein and his colleagues concluded that the important developmental changes in recall are in style rather than frequency of rehearsal (see also Cuvo, 1975; Kellas, McCauley, & McFarland, 1975).

Children can be trained to use this active rehearsal strategy, and their recall performance improves as a result, although age differences are rarely eliminated (Keeney, Cannizo, & Flavell, 1967; Kingsley & Hagen, 1969; Ornstein et al., 1977). What

Table 8.1 Typical rehearsal protocols for eighth-grade versus third-grade child

Word Presented	Rehearsal Sets	
	Eighth-Grade Subject	*Third-Grade Subject*
1. Yard	Yard, yard, yard	Yard, yard, yard, yard, yard
2. Cat	Cat, yard, yard, cat	Cat, cat, cat, cat, yard
3. Man	Man, cat, yard, man, yard, cat	Man, man, man, man, man
4. Desk	Desk, man, yard, cat, man, desk, cat, yard	Desk, desk, desk, desk

Source: From "Rehearsal and Organizational Processes in Children's Memory," by P. A. Ornstein, M. J. Naus, and C. Liberty, *Child Development,* 1975, *46,* 818–830. Copyright © The Society for Research in Child Development, Inc. Reprinted by permission.

changes in development is not children's ability to use a strategy, but their willingness to do so on their own. It is from findings such as these that John Flavell (1970) developed the idea of production deficiencies, discussed earlier in this chapter. Children have available to them techniques to improve their performance but fail to use those techniques when it would be beneficial to do so.

Organization One reason that active rehearsal may benefit memory is that organization among items—that is, relations in meaning—is noticed when items are rehearsed together (Ornstein & Naus, 1978). Organization in memory refers to the structure discovered or imposed upon a set of items that is used to guide subsequent memory performance. For example, in attempting to remember what items to buy at the grocery store, organizing the information by food categories (dairy products, meats, vegetables) or meals (Saturday's barbecue, Sunday's pot roast dinner) will help.

In a typical study of organization and recall, children are read a randomly ordered list of items that can be grouped into categories (for example, furniture, tools, and fruits). When children recall the information later, will they remember items from the same category together even though they were not originally presented together? Recalling items from the same category together has been referred to as **clustering,** and adults who display high levels of clustering in their recall typically remember more than those who display lower levels of clustering (G. H. Bower, 1970; Mandler, 1967). Developmentally, levels of recall and clustering usually increase with age, with preschool children's clustering often being at chance levels (Arlin & Brody, 1976; Furth & Milgram, 1973). Examples of recall responses of 5-, 9-, and 14-year-olds in a clustering experiment are shown in Table 8.2.

Organization in memory can be measured more directly by means of a sort/recall task, giving children the opportunity to sort items together into groups prior to recall. For example, Harriet Salatas and John Flavell (1976) gave first-graders a set of cards with 16 pictures, four each from four different categories. Children were told that they would be asked to remember the pictures later on, and that they should put them together in a way that would help them recall the pictures. Although these instructions would seem to bias children to organize

Table 8.2 Recall protocols for 5-, 9-, and 14-year-old children

Children were read 16 words, four words from each of four categories, in random order at a rate of one word every five seconds. After the last word had been read, children were asked to recall as many of the words as they could, in any order they wished.

Word list: dog, cat, horse, cow; table, chair, desk, couch; apple, grapes, peach, pear; gun, rifle, knife, sword

Age	Words Recalled	Recall Percentage	Clustering Score*
5	gun, knife, cow, peach, couch, cat	37.5%	.20
9	sword, rifle, apple, desk, dog, cat, cow, peach	50.0%	.43
14	horse, dog, cat, table, apple, peach, pear, desk, chair, gun, rifle	68.8%	.60

*Clustering is based on the formula $r/n - 1$ (Bousfield, 1953), where r corresponds to the number of word pairs recalled from the same category (for example, *horse, dog, cat* contains two pairs) and n corresponds to the total number of words remembered. This measure can range from 0 to 1.0.

the items by category, only 13 of 48 children (27%) did so to a significant degree. Other sort/recall studies, using similar instructions, have shown that children as old as 8 years often fail to organize items on the basis of meaning, placing items into groups randomly instead. Older children are more apt to group items on the basis of meaning and, as a result, show higher levels of recall (Best & Ornstein, 1986; Bjorklund, Ornstein, & Haig, 1977; Corsale & Ornstein, 1980). Yet when the instructions are changed slightly, stressing to children that they should group items on the basis of *meaning,* even preschoolers comply and demonstrate enhanced levels of memory performance (Corsale & Ornstein, 1980; Lange & Jackson, 1974; Sodian, Schneider, & Perlmutter, 1986). Clearly, these young children are capable of using the strategy; they just don't do it unless explicitly told to do so. As with rehearsal, training children to use an organizational strategy rarely eliminates age differences, however, and under most conditions, young children fail to generalize the strategy to new situations or new sets of materials (Bjorklund et al., 1977; Cox & Waters, 1986).

Other strategies Related to organization is the strategy of **elaboration**—associating two or more items by creating a representation of those items together. For example, if you needed to remember to buy a carton of milk on your way home from work, you could generate an image of a cow sitting on the hood of your car, or form a verbal elaboration such as *car*ton, so that when you see your car you'll think of a carton of milk. In both cases, the sight of your car should elicit the thought of milk. Most developmental research examining elaboration has used paired-associate procedures, in which children are given pairs of words and then asked to recall one word when given its mate. Elaboration tends not to be used spontaneously until adolescence (Pressley & Levin, 1977; Rohwer, Raines, Eoff, & Wagner, 1977), although, as with other mnemonics, young children can be trained to use it (Pressley, 1982).

Even if children don't use complex memory strategies spontaneously, this doesn't mean that they don't have strategies of their own. Even preschool children use some less complex strategies, although they may not be as effective in influencing memory behavior as the aforementioned mnemonics (Bjorklund & Muir, 1988; Wellman, 1988). One very simple strategy involves just trying hard. Preschoolers believe that one of the best things they can do to aid memory is to concentrate and try hard (Wellman, 1988; Wellman, Collins, & Glieberman, 1981). A more sophisticated and effective strategy used by 3- and 4-year-olds involves "looking at it real hard"—selectively attending to the target items (Baker-Ward, Ornstein, & Holden, 1984; Yussen, 1974)—including frequent reattending to the stimuli, a form of visual rehearsal (Wellman, Ritter, & Flavell, 1975).

Assessing memory strategies in more naturalistic settings, Judith DeLoache, Ann Brown, and their colleagues (DeLoache, 1986; DeLoache & Brown, 1983; DeLoache, Cassidy, & Brown, 1985; DeLoache & Todd, 1988) have reported memory strategies in children as young as 18 months. The procedure involves a hide-and-seek game that takes place in a child's own home. A toy is hidden in one of several locations and, following delays of several minutes, the child is asked to retrieve it. DeLoache and Brown report that young children engage in mnemonic behavior during the delay periods, including looking or pointing at the hiding place and repeating the name of the toy.

Based on the findings of DeLoache, Brown, and others, it seems clear that preschool children engage in some strategic behavior related to memory (Wellman, Fabricius, & Sophian, 1985). These strategies are not as effective as the strategies used by older children and often do not aid memory performance at all. However, Henry Wellman (1988) asserts that preschoolers' strategies are every bit as goal-directed as those of older children and are used in a wide range of situations.

Knowledge Base and Memory Development

Memory strategies are mental operations we perform on specific pieces of information. Other research has focused on the importance of the specific information that children possess. When studying age differences in strategies and other mental operations, does it make a difference what information children have stored in their minds to work with? Some scientists think so, proposing that specific knowledge—the child's knowledge base—is probably responsible for most of the mental differences between a 3-year-old and an adult (Carey, 1985).

As we saw earlier in this chapter, children who are experts in a specific area, such as chess, have longer memory spans when they are tested on information from their area of expertise (Chi, 1978). Some researchers have suggested that developmental differences in free recall are due as much to knowledge base as they are to strategies (Bjorklund, 1985, 1987b; Rabinowitz & McAuley, 1990). For example, in studies where children are asked to recall the names of their current classmates, performance is better than when they are asked to remember the same number of categorizable words (Bjorklund & Zeman, 1982). In one study of class recall, children were asked to give the names of their classmates in a specific order (row by row, for example) (Bjorklund & Bjorklund, 1985). Nearly all children gave the names they recalled in perfect order, yet left out just as many names as did children who were allowed to recall them in any order they wished. Children in a free-recall group followed a variety of schemes, but few followed them as perfectly as the instructed children. In other words, the use of an imposed strategy did not buy these children anything in the way of greater memory performance.

In other situations, having detailed knowledge can facilitate the use of memory strategies. The relationship between knowledge and strategy use was demonstrated in a study by Mary Zembar and Mary

Naus (1985). These researchers asked third- and sixth-grade children to rehearse out loud sets of words in preparation for a memory test. They varied the lists according to children's familiarity with the words, using a standard list (for example, *fern, astronaut, taco*), an easy list (for example, *shoe, doll, milk*), and a difficult list (for example, *limpet, galleon, rapier*). For the standard list, they found the usual: older children did better than younger in levels of recall and style of rehearsal. However, these differences were eliminated when the third-graders were given the easy list and the sixth-graders were given the difficult list. In effect, the memory ability of older children reverted back to that of younger children when they were asked to remember unfamiliar words (see Bjorklund & Muir, 1988; Folds, Footo, Guttentag, & Ornstein, 1990; Ornstein, Baker-Ward, & Naus, 1988).

When children are highly knowledgeable about a topic—whether chess, their classmates, or words—they are able to learn and remember information about that topic very well. In most situations, older children have more knowledge than younger children, and this could be the major reason for their superior memories and problem-solving abilities.

Why should having detailed knowledge about a subject result in improved memory performance? David Bjorklund and his colleagues have proposed that the better established information is in one's mind, the more easily it can be activated, bringing that information to consciousness (Bjorklund, 1987b; Bjorklund, Muir-Broaddus, & Schneider, 1990; see also Kee & Davies, 1990). Because older children usually know more than younger children about things in general, they require less in the way of mental effort to activate common word meanings, leaving them with more mental space or mental energy to spend on the recall of additional words or on other cognitive operations.

Knowledge plays a substantial role not only in memory, but in most other aspects of cognitive development as well. For example, as we'll show in the next chapter, reading comprehension is greatly affected by how much a child knows about the topic being read. Knowledge also plays a role in how successfully we communicate in our day-to-day lives. E. D. Hirsch (1987) has proposed that children (and adults) in modern American society lack the necessary knowledge base (what he refers to as "cultural literacy") to communicate effectively with one another. The role of knowledge in communication has important implications for education (see Box 8.5).

Children's Number and Arithmetic Concepts

Children begin learning arithmetic in kindergarten or the first grade. Before children can learn to add and subtract, however, they must first develop a basic concept of number, including conservation of number and counting.

Conservation of Number

Piaget (1965a) believed that the concept of number is reflected in conservation. Conservation-of-number tasks follow the same basic procedures as all of Piaget's conservation problems (see Chapter 7). Children are first shown a set of items—black jelly beans, for instance. They are then asked to select white jelly beans from a container until there are the same number of black and white jelly beans. Once the appropriate number of white jelly beans has been selected, the black and white jelly beans are arranged in two rows—one black bean for every white bean (see Figure 8.5). While the child watches, the experimenter then spreads out the line of white jelly beans so that it is longer than the line of black beans. Children are then asked if the two rows still have the same number of jelly beans. If children answer no, they are asked which row has more and why.

As with conservation in general, Piaget proposed three stages in acquiring conservation of number. In stage 1, children are unable to establish consistently a one-to-one correspondence between the two sets of items. In this example, stage 1 children would select too few or too many white jelly beans, or fail to arrange them in a one-to-one relationship with the black jelly beans. When two equal sets of jelly beans are established and one is made physically longer, stage 1 children will say that the longer, more widely spaced row now has more beans in it, being unable to ignore the perceptual differences between the two rows. In stage 2, children can establish an "intuitive one-to-one correspondence" between the

Box 8.5

Cultural Literacy: What Our Children Don't Know Can Hurt Them

Knowledge acquisition, which was the foundation of last generation's "little red schoolhouse," has fallen out of favor with this generation's educators. The specific content of lessons in social studies or literature, for example, are deemed of little significance. The emphasis today is on the teaching of specific skills—from the decoding of letters and words in the early grades to analytic reasoning in high school. As a result, over the past generation, our children's textbooks have included less and less of the information that is necessary for successful communication and that constitutes our unique heritage as Americans. Because of this, some believe that our children are heavy on skills and light on facts. It's as though we have taught them the latest techniques of tennis but forgot to provide them with tennis balls!

This situation was brought to public attention in a book titled *Cultural Literacy,* written by E. D. Hirsch, professor of English at the University of Virginia. In it, he examines the importance of being culturally literate—of having a broad background in the traditions, folklore, and history of American culture. Hirsch explains that effective communication requires a common knowledge on the part of all parties involved. Literate members of a society share a certain amount of relevant information, making it unnecessary for speakers to define precisely every term and phrase they use in order to be understood.

Hirsch has joined others who are alarmed at how little of the background necessary for cultural literacy young people seem to have today.

When the reports first surfaced, they were amusing—stories of high school and college students being unable to locate Cuba or the Soviet Union on a world map, of being unable to determine within 50 years when the American Civil War was fought, or of believing that people in Latin America speak Latin. But the reports became more numerous, and our initial amusement turned to embarrassment as evidence accumulated indicating that our young adults simply do not know many of the facts of history, geography, and literature that are central to our American heritage.

The More Children Know, the More They Can Learn

What's so important about knowing facts? Kids have enough to do without forcing them to learn long lists of presidents, state capitals, and dates. Information presented out of context is indeed dull and potentially an exercise in futility. We all recall memorizing long lists of facts for tests, only to forget them once the papers were handed in. However, when names, dates, and places are embedded in meaningful lessons, such information serves as the basis for later learning. The more children know, the more they *can* learn, because a child's prior knowledge provides the framework for gathering new information.

What Parents Can Do

The most important thing parents can do to foster cultural literacy in their children is simply to *talk* to them. Buying children fancy atlases and filling their bookshelves with the classics is no substitute for conversation. Dinner time provides a ready-made forum for topics of interest to all family members. What's new at work or at school? Did you hear about the family that just moved into the neighborhood? How are the Red Sox doing this year? Families that eat together talk together, and, assuming that dinner conversation goes beyond "pass the meat loaf," dinner time can be a great learning experience for both parents and children.

Another place where parent-child conversation can be readily practiced is the automobile. Children are a captive audience in the car, providing an excellent opportunity to share ideas. Forget the radio and just talk. Talk about what's important to your child, about what's important to you, about the weather, or about things you observe from the front seat of the car. Such conversations will not only give you the opportunity to impart important knowledge to your child, but will also help you get to know your child better.

Parents are limited in how much they can foster their children's intellectual development. Most thinking skills require a certain level of maturation and cannot (and, from our perspective, should not) be accelerated. Parents who are concerned about accelerating their child's educational progress could better spend their time enriching their child's cultural background rather than forcing skills that are too advanced for a child's cognitive maturity. Parents *can* have a major impact on their children's intelligence by presenting important facts in an interesting way and by fostering a love of learning.

Adapted from D. F. Bjorklund and B. R. Bjorklund. (September 1988). Babe Ruth Is Not a Candy Bar. *Parents Magazine,* Vol. 63, No. 6.

"Select from the jar the same number of white jelly beans as there are black jelly beans."

"Are there the same number of black jelly beans as there are white jelly beans?"

The row of white jelly beans is extended while the child watches.

"Are there now the same number of white jelly beans as there are black jelly beans? Which has more? Why?"

Figure 8.5 Conservation-of-number task

though performance deteriorated in the youngest children for arrays of six objects or greater. Children who counted items in arrays used a stable, repeatable order (that is, used the same number sequence each time they counted), with more than 90% of the 4- and 5-year-olds and 80% of the 3-year-olds using the same list of number words in the same order on all of their trials. Children sometimes used an idiosyncratic list of number words (for example, "one, two, six, eleventeen, twelveteen"), but they used this list consistently across arrays of varying size. Other researchers have shown that children are able to count (often accurately) before they can conserve, suggesting to some that learning to count is a necessary predecessor to conservation of number (Fuson, Secada, & Hall, 1983; Saxe, 1979). In summary, young children do possess limited knowledge about numbers and relations among numbers, but they are restricted to dealing with small quantities.

Children's Arithmetic Concepts

It's clear that preschool children have some concept of number; they can count and can determine which of two quantities is the larger. But when can children perform basic arithmetic tasks such as addition and subtraction? These skills are not formally taught un-

items in the two sets, but judgments of equivalence between the sets do not last long. In this example, they are able to select the right number of white jelly beans, but once that row is extended, they say that there are now more beans in the longer row. It is only the stage 3 child—corresponding to the period of concrete operations—who realizes that the number of jelly beans doesn't change when one of the rows is extended, but that changes in length of the row are compensated by equivalent changes in spacing of the jelly beans.

Children's Counting

There are a series of principles involved in counting, which gradually develop over the preschool years. For example, in one counting experiment (Gelman & Gallistel, 1978), 3-, 4-, and 5-year-old children were asked to tell the number of objects in a series of arrangements. All groups of children used one unique number name per object (for example, "four" was used to designate only one object), al-

The ability to count emerges gradually over the preschool years.

til the first grade in many schools. From a Piagetian perspective, they are skills that require concrete operational ability.

Piaget (1965a) proposed that addition and subtraction require inversion reversibility, something that is not achieved (according to Piaget) until about 7 years of age. For example, if 5 plus 3 equals 8, then, by the logical rule of inversion, 8 minus 3 must equal 5. According to Piaget, then, children should not be able to master arithmetic until they attain concrete operations, beginning around 7 years of age. More recent research, however, has shown that preschool children do add and subtract accurately, although they usually perform these operations "publicly," counting on their fingers or manipulating objects to arrive at an answer (Carpenter & Moser, 1982; Ginsberg, 1977).

Counting continues to be an effective way to add and subtract for children into the early school years, although different counting strategies are used. Perhaps the simplest strategy consists of counting from one to the first addend (in 3 + 5 = ?, the first addend is 3), then counting the second, then counting the two together (for example, "1, 2, 3 . . . 1, 2, 3, 4, 5, . . . 1, 2, 3, . . . 4, 5, 6, 7, 8"). This has been referred to as the **sum strategy,** and although it usually produces the correct answer, it takes a considerable amount of time to execute and is not very effective when large addends are involved (such as 23 + 5 = ?) (Baroody & Ginsburg, 1986; Siegler & Robinson, 1982).

A more sophisticated counting strategy develops in most children during the early school years. Now, instead of starting from 1 when faced with an addition problem, children start with the largest addend and count up from there. For example, given the problem 3 + 5 = ?, a child would start with 5, and count up three ("5 . . . 6, 7, 8"). This has been dubbed the **min strategy** because children count the minimum number of elements to arrive at an answer (Groen & Parkman, 1972; Groen & Resnick, 1977). By the second or third grade, many children no longer rely on overt counting methods but perform the calculations covertly, "in their heads."

With age and experience, children are able to use more sophisticated strategies to solve arithmetic problems. Counting-based procedures, such as the sum and min strategies, are replaced by **fact retrieval** strategies (Ashcraft, 1982, 1990; Ashcraft &

Fierman, 1982; Hamann & Ashcraft, 1985). For example, when given the problem 7 + 5 = ?, older children and adults need not start at 7 and mentally increment this by 5 to arrive at the answer. Rather, there resides in memory the knowledge that 7 + 5 = 12, and this fact can be retrieved just as any other fact in memory. Using patterns of reaction times (that is, how quickly they arrive at answers) to judge what strategies children of different ages are using on addition problems, Mark Ashcraft and Bennett Fierman (1982) concluded that by the fourth grade most children solve problems by retrieving facts directly from memory, just as adults do. Third-graders, however, were in a transitional stage, with about half the children solving problems via counting procedures and the remainder using fact retrieval. In general, with age and experience, more arithmetic facts become stored and can be accessed easily, without the need to execute effortful counting procedures.

The impression one may get from this research is of a steady improvement in arithmetic strategy use,

Table 8.3 Main arithmetic strategies used by children

Strategy	Typical Use of Strategy to Solve 3 + 5
Sum	Put up 3 fingers, put up 5 fingers, count fingers by saying "1,2,3,4,5,6,7,8."
Finger recognition	Put up 3 fingers, put up 5 fingers, say "8" without counting.
Short-cut sum	Say "1,2,3,4,5,6,7,8," perhaps simultaneously putting up one finger on each count.
Min	Say "5,6,7,8" or "6,7,8," perhaps simultaneously putting up one finger on each count beyond 5.
Count-from-first-addend	Say "3,4,5,6,7,8" or "4,5,6,7,8," perhaps simultaneously putting up one finger on each count.
Retrieval	Say an answer and explain it by saying "I just knew it."
Guessing	Say an answer and explain it by saying "I guessed."
Decomposition	Say "3 + 5 is like 4 + 4, so it's 8."

Source: From *How Children Discover Strategies,* by R. S. Siegler and E. Jenkins. Copyright © 1989 by Lawrence Erlbaum Associates, Inc. Reprinted by permission.

with children moving from sum to min to fact retrieval in a regular, stagelike progression. Such a view is not entirely accurate, however. At any given age, children use a variety of strategies to solve arithmetic problems, but the average sophistication of their strategies increases with age (Ashcraft, 1990; Bisanz & LeFevre, 1990; Siegler, 1987, 1990; Siegler & Jenkins, 1989).

This has been demonstrated in several studies by Robert Siegler and his colleagues (Siegler, 1988; Siegler & Jenkins, 1989; Siegler & Shager, 1984). In one study (Siegler & Jenkins, 1989), the development of arithmetic strategies in eight children was assessed over an eleven week period. Four- and 5-year-old children were selected who (a) could perform simple addition using counting methods, but (b) never used the min strategy.

Siegler and Jenkins found that all children used multiple strategies (see Tables 8.3 and 8.4) and that each child used a different combination of strategies. Over the course of the 11 weeks, however, children's strategies tended to become more sophisticated, so that children who started mainly by guessing or using the sum strategy progressed to using the min or fact-retrieval strategy.

One major aspect of the Siegler and Jenkins's study was children's discovery of the min strategy. At the beginning of the study, none of the children was using the min strategy; by the 11th week, seven of the eight children were using this strategy, and six of them could describe how they used it.

It is interesting to note that the first time children used the min strategy, and also on the problem immediately before it, they took much longer than average to arrive at a solution. Siegler and Jenkins speculated that the longer times spent on these problems meant that children were experiencing interference from alternative strategies. They also believe that new strategies require more mental effort than previously established ones, both of which will require more time and result in some hemming and hawing before arriving at an answer.

Metacognition

Metacognition refers to knowledge about one's own cognitions and the factors that influence think-

Table 8.4 Percent use, percent correct, and median reaction time (RT) for each arithmetic strategy

Strategy	Percent Use	Percent Correct	Median RT
Sum	34	89	10.8
Retrieval	22	89	5.0
Short-cut sum	17	85	13.2
Finger recognition	11	92	6.4
Min	9	86	9.0
Guessing	2	20	9.9
Count-from-first-addend	1	40	15.6
Unknown	4	71	—
TOTAL	100	85	9.4

Source: From *How Children Discover Strategies,* by R. S. Steigler and E. Jenkins. Copyright © 1989 by Lawrence Erlbaum Associates, Inc. Reprinted by permission.

ing. For every form of cognition, it is possible to think of a corresponding form of metacognition. Thus, for example, **metamemory** refers to one's knowledge about the working of one's memory, meta-attention refers to a knowledge of the factors that affect one's attention, and so on. Metacognition requires a conscious awareness. It's one thing to have complicated mental operations available for solving problems, but it's another thing to *know* that you have these operations, to know when to use them, and to know how effective they are in arriving at answers.

Person, Task, and Strategy Variables

John Flavell and Henry Wellman (1977) have described three major classes of metacognitive knowledge variables: person, task, and strategy. Person variables include a person's knowledge of his or her own abilities and the abilities of other people with respect to thinking—for example, a knowledge that you can solve certain problems faster with visual than verbal information, or that your grandfather remembers things from years ago more clearly than he does events from last week. Task variables involve knowledge of the requirements of tasks. Is there enough information provided to solve the task, or is more information needed? Is the task a familiar one that has been done before or a novel one that requires new ways of thinking? What variations in the task will make it more or less demanding? Strategy variables include a knowledge of what cognitive techniques one has available to solve a particular task and which strategies would be most appropriate for the task at hand. Does this task require my full concentration, or can it be accomplished with only a little study? What knowledge do I have that can be brought to bear on arriving at a solution?

Age Differences in Children's Metacognition

One robust finding of the cognitive-development literature over the past 20 years has been age differences in children's metacognitive knowledge. Metacognition has been investigated for a number of different cognitive domains, including memory (Flavell & Wellman, 1977; Schneider, 1985), imitation (Bjorklund, Gaultney, & Green, 1992), reading comprehension (Garner, 1990; Paris & Oka, 1986), attention (P. H. Miller, 1985), communication (Whitehurst & Sonnenschein, 1985), and self-monitoring (Wellman, 1977). Research findings include: the ability to distinguish important from unimportant aspects of a written story improves with age (Brown & Smiley, 1978); an understanding of the factors that influence attention increases developmentally (Miller & Weiss, 1982); and young children do not monitor well information they have in memory, causing them to predict poorly their memory performance (Wellman, 1977). In general, age-related differences have been found on person, task, and strategy variables, with children becoming more aware with age of their own knowledge and how it can be applied.

A good demonstration of developmental changes in metacognitive skills is seen in a study by Steven Yussen and Victor Levy (1975), in which children were asked to predict their own memory spans. Yussen and Levy presented children and college students with a set of 10 pictures, asking them to predict how many items they could recall in exact order (memory-span task); then they measured their actual recall. They found that 4-year-olds greatly overestimated their memory spans—estimating, on average, that they would recall slightly over 8 of the 10 items, whereas their actual recall was slightly greater than 3 of the 10 items (overestimation = 152%). Half the 4-year-olds predicted that they would recall all 10 items. Predictions were closer to reality for third-grade and college students (overes-

Box 8.6

An Author Is Born

Children frequently believe they are more competent and skilled than they really are. Take, for example, Nicholas, a 5-year-old boy who was visiting his grandparents' house and discovered a typewriter in the den. "Hey, what kind of computer is this?" he asked, and after his grandmother explained, he wanted to try it. While the adults visited in the next room, they could hear Nicholas typing busily. Soon he appeared, paper in hand, and gave it to his grandmother. "Here, *you* can read, Grandma," he said, "tell me what I wrote!" He knew that he couldn't read, but he still thought he could write. When she told him that it looked a lot like *The Three Billy Goats Gruff,* he was very happy and went back to the den to type another story (which, according to his grandmother, turned out to look a lot like *Peter Pan*). Later, Nicholas showed one of his stories to his grandfather, who had already been informed there was a new writer in the family. "Isn't this nice," his grandfather said. "It looks a lot like *The Three Billy Goats Gruff.*" Nicholas frowned and said, "You're just being silly, Papa, it's *Peter Pan!*"

Children's knowledge of their own mental abilities develops with age.

timation = 40% and 6%, respectively), and only 10% of third-graders and 2% of college students predicted perfect recall. After the memory test, the preschoolers were aware of their failure to recall according to their predictions, but many were unperturbed, saying things such as "If you gave me a different list like that, I could do it" (Yussen & Levy, 1975, p. 507).

How do we know what children know about the workings of their own minds? One straightforward way of finding out is simply to ask them. In a study by Mary Anne Kreutzer, Sister Catherine Leonard, and John Flavell (1975), kindergarten, first-, third-, and fifth-grade children were asked a series of questions about memory. For example, children were asked if they ever forget things, if it would be easier to remember a phone number immediately upon being told the number or after getting a drink of water, and if learning pairs of opposites (for example, boy-girl) would be easier or harder than learning pairs of unrelated words (for example, Mary-walk). Some kindergarten children asserted that they never forget things, and fewer than 50% believed that phoning the friend immediately would result in more accurate recall. About half the kindergarten and first-grade children believed that the arbitrary pairs would be easier or as easy to learn as the opposites.

The Relationship between Cognition and Metacognition

Good metacognition would seem to be important for good cognition, and many researchers have investigated this connection. For example, we have seen how training children to use strategies often improves their performance on memory and problem-solving tasks, but that the benefits of such training are often short-lived (see Bjorklund & Muir, 1988). A number of researchers have shown that strategy training is most effective, and generalization of the strategy to new situations most apt to occur, when training includes a metacognitive component (Leal, Crays, & Moely, 1985; Lodico, Ghatala, Levin, Pressley, & Bell, 1983; Ghatala, Levin, Pressley, & Goodwin, 1986; Paris, Newman, & McVey, 1982; Ringel & Springer, 1980). In other words, strategy instructions are most effective when children are made aware of how useful the strategies are to them, personally.

Given the impressive findings of these training studies, it seems reasonable that improvements in metacognition must be responsible for improvements in cognition: metacognition → cognition. Yet, an argument can be made that metacognition grows out of cognitive functioning: cognition → metacognition. That is, children first perform strategies effectively and then, as a result of hindsight, acquire knowledge about strategies.

Research aimed at elucidating the relationship between metacognition and cognition in development was conducted by John Cavanaugh and John Borkowski (1980) for the domain of memory. They administered extensive memory and metamemory interviews to children in kindergarten, first, third, and fifth grades and examined the relationship between metamemory and memory behavior. They reported that both metamemory and memory behavior increased with age, but that within a grade level, there was little in the way of significant relationships between the two factors. That is, at a given grade level, a child's level of metamemory was not a good predictor of that child's level of memory performance.

This does not mean that memory and metamemory are unrelated, only that the relationship is more complex than was originally believed. Contemporary researchers stress the bidirectional relationship between cognitive development and the development of metacognition (A. L. Brown, 1978; Flavell, 1978; Schneider, 1985). Metacognition is obviously an important component in children's cognitive development and certainly influences cognition; but the relationship also works in reverse, with competent cognition influencing metacognition. The two are intimately entwined, and the relationship varies depending on a child's age and the task involved.

Children's Theory of Mind

One characteristic of human beings is that we have a good deal of control over how we think and what we think about (or at least we *think* we do). How we direct our thought is a function, to some degree, of what we know about thinking. One aspect of children's metacognition that has received attention lately is **theory of mind**—how children conceptualize mental activity. As the child in the opening story of this chapter illustrates ("But Daddy, I don't know *how* to think!"), young children do not have the same understanding of mental processes as adults do.

One pioneer in this research has been Henry Wellman (1990). Wellman and his colleagues have demonstrated, for example, that preschool children misunderstand mental verbs such as "forget." For instance, 4-year-olds, told a story about a person who fails to find an object, say that person "forgot" the whereabouts of the object, even if the person didn't know its location ahead of time (Wellman & Johnson, 1979). In other research, preschoolers have been shown to be ignorant of the distinctions between remembering, knowing, and guessing (Johnson & Wellman, 1980). Yet preschool children are not totally out in left field when it comes to thinking about thought. For example, even 3-year-olds are able to distinguish real objects (such as chairs) from mental objects (such as wishes), and they also realize that mental activities can be about physically impossible things (such as a flying dog) (Wellman & Estes, 1986). Children as young as 2½ can carry out a simple deceptive strategy in a game, fooling a person into thinking something is so when it is not. Such deception indicates that they are aware of what another person is thinking and know that a false belief can be instilled in other people (Chandler, Fritz, & Hala, 1990).

State of the Art
Children's Eyewitness Testimony

At the Salem witch trials of 1682, children's testimony led to the execution of nearly 20 townspeople as witches or warlocks over a three-month period (Ceci, Ross, & Toglia, 1987). Juries in those days were all too willing to believe children's stories of people flying on brooms or transposing themselves into animals. Since then, however, children have generally not been welcomed into the courtroom as witnesses. Courtroom proceedings are very serious business, and children, by and large, have been viewed as incompetent witnesses (see Ceci, Ross, & Toglia, 1989).

Most adults still think that children are more suggestible and less accurate than adults (Ross, Dunning, Toglia, & Ceci, 1989). However, children are testifying in court in greater numbers than ever before because of the dramatic increase in cases involving children as victims of abuse or witnesses to domestic disturbances (Finkelhor, 1984). It has become increasingly necessary for children to testify in court, and this raises the issue of their competency as witnesses. Under what conditions can children's testimony be trusted? Conversely, how do adults, including jurors, view children as witnesses?

Memory Development and Children's Testimony

When children (or adults, for that matter) serve as witnesses, there are typically three features of memory involved (Brainerd & Ornstein, 1991; Ornstein, Larus, & Clubb, in press). First, for the most part, children are asked to recall information that was learned incidentally. In incidental memory, children are asked to recall events that they did not know ahead of time they were supposed to remember. Incidental memory is basically nonstrategic, in that no special preparation is involved in storing the information. Second, the testimony is usually about a very salient event. These events will likely be very meaningful, but also may be stressful and possibly even traumatic for a child. Third, there is usually a considerable amount of time between observing or experiencing an event and retelling it. As developmental psychologists, what do we know about children's *incidental* memory of *salient* and/or *stressful* events over *long* periods of time?

Unfortunately, the bulk of developmental research has focused on children's *intentional, strategic* memory for *nonsalient* and *nonstressful* events over *brief* periods of time—just the opposite of what is needed by courtroom experts. Nevertheless, some of what we have learned about memory development can be applied to children's eyewitness testimony, and newer research projects have been designed precisely to answer these questions.

For example, the role of children's knowledge (their knowledge base) greatly influences comprehension. The more children know about a topic, the more easily they can interpret and remember events related to that topic (Bjorklund, 1985; Chi & Ceci, 1987). This is particularly relevant in cases of child sexual abuse. According to Peter Ornstein, Deanna Larus, and Patricia Clubb (in press), "a child who does not understand what is happening to him or her will have little basis for subsequently remembering what was experienced. For example, when the targets of abuse are young enough to have almost no knowledge of sexuality, they will be unable to interpret what has happened and their memory will not be very accurate" (pp. 15–16).

Another factor influencing young children's recall is language. Young children may not see the same meaning in a question that an adult questioner does. Young children often have difficulty understanding the various types of questions (who, what, where, when), and interviewers may get the wrong answer, not because children don't have the information but because they don't understand the question (Ornstein, Larus, & Clubb, in press). Also, when questions are repeated for children, they may modify their responses, believing the interviewer is dissatisfied with previous answers (Siegal, Waters, & Dinwiddy, 1988).

Many of the factors that affect adult eyewitness testimony also affect children's testimony, presumably in similar ways. For example, the accuracy of recall diminishes the longer the delay, and accurate

How reliable are children as witnesses in court? What can be done to elicit the most accurate testimony?

recall can be enhanced by providing cues (that is, cued recall). Related to this last point is the issue of suggestibility. Even adults are suggestible under certain conditions, but there has been particular concern about the suggestibility of children.

How Suggestible Are Children?

Most recent research indicates that preschool children are indeed more suggestible than older children and adults (Ceci et al., 1987; Goodman & Reed, 1986; Ornstein, Gordon, & Larus, in press). For example, in a study by Gail Goodman and Rebecca Reed (1986), 6-year-olds performed as well as adults when asked nonleading questions about an event that occurred four or five days earlier (the correct recall of 3-year-olds was lower than that of both the adults and the 6-year-olds). When asked leading questions, however, both 3- and 6-year-olds performed more poorly than adults. In other research, recall of a visit to the doctor's office one and three weeks following the event produced relatively high levels of recall for both 3- and 6-year-old children (Ornstein, Gordon, & Larus, in press). When asked

misleading questions, both groups of children generally answered correctly, refusing to be swayed by the interviewer. However, 3-year-olds made a lower percentage of correct denials than 6-year-olds, indicating somewhat greater suggestibility for the younger children. Greater suggestibility for 3- and 4-year-olds compared to 5- and 6-year-olds was also found in a recognition (as opposed to recall) study by Stephen Ceci and his colleagues (1987).

One apparent reason for young children's greater suggestibility (when it is found) is related to the status of the interviewer. In one experiment (Ceci et al., 1987), preschool children were asked leading questions by either an adult or a 7-year-old child. As in other research, leading questions produced poorer memory than nonleading questions, but children were particularly susceptible to the leading questions when they were posed by an adult. These findings indicate that young children's suggestibility may be due, in part, to a desire to conform to the wishes of an adult.

In one series of studies by Alison Clarke-Stewart and her colleagues, preschool children watched a man posing as a janitor who either cleaned and arranged some toys, including a gender-specific doll, or played with toys in a somewhat rough and suggestive manner (Clarke-Stewart, Thompson, & Lepore, 1989; Goodman & Clarke-Stewart, 1991). About an hour later, the janitor's "boss" interviewed the children about what they had seen. With some children, the interviewer accused the janitor of playing with toys instead of doing his job, the suggestions of misbehavior becoming increasingly strong with each question. Two-thirds of the children followed the interviewer's suggestions, which did not correspond to what the children had actually seen. Moreover, when the children were questioned by their parents at the end of the session, they all stuck with the responses they had given the interviewer. In brief, children in this study were easily lead by a suggestive and accusative interviewer, and they did not alter their newfound interpretations when they were questioned later by their parents.

How Credible Are Child Witnesses?

How do adults perceive children as witnesses? It seems as though adults hold one of two theories about children as witnesses, depending on the nature of the event the child is testifying about: (a) children's inferior cognitive abilities make them less credible as witnesses; or (b) children's innocence makes them more credible than adults, and hence more credible as witnesses (Goodman, Bottoms, Herscovici, & Shaver, 1989; Ross, Dunning, Toglia, & Ceci, 1989).

When accurate testimony involves memory of specific events, such as identifying a robber or recalling an event that occurred some time ago, adults are reluctant to place much weight on a young child's testimony (Goodman et al., 1989; Goodman, Golding, Helgeson, Haith, & Michelli, 1987; Leippe & Romanczyk, 1987). However, in other situations, young children may actually be judged *more* credible than adults because of their lack of cognitive ability. For example, in a study by Gail Goodman and her colleagues (1989), college students read the account of a reputed sexual assault that occurred between a female and her male teacher. All college students read the same story, but the female in question was identified as either a 6-year-old, a 14-year-old, or a 22-year-old. Under these conditions, the 22-year-old was judged the *least* credible witness of the three, whereas the 6-year-old was the most believable. Apparently, many college students believed that the 6-year-old was too immature to concoct such a story, and therefore it must be true. Some comments of the college students were: "I don't think a child of 6 would have the knowledge about assault to be able to make it up unless it truly happened"; "I don't think her reasoning would be that advanced to plot out the sexual incident" (p. 16). In other cases, children are seen as more honest than adults because they have no reason to lie. For example, in a study that asked adults to judge the credibility of a witness who had seen cocaine in a neighbor's bedroom, an 8-year-old was judged a more believable witness than a 21-year-old (Ross, Miller, & Moran, 1987).

How a child behaves on the stand also influences how a person judges the credibility of a child witness. David Ross and his colleagues (1989) have shown that when children behave in a more confident, adultlike manner than expected for their age, their testimony is judged *more* favorably than that of an adult. However, when they behave as expected, like typical children, they are viewed as less credible. A related factor is children's speaking style. To the extent that children speak in less powerful ways than adults (more pauses, use of hedges such as "kind of" and "I guess"), they are viewed as less credible. But when they speak powerfully, they are considered equally as believable as adults (Nigro, Buckley, Hill, & Nelson, 1989).

The credibility of children as eyewitnesses is obviously a complicated issue, but an important one. Children are serving as witnesses in more and more trials, and adult judges and jurors must evaluate the merit of their testimony. Jurors do assess child witnesses differently than adult witnesses, and whether the reasons for the differences are justified or not, the legal system will be better served if we can find out what the actual differences are and what consequences they have for the cause of justice.

Summary

Both classical conditioning and operant conditioning can be demonstrated in early infancy. Behavior-modification techniques use operant-conditioning principles to shape and change behavior, but the desired behavior may decrease in frequency when the reinforcement is removed.

Albert Bandura's social cognitive theory, an extension of earlier social learning theory, is mainly a theory of how children operate cognitively on their social experiences. Bandura postulates five capabilities that contribute to development, all of which change with age: symbolization, forethought, self-regulation, self-reflection, and vicarious learning. Bandura believes that children have as much an effect on their environment as their environment has on them, and refers to such interaction as reciprocal determinism.

In social cognitive theory, observational learning involves four subprocesses, each of which changes with development: attentional processes, retention processes, production processes, and motivational processes. Imitation plays an important role in social and cognitive development throughout childhood. American children's TV viewing habits are established early. Educational programs such as "Sesame Street" have been shown to have positive effects on children's social and intellectual development. There is debate concerning the impact of television on children's school behavior, with recent research suggesting that watching television may not have the harmful effects previously proposed. Children are influenced by advertising, as reflected in their attempts to influence their mothers' supermarket purchases.

Research on the development of strategies indicates that sometimes children cannot take advantage of a strategy that is shown to them (mediation deficiency), and at other times they do not spontaneously use a strategy that they can be trained to use (production deficiency). In some situations, children will use a strategy spontaneously but will not realize any benefits (utilization deficiency).

Recognition memory is found even in newborns. Recall is more demanding, and developmental differences are frequently large on recall tasks.

Search techniques have been used to demonstrate recall memory in preverbal infants. The general inability of people to recall events from infancy and early childhood, known as infantile amnesia, is likely caused by the fact that information is represented differently by the infant and toddler than by the older child and adult.

The development of mnemonics, or memory strategies, is of critical importance to age changes in children's memory. In general, the use of strategies such as rehearsal, organization, and elaboration increases with age. Young children who do not use strategies spontaneously can be trained to use them, with corresponding improvements in memory performance, but children often do not transfer such strategies to new sets of materials. Age differences in children's content knowledge, or knowledge base, also contribute significantly to developmental differences in memory.

Children's concept of number is reflected in tests of conservation and counting. Children initially use highly effortful and external arithmetic strategies, such as counting on their fingers, and gradually progress to more efficient mental strategies, such as fact retrieval. Children use multiple strategies at any one time.

Metacognition refers to knowledge of one's own cognitions and the factors that influence thinking. Metacognition can be studied for any form of cognition and generally increases with age. The relationship between cognition and metacognition is bidirectional, with enhancements in one producing enhancements in the other. There are age differences in children's theories of mind, with young children conceptualizing mental activity differently than older children and adults.

Children are increasingly having to serve as witnesses in court proceedings. Many factors may influence children's eyewitness testimony, including their limited knowledge base and problems understanding the questions asked by an interviewer. There is debate concerning whether children are more suggestible than adults, with recent research indicating that preschool children may be particularly susceptible to the prestige of an adult interviewer. A number of factors affect how adults perceive children as witnesses, including the nature of the crime and the behavior of the child.

Key Terms and Concepts

learning
behaviorism
    classical conditioning
        unconditioned stimulus
        conditioned stimulus
    operant conditioning
        behavior modification
social learning theory
social cognitive theory
    symbolization
    forethought
    self-regulation
    self-reflection
    vicarious learning
    reciprocal determinism
observational learning

attentional processes
retention processes
production processes
motivational processes
deferred imitation
strategies
    mediation deficiency
    production deficiency
    utilization deficiency
memory
    recognition
    recall
        cued recall
        free recall
    infantile amnesia
    memory span
mnemonics (memory strategies)
    rehearsal
    overt rehearsal procedure
    styles of rehearsal
        passive rehearsal style

        cumulative rehearsal style
    organization
        clustering
    elaboration
knowledge base
    cultural literacy
conservation of number
sum strategy
min strategy
fact retrieval
metacognition
    person variables
    task variables
    strategy variables
    metamemory
    bidirectional metacognition/cognition
        relationship
    theory of mind
eyewitness testimony
    incidental memory
    suggestibility

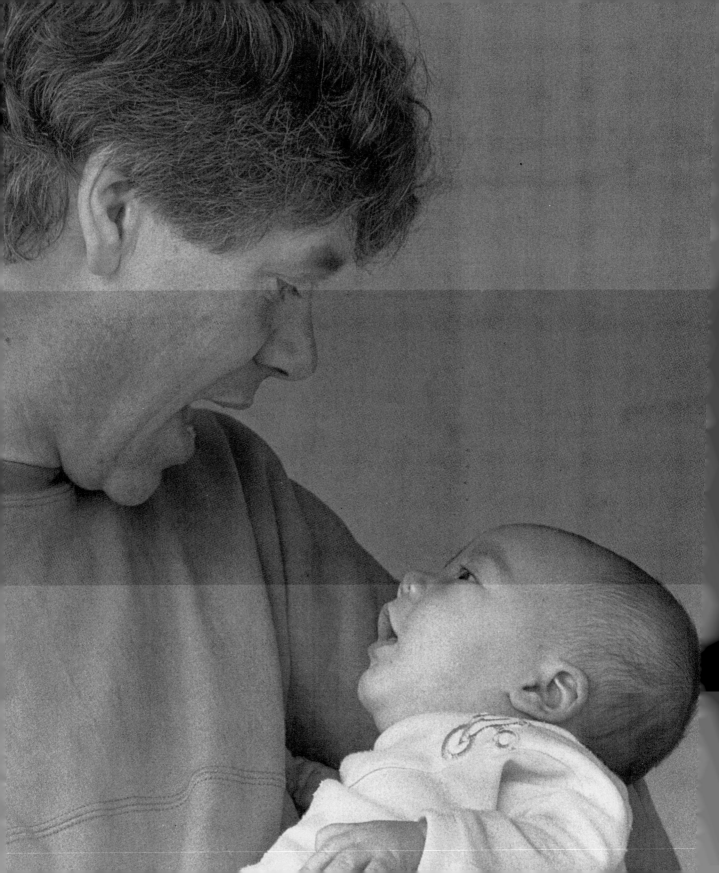

Language Development

9

The scene is a large bed, covered with a bright comforter. Two boys are lying across the bed. Nicholas is 6 years old; his brother, Jeffrey, is 10 months. Their mother's voice drifts in from another part of the house.

MOM: Nicholas, watch your brother while I put the clothes in the washer. Be careful, you know he can crawl over the edge of the bed. Okay?

NICHOLAS: Okay.

MOM: What? Did you hear me, Nicholas? Are you watching him?

NICHOLAS: (louder) OKAY! OKAY! I HEARD YOU!

JEFFREY: (looks at his brother, startled at the loud sound at first, then smiles) Ahhhh. Ahhhh.

NICHOLAS: (playfully) What are you laughing at?

JEFFREY: (smiles even wider) Ahhhhh.

NICHOLAS: Do you think that's funny?

JEFFREY: (giggles, kicks his feet) Ahhhh, ahhhh, ahhhh.

NICHOLAS: You're really weird, you know that?

JEFFREY: (giggles and kicks harder)

NICHOLAS: You are a weird, weird, WEIRDO. (slaps his hand on bed near his brother)

JEFFREY: (stares, startled for a few seconds, then smiles again) Daw, daw, daw.

NICHOLAS: WEIRDO! (slaps hand on bed again, harder)

JEFFREY: (laughs out loud)

NICHOLAS: WEIRDO! WEIRDO! WEIRDO! (slaps hand on bed three times)

JEFFREY: EEEEEEH! EEEEEH! (kicks feet down together to make the bed bounce)

NICHOLAS: (up on knees, jumping in rhythm) JEFF IS A WEIRDO! WEIRD WEIRD WEIRDO!

JEFFREY: DAW! DAW! DAW! (kicks heels into bed with great intensity)

MOM: Nicholas! What are you boys doing? Is Jeff okay? what's going on in there?

The obvious answer to this mother's question is that two brothers are playing on the bed, maybe a bit roughly, but it's a familiar scene. But something else is going on, too. Jeffrey is learning language, and Nicholas is teaching him. Surely neither is aware of this important process; they're just having fun on a Saturday morning. Their mother may not even notice; she's getting the laundry done and wondering about the condition of her bedroom. However, it is in these everyday scenarios that most of language learning takes place.

Babies as young as Jeffrey, who haven't yet spoken their official "first words," are well on the road to being fluent speakers of their native language. Adults and children, even as young as Nicholas, seem to know instinctively how to respond to babies' cues, how to present rhythmic, short phrases in high-pitched voices, and how to enter into the prelanguage "conversation" that allows babies to express themselves socially even before they know specific words. When families are together, there is usually more than one answer to the question "What's going on here?"

Language, more than any other single ability, is what distinguishes us from all other species. Children in all cultures acquire their mother tongue without the need of formal instruction. Language belongs to the class of innate abilities, such as sucking, grasping, and recognition of mother's odor, that are too important to be relegated to our conscious awareness and "free will." The reason for this seems to be that the evolution of language made human thought possible (Bickerton, 1990). The centrality of language to "humanness" requires that it be part of all groups of people and not subject to cultural peculiarities.

This chapter is about the development of language, the principal mode of human communication. Although a few nonhuman primates have shown simple language abilities (see Box 9.1), none has approached the level found in all normal humans. Language enables individuals to communicate on a daily basis, but it also does much more. Language allows us to share the experience of others without having to be there ourselves. We listen to the firsthand reports of others and gain information about events happening in other parts of the world without traveling there. We read the conclusions others have reached after a lifetime of experience and absorb the knowledge without living that lifetime. It is our ability to use language that has given us our dominance, for better or for worse, of the planet on which we live.

The Study of Language Development: A Brief History

Developmental psychology is a fairly new science, and language development is a fairly new topic of interest for that science. Although philosophers have long been interested in questions of language development, in-depth scientific study didn't begin until the 1960s. Since that time, however, children's language development has been one of the most popular research topics for developmental psychologists (Maratsos, 1983; Rice, 1989).

Behavioral Approaches

The earliest historical mention of language learning was in the fourth century A.D., when the philosopher St. Augustine wrote in his autobiography that he remembered learning language as a very young child. Adults around him, he recalled, would point to objects and repeat the names for them, and after many repetitions he learned the language (Bruner, 1983).

St. Augustine's view of language acquisition essentially prevailed for 16 centuries, anticipating the behavioral theories of the early and mid-1900s (Skinner, 1957). Behaviorists held that language, like any other behavior, is learned by instruction, practice, imitation, conditioning, and reinforcement. According to this theory, children learn the meanings of words as St. Augustine described—by associating them with certain objects or events that are present when the words are used (Staat, 1971). Other learning occurs by operant conditioning, they theorized, when parents reward their children for saying words correctly and punish or ignore them when they say words incorrectly (Mowrer, 1960).

In most of their research, the early behaviorists focused on *words,* not communication or grammatical structure. Moreover, they emphasized the parents as models of and reinforcers for language. The behaviorists actually paid relatively little attention to children, who for generations had been producing perfectly understandable original sentences and phrases they could not have possibly learned through conditioning and imitation, such as "all-gone sticky" to announce that their hands have been washed.

Many claims of the behaviorists have not stood the test of time. For example, although words can be learned via conditioning principles in the laboratory, there is little evidence that such structured techniques are used by parents at home; yet almost all children are fluent in their native language before they reach school age (Berko Gleason, 1985). Other research has shown that parents seldom comment to children about the grammatical correctness of their spoken messages, only the meaningfulness of them (Brown & Hanlon, 1970); and although new words are obviously learned by imitation, new grammatical forms (such as plurals or the past tense) are typically not imitated until children are able to produce them spontaneously (Bloom, Hood, & Lightbown, 1975). All this makes it very unlikely that a behavioral theory of language development is adequate.

Linguistic Approaches

With the many shortcomings of the behavioral approach, the stage was set for a revolution. In the late 1950s, Noam Chomsky (1957) declared that for the study of language acquisition, learning theory was dead. In its place, he offered a bold new theory. Children don't learn language the same way they learn to tie shoelaces; they learn language because it is a natural biological function of the human species. Language, he argued, was analogous to eating: we may exhibit different outward signs of these natural functions—eating rice and beans versus animal protein, or speaking English versus French—but the underlying structures of digestion and language are inborn.

Chomsky proposed that we acquire our native language via a **language acquisition device (LAD)** that is presumably located in the brain and programmed to recognize the **deep structure**—the underlying grammatical organization—of any language. Once the child is exposed to a sample of his or her native tongue, the LAD sorts out the rules of grammar and proper usage automatically, and the child is able to produce well-formed sentences regardless of his or her knowledge of the world or communication experience.

With Chomsky's revolution came an increased interest in language development and new ways of looking at old problems. In the late 1960s and early

1970s, the focus turned from the *structure* of language to the *function* of language. Developmental psychologists discovered the riches that the study of language development had to offer and became some of the first practitioners of the new discipline of developmental psycholinguistics. For example, Roger Brown and his colleagues did extensive work charting in detail the development of three children (Adam, Eve, and Sarah) from their first words through the early preschool years (see R. Brown,

Box 9.1

Some Apes Who Talk

Language, most people believe, is unique to humans. Yet this communication ability certainly originated in our evolutionary past. A number of researchers have suggested that chimpanzees and gorillas, as our evolutionary cousins, can reveal something about the origins of human language—that perhaps by studying them we can learn more about ourselves. To this end, they have attempted to teach language skills to nonhuman primates.

Viki
Viki, a chimpanzee, was born in the late 1940s and raised in the home of Keith and Catherine Hayes,

Viki

who thought that a chimpanzee raised in an environment similar to that of an American child might learn to speak English. After three years, Viki spoke only four words—"Mama," "Papa," "up," and "cup"—in a hoarse whisper that was difficult for people outside the "family" to understand. This was not surprising because the vocal tracts of chimps are dissimilar to humans' and their tongues don't move as well.

The experiment was not a failure, however. Although Viki didn't learn to speak very well, she did exhibit some signs of intelligence that chimpanzees were not known to possess. For example, she could sort a stack of photographs into two categories: humans and animals. (She always put her own picture in the "human" pile.) She also showed distinct signs of playing with imaginary toys, such as pulling an imaginary toy behind her on an invisible string while she marched around her cage. At the same time, the Hayeses' experiment demonstrated that a symbol system other than the spoken word would be necessary if researchers were to teach chimpanzees to use language.

Sarah
Sarah, a chimpanzee, was born in Africa in 1963 and came as an infant to the Missouri lab of David Premack along with Gussie, another infant chimpanzee. They were raised in a two-room apartment above Premack's office and were bottle-fed and diapered for several years by caretakers.

At age 5, Sarah and Gussie began formal lessons with the first of a series of trainers. Plastic chips of different shapes and colors that could be placed on a magnetic slate were used to represent words. The first words were names of fruit, such as "banana,"

1973).

Chomsky's theory provided the major theoretical impetus for much of the research during this time. The linguistic approach, as practiced both today and in the decades immediately following the publica- tion of Chomsky's theory, is focused on the *lan- guage* children learn to speak, not on the children themselves. Adherents of the linguistic approach be- lieve that every language has a structure—a set of rules that all who speak that language understand,

"apple," and "peach." If the chimp placed a plastic chip on the magnetic board, she would be given a piece of the fruit it represented. The next step was to teach names of familiar people (and chimps). Sarah learned to communicate with her trainer; Gus- sie never did. Sarah was used in the rest of the ex- periments that continued for the next 20 years.

Unlike other chimp language researchers, Pre- mack kept to highly structured lessons that paral- leled the development of speech forms in children. Sarah had lessons in the use of adjectives, conjunc- tions, and logical constructs. She did not "chat" with her trainers or have an opportunity to initiate conversation.

Washoe and trainer Roger Fouts

When Sarah reached full strength at sexual matur- ity, she was confined to her apartment/cage, where she lives today. She still has human companionship and can mutually touch and groom with her trainers, but her size, strength, and short temper make it im- possible for her to have the freedom she once knew.

Washoe and Loulis

Washoe, a chimpanzee, was born in Africa in 1965 and captured as an infant by animal traders. She was sold to the U.S. Air Force for the early trials of the manned space program, but was never used. Later she was offered to Allen and Beatrix Gardner at the University of Nevada for their language research program.

The Gardners raised Washoe in their home and taught her American Sign Language (ASL). The first nonhuman to learn sign language, she knows more than 130 signs. She became very attached to one of her trainers, a graduate student named Roger Fouts, and eventually came to live with Roger and his wife, Debbi, at the Psychology Department of Central Washington University in Ellensburg, Washington.

Today Washoe is 27 years old and is expected to live a normal life span of approximately 60 years. She is 4½ feet tall and weighs 135 pounds. Washoe lives with four other chimps in a series of cages connected by walkways and, because of her size and seniority, is the dominant chimp of the group. When her own baby died, she adopted one of the younger chimps, Loulis, as her son.

When Loulis joined the troop of chimps, the Foutses wanted to see if Washoe would teach him sign language. To make sure Loulis didn't learn it **(Continued)**

whether or not they are able to express them formally. As children gain experience with the language being spoken around them, they discover those rules for themselves. And once those basic rules are mastered, children can substitute words and create an endless number of sentences.

Most developmental psycholinguists following the Chomsky line believe that humans are biologically destined to use language. They offer as evidence the fact that all humans use language and that it develops similarly in all cultures and with very little or no formal training (McNeill, 1970).

Our understanding of language development was greatly enriched by Chomsky's theory. Liberated from the stranglehold of behaviorism, researchers were free to study language development in terms

Box 9.1 (Continued)

from anyone else, the human trainers were careful never to use sign language in his presence. Not only did Loulis learn Washoe's vocabulary, but incidents were recorded on videotape of Washoe actually teaching him the signs. In one incident, Washoe dragged a chair over to Loulis and signed "chair" over and over. In another incident, Washoe saw that Loulis wanted a candy bar that one of the trainers had. She took Loulis's hands and molded his fingers into the sign for "food." This evidence makes Loulis the first chimpanzee to learn sign language from another nonhuman and shows that chimps who have learned sign language know it well enough to pass it on to their children.

Nim Chimpsky

Nim, another chimpanzee, was raised by behavioral psychologist Herb Terrace. Nim was named as a joke after psycholinguist Noam Chomsky, whose theory was in direct opposition to the behavioral approach to language acquisition. Nim grew up like a child, wearing clothes and eating at a table. Over his first four years, a total of 60 teachers taught him sign language while video cameras recorded his progress.

Terrace analyzed the tapes to see if Nim's progress was similar to the language development of a child. On the surface it seemed to be, but upon closer study, Terrace concluded that Nim had simply learned to imitate his trainers and to perform properly for rewards—not to use signs to communicate his ideas in a mutually understood grammatical form. For example, as Nim got older and learned more words, his sentences got longer, much as a child's do. But when the longer sentences were analyzed, it became apparent that they were just longer strings of related and repeated words (for example, "Give orange me eat orange me give me eat orange give me you").

Other researchers have argued that Terrace's demonstration applies only to Nim Chimpsky—that another chimpanzee or another teaching method might produce other results.

Koko

Koko, a gorilla, was born in the San Francisco Zoo

Nim Chimpsky and trainer Herb Terrace.

Language

Babies are born
with the ability
to communicate
their needs and
to establish
social bonds.

Children are more adept than adults at learning second languages.

The pragmatics of language involves knowing that your message was heard and understood.

Communicative competence is firmly rooted by school age.

Being aware of the effect your communication has on others is a language skill.

The language of many deaf children is American Sign Language, which, unlike Signed English, is not based on the sounds of words.

By school age, children can use language to share their knowledge and interests with others.

Adults can foster a love of reading in children by reading interesting stories to them and by modeling reading themselves.

Until reading becomes effortless it cannot be pleasurable.

other than learning curves and acquisition rates. They could look at what the child was intending to express and why one word was learned more easily than another. The focus shifted to what the child was learning and why, not how quickly it was being learned.

But Chomsky's view was indeed a radical one, as extreme in one direction as learning theory had been in another. And although researchers had become dissatisfied with the behavioral approach, they had questions about the new biological approach as well. One researcher, George Miller, summed up the situation nicely: Now we have *two* theories of language acquisition, one *impossible* and one *miraculous* (Bruner, 1983). As research on language acquisition progressed through the 1970s and 1980s,

July 4, 1971. Koko is a nickname for Hanabi-Ko, which is Japanese for Fireworks Child. In 1972 she was acquired by Penny Patterson, then a graduate student at Stanford, who wanted to find out "everything about the mind of a gorilla." Patterson taught Koko sign language, but found that gorilla fingers are not as flexible as chimpanzee fingers, so she had to modify some of the signs. She calls Koko's method of communication GSL—Gorilla Sign Language.

Koko has learned more than 500 signs and has created combinations of signs to name objects and express feelings she has no sign for, such as calling a ring a "finger bracelet." Unlike Washoe, whose vocabulary consists of concrete objects, Koko uses abstract concepts such as "curious," "gentle," "mad," and "boring."

Koko, now 18, lives in Woodside, California, with Penny Patterson and a 15-year-old male gorilla named Michael, who also communicates in sign language. Their home is a set of trailers. Koko is the star of a children's book called *Koko's Kitten,* which features many beautiful photographs of Koko and tells of her request for a kitten as a Christmas gift. At the end of the true story, she receives a tailless Manx kitten, which she names All Ball. The story of Koko is so well known that when All Ball was run over and killed by a car, the event was reported in news magazines and on television.

Sherman and Austin

Sherman and Austin are two chimpanzees who live and work at the Yerkes Regional Primate Research Center at Georgia State University in Atlanta. They have been taught by Sue Savage-Rambaugh and Duane Rambaugh to communicate using symbols on a computer keyboard. Because some scientists theorize that language evolved for mutual problem solving, the Rambaughs have designed tasks for Sherman and Austin to perform that involve communicating with each other using symbols. For example, Sherman is given a jar of peanut butter that requires a can opener to pry off the lid. Austin, in another room out of sight, has access to various tools. Sherman has to use the computer keyboard to signal Austin that he needs a can opener. When the task is complete, Sherman and Austin have been taught to share the prize.

Koko and trainer Penny Patterson

so did disagreement concerning how best to approach the topic. In fact, one researcher has stated that by the end of the 1980s, language development was considered by some to be "the most contentious topic in developmental literature" (Rice, 1989, p. 149).

Research following the Chomsky tradition is thriving today, but so is research from many different perspectives. Many developmental psychologists now take an interactive approach, looking not just at the structure of a child's developing language, but also at the cognitive and social factors that influence language development and, conversely, at the role that language plays in cognitive and social development.

Interactive Approaches

Interactive approaches view the child's cognitive structures and social needs as interacting with the objects, people, and events in the environment to develop language. New language abilities, in turn, help develop new social and cognitive skills. This interactive perspective is well illustrated in the theorizing of Jerome Bruner (1983), who set out to fill the gap between "the miraculous and the impossible." He rejected the idea that language is encountered willy-nilly by the child and that the innate language acquisition device abstracts rules from this shower of spoken language. Instead, Bruner believes that language is carefully presented to children by the people around them. Not only is the content selected for the child's current abilities, but the presentation is executed to provide the best possible chance of learning.

How Children Acquire Language

Children gradually acquire their native language over the course of the preschool years. But what actually develops? Most obvious is vocabulary. Children go from three or four words in their vocabularies at age 1 to about 10,000 words by age 6 (M. Smith, 1926; Carey, 1977). Knowledge of word meanings is known as **semantics.** Semantics also includes the knowledge of the meaning of sentences and other utterances. Several other types of knowledge are also involved in language acquisition.

Syntax is the knowledge of sentence formation, or grammatical rules. **Morphology** is the knowledge of word formation. **Phonology** is the knowledge of how words are pronounced—how sounds are combined to make words and sentences. Finally, **pragmatics** refers to knowledge about how language can be used and adjusted to fit different circumstances, such as using different tones when speaking to small children versus adults, and using more formal words when speaking to teachers and grandparents than to same-age friends (Rice, 1989). All these types of knowledge are combined in a package called **communicative competence** (Hymes, 1972).

Early Nonlanguage Communication

Babies come into the world with a variety of abilities such as sucking, grasping, and turning their heads toward a nipple and away from a blanket covering their faces. They are also born with the ability to communicate with others to make their needs known and, more important, to establish the foundation of lifelong attachment bonds.

These and other early, well-formed abilities are not selected by chance; they are so vital to our survival that they must be present at birth. In some cases, such as sucking and head turning, the survival value is obvious. But early communication ability is also of crucial importance to human survival and development.

Adults' speech to infants   Communication implies an interaction between individuals, and researchers have investigated the role adults, especially mothers, play in early nonlanguage communication. Anyone who observes adults interacting with a baby will quickly realize that the adult end of the interaction involves a peculiar form of speech commonly known as "baby talk." ("Hello, Ben! How is the big boy today? Huh? How is Mama's big boy today? Did you go for a walk? Did you? Did you go for a walk with Daddy? Did you see the ducks? Did you? Did you see the ducks?")

Rochel Gelman and Marilyn Shatz (1977) studied the way mothers talked to their infants and found certain commonalities: high-pitched voices, short phrases, lots of questions, many repetitions, and exaggerated emphasis. This style has been termed **child-directed speech,** and is found in many cultures, in both men and women, and in children as

Adults rarely talk to infants the way they talk to older children or adults. *Source:* Reprinted with special permission of North America Syndicate, Inc.

young as 4 years. (Child-directed speech has also been referred to as "motherese," although research has shown that it is also practiced by fathers, babysitters, older siblings, and elderly gentlemen in supermarkets.)

How do adults and older children know child-directed speech? How have they learned what words to present to this particular infant and how to present them? Bruner (1983) suggests that people have a learning device in their brains that takes cues from a young child and interacts with the child's language acquisition device. Bruner suggests calling this the **language acquisition support system (LASS).**

Infants' reaction to human speech When infants hear human speech, they pay attention to the speaker; they become very quiet, face the speaker, and establish eye contact (Berko Gleason, 1985). Infants seem prepared to hear language from their first months. They seem to like to listen to language, and can be conditioned to change their sucking rate for the reward of hearing speech over a variety of other sounds tested (Butterfield & Siperstein, 1972; see Aslin, Pisoni, & Jusczyk, 1983, for an extensive review of infants' perception of human speech).

Not only do infants like human speech, they have a preference for who does the speaking. Infants prefer higher-pitched tones, such as women's voices, over lower-pitched tones, such as men's (Kearsley, 1973; Trehub, Schneider, & Endman, 1980). They recognize their mother's speech during the first few days after birth, and will change their sucking for the reward of hearing their own mother's voice over those of other women (DeCasper & Fifer, 1980).

Although infants cannot understand the words adults use to them, they do show a preference for child-directed speech. Four-month-old babies who have been taught to turn their heads to one side or the other to select which of two tapes they will listen to, prefer tapes of child-directed speech over conventional speech (Fernald, 1981; Fernald & Kuhl, 1981). The results of these and other studies suggest that the auditory system of newborns is prepared to process certain types of language, and that the singsong speech adults often direct to infants is no accident, but reflects the type of language infants most readily discriminate and attend to.

One other study worth mentioning here is that of William Condon and Louis Sander (1974). Condon and Sander presented evidence that newborns are prepared to respond selectively to human language. They reported that 1- and 2-day-old infants' movements were synchronized to speech sounds. It did not matter whether the language was English or Chinese; what was important was that it was language. Infants' movements were not synchronized to disconnected vowels or tapping sounds, suggesting to Condon and Sander that human infants have a template for recognizing human speech. Although provocative, these findings must be approached cautiously; subsequent research has not always yielded the same findings (see Dowd & Tronick, 1986). Nevertheless, coupled with infants' seemingly innate ability to discriminate many language sounds and their preferences for the human voice and child-directed speech, the research evidence indicates that the roots of language are planted firmly in biology.

Infants' social vocalization   If a mother talks to her 3-month-old baby, the behavior most likely to occur in the next 10 seconds is baby's vocalization. The second most likely behavior is baby's smile (Lewis & Freedle, 1973). During the first 6 months, infants vocalize along with speaking adults (Freedle & Lewis, 1977). By 7 or 8 months, babies will take turns vocalizing with an adult (Snow & Ferguson, 1977).

Babbling begins at 3 to 4 months and increases to 9 to 12 months, when it declines and one-word utterances begin. Rachel Stark (1979) described five stages of babbling (see Box 9.2). Sounds made during babbling vary widely, including sounds heard in the baby's native language and sounds that are not. Babbling sounds change with age. All this caused some early theorists to conclude from diary studies that babbling served as an exotic smorgasbord of universal language sounds from which infants selected those they heard in the language being spoken around them, while gradually eliminating those they didn't hear (Jakobson, 1968). This popular theory is still cited today by some, but recent research findings have not supported the early diary studies' data. Babbling does *not* contain all the sounds found in human language, only a small subset (Oller, 1980). The developmental changes in babbling reflect anatomic changes in the vocal apparatus more than approximations toward the sounds of one's native language (Ingram, 1989).

It has been suggested, however, that babbling plays a more important role in language development than just a poor attempt at spoken words (Sachs, 1977). Babbling may serve as a way to relate socially with family members long before the cogni-

Box 9.2

Developmental Stages of Infants' Babbling

Stage 1: Reflexive crying and vegetative sounds (0 to 8 weeks) Although infants can perceive a wide range of sounds, they are limited in the variety of sounds they can produce. Infants in stage 1 cry as a reaction to a distressed state and make various vegetative sounds associated with feeding and breathing, such as burps, coughs, and sneezes. One major reason for this limited repertoire is that their vocal apparatus is small and almost entirely filled by their tongue, leaving little room to make different sounds. As the infant's head and neck grow, a greater variety of sounds become possible.

Stage 2: Cooing and laughter (8 to 20 weeks) Infants at this age begin to make pleasant noises, especially during social interactions. These are mostly vowel sounds such as "oooh" and are termed cooing because they resemble the sounds made by pigeons. A few of the sounds will also contain some consonants such as *g* and *k*. Crying decreases and takes distinct forms that convey meaning to caregiv-ers—discomfort, call, and request. Sustained laughter appears.

Stage 3: Vocal play (16 to 30 weeks) This is a transition between cooing and true babbling. Infants begin to utter single syllables with prolonged vowel or consonant sounds.

Stage 4: Reduplicated babbling (25 to 50 weeks) True babbling sounds appear, such as "bababa" and "nanana." Consonant-vowel patterns are repeated, and playful variations of pitch disappear. This type of vocalization is not just a response to caregiver's social interaction, but often occurs when no one is present.

Stage 5: Nonreduplication babbling and expressive jargon (9 to 18 months) Babbling consists of many nonrepeated consonant-vowel patterns. Jargon babbling is strings of sound filled with a variety of intonations and rhythms to sound like meaningful speech.

Source: From "Prespeech Segmental Feature Development," by R. Stark. In P. Fletcher and M. Garman (eds.), *Language Acquisition.* Copyright © 1979 by Cambridge University Press. Reprinted by permission.

tive system is able to appreciate the intricacies of language—that certain sounds made in certain orders symbolize certain specific ideas.

Evidence for this is that, although *sounds* of babbling don't gradually come to approximate speech, the *intonation* of babbling does. Infants begin to "converse" in many ways that do not involve words, but rather the conventions of speech. They develop the ability to take turns (Snow & Ferguson 1977), match the speaker's tone of voice, pause between strings of syllables, end phrases with upward or downward inflections (Tonkova-Yompol'skaya, 1969), and match the pitch of adults speaking to them—higher for mother, lower for father (Lieberman, 1967).

The Second Year (12 to 24 Months)

Children show the beginnings of true language ability around the age of 10 to 13 months. It is at this time that they speak their first words that can be understood by family members and that consistently have the same meaning—for example, saying "dada" frequently to refer to the male parent and not to request a cookie or address the family cat.

Over the next six months or so, children increase their vocabularies a few words at a time, but their speech consists of one-word expressions. The words they acquire usually refer to familiar people, toys, and food (Nelson, 1974). The pronunciation of these first words often contains "errors," relative to adult speech, but an individual child's errors are often similar among groups of words. Furthermore, these errors in pronunciation seem to drift from one set of sounds to another, with children sometimes producing correct sounds at an early age and drifting to incorrect sounds in later months. For example, one child pronounced "turtle" correctly at 15 months and then as "kurkel" at 18 months (de Villiers & de Villiers, 1979).

As children's correct pronunciation of words slowly develops, so does their correct use of words. Using words properly is not easy, and many errors are made along the way. Researchers who have analyzed these early errors find that one common pattern is to use **overextensions**—stretching a familiar word beyond its correct meaning. An example of an overextension is using "doggie" to refer to the neighbor's cat, a pony, or any small four-legged mammal (Thompson & Chapman, 1977).

Many developmental psychologists argue against the concept of "error" in children's early language use, pointing out that practices such as using overextensions result in having adults provide the correct words and can be very effective learning devices. In the above example of a child overextending "doggie," the parent might respond, "That's not a *doggie,* it's a *kitty*" (Clark & Clark, 1977). The adult might also add other information, such as "We have a doggie at home, don't we? But this one is a kitty." Or "Doggies say 'woof-woof,' don't they? Kitties say 'meow.' Can you say that?"

Although children at this age express limited words and ideas, they are capable of understanding much more. It is estimated that by the time children speak their first word, they understand approximately 100 (Benedict, 1979). This brings us to the distinction between **productive language**—the language children can actually produce, or speak—and **receptive language,** the language that children can understand. Throughout development, receptive language exceeds productive language, even for adults.

Around 18 to 24 months, children know a few dozen words and begin putting them together, a few at a time, into short sentences or phrases. Again, the

Throughout childhood, children are capable of understanding more words than they actually use in speech.

words they know are those that are important to them, such as actions (what happened and who did it), possession (what belongs to whom), location (where people and objects are), recurrence (requesting "more" or "again"), naming (familiar people and objects), and nonexistence ("all gone") (de Villiers & de Villiers, 1979).

Another way toddlers get the most meaning from their limited language abilities is by using gestures and intonations to supplement their sparse sentences. "MOMMY!" can be a clear cry of distress, whereas "Mommy?" can be the initiation of a light conversation. Add a little hand waving and an empty cup and "Mommy" becomes a request for a drink refill. And coming from behind a chairback, "Mommy" can be the beginning of a round of peek-a-boo.

We know a toddler who gets his mother's attention by climbing up next to her on the sofa, putting one hand on each of her cheeks, and turning her face toward his as he finally says "Cookie?" And another 2-year-old in our family tells her parents that she doesn't want any more milk by giving a negative head shake as she says "More milk."

In their short tenure as language users, 2-year-olds have learned pragmatics, too—adjusting language to circumstances. They know to watch their listener for signs that they are being understood (Wilcox & Webster, 1980). They know they must be close to their listener in order to be heard and that if they are not close, they must speak louder (Wellman & Lempers, 1977).

The Preschool Years (2 to 5)

During the next three years, children's language develops from baby talk to adultlike communication—surely a most impressive feat to the college student struggling with first-year French. Yet children accomplish this with little formal instruction, only their day-to-day interactions with language-using adults and older children.

Longer sentences, more meaning   Children increase their vocabulary dramatically during these years, learning an average of a dozen new words a day. By school age, children know between 8,000 and 14,000 words (Carey, 1977). At the same time, they increase the length and content of their sen-

tences. Instead of asking to go outside by saying "Outside, Daddy?" the older preschooler can say "Will you go outside and play with me, Daddy?" It's unclear whether this reflects an increase in memory ability or the addition of "filler words," such as *will* and *with,* to their vocabularies.

The increase in sentence length is such a strong developmental trend that many researchers use a child's **mean length of utterances (MLU)** as a good measure of how far a child has developed linguistically. MLU is measured by recording a child's speech over a period of time and computing the average number of **morphemes,** or meaningful language units per utterance. Morphemes include words (such as *shoe, run,* and *help*) and word endings (such as *-s, -ing,* and *-ed*) that make nouns plural or alter the tense of a verb.

Children's language develops in more ways than simply adding words to their vocabularies and lengthening their sentences. They also learn to express more subtle meanings with their words, such as adding *-s* to a noun to mean more than one and adding *-ed* to a verb to mean the action took place in the past. Roger Brown (1973) identified many of these morphemes, or additions that give special meanings to words, and analyzed the speech of three unacquainted children (Adam, Eve, and Sarah) to determine the order in which they appear. He found 14 morphemes that occurred in almost the same order for the three children in his sample (see Table 9.1). Later research by Jill and Peter de Villiers (1973) extended these findings to 21 other preschoolers and found a high correlation between their sample and Brown's.

Overregularization   Many of the morphemes children learn are word endings. For example, 2- and 3-year-old children learn that adding an *-s* to the end of a word makes it plural and adding an *-ed* makes a verb past tense. Once children learn these rules, they tend to apply them, even when it is not correct to do so. This is referred to as **overregularization.** For example, once children learn the *-ed* rule, they often apply it incorrectly to words they previously used properly, such as *goed* (or *wented*), *drinked,* and *runned.* Children who have been saying *feet, mice,* and *cups of sugar* may suddenly and consistently switch to *foots* or *feets, mouses* or *mices,* and *cup of sugars.* They have learned a rule for regular

Table 9.1 Mean order of acquisition of 14 morphemes for three children

Morpheme	Example	MLU per Child		
		Adam	Eve	Sarah
1. Present progressive	sing*ing,* walk*ing*	2.5	2.5	2.5
2. & 3. in, on		2.5	2.5	2.5
4. Plural, regular	apple*s,* shoe*s*	2.5	3.0	2.0
5. Past, irregular	*went, saw*	3.0	4.0	2.5
6. Possessive	Eve*'s,* hers	3.5	2.5	2.5
7. Uncontractable copula	The dog *is* big.	3.0	4.0	3.0
8. Articles	*a, the*	3.5	4.0	3.0
9. Past, regular	talk*ed,* throw*ed*	4.0	3.0	4.0
10. Third person, regular	he run*s,* she swim*s*	4.0	4.0	3.5
11. Third person, irregular	he *does,* she *has*	3.5	4.0	4.0
12. Uncontractable auxiliary	I *am* going.	4.0	4.0	4.0
13. Contractable copula	The dog*'s* big.	4.0	4.0	4.0
14. Contractable auxiliary	I*'m* going.	4.0	4.0	4.0

Source: Reprinted by permission of the publishers from *A First Language: The Early Stages,* by Roger Brown, pp. 271, 274, Cambridge, Mass.: Harvard University Press, copyright © 1973 by the President and Fellows of Harvard College.

words and generalize it to irregular words. Apparently, having a history of being understood is not so potent a motivator for using a certain form of language as is the acquisition of a rule and its generalization to all situations where it might apply. Similar patterns of overregularization have been observed in a wide variety of languages, indicating that children around the world approach the problem of language acquisition in a similar way (Slobin, 1970).

Negatives Early in the preschool years, children learn the power of negatives. In fact, many problems during the so-called "terrible twos" spring from the new knowledge that they can have thoughts and wishes that don't necessarily reflect those of their parents, and that they can express them by using negatives. Early use of negatives involves tacking "n" words onto positive phrases, such as "*no* drink milk" or "*not* bath, Mommy." Later they learn negative verb forms such as "I *don't* want more milk" and "I *won't* take a bath, Mommy" (Bellugi, 1967).

Questions Similarly, questions develop from adding a raised intonation at the end of declarative sentences, such as "Brittany go outside, Mommy?" to more adultlike forms such as "Can I go outside, Mommy?" Sometime during the third year, the "wh" questions begin: "Where's daddy?" "What's this?" and the all too common "Why?" (R. Brown, 1968).

More significant to developmentalists is the child's growing ability to *answer* "wh" questions. *Who, what,* and *where* refer to people, objects, and locations, and are easily answered by young toddlers. For example, "Where's Mommy?" requires a simple response of "outside" or "in the kitchen." In contrast, *when, which, how,* and *why* require more difficult concepts and language ability. For example, asking a toddler "When did Daddy go to work?" or "Why did you leave the door open?" could result in great frustration for both adult and child (de Villiers & de Villiers, 1978).

Another fact of language life involves pragmatics. Children need to learn that sometimes a question is not a question, as in "How many times do I have to tell you to leave that alone?" and "Why do you insist on carrying that blanket everywhere?" Evidently, children learn from the speaker's tone of voice that these are really statements, because even young preschoolers seldom mistake them for questions

Two-year-olds, busy exploring their world, want to know the word for each new discovery.

(de Villiers & de Villiers, 1978). Conversely, questions can sometimes be hidden in statements, such as asking a babysitter for a bedtime extension by saying "Mommy always lets me watch 'The Simpsons'" (Reeder, 1981).

Word relationships   Late preschool brings another major change in children's language development. Although they have known and used the terms *big, little, tall,* and *short,* they now learn how to use them in relation to each other. A toy may be little in comparison to the child, but big in comparison to another toy.

Asking children which of two sticks is *long* and which is *short* is an easy task if both sticks are the same thickness, but if one is thicker than the other, young children are confused. The same is true with other comparisons such as short/tall, deep/shallow, small/large, wide/narrow. First children learn that the words are opposites, then they learn what physical dimensions they refer to (Carey, 1977).

By the age of 3, most children can understand and express the relational concepts I/you, your/my, yours/mine, this/that, and here/there (Clark & Clark, 1977).

Relating events in sentences   Around the age of 3, children can relate two ideas by connecting them with *and.* Instead of stringing together short sentences—"I went outside. I played on the swing."—they can now say "I went outside and played on the swing." Later they can use other conjunctions, such as *but, because,* and *while,* giving them new ways to express more complex relationships between ideas than just tacking them together with *and* (de Villiers & de Villiers, 1978). There is quite a difference in meaning between "Mommy got mad *and* Daddy was late" and "Mommy got mad *because* Daddy was late."

Passive sentences   Late in the preschool years, around 5 or 6, children learn about passive sentences. In active sentences, the word order tells the

Box 9.3

When Children Ask "Why"

Some children we know, around the age of 2, began to use "why?" and "what?" in response to many things adults said to them. One child, after being told by her father that she couldn't go outside, asked "Why?" He told her it looked as though it was going to rain soon. She responded "Why?" again, and he told her about the dark clouds gathering to the west. Her third "Why?" brought an explanation of the evaporation/precipitation cycle, and by her fourth "Why?" he was sure he had a scientific genius for a daughter. His wife burst his bubble by suggesting that perhaps their daughter was just interested in listening to Daddy talk. She had learned that "why?" was a magic word that caused adults to take a deep breath and explain *something* at great length.

Another child of 2 had her mother consulting the pediatrician about possible hearing impairment because she responded "What?" after everything her parents said to her. Again, it seems this child was using a "wh" word to extend conversations. When a parent said "Where is your bunny?" she would respond with "What?" This caused the adult to elaborate: "Your bunny, you know, the pink bunny that Grandma gave you? Where is it?" A second "What?" would bring another round of adult conversation: "Did you leave your bunny in the car when we went to the store? I hope you didn't leave it in the store."

This usage of "wh" words at an early age does not indicate acquisition of the concept of questions and answers. What it does illustrate is how social needs can advance ahead of true language abilities. Preschoolers like to converse with others and seldom let minor details, such as lack of language ability, get in their way.

story: "John hit the ball." Passive sentences—"The ball was hit by John"—take away that cue, and young preschoolers get confused (Goodz, 1982). Interestingly, children first learn to interpret passive sentences when the verb refers to some observable event, such as "The horse *was kicked* by the cow." Later they learn passive sentences with less observable verbs, such as "Tommy *was remembered* by the teacher."

Language development in later childhood Language development does not stop at 5, of course. What develops most obviously over childhood and into adulthood is vocabulary, as children acquire more abstract words and words that are heard infrequently in speech but appear more often in written text. The structure of children's language also increases in complexity, but the differences between the grammar used by 6- and 7-year-olds and by adults are subtle and minor. For example, school-age children still must master subject/verb agreement ("They were going" instead of "They was going") and the proper use of personal pronouns ("He and she went" instead of "Him and her went"). In general, however, the basic grammatical structure of school-age children's sentences varies little from that of adults' (Dale, 1976).

This does not mean that the whole package of communicative competence is adultlike by the time a child starts school. Although children may have acquired the basic structure of language and know enough words to make most of their wants and feelings known, their ability to communicate continues to develop. Communicative competence also involves social and cognitive skills, which have their own developmental progression and will be discussed later in this chapter.

Factors That Affect Language Development

Most scientists today agree that humans are biologically programmed to acquire language, and that language acquisition requires an environment in which the language is spoken. But the details of precisely how language is acquired are unknown, and there is considerable debate on the role of the environment (mainly parents) in language acquisition. Although much is known about the factors that influence language development, much still needs to be learned. This is fertile ground indeed where a future scientist could make important contributions.

Cognitive Skills

What types of abilities in a young child are important to language learning? One of the most important is level of cognitive development. Before children can use words to express ideas, they need ideas to express. Comparison of children's early cognitive progress with their language ability makes this relationship evident. Children first develop thinking skills through their actions on their environment. During the same period, their first words emerge, usually naming those people and objects they have experience with, such as "mama" and "cookie." Later, when children acquire the concept of object permanence (knowing that an object still exists even though it has been hidden), they begin using phrases such as "all gone" and "more."

This does not mean, however, that language development simply reflects a child's cognitive development. Although some components of language development occur close to the same time as corresponding components of cognitive development, research has not indicated a pattern of broad, pervasive relationships (Rice, 1989). And another problem is that although some cognitive development milestones occur close in time to some language development milestones, sometimes the language abilities develop first, making it difficult to conclude that progress in thinking *causes* progress in language development.

What we do know, however, is that the development of thought interacts with the development of language. Young children experience objects in the environment and learn about the world through these experiences. Part of their experience with these actions and objects involves hearing the words for them and, later, saying the words for them. Objects and actions come to be represented in the mind by words.

By school age, children's vocabularies have increased dramatically, and so have their thinking skills. Not only are they adept at expressing their thoughts and knowledge through language, they can

School children use language skills to share their thoughts and knowledge with each other.

also use language to help them work with thoughts and knowledge—to remember facts, organize related thoughts, and solve complex problems. Cognitive abilities aid language development, and language abilities aid cognitive development (Rice, 1989).

Social Skills

Children develop language not only to represent thoughts, but also to interact with family members and friends. In fact, some argue that all human learning involves social interaction, especially language acquisition (see Chapter 11).

Infants are born with basic components of social skills, such as making eye contact with adults and responding to human language, particularly child-directed speech. As early social skills develop, so do various forms of communication, including language. Again, it is an error to conclude that developing social skills *cause* language development. Rather, the children's expanding social world interacts with their increased language ability, and both grow as a result.

So important is this social aspect that autistic children, who are diagnosed by their "apparent lack of wish or intention to communicate with others" (Prior, 1984), are among the most pervasively handicapped. Severely autistic children do not seem to make distinctions between people and objects, not responding to attempts at social interaction or communication. Even autistic children who are able to speak show deficits in the pragmatics of language—the social component of communication. They have difficulty understanding facial expressions, gestures, intonations, and situations surrounding the use of language (Fay & Schuler, 1980).

Perceptual Systems

Language cannot develop without the necessary physical structures. A child must have the ability to express and receive messages, both spoken and written. This usually involves acuity (normally functioning systems for vision, hearing, speaking, and writing), discrimination (telling the difference between sounds and letters, and between various orders of sounds and letters), and association (being able to attach meanings to the sounds heard or the letters written).

Language acquisition in deaf children Much research has been done on language acquisition of deaf and hearing-impaired children. Deaf babies begin to babble at the same time hearing babies do, but the behavior drops out if no responses are heard. Babies who are partially deaf or who are fitted with hearing aids in the early months are capable of acquiring spoken language along the same course as hearing infants. Deaf and hearing-impaired children also have problems acquiring written language, because the alphabetical/phonetical system is based on how words sound (de Villiers & de Villiers, 1978).

Although one would think that deaf children with hearing parents should acquire language more easily than deaf children with deaf parents, this is not the case. One reason is that deaf parents are able to communicate with their infants from birth, whereas hearing parents must either learn some form of sign language as a second language before they can communicate with their deaf child or wait until their child begins school (Sacks, 1990).

A second reason deaf infants of hearing parents are at a disadvantage is that the predominant sign language taught in North American schools is *signed English,* which involves spelling out words according to how they sound—a difficult task for hearing adults and an impossible one for deaf infants and toddlers. In contrast, the native language of deaf

Box 9.4

Social and Language Development in Blind Infants

The importance of infant vision for the development of social relationships has been explored in studies of mother-infant interaction in blind babies. In her study of babies' early "smile language," Selma Fraiberg (1971) found that blind infants do not smile as frequently and as regularly to the sound of their parents' voices during the first three months as sighted babies do, and when blind infants do smile, it is often muted and seldom "joyous and ecstatic" like the smiles of sighted babies this age. The smiles of blind babies usually occur in response to their parents and are not used to initiate social exchanges. It seems that "joyous" smiling and starting smile "conversations" depend on visual stimuli to begin them and to reinforce them for future recurrence.

Blind babies develop vocal communication along the same course as sighted babies, but they are generally quieter. They seldom engage in "self-entertainment" vocalizing, vocalize to greet someone, or initiate vocal dialogues (Fraiberg, 1974). Fraiberg suggests that the lack of eye contact may cause parents to vocalize less to blind babies, which causes decreased vocalizations in return.

Parents of blind babies report feeling that their babies don't "know" them, that they are perplexing and unresponsive, and that it's hard to know what they want. Fraiberg (1974) suggests the problem is due to blind babies' not communicating with their eyes and parents' understandable inability to interpret their "hand language." She and her colleagues studied videotapes of blind babies and identified hand movements that signaled interest in certain toys (10 months), a request to be given something (8 months), and a request to be picked up and held (12 months). They also noticed blind babies' hands exploring mothers' hands and faces during feeding (2 to 5 months). Fraiberg trained the mothers in her research project to "read" these signals from their babies and to respond in ways the babies could understand.

Another finding in Fraiberg's (1974) project was that blind babies can recognize their parents' faces by touch at 5 to 8 months of age. When a stranger picks them up and they feel the unknown face, they react with fear much as sighted babies do when they *see* a stranger's face. And of course, the feel of the parent's face brings comfort again.

individuals in North America is **American Sign Language (ASL),** a language of signs that directly conveys meaning without requiring a knowledge of word sounds (Sacks, 1990).

Deaf infants who are responded to in ASL develop that language along the same course that hearing children follow in developing spoken language (Bellugi & Klima, 1972). In fact, deaf children learning ASL from their parents learn signs for some things earlier than hearing children learn to say the corresponding words. One reason is that some signs —such as those for "eat," "sleep," and "drink"—are based on action instead of arbitrary, abstract sounds. Another reason is that it is easier for young children to produce some signs with the hands than to produce the corresponding words with the vocal apparatus (Moores, 1974; Sacks, 1990).

The role of vision in early parent-child communication   Vision plays an important role in early parent-child communication. We know that babies can see at birth and that faces are one of the things they prefer to look at from an early age. Eye contact between infants and their mothers can be an important factor in developing social relations. In fact, researchers who studied 3-month-old infants and their mothers reported a social interaction of eye-contact episodes that resembled adult conversational turn-taking (Jaffe, Stern, & Perry, 1973). In the early months, some infants vigorously seek out eye contact with their mothers, while others do not. Some mothers are more responsive than others to this behavior. By 4 to 6 months, a pattern of eye contact is established for each mother/infant pair, and that pattern predicts an infant's attachment to the sight of his or her mother's face (Robson, 1967).

Role of Parents

Clearly parents play a significant role in children's language development. But what is that role, and how do they play it? Much research has focused on how parents talk to young children, using the special form of language known as child-directed speech.

A number of researchers have analyzed the features of child-directed speech and have found it to be simpler, more redundant, and better formed than speech to adults (Snow, 1977). Elisa Newport (1975), who studied 15 mother/infant pairs, found that grammatical errors occurred only

Even 4-year-olds use a different style of speech with young toddlers than they do with other children and adults.

once in every 1500 utterances. This finding challenges Chomsky's argument that the seat of language acquisition must be in the child because the language directed to children by adults is distorted and ungrammatical.

People do speak differently to small children than they do to other adults. The use of child-directed speech has been observed in both black (Drach, 1969) and white (Snow, 1977) cultures in the United States, among Luo and Samoan cultures (Blount, 1972), among speakers of Chinese and German (Grieser & Kuhl, 1988), and even among 4-year-olds (Shatz & Gelman, 1973).

How do we learn child-directed speech? One explanation is Jerome Bruner's (1983) language acquisition support system (LASS), the prewired device adults presumably have that detects the features of the infant and responds with simplified speech. Another explanation is that infants give feedback to this type of speech, reinforcing the parents' efforts with sustained attention, smiles, and vocal responses (Glanzer & Dodd, 1975; Shipley, Smith, & Gleitman, 1969).

Closer analyses have shown that parents have a fine-tuned ability to sense their child's changing communicative abilities and adjust their speech input to fit (Snow, 1977). Toni Cross (1977) studied 16 mothers and their infants, ages 19 to 32 months, comparing the mothers' child-directed speech with the infants' language abilities. She found that as infants progressed in communication ability, mothers used more new words, nonrepeated words, references to past and future events, and longer utterances. They also used fewer expansions of children's utterances, questions, self-repetitions, and references to the child's activity. Although these changes were related to the child's language ability in general, they were most strongly related to measures of the child's receptive language abilities. Cross interpreted this as evidence that mothers are capable of monitoring their child's overall psycholinguistic abilities rather than simply their levels of spontaneous speech.

The role of parents in their children's language acquisition is clearly important and one in need of further investigation. Topics recently proposed for research in this area include language acquisition in cultures that do not use child-directed speech, investigations of other social facilitators of language (besides child-directed speech), the role of parent/child book reading in the development of vocabulary, and parent practices that may actually inhibit language acquisition, such as commands, corrections, and directive instructions (Snow, 1986).

Is There a Critical Period for Learning Language?

Almost without exception, adults learn things more easily than children. This truism is apparent in our school system. Children first starting school are not expected to master complicated material. In fact, some theorists argue that expecting too much in the way of intellectual mastery in young children is not only foolish, but emotionally harmful (Elkind, 1987). Young children just don't have the mental capacity to acquire and understand information that an older child or adult has.

This general rule has one major exception, however, and that is language development. Children are better at acquiring both first and second languages than are adults. The cognitive system of the child is particularly well suited to the demands of language learning. As a result, many researchers have suggested that there is a critical period for learning language—that children must be exposed to language early in life if they are ever to master it.

Eric Lenneberg (1967) proposed that language learning occurs exclusively or primarily in childhood. With age, the nervous system loses its flexibility, so that by puberty the organization of the brain

is fixed, making language learning difficult. There has been much evidence consistent with this position, including differences between adults and children in recovery from language-specific brain damage (see Chapter 5) and behavioral studies examining language acquisition in older children who were severely deprived early in life (Curtiss, 1977).

More recent research by Jacqueline Johnson and Elisa Newport (1989) has examined second-language learning as a function of age. They tested 46 native Chinese or Korean speakers who had emigrated to the United States and learned English as a second language. These people ranged in age from 3 to 39 years and had lived in the United States between 3 and 26 years when they were tested.

Johnson and Newport reported that their subjects' proficiency in English was related to the age when language training began: people who learned their second language early in childhood showed greater proficiency as adults than people who learned later in childhood (see Figure 9.1.). Note, however, that the decline in English proficiency was gradual. Similar results have recently been reported for deaf people learning American Sign Language as their first language (Newport, 1990). These data ne-

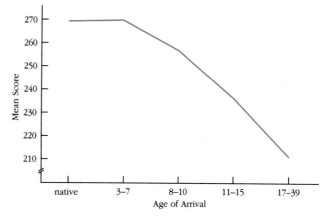

Figure 9.1 Relationship between age of arrival in the United States and score on a test of English grammar. *Source:* From "Critical Period Effects in Second Language Learning: The Influence of Maturational State on the Acquisition of English as a Second Language," by J. S. Johnson and E. L. Newport, *Cognitive Psychology,* 1989, *21,* 60–99. Copyright © 1989 by Academic Press. Reprinted by permission.

cessitate a modification of the critical period hypothesis for language development, indicating that there is a gradual decline in a person's ability to acquire a second language throughout childhood, rather than a sharp discontinuity at puberty.

It is clear that the cognitive system of the young child is especially suited for language learning, of both a first and second language. This ability is gradually lost over childhood, and although adults are able to acquire a second language, they rarely attain the same proficiency that is achieved when language is acquired in childhood.

Learning to Read

Unlike spoken language, which children acquire spontaneously just by living in a human culture, reading must be taught. And although all normal children learn to be proficient speakers of their mother tongue, not all learn to be proficient readers.

Stages of Reading

Learning to read involves the acquisition of a set of skills, each built upon the preceding ones. Jeanne Chall (1979) has proposed five stages in the development of proficient reading, ranging from the prereading skills of the preschool child to the highly skilled reading of the adult.

In stage 0, covering the years before a child enters first grade, children must master the prerequisites of reading, most notably learning to discriminate the letters of the alphabet. In one study, for example, kindergarten children's ability to name letters predicted their later reading achievement scores in the second and third grades (deHirsch, Jansky, & Langford, 1966). By the time children enter school, many can already "read" some words, such as *Pepsi, McDonalds,* and *Pizza Hut.* These popular symbols, flashed at children from the television and seen repeatedly along the highway or on the dinner table, indicate that they can tell the difference between patterns of letters, even if they are unable to "sound out" the words. Children's knowledge of letters and single words is generally better than it was several generations ago, in part because of children's television shows such as "Sesame Street."

Stage 1 covers children's first year of formal reading instruction. It is in first grade that children learn **phonological recoding** skills—the skills used to translate written symbols into sounds and thus words. This is followed in the second and third grades by stage 2, in which children learn to read fluently. By the end of third grade, schoolchildren have mastered the letter-to-sound correspondence and can read most words and simple sentences they are given. But reading is effortful for these children, in that the process of identifying individual words requires so much of their limited mental resources that they often do not comprehend much of what they read. Still concentrating on what individual sets of letters mean, they are not very skilled at putting the words together to abstract the broader meaning of the text.

The change from "learning to read" to "reading to learn" begins in stage 3, spanning grades four through eight. Children can now more readily acquire information from written material, and this ability is reflected in the school curriculum. Children in these grades are expected to learn from the books they read. Instruction is not limited to what the teacher tells them, but also includes what the children read. If children have not mastered the "how to's" of reading by fourth grade, progress in other subjects may be difficult.

Stage 4, beginning in the high school years, represents truly proficient reading. Children at this level are increasingly able to comprehend a variety of written material and to draw inferences from what they read.

Based on this brief description, it would appear that learning to read develops along with children's general cognitive abilities, not their spoken language ability. Reading is built on a well-established language system and develops alongside general cognitive development.

Cognitive Development and Reading

Prereading skills   In addition to letter discrimination, an early skill that predicts good reading in later years is phonemic awareness—the understanding that words consist of separable sounds. Such awareness is generally not available to preschool children. In one study (Liberman, Shankweiler, Fischer, & Carter, 1974), 4- and 5-year-olds were taught to tap once for each sound in a short word—for instance, twice for *at* and three times for *cat*. Although the children presumably understood the task, their performance was poor, with none of the 4-year-olds (and only a few of the 5-year-olds) performing it accurately. Although this task may seem trivial, it predicts children's early reading achievement quite well (Liberman & Shankweiler, 1977). Other aspects of phonological awareness, such as children's abilities to detect rhymes, also develop slowly over the preschool and early school years and also predict remarkably well children's later reading skills (Bryant & Bradley, 1985; Wagner & Torgesen, 1987; Stanovich, Cunningham, & Cramer, 1984). Recent research has shown that children's sensitivity to rhymes leads to awareness of phonemes, which in turn affects reading, presumably making it easier for children to recognize written words that both sound and look alike, for example, *cat* and *hat* (Bryant, MacLean, Bradley, & Crossland, 1990).

Identifying words The reason that phonological awareness is such a good predictor of early reading, of course, is that early reading generally involves sounding out words. This process of phonological recoding is the basis of the majority of reading instruction programs in the United States today (the phonics method). Children are taught the sound of each letter and how to combine these sounds, blending them into words.

Truly proficient reading is achieved not by sounding out each letter, but rather by directly retrieving the meaning of the whole word from memory (whole-word, or visually based, retrieval). Think for a while about how you read. Very few college students sound words out, letter by letter; they simply "know" the meaning of a word when they see it. Adults and older children who read phonetically are not good readers. The amount of mental effort it takes to process a single word by this method is tremendous, making it unlikely that much meaning will be obtained from what is read. Yet without phonological recoding skills, we would be limited to reading only words we have learned before. Thus, phonological skills seem necessary if one's reading ability is to advance.

The key to proficient reading, then, is automatization—the effortless retrieval of word meaning. Being able to access the meaning of words, expend-

Children begin reading phonetically, but before it can become a pleasurable pasttime it has to become automatic.

ing little or none of one's limited resources in the process, is critical for skilled reading. When too many mental resources are used just identifying individual words, there will be too few resources left to piece the words together and understand the greater meaning of the text. Robert Siegler (1988) has suggested a model of how children come to retrieve words automatically. He proposed that children's first choice for a strategy of word identification is visually based retrieval (or fact retrieval, as he calls it). Such a process is done automatically. If the word is not sufficiently familiar to children so they can retrieve its meaning directly, they fall back on more effortful strategies—in this case, phonological recoding. As children become more experienced with the words they read and better able in general to automatize processing, reading becomes more proficient.

Comprehension Reading involves more than just identifying words; it involves understanding stories, instructions for operating a VCR, and child-development textbooks, among other things. Children must relate the meanings of individual words and sentences to abstract the broader meaning that a written text intends. This process is referred to as reading comprehension.

One factor that limits children's comprehension is the amount of information they can hold in short-term memory at any one time. Meredith Daneman and her colleagues have proposed that information must be retained in working memory as long as possible so that each newly read word in a passage can be integrated with the words and concepts that preceded it. Younger or less proficient readers have less available mental capacity to store and maintain information in working memory because they need to devote so much capacity to identifying and understanding words. Daneman and her colleagues showed that listening span, defined as the number of successive short sentences that could be recalled verbatim, correlates significantly with comprehension for people ranging from preschoolers to college students (Daneman & Blennerhassett, 1984; Daneman & Carpenter, 1980; Daneman & Green, 1986).

Another critical factor in reading comprehension is the knowledge an individual has of the material being read. As we saw in Chapter 8, having detailed knowledge of a topic permits one to process information about that topic more efficiently (Bjorklund, Muir-Broaddus, & Schneider, 1990). This is especially true in reading comprehension.

Richard Anderson and his colleagues (Anderson, Hiebert, Scott, & Wilkinson, 1984) have defined reading as "a process in which information from the text and the knowledge possessed by the readers act together to produce meaning" (p. 8). In other words, "reading is a constructive process" (p. 9), in which the background knowledge that one brings to a text interacts with what is written on the page to produce understanding. They cite considerable evidence from the research literature to support this view. In one study, for example, second-graders who were equated in reading skill were tested for their knowledge of spiders and then given a passage about spiders to read (Pearson, Hansen, & Gordon, 1979). Children who knew more about spiders at the outset were better at answering subsequent questions about the passage, especially questions that involved reasoning. Instructional efforts aimed at

increasing background knowledge have also been found to enhance reading comprehension (Hansen, 1981; Hansen & Pearson, 1983; Omanson, Beck, Voss, & McKeown, 1984).

In more recent research done in Germany, Wolfgang Schneider, Jochamin Körkel, and Franz Weinert (1989, 1990) compared the text comprehension of soccer expert and soccer novice third-, fifth-, and seventh-grade children on stories related to soccer. They also classified children as successful learners versus unsuccessful learners based on their classroom grades in German and mathematics and performance on IQ tests. This led to four groups of children at each grade: soccer experts/successful

Children who perform poorly in school sometimes do better when lessons are taught in terms of something they know a great deal about, such as baseball or soccer.

Box 9.5

Learning to Write

Although many language-users cannot express their native language in writing (nor read it), these skills are important in a technological society. In fact, some believe that members of our literate society have not fully acquired language unless they are able to read and write (Perera, 1986).

Children's writing is not simply adult writing in less complex form; rather, like children's speech, it represents different concepts and structures (Kress, 1982). By studying children's writing at different ages, we can see how thinking affects writing and how the ability to write begins to influence thinking.

Writing begins much later than speech production, of course. Toddlers are not physically coordinated enough to hold writing instruments and, more important, have little idea that marks on a paper represent ideas. However, some beginnings can be seen in children's drawings, which begin around the age of 2.

By the late preschool years, children know about writing: they see others doing it, they know its purpose, and they are able to imitate the physical procedures. This is usually all that is necessary for a child this age to feel confident enough to "write." Researchers who have asked children this age to write certain words have found some interesting results. For example, they write words for big objects (such as *elephant*) in big letters and, when given a choice of pen color, will write words for red objects (such as *tomato*) in red ink. Other kids have been found to write the names for round objects (such as *wheel*) in symbols that form a circle on the paper and the names for flying objects (such as *bird* and *plane*) high at the top of the page. Young children know that long-sounding words should be long-looking words and that short-sounding words should look short.

In the early school years, between ages 5 and 7, children's writing is usually limited to learning how to form letters and copy the writing of adults. Between ages 7 and 9, kids learn to do independent writing, and what they write is very similar to what they say. Between ages 9 and 12, children begin differentiation: they write in a different form than they speak. Writing becomes a channel of expression with different constructions and forms than speech. After age 12, children are capable of developing

The development of children's writing ability leads to more mature thinking, which in turn results in improved writing.

their own, individual styles of writing. They can express their emotions in writing, and in many ways see writing as the preferred form of communication (Kroll, 1981).

Writing assists in thinking. Many adults feel that a different part of their intellect is tapped through writing than through speaking. In fact, developmental psychologist Jerome Bruner tells us, "Some people write to find out what they think, I among them" (1983, p. 9). Many adults in literate societies never reach this stage of thinking and writing, however. One of the problems seems to be manual dexterity. Until the physical act of writing becomes effortless (automatic), children are not free to become fluent writers (Kroll, 1981). For this reason, some educators are promoting the use of typewriters and word processors for elementary school children who have difficulties with handwriting—although this has met with criticism from traditionalists who stress writing as one of the "three Rs."

learners, soccer experts/unsuccessful learners, soccer novices/successful learners, and soccer novices/unsuccessful learners. Children were then read a story about soccer. Care was taken to ensure that most parts of the story would be easily understood even by the soccer novices. Children were then asked questions about the story or were asked to recall the story. The average number of idea units children remembered from the soccer story is presented in Figure 9.2, collapsed across grades. Not surprisingly, expert children performed better than did novice children. What may be surprising, however, is that a child's learning ability did *not* influence performance: the soccer expert/unsuccessful learners remembered more than did the soccer novice/successful learners. In other words, what children knew about soccer determined how well they performed, independent of their general learning ability (see also C. H. Walker, 1987; Recht & Leslie, 1988). Knowledge, then, clearly makes reading more accurate and meaningful. It also makes reading less effortful, in that knowledge provides the reader with ready-made inferences and interpretations.

Another factor related to reading comprehension is the ability to monitor one's understanding of a text and to adjust reading strategies accordingly (Brown & Smiley, 1978; Paris & Oka, 1986). Good readers easily recognize when they don't comprehend something they are reading. They then take the necessary action to rectify the situation: rereading a sentence, reading more slowly, checking back a few lines to see if some important information may have been missed, or perhaps consulting a dictionary. Children do not approach these higher-order skills until the high school years, and many people never develop them fully. Comprehension-monitoring skills generally improve with age and experience (Baker, 1985; Garner, 1990; Markman, 1977) and can be further improved with instruction (Palincsar & Brown, 1984).

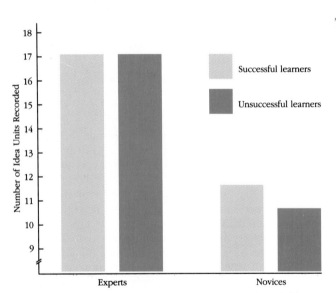

Figure 9.2 Number of idea units remembered about a soccer story. *Source:* Adapted from "Expert Knowledge, General Abilities, and Text Processing," by W. Schneider, J. Körkel, and F. E. Weinert. In W. Schneider and F. E. Weinert (eds.), *Interactions Among Aptitude, Strategies, and Knowledge in Cognitive Performance.* Copyright © 1990 by Springer-Verlag. Reprinted by permission.

The Development of Communication Skills

As children's language becomes more complex, their ability to communicate their needs, wants, and ideas via speech increases. Vocal communication is nothing new for the toddler; from the first months of life infants have used cries and coos to communicate with adults and to modify the behavior of their parents. With the advent of language, however, communicative power increases substantially. Children can express complex ideas—specifying in words, for example, exactly what they would like to eat and which shirt they would like to wear. They can also comprehend adult speech and, through language alone, understand that they must return their toys to their room and stop feeding M & Ms to the dog.

There's more to effective verbal communication than just words, however. A responsive listener will provide a speaker with nonverbal cues (such as nods, gazes, and smiles) and say "yes" and "uh-huh" at appropriate times to make it clear that the message is being understood. These skills also increase with age, but even 2-year-olds use many of these tactics when listening to an adult (Miller, Lechner, & Rugs, 1985). Despite the seeming communicative sophistication of many preschoolers, effective communication between adult and child, or between

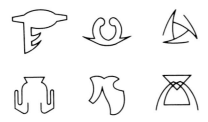

***Figure* 9.3** Abstract stimuli used in a communication task. Children are to tell another child which abstract form to select by means of language alone. *Source:* From "Referential Communication in Nursery School Children: Method and Some Preliminary Findings," by S. Glucksberg, R. M. Krauss, and R. Weisberg, *Journal of Experimental Child Psychology,* 1966, *3,* 333–342. Copyright © 1966 by Academic Press. Reprinted by permission.

child and child, is variable. Many messages that are within the grammatical competence of a child are simply not understood. Also, young children often have difficulty in conveying exactly the right message to another child and frequently are unaware that their message was inadequate.

Preschool children have a difficult time taking the perspective of another (see Chapter 7), and this is reflected in their use of language. For example, when trying to communicate specific information to another child, preschoolers often give incomplete information and use idiosyncratic descriptions of objects. In one study by Sam Glucksberg and his colleagues (Glucksberg, Krauss, & Weisberg, 1966), 4- and 5-year-olds were placed on opposite sides of a table so that they could not see one another. Visible to each child was an array of abstract forms (see Figure 9.3). The child's task was to communicate to another child which form to choose. Although the children were apparently highly motivated to do the task, they rarely performed well. Rather, the speaker frequently gave incomplete instructions (for example, "Pick the red one" when there were several red objects) and used idiosyncratic descriptions of objects (for example, "Pick the one that looks like Mommy's shirt"), providing the listener with little useful information on which to base a decision. More recent research indicates that young children are not completely egocentric with respect to lan-

guage, but their self-centered perspective can cause problems when communication of specific ideas is called for.

Several researchers have investigated the development of **metacommunication**—children's knowledge of their own communicative abilities (Evans, 1985; Flavell, Speer, Green, & August, 1981). To what extent are children able to monitor their own speech? Are children aware of what they are saying and that, at times, they may not be providing the listener with adequate information to be properly understood? Again, young children tend to display deficits here. Young children's speech exhibits a higher incidence of omissions and ambiguities and requires greater contextual support to be comprehended than does the speech of older children (for reviews, see Shatz, 1983; Whitehurst & Sonnenschein, 1985).

Preschool children are not totally devoid of metacommunication skills, however. Marilyn Shatz and Rochel Gelman (1973) observed the speech of 4-year-old children when they talked to adults, to other 4-year-olds, and to 2-year-olds. They found that these children modified their speech to the 2-year-olds, using different tones of voice and shorter sentences, much as adults do.

The findings of Shatz and Gelman (1973), among others, suggest that young children do have metacommunication skills. However, as with many newly acquired skills, communication abilities seem to develop first in highly specific, familiar situations and are easily disrupted. With age, children display their communicative skills in increasingly diverse contexts, generalizing what they know to new and unfamiliar settings.

Language and Thought

When people think about thinking, they usually do so in terms of language. For most people, thought without language is unthinkable. Although language is not our only means of thought, it is certainly the basis for much of our cognitive processing.

The connection between language and thought is not a constant one but develops over childhood. Jerome Bruner (1966) argued that preschool children, although possessing language, represent their world in terms of images. Not until the early school

Wharf

years do children begin to use language as a tool for thought.

The developmental relationship between language and thought was investigated earlier in this century by the Soviet psychologist Lev Vygotsky (1962, originally published in 1934). Vygotsky believed that thought and speech have different roots in development and that the two are initially independent. However, with development, thought and speech merge: thought becomes verbal, and speech becomes rational. It is this developmental relationship between language and thought, particularly during the stages when the two cross, that has attracted the interest of many contemporary psychologists.

Vygotsky was particularly interested in the role of **egocentric speech,** or **private speech,** in affecting children's thought. Private speech is overt language that is carried out with apparent satisfaction, even though it does not communicate. It can be observed when children are alone or in social settings.

An example of private speech is the **collective monologues** described by Piaget (1955). In collective monologues, two (or more) children will be talking *about* some common activity, but not necessarily talking *to* one another. Take, for example, the "conversation" we overheard not long ago of two 5-year-old boys. Michael described how his Ghostbuster was going to drive Ecto-1 over to Jimmy and catch some ghosts in his ectoplasm containment trap. Jimmy commented that his Ghostbuster had been slimed and he had to hurry back to the fire station (Ghostbuster headquarters). The conversation continued for some time, with both boys moving their toys and describing their actions; but what one boy said appeared to have little to do with what the other said or did.

Vygotsky believed that private speech plays a specific role in children's thought and problem solving. Language can serve to guide children's behavior (and thus their thought), but young children cannot yet use language covertly, "in their heads." In order to guide their own behavior through language, they must talk out loud to themselves. With development, children become able to use **inner speech.** In other words, private speech serves as a **cognitive self-guidance system** and then goes "underground."

In contrast to Vygotsky's view of the role of private speech in cognitive development is that of Jean Piaget (1955), who believed that the egocentric speech of preschoolers reflects their general egocentric perspective of the world. As children become increasingly able to decenter their cognition and perception and see the point of view of another, private speech decreases. For Piaget, private speech plays no functional role in cognitive development but is merely symptomatic of ongoing mental activity.

In an early study designed to investigate these conflicting views, Lawrence Kohlberg and his colleagues (Kohlberg, Yaeger, & Hjertholm, 1968) proposed that private speech can be classified according to its function, and that it has different functions at different ages. The earliest form of private speech serves only as self-stimulation and word play. This is followed by children's speech describing their action but not directing their behavior. In a third stage, overt speech serves to direct problem solving. This self-regulatory function of speech evolves into inaudible mutterings as speech becomes covert verbal thought.

Young children often have a difficult time keeping their thoughts to themselves. *Source:* DENNIS THE MENACE® used by permission of Hank Ketcham and © North America Syndicate, Inc.

In a series of experiments assessing children's private speech while solving problems, Kohlberg and associates reported that the incidence of word play and simple descriptions decreased with age, whereas private speech used to guide performance increased over the preschool years, peaking between the ages of 6 and 7 and declining thereafter. This trend was accompanied by an increase in inaudible mutterings with age, peaking between 8 and 10 years. They interpreted these findings as supporting Vygotsky's position, with the self-guidance function of private speech varying with age and eventually giving way to covert inner speech. Furthermore, they found that the incidence of private speech to guide task performance peaked earlier for brighter children, suggesting that intellectually more advanced children go through this sequence sooner than average or less bright children. Recent research has generally supported the findings of Kohlberg and his colleagues, providing strong evidence for Vygotsky's theory of a developmental relationship between language and thought (Berk, 1986; Berk & Garvin, 1984; Frauenglass & Diaz, 1985).

State of the Art
Stamping Out Illiteracy

In an earlier section of this chapter, we presented information about how children learn to read. This may have given the impression that reading is something that develops like most other cognitive abilities—pretty much on schedule for most children in most environments. This, of course, is not the case. Illiteracy is a serious problem in the United States.

If this seems surprising, you are not alone in your puzzlement. Reading does not involve a new language, but merely encoding written symbols corresponding to the language already known. The symbols of reading—letters and the words they form—are concrete: you can see them and point to them, unlike spoken language, which must be listened to and remembered. The symbols for reading are uniform in print, not flavored by individual accents and tones of voice. Reading takes place at a later age than language acquisition and is taught largely in a school setting by experts. Yet it is estimated that 60 million adults in the United States—one third of the population—cannot read well enough to function as full members of society (Kozol, 1985). The question is well stated by psychologist Fitzhugh Dodson (1981, p. 20):

> If little kids are so smart that they can figure out the structure of very complex languages, why do we have so many reading problems in American schools and so many nonreaders in America? Are our children brilliant between the ages of nine months and two years, and do they suddenly become stupid when they enter the door of the schoolhouse at age six? Obviously not.

Knowing how reading develops can give us some insight into how we can make children better readers. The problems of illiteracy and semiliteracy cannot be solved by psychologists, or even educators, alone; the reasons for widespread reading difficulties are social and economic as well. There is no single answer to the question "How do we stop illiteracy?" But based on our knowledge of the science of reading and child development, we do feel comfortable making a few suggestions.

1. *Educate the parents.* The most important persons in helping children acquire language are parents. The job they do is in the day-to-day interactions with their children, not in formal lessons. Parents need to incorporate reading into their repertoire of family activities. They need to read themselves as role models, and they need to read to their children. Yet according to the National Commission on Excellence in Education, about 25% of all parents are unable to read to their children, and 33% are unable to read well enough to help with homework or understand written messages from their children's schools.

2. *Turn off the television set.* Dodson (1981) names television viewing as the number one enemy of reading, especially for children. By the time an average American child graduates from high school, he or she will have spent 22,000 hours watching television (compared to 10,000 hours in school). Although debate abounds over whether television has a negative effect on children's behavior because of its violence and commercialism, there is no question

Parents and other adults who are important to children should provide interesting alternatives to television.

that television takes up time that could be spent in other activities. Parents (and grandparents and day-care workers) should not only limit television time for children, but offer interesting reading material as an option, maybe with adult interaction involved.

3. *Don't dwell on the good old days of education.* They weren't so good. Statistics from last generation's schools did not include a good number of minority children, and test scores reflected only the middle-class majority who took the college preparatory tests. Some people believe that the illiteracy rate hasn't changed much; we just aren't hiding it as well these days.

4. *We need better primary teachers.* This means higher pay for teachers in general, and a pay structure that doesn't favor upper grades and noninstructional personnel.

5. *Don't rush kids to read.* There is no evidence that children who learn to read early (before 6) have any long-lasting advantage over children who learn to read late (after 7). However, there is evidence that early formal instruction can cause problems. David Elkind (1981) tells us that children who are forced to read often have more reading difficulties, and even though they may be able to read, they don't enjoy reading and don't do so unless it's part of a school assignment.

Summary

Behavioral approaches to language development proposed that language is learned as are any other complex phenomena—namely, by reinforcement, association, and imitation. The linguistic approach, based on the theorizing of Noam Chomsky, proposed that children are born with a language acquisition device (LAD), and all that is needed for language acquisition is exposure to speech. Many developmental psychologists today hold an interactionist viewpoint, examining the interplay between language, cognitive, and social development.

Infants are biologically wired to communicate, through both vision and sound. Young infants are responsive to human speech and are especially responsive to the high-pitched, repetitive child-directed speech used by most people when talking to infants. Infants' vocalizations (babbling) change in form from 3 to about 18 months and serve to foster parent-infant social relations as well as later language development. Children usually speak their first words around 10 months and often make over-extensions, applying a word beyond its correct meaning. Children's vocabularies increase over the next few months, and children say their first two-word sentences at about 18 months. These sentences become longer and more complex as children develop, making mean length of utterances (MLU) a good indicator of language development in preschool children. Children seem to learn rules and overregularize irregular words to fit these rules (such as *goed* and *mouses*). Regular age-related changes are seen in forming plurals and past tenses, forming negatives, asking questions, using relational terms, relating events in sentences, and using passive sentences. By the time children are 6 or 7 years old, the structure of their language is very similar to that of an adult.

Various factors—cognitive, social, perceptual, and environmental—influence language acquisition. Level of cognitive development is related to level of language use, although no clear-cut cause-and-effect relationship can be discerned at this time. Deaf infants acquire sign language in much the same fashion as hearing children acquire spoken language; blind infants vocalize less, presumably because their parents talk to them less. Parents modify their speech to children as a function of how sophisticated the child's language is. Both first and second languages are learned more easily by younger than older children, suggesting a critical period for language learning.

Chall has described five stages of learning to read: (1) the prereading skill of letter identification, (2) phonological recoding in the first grade, (3) fluent but effortful reading in grades two and three, (4) "reading to learn" in grades four through eight, and (5) proficient reading in high school and beyond. Reading comprehension involves a series of processes, all of which develop with age and experience.

Research on children's communication has shown that preschool children display poor communication and metacommunication skills, being generally unaware of factors that influence comprehension of messages. However, some researchers have shown that young children's language is not as egocentric as Piaget contended and that the roots of metacommunicative competence can be found in 2-year-olds.

Research into the developmental relationship between language and thought has concentrated on the self-regulatory role of speech. Vygotsky proposed that egocentric, or private, speech has a special role in guiding children's thinking and behavior. Young children's private speech serves as a cognitive self-guidance system and is eventually replaced by covert verbal thought. Recent research provides support for Vygotsky's theory.

Despite our knowledge of the process of learning to read, many children never learn to read well, and many adults are functionally illiterate. Some suggestions are provided to help children's reading.

Key Terms and Concepts

behavioral approaches
linguistic approaches
    language acquisition device (LAD)
    deep structure
interactive approaches
communicative competence
    semantics
    syntax
    morphology
    phonology
    pragmatics
child-directed speech
language acquisition support system (LASS)
overextensions
productive language
receptive language
mean length of utterances (MLU)
    morphemes
    overregularization
    American Sign Language (ASL)
stages of reading
    phonological recoding
phonemic awareness
reading comprehension
    comprehension monitoring
metacommunication
egocentric (private) speech
    collective monologues
    inner speech
    cognitive self-guidance system
illiteracy

Individual Differences in Intelligence

Katie and Jason were sister and brother, born one year apart and sharing very similar genetic and environmental backgrounds. They were both in middle school when their school district started a special class for intellectually gifted children, and both were nominated to be tested for possible placement in this program. Their parents were college educated and very involved in the children's academic progress. Katie and Jason both had good grades and were involved in sports and student council activities. They were well-disciplined kids and had lots of friends. Yet Jason passed the screening tests with flying colors—one of the highest IQ scores in the school—while Katie's test results were surprisingly low—quite inconsistent with her grades and class leadership.

When the results were given to Katie and Jason's parents, they were aware of a potential problem—not Katie's lower intelligence, but how Katie would feel about her test results and her failure to qualify for the gifted program. Katie and Jason had always had such a good relationship, and despite their close ages, their parents had always avoided comparisons. However, this situation was highly volatile, and they were concerned.

Katie broke the ice and brought up the subject herself. One evening when Jason was at baseball practice, she told her parents that something was bothering her. She explained that although her parents had always told her to do her best at everything, she had intentionally given wrong answers during her IQ test session. Now she was having second thoughts about it and was afraid her parents would be disappointed in her.

Her parents were puzzled. Why had she done that? She explained, somewhat tearfully now, that her friends had told her that if she qualified for the gifted program it would conflict with cheerleading practice and she would have to resign from the team. Katie explained that she had looked at the psychologist's scoring sheet and saw red lines he had drawn across each column at different levels. She made sure she didn't answer any questions correctly once they got down to that line on the answer sheet. She had guessed that the red line meant that correct answers beyond showed "gifted" intelligence.

Much later, Katie's parents were able to talk about this incident with some humor. What is intelligence, anyhow? If it is simply a score on a test, their two children were quite different. But if intelligence is taking action to achieve some desired goal, then it would be difficult to judge which child showed more of it—Jason, who was highly motivated to do well in everything he tackled, or Katie, who decoded the psychologist's scoring method and deliberately gave incorrect answers because she wanted to be a cheerleader.

Intelligence is an elusive concept. When we speak of intelligence, we typically refer to differences among individuals in thinking or functioning effectively in the world. In this chapter, we will examine the concept of intelligence as it relates to children. We will look at its measurement, the extent to which it is stable over time, and the degree to which it is influenced by environmental factors. We will also look at some new theories of intelligence and see how they differ from the traditional approach, and in the final section of the chapter, we will take a brief look at some ideas about how intelligence evolved in the species.

Measuring Intelligence

A History of Controversy

Intelligence has long been recognized as a critical component of human success, and scientists of the 19th century devised methods to measure it. Anatomists such as Paul Broca proposed a direct relationship between brain size and intelligence (see Gould, 1981). Broca and others "discovered," among other things, that men had larger skulls than women, providing "proof" for the investigators' biased assumption that men were smarter than women. In making these comparisons, however, they failed to consider differences in body size. Men are larger overall than women, and when differences in body size are considered, the sex difference in skull size disappears (or even slightly favors women).

Not surprisingly, the skull capacity/intelligence relationship was eventually discredited. However, cultural biases concerning who is intelligent and who is not continued to affect how measures of intelligence were interpreted. A good example is found in the Army IQ tests developed during World War I. This was the first large-scale testing of intelligence and was given by the United States Army to 1.75 million men. Two forms of the tests were constructed: the Army Alpha test, a paper-and-pencil test used for recruits who could read English; and the Army Beta test, used for recruits who were not fluent in English. Not surprisingly, assessment procedures were lax, making the accuracy of the tests highly questionable (see Gould, 1981). Despite the many difficulties, the findings of the tests were regarded as reliable, perhaps because they confirmed the preconceived biases of the researchers. The results showed lower levels of intelligence for blacks and the more recently arrived immigrants from southern Europe than for native-born whites and those who had lived in the country for longer periods of time (mostly of northern European origin). Table 10.1 presents the average mental age of recruits as a function of years of residence in the United States. Rather than question the testing procedures, particularly for non-English speakers, or consider that differences in cultural experiences could be responsible for the pattern of results, researchers proclaimed that the more recent immigrants to the country were innately less intelligent than the earlier immigrants (Brigham, 1923). Clearly, the pre-existing belief that intelligence was innate and had been measured accurately by the Army IQ tests, coupled with not-so-subtle racial prejudice, determined how the results were interpreted.

Controversy flared again with accusations of fraud against British psychologist Sir Cyril Burt. Burt was a strong proponent of the genetic basis of intelligence. In a series of studies, he demonstrated that the IQs of identical twins who had been separated

early in life were remarkably similar, even though they were raised in different environments. The results, clearly supporting a strong genetic view of intelligence, were seriously questioned shortly after his death in 1971. Burt had published studies comparing IQ scores in three different groups of separated twins, and the numerical results in all three studies were exactly the same—a coincidence so unlikely as to be considered impossible. Moreover, no records could be found of research associates who had purportedly worked with Burt and administered the IQ tests. They were phantoms, apparently invented by Burt to advance his genetic thesis (see Kamin, 1974).

For the most part, the field has recovered from the shock of Burt's fraud. Research over the past 15 years has investigated both genetic and environmental influences on intelligence, and each camp has impressive research findings to support its claims. There is no straightforward answer to the nature/nurture issue for intelligence. In order to get an accurate picture of the nature of human intelligence, it is necessary to examine biology and environment in interaction. This is an exciting area of study, full of social and political ramifications.

Defining Intelligence

Everybody "knows" what intelligence is. We can use the term effectively in conversation, confident that another person will know what we mean. Yet when forced to be more specific, agreement among both professionals and nonprofessionals alike often disappears. In the broadest sense, intelligence refers to acting or thinking in ways that are goal directed and adaptive (Sternberg & Slater, 1982). Although this definition permits much leeway, there seems to be some general agreement about the common characteristics of intelligence. Based on interviews with both professionals and ordinary citizens, Robert Sternberg and his associates (Sternberg, Conway, Ketron, & Bernstein, 1981) found that people believe that intelligence involves three main sets of skills: (1) practical problem-solving ability—getting to the heart of a problem, interpreting information accurately, and reasoning logically; (2) verbal ability—speaking and writing clearly; and (3) social competence, being curious and sensitive to the needs and desires of others.

Table 10.1 Average mental age of World War I recruits as a function of years of residence in the United States (based on U.S. Army Alpha and Beta tests)

Years of Residence	Average Mental Age
0–5	11.29
6–10	11.70
11–15	12.53
16–20	13.50
20+	13.74

Source: From *The Mismeasure of Man,* by S. J. Gould, p. 221. Copyright © 1981 by W. W. Norton & Co., Inc. Reprinted by permission.

Most people define "intelligence" to include practical skills as well as social and verbal competence.

The Psychometric Approach

How does one measure problem-solving ability, verbal skills, and social competence? The major approach to assessing individual differences in intelligence since the dawn of psychology has been the **psychometric approach,** and the best known product of this approach is the IQ test.

Psychometric theories of intelligence rest on the assumption that intelligence can be described in terms of mental **factors** and that tests can be constructed that reveal individual differences in these factors. A factor is a set of related mental skills that affect thinking in a wide range of situations. For example, a verbal factor can be tapped by tests measuring a variety of verbal skills, such as vocabulary and reading comprehension.

Factors are determined by statistical tests known as **factor analysis.** Depending how the analysis is done and how the tests are constructed, the number of factors proposed to describe human intelligence

ranges from 1 to 180. Charles Spearman's (1927) theory is perhaps the most straightforward, and his ideas on the nature of intelligence continue to be influential today. He proposed that intelligence can be viewed as existing on a single dimension, not as being some multifaceted phenomenon. He labeled this general factor **g,** and he hypothesized that people who perform intelligently in one situation can be expected to perform intelligently in others.

At the other extreme, J. P. Guilford's (1967, 1988) **structure-of-the-intellect** theory includes, in its latest formulation, 180 unique intellectual factors organized along three dimensions (see Figure 10.1). One dimension is composed of six types of mental

Content

Visual
Auditory
Symbolic
Semantic
Behavioral

Products

Units
Classes
Relations
Systems
Transformations
Implications

Operations

Evaluation
Convergent production
Divergent production
Memory retention
Memory recording
Cognition

Figure 10.1 Guilford's structure-of-the-intellect model. *Source:* From "Some Changes in the Structure-of-the-Intellect Model," by J. P. Guilford, *Educational and Psychological Measurement,* 1988, *48,* 1–4. Reprinted by permission.

operations; a second dimension includes five types of content on which the operations function; the third dimension has six types of products that result from applying a given operation to a particular content. By looking at combinations of these three factors, one can examine specific types of intelligence.

Other theories exist between these extremes. One influential theory is that of Raymond Cattell (1963, 1971), who proposed both a general intellectual factor similar to Spearman's *g* and two second-order factors that he called **fluid abilities** and **crystallized abilities.** Fluid abilities are biologically determined and are reflected in tests of memory span and most tests involving spatial thinking, whereas, crystallized abilities are best reflected in tests of verbal comprehension or social relations, skills that are more highly dependent on cultural context and learning experiences.

IQ Tests

Intelligence testing is so prevalent in our society that it is virtually impossible for a child to graduate from high school without having had at least one IQ test and more than a dozen other tests of more specific academic aptitudes. In a fitting comment on our times, when *Science 84* (1984) listed the 20 most influential scientific discoveries of our century, the IQ test was right up there with plastics, antibiotics, and television.

The first IQ test was developed at the turn of the century in France by Alfred Binet and Theodore Simon (1905, 1908) to predict children's school performance. Binet's original scale was modified in 1916 by Lewis Terman, a researcher at Stanford University, producing the **Stanford-Binet.** The test has gone through revisions from time to time, the most recent (fourth edition) being in 1986 (Thorndike, Hagen, & Sattler, 1986). The test has been standardized on large samples and is individually administered by trained examiners using exact procedures. The current version consists of 15 subtests, organized in three levels (see Table 10.2).

The Stanford-Binet is not the only IQ test readily available today. Some paper-and-pencil tests can be given to large groups of children at a time. However, the Stanford-Binet remains one of the two standards by which other IQ tests are measured. The other standard consists of the three intelligence scales

Table 10.2 Three-level hierarchical model of Stanford-Binet

g			
Crystallized Abilities	*Fluid-Analytic Abilities*		*Short-Term Memory*
Verbal Reasoning	*Quantitative Reasoning*	*Abstract/Visual Reasoning*	
Vocabulary	Quantitative	Pattern analysis	Bead memory
Comprehension	Number series	Copying	Memory for
Absurdities	Equation	Matrices	sentences
Verbal relations	building	Paper folding	Memory for
		and cutting	digits
			Memory for
			objects

Source: From *The Stanford-Binet Intelligence Scale (4th Edition): Guide for Administering and Scoring,* by R. L. Thorndike, E. P. Hagen, and J. M. Sattler. Copyright © 1986 by Riverside Publishing Company. Reprinted by permission.

The Stanford-Binet is an individually administered IQ test that consists of 15 subtests and assesses three levels of abilities.

developed by David Wechsler: the Wechsler Pre-school and Primary Scale of Intelligence–Revised (WPPSI-R), the Wechsler Intelligence Scale for Children–Revised (WISC-R), and the Wechsler Adult Intelligence Scale–Revised (WAIS-R). The **Wechsler scales,** like the Stanford-Binet, have been standardized on large samples and are individually administered by trained examiners.

The three Wechsler IQ tests have also been revised several times since their inception in the 1940s, and a new version of the WISC—WISC III—has recently been published. Each test consists of a series of subtests that are organized into two factors: verbal abilities and performance abilities. Wechsler (1974) noted that the division of verbal and performance tasks reflects "two principal modes by which

human abilities express themselves" (p. 9), while acknowledging that mental abilities could also be classified in other ways.

Table 10.3 shows lists of the WISC-R subtests, with examples of questions similar to those that appear on the test. Box 10.1 describes how IQ tests are constructed and how IQ scores are determined.

Alternative Conceptions of Intelligence

The IQ test is the most important product of the psychometric approach to intelligence, which has dominated the study of intelligence throughout this century. However, there have been many critics of

---

Table **10.3** Subtests of the WISC-R

VERBAL IQ

Information
  Children are asked questions assessing their general world knowledge. *Examples:* "How many pennies make a dime?" "What do the lungs do?" "What is the capital of Italy?"

Similarities
  Children are read two words and asked to tell how they are alike. *Examples:* pear-peach; inch-ounce; snow-sand.

Arithmetic
  Children are given arithmetic problems. The easiest involve counting, addition, and subtraction using physical prompts. For example, a child may be shown a picture of 9 trees and asked to cover up all but 5. More complex problems are read aloud. *Examples:* "Joyce had 6 dolls and lost 2. How many dolls did she have left?" "Three girls had 48 cookies. They divided them equally among themselves. How many cookies did each girl get?"

Vocabulary
  Children are read words and asked to tell what each word means.

Comprehension
  Children are asked questions tapping their knowledge of societal conventions and what is appropriate behavior in a variety of situations. *Examples:* "What are some reasons we need soldiers?" "What are you supposed to do if you find someone's watch in school?" "Why is it important to have speed limits on roads?"

Digit Span
  Children are read digits at a rate of one per second and asked to repeat them back in exact order. This is followed by a backward digit span test, in which children must repeat the numbers in the

reverse order in which the examiner spoke them. This is an optional test.

PERFORMANCE IQ

Picture Completion
  Children are shown black-and-white pictures and asked to determine what important part of each picture is missing.

Picture Arrangement
  Children are given a series of pictures in a mixed order and asked to arrange them so that they tell a sensible story.

Block Design
  Children are given 9 cubes colored red on two sides, white on two sides, and red/white on two sides. They are shown designs and asked to reproduce them using the 9 blocks. Bonus points are given for fast response times.

Object Assembly
  Children are given pieces of a familiar object in scrambled order and asked to put the pieces together to make the object. Bonus points are given for fast response times.

Coding
  Children are shown a key of simple geometric figures (triangle, square, and so on), each associated with another symbol (cross, vertical line, and so on). Children are to make the appropriate mark (cross, vertical line) below each of 45 randomly arranged figures without skipping any. Bonus points are given for fast response times.

Mazes
  Children are shown mazes drawn on paper, and asked to draw their way out of the maze. This is an optional test.

Note: The examples provided here are *not* items from the WISC-R but are similar in form to items found on the WISC-R.

the psychometric approach to intelligence, and it does have competitors. Two popular contemporary theories of intelligence that challenge the psycho- metric approach are Robert Sternberg's triarchic theory and Howard Gardner's theory of multiple intelligences.

Box 10.1

Constructing IQ Tests

All IQ tests are standardized. This means that possible questions have been given to a large number of children in various age, racial, and social groups. Questions that are found to discriminate between children of different ages are kept in the test, whereas questions that are found to be too easy or too difficult are removed. For each age group, the average number of questions answered correctly by half the children is computed. For example, items passed by 50% of the 8-year-olds in the standardization sample would reflect the number of items an average 8-year-old should be able to pass.

Historically, the relationship between the number of items passed and the age of the child was expressed as a ratio, or quotient, of one's mental age to one's actual (or chronological) age (hence the term *intelligence quotient,* or IQ). A child's mental age corresponds to the number of test items he or she passes. If a child passes the number of items equal to the number passed by an average 12-year-old, the child's mental age would be 12 years. The child's mental age is then divided by his or her actual age, and the result is multiplied by 100. Thus, a 10-year-old child with a mental age of 10 years has an IQ of 100 (10/10 × 100). A 10-year-old with a mental age of 9.5 years has an IQ of 95 (9.5/10 × 100), and a 10-year-old with a mental age of 12 has an IQ of 120 (12/10 × 100).

The concept of mental age has received substantial criticism in recent years (see Sattler, 1988; Wechsler, 1974) and has been replaced by the **deviation IQ.** Children's performance is compared to that of children their own age and not to the performance of older or younger children. Because of this, tests can be constructed so that the statistical characteristics of IQ are the same at each age level.

Modern tests are constructed so that IQ scores exhibit a normal distribution with specified statistical properties. The distribution of IQ scores for the WISC-R (Wechsler, 1974) is shown in Figure 10.2. As can be seen, children with scores of 100 have IQs equal to or greater than 50% of the population (of children their own age). Children with scores of 115 have IQs equal to or greater than approximately 84% of the population. Thus, by knowing a child's IQ score, one knows where that child stands intellectually relative to agemates.

There is nothing magic about the IQ test. It does not necessarily measure innate intelligence, nor does it necessarily reflect a value that will stay with an individual throughout his or her lifetime. In fact, although IQ does correlate significantly with academic success and occupational status, many argue that it is limited in the type of mental functioning it measures. To equate an IQ score with a child's mental ability is woefully inadequate.

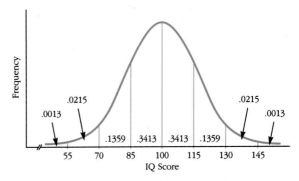

Figure 10.2 Theoretical distribution of WISC-R IQ scores

Sternberg's Triarchic Theory of Intelligence

Robert Sternberg's (1985) **triarchic theory** describes intelligence in terms of three subtheories: the contextual, the experiential, and the componential.

The **contextual subtheory** holds that intelligence must be viewed in terms of the context in which it occurs. What are intelligent behaviors for the middle-class American schoolchild may not be considered intelligent for the inner-city youth or the Guatemalan farm boy. Basically, the contextual subtheory is one of **cultural relativism:** intellectual skills that are critical for survival in one culture may not be so important in another (see also Ceci, 1990).

The **experiential subtheory** is concerned with how prior knowledge influences performance. More specifically, the subtheory examines the ability to deal with novelty and the degree to which processing is automatized (so that it involves relatively little mental effort). Both skills are highly dependent upon experience. A stimulus is novel when it differs in some way from what is already familiar (Rheingold, 1985). People who deal with novelty easily will be able to apply their past knowledge in new situations to solve problems. They are able to compare the new situation to what they already know and use this knowledge to their advantage.

With respect to making processing automatic, newly acquired skills usually require substantial experience before they can be used effortlessly (Shiffrin & Schneider, 1977). Take reading, for example. Young children often labor over every letter, carefully sounding out each word. With years of practice, many of the skills involved in reading become automatic (or nearly so), resulting in more proficient performance. Sternberg proposes that how people respond to novelty and the ease with which they can make mental processes automatic are important and universal aspects of intelligence.

The importance of such skills is apparent in any occupation. For example, the installation of three ceiling fans in our home by an experienced electrician was a lesson in dealing with novelty. We had attempted to do the job ourselves and, after failing miserably, called two different electricians to the house who also failed. The third electrician, a semi-retired man, was different, however. He approached the problem cautiously, and, after nine hours of running into more obstacles than we knew existed in the walls and above the ceilings, the task was done. When we expressed our admiration for a job well done, the electrician commented, "Any yahoo can lay wire in a straight line. It only takes brains when things don't go as you planned."

The **componential subtheory** is Sternberg's information-processing model of cognition. Briefly, Sternberg proposed several components of information processing: knowledge-acquisition components, which get information into the system; performance components, which make comparisons between information and get information out of the system; and metacomponents, which monitor how the other components are doing.

Sternberg's theory is an attempt to go beyond earlier, single theories. The contextual subtheory points out the relativity of intelligence by emphasizing the importance of specifying what constitutes intelligent behavior. Alone, such a theory is incomplete, for it is almost impossible to make comparisons among people with different experiences. Everything is relative, and as such, intelligence can be studied only from the perspective of a particular culture or subculture. However, the experiential subtheory specifies what types of tasks are most apt

"YOU CAN'T BUILD A HUT, YOU DON'T KNOW HOW TO FIND EDIBLE ROOTS AND YOU KNOW NOTHING ABOUT PREDICTING THE WEATHER. IN OTHER WORDS, YOU DO TERRIBLY ON OUR I.Q. TEST."

Many argue that IQ tests are biased. *Source:* © 1987 by Sidney Harrison, *American Scientist Magazine.*

to tap intelligence (those with a degree of novelty and those requiring automatic processing), and the componential subtheory provides the universal mental mechanisms by which knowledge is acquired and manipulated. Together, the three subtheories provide a framework for understanding intelligence and its development that, in many ways, is broader and more inclusive than psychometric theories.

Gardner's Theory of Multiple Intelligences

Howard Gardner's (1983) **theory of multiple intelligences** proposes that intelligence is composed of separate components, or modules, much like the factors used in the psychometric approach. His theory differs, however, in that it relies heavily on neuropsychological evidence for the existence of seven relatively independent "frames of mind": (1) linguistic, (2) logical/mathematical, (3) musical, (4) spatial, (5) bodily-kinesthetic, (6) interpersonal, and (7) intrapersonal. Linguistic and logical/mathematical intelligences are highly valued in technological societies such as ours, and people high in these types of intelligence are generally viewed as being "smart." Musical intelligence is usually associated with the composition or performance of music, and spatial intelligence involves the ability to perceive form, solve visual problems, and get around effectively in one's environment. Bodily-kinesthetic intelligence refers to control of one's body, as epitomized by athletes of exceptional ability. The two forms of personal intelligence involve knowing how

Some theorists believe that our definition of intelligence should be broadened to include musical and physical abilities.

to deal with others (interpersonal) and knowledge of self (intrapersonal).

What is Gardner's basis for this particular classification? He points to many studies demonstrating that brain damage to specific areas can lead to specific types of intellectual deficits. Further evidence comes from savants—mentally retarded people who have extraordinary talents in specific areas, such as music, painting, or mathematical computation. The very existence of savants suggests that these abilities are independent and based in biology.

Gardner proposes that different forms of intelligence vary in importance in different cultures and historical periods. For example, in a hunting society, physical dexterity and an ability to locomote effectively are more important than numerical computation. In medieval Europe's apprenticeship system, emphasis was placed on bodily, spatial, and interpersonal abilities, whereas 400 years later, in today's Western society, the emphasis is on linguistic and logical/mathematical skills (Gardner, 1984a). Thus, Gardner views the cultural aspects of intelligence to be of utmost importance: different cultures will value different types of intelligence. Moreover, Gardner argues that our society's reliance on IQ tests to classify children in terms of intelligence does a great disservice to many of them and to society itself. Because of the emphasis on linguistic and mathematical abilities, children gifted in other areas, such as working with their hands, are often "thrown on society's scrap heap" (Gardner, 1984a, p. 76), instead of receiving the education that could enhance their special abilities.

Gardner argues for the exclusion of intelligence and aptitude tests from our schools because they measure only two types of intelligences while ignoring other, equally important types. Gardner is not opposed to intellectual assessment in general, however. He advocates the development of measures that would evaluate all seven types of intelligence.

Gardner proposes that we recognize seven areas of intelligence, believing that culture determines which areas are valued most highly.

He believes that such assessments should be done early so that intellectual strengths can be discovered and developed through education. Although Gardner believes that each form of intelligence has its origins in biology, he also believes that they are flexible and can be enhanced by education.

Gardner and his colleagues have implemented some of these ideas in a preschool program called Project Spectrum (Gardner & Hatch, 1989; Wexler-Sherman, Gardner, & Feldman, 1988). The curriculum for 4- and 5-year-old children is based on the various domains of intelligence in Gardner's theory. Assessment of children's abilities in each of these domains extends naturally from the curriculum, making the assessment ecologically valid for children. Children are given substantial freedom to explore within the preschool environment, being encouraged, but never forced, to experience all of the content areas. Based on observations in the preschool, 15 different subskill areas have been identified within the framework of Gardner's theory (see Table 10.4). Clear distinctions are noted among children in each of these areas, bolstering the claim that each represents a distinct form of intelligence (Wexler-Sherman et al., 1988).

Although there has not yet been a rigorous experimental test of Gardner's theory, preliminary results are available. Gardner and Hatch (1989) report two small-scale studies—one with a group of 20 preschool children and another with a group of 15 kindergarten and first-grade children—using an assessment procedure developed to evaluate each of the seven intelligences. They found that the preschoolers did not perform at the same level on the various tasks, but showed distinct intellectual profiles, as predicted by the theory. Similar findings were reported for the kindergarten children. The 5 first-grade girls, however, showed no intellectual weaknesses and many strengths (only 2 first grade boys were tested). Given the small sample sizes, no definitive conclusions can be reached; but the data, at least from the younger children, are consistent with Gardner's theory. More important, they indicate that an assessment measure can be constructed and that the theory is testable.

Alternatives to IQ Tests

Few people, even among psychometricians, would argue that IQ tests accurately measure intelligence. Yet there is general agreement that the tests do mea-

Table 10.4 Types of intelligences and examples of tasks used for evaluation in Project Spectrum

Type of Intelligence	Tasks	Examples
Music	Production	Singing familiar and novel songs
	Perception	Identifying patterns of bell chimes
Language	Narrative	Telling a story from pictures on a storyboard
	Descriptive	Reporting a sequence of events
Numbers	Counting	Counting moves in a board game
	Calculating	Creating a notational system, performing mental calculations, and organizing number information in the context of a game
Visual Arts	Drawing	Making pictures
	3-D	Working with clay
Movement	Dance	Responding to rhythm and performing expressive dance movements
	Athletic	Maneuvering through an obstacle course
Science	Logical inference	Playing treasure hunt games
	Mechanical	Using household gadgets
	Naturalistic	Observing, appreciating, and understanding natural phenomena in classroom "Discovery Area"
Social	Social analysis	Playing with scale model of classroom
	Social roles	Interacting with peers

Source: Adapted from "A Pluralistic View of Early Assessment: The Project Spectrum Approach," by C. Wexler-Sherman, H. Gardner, and D. H. Feldman, *Theory into Practice,* 1988, *27,* 77–83. Reprinted by permission.

sure something important that is close to our understanding of intelligence. Moreover, the IQ test has been part of our culture for most of this century, and its easy availability to educators and researchers makes it, to many, the best of all possible measures.

But the IQ test has its detractors, with Sternberg and Gardner perhaps the two most prominent and vocal. At the same time, however, they differ with each other. Gardner (1984b) complains that Sternberg's account of intelligence is not sufficiently different from the psychometric account, in that it leaves room for a general intellectual factor similar to Spearman's *g*. Sternberg (1984) counters that it is too early to compare the two theories because there have been no experimental tests of Gardner's theory.

It is too early to judge the ultimate merit of Sternberg's and Gardner's approaches to the study of intelligence or to predict if either will replace the psychometric approach. Both theories have stimulated much research and discussion among psychologists and educators in the brief time since their publication. Regardless of their theoretical merits, however, intelligence testing is big business, and the theory that produces a reliable test is the one that will likely win the hearts and minds of the educational establishment. The promise of such a test (Gardner refers to it as an assessment) has yet to be fulfilled. Future work will determine whether these new theories can explain the vagaries of intelligence better than older theories, and whether tests based on these theories can be constructed and made available for wide distribution.

Stability of IQ over Infancy and Childhood

Most of us like to believe that the world we live in is relatively stable and predictable. This goes for intelligence, too. We generally assume that bright children grow up to become bright adults. We don't expect a smart 7-year-old to turn into a dullard at 12, nor do we expect an 8-year-old who can barely remember his phone number to turn into a genius by age 10. But these are empirical questions. How stable are individual differences in intelligence over time? Can adult intellectual functioning be predicted from intelligence tests administered at age 12? At age 6? In infancy?

Measuring Stability

What do we mean by stability? Surely we do not mean that intelligence stays the same; many of the preceding chapters have dealt with ways in which all children develop intellectually over time. Stability, as used here, refers to how constant over time an

Box 10.2

Passing the SATs without Reading the Questions

Although IQ tests are the crowning glory of the psychometric approach, achievement tests such as the Scholastic Aptitude Test (SAT) have become a staple of the American educational system. The SAT is taken by hundreds of thousands of college-bound students annually and consists of two major sections—verbal and quantitative—each assessing a variety of language and mathematical skills predictive of success in college.

One section of the verbal portion of the SAT is a reading comprehension task. On this task, students read short texts and then answer multiple-choice questions about them. This task is designed to measure students' ability to read and understand English prose passages. But does it? In a recent experiment, college students were given the multiple-choice questions from reading comprehension sections of the SATs and asked to guess the right answers

without reading the text (Katz, Lautenschlager, Blackburn, & Harris, 1990). Their performance was compared to that of a group of college students who read the corresponding text before answering the questions.

The researchers reported that students not given the passages to read performed similarly to students with the passages. That is, students who depended on their prior knowledge to answer the questions did comparably to students who based their answers on the passages they read. Reading comprehension performance was related to how well students did on the overall verbal subtest of the SAT. These findings suggest that performance on the reading comprehension section of the SAT is not tapping reading ability, but rather some other general verbal abilities.

individual stays relative to others on measures of intelligence. It is measured by correlations of rank order. For example, if a group of children are given IQ tests at age 5, they can be ranked in terms of their IQ scores from highest to lowest. If that same group is tested again at age 10, we can compare the rank orders of children at the two points in time. If the rankings are similar, the correlation will be positive and high. (A perfect positive correlation is +1.0.) If there is no stability of individual differences in IQ between ages 5 and 10, the correlation will be close to zero, which reflects chance.

Predicting Later Intelligence from Infancy

Can childhood and adult intelligence be predicted from infancy? Stated another way, is intelligence stable over infancy and childhood? For most of the cen-

Box 10.3

Education of the Gifted: Meeting the Challenge

Dr. David Goldstein
Director of Research and Development
The Talent Identification Program at
Duke University

Few would question the statement that a nation's richest resource is its children and youth. Yet the 3% to 5% of American children who are most intellectually capable—those with IQ scores above 130 or standardized test scores above the 97th percentile—are seriously underserved. These gifted and talented children come from all ethnic, economic, social, and geographical segments of our society. They typically have an advanced vocabulary, broad interests, in-

tense powers of concentration, exceptional memory, a seemingly effortless mastery of concepts and skills, and a high activity level. Their classroom performance is often, but not necessarily, high. Motivation is usually intense, but may be sporadic or focused on unusual topics. Their demonstrated ability in one or more areas is typically outstanding.

Of great surprise to many is the fact that only half the gifted children in the United States have been identified as such by parents, teachers, psychologists, or pediatricians. Many parents underestimate their children's abilities; they have difficulty accepting that their child is gifted rather than "just bright," believing one must be a genius to be considered gifted. As a result, only a limited number of the nation's gifted children are being provided with suitable opportunities to develop their unique capabilities.

Too often gifted students, particularly those not yet formally identified, are significantly underachieving in school. Some studies suggest that at least 10% of gifted students become high school dropouts. Gifted children often feel bored with school or different from their classmates; some experience severe feelings of depression and alienation. Such problems are more easily handled when parents and professionals realize that the gifted have special needs and seek to provide the necessary attention and services to guide and support these children.

(Continued)

tury, this question has been addressed through the correlation of scores on sensorimotor tests (Bayley, 1969; Brazelton, 1973; Gesell & Amatruda, 1954). These infant tests are constructed in a way similar to the IQ tests, with a score of 100 representing average performance of an infant at any age. Rather than an IQ score, however, infant tests typically produce a **DQ** score, which stands for **developmental quotient.** Although the constructors of infant tests hold a variety of theoretical views, their tests contain quite similar items. (For sample items from the Bayley Scales of Infant Development, see Table 10.5.)

Will babies who score high on these DQ tests also score high on later IQ tests? The results of several decades of research are relatively consistent, and negative. Joseph Fagan and Lynn Singer (1983)

Box 10.3 (Continued)

Unfortunately, the assumption is widespread that special attention for the gifted is unnecessary (or worse, that it will create an "elitist" group). Statements reflecting this attitude are widespread: "A bright mind will find its own way." "Gifted children can make it on their own; they just need to fit in like everybody else." In truth, gifted children need and deserve our understanding and emotional support, as well as challenging educational opportunities, if they are to develop their talents to the fullest and become contributing members of society.

One organization that is devoted to the identification, support, and development of exceptional academic talent is the Talent Identification Program (TIP) at Duke University. Covering 16 states in the Southeast, Midwest, and Southwest, TIP identifies the brightest children at an early age and works to develop their potential to the fullest. TIP was founded in 1980 by Professor Robert Sawyer of Duke University and is currently one of four programs of its kind in the nation. To nurture the students' talents throughout their middle and high school years, TIP provides them with various services, including recognition ceremonies, an extensive *Educational Opportunity Guide,* a By-Mail Program, Advanced Placement course materials, and—for truly exceptional students—a summer residential program on the Duke University campus.

The summer residential program at Duke offers intensive, fast-paced courses in the humanities, social sciences, natural sciences, mathematics, and computer science. To qualify, a student must have attained, as a seventh-grader, a score on the SAT math test of 550 or higher or a score on the SAT verbal test of 500 or higher (or equivalent scores on the ACT). These scores are higher than those earned by roughly two-thirds of college-bound high school seniors! Students enroll in a single course during a three-week term. Under the direction of talented and encouraging instructors, participants generally complete the equivalent of a year of high school or a semester of college-level work in the subject. In 1990 more than 1000 students attended the summer program at Duke or at one of three overseas sites.

TIP is also actively engaged in research to increase our understanding of the nature of giftedness. Some of the topics under investigation include the role of family variables and biological factors in the development of academic talent and sex differences in mathematical and spatial abilities.

Although organizations such as TIP, and other major programs such as the Center for the Advancement of Academically Talented Youth (CTY) at the Johns Hopkins University and the Connie Belin National Center for Gifted Education at the University of Iowa, have done much to advance the cause of serving our nation's gifted and talented youth, much more needs to be done so that our most precious resource—the talent of our youth—is not wasted.

Reprinted by permission.

Table 10.5 Bayley Scales of Infant Development: Sample items

Items typifying infants between 1 and 3 months	in response to "bye-bye" or clapping hands in response to "pat-a-cake"?
Responds to sound of bell	Puts cube in cup on demand
Regards red ring	Will infant place a cube in a cup when requested to do so?
Does infant attend to a red ring suspended by string 8 inches from infant's eyes?	Stirs with spoon in imitation
Vocalizes once or twice	Will infant imitate the examiner who makes a stirring motion in a cup?
Does infant coo, gurgle, squeal during examination period?	Attempts to scribble
Circular eye coordination: red ring	After examiner demonstrates scribbling on a piece of paper, will infant attempt to scribble when given the chance?
Does infant follow circular path of red ring moved above infant's eyes?	Turns pages of book
Social smile	
Does infant smile or laugh in response to smile from examiner?	*Items typifying infants between 14 and 17 months*
	Spontaneous scribble
Items typifying infants between 5 and 7 months	Will child attempt scribbling before it is demonstrated by examiner?
Smiles at mirror image	Says two words
Turns head after fallen spoon	Does child say two recognizable words during the interview?
Does infant turn head in direction of a spoon that falls to the floor and makes a noise?	Shows shoes or other clothing
Interest in sound production	Will child point to his or her shoes in response to question "Where are your shoes?"
Does infant intentionally use objects to make noise?	Builds a tower of three cubes
Picks up cube deftly and directly	Attains toy with stick
Does child pick up small cube?	When small toy is placed out of reach of child, will child use stick to attempt to obtain it?
Vocalizes four different syllables	
Items typifying infants between 9 and 12 months	
Responds to verbal requests	
Can child perform some act upon request, such as waving	

Source: Adapted from *The Bayley Scales of Infant Development,* by N. Bayley. Copyright © 1969 by The Psychological Corporation. Reproduced by permission. All rights reserved.

summarized the results of studies examining the relationship between DQ tests of sensorimotor development and later IQ for both normal and high-risk samples as a function of age of testing (both in infancy and in childhood). The correlations, shown in Table 10.6, are of a moderate magnitude for high-risk infants; other research has shown that these tests predict well children who are apt to show delayed development (see Siegel, 1989). But for normal infants, the correlations are uniformly low—the average correlation between infant tests and IQ at age 6 is .11—raising questions as to what exactly these tests measure.

In the past decade, new measures of infant intelligence have been found that correlate significantly better with later IQ than do infant DQ tests. Rather than looking at infants' performance on sensorimotor tasks and overall DQ test scores, researchers

have looked for specific cognitive processes in infancy. Tests of infant perception—specifically, those involving habituation and dishabituation (discussed in Chapter 6)—have been found to predict childhood IQ far better than DQ tests.

Research examining the relationship between childhood IQ scores and measures of habituation and dishabituation has produced consistently high correlations. Marc Bornstein (1989), summarizing the results of these studies, reported average correlations between childhood IQ and infant habituation scores of .49, and between childhood IQ and infant dishabituation scores of .46. Studies published since Bornstein's review have yielded comparable findings (Rose, Feldman, & Wallace, 1988; Rose, Feldman, Wallace, & McCarton, 1989; Slater, Cooper, Rose, & Morison, 1989). Although these correlations are still only moderate, they are substantially higher

Table 10.6 Median correlations between infant DQ tests and later IQ scores for normal and high-risk samples

| Infant Test (Months) | Normal Sample | | | | High-Risk Sample | | | |
| | Age at Follow-Up Test (Years) | | | | Age at Follow-Up Test (Years) | | | |
	3	4–5	6+	Mean	3	4–5	6+	Mean
3–4	.04 (4)*	.06 (2)	.07 (3)	.06	.14 (2)	.08 (4)	.07 (2)	.10
5–7	.25 (14)	.20 (5)	.06 (6)	.15	.27 (5)	.24 (13)	.28 (3)	.26
8–11	.20 (8)	.23 (5)	.21 (3)	.21	.29 (6)	.23 (10)	.29 (6)	.27
Mean	.16	.16	.11		.23	.18	.21	

*Numbers in parentheses represent number of studies in each median correlation.
Source: From "Infant Recognition Memory as a Measure of Intelligence," by J. F. Fagan III and L. T. Singer. In L. P. Lipsitt and C. K. Rovee-Collier (eds.), *Advances in Infancy Research, Vol. 2.* Copyright © 1983 by Ablex Publishing Corporation. Reprinted by permission.

than the correlations between infant DQ tests and later intelligence.

Why should these measures of infant information processing predict later intelligence? The primary reason seems to be that mental processes in habituation and dishabituation are the same as the processes used by older children in more complex cognitive tasks (Bornstein, 1989; Fagan, 1984). Habituation and dishabituation involve the ability to detect similarities and differences among stimuli, memory, and the formation of mental concepts—abilities central to thinking at any age. When cognition is based on the same underlying mental processes at different ages, stability of individual differences can be expected (Bjorklund, 1989; McCall, Eichorn, & Hogarty, 1977).

Yet the cognitive abilities involved in infant habituation and dishabituation reflect only part of the picture of infant intelligence. Environment can also play a substantial role in influencing intelligence. Marc Bornstein and his colleagues (Bornstein, 1989; Tamis-LeMonda & Bornstein, 1989) demonstrated that the quality of mother-infant interaction predicted childhood intelligence at age 4, independent of infant habituation rates. In other words, how parents interact with their babies has an important influence on their children's intelligence above and beyond the basic information-processing skills measured by habituation rate. This means that intelligence is a multifaceted thing, and we must interpret very cautiously any global pronouncements concerning its development.

Predicting Adult IQ from Childhood Data

Although infant DQ measures do not predict later IQ well, the stability of individual differences in intelligence as measured by IQ increases dramatically by age 2. Table 10.7 summarizes the findings of two longitudinal studies (Bayley, 1949 and Honzik,

Table 10.7 Correlations of childhood and adult IQ scores by age at childhood testing

Age at Testing	Honzik et al. (1948)	Bayley (1949)
1 year	—	−.14
2–3 years	.33	.40
4–5 years	.42	.52
6–7 years	.67	.68
8–9 years	.71	.80
10–11 years	.73	.87
12–13 years	.79	—
14–15 years	.76	.84

Source: From "Consistency and Variability in the Growth of Intelligence from Birth to Eighteen Years," by N. Bayley, *Journal of Genetic Psychology,* 1949, *75,* 165–196. Reprinted with permission of the Helen Dwight Reid Educational Foundation. Published by Heldref Publications, 4000 Albemarle St., N.W., Washington, D.C. 20016. 1948 data from "Stability of Mental Test Performance between Two and Eighteen Years," by M. P. Honzik, J. W. McFarlane, and L. Allen, *Journal of Experimental Education,* 1948, *17,* 309–324.

MacFarlane, & Allen, 1948) and presents the correlations between scores on intelligence tests given to a group of individuals at various times between 1 and 18 years of age. The correlations with adult IQ rise rapidly until early childhood and are relatively stable from around age 8 on. In fact, Claire Kopp and Robert McCall (1982) have stated that "following age 5, IQ is perhaps the most stable, important behavioral characteristic yet measured" (p. 39).

Why should there be such a high degree of stability in IQ over childhood, especially when predictions from infant psychometric tests are so poor? In all likelihood, the increased stability of IQ beginning around age 2 is due to the common, symbolic basis for thought at different ages. According to Piaget, there is a qualitative change in thinking that occurs sometime between 18 and 30 months of age. Children become symbol users and remain symbol users throughout their lives. The ability to access and manipulate symbols is a central aspect of most if not all intelligence tests from the age of 2 on. As with the prediction of childhood IQ from habituation/dishabituation rates in infancy, stability of individual differences can be expected when cognition at different ages is based on the same underlying mental process—in this case, on the use of symbols.

Experience and Intelligence

The relative stability of intelligence over childhood, with moderate degrees of stability found from infancy, has been interpreted by some theorists to reflect an underlying intelligence factor (*g*), presumably genetic in nature (Fagan, 1984). Needless to say, other theorists disagree. However, even if they were right, intelligence is also greatly influenced by experience.

Establishing Intelligence

Extreme environments can have drastic effects on intelligence. Studies with laboratory animals clearly show that social, emotional, and intellectual functioning is greatly impaired when animals are raised in restricted environments (Greenough, Black, & Wallace, 1987; Harlow, Dodsworth, & Harlow, 1965). Although such lab experiments cannot be done with children, some naturalistic studies have been done in institutions and homes, assessing the consequences of growing up in impoverished environments.

Institutionalization studies Several **institutionalization studies** conducted during the first half of the 20th century examined the effects of maternal deprivation, where infants had been separated from their mothers and raised in overcrowded and understaffed institutions (Dennis, 1973; Skeels & Dye, 1939; Spitz, 1945). Wayne Dennis (1973) contrasted the outcomes for children reared in an orphanage in Beirut, Lebanon, and infants placed in adoptive homes. At the orphanage, a charity-run institution for illegitimate children, infants received little direct stimulation in the form of play or other social interactions. They remained in small cribs much of their day, without toys and with sheets hung on the sides of their cribs, blocking their view of nursery routine. Life was more varied for older children, but opportunities for intellectual stimulation were minimal, as was adult-child interaction. Furthermore, many of the primary caretakers, "graduates" of the orphanage themselves, were characterized by low IQs and a general unresponsiveness toward their young wards.

Dennis reported that infants who remained institutionalized displayed signs of severe retardation within their first year, and that their average IQs by age 16 ranged between 50 and 80. In contrast, infants who left the orphanage for adoptive homes before the age of 2 regained normal intellectual functioning, having average childhood IQ scores of about 100. Children adopted following their second birthday also demonstrated childhood gains in intellectual performance, but performed several years below their age level.

Home studies Beginning in the late 1960s, researchers began evaluating parent-child interaction patterns in the homes of preschool children. Several studies demonstrated significant differences between middle-class and working-class families with respect to parenting styles. Middle-class parents were more apt to talk to their children, teach them intellectual tasks, and permit them opportunities to explore the environment (Tulkin & Kagan, 1972).

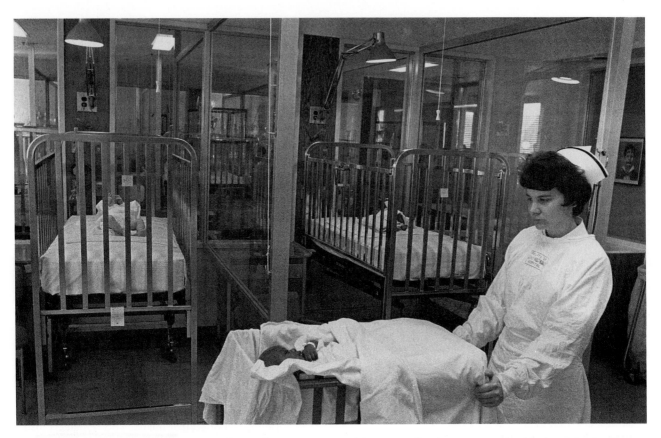

In the early part of this century, infants whose parents could not care for them were raised in large institutions.

Although it was assumed that these differences in parent-child interaction were responsible for differences in intellectual performance, this can only be determined through longitudinal studies. One of the more impressive longitudinal projects evaluating quality of parent-child interactions and later intelligence is that of Bettye Caldwell, Robert Bradley, and Richard Elardo. They developed an inventory for assessing the quality of the home environment called the Home Observation for Measurement of the Environment (HOME) (Caldwell & Bradley, 1978). The HOME scale is divided into six subscales (see Table 10.8) and is used to code aspects of a child's home environment that relate to intellectual development.

Studies in which researchers coded mother-child interactions in the home using the HOME scale revealed moderate correlations (.30–.60) between HOME scores and IQ measures (Bee et al., 1982; Bradley & Caldwell, 1976, 1980; Elardo, Bradley, & Caldwell, 1977). More specifically, mothers who were emotionally and verbally more responsive to their infants, who provided more play materials for their children, and who were generally more involved with their infants at 6 and 24 months of age had children with higher Stanford-Binet IQ scores at 54 months than did mothers who provided less stimulation for their youngsters (Bradley & Caldwell, 1976). Table 10.9 presents the correlations between 6-month and 24-month HOME scores and 54-month IQ scores for children in the Bradley and Caldwell (1976) study.

More recent research using the HOME scale has demonstrated that descriptions of the home environment during the first two years of life predict reasonably well academic performance at age 11 (Bradley, 1989). However, a beneficial early environ-

Table 10.8 Subscales and sample items from the HOME inventory

I. *Emotional and Verbal Responsivity of the Mother*
Examples: Mother spontaneously vocalizes to child at least twice during visit (excluding scolding).
Mother responds to child's vocalizations with a vocal or verbal response.
Mother caresses or kisses child at least once during visit.

II. *Avoidance of Restriction and Punishment*
Examples: Mother does not shout at child during visit.
Mother neither slaps nor spanks child during visit.
Mother does not interfere with child's actions or restrict child's movement more than three times during visit.

III. *Organization of the Physical and Temporal Environment*
Examples: Someone takes the child to the grocery store at least once a week.
When mother is away, care is provided by one of three regular substitutes.
The child's environment appears safe and free of hazards.

IV. *Provision of Appropriate Play Materials*
Examples: Child has a pull or push toy.
Mother provides toys or interesting activities for child during interview.
Provides toys for literature and music (books, records, etc.).

V. *Maternal Involvement with the Child*
Examples: Mother tends to keep child within visual range and to look at child often.
Mother talks to child while doing her work.
Mother structures child's play period.

VI. *Opportunities for Variety in Daily Stimulation*
Examples: Father provides some caregiving every day.
Mother reads stories to child at least three times weekly.
Child has at least three or more books.

Source: Adapted from *Home Observation for Measurement of the Environment,* by B. M. Caldwell and R. H. Bradley. Copyright © 1978 by University of Arkansas. Reprinted by permission.

ment is not apt to have long-term consequences if later environments are less supportive. That is, when the childhood environment is stable, patterns of development are usually stable; when the childhood environment is constantly changing, patterns of intellectual development are also apt to change (Bradley, 1989). Thus, not only is a stimulating early environment important for sound intellectual development, but so is its continuity and stability (see also Clarke-Stewart, 1973; White, 1978; White, Carew-Watts, Barnett, Kaban, Marmor, & Shapiro, 1973).

A word of caution is warranted before concluding that competent parenting causes children to be more intelligent. For example, Burton White (1978) has quite sensibly argued that placing children behind barriers, such as in a playpen, for long periods hinders cognitive development. Although we suspect that there is much truth to this statement, the role of the child must also be considered. Some children are easier to keep in a playpen than others; they are content sitting and playing with a few favorite toys and rarely complain about their confinement. Other children make it very difficult for Mom or Dad to make frequent use of the playpen, letting their parents know in no uncertain terms that life behind bars is not for them. The end result may be the same: the child given more freedom to explore develops more quickly than the child who spends more time in the playpen. What must be kept in mind is that children play a crucial role in affecting

Table 10.9 Correlations between Stanford-Binet performance at 54 months and scores on the HOME scale at 6 and 24 months

Home Observation for Measurement of the Environment	Correlations	
	6 months	24 months
1. Emotional and verbal responsivity of mother	.27	.50**
2. Avoidance of restriction and punishment	.10	.28*
3. Organization of physical and temporal environment	.31*	.33*
4. Provision of appropriate play materials	.44**	.56**
5. Maternal involvement with child	.28*	.55**
6. Opportunities for variety in daily stimulation	.30*	.39**
Total score	.44**	.57**
Multiple correlation[a]	.50*	.63**

[a]This represents the correlation of all HOME subscales with Binet scores.
*$p < .05$.
**$p < .01$.
Source: From "The Relation of Infants' Home Environment to Mental Test Performance at Fifty-four Months: A Follow-up Study," by R. H. Bradley and B. M. Caldwell, *Child Development,* 1976, *47,* 1172–1174. Copyright © The Society for Research in Child Development, Inc. Reprinted by permission.

Loving, involved parents and a stimulating home environment are important to the intellectual development of preschoolers, and of older children as well.

their own development, in part by influencing how their parents treat them. Thus, parents' influence must be evaluated in terms of a continuous transaction between children and their parents, both of whom are changed as a result of the interactions.

Modification of Intellectual Functioning

Clearly, a child's early environment can affect individual differences in intelligence. A related series of questions concerns the extent to which intelligence can be modified. Is intellectual functioning set by early experience, or can it be changed, for better or worse, by later experience?

One of the earliest studies to demonstrate reversibility in the effects of a nonsupportive early environment was reported by Harold Skeels (Skeels, 1966; Skeels & Dye, 1939). A group of infants living in an overcrowded and understaffed Depression-era orphanage were showing signs of retardation, apparently due to their stimulus-deprived environment. One group of infants (the experimental group, average age 19 months, average IQ 64.3) was transferred to a residential facility for mentally retarded adults and placed with the brighter women residents. A contrast group was chosen from children who remained in the orphanage until at least age 4; their average IQ at 18 months was 86.7. The children in the experimental group received loving attention from the mentally retarded women. In almost every case, a single adult became closely attached to a child, resulting in an intense one-to-one relationship that was supplemented by less intense but frequent interactions between the child and other adults. Children in the experimental group remained in the institution for the mentally retarded for an average of 19 months, after which they were placed in foster homes or with adoptive parents.

When tested again at approximately age 6, the average IQ score for children in the experimental group was 95.9, an increase of more than 32 points, whereas the average IQ of children in the contrast group had dropped to 66.1 points, a decline of more than 20 points. Skeels followed these individuals into adulthood. The experimental subjects represented a normal range of economic levels and educational attainment (high school education). In comparison, the subjects in the contrast group were all in the two lowest socioeconomic levels and had, on average, a third-grade education. Although IQ tests were not given to the subjects as adults, IQ scores were available for some of the 28 children of the experimental subjects. IQs of these children ranged from 86 to 125, with an average of 103.9. In general, the experimental group, who started life with very low IQs due to severe disadvantage, had become, by a variety of intellectual, occupational, and social standards, normal.

Other evidence for the reversibility of the effects of negative early experience comes from observations of children removed from neglectful homes. One of the best-documented studies of the mental growth of isolated children is that of Jarmila Koluchova (1972, 1976). Monozygotic twins, who were physically and psychologically normal at 11 months, experienced abuse, neglect, and malnutrition until discovered at the age of 7 years. The children had no language ability and an estimated mental age of 3 years. They were placed in foster care and given an educational program in the hopes they would attain some semblance of normal intelligence. The program was far more successful than originally expected, with the twins having IQs of 93 and 95 by 11

years of age and 101 and 100 by 14 years (see also Clarke & Clarke, 1976; Davis, 1947; Mason, 1942).

More recent studies have looked at the progress of malnourished and socially deprived children from Southeast Asia adopted by American couples (Clark & Hanisee, 1982; Winick, Meyer, & Harris, 1975). The results of these studies indicate that, two years later, these children showed no signs of their early deprivation.

The Evolution of Human Intelligence

As it was for all other species, the task of our ancestors was to survive—to find food, defend against predators, reproduce, and raise offspring to adulthood so they could continue the life cycle. What is unique about humans is that, more than any other species, we have developed a flexible intelligence as our primary means of survival. Other animals evolved thick fur, sharp claws, specialized teeth, and swift speed as means for adapting to their environments. Humans, above all others, developed an intellect and an ability to learn that resulted in the creation of culture, morality, and eventually, ecological dominance over the globe. What were the pressures that caused this development, and how is our intelligence today used for adapting to the demands of the many varied environments in which we find ourselves?

Although we cannot present a precise picture of the evolution of human intelligence, we can say with confidence that one of the most influential factors was the fact that humans are social creatures. Many contemporary researchers believe it was social pressures that made it necessary for our species to evolve intellectually, as much as or even more than pressures to locate food or avoid predators (Alexander, 1989; Byrne & Whiten, 1988; Crook, 1980; Humphrey, 1976).

From Apes to Humans

Biochemical analyses reveal that humans share approximately 99% of their DNA with chimpanzees and gorillas (Gribbin & Cherfas, 1982). By estimating the rate of mutations over time, biochemists have determined that humans, chimpanzees, and gorillas shared the same ancestor as recently as 5 to 8 million years ago. Our earliest ancestor that was distinct from the chimps and gorillas has been called *Australopithecus afarensis*. These were small animals, the females being about 3.5 feet tall, who walked upright, much as modern humans do, but had small skulls that were more apelike than human. From the fossil skulls, we know that *Australopithecus afarensis* had a small cranium (about 400 cc), and it follows that they also had small brains. There is no evidence that these animals used tools or possessed language (see Box 10.4).

The earliest member of the *Homo* (true human) genus lived about 2.5 million years ago and has been termed *Homo habilis*. These were brainier animals (brain size about 650 cc) who used primitive stone tools. Casts of *Homo habilis* skulls reveal a developed Broca's area, one of the primary language areas in modern humans, suggesting that they may have possessed primitive language abilities. Next to evolve was *Homo erectus*, appearing about 1.6 million years ago. These animals had still larger brains (about 900 cc), with greater development in Broca's area, and they used fire and more complex stone tools. *Homo erectus* became extinct about 250,000 years ago and was replaced by archaic *Homo sapiens*, who had characteristics of both *Homo erectus* and modern *Homo sapiens*. Modern humans with large brains (about 1300 cc) appeared on the scene within the past 100,000 years (Eccles, 1989; Lewin, 1988).

The Development of Intelligence

Many factors cause a species to evolve, but the most pervasive is a changing environment. When environments change, as they did on the African continent between 5 and 6 million years ago, species must make modifications if they are to survive. One option is to maintain its current lifestyle and relocate to more hospitable areas. A second option is to stay put and, over long periods of time, evolve to fit the new environment.

Human evolution occurred hand in hand with the development of several abilities: upright walking, larger skull capacity, functional language, food gathering, and tool invention. From time to time, each of these has been hypothesized as causing human evolution. However, many contemporary scholars believe that human intelligence is the product of social forces (Alexander, 1989; Byrne & Whiten, 1988; Humphrey, 1976; Crook, 1980)—that language and intelligence evolved to help individuals understand their social world. The ultimate purpose of a brain is to create a form of reality that permits an animal to function in its world. The greater social complexity of hominid groups resulted in a "need for a keener conscious awareness of ourselves so that we could understand—and perhaps manipulate—others better" (Lewin, 1988, p. 174).

One consequence of increased social complexity in a group is the need for greater cooperation among members. It increases the likelihood of success in hunting and food gathering, and also in competition with other groups. During the course of evolution, groups of hominids who failed to cooperate could find themselves victims of other, better organized (that is, more cooperative) groups. This, of course, was the beginning of the "us versus them" feelings that persist today in modern humans.

What type of intelligence must develop in order to deal with these new social pressures? One useful mental tool is self-consciousness, an ability to experience one's own feelings and behavior. Being self-conscious also puts us in a better position to interpret and predict the feelings and behaviors of others, a valuable tool for a social animal (Hum-

Table 10.10 Suggested evolutionary line of *Homo sapiens*

Years from Present	Species	Average Brain Capacity
100,000	Modern *Homo sapiens*	1300 cc
300,000	Archaic *Homo sapiens*	1300 cc
1.6 million	*Homo erectus*	900 cc
2.6 million	*Homo habilis*	650 cc
3.5 million	*Australopithecus afarensis*	400 cc

phrey, 1976). With some idea of what other people are thinking, we can use that information to our own advantage.

Another related intellectual skill is deceit. Deception has been observed in chimpanzees and baboons—for example, one animal luring others away from a source of hidden food (Byrn & Whiten, 1988).

Being able to hide one's true feelings and to act trustworthy and kind when one's real motives are less than friendly, is a consummate political skill, and one that likely developed via its success over 3 million years of evolution (Alexander, 1989).

The social pressures of cooperating and competing with other members of the group can be seen as

Box 10.4

Lucy

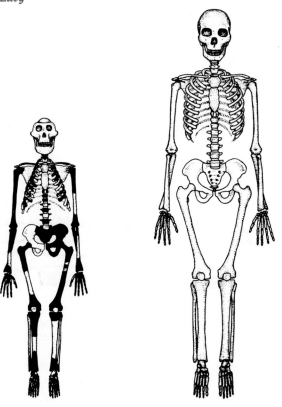

A. afarensis   H. sapiens

Donald Johanson was leading a team of paleoanthropologists in the Afar region of Ethiopia in quest of fossils that would shed light on the origins of our own species. During their digs they came across the fossil remains of a remarkable creature—a direct ancestor of the human race that was determined to be more than 3.5 million years old. Of course, only fragments of the skeleton were found, but enough pieces were discovered to learn much about this ancient animal. First of all, it was a female. She was given the name Lucy, after a Beatles song heard on the radio the night of the discovery ("Lucy in the Sky with Diamonds"). She stood about 3.5 feet tall and definitely walked upright, just as modern humans do—a gait very different from the knuckle-walking of chimpanzees and gorillas. Her great age, based on the known age of the rocks in which she was found, pushed back the direct descendants of *Homo sapiens* by a million years. Johanson and his colleagues recognized Lucy as an *Australopithecine,* an extinct species directly related to modern humans that had been initially discovered in South Africa in 1925. Other, equally ancient *Australopithecine* fossils have since been found in and around the area where Lucy was unearthed, confirming that this small-brained, upright walker, deserves a special place in our species' evolutionary history.

Figure 10.3 Comparison of Lucy (*Australopithecus afarensis,* left) and modern *Homo sapiens.* The black areas on Lucy's skeleton indicate the fragments actually recovered. The skull should also be black, but has been left clear to reveal detail. *Source:* From *Lucy: The Beginnings of Humankind,* by D. C. Johanson and M. A. Edey. Copyright © 1982 by Warner Books, Inc. Reprinted by permission.

the driving force of human intelligence. Humans are more intelligent than necessary to eke out an existence in the rain forests of Africa. Our intelligence developed not so much to meet the demands of a hostile external environment, but to meet the demands of hostile members of our own species. According to Richard Alexander (1989), hominids essentially evolved a new hostile force of nature—themselves.

Intelligence and Culture

Human intelligence evolved in a social setting. Our dependence on other members of the species for survival requires that we form alliances and cooperate with one another. In striving for social rank and status, we achieve advantage primarily through social skills and intellectual accomplishments rather than physical prowess (Crook, 1980). Human social skills are learned, and human intelligence is developed within a social system.

Parents in all cultures strive to raise successful children—children who will produce other children and who will enjoy high status and receive the benefits available from their culture. Children are reared in social settings in which they acquire the intellectual and social skills necessary for future success. Because human culture and the skills consid-

A tongue-in-cheek view of the evolution of human intelligence. *Source:* © 1982 by Sidney Harris, *American Scientist Magazine.*

ered desirable within a culture are so variable, intelligence must be flexible. And for this reason, intelligence must be evaluated from the context of the culture in which it develops (see Chapter 11). Human intelligence evolved as a function of social pressures, and so it should not be surprising that intelligence is also developed for each individual child in a social context.

State of the Art
IQ Tests and Minorities

Minority children in the United States consistently score lower on IQ tests than white, middle-class children. In one respect, this should be expected, because IQ tests do their best job predicting school success and minority children often perform more poorly in school than their majority counterparts. But does this mean that minority children are less intelligent than children from the majority? Posing this question requires one to evaluate what is meant by intelligence and the extent to which IQ tests assess it.

There have been many critics of IQ testing, especially when it comes to evaluation of minority children's intelligence. The tests, state many critics, are based on skills and knowledge deemed important by the majority culture. Children from minority homes may not share the same values or have access to the same knowledge that middle-class children do, making the test culturally biased. There is a strong movement today pushing the idea that intelligence can be meaningfully assessed only within the culture in which a child lives (Laboratory of Comparative Human Cognition, 1983; Miller-Jones, 1989; Rogoff, 1990; see Chapter 11). Thus, although IQ tests may measure accurately some aspects of intelligence for children from the majority culture, they do not assess intelligence adequately for minority children. Moreover, the rigorously standardized nature of IQ tests may be a detriment to minority children because the tests must be administered in a constant format. The examiner cannot provide feedback to a child and usually cannot probe answers to determine if a child has more knowledge than reflected by an initial response. If minority children have different expectations of what type of answers

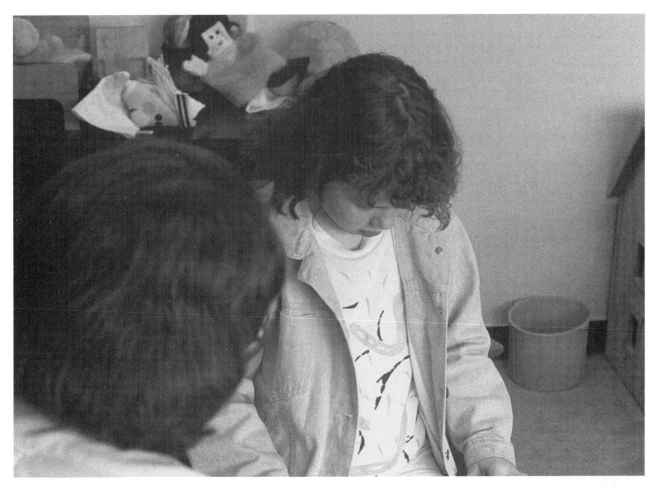

Some children may be unfamiliar with standardized test situations, and uncomfortable with them, resulting in lower scores.

the examiner is looking for, their competencies will be masked by the requirements of standard test administration (Miller-Jones, 1989; Sattler, 1988).

Dalton Miller-Jones (1989) provides several examples of how a 5-year-old black child's performance on an IQ test may be underestimated by the standardized nature of the test:

> *Tester:* "How are wood and coal alike? How are they the same?"
> *Child:* "They're hard."
> *Tester:* "An apple and a peach?"
> *Child:* "They taste good."

> *Tester:* "A ship and an automobile?"
> *Child:* "They're hard."
> *Tester:* "Iron and silver?"
> *Child:* "They're hard."

These answers all earn a score of zero, but does this mean that the child does not know the conceptual relation between iron and silver or between an apple and a peach? By the rules of the test, no feedback can be provided, and the child must guess what type of answer the examiner wants. There is nothing incorrect about the child's answers to these questions, but they do not fit the test makers' conceptions. They also do not likely exhaust this child's knowledge of the relations between these objects, but the test format precludes finding this out.

Other aspects of test administration also influence minority children's performance on IQ tests. The testing situation, for example, with a child sitting quietly across the table from an adult and answering a series of questions, may be more familiar and comfortable to a middle-class child than to a low-income or minority child. Also, in most testing situations, the examiner belongs to a different ethnic group and social class than the minority child, adding further to the discomfort and novelty of the testing situation. Jerome Kagan (1969) cites evidence that IQ scores of inner-city black children are higher when they are interviewed over a series of days, giving them time to acclimate to the test situation.

Not everyone agrees that there is bias against minority children in mental testing, of course (Jensen, 1980). Despite all the criticism, the tests are cost efficient and widely (though not universally) accepted by both educational professionals and the public (Snyderman & Rothman, 1987). Yet most people acknowledge that we could do a better job in assessing minority children's intelligence and achievement. Miller-Jones (1989) makes five recommendations for improving minority assessment:

1. When assessing any area of intelligence, it is important to specify the cognitive processes that may be involved in the task or elicited by the stimuli.
2. Multiple tasks with different materials should be used with the same individual.
3. Tests must be appropriate for the culture from which the child comes.
4. The connection must be validated between the cognitive operations assessed by a test and the attainment of school-related concepts such as arithmetic and reading.
5. Procedures must be developed that permit an examiner to probe for the reasoning behind a child's answers.

Summary

Most people, professionals and public alike, believe that intelligence involves components of practical problem-solving ability, verbal ability, and social competence. Views concerning the nature of intelligence have changed over the years, with issues of intelligence being closely tied to politics.

Individual differences in intelligence have most often been evaluated by the psychometric approach, which describes intelligence in terms of mental factors. The number of factors proposed to describe intelligence has varied from 1 (Spearman's g) to 180 (Guilford's structure of the intellect).

The psychometric approach has had its greatest impact in the form of the IQ test. The principal IQ tests are the Stanford-Binet and the three IQ tests developed by Wechsler (WPPSI-R, WISC-R, and WAIS-R). IQ tests are based on large samples of individuals and constructed so that the average IQ at any age is 100. Alternative approaches to intelligence have been suggested, including Sternberg's triarchic theory and Gardner's theory of multiple intelligences. Sternberg proposes three subtheories: the contextual, the experiential, and the componential. Gardner, relying heavily on neuropsychological evidence, postulates seven distinct forms of intelligence: linguistic, logical/mathematical, musical, spatial, bodily-kinesthetic, interpersonal, and intrapersonal. Both Sternberg and Gardner take a perspective of cultural relativism, believing that different cultures value different types of intelligence.

Stability refers to the degree to which differences in the rank order of individuals remain constant over time. DQ, or developmental quotient, tests given in infancy do not predict later childhood IQ, although infants' rates of habituation and dishabituation do predict later IQ to a moderate degree. Intelligence is multifaceted, and other factors in infancy (such as rearing environment) also predict later intelligence. IQ is highly stable over childhood into young adulthood.

Lack of stimulation, such as found in Depression-era institutions, leads to social, emotional, and intellectual deficits. Patterns of child rearing are also related to children's levels of intelligence, with middle-class mothers often providing their children with experiences that are more conducive to fostering intellectual development than low-income mothers. Research has shown, however, that early, environmentally induced retardation can be reversed under certain conditions.

Many contemporary scholars believe that social pressures from other members of the species were responsible for the ever increasing intelligence in the line that led to *Homo sapiens,* with language and intelligence evolving to help individuals understand their social world.

It has been demonstrated that IQ tests are culturally biased, with minority children often misinterpreting the testing situation.

Key Words and Concepts

intelligence
psychometric approach
factors
factor analysis
Spearman's *g*
Guilford's structure of the intellect
fluid abilities
crystallized abilities
IQ tests
Stanford-Binet
Wechsler scales
deviation IQ
Sternberg's triarchic theory
contextual subtheory
cultural relativism
experiential subtheory
componential subtheory
knowledge-acquisition components
performance components
metacomponents
Gardner's theory of multiple intelligences
stability (of intelligence)
DQ (developmental quotient) tests
habituation/dishabituation
institutionalization studies

Culture,
Schooling,
and Cognition

In the 1930s, A. R. Luria studied the thinking styles of people in Uzbekistan, a remote area of the Soviet Union. These people were farmers who could not read or write, and had no formal schooling. In one task, Luria (1976) presented people with four drawings of common objects, three from one category and one from another, and asked them to select the one that didn't belong with the other three. Box 11.1 shows some of the items presented and one 39-year-old man's responses.

No doubt American and European college students would answer these items differently, quickly selecting the log, the child, and the bird. But what type of cognitive system do the Uzbekistani's answers reflect? Despite repeated attempts by the investigators to point out the conceptual relations among the objects, this man and his fellow Uzbekistanis were unable to see the categorical relations among groups of common objects. Their thinking was based firmly in the concrete world: It is good for the boy to work with the men, and why have all those tools if there's nothing to cut? Such thinking is similar to that observed in 5-year-olds growing up in the technological cultures of North America and Western Europe. Yet we would not wish to suggest that this man had the intelligence of a 5-year-old. Far from it. He and the many others who responded in a similar fashion were successful adults in their culture. Their brains and nervous systems were no doubt similar to ours, but their thinking is clearly different from ours, and it is culture that is responsible for those differences.

What is it about the society one is raised in that accounts for differences in thought processes? And how do the child-rearing practices of a culture influence the types of thinkers its members will become? One major difference between cultures that surely influences cognition is the technological tools that are used to aid problem solving. Cultures that use computers, an alphabet, and calculus will certainly require a different cognitive system than cultures that rely on knotted ropes to keep numerical records and the position of stars for navigation. An

Box 11.1

Testing Uzbekistanis: Sample Responses

1.

Q: Which one doesn't belong with the other three?
A: They're all alike. I think all of them have to be here. See, if you're going to saw, you need a saw, and if you have to split something you need a hatchet. So they're *all* needed here.

2.

Q: Which one doesn't belong with the other three?
A: Oh, but the boy must stay with the others! All three of them are working, you see, and if they have to keep running out to fetch things, they'll never get the job done, but the boy can do the running for them. . . . The boy will learn; that'll be better, then they'll be able to work well together.

3.

Q: Which one doesn't belong with the other three?
A: The bird doesn't fit here. . . . No . . . this is a rifle. It's loaded with a bullet and kills the bird. Then you cut the bird up with a dagger, since there's no other way to do it. . . . What I said before about the bird was wrong! All these things go together.

Source: Luria, 1976, pp. 55–57.

economy in which each family provides for its own necessities through hunting and gathering food calls for a different cognitive system than one that relies on bartering or one in which goods are purchased at stores with currency and credit cards.

What is unique about human cognition is its flexibility: we are able to modify our thought processes and behavior to meet the particular demands of our environment. All groups of humans are capable of achieving the abstract thought so valued in technological societies. But that is only one intellectual system, and one that is not necessarily adaptive to all cultures. Other cultures, such as 1930s Uzbekistan, are successful using concrete thought and functional relationships.

In this chapter, we will investigate the role of culture in shaping cognitive development. The effects of culture on development are most easily appreciated when we look at the practices of other societies and compare them to our own. We will examine the close link between culture, cognition, and child rearing, and look at the role of formal education in affecting thought processes.

Cultural Differences in Cognition

There is no debate that people from different cultures think differently. The greatest differences in cognition are found between people in traditional cultures, where there is no formal schooling, and people in technological cultures, where most of childhood, and often part of adulthood, is spent in one type of school or another.

These cognitive differences have their beginnings early in childhood. For example, although the sequence of development through Piaget's sensorimotor stages is the same across cultures, infants from sub-Saharan Africa often progress through these stages faster than Western infants (Munroe, Munroe, & Whiting, 1981; Super, 1981). Differences in the rate of attaining concrete operations, as defined by Piaget, have also been repeatedly observed, with most studies finding a slower rate of development for nonschooled children relative to schooled children (Dasen, 1977). The most substantial cultural differences, in Piagetian terms, have been found in the attainment of formal operations, a mode of thinking that seems to be manifested only

by children who receive substantial levels of formal education (Goodnow, 1962; Laurendeau-Bendavid, 1977). In fact, when Piaget (1972) found evidence that nonschooled children did not attain formal operational thought, it caused him to modify his theory, stating that this stage may not be universal but rather dependent upon specific experiences.

Consistent cultural differences have also been found in non-Piagetian tasks, most notably memory and classification. With respect to memory, unschooled children seem to rely on rote memorization, failing to use strategies such as rehearsal and organization that develop over childhood in Western culture (Rogoff, 1990; Wagner, 1981). In classification tasks, subjects are asked to group objects or pictures that "go together" and, usually, to supply a justification for their choice. By age 7 or 8, Western children typically group together objects that are members of the same conceptual category—for example, placing all pictures of tools in one group, food items in another, and animals in a third (Bjorklund, 1985). Children and adults from traditional cultures, however, are more apt to sort objects into functional groupings, reflecting how these objects might be used or found in a real-life setting—for example, putting pictures of a knife and an orange together, explaining that you can cut the orange with the knife. The example from Luria (1976) provided at the beginning of this chapter clearly reflects this pragmatic approach. A bird must be grouped with the rifle, bullet, and dagger; otherwise the weapons have no function. The bird ties the other three objects together into a coherent and meaningful scheme.

Origins of Cultural Differences

What are the origins of these differences? One discarded theory is that cultural differences are a result of genetics: people of different cultures usually represent different gene pools; and, according to genetic theories, the differences observed in cognition can be attributed to heredity. This theory was popular a century ago, but no serious scholar of cultural differences holds this view today. For one reason, research has clearly shown that as an individual's culture changes, so does his or her cognition. For example, as a result of formal education, the peasants of Uzbekistan studied by Luria (1976) showed marked changes in thinking style, becoming more

European in their thought processes. Other research has shown that people from traditional cultures are able to classify objects according to conceptual criteria—they just don't think that it's a very intelligent way of doing things. In a study of Kpelle farmers in Liberia, for example, adults consistently sorted objects into functional groups (for example, knife with orange, potato with hoe) rather than conceptual categories (potato with orange, hoe with knife). This, many farmers stated, was the wise way to do it. When asked how a fool would do the task, the farmers classified the objects into neat conceptually based piles, exactly as Westerners do (Glick, 1975).

As we've said repeatedly, perhaps the most magnificent thing about human cognition is its flexibility. A newborn infant may grow up to become a navigator, sailing the South Pacific using stars, currents, and water conditions to guide his course over hundreds of miles; or that same infant may become a proficient hunter, a shaman, a weaver, a Koran scholar, or a computer analyst—all as a function of the culture in which he or she grows up. Within any culture there will be individual differences in abilities, some genetic in origin, making some children more likely candidates than others for certain occupations available to them. But the potential to succeed in any human culture is present in all groups of people. The cognitive differences between cultures are due not to differences in heredity, but to differences in environment, beginning from the earliest time of life.

If the origin of intellectual differences among cultures is environmental, how is it that environment influences cognitive development? One possibility is that experiences during childhood affect a person's entire cognitive system. In this view, people from a traditional society consistently approach problems in a similar way; their entire thought processes are different from those of people reared in a technological society. An alternative theory is that cognition is context specific; individuals have a variety of mental processes available, but the particular context in which a cognitive task is performed will determine how that task is accomplished. This approach is consistent with the knowledge-base theory of cognitive development (see Chapter 8)—that children will approach problems differently as a function of how much task-relevant knowledge they have—and Sternberg's and Gardner's theories of intelligence

(see Chapter 10). Current research clearly favors explanations that consider specific environmental contexts to be important for cultural differences in cognition.

The Cultural Context of Development

Cognitive development is inseparable from the context in which it occurs, and this context is determined by the economic, family, and religious values provided by one's culture (Laboratory of Comparative Human Cognition, 1983; Rogoff, 1990; Rogoff & Morelli, 1989). When assessing cognitive development, it is essential to appreciate the circumstances in which children are being evaluated and compare them to conditions of their daily lives. For example, research done with Western children in a laboratory setting typically involves questioning them about what they know. Children are asked to remember a list of words, to classify objects into groups, to tell the meaning of words or pictures, or to interpret a story. Children from traditional cultures frequently do poorly on such laboratory tasks. In most cases, the reasons for their poor performance have less to do with intellectual ability than with the context of the tasks.

Children who attend school are accustomed to answering the questions of teachers and parents. They find no incongruity in being asked to think about things that have no immediate relevance to them or to tell adults answers to questions that the adults surely must know themselves (see Rogoff, 1990). In fact, formal education requires children to think about things upon request, not only when there is a clear practical goal for such thinking. Because of their school experiences, Western children understand experimenters' requests and will perform the required operations as they do similar school tasks. Nonschooled children, on the other hand, may not be accustomed to thinking out of context or providing adults with information that the adults surely already know. Thinking serves particular purposes, and the purpose of laboratory activities may escape children and adults from traditional societies. Moreover, the social values of a culture may influence how children perceive a task and what they consider to be appropriate answers. For example, in many cultures, it is impolite for children to act as if they know more than an adult, and answering an adult's simple questions may be viewed as a social transgression. Similarly, in cultures where adults do not ask children questions for which they themselves already know the answers, an experimenter's question may be viewed as a trick or riddle, requiring something other than the obvious reply (Irvine, 1978; Rogoff & Mistry, 1985).

There is ample evidence that people from nontechnological cultures possess greater intellectual skills than many laboratory tests reflect, and that these skills are revealed when the materials or contexts are changed to bring the evaluation situation more into line with typical practices of their culture. Research has found this to be the case for Piagetian, memory, and mathematics tasks.

Piagetian tasks   As noted previously, concrete operations are often attained at later ages by nonschooled as opposed to schooled children (Dasen, 1977; Greenfield, 1966). However, cultural differences in how the tasks are presented can greatly influence children's performance in these experiments. In many studies, for example, children from traditional cultures are tested either through interpreters or in their second or third language (see Nyiti, 1982). This contrasts sharply with the way American or European children are tested and makes it difficult to interpret the differences found between groups.

In a study of conservation, Raphael Nyiti (1982) compared two groups of Canadian children: white, English-speaking Europeans and Micmac Indians. The Indian children attended school, where they learned English, but spoke their native language (Micmac) at home. Both the European and Indian children were given a series of conservation tasks, following standard Piagetian procedures. The European children were all tested in English. The Indian children were divided into two groups: half were tested in English by a European, and the other half in Micmac by a Micmac Indian. There was no difference in how European and Indian children performed on the tasks when tested in their home language—European children in English and Indian children in Micmac. However, when the Indian children were tested in English by a European examiner, they gave much shorter and less complete answers and were significantly less likely to be classified as conservers than their European counterparts.

These results suggest that certain aspects of cognitive development as described by Piaget are universal and that concepts such as conservation develop on a predictable schedule in all cultures (Nyiti, 1982). This truism can be overlooked, however, if one is not mindful of the cultural context in which performance is assessed.

Memory   Children and adults who have not attended school perform poorly on memory tasks in which they are asked to remember unrelated pieces of information. They are much less apt to use memory strategies, such as rehearsal or organization, than are schooled children (Rogoff & Mistry, 1985; Wagner, 1981). The picture is far different, however, when the memory task is embedded in a meaningful and structured context. Whereas only schooled children are familiar with the task of recalling lists of isolated information, people from all backgrounds need to remember contextually relevant information (Rogoff, 1990). When tests are structured so that people must recall organized prose (as in a story) or items from spatially organized arrays (as in familiar scenes), few cultural differences in memory performance are found (Mandler, Scribner, Cole, & DeForest, 1980; Neisser, 1982).

A particularly clear demonstration of the importance of cultural context in memory performance is provided by a study by Barbara Rogoff and Kathryn Waddell (1982). Previous research had shown that Guatemalan Mayan children's memory for lists of items was significantly worse than that of American children of the same age (Kagan, Klein, Finley, Rogoff, & Nolan, 1979). Rogoff and Waddell showed 9-year-old Guatemalan Mayan and U.S. children three-dimensional, culturally appropriate scenes of a model town. A total of 20 objects, such as animals, cars, people, and household items, were placed in the scene, and children were asked to remember the objects and their locations. The 20 objects were then mixed into a pool of 80 objects, and, after a brief delay, the children were asked to reconstruct the scene. In contrast to the earlier list-learning experiment, the Mayan children actually performed slightly better than the U.S. children on the reconstruction task. These results clearly indicate that the unschooled, rural children's poor memory performance on the list-learning tasks was due not to deficient memory abilities, but rather to the context in which memory was studied.

Mathematics   Kpelle children in Liberia have a particular problem mastering mathematics in Western-style schools. Specific perceptual deficits, linked to their home environments, were hypothesized to account for their difficulties. Kpelle children do not discriminate geometric forms well, and such problems were attributed to a lack of perceptual stimulation (Laboratory of Comparative Human Cognition, 1983). Judy Gay and Michael Cole (1967) argued that Kpelle children did not lack perceptual experiences, but merely had different ones than American children. The researchers thought that by examining the daily lives of the Kpelle, they could discern mathematically relevant experiences and possibly use them to improve instruction in Western-style mathematics.

Gay and Cole found that the Kpelle had no single form of measurement that was used for a variety of commodities. However, they did have a consistent way of measuring rice. Rice is the only cash crop for Kpelle farmers, and buying and selling rice is a very important part of their culture. Gay and Cole evaluated Kpelle farmers' ability to estimate the amount of rice in bowls of varying size and compared their performance to that of Americans. The Kpelle were consistently more accurate in this task than Americans, reflecting a mathematical competence not apparent in previous tests.

As with the findings for conservation and memory, people from traditional cultures can perform well on cognitive tasks when their familiarity with the test materials and the testing context are taken into consideration. The typically poor performance of unschooled people on many cognitive tests reflects not a general lack of ability but specific difficulties that can often be overcome by changing aspects of the testing situation.

Child-Rearing Practices, Culture, and Cognitive Development

The overriding theme of this chapter has been that cognitive development is inseparable from its cultural context. Culture is transmitted to children by their parents and other members of society. It is within the adult/child interchanges of daily life that children's intellectual processes are developed to handle the tasks and problems pertinent to their particular surroundings. Parents may not be conscious of their instructional techniques, but cultural practices of child rearing are usually well suited for the type of life children can expect to face as adults.

A theory emphasizing this sociocultural viewpoint that has gained popularity in recent years is that of the Soviet psychologist Lev Vygotsky (1978; Werstch, 1985). Vygotsky, writing in the 1920s and 1930s, emphasized that development was guided by adults interacting with children, with the cultural context determining to a large extent how, where, and when these interactions would take place. Vygotsky proposed that cognitive development occurs in situations in which a child's problem solving is guided by an adult. Adults serve as models for children and guide them to appropriate solutions in situations in which the child is not quite able to reach a solution independently. This is the **zone of proximal development,** defined by Vygotsky as the difference between a child's "actual developmental level as determined by independent problem solving" and his or her level of "potential development as determined through problem solving under adult guidance or in collaboration with more capable peers" (Vygotsky, 1978, p. 86). In other words, children learn best at a level between their current ability and their ability when assisted by an adult. It is within this zone that adults can do the most effective teaching. The skills of the child continue to develop, of course, requiring constant modification on the part of the adult. Thus, the sociocultural approach is by necessity dynamic—ever changing—with both adults and children progressing as a result of their repeated transactions (Saxe, Guberman, & Gearhart, 1987).

Adults' interactions with children vary depending on their culture. Although child rearing in all cultures may take advantage of the zone of proximal development, what is taught will depend on what roles the child is expected to play in society. Barbara Rogoff (1990) has viewed the transaction between children and adults as reflecting an "apprenticeship in thinking," with novice children improving their "skills and understanding through participation with more skilled partners in culturally organized activities" (p. 39). All the responsibility for the apprentice-

In Thailand a child's apprenticeship in thinking may include woodcarving lessons.

ship is not placed on the adults, however. Children may actively place themselves in positions to learn, prompting adults to increase the level of instruction as they become increasingly competent.

The idea of apprenticeship may seem reasonable in cultures where children are integrated early into the daily activities of adult life, such as the agrarian Mayans of Guatemala and Mexico or the !Kung of Africa, whose hunting and gathering lifestyle has remained virtually unchanged for thousands of years. But this idea is not as easily grasped when applied to a culture such as our own. Many school-age children in our culture do not even know what their parents do for a living and may never have seen their parents "in action" at their jobs. Moreover, our children are generally excluded from adult activities, spending much of their day segregated from adults. In other cultures, for example, children sleep in the same room as their parents throughout childhood and babies never leave home unless they are strapped to their mothers' backs.

Many aspects of cognitive development in Western culture have been shifted from parents to professional educators, whose job it is to teach cultural knowledge and skills to children. Yet much learning certainly transpires between parent and child in technological societies, particularly during the preschool years. In many ways, these transactions are designed to prepare children for the schooling that will follow. As noted previously, formal education in North America and Europe requires children to respond to questions from adults who already know the answers. It also involves learning and discussing things that have no immediate relevance—knowledge for knowledge's sake. Such context-independent learning, foreign to many cultures, is fostered in infancy and early childhood in our own culture. For example, parents of young children frequently prompt them to name objects or to recall recent events (Rogoff, 1990). Take, for instance, the following interchange between 19-month-old Brittany and her mother:

Mother: "Brittany, what did we see at the park?"
Brittany: "Babysing."
Mother: "That's right, the baby swing. And what else?"
Brittany: (shrugs)
Mother: "A slide?"
Brittany: (smiling, nods yes)
Mother: "And what else is at the park?"
Brittany: (shrugs)
Mother: "A see . . ."
Brittany: "See-saw!"
Mother: "That's right, a see-saw."

This type of interchange is not at all unusual for a mother and child from mainstream America, and it is a good example of Vygotsky's zone of proximal development. Brittany, in this case, was learning to recall specific objects with her mother's help. But she was also learning the importance of remembering information out of context (mother and daughter were in their living room at the time, miles from the park). Brittany was learning that she could be called upon to state facts to her mother that her mother already knew; and that she could depend upon her mother to help provide answers when she was unable to generate them herself.

Another way parents in technological cultures prepare their children for formal education is by talking to them. In North America, and most of the developed world, parents talk to their young children, including them as conversational partners. Although the type of language environment children are exposed to does influence their language development (Moerk, 1986), children around the world acquire language at about the same time, even in cultures where they are "seen and not heard." Children who are not included as conversational partners by adults may not be prepared for the type of language interaction used in school. These children may become proficient users of language in their own community, but be perceived as language deficient at school (Rogoff, 1990).

Schooling, Culture, and Development

We have seen that formal schooling has a profound influence on how children think. Children who attend school learn to divorce their thinking from specific contexts. They can classify information on the basis of conceptual rather than functional criteria, reason about things of which they have no prior knowledge, and use strategies to learn and remember information. They can do all this while sitting in

Box 11.2

Kids and Work

One of the biggest communication gaps between parents and children involves what Mom and Dad do for a living. Of course, most school-age kids can give a quick answer, such as "architect" or "financial consultant," but few can describe what their parents' jobs entail or what a typical day is like "at work." Understanding their parents' jobs is one way children learn about the adult world—a world they will be making their own decisions about all too soon.

Difficulties children have understanding what their parents do for a living are partly due to the abstract nature of many jobs today. Although some jobs are self-descriptive, such as milkman, letter carrier, and auto mechanic, others have titles that don't really tell a child much about what Mom or Dad actually does—for example, systems analyst, technical advisor, and assistant production manager. Even if our kids understood these titles, they would have trouble knowing what it is we

analyze, advise, or manage because we often deal in intangibles such as information, market activity, and interest rates.

Putting our jobs into terms our children can understand is sometimes a challenge. One suggestion is to tell your children what you do on the job during an average day. To make it more real, compare your schedule with theirs. Tell them what you are doing at work while they are having math class or lunch. For example, if Dad is a land surveyor, he could explain that he drives to the office and meets with the engineer first thing in the morning. Then he and the rest of his crew pack up the truck with the equipment and go out to the job site. This may not be as interesting as telling about the day you found an alligator in a pond when you were surveying a golf course, but it's more typical.

If possible, take your children to your workplace for a visit. If that's not possible, perhaps you could bring home some of the equipment you use on the job.

Tell your children about your past jobs. Did you start working with the same company and advance to your present position? Did you start in some other job area and decide to make a change? If so, why? Did you spend several years in college or in a training program to get the job you have? What did you want to be when you were their age? How did you decide to be in the job you have now?

Let your children know about the high points and low points of your job—the big contracts you won (and lost) and the goals you have for the future.

Not only will kids be learning important lessons about the world, but they will be getting to know their parents as interesting individuals with talents and concerns focused outside as well as inside the family circle.

Source: Adapted from D. F. Bjorklund and B. R. Bjorklund. (July 1988). Kids and Work. *Parents Magazine,* Vol. 63, No. 7.

Box 11.3

Family Differences

Kids think that all families are pretty much alike—until the age of 7 or 8, that is. Around this age, children begin to realize that other families may be a bit different from their own. Not all fathers are teachers. Not all mothers work at hospitals. Some grandparents speak Spanish. And some older brothers wear earrings.

During the middle years, children begin to expand their social territories. They are no longer limited to playing in their own yard with their siblings or with the children of their parents' friends. They venture out to school and playgrounds and meet other kids their age with diverse family backgrounds. At the same time, they are learning important lessons about themselves by making comparisons between themselves and others. Call it "social networking" or "forming pecking orders," kids want to know where they fit in the society of children. Part of this involves noticing the similarities and differences in their friends and their friends' families.

This can be a difficult time for parents as they listen to long accounts of what other families do that theirs do not. If parents stress nutrition, they will hear about families who seem to live at fast-food restaurants and think of french fries as a staple. Parents on strict budgets will hear about families that spend money like there's no tomorrow. And if parents have raised their children in a particular religion, they are certain to be told about families that have never set foot in a church or synagogue and who spend Sunday mornings at the beach.

Parents must keep in mind that, in most cases, children are sharing information with them, not challenging their values. They are seeing the world in a little different light and want parents to know about their new discoveries.

Parents should attempt to be interested in their children's discoveries about other families. They can ask questions and share similar facts about their own friends. If children mention a vegetarian family, parents can listen with interest. They can ask about their reasons and about the details of their diet.

Parents should not isolate children from different viewpoints. Being exposed to new ideas is good for children. It helps them learn about others and, more important, about themselves. Different ideas don't confuse children but enrich them. Pointing out the different customs of other people and speaking of them positively tells children that diversity has its benefits.

Parents can provide children with information about children from different cultures. It's always a good idea to capitalize on children's newfound interests. Parents should follow their lead. Introducing them to foods and traditions of other countries can lead to tolerance for differences. When eating at a Chinese restaurant, parents can ask the waiter to explain what it means to be born in "the year of the rabbit," and discuss the Chinese calendar. They can take their children to local ethnic festivals where people wear traditional outfits and serve traditional fare. And parents can make a point of watching television programs with their children that show people from other parts of the world. They may never meet an Afghan sheepherder, but understanding that such people exist and have a unique lifestyle may help them view children in their own backyard who differ less drastically in a more favorable light.

When families celebrate cultural diversity, children gain both an understanding of others' customs and an appreciation of their own.

Source: Adapted from D. F. Bjorklund and B. R. Bjorklund. (August 1987). Family Differences. *Parents Magazine*, Vol. 62, No. 8.

a classroom, even though the things they are asked to learn about may be thousands of miles and hundreds of years distant from them. Such context-independent thinking is necessary in a technological society, where literacy is important and where commodities are bought and sold using checks, credit cards, and electronic transfers from one bank account to another. This style of thinking is less critical, and may even be counterproductive, in traditional cultures, where learning and thinking are directly related to everyday events.

The distinction between schooled and unschooled societies is an important one, but there are also important differences among cultures where schooling is practiced. The cultural values expressed by schools and parents vary, as do educational practices.

Cultural Effects on Schooling

The intellectual demands of all technological cultures require that children be formally educated. However, a culture's views on education and beliefs about development will influence the type of schooling children receive and the context in which children are educated.

In recent studies, differences in American and German attitudes toward intellectual development have been linked to differences in strategy use (Carr, Kurtz, Schneider, Turner, & Borkowski, 1989; Kurtz, 1990; Kurtz, Schneider, Carr, Borkowski, & Rellinger, 1990; Schneider, Borkowski, Kurtz, & Kerwin, 1986). In these studies, second- and third-graders in Germany and the United States were trained to use a memory strategy (specifically, to recall related items together in clusters; see Chapter 8). Prior to training, children were given a battery of tests assessing their verbal and nonverbal intelligence, academic self-esteem, metamemory, spontaneous use of strategies, and attributional beliefs about learning (whether they attribute success and failure to luck, effort, or inherent ability). The children's parents and teachers also answered questionnaires on their beliefs about children's academic success or failure and the extent of instruction or encouragement of strategic thinking that occurred in the home and school.

An initial finding was that the German children were significantly more strategic on their own than the American children, although the American children did benefit from the memory training. However, despite the German children's superiority on the memory task, the American children had more positive academic self-esteem and were more apt to attribute academic outcomes to effort (hard work) than the German children, something that has been associated with improved academic achievement (Dweck & Leggett, 1988). The German children were more apt to believe that their success or failure in school-related tasks was due to ability (inborn traits). A replication of this study (see Kurtz, 1990) found that American children who believed in effort performed better than American children who held other views, but German children who believed in natural ability performed better than German children who held other views. These results suggest that the relation between belief in effort and higher academic achievement, found in other studies of American children, is culturally dependent—holding only for a particular culture.

The cultural differences found between German and American children in strategy use and attribution of success could be traced to the behaviors and attitudes of their parents and teachers. German parents gave children more direct strategy training, bought them more games that required strategic thinking, and checked their homework more than did the American parents. German teachers reported more direct strategy instruction than did American teachers (Carr et al., 1989; Kurtz et al., 1990). German parents and teachers were more likely to attribute children's academic performance to ability, whereas their American counterparts were more likely to attribute it to effort.

Perhaps the most extensive studies of cultural differences in the effects of schooling have been conducted by Harold Stevenson and his colleagues, contrasting school achievement in Oriental and American children (Stevenson & Lee, 1990; Stevenson, Lee, & Stigler, 1986; Stevenson, Lee, Stigler, Lucker, Kitamura, & Hsu, 1985; Stigler, Lee, & Stevenson, 1987). Much has been written lately in the popular press about Chinese and other Oriental children's superior academic performance relative to American children, especially in mathematics. Figure 11.1 shows the mathematics test performance of first- and fifth-grade children in the United States

(Minneapolis), Japan (Sendai), and Taiwan (Taipei). As can be seen, the American children performed poorly relative to both Oriental groups, and the differences were quite substantial as early as the first grade. The magnitude of the performance gap suggests differences in school systems, but the fact that this gap is found so early also points to differences in the home.

What aspects of the culture account for these findings? One difference is in parents' attitudes and behavior regarding education and child rearing. As we have seen, American parents are more apt to attribute their children's academic performance to effort than are German parents; this tendency to emphasize effort and hard work is even more apparent in Japanese and Chinese parents. Japanese mothers, for example, are more apt to believe that their children's academic performance can be improved than are American mothers. These Japanese women also take personal pride in the success of their children

and require their children to establish regular study habits. They are less likely to be satisfied with their children's academic performance and they set higher academic standards for their children than American mothers. At the same time, the Buddhist, Confucian, and Shinto traditions of Japan, which value order, intellectual growth, and social good, may contribute to a cultural setting that is geared for success in school.

Because of Japan's cultural traditions, children also spend more time in school and devote a higher percentage of their school time to academic activities than do American children. For example, whereas the average school year in Minneapolis is 174 days, it is 230 days in Taipei and 243 days in Sendai (Stevenson & Lee, 1990).

First-generation Oriental-American children perform better in school, on average, than white or black native-born Americans. A major reason for this difference is the attitudes that Chinese- and Japa-

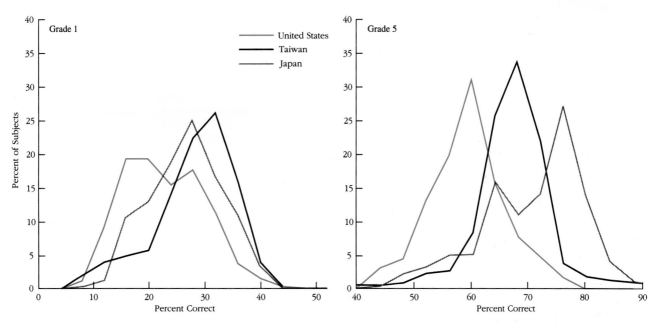

Figure 11.1 Frequency distributions of mathematics scores for first- and fifth-grade children in the United States, Japan, and Taiwan. *Source:* From "Context of Achievement," by H. W. Stevenson and S. Y. Lee, *Monographs of the Society for Research in Child Development,* 55 (Serial No. 221.) Copyright © The Society for Research in Child Development, Inc. Reprinted by permission.

Academic performance in Japan is higher than in the United States because of cultural traditions, parental attitudes, and school curriculum.

nese-American parents have toward education. For example, in a study by Chin-Yan Cindy Lin and Victoria Fu (1990), the child-rearing practices of Caucasian-American parents were compared with those of Chinese parents in Taiwan and immigrant Chinese parents living in the United States. They reported that both the immigrant Chinese and the Taiwanese parents rated higher on parental control, encouragement of independence, and emphasis on achievement than did Caucasian-American parents. Cultural attitudes of Chinese-American parents exert an influence on their children's educational attainment, which is likely responsible for the academic edge these children have in American schools.

After looking at the Chinese and Japanese educational systems, it might be tempting to conclude that American children can easily catch up merely by increasing the number of days they spend in school. Stevenson and Lee (1990) caution that a simple extension of the school day or school year is not the answer. In fact, although the Chinese and Japanese fifth-graders spent more hours per week in school than the American children, the school day for first-graders in both Taipei (4 hours) and Sendai (5 hours) was shorter than in Minneapolis (6 hours), reflecting an awareness of the attentional limitations of these young children.

A common observation by Westerners in Oriental schools is how attentive the children are. Such intense concentration is attributed in part to the fre-

quent opportunities children have for vigorous play provided by between-class breaks. In both Taipei and Sendai, the school day was highly structured, with 40- to 45-minute classes followed by 10- to 15-minute breaks. Children in the Minneapolis schools had no more than two recesses per day, whereas first-graders in the two Oriental schools had four, and fifth-graders had between five and eight. Thus, although Chinese and Japanese children do spend more days and more hours in school than American children, their school day is structured differently, providing them more physical exercise as well as more academic experiences.

Before concluding that the Japanese educational system is superior to the American, it must be remembered that the two educational systems have evolved within different cultures. The system that works for the Japanese cannot simply be transported to the United States and expected to work. The creativity that is permitted (and often encouraged) in many American schools, for example, and the young intellectual maverick, so valued in American universities, would be lost in a Japanese system that emphasizes conformity and respect for age. This is not to say that the poor performance of American children in mathematics, geography, and the sciences, relative to children in other developed countries, is inevitable or acceptable. What it does mean is that a country's educational problems must be solved within that country's culture and cannot be solved simply by importing a system that evolved elsewhere.

Schooling and Cognitive Development

There should be little question that schooling makes a difference in how a child thinks. In our day-to-day experience, children who attend school are brighter than children who don't, and children in more advanced grades are smarter than children in lower grades. But children in higher grades not only have more school experience than children in lower grades, they are also older. Does attending school actually make a difference in cognitive development above and beyond the effect of age?

Schooling versus age effects on intelligence   This question was addressed by Frederick Morrison (1991), who looked at the effects of one year of age versus one year of schooling on the cognitive per-

Culture

Chinese preschoolers quickly learn that cooperation is highly valued in their society.

Cultural experiences determine whether a child develops the thinking skills necessary to becoming a proficient Fijian fisherman, Yugoslavian factory worker, or Cambodian Buddhist monk.

Although these children all live in Israel, their lives differ greatly. But the Arab children (top) and the Israeli child (bottom) have all learned to live with the constant threat of violence.

In Kenya, as elsewhere, growing up in a rural environment is very different from childhood in the city.

The classroom experience is similar for these Cuban children and schoolchildren everywhere.

formance of groups of children just beginning school. In this study, children who had just missed the cutoff date for entering first grade were compared to children who were close to their age but had just made the cutoff date. Following a year of school (kindergarten for one group, first grade for the other), the children were compared on a series of cognitive tasks. Despite being nearly identical in age, children in the first grade showed more advanced cognitive skills, including memory, language, and reading skills, than did the kindergarten children. Similar results have been found for intelligence test scores and school achievement of fourth-, fifth-, and sixth-grade children (Cahan & Cohen, 1989), with children in the higher grade scoring better than children the same age in the lower grade. These findings clearly show that IQ and related cognitive skills are strongly associated with schooling (see also Ceci, 1991).

These results may not be surprising; after all, we expect education to produce smarter children. But they force us to question the concept of intelligence as measured by IQ tests. IQ tests are age-based; the norms change as a function of age, not grade. The results of the research cited here indicate that not only should age be considered in computing an IQ score, but so also should school experience (Cahan & Cohen, 1989). Moreover, the idea that some intelligence tests can be "culture fair" (that is, used in any culture without yielding biased results) must be questioned. One of the tests used by Cahan and Cohen was the Raven's Progressive Matrices Test, which its authors claim produces "an index of intellectual capacity whatever [a person's] nationality or education" (Raven, Court, & Raven, 1975, p. 1). The effects of one year's schooling were twice as large as the effects of one year of age on the Raven's Test, seriously calling into question the "fairness" of such a test when assessing children from cultures where there is no formal education.

The costs and benefits of academic preschools Although schooling clearly has a positive effect on cognitive development independent of age, this does not necessarily mean that children should begin formal education as early as possible. There is a tendency among many families in the United States to "push" their young children with respect to formal education. Many preschool programs have academic curricula, preparing 3- and 4-year-old children for the rigors of school. The logic behind such programs is that education in a technological society cannot begin too soon. These parents believe that if children can be taught in preschool the important skills used in reading and arithmetic, they will have an intellectual advantage when they enter first grade.

Some critics have challenged this reasoning, however, including David Elkind (1987), who believes that academic preschool programs amount to miseducation. Young children lack the cognitive capacity to master the academic skills taught in these programs, and the overall result is unnecessary stress with no long-term benefits. Despite the importance of this issue, there has been surprisingly little research on it. A notable exception is a recent study by Marion Hyson, Kathryn Hirsh-Pasek, and Leslie Rescorla (1989), in which they assessed 4-year-old children attending prekindergarten programs. Children were given tests of academic skills, creativity, social competence, and emotional well-being at the end of the prekindergarten program and again following kindergarten. Parents were also interviewed concerning their attitudes toward education and their expectations for their children's academic achievement. The preschool programs were classified as academic or nonacademic. Not surprisingly, parents who stressed education placed their children in the more academic schools.

At the end of the preschool program, children whose parents stressed education scored higher on the tests of academic skills (such as knowledge of letters, numbers, and shapes) than did children whose parents placed little stress on academics. There was no difference, however, on more general measures of intellectual competencies. The type of school children attended was less important in influencing academic skills than were parents' attitudes toward achievement. Thus, there is an academic advantage associated with an early environment that stresses achievement. This effect was not maintained, however. By the end of kindergarten, there were no differences in academic skills attributable either to parents' expectations or to preschool experience.

With respect to creativity, children who attended the academic preschools were judged to be *less* creative. Hyson and colleagues suggested that creativity during the preschool years may be enhanced by environments that encourage playfulness and minimize adult control. There was no difference in social competence between children who attended the academic and nonacademic schools, but children in the academic programs did show greater signs of test anxiety and had a more negative attitude toward school at the end of kindergarten than did children from the nonacademic schools.

In general, Hyson et al. (1989) found that there were no long-term benefits of an academically oriented preschool program, and there was some evidence that such programs may actually be detrimental. They concluded:

> For many middle- and upper-middle-class children, a strong emphasis on formal academic learning in the preschool years appears unnec-

essary. In our study, academic skills were acquired by virtually all children by the end of kindergarten regardless of family or preschool emphasis, and broader intellectual abilities such as those tapped by Raven's Progressive Matrices were not enhanced by structured academic programs. In summary, our results indicate that the effort spent on formal, teacher-directed academic learning in preschool may not be the best use of children's time at this point in their development. (p. 15)

Although the results of this study must be considered tentative, they are consistent with the view that cognitive development during the early years of life

Box 11.4

Is Your Child Ready for School?

First grade has always been a time when there is a wide range of variation in children's cognitive abilities. Some are reading, doing arithmetic, and demonstrating the social maturity to work unsupervised on paper-and-pencil tasks for more than an hour. Others think that "elemeno" is the name of a single letter of the alphabet, can't consistently count past 10 with any degree of accuracy, and have a difficult time sitting still for more than two minutes. Somehow, first-grade teachers must consider the wide range of intellectual, social, and emotional abilities possessed by their 6-year-old wards and still teach them the skills dictated by the state legislature and the local school board. This is more easily said than done, and many children get trampled in the process.

Dr. Louise Ames, associate director of the Gesell Institute in New Haven, Connecticut, says that early school is

Parents and teachers can decide together whether or not a child is ready for the rigors of first grade.

is best accomplished outside a formal, teacher-directed environment. Young children's cognitive systems are immature, and because of this, learning and development may take place best in unstructured settings. The skills of young children are different from the skills of older children and may be ideally suited for the learning they need to do at this time in their lives. These findings suggest that children should not be hurried through a childhood that has purposes in and of itself (Bjorklund & Green, 1992).

Related to the issue of early academic programs is the issue of school readiness. The demands made of children in the early school years require a cognitive system that not all 5- and 6-year-olds possess. In other words, there is a certain level of readiness that is required to meet the demands of the early grades, and some children have not reached this level when the calendar says it is time for them to begin school. The issue of school readiness is discussed in Box 11.4. The suggestion we make—that many young children could benefit from delaying entry into first grade—is controversial, but we believe the issue is an important one, and one that deserves attention from policymakers in the decade ahead.

Educational Enrichment for Low-Income Children

A consistent finding in the United States is that minority children from poverty homes do not perform

getting "infinitely more difficult for children. Kindergarten today is taught like first grade was 20 years ago. Kindergarten is so much harder for children than it used to be."

Many children, of course, do fine in kindergarten and first grade, but many do not. We are often quick to blame the child for this, when, in many respects, it's the school we should be examining. A curriculum that is too difficult for a 5- or 6-year-old is bound to produce failure, and some children need an extra year or so of "just developing" before they are ready for the demands of modern American schools. If they can be saved from the experience of early failure, they quite possibly can be saved from later failure and the accompanying feelings of low self-esteem and poor self-confidence.

Too-early entry into school affects not only children's intellectual development, but also their emotional and social development. James Uphoff of Wright State University and psychologist June Gilmore cite research evidence that "fall" and "summer" children who start school on schedule and are the youngest in their class fare far less well in school than do children with the same birthdays who start school a year later. And these effects can influence children far beyond their early school years. Uphoff and Gilmore report negative long-term effects of early school placement, including increased drug dependency, deviance in school, and generally poor social and emotional adjustment. One startling, though preliminary, finding concerns the incidence of suicides in young people (25 years and younger). Uphoff and Gilmore reported that "fall" and "summer" children in one Ohio school district were overly represented among youth suicides.

Transition programs are an attractive option available to parents in many communities for "unready"

children. These include prekindergarten programs, for children who are old enough to start school but not yet developmentally ready for conventional kindergarten, and pre-first-grade programs, for children who have completed kindergarten but who are not up to the rigors of first grade.

With regard to school readiness, early childhood specialist Dr. Linda Coffey offers the analogy of a prize orchid she had grown that she wanted to use as a centerpiece for an important dinner party. When the orchid had not opened the day before the party, she gently pulled at the petals, trying to give it a boost. The next morning she found a wilted mess. Some kids, like orchids, need to grow a little more before they are ready to bloom. Pushing them too fast will do more harm than good.

Source: Adapted from D. F. Bjorklund and B. R. Bjorklund. (June 1988). Is Your Child Ready for School? *Parents Magazine*, Vol. 63, No. 6.

Children from impoverished homes often have problems in school that are due to lack of money, family stress, and parental attitudes toward education.

as well in school as do middle-class children. Such children begin school at a disadvantage, and the discrepancy between poverty and middle-class children usually increases over the years.

In Chapter 10, we discussed the role of parents in influencing intellectual development. Parents who talk to children, provide them with opportunities to explore, and raise them in a structured environment have children who score higher on IQ tests and do better in school. Parents from poverty homes are less likely (and less able) to provide the type of home environment conducive to academic excellence. Reasons for this are many, including lack of

financial resources, greater stress and instability in the home, and importantly, different cultural beliefs and values about intelligence and education.

Steven Tulkin and Jerome Kagan (1972) interviewed working-class and middle-class mothers of infants, asking their opinions about child rearing and intelligence. They found some interesting contrasts that may account, in part, for some of the intellectual differences often found between these groups. One difference was in speaking to children. The middle-class mothers felt comfortable talking to their 11-month-old babies, and said so. In contrast, many working-class women believed it unnecessary to talk to children until they start talking themselves and considered it socially inappropriate to talk to a preverbal child. Differences in attitudes corresponded to differences in behavior during an observation period: middle-class women talked to their babies more than twice as much as working-class women. Mother's verbal input is an important factor in language development, even at this early age (see Chapter 9). A second difference was in their view of intelligence. Middle-class women were more apt to believe that they had an impact on their child's developing intellect. They believed that intelligence is something modifiable and that they, as mothers, could have a positive influence. The working-class mothers were more apt to believe that intelligence is something inborn and that parents have relatively little influence on its development.

Given such differences in attitudes and behavior, it is not surprising that children from lower socioeconomic status homes do poorly in school. It is important for society to provide all children with adequate education, and since the 1960s, special programs have been designed to provide educational enrichment to low-income children. One of the earliest large-scale programs was Head Start, which is still in existence. Head Start was designed to provide low-income children with medical, nutritional, and educational enrichment during the preschool years. The hope was that compensatory education, or enrichment programs, prior to kindergarten would eliminate differences between low- and middle-socioeconomic status children when they enter school and that this equality would continue through the school years.

As a social program, Head Start is a success; as an experiment, however, it is very difficult to assess (Haskins, 1989). For this reason, we will review

Head Start, begun in the 1960s, offers preschoolers in poor families medical, nutritional, and educational enrichment.

some smaller-scale enrichment projects that have been carefully designed, permitting an evaluation of the components of compensatory educational programs.

The effects of preschool enrichment programs There is no question that children from low-income homes can benefit from educational enrichment programs. Preschool programs have raised the IQs of participants by 10 to 15 points over the course of the program (Bereiter & Engelmann, 1966; Klaus & Gray, 1968; Ramey, Campbell, & Finkelstein, 1984; Ramey, Lee, & Burchinal, 1989). These experimental programs varied considerably in the organization of their curricula, ranging from programs based on Piagetian theory to those using behavior modification techniques as advocated by B. F. Skinner and other behaviorists. What most programs did have in common was an emphasis on language and problem-solving skills, along with a low student/teacher ratio that permitted substantial individual attention to children. Generally, the greatest gains were demonstrated by children in the more rigorous, highly structured programs. In some programs, large gains in IQ were noted relative to control subjects and to

children's performance before they entered the programs (Bronfenbrenner, 1974; Klaus & Gray, 1968). In other studies, in which intervention began shortly after birth, children demonstrated high IQs relative to control subjects at every age tested and never needed compensation for below-average intellectual achievement (Ramey et al., 1989).

Long-term benefits of enrichment programs How long do these positive effects last? Once children have participated in compensatory education programs and raised their IQs to middle-class standards, do they maintain these gains in school? Unfortunately, once the program ends, the intellectual benefits begin to decline. The initial gains in IQ and academic performance shown by graduates of these preschool programs were slowly lost; by the end of the fourth grade, levels of intellectual attainment were comparable between children who had participated in the programs and those who had not (Bereiter & Engelmann, 1966; Klaus & Gray, 1968). In fact, the lack of long-term consistency in intellectual achievement caused Arthur Jensen (1969) to conclude that compensatory education had failed and to question whether intelligence can be altered significantly by early intervention.

Despite these findings, researchers were not ready to dismiss the effect of early enrichment on the later intellectual functioning of low-income children. Several investigators inquired into the long-term consequences of the preschool experience. Perhaps the most ambitious of these projects to date is that of Irving Lazar and his colleagues (Lazar, Darlington, Murray, Royce, & Snipper, 1982), who collaborated with the investigators of 11 compensatory preschool programs. Graduates of these programs ranged in age from 9 to 19 years at the time of the follow-up. Assessments were made of their IQs, academic achievement (as measured by standardized tests), school competence (as measured by assignment to special-education classes and retention in grade), and children's attitudes concerning their school performance and their likelihood of future success.

Although different programs yielded slightly different patterns of results, the findings for the 11 programs were relatively consistent. With respect to levels of IQ and academic achievement, compensatory preschool programs had little long-term effect. Although the programs had an initial impact on chil-

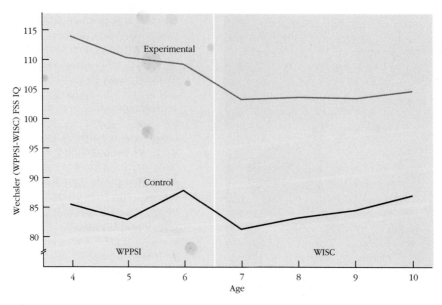

Figure 11.2 The Milwaukee Project: mean IQs of experimental and control groups, 48 to 120 months. *Source:* From *The Milwaukee Project: Preventing Mental Retardation in Children at Risk,* by H. L. Garber. Copyright © 1988 by the American Association of Mental Retardation. Reprinted by permission.

dren's IQs, few reliable differences were found by age 10 between poverty children who had attended the programs and those who had not (see also Miller & Bizzell, 1984).

The findings were more encouraging for school competence. For example, the median rate of assignment to special-education classes was 13.8% for children who had participated in compensatory preschool programs, compared to 28.6% for poverty children who had not. (The savings in tax dollars here alone justified the cost of the programs.) Although less dramatic, there were also significant differences in the percentage of children held back in grade: a median of 25.8% for program participants versus 30.5% for other poverty children. Differences were also found in children's attitudes toward achievement. Compensatory program graduates were more apt to give reasons for being proud of themselves that were related to achievement, and their mothers felt more positive about their children and their chances for success than did the mothers of control subjects. As a result, graduates of compensatory education programs may be more apt to succeed economically in the years to come than similar children who do not participate.

There is also some tentative evidence that high-quality preschool programs can have an impact on other areas of children's lives. In a recent review of preschool intervention programs, Ronald Haskins (1989) cited several programs whose participants grew up to be less involved in crime and the welfare system and had lower rates of teenage pregnancy and higher rates of employment than similar children who did not attend the program. Haskins cautions, however, that these results are not found in all programs; they reflect the effects these programs *can* have on children's lives, not necessarily what they do have.

In sum, most of the long-term benefits of the compensatory preschool programs were noncognitive, involving social factors rather than intelligence (as measured by IQ scores). These findings suggest that intellectual gains made during the preschool years will be lost if the program responsible for the gains is not continued into the school years. Once intellectual competence is attained, it must be maintained. Apparently, the environment for most of the low-income children in these studies was not sufficiently supportive to maintain the level of intelligence established during the preschool years.

One compensatory study that did find long-term intellectual benefits of preschool intervention was the Milwaukee Project (Garber, 1988). Howard Garber and his colleagues worked with a small sample of inner-city children who were at high risk for mental retardation. Twenty experimental and 20 control families, living in the most economically disadvantaged area of Milwaukee, participated in the study. All mothers had a WAIS IQ of 75 or less. For families assigned to the experimental group, a paraprofessional infant caregiver visited the home three days a week for 3 to 5 hours per day. The experimental mothers participated in an education and rehabilitation program for a month and received 26 weeks of paid, on-the-job vocational training. Their infants attended a stimulation program beginning at 3 months that continued until they entered first grade at about the age of 6.

The average Wechsler (WPPSI and WISC) IQs for the experimental and control groups, measured each year between 4 and 10 years of age, are shown in Figure 11.2. As can be seen, the difference between the two groups was large and significant at the termination of the program (6 years, experimental = 109; control = 85). Differences in IQ remained relatively stable for both groups over the next four years, with the experimental children maintaining their advantage relative to the control group (10 years, experimental = 104; control = 86). IQ tests were also administered at ages 12 and 14 years, and the experimental group still held an advantage (14 years, experimental = 101; control = 91). The long-term benefits found for IQ, however, were not found for school achievement. Although the experimental children showed an advantage in school performance over the early grades, by the fourth grade the

Box 11.5

Education Begins at Home

Beginning about age 6, going to school is what children "do." It's the closest thing they have to a job. School not only serves as their major source of education, but also provides them a social laboratory where they learn how to get along with agemates. The importance of school in the life of a child is undeniably great, and because of its impact parents have a right and obligation to be involved in what transpires in the classroom.

In fact, there is a quiet trend in progress in this country as a greater number of parents choose to take a more active role in their children's education. Although a small minority of parents have gone to the extreme of undertaking the entire education process themselves in their homes, most have chosen to work within the

system, trying to make the schools more responsive to their family's views. Some have gone as far as taking local school districts to court, most often over issues of textbook selection.

Regardless of whether one agrees or disagrees with the particulars of these examples, there is a deeper implication here for parents of elementary school children. School is no longer viewed as a magic kingdom of "experts" to whom parents send their children without question or comment to be educated as "they" see fit. Parents today are more knowledgeable and better educated than any generation before. They are aware of the importance of early education, and they often approach school as a consumer would, to make sure they get the most for their education dollar.

And how do school personnel feel about this new involvement? Many are tickled pink. After years of facing apathetic parents and feeling like glorified babysitters, many teachers and administrators welcome the renewed interest parents have taken in their professionalism.

It's sometimes difficult to know where to start, however. What can parents do to become more active in their children's education? The following list may help.

Exactly what does the school have to offer? Parents should talk to the administrators and the teachers. They should ask questions, LISTEN to the answers, and share their concerns. Often there are options available for parents who take the time to ask.

What avenues do parents have for **(Continued)**

two groups both scored below national averages on standardized tests and were generally indistinguishable from each other.

The major factor accounting for the disappointing long-term effects of compensatory education appeared to be the quality of the home environment following the end of the program. Children in the experimental group who lived in more stable and stimulating homes maintained higher IQs than did other children in that group who lived in less supportive environments (Garber & Heber, 1981). The significance of the home environment for intellectual performance caused Garber (1988) to question the long-term prospects for early intervention: "In each developmental period, however, subsequent to infancy (0 to 3 years), although it is possible to maintain normal IQs, it also seems that this can be accomplished only with increasing difficulty. To the extent that this is true, it suggests most simply that there

are limits to the performance benefits we can expect from an early intervention treatment" (p. 403).

What if compensatory preschool programs were extended into the early elementary school years? Might there then be long-term effects of early education? To investigate this question, Wesley Becker and Russel Gersten (1982) examined the academic performance of fifth- and sixth-grade children who had participated in Project Follow Through, a program designed to take over after preschool, when Project Head Start left off. In Project Follow Through, low-income children are provided with compensatory education through the third grade. Becker and Gersten evaluated the effectiveness of five different Follow Through programs, comparing participants' performance with that of children in control groups and also with national norms on a series of achievement tests.

Children in the study were given portions of the

Box 11.5 (Continued)

---

input? Many schools have parents serving on community advisory boards and textbook selection committees. Unfortunately, small school districts often forfeit their votes on statewide decisions for lack of interested parents to serve on these committees.

If parents feel something is lacking in their child's school, what can they contribute? Parents can share their own talents and knowledge by giving an hour of their time one day a week. They can lend some books on a special topic from their own library. They can lead the class in aerobics each morning instead of working out alone.

If parents feel something is being taught at their child's school that they don't like, or taught in a way they don't agree with, what can they do about it? If discussing the problem

with school officials doesn't help, parents can see if there are other families who feel as they do. If so, they might convince the school to offer an alter-

Parents need to know both what is going on in their children's classrooms and what to do if they don't like what they find.

native class that's more acceptable. If that fails, they can ask for assistance in setting up a home-school class for their child in a particular subject. Many teachers and administrators will suggest alternative textbooks and lesson plans that will let a child keep pace with classmates while having lessons in that particular subject at home.

School was never intended to be the sole source of education for children. Children spend approximately 30 hours a week in school. That leaves about 65 waking hours for parents to have an influence. Whenever possible, parents should try to fill those hours with interesting activities and opportunities for learning.

Source: Adapted from D. F. Bjorklund and B. R. Bjorklund. (October 1987). Learning Begins at Home. *Parents Magazine,* Vol. 62, No. 10.

Table 11.1 Mean percentile for children participating in Project Follow Through on subtests of the Wide Range Achievement Test (WRAT) and the Metropolitan Achievement Test (MAT)

Time of Test	WRAT Reading	MAT Reading	MAT Math	MAT Spelling
Last year of Follow Through grade 3	63rd	38th	62nd	47th
After completion of Follow Through grade 5	53rd	22nd	29th	37th
grade 6	38th	20th	27th	37th

Source: Adapted from "A Follow-up of Follow Through: The Later Effects of the Direct Instructional Model on Children in Fifth and Sixth Grades," by W. C. Becker and R. Gersten, *American Educational Research Journal,* 1982, *19,* 75–92. Copyright © 1982 by the American Educational Research Association. Adapted by permission of the publisher.

Wide Range Achievement Test (WRAT) and/or the Metropolitan Achievement Test (MAT). Significantly better performance was found for the Follow Through children than the control children at both the fifth and sixth grades—two and three years after the compensatory program had ended. Most striking were differences in reading level on the WRAT and differences on the spelling and math problem-solving subscales of the MAT, all in favor of the Follow Through children. Of 180 statistical comparisons made between the control children and Follow Through children from the five different programs, 76 comparisons favored the Follow Through children, whereas only 2 favored the Control subjects (102 comparisons showed no significant difference between the two groups). Thus, compensatory education programs that are continued into the primary grades also continue the beneficial effects on academic achievement.

Becker and Gersten also compared the performance of the Follow Through children with the national norms on the WRAT and MAT. Mean percentile rank for the Follow Through children for tests given in the third, fifth, and sixth grades are presented in Table 11.1 for WRAT Reading, MAT Reading, MAT Math, and MAT Spelling subscales. The most striking aspect of these data is the steady decline in relative score as a function of grade. These high-risk children were performing close to or above the national average (50th percentile) on three of these four tests in the third grade (the exception being MAT Read-

ing, which was at the 38th percentile). Two years after leaving Follow Through, only the WRAT Reading was comparable to the national average, and this declined to the 38th percentile by the sixth grade. Thus, although the Follow Through children maintained an academic advantage relative to matched sets of high-risk children with no compensatory education, they showed a decrease relative to children in the general population after the program ended. Again, the immediate social and educational benefits of the program were significant; however, as with the findings of Lazar et al. (1982), intellectual gains diminished once children left the program.

What's the big deal about getting minority children to do well on tests that favor the cultural majority? After all, the skills that these tests evaluate may not tap pure intelligence and are surely culturally biased. However, they *do* reflect the skills necessary to succeed economically in the United States, and if the cycle of poverty is to be broken, it will be through education. There are no easy answers.

State of the Art
The New Immigrants

The United States is a nation founded and populated by immigrants and their descendants. The American culture has evolved from the variety of cultures brought to these shores from every corner of the world, and many believe that this is the secret of America's success.

As we approach the next century, many Western nations are facing the twin problems of decreasing birthrates and increasing average population age. The eldest countries, based on average population age, are Germany, the Netherlands, and the Scandinavian countries, with the United States not far behind. However, of all the aging nations (including Japan), only the United States has liberal immigration policies.

Hope for the Future

In 1988, the United States admitted 643,000 legal immigrants—more than all other countries in the world combined. Labor economists believe that the United States will be able to fill new jobs and remain economically sound because of its continuing liberal immigration policies.

According to the Hudson Institute, a Washington-based research organization, the proportion of immigrants in the American labor force was 7% in 1985. It is projected to increase to 22% by the year 2000—more than tripling in 15 years. Residents of south Florida, southern California, and New York, among others, can attest to the change in their areas already. In south Florida, Broward County schools registered more than 400 children per month at their foreign language schools (Brecher, 1990). By anyone's estimate, the 21st century will find white, native-born Americans a minority in the United States.

But the impact of immigration is not fully expressed by numbers; the new immigrants, of course, have families. Children from a diversity of cultures are joining our neighborhoods and our schools. What effect does their presence have on native-born children? And what effects do their immigration have on children who were born here?

Culture Changes for Immigrant Children

Emotional problems   Adjusting to a new culture is not easy for today's immigrant children. Not many

Bilingual schools in the United States are attended by students from many countries who speak a number of languages. Classmates here (from left to right) are Michelle from Haiti, who speaks Creole; Alex from Brazil, who speaks Portuguese and Spanish; Lisandro from El Salvador, who speaks Spanish; and Priscilla from Brazil, who speaks Portuguese.

families come to this country for a simple change of lifestyle. They come because of war, economic chaos, and political tyranny. Immigrant children often carry the scars of that past with them into the new American culture. Native American kids may think of trauma as not getting the right kind of bike for Christmas; the Cambodian child sitting at the next desk in school might equate trauma with seeing one's parents murdered (Olsen, 1988). Many immigrant children bring memories of mentally shattered parents, wartime horror, and severe deprivation. School counselors have not been trained to deal with these types of problems, especially in 20-some different languages.

Once children arrive in the United States, they face new problems. The Center for Human Rights and Constitutional Law tells us that some 5500 children per year are detained at the U.S. border until INS officials determine whether or not they are eligible to enter the country. Unaccompanied children from 3 to 17 can be released on bail only to a parent, close relative, or legal guardian (adults who may be unwilling to submit themselves to INS scrutiny). The result can be months spent in detention centers, which are not licensed or regulated, while waiting for INS hearings. Many human rights groups are working to improve the immigration experience for children coming to the United States.

Education lag   Immigrant children often have tremendous gaps in their education, and when they arrive not speaking English, they lose ground for the three years it takes them, on average, to become fluent (Brecher, 1990). Most large school systems have special bilingual centers where children can be taught academic lessons in their native language in addition to learning English.

Adjusting to cultural diversity   Surprisingly enough, one of the big changes immigrant children have to make in adapting to American culture is adjusting to the large number of different nationalities and ethnic groups they find here. Most immigrant children come from countries with only one major culture, and they find it difficult to adjust to the multicultural society we take for granted. Just because immigrant children are "foreign" doesn't mean they can adapt easily to other "foreigners."

Adjusting to American customs   Adjusting to American customs is especially difficult when parents are

Immigrant children often adjust more quickly than their parents to American customs.

unsure of themselves also. Frequently, immigrant children master the new language and culture before their parents do; the result is an upside-down type of socialization, with adults depending on their children for explanations and translations. And parent-teacher communication, so central to American education, doesn't work well when parents don't know the rules and can't read the notes the teacher sends home.

Culture Changes for Native-Born American Children

Family attitudes of Americanism Immigrant children aren't the only ones who need to adjust to our changing population mix. Native-born American children are having problems, too. Many white American parents have long seen themselves and their families as mainstream Americans. They con-

sider everyone else as semi-Americans and treat "equality as a benevolence granted to minorities rather than an inherent right" (Henry, 1990, p. 30). Black families often have their own problems with the new immigrants. Many feel that they have fought so long for a piece of the American dream, and now they are being passed over as other minorities rush in through the doors opened by the civil rights movement. When schoolchildren are the first in their families to encounter the newcomers, they feel torn between their parents' ideas and their own experiences.

Being monolingual Most native-born American children speak only English, and so do their parents. Whereas immigrants of former times eagerly adopted the language in order to merge into the melting pot, today's immigrants aren't so eager. Although many learn English and use it as a second language, others argue that their language is part of their ethnic heritage and that there is nothing so American about English, either.

About half the non-English-speaking children beginning kindergarten in Dade County, Florida, were born in the United States. The philosophy among Cuban-American parents is to teach them Spanish at home and then let the schools teach them English. The result is children fluent in two languages, having learned both from native speakers. Some native-born American parents have responded to this, not by insisting that their children be taught a language other than English, but by voting to pass various types of English-only laws in 16 states.

Changes in school curricula   "History belongs to those who write it," an old saying goes, and history in American schools has been written by Western European Christian men. Now that this group is in a minority, educators and textbook writers are revising lessons to include a wider range of ethnic roots, many religions, and both genders.

Cultural Tossed Salad?

Few countries in recorded history have been able to contain diverse populations and still survive. It is clear that our population will not merge into a melting pot of generic Americans, but can we continue to exist in our diverse little groups as a type of cultural tossed salad? Optimism runs high in some quarters. America is unique among other multiethnic countries because it was founded primarily by voluntary emigration, and the new immigrants of today are just as hopeful and ambitious as the European immigrants of yesterday.

For older Americans who were raised in a world where native-born whites were the majority, the new immigrants are frightening harbingers of a future full of uncertainty. However, for our children, the new America is the only one they know, and it's here.

Summary

Cultures differ substantially in thinking styles, especially schooled versus unschooled cultures. These differences are not genetic but are related to the cognitive demands made by the culture. Cognition is context specific: certain cognitive skills develop in the particular contexts in which they are practiced. Social-value and language differences can result in cultural differences on Piagetian tasks such as conservation, but unschooled children can often solve such problems when the testing situation is adjusted for their culture. Differences in memory performance have been found between children in schooled and nonschooled cultures, but these differences disappear when the memory task is embedded in a meaningful context. Similarly, the mathematics performance of people from traditional cultures, usually much poorer than that of people from technological societies, can be improved when their familiarity with the test materials and the context of testing are taken into consideration.

Child-rearing practices are greatly influenced by culture, and these practices determine, to a large extent, the pattern of cognitive development. Vygotsky proposed a sociocultural theory of cognitive development, emphasizing that development is guided by adults interacting with children, and that cultural contexts determine how, when, and where these interactions take place. He defined the zone of proximal development as the area between a child's actual developmental level and his or her potential level when aided by adults. It is within this zone that adults can most effectively teach children.

Cognitive abilities vary as a function of culture even in those societies that require formal education, with different values and educational practices affecting children's academic performance. Differences in educational practices between countries (Japan and the United States, for example) are a function of differences in culture, and educational reform cannot be achieved simply by importing a system that evolved elsewhere.

Attending school produces enhanced cognitive development above and beyond the effects of age. Children who attend preschool programs that stress academics show some short-term intellectual gains, but demonstrate no long-term gains and have a less positive attitude toward school than children who attend nonacademic preschool programs.

Children from low-income homes usually do poorly in school relative to children from middle-class homes, in part because of differences in child-rearing patterns. Compensatory preschool programs, designed to eliminate academic differences between low- and middle-class children, have had considerable short-term success. However, follow-up data indicate that many of the gains shown by these children are lost after the program ends. Once intellectual accomplishments are established, they must be maintained by subsequent environments.

Immigration to the United States is expanding and rapidly changing the face of America. Immigrant children have difficulties adjusting to our society and are forcing changes in the American education system. The population changes in the United States require native-born Americans to adjust also.

Key Terms and Concepts

context specificity
sociocultural view
    zone of proximal development
school readiness
preschool enrichment programs
    Head Start
    The Milwaukee Project
    Project Follow Through

Four

Becoming a Social Being

Attachment: The First Relationship

12

It was to be their first child, and the young couple in the delivery room had been looking forward to this event for the past nine months. They had read all the how-to books and articles they could find about pregnancy, birth, nursing, and parenting. Childbirth was to be drug free, with the husband coaching his wife through labor, and the parents-to-be insisted that their new son or daughter be placed on the mother's belly immediately after birth. But there were unforeseen complications at the last minute, resulting in a Caesarean section delivery and an anesthetized mother.

Hours later, both mother and her new son were doing fine, but the woman was nonetheless distraught. She had not had the skin-to-skin contact with her newborn, and wouldn't get to handle her son until nearly 12 hours after delivery. She feared that she had missed the critical time for establishing a close mother-child bond, and that her relationship with her infant son would be less rewarding because of this.

This woman has good reason to be upset. She has missed a moment that she and her husband had planned for and anticipated for nearly nine months, and one that cannot be made up later on. But is her fear justified that missing this experience will have permanent consequences? Has she missed a critical time that will forever affect her relationship with her child? As we shall see, research evidence suggests otherwise.

Psychologists today agree that social relationships begin at birth, and even before. Human infants and their mothers are predisposed toward one another like opposite poles of a magnet. Humans have a prolonged immaturity, making children dependent upon their parents for an inordinately long time. Dependence in infancy is total. It is months before infants can crawl, and years before they can fend for themselves in even the most elementary ways. It is important for the infant (and the species), therefore, that an emotional attachment be made as soon as possible between mother and child.

In this chapter, we will look at the establishment of attachment and the development of social relationships, how these relate to emotional development, and what role biology plays in the process. We will focus on infant-mother attachment, beginning at birth and continuing into adulthood, and examine the effects of secure or insecure early attachment on later social, emotional, and intellectual behaviors.

The Nature of Infant-Mother Attachment

Attachment refers to a close emotional bond between a child and his or her caregiver. The significance of attachment should be obvious. Infants who are attached to their mothers increase their chances of survival. This is true not only for humans, but also for many other species that are born immature, including ducks, geese, sheep, monkeys, and chimpanzees. Moreover, the social nature of human existence depends on learning, and infants and children who stay close to their parents are in a good position to learn the ways of their society. The consequences of attachment extend far beyond infancy. Sigmund Freud (1938), for example, considered the attachment between an infant and its mother to be the basis for all later social relations.

The survival of our species has depended on the establishment of strong emotional bonds between mother and child.

Attachment is typically measured by some combination of three factors: proximity behavior, distress upon separation, and the extent to which the mother (or attachment figure) can soothe a distressed infant. Proximity behavior—how close infants stay to their mothers—is a useful measure for species or individuals who can locomote well, but is less useful for species such as humans who do not get around on their own until months after birth. Distress upon separation (sometimes referred to as separation anxiety) typically occurs when the infant and mother are in an unfamiliar situation and the mother leaves. In humans, such separation distress is not typically found until between 8 and 10 months (Schaffer & Emerson, 1964) and is highly variable, with some children showing little more than a whimper and others shrieking uncontrollably. One of the most frequently used measures of attachment in humans is the ability of a parent to calm a distressed infant (Ainsworth & Wittig, 1969).

The Origins of Attachment

Based on the behaviors just described, infant-mother attachment in humans would appear to occur sometime during the second half of the first year. However, the roots of attachment are firmly planted in the early months of life. Social give-and-take between infant and parent occurs from birth. Parents are responsive to their infants' cries, coos, smiles, and movements, and infants respond in turn to their parents' attention. The interactions that occur during feeding or diaper changing serve as the basis for later social relationships. Although infants during the first couple of months are not socially sophisticated, neither are they socially incompetent, and they do behave in ways that increase the likelihood of social interaction between themselves and their parents. By 3 or 4 months, their ability to understand physical relations and cause and effect changes, and so does their ability to understand social relations.

How is the mother-infant bond established? Psychoanalytic and learning theories suggested that infants become attached to people who feed them (A. Freud, 1946). However, research with rhesus monkeys in the 1950s by Harry Harlow and his colleagues seriously questioned the validity of the feeding-attachment claim (Harlow & Zimmerman, 1959). Harlow separated infant monkeys from their mothers shortly after birth and raised them with in-

In Harlow's research, infant monkeys were raised in a cage with a wire mother and a cloth mother. Although they received food from the wire mother (left), they clung to the cloth mother (right) when frightened or distressed.

animate surrogate "mothers." Some monkeys were raised in a cage with a surrogate mother that was a wire cylinder containing a hole in the chest area in which a bottle could be placed. The baby monkeys quickly learned to nurse from these wire mothers. When monkeys who had been raised by a wire mother were placed in cages where both a wire and a cloth-covered mother were available to them, they spent an inordinate amount of time clinging to the cloth mothers, even though the wire mother still fed them. Furthermore, in situations where the monkeys were frightened, they would run to the cloth mother which, much as a real mother, would serve to lessen their fear. Clearly, infant monkeys preferred the object of "contact comfort" over food. Something more complex than feeding was responsible for establishing attachment in these animals.

Infants are born into a social world and it would make sense, from an evolutionary perspective, for them to be prepared to perceive and respond to social stimuli. Research findings over the past 25 years clearly point to this conclusion. As we noted in Chapters 4 and 6, human infants are not born as blank slates, but from their earliest days have things they prefer to look at, smell, and hear. From shortly after birth, infants are attentive to stimuli that move, have areas of high contrast, and consist of curved rather than straight lines (Haith, 1966; Ruff & Birch, 1974; Salapatek & Kessen, 1966)—all characteristics of the human face. Perceptual biases are not limited to vision, but are found for other senses as well. Infants prefer the voices of women over men (Trehub, Schneider, & Endman, 1980) and display a preference for their mother's voice over that of another woman within their first week of life (DeCasper & Fifer, 1980). Within the first two weeks, infants show a preference for their mother's odor over another woman's (MacFarlane, 1975). These and other early preferences mean that babies are oriented toward human contact; they may also help support the behavior of adults who interact with them. Attending to and caring for an infant is more rewarding when the infant responds positively to the adult's social gestures.

Extending work from animals, John Bowlby (1969, 1973) proposed that there is a sensitive period during which an infant is most apt to form an emotional attachment to its mother. In humans, this is during the latter half of the first year of life (6 to 12 months), although experiences both earlier and later in development also contribute to this attachment. Bowlby proposed that human newborns have certain biological tendencies that keep them close to their mothers—including motor reflexes, such as the grasp, and perceptual reflexes, such as a preference to look at the human face.

Equally important, however, are dispositions adults have to respond to infants. Bowlby proposed that, through evolutionary adaptiveness, adults are predisposed to attend to infants' signals, including crying, smiling, and babbling. Although human infants today who stray from their mothers may no longer encounter hungry predators, secure infant-mother attachment continues to be important to infants' psychological well-being (Ainsworth, Blehar, Waters, & Wall, 1978; Bowlby, 1969). Bowlby proposed that both infants and parents are prepared by biology to establish this important social relationship.

Similar to Bowlby's assertion that human adults are biologically prepared to respond to infants' social signals is Konrad Lorenz's (1943) observation that caretaking behaviors are triggered by infants' immature features. Lorenz noted that infants of many species share certain characteristics, including a head that is proportionally larger than the body, a

Human and canine infants share many features that adults find endearing.

Figure 12.1 Facial features of infants and adults of various species. *Source:* Lorenz, 1943.

forehead that is large in relation to the rest of the face, large eyes, round cheeks, a flat nose, and short limbs (see Figure 12.1). Most adults find this combination of characteristics appealing, or "cute." These features are found not only in infants, but also in lovable cartoon characters (Mickey Mouse), dolls, and make-believe movie creatures (E.T.).

The Bonding Experience

Bonding refers to the mother's "falling in love" with her infant. The concept of bonding was popularized by Marshall Klaus and John Kennell (1976, 1982), who demonstrated that women who had close physical contact with their newborns immediately after birth, and who continued to have an extra amount of contact with their infants in the days and weeks following birth, had more positive interactions with their infants over the course of the first

year than did women who had a usual amount of contact. In some cases, the effects were found to persist for months and even years. In one study, infants born of mothers from poverty homes were less likely to be victims of abuse when they received extra handling by their mothers in the days following birth (O'Connor, Vietze, Sherrod, Sandler, & Altemeier, 1980). Based on these and other data, Klaus and Kennell (1982) proposed that the period shortly after birth is a sensitive one, during which contact between mother and infant serves as the basis for later attachment. Popularization of the research of Klaus and Kennell led many to believe that bonding has the quality of super glue—it works fast and holds strong. Unfortunately, this implied to many that a mother who missed the early skin-to-skin contact with her newborn missed a critical stage in the development of the mother-child relationship.

It should be clear, however, that early physical contact is not necessary for a healthy parent-child relationship to develop. For several generations, childbirth practices in North America and parts of Europe involved anesthetized deliveries, resulting in unconscious new mothers and groggy newborns. However, secure attachments were still formed.

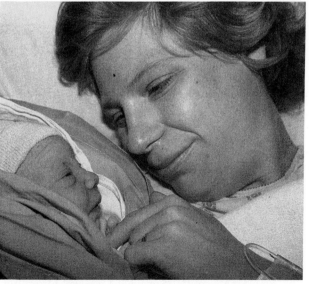

One road to secure attachment is infant-mother bonding: "falling in love" with one's infant shortly after birth.

Close parent-child attachments are also established between parents and their adopted children, even though their first contact may not occur until months after birth. These examples show the versatility of our species: we are able to establish positive social relationships under a variety of conditions our ancestors could not have even dreamed about.

There has been substantial criticism of Klaus and Kennell's position, much of it focused on bonding as a phenomenon that occurs suddenly, shortly after birth (Goldberg, 1983; Lamb, 1982; Lamb, Campos, Hwang, Leiderman, Sagi, & Svejda, 1983). For example, in much of the bonding research, the mother's motivation has not been taken into consideration. Women who seek out the bonding experience are likely to have different attitudes about babies and child rearing than women who do not (Goldberg,

1983), and it may be this attitude, rather than the event, that is the principal factor in attachment. In fact, in a study that controlled for mothers' motivation for having the bonding experience, no differences in mother-infant interactions were observed between mothers who had the critical skin-to-skin contact and those who did not (Svejda, Campos, & Emde, 1980).

Does bonding at birth serve as the basis for secure attachment during the first year of life? One way of examining this question is to look at premature infants who, for medical reasons, are separated from their mothers at birth and who receive little direct contact from their parents over the course of the first month. A study by Sara Rode and her colleagues (Rode, Chang, Fisch, & Sroufe, 1981) compared the quality of attachment at 12 months of age between a

Box 12.1

A Tale of Bonding

Karen K.

I delivered twin boys, by Caesarean section, on schedule. I was medicated for the surgery, so I didn't see my babies at birth. Half an hour after surgery I was still sluggish, but the nurses brought me Richard, whom I held. There were medical problems with the other twin, Danny, and he was sent to another hospital for immediate treatment. I was in the hospital for three days, where I had Richard "on demand." I nursed him, and had him with me about 12 hours a day. I was nervous about being a mother, and about nursing in particular. After the third or fourth time, however, Richard and I became comfortable with each other, and we started to develop a real mother-son relationship. I got to know him, what he liked, his schedule, and we interacted easily.

I've read about bonding, and it started in the hospital. But it wasn't complete until I took Richard home. Within a couple of days, I really fell in love with him. And it really is like being in love. You always want to be together. It's a physical feeling. You don't want to be apart. If I was away from him for a while, I needed him back.

Danny was in neonatal care at a hospital two hours from home. I first saw Danny five days after he was born, and didn't get to hold him until he was one week old. Even then, I was able to visit only about one hour every day.

When I first held Danny, it was like holding someone else's baby. I didn't know him at all. After he came home, I made a special effort to spend extra time with Danny. Although it was really hard at first, within two weeks I developed the same strong feelings toward Danny that I had for Richard. The two boys really are different. Danny was a better nurser, and I think that helped me form a relationship with him after being separated for more than a week.

The close contact I had with Richard, seeing him every day from birth, made it a lot easier to become attached to him. But I eventually felt that way about Danny; it just took longer. The feelings were very strong, and it certainly made me a believer in biology.

group of premature infants who had been hospitalized for their first month and a group of full-term infants who had not. They reported no differences in quality of attachment, suggesting that the bonding experience is not necessary for developing secure infant-parent attachment.

Klaus and Kennell (1982, 1983) readily admit that too much emphasis has been placed on bonding as an instantaneous experience that happens shortly after birth. They further admit that the effect of such bonding may be short-lived. More important, they propose, is the extended contact between mother and infant over the first weeks of life. Such extended contact, with the mother and infant confined together while others care for the pair, is characteristic of 98% of the traditional hunter/gatherer cultures anthropologists have studied (cited in Klaus & Kennell, 1982), and this practice, Klaus and Kennell believe, contributes to a healthy mother-child relationship. Although attachment *can* occur without such early experience, the bonding experience can be rewarding for those women who desire it. In fact, it may be particularly helpful for women from poverty and stressed environments, since it fosters a strong relationship between mother and child.

The Development of Attachment over Infancy

If attachment doesn't develop instantaneously from early mother-child contact, how does it develop? The simple answer is that it develops as all other social relationships do—as a function of social interaction over time. But attachment is different from other social relationships, if only because it develops in infancy and constitutes a child's first enduring relationship. Thus, we should not be surprised that infants are born prepared to become attached, or at least to make efforts in that direction.

Learning to Predict and Control

Attachment in infancy develops along with and as a function of a child's cognitive abilities. Babies are learning to control their own bodies and to control events in the outside world. According to John Watson (1973), infants perform contingency analyses, trying to determine whether something in the environment is contingent upon something they have

done. After repeated exposure to similar events, infants can predict what will happen when they act in one way or another, and they begin to be able to exert some control over the events. It should not be surprising that the social actions of people, particularly Mom and Dad, constitute important events in infants' lives, and that they attempt to gain some control over the behavior of these important people.

Because of young infants' limited attention and memory skills, they have a difficult time performing contingency analyses during the first couple of months. Watson proposed that when infants reach about 3 months of age, they and their caregivers begin "the game," which is an important and universal mechanism in the establishment of attachment. It begins with an adult playing with the infant. For example, every time the baby wiggles his leg, his mother kisses his belly; or every time the baby smiles and makes eye contact, his mother smiles back and says something. This becomes "the game" when there are contingencies between the child's behavior and the adult's responses. The game is repeated, often with variations, because the reactions of the infant are as rewarding to the adult as the adult's are to the infant.

The Quality of Attachment

Infants' knowledge of their caregivers extends beyond the game, of course. But what remains important throughout infancy is children's ability to predict and control aspects of their parents' behavior. Mary Ainsworth and her colleagues (Ainsworth, 1979; Ainsworth, Blehar, Waters, & Wall, 1978) have proposed that attachment develops as the result of mothers' responding contingently to their infants' signals of physical and social needs. More specifically, Ainsworth and her colleagues talk about differences in the quality of attachment as a function of mothers' sensitivity to their babies' signals.

Ainsworth and her colleagues developed the **Strange Situation** to assess quality of attachment (Ainsworth & Wittig, 1969), and this procedure has been used widely since its inception (Ainsworth et al., 1978). Briefly, the Strange Situation begins with a mother and her infant, between the ages of 12 and 18 months, entering a small room (although fathers and infants of other ages are sometimes tested, too). The mother interests the infant in some toys and allows the child to explore or play freely. This is followed by a series of 3-minute periods of various activities by the adults in the study. First, an unfamiliar adult enters the room, talks to the mother, and interacts with the infant. Three minutes later, the mother goes out of the room, leaving the child with the stranger. Finally, the mother returns. The behaviors that are most important for evaluating attachment are those of the baby when the mother returns. Based on babies' responses, Ainsworth and her colleagues developed three attachment classifications: secure, insecure–anxious/resistant, and insecure–anxious/avoidant.

About 70% of the babies tested are classified as **securely attached.** These infants actively explore while in the room alone with their mothers and become upset when their mothers leave them. When mother returns, a securely attached baby will often run or crawl to her, greeting her warmly. The mother is able to soothe the child, so much sometimes that the child returns to play with the stranger.

About 10% of the babies tested are classified as **anxious/resistant.** These infants appear anxious even when with their mothers, and tend not to explore much. They become very distressed when the mother leaves, but are ambivalent and display anger on her return. They stay near the mother after she returns, but resent her earlier departure and often resist her attempts at contact. These babies are wary of the unfamiliar adult, even when the mother is present.

About 20% of the babies tested are classified as **anxious/avoidant.** Like the anxious/resistant babies, they explore the environment only minimally. But unlike the anxious/resistant babies, they show little distress when their mothers depart, avoid contact with the mother when she returns, and usually don't show wariness of the stranger, although they may avoid the stranger much as they do the mother.

These patterns of attachment have been studied cross-culturally, with securely attached infants being the majority in all cultures studied (van IJzendoorn & Kroonenberg, 1988). There is some cultural variability, however: the anxious/avoidant classification is more common in Western Europe, the anxious/resistant is more common in Japan and Israel, and the U.S. distribution falls between the two extremes. Despite these differences, variability is often greater within than between cultures, with factors such as socioeconomic status and stress contributing to this variability (van IJzendoorn & Kroonenberg, 1988; Vaughn, Egeland, Sroufe, & Waters, 1979).

More recent research has questioned the adequacy of Ainsworth's attachment groups, noting that the behavior of many infants does not fit easily into her three categories. Mary Main and Judith Solomon (1986) suggested adding a new classification to Ainsworth's system: **disorganized/disoriented.** Unlike those in the three standard classifications, disorganized/disoriented infants show no coherent strategy for dealing with stress during separation and reunion in the Strange Situation. It was for this reason that some infants in past studies were labeled "unclassified" or forced into one of the other three categories.

Disorganized/disoriented infants seek to be close to their mothers in distorted ways, often showing patterns typical of secure, avoidant, and/or resistant infants simultaneously (for example, strong approach to the mother followed by strong avoidance). They may sometimes look dazed and disoriented upon reunion with their mothers. They may freeze in the middle of movement, approach her backwards, or wait an inordinate amount of time before deciding to approach her. Unlike secure, resistant, or avoidant infants, disorganized/disoriented infants seem to have developed no consistent way of handling separation and reunion with their mothers.

Because the disorganized/disoriented classification category is new, it has not been used frequently; nor has it been accepted without some controversy. Yet the little research that has been done using this new classification scheme has been provocative, particularly regarding children from highly stressed homes. Some of this research will be discussed in the State of the Art section at the end of this chapter.

Mothers' behavior and quality of attachment • Ainsworth and her colleagues (1978) have shown that mothers of securely attached infants are more responsive to their babies' emotional signals, encourage them to explore, and seem to enjoy close contact with them. These women respond appropriately and reliably to the cues their babies send, and their babies are able to predict reasonably well what to expect in various situations. Mothers of anxious/resistant infants are also interested in their babies, but they frequently misinterpret their infants' signals. They are "out of synch" with their babies' schedules and are often inconsistent in the enthusiasm they show toward their babies (Ainsworth, 1979). Mothers of anxious/avoidant infants show a lack of interest in their babies—often an overt re-

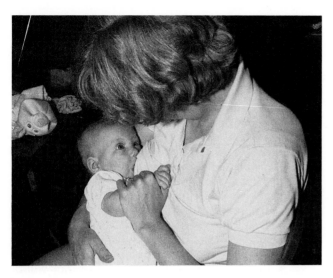

A mother who understands her baby's needs and responds reliably to cues teaches trust and fosters strong bonds.

sentment. They are generally unresponsive to their infants' signals (Ainsworth, 1979). Of course, Ainsworth's predictions do not hold up for all mothers and infants, but there is clear evidence that how mothers respond to their infants over the first year of life greatly influences the quality of attachment (see Pederson, Moran, Sitko, Campbell, Ghesquire, & Acton, 1990).

Ainsworth's ideas about the importance of mothers' behavior for quality of attachment find support in the ideas of Erik Erikson (1968), who extended Freud's theory of psychosexual development to include a significant psychosocial component (see Chapter 15). Erikson proposed that infants who receive warm maternal care develop a sense of basic trust. Like Ainsworth, Erikson stressed the importance of babies' learning that people in the world are predictable and dependable and that their parents can be trusted to keep them safe. Infants who do not receive such loving and predictable care develop a sense of mistrust. Although developing a sense of trust or mistrust during infancy does not destine a child to good or poor psychological adjustment, it does significantly affect later development, establishing patterns that may be difficult to reverse.

Characteristics of infants and quality of attachment

It should not be surprising that characteristics of infants as well as of mothers influence quality of attachment. For example, infants described as "difficult" (irritable, unresponsive, and irregular in their schedules of feeding and sleeping) are apt to be classified later as insecurely attached (Waters, Vaughn, & Egeland, 1980). Similarly, babies who are low in sociability at 3 months (more toy-oriented than people-oriented) are more likely to be classified as anxious/avoidant at 1 year (Lewis & Feiring, 1989). The link between infant temperament and quality of attachment is not a straightforward one, however, as evidenced by several studies that have failed to find this relationship (Weber, Levitt, & Clark, 1986).

There is also evidence that a baby's attractiveness affects maternal behavior, with more attractive infants being cuddled more and receiving more face-to-face interactions with their mothers (Barden, Ford, Jensen, Rogers-Salyer, & Salyer, 1989; Field & Vega-Lahr, 1984). In most cases, mothers of unattractive or facially deformed babies report no difference in their feelings or reactions toward their infants than mothers of attractive or normal babies, but there is a difference in their behavior (Barden et al., 1989). This does not mean that the infant is responsible for attachment; but it does mean that the process is a dynamic and transactional one, with both infant and mother interacting and changing over time to produce their own pattern of attachment.

The Consequences of Secure (and Insecure) Attachment

Attachment has long been recognized as important for psychological development. John Bowlby (1958, 1969, 1973), the father of the modern study of human attachment, noted that hard-core delinquent boys often shared one thing in common: they had never formed a warm attachment in infancy, making it difficult for them to form healthy social relations later in life and giving them a dissocial perspective on the world. Bowlby proposed that infants are biologically adapted to form attachments during their first year. If an attachment is not made during this time, it may be difficult or impossible to form one later, leading predictably to social and personality problems in later life.

Attachment and dependency Ainsworth proposed that infants who are securely attached are more in-

Securely attached children show more independence and confidence, and explore more than those who are insecurely attached.

dependent than infants who are insecurely attached (both anxious/resistant and anxious/avoidant). This may seem contradictory at first: it is easy to think of attachment as dependence, but in fact it is just the opposite. Securely attached infants are more likely to leave their mothers' sides to explore the world around them than are insecurely attached infants (Ainsworth, Bell, & Stayton, 1971; Ainsworth et al., 1978; Hazen & Durrett, 1982). They have learned that they can depend upon their mothers and, when exploring, frequently look back or return to their mothers, showing them things they have discovered in their travels (Rheingold & Eckerman, 1970). They are able to use their mothers as a secure base for exploration, confident that if anything should go wrong, mother is nearby to help. This increased independence and exploration produces a more confident child, and possibly one who is more intellectually competent.

Attachment and self-concept   Research has shown a relationship between security of attachment and children's sense of self. Bowlby (1969) proposed that children form mental representations, or "working models," of their attachment figures as a result of repeated experiences with them. These representations are closely intertwined with children's self-concept. Thus, according to Bowlby, it is through the attachment relationship that children develop a sense of self. A study by Jude Cassidy (1988) found that children described as securely attached to their mothers at age 6 had better self-images than insecurely attached children. Securely attached 6-year-olds described themselves in a positive light, but were still able to evaluate their own strong and weak points. According to Cassidy (1988), "the working models of these children and of their attachment figures appear to lead to a sense that they will be accepted despite flaws" (p. 130).

Attachment and social relationships   The quality of attachment is also associated with the quality of a child's other social relationships. Children learn how to interact with others by how they interact with their parents. Securely attached children develop a "working model" of their parents as being responsive and receptive and see themselves as being worthy of love (Bowlby, 1973; Bretherton, 1985). These children are more likely to expect positive experiences when they interact with others, relative to insecurely attached children. Evidence of this has been found by several researchers, who report that children classified as securely attached have more positive interactions with and are better liked by their peers (Cohn, 1990; LaFreniere & Sroufe, 1985; Pastor, 1981). Securely attached children are also rated by their parents and/or teachers as having fewer behavior problems than insecurely attached children (Erickson, Sroufe, & Egeland, 1985; Lewis, Feiring, McGuffog, & Jaskir, 1984).

Although these findings clearly show how important secure attachment is to later social and personality development, this does not mean that being insecurely attached as an infant dooms a child to a life of unpopularity and behavior problems. For example, several studies found that attachment is related to later emotional well-being only for boys (Cohn, 1990; Lewis et al., 1984). In their study of mental illness in 6-year-olds, Michael Lewis and his colleagues (1984) found that other life-stress and family factors were as important as quality of early

Children who are securely attached play better with their friends and are more popular with their peers than children who are insecurely attached.

attachment in predicting the emotional problems of a child: "The findings suggest that although a child's attachment relationship plays an important role in the development of psychopathology, the child is neither made invulnerable by an early secure attachment nor doomed to psychopathology by an insecure attachment" (p. 123).

The effect of attachment classification on children's social behavior was nicely illustrated in a study by Kathryn Park and Everett Waters (1989), who looked at interactions between pairs of best friends as a function of security of attachment. Preschoolers (average age 4 years) were observed in pairs, each child playing for about an hour in a room with his or her best friend. Half of the pairs were children who were both securely attached to their mothers. In the other pairs, one child was securely attached, and the other was insecurely attached.

The interaction between preschool friends was significantly different depending on their attachment classification. The picture one gets is of a much less harmonious friendship when one of the children is insecurely attached. Both types of friends had the same amount of disagreement and conflict; however, the secure/secure pairs resolved them in different ways than the secure/insecure pairs:

Patterns observed in secure/secure pairs
Negotiate a fair settlement.
Negotiate peacefully to settle issues.
Reach agreement easily.

Be responsive to partner's suggestion.
Comply with another's request.
Endorse another's attitude or preference.
Respond to protests and complaints.
Share secrets.

Patterns observed in secure/insecure pairs
Respond to challenges and dares.
Use direct rather than indirect strategies to win toys from each other.
Grab and take possessions rather than ask permission first.
Be verbally aggressive.
Verbally reject and be angry with partner.
Source: Park and Waters, 1989.

These findings, along with those cited previously, clearly demonstrate the significance of secure attachment for relationships beyond the mother/child pair.

Attachment and cognition Studies have shown a relationship between the amount and quality of mother-infant interaction during the early months and later scores on IQ or other standardized tests (Coates & Lewis, 1984; Cohen & Beckworth, 1979; Olson, Bates, & Bayles, 1984). A relationship has also been found between quality of attachment and exploration behavior, with securely attached infants exploring new environments more than insecurely attached infants (Ainsworth et al., 1971; Ainsworth et al., 1978; Hazen & Durrett, 1982; Main, 1981). Studies looking at the effects of early attachment on later cognitive performance have found that children who were classified as securely attached at 18 months showed better problem-solving behavior at age 2 (Matas, Arend, & Sroufe, 1978), were more socially competent, self-directed, and attentive at age 3.5 (Erickson, Sroufe, & Egeland, 1985; Waters, Wippman, & Sroufe, 1979), and were more curious, flexible, persistent, and resourceful in problem situations, and in better control of their impulses and feelings, at age 5 (Arend, Gove, & Sroufe, 1979), all relative to children who had been classified as insecurely attached.

The Stability of Attachment

These research results clearly point to a relationship between quality of early attachment and later social and cognitive competence. However, one must be cautious in interpreting the relationship. It is unlikely that being securely attached at 18 months

Securely attached infants become competent children because their parents continue to be sensitive and responsive to their changing needs.

caused children to be more socially competent or intellectually advanced at age 5. Rather, securely attached 18-month-olds received greater support from their families in exploring the environment and felt secure and comfortable doing so. As these children grew older and their motor and cognitive skills became more advanced, they continued to receive support from their parents. That is, there was continuity of parenting styles over time. Children who had sensitive and responsive parents at 6, 12, and 18 months usually had sensitive and responsive parents at 3 and 5 years (Arend et al., 1979). The same parental qualities that promoted secure attachment in infancy also promoted the development of other abilities during childhood.

Research evidence supports this contention. In studies with middle-class samples, most children classified as secure (or insecure) at 12 months were classified similarly at 18 or 20 months (Main & Weston, 1981; Owen, Easterbrooks, Chase-Lansdale, & Goldberg, 1984; Waters, 1978). In a more recent study, Mary Main and Jude Cassidy (1988) assessed the stability of attachment from infancy to age 6, using a method similar to Ainsworth's Strange Situation. Six-year-olds and their mothers were separated for an hour, during which time they were inter-

viewed. Following the interview, the pair was reunited, and their behaviors were evaluated in terms of security of attachment. Main and Cassidy (1988) reported that 84% of the children were classified the same at 6 years as they had been at 12 months, confirming the stability of attachment behaviors over the preschool years.

Somewhat different results are obtained, however, when stability of attachment is examined in less stable families. Byron Egeland and Alan Sroufe (1981) reported that attachment classification for a group of 12-month-old infants who were receiving excellent care was the same at 18 months in 92% of the cases. In contrast, attachment classification was much less stable (only 52%) for a group of infants who were being neglected or abused. Thus, when the environment is stable, quality of attachment is also likely to be stable over time; when the environment is disruptive and unpredictable, however, changes can also be expected in the quality of attachment. Despite the greater variability in the stability of attachment in high-stress homes, it is worth noting that the quality of attachment for a majority of children, even in these families, is stable over time.

Attachment beyond Infancy

Although quality of attachment is stable for most children, the character of attachment must change with age. The behaviors that reflect secure attachment in a toddler, for example, will be greatly different from those reflecting secure attachment in a 10-year-old. One approach to studying changes in attachment over time is to look less at specific behaviors and more at the "working model" of attachment that underlies the behavior. As noted previously, John Bowlby (1973) and others have proposed that attachment involves a psychological organization, or working model, that resides within a person. In other words, attachment behaviors reflect some enduring cognitive representation of feelings of security, social relations, and mechanisms to foster closer proximity with one's attachment figure.

Inge Bretherton (1980, 1985) has constructed an internal working model of attachment consistent with the theories of Bowlby and others (see Figure 12.2). As in any information-processing model, information from the external world must be monitored and compared with information the individual already has. Children must evaluate the information ("Is this a potentially dangerous situation?"), deter-

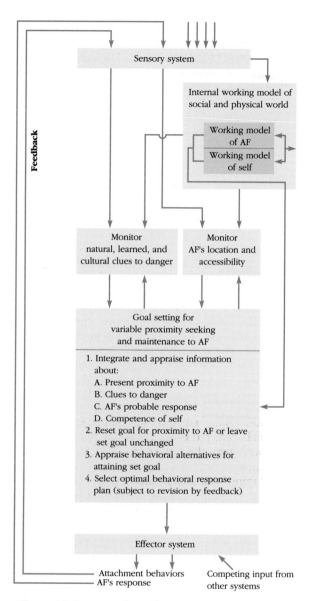

Figure 12.2 Internal working model of the attachment system (AF = attachment figure). *Source:* From "Attachment Theory: Retrospect and Prospect," by I. Bretherton. In I. Bretherton and E. Waters (eds.), "Growing Points of Attachment Theory and Research," *Monographs of the Society for Research in Child Development,* 1985, *50,* (Serial No. 209). Copyright © The Society for Research in Child Development, Inc. Reprinted by permission.

mine the accessibility of their attachment figure (AF in Figure 12.2), integrate that information, generate a goal or plan, select an appropriate response, and then emit the desired behavior. All of this decision making is done in the context of what children know about themselves and about their attachment figures, which, of course, changes with experience. Attachment, when seen from this viewpoint, develops not only as a function of the quality of social interaction between a mother (or father) and child, but also as a function of the changing mental model the child carries in his or her head.

Recent research has used working models of attachment to assess attachment in older children (Bretherton & Ridgeway, 1987; Cassidy, 1987; Kaplan, 1987; Main, Kaplan, & Cassidy, 1985), adolescents (Kobak, 1987), and adults (Main, 1987; Main et al., 1985). For example, in some experiments, children are shown a series of photographs of other children being separated from their parents. Some pictures reflect nonstressful situations (for example, parents kissing their child good-night), whereas others are more stressful (for example, parents leaving their child on the first day of school, for a weekend trip, and for a two-week trip). Children are asked what they think a child their age would feel and do in the situations shown in the photographs. Children's responses to these questions are evaluated in terms of emotional openness, the extent to which they express their feelings (the child in the photo would feel lonely, sad), and the extent to which they display distress during the task. Longitudinal research using this technique has shown that the quality of attachment at 12 months is related to emotional openness at age 6 (Kaplan, 1987; Main et al., 1985). The behaviors measured at age 6 in this study are quite different from those measured at 12 months with the Strange Situation; yet there seems to be a single underlying structure connecting the two. This structure is thought to be the mental model children have for their attachment figure.

Responses to situations will change over time as children's cognitive abilities change and as they venture out into the world more and more on their own. However, there is a continuity in the internal working model of attachment. Early experiences are integrated into this model and influence the perception of later experiences. The behaviors may vary considerably, but the mental model governing them traces its roots back to the earliest days of life.

Fathers and Attachment

Until recently, most research on parent-infant attachment had been done with mothers; fathers were the "forgotten contributors to child development" (Lamb, 1975). Fathers traditionally have had little role in caring for infants, and even today spend much less time interacting with infants than do mothers (Belsky, Gilstrap, & Rovine, 1984). Still, fathers today are playing an increasing role in the care of their infants. Recent research shows that they are quite competent (Parke & Sawin, 1980) and form attachments to their babies much as mothers do (Lamb, 1981).

Mothers' and fathers' interaction styles differ, however. Mothers more frequently take the role of

---

Box 12.2

Attachment Eight Years Later

Secure attachment develops when parents are sensitive to the wants and needs of their children. Parents learn to read the physical and social cues their children give them and to respond accordingly. This gives children a knowledge that their parents are people who will behave predictably toward them and who can be depended upon in a pinch.

How different are things for older children and their parents? School-age children are certainly more independent than toddlers, but they still require parents' sensitivity in reading their signals. Although verbal, school-age children are more complex than toddlers, and reading their moods requires as much sensitivity and attentiveness as it did when they were babies. The unusually quiet 9-year-old may be pondering an exciting lecture on the Aztecs from social studies class, brooding over a disagreement with a friend, or just be tired. A parent's job isn't necessarily to make the child talk, but to be sensitive to the child's mood and receptive to subtle cues that invite discussion. These are skills not so different from those needed eight years earlier.

Secure attachment during childhood implies a basic respect for children's own needs and individuality. Parents are often disappointed when a child's interests don't follow their own. The ardent baseball fan whose 10-year-old son prefers reading mystery stories to playing first base may not be enthused about his son's avocation, but should respect his choice. A basic respect for children and their interests goes a long way in fostering secure attachment during the school-age years.

Another thing that doesn't change all that much from infancy is children's need to use parents as a secure base from which they can explore the world. However, the nature of children's exploring changes dramatically over the years, and with it the nature of the secure base. Infants and toddlers need Mom or Dad available to run to, to physically hold them and protect them. You see much less of this among 7- and 8-year-olds. Parents can instill feelings of security without being physically present but by being only a phone call away. In many families, children come home after school to an empty house. A note on the refrigerator, a phone call at 3:00 sharp, or a message left on a tape recorder may be all that's needed to remind children that Mom and Dad are not too far away.

As our children continue to separate themselves from us, they develop new skills. They often like us there to watch, assuring them that we're available and that we approve of their new accomplishments. Nine-year-old Allen calls to his mother to watch as he practices his jump shots on the basketball court in the driveway. Fourth-grader Debbie searches on tiptoes for her parents in the audience during her chorus recital, smiling broadly and waving excitedly when she finally finds them in the crowd. Although there are many activities that parents and children of this age can share, sometimes parents can do the most by just sitting, watching, and approving.

Growing up so often means physically moving away from parents. But it does not have to mean a lessening of the emotional bond between parent and child. The *character* of attachment changes over time, but the *quality* of the relationship can be maintained and even strengthened.

Source: Adapted from D. F. Bjorklund and B. R. Bjorklund. (February 1987). Attachment 8 Years Later. *Parents Magazine,* Vol. 62, No. 2.

Fathers, traditionally left out of attachment research, also form secure bonds with their infants.

primary caretaker. They are more apt to hold and soothe their babies, to play traditional verbal games such as peekaboo and pat-a-cake, and to care for their babies' needs. Fathers are more apt to play physical games with their babies, involving unexpected reactions and stimulation (Lamb, 1981; Kotelchuk, 1976). Not surprisingly, babies often prefer their fathers at playtime and their mothers when they are distressed (Clarke-Stewart, 1980; Lamb, 1981).

When Children Don't Form Attachments

What happens when infants do not form attachments? Granted, such situations are rare, but they do exist, and learning about these exceptions can teach us more about the norm. In fact, much of the research interest today in infant-mother attachment stems from observations earlier in this century of orphanage-reared infants who were deprived of proper mothering and developed poorly as a result. Such research took advantage of naturally occurring conditions and assessed the role of deprivation in ways that could never be done in controlled experiments with children. Experiments have been done with animals, however, and together with the study of deprived human infants in institutions, they give us a picture of the role early social contact plays in development.

Institutionalization Studies

Earlier in this century, orphanages (or foundling homes) existed in much of the world as places where children were raised institutionally. Most children in orphanages came from poverty backgrounds, having parents who could not afford to support them. Others carried some "stigma of birth," such as being illegitimate or of mixed race. Although the intent of these institutions was benevolent, they were typically overcrowded and understaffed and provided infants and children with only minimal care. The term **hospitalism** was used to describe the deteriorating effect of long-term confinement to hospitals or similar institutions, particularly for infants. Rene Spitz (1945) noted that turn-of-the-century foundling homes in Germany and the United States frequently reported death rates ranging from 30% to 90% for infants under 2 years. These babies, though presumably receiving adequate medical attention, were highly susceptible to the deadly diseases that afflicted infants during those preantibiotics days. Equally compelling were the psychiatric problems faced by surviving infants.

The typical foundling home had many infants living together in a ward with few staff members. The underfunded institutions usually provided infants with adequate nutrition and regular medical attention, but toys in the cribs were rare, as were other forms of stimulation. A practice of many of these institutions, for sanitary reasons, was to place sheets over the sides of cribs. This, of course, prevented infants from seeing anything of interest. They were fed and diapered on regular schedules, but the attention they received from the overburdened staff was minimal. They were typically held only during these maintenance times (Dennis, 1973; Provence & Lipton, 1962; Skeels, 1966; Spitz, 1945).

The effects of institutionalization   The results of such early living conditions were increased susceptibility to illness; retarded physical, mental, and social development (Dennis, 1973; Provence & Lipton, 1962; Skeels, 1966; Spitz, 1945); and, in some cases, death (Spitz, 1945). The effects of social deprivation appeared early, within the first two or three months of life. Infants as young as 2 months did not know how to be held; they did not adjust their bodies well to the arms of an adult. Sally Provence and Rose Lipton (1962) describe 2- and 3-month-old institutionalized infants as feeling "somewhat like sawdust dolls; they moved, they bent easily at the proper joints, but they felt stiff or wooden" (p. 56). Signs of retardation and inappropriate social reactions to adults increased over the first two years, although these signs decreased some as children became able to move around on their own and were removed

from nurseries to wards for older children (Provence & Lipton, 1962; Skeels, 1966).

Long-term effects of institutionalization   The effects of spending their early years in institutions persisted long after children were removed from the foundling homes and placed in adoptive or foster homes. For example, Provence and Lipton (1962) followed into the preschool years a small group of institutionalized infants who had been placed in foster homes, most between 18 and 24 months of age. Provence and Lipton commented on the considerable resilience and capacity for improvement that these children showed, while noting that early institutionalization still caused long-term problems. These children, though relating to other toddlers, did not form strong personal attachments to other children or to adults. Their emotional behavior was described as "increasingly impoverished and predominantly bland. . . . One gained the impression on watching them that they had largely given up on their efforts to initiate a contact with the adult" (p. 145). These children continued to improve, socially and intellectually, over the preschool years, so that many looked, on casual observation, like normal children. But closer examination revealed problems in forming emotional relationships, control of impulses, language development, and flexible problem solving. In testing situations with adults, the children rarely sought assistance from their foster mothers, nor did they frequently turn to their foster mothers for comfort when distressed. This pattern is reminiscent of anxiously attached infants as described by Ainsworth and her colleagues.

Similar findings of emotional and intellectual deficits were reported by William Goldfarb (1945, 1947), who compared children placed in foster homes during their first year (foster children) with children who had lived in a foundling home for approximately three years before being placed in foster homes (institution children). A most compelling finding was the observation that institution children, through the age of 12, did not easily establish personal relationships. They showed no close attachments to their foster parents, had difficulty relating to family members and peers, and were generally loners. Three years of institutional life had made a powerful imprint on these children, one that continued to affect them nine years later.

Animal Studies

The unfortunate conditions of the foundling homes of earlier decades provided an opportunity to examine the consequences of social deprivation in human children. Yet, for understandable ethical reasons, these studies lacked the rigor of well-designed experiments. Social-deprivation experiments have been done with animals, however, and the findings serve to bolster those of the institutionalization studies.

Studies isolating dogs from all social contact immediately after weaning have shown that the isolates often display strange behavior, particularly when it comes to relating to humans or other dogs (Fuller & Clark, 1966). The most influential animal work of this type, however, was done by Harry Harlow and his colleagues (Harlow, 1962; Harlow, Dodsworth, & Harlow, 1965; Harlow & Harlow, 1977), who separated rhesus monkeys from their mothers shortly after birth and raised them in isolation from other monkeys.

The effect of isolation for six months was extremely abnormal social and sexual behavior that persisted into adulthood. When placed in colonies with other monkeys, animals isolated for six months avoided peers, preferring to play alone. When attacked by other monkeys in bouts of aggressive play, the isolates would frequently cower, accepting the abuse without fighting back. As adults, they were generally inadequate sexual partners, seeming to know they were supposed to do *something* but not knowing quite what that something was. As debilitating as six months of social isolation was for these animals, the effects were even more extreme for monkeys isolated for 12 months.

Some of the female isolates did succeed in conceiving and delivering infants, but, not surprisingly, they turned out to be horrendous mothers (Harlow, Harlow, Dodsworth, & Arling, 1966). These "motherless mothers" frequently refused to nurse their offspring and sometimes physically abused them. Several babies were killed, and others had to be removed from their abusive mothers. One somewhat surprising finding concerned the mothers' behavior toward their second or third offspring. These "motherless mothers," who were abusive or at best neglectful with their first babies, became adequate mothers for their later infants. Presumably, the first-born infants socialized their mothers, teaching them

something about social relationships. Nevertheless, they continued to show abnormal social and sexual behavior toward other adult monkeys.

Reversibility of the Effects of Social Deprivation

The results of long-term institutionalization and social deprivation, in both humans and animals, are retarded intellectual development and maladaptive social behavior. Institutionalized children are typically withdrawn, wary of adults, aggressive, and have difficulty forming social relations. They carry these behavior patterns and attitudes with them into new environments, where adults and other children react to their behavior. Children who are distant, emotionally cold, and prone to temper tantrums do not endear themselves to the people who interact with them. As a result, people often respond to these children in a way that serves to maintain their maladaptive behavior. That is, it is not so much that their early experiences directly cause children to be socially withdrawn at age 12, but that the pattern of behavior established in the institution becomes maintained through repeated interactions with other people. From this transactional perspective, children's dispositions influence how others respond to them, which in turn affects their subsequent behavior.

The clearest demonstration that a radical environmental change can modify the effects of long-term social deprivation comes from the work of Stephen Suomi and Harry Harlow (1972) with isolated rhesus monkeys. Monkeys raised for six months in social isolation were placed in cages for one hour a day, five days a week, for 26 weeks, with a "therapist" monkey. The therapist monkey was 3 months old at the beginning of the experiment. This age was chosen because 3-month-old monkeys are physically active, but socially immature. An older, more experienced monkey would know that the isolate's behavior was abnormal and treat it accordingly, either ignoring the animal or acting aggressively toward it. The younger "therapist" monkeys, however, did not realize that the withdrawn, often fearful behavior of the isolates was bizarre. They directed their actions toward the isolates, initially by climbing on and over them, trying to elicit some social behavior from their cagemates.

Imagine how difficult it is to ignore a small monkey climbing all over you. Thus, the first therapeutic thing that the younger monkeys did was to break down the isolates' self-directed behavior. Then, over the weeks of the experiment, the therapists and isolates developed social behaviors together. The therapist monkeys spent most of their days in a monkey colony where they developed normal social behavior. They in turn "taught" the isolates how to be social during their one-hour sessions. The result was that when isolates were introduced into a monkey colony at 12 months, they behaved normally. What was once thought to be a permanent disability was reversed when the conditions of the environment appropriately matched the needs of the socially deprived animal. In this case, the best therapist was not a more sophisticated animal, but a socially naive one who would not recognize and react to the abnormal behavior the isolate brought to the situation. Subsequent research using the same paradigm demonstrated reversibility in monkeys isolated for 12 months (Novak, 1979).

Reversibility of social deprivation has also been reported for humans. In Chapter 10, we discussed cases in which socially deprived children placed in adoptive homes or given special educational programs attained normal levels of intelligence (Clark & Hanisee, 1982; Koluchova, 1972; Winick, Meyer, & Harris, 1975). Audrey Clark and Jeanette Hanisee (1982), studying socially deprived children from Southeast Asia adopted by American families, found evidence not only of intellectual gains but also of social adjustment. These children, who were malnourished and socially deprived for most of their first two years of life, were given the Vineland Social Maturity Scale at approximately 4 years of age, two years after being adopted. Their average score was 137 (100 being the national average)—clear evidence of above-average social adjustment.

One of the most dramatic examples of reversibility of the effect of early social deprivation is the work by Harold Skeels (1966; Skeels & Dye, 1939), discussed in Chapter 10 with respect to the modification of intelligence. As you will recall, children (average age 19 months) were removed from an orphanage and placed with women in a home for mentally retarded adults, where they received loving attention from the women. In almost every case, a child formed a close attachment to one particular person, and this attachment served as the basis for social relationships with other women on the ward. The change in intelligence and general social behavior was remarkable, with most children functioning at normal levels by age 4 and being placed in foster or adoptive homes. A 20-year follow-up showed that this small group had developed normally, attaining an average level of education, economic success, and social adjustment. Most were married and had children. The severe effects of social deprivation had been reversed at the hands of loving, mentally retarded women.

The Skeels study is somewhat analogous to the "therapist monkey" study by Suomi and Harlow (1972). In the Skeels study, mentally retarded women may have provided the children with stimulation they might not have had at the hands of more mature caretakers. Chances are, the characteristics of the orphanage children would not have seemed normal to most adults. Most well-meaning adults who interact with a child expect some response in return. Children who are nonresponsive and generally lethargic tend not to receive continued attention from adults, particularly adults from stressed environments (Sameroff & Chandler, 1975; Zeskind, 1986). It is difficult to shower attention on children who do not respond, and this might be especially true of an overburdened institution staff. But because of the limited mental capacity of the retarded women (and probably unlimited time to spend), their attention may have been repeatedly directed to the children, even in the absence of normal social responses from them. Following months of such contact and loving stimulation, the children became more responsive, much as the isolate monkeys did.

State of the Art
Attachment in Families in Crisis

The orphanages and children's homes of past decades no longer exist. But the absence of overcrowded orphanages does not mean that all home-reared children become securely attached. Many parents leave their infants in low-cost, low-quality day care, where they spend the better part of their day with overworked, nonresponsive employees. Long working hours, financial problems, single parenthood, immaturity, and inexperience all produce family stress that can translate into frustration, depression, and anger—all of which take a toll on parenting ability. And the inability to function as an adequate parent is by no means limited to low-income, single-parent families. All levels of our society have their share of dysfunctional families, whether because of substance abuse, psychiatric problems, or other inabilities to cope with day-to-day responsibilities. Each of these factors can have profound effects on the quality of mother-infant attachment, and thus on the social, emotional, and intellectual development of the child.

Attachment and Families in Crisis

Recall from our earlier discussion that about 70% of infants tested in Ainsworth's Strange Situation are classified as securely attached. These numbers change, however, when infants from low-income, often unstable homes are tested. For example, Byron Egeland and Alan Sroufe (1981) reported that only 55% of infants from a poverty sample were classified as secure at 18 months, and that these infants were more likely to change their attachment classification over a six-month period than infants from middle-class homes. The fact that poverty homes produce a greater proportion of insecurely attached children suggests that entire school systems may soon be flooded with anxiously attached children as the number of urban poor swells. Larry Aber, director of the Barnard Center for Toddler Development at Columbia University, estimated that of the 100,000 4-year-olds in New York City, perhaps 50% are insecurely attached (Karen, 1990). Given the long-term consequences of insecure attachment,

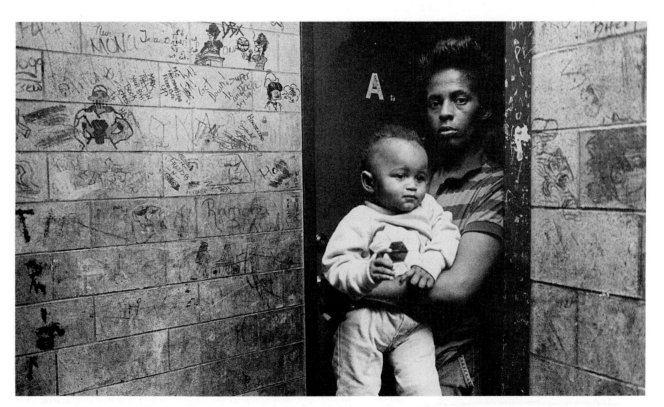

The stress of being a poor single mother can hamper secure mother-infant attachment. Intervention programs can help.

the matter is of extreme importance, having implications for the behavior of these children as they grow to maturity, including such socially important issues as drug abuse, teenage pregnancy, and delinquency.

Poverty in itself, of course, does not cause insecure attachment. In fact, we should probably look at the data and be impressed that more than 50% of low-income families have infants who are securely attached. More critical are families in which children are abused or neglected. Infants from homes where abuse or neglect has occurred (either to them personally or to older siblings) are more apt to be classified as insecurely attached than are nonmaltreated infants from similar backgrounds (Egeland & Sroufe, 1981; Schneider-Rosen, Braunwald, Carlson, & Cicchetti, 1985). Abused and neglected children are more likely to be classified as having disorganized/disoriented attachment, showing no consistent set of attachment-related behaviors in the Strange Situation test (Carlson, Cicchetti, Barnett, & Braunwald, 1989; Lyons-Ruth, Connell, Grunebaum, & Botein, 1990; O'Connor, Sigman, & Brill, 1987). In the study by Vicki Carlson and her associates (1989), 82% of the abused or neglected infants (average age 13 months) were classified as disorganized/disoriented, compared to only 19% of control infants.

Why should there be such a high proportion of disorganized/disoriented infants in these samples of abused and neglected infants? First, the care received by maltreated infants (or infants in homes where maltreatment has occurred) lacks consistency (Egeland & Sroufe, 1981; Cicchetti & Rizley, 1981); maltreating parents switch from overstimulation to understimulation (Carlson et al., 1989), a pattern that has been associated in the past with avoidant attachment (Belsky, Rovine, & Taylor, 1984). Second, Mary Main has suggested that fear is one of the main characteristics of a disorganized/disoriented attachment pattern, and fear must be a common experience for maltreated infants (Main & Hesse, in press). Feelings of fear combined with the desire to approach a parent produce conflicting motivations, which may account in part for infants' disorganized behavior during the Strange Situation. Third, mothers who maltreat infants may suffer from other clinical syndromes, notably depression (Carlson et al., 1989).

Maternal Depression and Attachment

Recent research has demonstrated that children of depressed parents are at risk for psychopathology because parental depression leads to disruptions in the family environment and parent-child interactions (Dodge, 1990; Rutter, 1990). Research has shown that depressed mothers present their children with a confusing interaction style, making it difficult for children to predict their mothers' behavior and the impact of their own actions (Zahn-Waxler, Cummings, McKnew, & Radke-Yarrow, 1984). Recall that, according to Ainsworth, if parents are responsive to their children's social and physical needs, their children develop a sense of control over their behavior and environment, and this leads to secure attachment. Conversely, if infants of depressed mothers do not develop this sense of predictability and control, it can lead to insecure attachment.

In addition to lack of predictability, depressed mothers typically provide less stimulation and spend more time interacting with their infants in negative states, such as anger (Field, 1984; Field, Healy, Goldstein, & Guthertz, 1990). Their infants, in turn, are fussier and less responsive, have lower activity levels (Field, 1984), all of which serves to maintain the generally negative interaction style of the depressed mothers.

One recent study has demonstrated a link between depression in low-income families and attachment classification. Karlen Lyons-Ruth, David Connell, Henry Grunebaum, and Sheila Botein (1990) found that infants of depressed mothers were more likely to be classified as disorganized/disoriented (61%) than were infants of nondepressed mothers from similar backgrounds (34%). More significantly, however, their study also included a treatment group for high-risk infants. Within this group, 32% of the infants had been maltreated, and 65% had mothers who were depressed. Each family in this group was visited regularly by a paraprofessional—a mother from the same low-income community who had received special training. These women used a toy-demonstration procedure to facilitate developmentally appropriate interactions between mothers and their infants, and also attended to the family's social service needs. In addition, the family was visited weekly by master-level psychologists, who also conducted weekly group meetings. The goals of this treatment program were:

1. to create an accepting and trusting relationship between the mothers and the service providers;
2. to increase the family's competence in obtaining resources to meet basic needs, including social, financial, health, and educational services;
3. to demonstrate and reward more interactive, positive, and developmentally appropriate exchanges between mother and infant, stressing the mother's role both as teacher and as a source of emotional support for her infant; and
4. to decrease social isolation from other mothers by encouraging attendance at weekly parenting groups or monthly participation in a drop-in social hour.

Source: From "Infants at Social Risk: Maternal Depression and Support Services as Mediators of Infant Development and Security of Attachment," by K. Lyons-Ruth, D. B. Convell, H. U. Grunebaum, & S. Botein, *Child Development,* 1990, *61*, 85–98. Copyright © The Society for Research in Child Development, Inc. Reprinted by permission.

The average length of treatment was 13 months, with a range of 9 to 18 months. When infants were tested again at 18 months, 61% of those in the treatment group were classified as securely attached, compared to 23% of untreated infants.

These findings not only demonstrate a connection between depression, maltreatment, and security of attachment; they also reveal that harmful patterns

Box 12.3

Parental Leave around the World

Denmark   Mothers are given 14 weeks of paid leave after childbirth, then the couple is given the option of an additional 10 weeks of either maternal or paternal leave.

Finland   Maternity/paternity leave consists of 70 working days at full pay, 188 working days at about 70% pay, and unpaid leave for up to 3 years. Mothers who stay home with their children receive a supplement for their first child equivalent to about 25% of Finland's average family income and slightly less for the following children.

France   Working women are paid 84% of their salaries during a 16-week maternity leave.

Israel   New mothers get 12 weeks' paid leave and 40 weeks' unpaid leave.

Japan   Mothers are given 14 weeks of maternity leave, but most quit work to care for their babies.

Poland   Mothers can take 3 to 6 months off after childbirth with full pay, and parental leave with a portion of pay is available until the child is 3.

Soviet Union   Women are given 4 months' maternity leave at full pay followed by 25% pay until the baby is 1 year old. There is no paternity leave.

Sweden   A working mother is paid 90% of her salary during a 6-month maternity leave. She can then extend it another 6 months, or the father can take a 6-month parental leave.

United States   There is no national child-care policy and no national policy of parental leave.

Source: Adapted from *International Society for the Study of Behavioral Development Newsletter,* 1989, *2*, pp. 4–8.

established during the first year of life can be modified with intervention. In addition, Lyons-Ruth and associates reported significant improvements for treated infants on a test of infant mental development. These results show the resiliency of infants, who are able to overcome negative home environments with the help of social services within the home. With assistance, patterns of family interaction can change, and with them so can the security of a child's attachment to its parents and all the positive consequences that come with it.

The need for social programs to assist families in crisis when children are young should be obvious. Such programs, enhancing the chances of secure attachment between parent and child, can result in significant savings—financial, social, and emotional. Some scientists and policy makers believe that secure mother-infant attachment is sufficiently important that it should be addressed at the national level (Phillips, McCartney, & Scarr, 1990). Many businesses agree, and, realizing that secure parents make productive employees, have parental leave policies, giving mothers time to form attachments with their infants without fear of losing their jobs. Many countries, recognizing the importance of establishing secure attachment in infancy, have national parental leave policies (see Box 12.3). The United States, however, has no national parental leave policy, making it an exception among industrialized countries.

Summary

Attachment refers to the close emotional bond between a child and his or her caretaker. Infants are born with many perceptual abilities that bias them to become attached.

Bonding refers to the mother's "falling in love" with her infant. Although it has been suggested that bonding occurs as a result of skin-to-skin contact immediately after birth, research has shown that bonding can develop more gradually and that infants who do not have the "bonding experience" can still form close attachments with their parents. Beginning around 3 months, infants and their caregivers begin "the game," in which clear contingencies exist between the infant's behavior and an adult's responses, fostering the infant's sense of control, its relationship to another person, and attachment.

Mary Ainsworth and her colleagues proposed that how mothers respond to their infants affects the quality of attachment. Using the Strange Situation, Ainsworth described three attachment classifications: secure, anxious/resistant, and anxious/avoidant. Secure attachment results when mothers are responsive to their babies' emotional signals, encourage them to explore, and enjoy close contact with their infants. Securely attached infants are more independent, have a better self-concept, have more positive social relationships, and show greater cognitive skills, relative to insecurely attached children. Attachment classification tends to be relatively stable over time, but this presumably reflects continuity of parenting styles over time. Recent research has looked at attachment beyond infancy, and between infants and fathers.

Institutionalization studies demonstrate the importance of early social contact for later emotional well-being. Infants raised in overcrowded and understaffed orphanages showed retarded physical, social, and emotional development, which were often maintained into adolescence and adulthood. Similar interpretations have been derived from animal studies, in which animals are deprived of social contact early in life. Other studies, with both animals and humans, have shown that the negative effects of early deprivation can be reversed under certain conditions.

Recent research has examined attachment in families in crisis. Infants from stressed homes are more apt to be classified as insecurely attached, as are maltreated infants. A new attachment classification, disorganized/disoriented, has been developed to describe the attachment behavior of many high-risk infants. Infants from homes where abuse or neglect occurs, or where the mother is clinically depressed, are more likely to be classified as disorganized/disoriented than other infants. The maladaptive parenting style of abusive, neglectful, or depressed mothers can be modified with intervention, and their children's quality of attachment changed for the better.

Key Terms and Concepts

attachment
bonding
contingency analyses
    the game
quality of attachment
    Strange Situation

secure attachment
anxious/resistant attachment
anxious/avoidant attachment
disorganized/disoriented attachment
stability of attachment
internal working model of attachment
institutionalization studies
    hospitalism

posed a number of different ways to classify parenting styles, but the most successful classification has been that of Diana Baumrind (1967, 1971, 1973), who has found that most parents can be described as using one of three general styles: **authoritarian permissive,** or **authoritative.**

Authoritarian parents expect absolute obedience. They establish the rules and expect their children to obey them without question. They frequently enforce the rules by physical punishment and withdrawal of affection.

Permissive parents, in contrast, generally exert little control over their children. In these families, children pretty much do what they want, receiving little guidance or direction from their parents. Most permissive parents are warm and involved with their children, but some are detached and uninvolved.

Authoritative parents are those who set clear standards but enforce their rules with warmth and explanations. Authoritative parents will often listen to their children's justifications for their behavior or reasons for their requests, and sometimes make exceptions accordingly. They value conformity along with self-reliance and take into consideration children's uniqueness when setting and enforcing rules.

It should not be surprising that these general parenting styles are associated with different characteristics in children (see Table 13.1). Children of

Authoritarian parenting features iron-clad rules, harsh criticism, and, often, physical punishment.

authoritarian parents tend to be withdrawn, irritable, and indifferent to new experiences (Baumrind, 1967). These children often have low self-esteem (Coopersmith, 1967), are more apt to be rejected by their school peers (Pettit, Dodge, & Brown, 1988), and when physical punishment is used to enforce the rules, are apt to be highly aggressive and bully others (Olweus, 1980).

Permissive parents, at first glance, may seem to be the ideal. After all, children are seldom criticized or reprimanded, and if the parents are warm and loving, who could ask for anything more? But freedom that exceeds what is appropriate for a child's developmental level can be confusing and frightening. Without proper guidance from parents, young children cannot learn to regulate their own behavior. Self-control and self-discipline are not attained if parents fail to set rules or enforce them. Research shows that children of permissive parents tend to be impulsive and aggressive, often acting out of control. In one study, a generally permissive style of parenting during the preschool years predicted later drug use in adolescent girls (Block, Block, & Keyes, 1988).

Table 13.1 Authoritative, authoritarian, and permissive parenting styles

Type	Parent Behavior	Child Characteristics
Authoritative	Controlling; demanding; warm; receptive; rational; verbal give-and-take; values discipline, self-reliance, and uniqueness	Independent; socially responsible; self-controlled, explorative; self-reliant
Authoritarian	Stricter control and more critical evaluation of child's behavior and attitudes; little verbal give-and-take; less warm and more emotionally detached	Withdrawn; discontented; distrustful of others
Permissive	Noncontrolling; nondemanding; little punishment or exercising of power; use of reasoning; warm and accepting	Lacking in self-reliance, self-control, and explorative tendencies

Box 13.1

Discipline and Children: Some Things to Keep in Mind

Usually when parents think of discipline, they think of problems. "What can I do to *discipline* my child when he persists in calling the next-door neighbor doo-doo head, or when he threatens his little sister with physical violence?" "How can I get my daughter to go to bed at night without fussing or stop her from making a scene in the grocery store when we pass through the candy aisle?" Handling these situations involves doing something to remedy an immediate crisis. When parents think of discipline only in these terms, it's what we refer to as "crisis parenting."

True discipline, however, entails much more than dealing with behavioral emergencies. In fact, discipline is most effective when it is viewed as the result of a continuous interaction between children and parents over time. We teach our children to *become disciplined*—to develop self-discipline—by dealing with them lovingly and consistently on a day-to-day basis and by setting good examples for them to emulate. Discipline should be viewed as "rules to live by" and not simply as a bag of tricks to make a child comply in specific, problem situations. Discipline is part of a lifestyle. Disruptive and problem behaviors have a history; they don't arise out of the blue. Understanding that problem behavior is often the re-

Parents who think of discipline only in problem situations are practicing "crisis parenting."

sult of patterns firmly established in infancy can help parents avoid problem situations, modify undisciplined lifestyles, and handle immediate crises with a minimum of strife.

Developing a disciplined lifestyle requires considerable effort on the part of parents. It involves thinking about the kind of life you want to live and the kind of children you want to raise. It involves evaluating your own childhood, keeping what you think is valuable, and weeding out or updating the rest. It involves firming up your adult life so you can be a positive role model for your children. It involves many long talks with your spouse about making definite family rules. It also involves the risk of "looking human" to your family when you fall short of perfection. And once all that is in place, it involves periodic checking to make sure everything is running smoothly and to make the inevitable corrections when everything is not.

A disciplined child is a child responsible for his or her own actions and in control of his or her own behavior. We believe that the goal of parenting should be to raise a competent, independent adult and that this process begins in infancy. One of the greatest gifts parents can give their children is self-discipline—control over their own lives. Such a gift is most easily given with warmth, love, and respect for the child as an individual.

Two Views of Parenting

Parents too often view child rearing, and discipline in particular, as imposing their will upon their children. From this point of view, children are little lumps of clay and parents are the sculptors. Such a view places all the responsibility on the artist and none on the raw material.

On the other hand, some parents believe that child rearing is more like gardening. Nature provides the necessary sun and soil and seed, and the parent is little more than the attentive gardener whose job it is to water them and watch them grow. This view places most of the responsibility on the child, leaving parents hopeful that they have been entrusted with a well-bred seedling who won't grow out of control.

Not surprisingly, the truth lies somewhere in the middle. Parents are truly the most significant shapers of children's lives. Yet the child comes into the world with a unique biology that forms the basis of his or her personality. Some babies are easily soothed, whereas others must be danced around the living room most of the evening before calming down; some love being held, whereas others tolerate cuddling only long enough to be fed. These dispositions—personality traits, if you will—influence how children interpret and respond to their world, and to their parents in particular. Yet children, regardless of their biology, are influenced by the efforts of parents. Children and parents have a relationship that is like a continuous dance, with one partner adjusting his steps to the moves of the other.

Discipline and Development

Children at different ages require different types of behaviors from their parents. They have different ways of understanding their world, and thus different ways of perceiving what their parents do. The techniques used to control the behavior of a 1-year-old will simply not be adequate for controlling the behavior of a 2- or 3-year-old. Children change over time, and this requires that their parents change.

Some of the most persistent problems in child rearing during the early years can be traced to parents' difficulty dealing with or understanding the developmental level of their children. Children become more competent and demand more independence, but parents frequently have difficulty dealing with children's newfound abilities. Some of the fiercest battles are fought in children's "war of independence." On the other hand, parents often expect more of children than they are capable of producing. Such overestimation of children's abilities is another frequent source of conflict and one that can be avoided if parents are alert to the developmental level of their children.

Discipline, Love, and Respect

Raising a disciplined child is best accomplished in an atmosphere of love and respect. Children who are rarely taken seriously—whose ideas are not

Family discipline involves mutual love and respect. Rules are necessary, but should be made with each child's developmental level in mind.

listened to and who are repeatedly told without justification to comply—do not see the merit of discipline. The child whose rationale is "I'll behave so I don't get into trouble" does not develop respect for adults. When the opportunity comes to break the rules without being "caught," he or she will do so.

On the other hand, children whose ideas and feelings are respected, who are listened to and who sometimes get their way when their arguments are sound, see their parents as reasonable people worthy of respect. The rules laid down by their parents are not always agreeable, but they are not capricious either. As all children do, they will argue and disobey, but they will also develop an appreciation for their parents' judgments and the merits of a disciplined lifestyle. Of course, they can't articulate this, but children who are accorded respect will learn respect for others in the process, and are more apt to internalize those "rules to live by."

Source: From *Parent's Book of Discipline* by B. R. Bjorklund and D. F. Bjorklund. Copyright © 1990 by Gruner and Jahr USA, Publishing. Reprinted by permission of Ballantine Books, a Division of Randam House, Inc.

Not surprisingly, children of authoritative parents fare best. These children are more independent and socially responsible than the children of either authoritarian or permissive parents. They tend to be self-reliant, self-controlled, and curious. They get along well with other children (Pettit et al., 1988), have high self-esteem (Coopersmith, 1967), perform well academically (McCall, Appelbaum, & Hogarty, 1973; Steinberg, Elmen, & Mounts, 1989), and, as adolescents, have a healthy psychological orientation toward work (Steinberg et al., 1989). In fact, most popular books written for parents about child rearing and family discipline, despite their varied approaches, advocate a healthy degree of control in a warm, loving relationship—characteristics of the authoritative parent (Bjorklund & Bjorklund, 1990; Dodson, 1977; Rosemond, 1981; Samalin, 1987; for a different view, see Dobson, 1970).

How a society raises its children is a function of what type of adult it wants to produce. It may seem obvious that a self-reliant, independent, exploring, and trusting person would be the most competent adult, and this is very likely true for middle-class American society. But is it also true for Japanese, German, and Iraqi children? Is it true for American children growing up in areas of urban poverty or on Indian reservations? Maybe not. Certainly there is great variability in what constitutes an "effective adult" in different cultures (and subcultures) around the world; when evaluating the best way to rear children, one must keep in mind the skills and attitudes that will serve them best, both in their immediate environments and when they grow up (see Baumrind, 1972).

Factors That Influence Parenting Style

Why are some parents authoritative, others authoritarian, and still others permissive? Jay Belsky (1984) has proposed a model in which a number of different factors interact to determine parenting style (see Figure 13.1). The parent's personality—as shaped by his or her own developmental history—to a large extent determines parenting style. But personality is also affected by other factors, including the marital relationship, work, and social support. Each of these factors can affect parenting indirectly by influencing the parent's personality; they can also have a more direct effect on specific parenting practices. Last, but not least, are the characteristics of the child. Different types of children bring out different responses in parents, thus making the child an important component in how he or she is treated.

The only modification we would suggest to this useful model is the effect of the child's own development on parenting. As children develop, they present different demands to their parents, requiring changes in how parents behave. In some cases, these developmental changes can result in changes in parenting practices.

Parents' emotional adjustment   There is considerable evidence in support of Belsky's theory. Psychologically mature and healthy people are more likely to show effective parenting skills than less well adjusted people. As we saw in the last chapter, mothers suffering from depression are often ineffective parents, having infants who are insecurely attached (Dodge, 1990). Research has shown that depressed

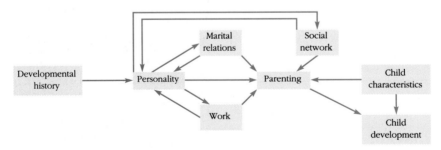

Figure 13.1 Belsky's model of the determinants of parenting. *Source:* From "The Determinants of Parenting: A Process Model," by J. Belsky, *Child Development,* 1984, 55, 83–96. Copyright © The Society for Research in Child Development, Inc. Reprinted by permission.

Happily married parents provide positive parenting and are most apt to have well-adjusted children.

mothers of older children often use disruptive, hostile, and rejecting child-rearing practices, and that children's temperaments influence parents' perceptions and behavior toward them (see Belsky, 1984).

Parents' marriage Belsky (1984) proposed that marriage is the principal support system for parents. There is ample evidence linking marital problems with use of physical punishment, infrequent use of reasoning as a discipline style, and generally negative outcomes for the children (see Emery, 1982). Recent research has shown that even *premarital* satisfaction with an eventual mate predicts aspects of parenting and how well children function in the family (Howes & Markman, 1989). Other research has shown that husbands and wives who generally agree about parenting styles have more congenial homes that are conducive to good parenting and have children who are intellectually and socially competent (Block, Block, & Morrison, 1981; Vaughn, Block, & Block, 1988). A recent study suggests that it

may not be agreement per se that is so important; rather, husbands and wives who agree on child rearing tend to have more positive parenting skills than do husbands and wives who disagree (Deal, Halverson, & Wampler, 1989).

Social support Research evidence cited by Belsky (1984) clearly showed that "the availability of significant others and the support received from them exert a beneficial impact on parent-child relations" (p. 88). Having an extended family or a network of friends provides the parent (particularly the mother) with a source of emotional support and important knowledge about child rearing that serves, in many cases, to influence specific parenting behaviors (Stevens, 1988). In one recent study, friendships and community support influenced mothers' perceptions and reactions to daily child-rearing hassles to a greater extent than did support from husbands (Crnic & Greenberg, 1990).

Economic stability It is also clear that poverty, loss of a job, or other significant life stressors influence the quality of parent-child interactions. In a recent review of the effects of economic hardship on parenting in black families, Vonnie McLoyd (1990) noted that "mothers who are poor, as compared to their advantaged counterparts, are more likely to use

An extended network of family and friends provides parents with advice and emotional support.

power-assertive techniques in disciplinary encounters and are generally less supportive of their children. They value obedience more, are less likely to use reasoning, and are more likely to use physical punishment as a means of disciplining and controlling the child" (p. 322).

Although such effects are associated with long-term poverty, there is also evidence that parents become more irritable, hostile, and depressed as a result of economic loss and, as a consequence, react toward their children in punitive and erratic ways (Conger, McCarty, Yang, Lahey, & Kroop, 1984; Lempers, Clark-Lempers, & Simons, 1989; see also McLoyd, 1990). One study of adolescents in a Midwestern farming community that was experiencing hard times found a connection between economic hardship, parents' behavior, and adolescents' functioning (Lempers et al., 1989). As a result of economic hardship, parents became less nurturant and less consistent toward their children. These changes resulted in feelings of depression and loneliness in many adolescents that were associated, in turn, with delinquency and drug use.

Parenting practices and antisocial behavior Adolescent delinquency has long been associated with deficiencies in parenting (see Patterson, DeBaryshe, & Ramsey, 1989). G. R. Patterson and his colleagues (Patterson, 1986; Paterson et al., 1989) argue that children learn antisocial behavior in the home as a direct result of their parents' child-rearing practices. In families characterized by coercive parenting, children learn to use aggression or other forms of disruptive behavior to get what they want from their parents and siblings. They may be punished for their behavior, but they often get their way, learning that negative behavior has its rewards. Sometimes what they want is a reduction in conflict between their parents; by displaying aggressive or aversive behavior, children may stop the fighting, even if it means that they become the target of conflict themselves. In such families, coercive behaviors are functional, making it possible to survive in a highly aversive environment.

In the process of learning aversive control of family members, many children in dysfunctional families also fail to learn adequate positive social behaviors. They are not only highly aggressive and aversive but also socially unskilled, and as a result, they find themselves rejected by their school peers. These children frequently perform poorly in school as their noncompliant and undercontrolled behavior interferes with learning. In the classroom, antisocial children spend less time on the task at hand, are deficient in academic skills, and are less likely to complete homework assignments (see Patterson et al., 1989). They don't fit comfortably with well-behaved, academically oriented children, so they become friends with other children like themselves, who encourage or model antisocial acts. All the while, of course, children continue to live in the same family where the cycle of aversive behavior began and where, in all likelihood, the inept parenting styles continue—all further reinforcing the antisocial behavior of these adolescents. Figure 13.2 shows this progression of antisocial behavior, begin-

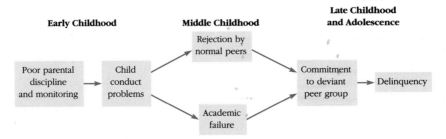

Figure 13.2 A developmental progression for antisocial behavior. *Source:* From "A Developmental Perspective on Antisocial Behavior," by G. R. Patterson, B. D. DeBarsyche, and E. Ramsey, *American Psychologist,* 1989, *44,* 329–335. Copyright 1989 by the American Psychological Association. Reprinted by permission.

ning with poor parental discipline and ending in delinquency.

Child Abuse

At the extreme of poor parenting are those who abuse or neglect their children. Abuse takes many forms, including physical battering, sexual assaults, forced labor, and emotional maltreatment. Neglect includes abandonment and failure to provide adequate clothing, housing, medical treatment, or nutrition. The frequency of abuse and neglect is difficult to document, because much of it occurs in the privacy of the home. What we do know is that the inci-

dence of *reported* child abuse is on the rise (see Figure 13.3) and is now well over 2 million cases annually in the United States.

The Consequences of Child Abuse

Abused children show a wide range of emotional and behavioral responses. Often they are highly aggressive, have difficulty with peer relationships, have poor social cognitions, are depressed, and perform poorly on cognitive tasks (see Emery, 1989). Carol George and Mary Main (1979; Main & George, 1985) compared the social behavior of ten abused toddlers with that of ten other toddlers who came from stressed homes but who had no history of abuse. In one study (George & Main, 1979), abused toddlers

Box 13.2

A Little History

From ancient times, children have been the responsibility of their parents, and society has been reluctant to legislate how parents raise their children. Homes for sick and abandoned children began to appear in Europe in the 1600s and 1700s, and child labor laws were passed in 1836 and 1842 in Massachusetts and Connecticut, respectively, "as the result of the evils of child labor and industrialization" (Nazario, 1988). Yet, in the United States, there were no laws that specifically related to child abuse by parents. One of the first organizations to come to the aid of children was the American Society for the Prevention of Cruelty to Animals, when, in 1874, the plight of a little girl named Mary

Ellen was brought to their attention in New York.

"As recounted by the New York SPCA, a church worker, while visiting an aged woman in a tenement house, learned of little Mary Ellen, who was beaten daily by her stepmother. She was told that the child was chained to her bed, was fed bread and water, and was seriously ill from all the mistreatment.

"The woman's efforts to obtain help for Mary Ellen proved unavailing. Neither the police, the district attorney's office, nor any of the agencies to which she turned for help was able or willing to go to Mary's aid.

"In sheer desperation the woman appealed to Henry Bergh, who had previously established the American

Society for the Prevention of Cruelty to Animals. She pointed out that should an animal be abused as this child was, the ASPCA would intervene to rescue the animal and punish the offender. She appealed for his help on the ground that Mary Ellen was a member of the animal kingdom.

"On this specious argument the SPCA took action and, after an investigation, the parents were hailed into court. So emaciated and abused was the child that she was brought into court on a blanket. The child was removed from the parents' custody, and they were given a term in the penitentiary." (Quoted from Nazario, 1988, pp. xx–xxi.)

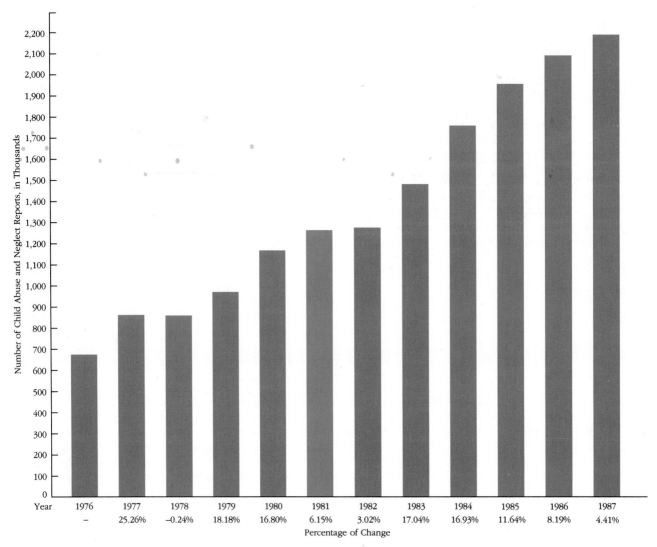

Figure 13.3 Number of child abuse and neglect reports in the United States, 1976–1987. *Source:* American Association for Protecting Children (1989). *Highlights of Official Aggregate Child Neglect and Abuse Reporting,* 1987. Denver: The American Humane Association. Reprinted by permission.

were more aggressive toward peers and caregivers than were nonabused toddlers. They were more withdrawn and less likely to approach caregivers, especially when the caregiver made a friendly gesture toward the child. When abused children did approach a friendly caregiver, they were more likely to do so from the caregiver's side or back, or in some cases, turn around and backstep toward the

caregiver. In a second study (Main & George, 1985), abused toddlers responded to the distress of other children in disturbing ways. Nonabused toddlers reacted to distress in peers with simple interest or with empathy and sadness. Abused children, however, showed no concern for the distress of another child; often they attacked the distressed child or showed inappropriate emotion, such as fear or anger. Three

of the abused toddlers both attacked and attempted to comfort distressed peers. Given this behavior—some of which might be adaptive in an abusive home—it is easy to see how these children would become unpopular, both with their peers and their caregivers. Their aggressiveness, lack of empathy, and inappropriate social responding would serve to isolate them from others and maintain their maladaptive social behavior.

Although most research on the behavior of abused and neglected children has concentrated on preschoolers, the effects of abuse are felt by older children as well. Joan Kaufman and Dante Cicchetti (1989) interviewed school-age children who had been neglected or physically or emotionally abused. They reported that the maltreated children had poorer self-esteem and social skills than did control children, and were also more withdrawn. They found few differences among the three types of maltreated children, with the exception that physically abused children were more aggressive than neglected or emotionally abused youngsters. Kaufman and Cicchetti proposed that the lower self-esteem of maltreated children results in negative expectations when they try to enter peer groups. Their poor self-esteem and expectations of failure thus become self-fulfilling prophecies.

Who Are the Abusers?

Few parents can claim that they have never hit or spanked their child, yet few cross over the line to criminal abuse. Why do some parents abuse their kids while most others do not? Most cases of abuse do not seem to be the result of a specific form of mental disorder in the parent. Rather, the factors that influence effective and ineffective parenting in the normal range also seem to influence parenting at the extreme (Emery, 1989). Thus, the model proposed by Belsky (1984), emphasizing personality factors, situational factors (such as quality of marriage and social support), and characteristics of the child, may also describe the processes involved in most forms of abusive parenting.

It has long been recognized that child abuse runs in families: parents who abuse their children were likely abused by *their* parents. Recent research has confirmed clinical observations, demonstrating quite convincingly that people learn parenting skills, even abusive ones, from their parents (see Emery, 1989). Although abuse is found in all segments of society, it is reported more frequently among the poor, who experience substantial amounts of chronic stress in their lives, which, as we have seen, is related to authoritarian parenting styles.

Many abusive parents seem to show a lack of empathy and an inability to differentiate emotional signals in infants and children. For example, in a study by Ann Frodi and Michael Lamb (1980), abusive and nonabusive women were shown videotapes of infants displaying different behaviors (such as smiling and crying). The women described their emotions while physiological measures of their reactions to the videotapes were recorded (for example, changes in heart rate and blood pressure). Frodi and Lamb found that the abusers responded to the infants' cries with increased physiological arousal and described more aversive feelings than did the nonabusers. They also continued to show physiological arousal to a smiling infant, whereas the nonabusers were more relaxed. In other words, the abusive mothers found any social cue from an infant aversive, and it is aversive cues that are most apt to lead to aggression.

Abusive mothers have also been shown to feel more out of control concerning child rearing than nonabusive mothers. They believe that they can do little to prevent their child's aversive behavior, such as persistent crying, but believe that their child can control such behavior (Bugental, Blue, & Cruzcosa, 1989).

Who Are the Abused?

Some children are at higher risk for child abuse than others. Children living in impoverished and stressful environments are more likely to be victims of abuse, because it is under such conditions that physical punishment is more apt to be used (Egeland et al., 1988). But abusive parents seldom abuse *all* their children; many single out one child for abuse. Thus, child abuse, too, must be viewed from a transactional perspective. As in normal parenting, characteristics of the child interact with those of the parents (and other environmental factors) to produce a particular pattern.

Children who are singled out for abuse have been found to be more sickly than nonabused children, with the illness occurring before the abuse (Sherrod, O'Connor, Vietze, & Altemeier, 1984). Similarly, children born prematurely are more likely to be abused sometime during childhood than full-term children (Martin, Beezley, Conway, & Kempe, 1974). The reason may lie in the characteristics of unhealthy infants. Recall that abusive mothers are more likely than nonabusive mothers to find the cries of infants aversive (Frodi & Lamb, 1980). The cries of most premature or sickly infants truly are more aversive (Zeskind, 1986); abusive parents presumably react even more strongly to them, and these aversive feelings persist even after the sickly cries have disappeared. Sickly children, or children who have an

especially difficult temperament, may be singled out by stressed parents because their behavior is so irritating—making them the whipping boys (or girls) for dysfunctional families.

Ending the Cycle of Abuse

Although child abuse does seem to be passed down from one generation to the next, most people who were abused as children do not become abusive parents, even under stressful conditions. Byron Egeland, Deborah Jacobvitz, and Alan Sroufe (1988) have looked at mothers who were abused as children and compared those who later abused their own children (the continuity group) with those who did not (the exception group). Women in the exception group were more likely to have had some supportive adult they could rely upon during their own childhood and were more likely to have had some type of therapy; they also reported better relationships with their husbands and fewer stressful life events than did women in the continuity group (see Table 13.2). Egeland and his colleagues concluded that although early relationships have a strong impact on later parenting behavior, change is possible. If women abused as children can improve their self-esteem, develop a trusting relationship (possibly through therapy), and receive social support, the cycle of abuse can be stopped.

Table 13.2 Some characteristics of relationships experienced by "Continuity-of-Abuse" and "Exception" groups of women

	Groups	
	Continuity (n = 18)	Exception (n = 12)
Supportive adult during childhood	3 (17%)	8 (67%)
Extensive therapy	0 (0%)	4 (33%)
Relationship with mate:		
Intactness	0 (0%)	6 (50%)
Stability	0 (0%)	6 (50%)
Satisfaction	9 (50%)	10 (83%)
Physical abuse	11 (61%)	2 (17%)

Source: From "Breaking the Cycle of Abuse," by B. Egeland, D. Jacobvitz, and L. A. Sroufe, *Child Development,* 1988, *59,* 1080–1088. Copyright © The Society for Research in Child Development, Inc. Reprinted by permission.

Coping with Family Transitions

Families differ from culture to culture, but the ideal American family, at least in this century, is the nuclear family: husband, wife, and minor children. Life in the 1990s, however, is not as simple as it used to be. Over the past 30 years, the incidence of divorce has increased dramatically, and it is estimated that one in every three children today will experience divorce over the course of childhood (Nazario, 1988). About 90% of the children of divorce live with their mothers in single-parent homes. About 75% of divorced mothers remarry, meaning that many of these children will eventually become part of a stepfamily. The incidence of divorce is higher, however, for once-divorced people, making it possible that these children will go through yet another transition sometime before they reach adulthood. What are the effects of these transitions on children? And what are the factors that lead to their positive or negative adjustment?

Children's Adjustment to Divorce and Remarriage

Children of divorce, on average, display more behavior problems, more psychological distress, and lower academic achievement than do children from nondivorced families (Allison & Furstenberg, 1989; Guidubaldi & Perry, 1985; Hetherington, Cox, & Cox, 1985; Wallerstein, Corbin, & Lewis, 1988). When divorce occurs, children usually show poor initial adjustment, in part because of the high degree of conflict between the parents both before and after the divorce, and also because divorce often results in a significant reduction in economic level and substantial economic stress for mothers and children (Wallerstein & Kelly, 1980).

Children's initial reactions to divorce may include anger, resentment, anxiety, depression, regression, sleep disturbances, and even guilt (Hetherington, Stanley-Hagan, & Anderson, 1989; Wallerstein et al., 1988). They may grieve for the absent parent and defy the remaining parent's rules and requests. Within the two-year period following divorce, most parents and children show signs of good adjustment, particularly when compared to the period immediately following the divorce (Hetherington et al., 1982; Wallerstein et al., 1988). Not all children adjust well, however, with boys typically

showing the most problems (Guidubaldi & Perry, 1985; Hetherington et al., 1982). In a longitudinal study by E. Mavis Hetherington, Martha Cox, and Roger Cox (1982, 1985), boys from divorced homes showed more antisocial, acting-out, coercive, and noncompliant behaviors at home and at school than did boys from nondivorced homes two and six years following divorce. These boys also had difficulty with peer relations and school achievement. Girls from divorced homes, in contrast, were functioning relatively well. Carol MacKinnon (1989), looking at the quality of interaction between siblings from intact versus divorced homes as a function of age and sex, found that older boys from divorced homes were particularly negative, noncompliant, and abusive, indicating once again the greater vulnerability of boys to the breakup of their parents' marriage.

There is some suggestion that the poorer adjustment of boys to divorce may be a reaction not to divorce per se, but to marital conflict in general. Jeanne Block, Jack Block, and Per Gjerde (1986) evaluated the personalities of a large number of chil-

Children's problems in adjusting to their parents' divorce may reflect events that happened before the divorce.

dren, some of whose parents subsequently divorced. They reported that many of the behavior and personality problems others have found in boys from divorced homes (for example, aggression and poor impulse control) were found in boys years *before* their parents divorced, presumably as a consequence of marital and family conflict.

Although boys show poorer adjustment to divorce than girls, the reverse is true for remarriage. Because most children of divorce live with their mothers, it is the mother's remarriage that is usually investigated rather than the father's. In the study by Hetherington and her colleagues (1985), girls showed increased behavior problems after their mother's remarriage, whereas boys' behavior problems decreased. Many girls in single-parent homes have considerable freedom and responsibility and develop a close, adultlike relationship with their mothers; thus, they see remarriage as a threat to both their independence and their relationship with their mothers. These feelings, it seems, are only slightly influenced by the stepfather himself; Hetherington (1989) reports that a daughter's rejection of her stepfather was not related to how hard he tried to get along. Boys, in contrast, may have less to lose with a new stepfather and much to gain, in that he may get the boy's mother "off his back."

What Factors Lead to Good or Poor Adjustment in Divorced and Remarried Families?

What are some of the factors that influence how well a child will react to family changes brought about by divorce? One factor is age. In the longitudinal study by Judith Wallerstein and her colleagues (Wallerstein et al., 1988; Wallerstein & Kelly, 1980), children of preschool age showed the greatest stress immediately following divorce. In a ten-year follow-up, however, these same children were the best adjusted, or "least burdened," relative to children who were older at the time of the divorce (Wallerstein et al., 1988; see also Hetherington, 1989).

As in intact homes, the amount of stress, presence or absence of social support, and personality characteristics of both parents and children interact to produce adaptive or maladaptive behavior patterns (Hetherington, 1989). For example, in the studies by Hetherington and her colleagues, children with "difficult" temperaments showed increased behavior

problems with increases in stress. The relationship was not as straightforward for children with easy temperaments, however. For these children, an intermediate amount of stress led to the best adjustment; having some practice solving moderately stressful problems in a supportive environment gave them more patience, more persistence, and more flexibility on problem-solving tasks and in social relations (Hetherington, 1989). This finding is consistent with the theorizing of Michael Rutter (1987), who proposed that "inoculation against stress may be best provided by controlled exposure to stress in circumstances favorable to successful coping or adaptation" (p. 326). Rutter's idea of "inoculation against stress" holds true for children in all types of families—married or divorced. Hetherington's data indicate, however, that the value of these early experiences in dealing with stress depends on a child's temperament.

Perhaps the single most important factor in determining a child's long-term response to divorce and remarriage is quality of parenting. As with intact families, children adjust best when their parents practice authoritative rather than authoritarian or permissive parenting. The longitudinal study by Hetherington and her colleagues found that authoritative parenting, characterized by warmth and firm but responsive control, was associated with positive social adjustment and low rates of behavior problems. The one exception to this pattern, Hetherington (1989) reported, was for stepfathers in the first two years following remarriage: apparently, *any* attempt by the stepfather to take control of family discipline was met with hostility by the children, especially when remarriage occurred when the children were in early adolescence (between 9 and 15 years). After two years, however, authoritative parenting by the stepfather was associated with fewer behavior problems and greater acceptance by their stepsons but not their stepdaughters. The best strategy for stepfathers in gaining the acceptance of their stepchildren appears to be to establish a positive relationship with the child before taking an active role in discipline and decision making. According to Hetherington and her colleagues (1985), "the most successful stepfathers appear to be those who offer emotional support to the mother and support her in her disciplinary role, rather than those who try to take over the role of disciplinarian or who remain uninvolved" (p. 529).

What, then, can we say about the effects of divorce on children? These transitions are stressful and result in behavior and psychological problems for children. Most children adjust within two years, but many carry the scars of a disrupted family life for years. Judith Wallerstein and her colleagues (1988) question whether the long-term effects of marital disruption are due to the divorce per se; rather, they see lasting damage as the result of ineffective parenting, economic hardship, continued conflict between the parents, and "the flawed and tragic role models provided by parents who fail over many years to reconstitute or stabilize their lives" (p. 212). E. Mavis Hetherington (1989) sees a complex combination of factors involved in children's adjustment to family transitions: "depending on the characteristics of the child, particularly the age and gender of the child, the available resources, subsequent life experiences, and especially interpersonal relationships, children in the long run may be survivors, losers, or winners of their parents' divorce or remarriage" (p. 13).

State of the Art
Making Quality Day Care Available for American Children?

In 1986, for the first time in history, a majority of American families required child-care services to support parental employment. A decline in real income between 1973 and 1988 has meant that both parents now have to work in order for many families to live the way they did previously with only one wage earner. The situation is even more critical for the growing number of single parents, including mothers of infants—more than half of whom are now employed outside the home (Clarke-Stewart, 1989). Nor is this likely to be a temporary situation. The declining population of working-age people in the United States is predicted to result in more working parents, not fewer.

Day care has become a fact of life for most American families and a focus of research for developmental psychology. The issue today is more complex than day care versus mother care. What are the effects of day care on attachment, on social adjustments, on intellectual competence? What is quality

Economists predict that an increasing number of families will use day care.

day care, and how do we make it available for all children? If there are risks to young children from day care, how do we improve day care to minimize them? And what types of day-care arrangements leave policies are best for new parents and their infants?

The Effects of Day Care on Children

After reviewing the wealth of research on the topic of day care versus mother care, Sandra Scarr, Deborah Phillips, and Kathleen McCartney (1990) conclude that "there is near consensus among developmental psychologists and early childhood experts that child care per se does not constitute a risk factor in children's lives; rather, poor quality care and poor family environments can conspire to produce poor developmental outcomes" (p. 30). Yet "near consensus" is not total, and some researchers, looking at the same data, see evidence of negative, long-term emotional effects on children as a result of prolonged day-care experience (Barglow, Vaughn, & Molitor, 1987; Belsky, 1986). Concerns about the effects of day care have centered primarily on three areas: infants' attachment to their mothers, children's later social adjustment, and intellectual competence (Clarke-Stewart, 1989; Scarr et al., 1990).

Day care and attachment   Early research had demonstrated that children reared in orphanages showed deficient social, emotional, and intellectual skills; based on that work, concerns were raised that repeated daily separations between mothers and infants would weaken the infant-mother bond and lead to poor emotional adjustment (see Scarr et al., 1990). Initial research seemed to put this concern to rest, however. Infants attending day care did form bonds with their caregivers, but these bonds did not replace or interfere with infant-mother attachment; infants still preferred their mothers to their substitute caregivers (see Belsky & Steinberg, 1978; Clarke-Stewart & Fein, 1983; Etaugh, 1980).

More recently, the focus has shifted to differences in the *quality* of infant-mother attachment as a function of whether mothers work or not. K. Allison Clarke-Stewart (1989) examined the 17 published studies that evaluated the quality of attachment between children and their mothers using the Ainsworth Strange Situation. She reported that infants whose mothers worked full-time were more likely to be classified as insecurely attached (36%) than infants whose mothers did not work or who worked only part-time (29%). With a sample of 1247 mother/infant pairs, this 7% difference was significantly greater than expected by chance. Nonetheless, the difference is small, and Clarke-Stewart (1989) suggests it may be due to the fact that infants attending day care may not feel as anxious about separating from their mothers in the Strange Situation as stay-at-home infants. In fact, when mothers, teachers, or observers rate quality of attachment in daily settings, no differences have been found between infants of working and nonworking mothers (Belsky, 1988). Even if the attachment differences between the infants of working and nonworking mothers are real, they are not substantial and, according to Sandra Scarr and her colleagues (1990), do not constitute evidence of greater risk.

Day care and social adjustment   Some studies report no differences in social competence between day-care and home-care children; some report greater social competence for children who attend day care; others report higher social competence for home-care children (see Scarr et al., 1990). This mixture of results should not be surprising, considering the complexity of the issues involved. One common finding, however, is that children with day-care experience tend to be more aggressive with peers and less compliant with parents than do non-day-care children (Haskins, 1985; Schwarz, Krolick, & Strickland, 1973). Clarke-Stewart (1989) suggests that this pattern does not reflect social maladjustment, but rather the fact that children who have been in day care are more likely to think for themselves and less willing to comply with adults' arbitrary rules. "Children who have spent time in day care, then, may be more demanding and independent, more disobedient and aggressive, more bossy and bratty than children who stay at home because they want their own way and do not have the skills to achieve it smoothly, rather than because they are maladjusted" (p. 269). On the positive side, children who spend their infancy in day care tend to be equally or more socially competent than children without day-care experience (see Clarke-Stewart, 1989).

Day care and intellectual competence   Although many studies find no differences in intelligence between day-care and home-care children (see Scarr et al., 1990), when differences are found, they typically favor children who attend day care (Clarke-Stewart & Fein, 1983). Intellectual advantages are frequently found for children attending preschool enrichment programs, designed to provide intellectual stimulation for children from disadvantaged homes (Burchinal, Lee, & Ramey, 1989; see also Chapter 10), although advantages are also found for middle-class samples. The intellectual head start, however, is typically short-lived. When home-care children enter school, they quickly catch up to the children with day-care experience, making any advantage from day care a transitory one (Clarke-Stewart & Fein, 1983).

What Is Quality Day Care?

In general, it seems, the effects of day care on children do not last long (such as the differences in intellectual functioning), are small in magnitude (such as differences in quality of attachment), or are compensated by other factors (such as greater aggressiveness and disobedience associated with greater social maturity and independence). But all these are only *average* effects. Just as there are differences between families in the quality of parent-child interactions, so too are there differences in the quality of day-care services. In addition, differences in the behaviors and attitudes of parents and the temperaments of children can affect the type of experience children have in day care.

Scarr and her associates (1990) listed three features of day care that are associated with the quality of a child's experience: caregiver/child ratio, group size, and caregiver training and experience. A ratio of one caregiver for four or fewer children ensures greater physical safety and more individual attention (talking and playing). Similarly, the fewer children there are in a day-care group, the more social and intellectual stimulation children receive. Children in large groups have been found to be more apathetic and distressed (Bruner, 1980; Howes & Rubinstein, 1985). And not surprisingly, the number of years of child-related education and work experience a day-care worker has is related to "increased responsivity, positive affect, and ability to provide socially- and intellectually-stimulating experiences" (Scarr et al., 1990, p. 31). In one recent study, 4-year-olds who attended high-quality day care had more friendly interactions with peers and fewer unfriendly ones, were rated as more socially competent and happier, and were less likely to be regarded as shy by their peers, relative to 4-year-olds who attended low-

Day-care quality depends on adult-to-child ratio, the size of groups, and the extent of workers' experience and education.

quality day care (Vandell, Henderson, & Wilson, 1988).

Another important factor in a child's day-care experience is the stability of day-care arrangements (Cummings, 1980; Howes, 1988; Howes & Olenick, 1986). Children's social and language development is hindered when they change day-care settings frequently or when they experience a "revolving door" of caregivers. Yet the turnover rate for child-care workers is alarmingly high—in part, at least, because of low pay, lack of benefits, and stressful work conditions (see Scarr et al., 1990).

Parents who choose (or who can afford) high-quality day care for their children differ in many ways from parents who place their children in lower-quality day care. Carrollee Howes and her col-

Box 13.3

Day Care in Other Countries

Australia   Balancing jobs and child care is a problem for 49% of Australia's work force. There is no national policy, however, and day-care programs have not kept up with demand.

Canada   Government recently funded the National Day Care Survey to determine what was available and what was needed. Canadian researchers are continuing a long tradition of studying the effects of day care on children and presenting their findings to government policy makers.

Denmark   Public day-care facilities provide for 44% of children under 3 and 69% of those between 3 and 5. Costs are as low as $115 per month. Waiting lists are long, so the government also pays women to care for children in their homes.

Finland   More than 80% of women are in the labor force, and 35% to 50% of children under 7 are in day care. Day-care costs are based on family income, and quality of day care is high. Kindergarten programs are based on child-development research. Local authorities monitor day-care centers, kindergartens, and homes of babysitters.

France   Almost 1500 creches, most of them government-run, care for more than 79,000 children. They are open 11 hours a day and cost between $3 and $17 per day. Because there is such a waiting list, the government gives parents up to $340 a month to hire child-care help at home. There are also centers that care for children for a few hours at a time and mothers who care for other people's children in their homes.

Germany (West)   One-third (33%) of mothers with preschool children work outside the home. In large cities, the percentages are 40% to 50%. The percentage of single parents doubled between 1977 and 1987. However, publicly supported day care is available for only 1.5% of all preschoolers. The government supports the idea of day care, but has not provided funds. There is substantial debate over the effect of day care on children. All this has resulted in parents' organizing their own cooperatives with little public funding.

India   There is no national day-care policy. Approximately 20% of affluent women work, entrusting their children to maids and mothers-in-law; 40% of middle-class women work, leaving their children with family members (unmarried sisters-in-law or mothers-in-law); 70% of less wealthy women work, either taking their children with them or leaving them unattended.

Israel   A total of 900 government day-care centers charge between $27 and $90 a month, depending on family income. Of 240,000 Jewish preschoolers, 24% are in day care. Few Arab families use day care.

Italy   Approximately 35% of mothers with preschool children are in the labor force. Often moth-

leagues (Howes, 1990; Howes & Stewart, 1987; Howes & Olenick, 1986) have described the lives of parents who place their children in lower-quality day care as "more complex"; these parents experienced more stress, made more changes in child-care arrangements, were less involved with their children at home, and used less effective parenting practices than did parents choosing higher-quality day care. But even when these family characteristics were controlled, children attending high-quality day care showed more sophisticated social behavior than did children attending lower-quality day care (Howes & Stewart, 1987), indicating that the quality of day care does have a significant influence on children's development over and above home environment.

---

ers work part-time to avoid putting their children in day care, but there are many exceptions among disadvantaged families. Day care is not as much of a problem because of the traditional family network of social support for young parents and the general political interest in child-rearing issues.

Japan The number of working married women has quadrupled in the past 20 years. However, traditional ideas still prevail, and working mothers are also responsible for all duties inside the home. There are 23,000 licensed day-care centers and many unlicensed ones. Many do not accept newborns, and the better ones have long waiting lists. There is no government policy on child care.

Nigeria All women work in Nigeria, whether in paid jobs or on farms. Rural women work with babies strapped to their backs. In the past, rural Nigerian working women lived in compounds and pooled child-care responsibilities; however, urbanization and the need for paid employment have reduced the effectiveness of extended families. The government of Nigeria does not accept any responsibility for child care; as a result, urban day-care centers vary in quality and cost. UNICEF operates several experimental day-care centers, which also provide medical and nutritional help.

Poland Day care has a long tradition in Poland, beginning after World War II. Creches are available for children from 3 months to 3 years, and nurseries and kindergartens for children 3 to 7. These facilities are supervised by the central government. In the 1950s, it was found that children in day-care institutions were developing differently than children at home, exhibiting lower levels of speech development and sensorimotor activity. Improvements were made in the 1960s, and now no such effects are found; in fact, some day-care children show better development than their peers raised in average and below-average home environments.

Turkey Women now constitute 36% of the working population, although 85% of them work in agriculture settings. Only 1% of Turkish preschoolers are in day-care or nursery programs. Most young children of working women are cared for by their grandmothers, and others by inexpensive household helpers (usually women) who serve as babysitters. No national policy exists, but the government is working with scholars and UNICEF to develop a national child-care policy in the 1990s.

United Kingdom As in the United States, children are seen as a private responsibility. Nevertheless, more than 29% of mothers with preschool children are in the work force, and this percentage is expected to increase. Child care facilities vary greatly in quality, which means that the effects on children also vary greatly.

Source: Adapted from *International Society for the Study of Behavioral Development Newsletter,* 1989, *2,* pp. 4–8.

High-quality day care can be difficult to find and afford. *Source:* DOONESBURY Copyright 1987 by G. B. Trudeau. Reprinted with permission. All rights reserved.

The impact of day care may also depend on parental attitudes. For example, mothers who want to work but feel obligated to stay home with their children have more child-rearing difficulties, stress, and depression than do other women (Hock & DeMeis, 1990; Stafford, 1984; Yarrow, Scott, deLeeuw, & Heinig, 1962). Maternal attitudes, child characteristics, and maternal employment interact, so that women who want to work and place their children in day care develop a different relationship with their children than do other women (McBridge & Belsky, 1988).

Although, as we've seen, there are many factors that influence the type of experience a child has in day care, generally speaking, quality day care represents no risk to children. One problem, of course, is that quality day care is expensive. The United States has no national policy on child care and has made no commitment to providing quality child care for all families that need it. It is too late to tell mothers to stay at home with their children. As K. Allison Clarke-Stewart (1989) writes, "Maternal employment is a reality. The issue today, therefore, is not whether infants should be in day care but how to make their experiences there and at home supportive of their development and of their parents' peace of mind" (pp. 271–272).

Summary

Parenting style refers to general and relatively stable ways in which parents interact with their children. Three major parenting styles have been proposed: authoritarian, permissive, and authoritative. Authoritarian parents expect absolute obedience, often use physical punishment, and express hostility toward their children. Permissive parents exert little control and are usually (but not always) warm toward their children. Authoritative parents set clear standards and enforce rules with warmth and explanations. Children of authoritative parents are more independent, curious, responsible, and socially competent than children of authoritarian or permissive parents. Multiple factors influence parenting style, including developmental history of the parents, marital satisfaction, social support, and the temperament and developmental level of the child. Poverty and other life stressors are associated with an authoritarian parenting style, and this has been linked to delinquency in adolescence.

The reported incidence of child abuse has risen dramatically in the United States over the past several decades. Abused children tend to be highly aggressive, have difficulty with peer relations, have poor social cognitions, be depressed, and perform poorly on cognitive tasks. Factors that influence parenting in the normal range also seem to influence parenting in cases of child abuse. Women who were abused as children are more likely to stop the intergenerational cycle of abuse if they have had some supportive adult they could rely upon during childhood or if they have sought therapy.

Almost all children show some negative reactions immediately after their parents divorce, including anger, resentment, depression, and even guilt. Most children show good adjustment within two years following the divorce, but many do not. Boys are especially affected by divorce, but girls are more adversely affected by their mother's remarriage.

There is some evidence that boys' negative reactions to divorce is not to the parental separation per se, but rather to more general parental conflict. Many of the same factors that influence a child's psychological adjustment in intact families also affect how well children adjust to divorce and remarriage.

Day care is widely used in the United States today. The effects of day care on quality of attachment, social adjustment, and intellectual competence are small and short-lived. Quality of day care is associated with caregiver/child ratio, group size, and caregiver training and experience. A child's day-care experience is also influenced by the stability of day-care arrangements, parental involvement with children in the home, and parents' attitudes toward day care and maternal employment.

Key Terms and Concepts

parenting style
    authoritarian parenting style
    permissive parenting style
    authoritative parenting style
child abuse

Interacting with Others

14

"Today everybody's going to Mary Ann's party in the group. I'm sort of the one that gets left behind. I'm not invited to the party so I won't do anything on the weekend. Anywhere the whole group goes, I don't. . . . I'm just the person that gets left back. Maybe they don't realize that I get left, that I'm here, but it happens all the time" (sixth-grade girl, from Hayden, Tarulli, & Hymel, 1988, quoted in Asher, Parkhurst, Hymel, and Williams, 1990).

During their first years, children's lives are centered around their families. But as children grow, other children come to play an increasingly important role in their lives. In fact, Steven Asher (1990) has suggested that friends may play a more important role in the lives of children today than they did in earlier times. In the United States, with more mothers working and the prevalence of single-parent homes, children enter organized peer groups earlier in preschools and day-care centers, and many school-age children spend their after-school hours in similar organized groups.

But, as the quote that opens this chapter reflects, the joys of carefree play and close friendships are not shared by all children. Some get left out, and sadness and loneliness result. The lessons children learn in play with their friends serve as the basis for adult relationships. Children who are neglected or rejected by their peers are also learning important lessons that may follow them into adulthood. In addition, not all peer interaction is pleasant. Conflict seems to be a necessary product of peer interaction, and aggression is a common childhood response to conflict.

In this chapter, we examine some important aspects of children's interactions with other children. We look first at peer relations, children's friendships, and factors that contribute to a child's popularity and social standing, then at peer groups, prosocial behavior, and aggression. We end the chapter with some new findings about schoolyard bullies and their victims.

The Development of Peer Relations

When do peer relations begin? Do babies truly interact with one another? Do toddlers have friends? The answers depend, to a certain extent, on what we mean by "relations," "interact," and "friends."

Peer Relations Early in Life

Infants under 1 year of age rarely have the opportunity to interact with one another. Until their locomotive skills develop enough so they can move to or from another child, their peer relations are limited to situations in which an adult places one infant close to another. Such opportunities do arise in day-care centers and research laboratories (Eckerman, Whatley, & Kutz, 1975); when they do, some form of interaction tends to occur. For example, 3- and 4-month-old infants will reach out and touch one another, and 6-month-olds will smile and vocalize to each other (Dufree & Lee, 1973). As babies get older and can crawl, they will mutually explore each other's eyes, ears, and mouths. They will gaze at another baby much as they gaze at adults, often smiling or vocalizing as they do. But infant-infant interaction is infrequent, even when the opportunities are there (Becker, 1977; Eckerman et al., 1975). In a day-care setting, for example, infants are seven times more likely to interact with an adult than with another infant (Finkelstein, Dent, Gallagher, & Ramey, 1978).

The term *relation* usually implies some long-term social commitment, with some implicit, general rules about how one behaves toward another. According to Robert Hinde (1979), a relationship involves a series of interactions such that "the behavior of each takes some account of the behavior of the other" and "each interaction is affected by interactions in the past and may affect interactions in the future" (p. 14). In this sense, there are no peer relations among infants. We thus concur with Willard Hartup (1983) that "peer relations exist in babyhood in only the loosest sense" (p. 114).

Peer Relations in Toddlerhood

Life changes dramatically for children once they learn to walk. They can now get to places and into things they could not even dream of before. Toddlers still spend the vast majority of their time with adults rather than other children, and this seems to be true in most if not all cultures (see Hartup, 1983).

As more toddlers are placed in day care, the opportunity for peer interaction increases. The fact that

Family

Large extended families provide information and emotional support to young parents.

Children who were securely attached as infants have an advantage in social and intellectual development through the school years.

Infants learn a sense of trust from interacting with their parents that is the basis of social relationships throughout their lives.

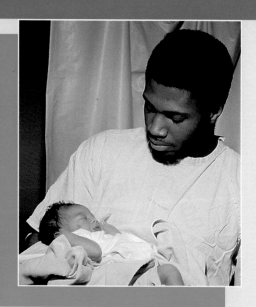

The attachment between children and their parents doesn't end with infancy, but grows and changes as they do.

How parents raise their children often reflects how they were raised by their own parents.

Couples who are happy in their marriage are usually successful in their parenting roles.

The extended family is very important to Japanese culture.

Children can form relationships with grandparents, babysitters, and daycare workers without diminishing their attachment to their parents.

The flexibility of human attachment lets adoptive parents establish strong bonds with their children even if their first contact was months after birth.

Toddlers enjoy each other, but these relationships are not what they will later experience as friendships.

of their time together is spent with toys or other objects (Eckerman et al., 1975). But social interaction involves taking turns and adjusting one's behavior to that of another person. Do toddlers show evidence of these more sophisticated social behaviors that serve as the basis for friendship?

To some extent, they do. For example, in research by Hildy Ross and Susan Lollis (1989), 20- and 30-month-olds were paired with other children the same age and observed in a series of interactions in their homes. The children did not know each other initially, but became acquainted over a four-month period. Ross and Lollis reported that relationships emerged over time. As the two children came to know each other, they changed their behavior to match that of their peer, a process known as **reciprocity.** According to Ross and Lollis (1989), "the willingness of two children to continue any positive interaction . . . was part of a mutual pattern that existed within a special relationship and that remained consistent over time" (p. 1089). In other words, the toddlers were reacting to another child in a special way, and not treating all children the same.

When given the opportunity, as in play groups or day care, toddlers do interact with other toddlers, behave reciprocally with some special children, share good times more with some children than others, and stay in closer proximity to some children than to others (Howes, 1988; Ross & Lollis, 1989). Other children can be a nice addition to a toddler's life, but toddlers rarely seek them out. They do possess some rudimentary social skills that aid peer relations, but these fall short of what most of us think of as friendships.

children are in a group, however, does not mean that they will interact. In fact, when toddlers are observed together, they spend the majority of their time in solitary activities (Bronson, 1981; Mueller & Brenner, 1977). The amount of social contact among toddlers is greater for children who are well acquainted with one another, but even in these situations, children this age spend about half their time playing alone (Rubenstein & Howes, 1976).

When toddlers do interact, what do they do? For older toddlers (between 18 and 24 months), some

Peer Relations during the Preschool Years

During the preschool years, loosely defined as ages 2 to 5, the amount of social contact between children increases considerably (Parten, 1932). For example, in a longitudinal study that observed children at four-month intervals from 16 to 32 months, researchers counted the total number of acts a child performed that were imitated or coordinated with those of a peer (Eckerman, Davis, & Didow, 1989). They found that as children grew older, the number of coordinated acts and imitations increased (see

Figure 14.1). This increase was gradual between 16 and 24 months, then increased sharply at 28 months. Sharing and expressions of sympathy also increase over the preschool years (Hartup & Coates, 1967; Strayer, Wareing, & Rushton, 1979), although even many 5-year-olds find the concept of sharing a difficult one to grasp.

Social conflicts also increase over the preschool years. It is interesting to note that preschoolers who are friends fight with one another just as much as preschoolers who are only acquaintances. The conflicts, however, tend to be less intense between friends and are more likely to result in equal or almost equal outcomes for both children involved than conflicts between nonfriends (Hartup, Laursen, Stewart, & Eastenson, 1988).

Preschoolers also engage in substantial amounts of rough-and-tumble play, a term that refers to good-natured tussling and chasing. Rough-and-tumble play is more frequent among boys (especially the contact type, such as wrestling), although girls also engage in it, especially the noncontact type (for example, chasing) (Humphreys & Smith, 1984).

Many children during the preschool period still spend much time playing alone or engaged in what has been termed **parallel play.** Parallel play consists of two or more children playing near one another, possibly involved in similar activities (for example, building castles in a sandbox), but not engaged in mutual or cooperative play (Rubin, Watson, & Jambor, 1978). In an earlier chapter, we discussed

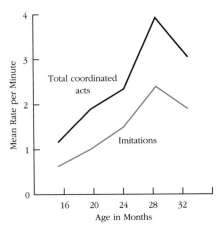

Figure 14.1 Toddlers' coordination of actions with peers and imitation of other children: age-related changes from 16 to 32 months. *Source:* Adapted from "Toddlers' Emerging Ways of Achieving Social Coordinations with a Peer," by C. O. Eckerman, C. C. Davis, and S. M. Didow, *Child Development,* 1989, *60,* 440–453. Copyright © The Society for Research in Child Development, Inc. Reprinted by permission.

Piaget's (1955) observations of children's language during parallel play. Two boys, for example, may be playing with trucks, each talking about his truck and what he is doing. Although, at first glance, it appears as if these children are playing with each other, a closer look reveals that neither child's "conversation" includes the other child. Piaget referred to such "conversations" as collective monologues. The children would not be so vocal if they were not playing side by side; thus, the social situation influences their behavior. But interaction is minimal, and the situation can best be described as "semi-social."

Semi-social parallel play may lead children into more cooperative social play. For example, Roger Bakeman and John Brownlee (1980) found that preschoolers often move from parallel play to cooperative play during the course of a play session. They suggested that parallel play may serve an unconscious strategy or technique that gives children access to more socially oriented activities.

Peer Relations in School-Age Children

Perhaps the biggest contribution to improving peer relations from the preschool to the school years is a

Between the ages of two and five, children develop such social behavior as sharing, imitation, sympathy, and coordination of activities.

child's cognitive development. Between the ages of about 5 and 7 years, children become increasingly able to take the perspective of another (see Chapter 15). They are better able to remember the rules of games, to understand the need for taking turns, and to communicate their ideas through language.

Even during the preschool years, children tend to segregate themselves into same-sex groups, but this tendency increases during the school years (Maccoby & Jacklin, 1987). Preference for same-sex friends and play groups is not something unique to Western culture, but is found universally (Edwards & Whiting, 1988). Parents and teachers seem to foster same-sex interaction early (Lewis, Young, Brooks, & Michalson, 1975), but boys and girls also differ in how they play: boys engage in more rough-and-tumble play and center their interactions on movable toys, whereas girls are more apt to engage in dramatic play and table activities. In fact, there is

some suggestion that girls actively avoid contact with boys because of their roughness (Haskett, 1971). Also, from the preschool years through adolescence, girls are more apt to play in smaller groups than boys (Lever, 1976). Such observations led Eleanor Maccoby (1988) to suggest that biologically based differences in play style may contribute to sex-segregated play groups.

Rough-and-tumble play is less frequent during the school years than during the preschool years, but it is not absent. Anne Humphreys and Peter Smith (1987) observed 7-, 9-, and 11-year-olds on their school playground and found that rough-and-tumble play occupied about 10% of their time. It was more frequent in boys than in girls and occurred in a friendly, nonaggressive manner. At times, however, rough-and-tumble play can lead to real fighting, especially when an unpopular or rejected child engages in it (Pellegrini, 1988). In Anthony Pellegrini's

The tendency of children to play in same-sex groups becomes stronger during the school years.

research, rough-and-tumble play typically led to games for popular children, but led to fights for unpopular ones.

Not all conflict results in fighting, of course, but it is safe to say that all friendships involve conflict. In fact, Piaget (1965b) proposed that it is through play and interaction with peers that techniques for resolving conflict develop. Investigating this issue, Janice Nelson and Frances Aboud (1985) assessed changes in children's social knowledge as a result of discussing interpersonal issues with a friend or a nonfriend acquaintance. Third- and fourth-grade children were first given a pretest of social knowledge. The questions raised social/moral dilemmas, such as:

> "What are you supposed to do if you find someone's wallet in a store?"
> "What is the thing to do if a boy (girl) much smaller than you starts to fight with you?"

Box 14.1

Gender and Friendship

We asked some elementary school children who their friends were, boys or girls, and why they liked playing mostly with one sex as opposed to the other. Here are some of their responses:

What Girls Had to Say

Lynsey (age 7) Girls like to talk about things girls like, and boys like to talk about things boys like. Some girls are interested in what boys like, and some boys like to talk about things girls like. Girls can share different ideas than boys, and boys will share different ideas than girls.

Nicole (age 8) Girls—they are most like you.

Maggie (age 8) Mostly girls. Boys are so rowdy. And when you have braces, they call you "tinsel teeth" and "metal mouth." And they yell and things like that.

Julie (age 9) I like girls best. Girls compliment you on things—and they're, like, really nice.

Francine (age 9) Girls. You can tell your feelings to them. You can tell them secrets and they won't tell.

Tracy (age 9) It's hard to say because I have a lot of friends, girls and boys. I like to play sports, so I play with the boys outside. And in the classroom I sit with the girls.

Rhodine (age 10) Girls are nice. They're not as rough as boys. They share things. They help you. Boys are rough. I didn't like to play with boys when I was little, but I think I'll like them better when I'm older. Maybe they'll be nicer.

What Boys Had to Say

Scott (age 6) I like to play with boys best. Boys normally want to play Nintendo. We'll ride bikes, jump ramps, and ride through piles of dirt. And we do karate fights together. All girls do is sit around and do nothing. They boss you around, especially when it comes to sisters.

Mitch (age 8) Mostly boys. I don't know why. I've just known them for a long time.

Troy (age 8) I usually just hang out with boys more than girls. Because they like to do the same stuff as I do.

Adam (age 9) Mostly boys, because they're more fun to play with. They're more active.

Stephen (age 9) Girls just sit and play cards. Boys would go outside and do something, like wrestling. Girls wouldn't do that. When I was a little kid, I'd play with anyone—boys or girls—because I just wanted to play. I guess I was bored.

Kurt (age 9) Boys most of the time, except when they get a little overreacted and try to beat you up. Girls are a little nicer than some boys, but they don't do the same stuff as boys. They're always playing house or something like that with their Barbie dolls.

Harris (age 10) Boys—they're more active. They're not afraid to climb stuff and go into the woods and forests and do dangerous things. Sometimes boys are mean. Girls are always nice. But girls will scratch you if they get mad at you. I used to think they would bite.

Rough-and-tumble play is common among boys, and may be one reason girls prefer to play with other girls.

Children were then paired with either a friend or a nonfriend acquaintance from their school class and asked to discuss one of the questions from the pretest. Following this, each child was asked individually for a solution to the problem he or she had been discussing.

Friends were more critical of each other during their discussions than were nonfriends, but they were also more likely to provide detailed reasons for their own point of view. Pairs of friends changed the most in terms of social knowledge as a result of their discussions. When friends disagreed, their ultimate solutions to the dilemmas were more mature than when nonfriends disagreed. In other words, healthy social conflict between friends resulted in greater growth in social knowledge than did conflict between nonfriends.

Friends, of course, become increasingly important to children during the school years. Willard Hartup (1983) has likened the attachment among friends to that between mothers and their children. "Friendships maintain proximity or contact with the other person; separation is disturbing. Friends provide a sense of security in strange situations that acquaintances do not . . . ; children enjoy their friends, trust them, and receive pleasure from them" (p. 137).

What constitutes a friend and what children expect of friendship change over the school years. Brian Bigelow (1977) evaluated the essays of Scot-tish and Canadian children, ages 6 to 14 years, on what they expected in their best friends that was different from what they expected from other acquaintances. Bigelow found that friendship expectations evolved in three stages. In the first stage, characterizing the youngest children, friends were those who participated in shared activities and who lived nearby. In stage 2, friendship was viewed as following agreed-upon rules, such as loyalty and commitment. The third stage involved empathy, understanding, and self-disclosure: friends share unconditional positive regard and intimate communication. During this stage, Bigelow found, the personality characteristics of another person are important in determining who is likely to be a friend.

Popularity and Social Status

Social status is something most of us associate with adulthood. People differ in the perceived importance of their jobs, the neighborhoods in which they live, the amount of money they make, and the status symbols they possess. But adults do not hold a monopoly on social status. Within any group of children, there are some who are more popular or have greater social impact than others.

Popularity and social impact Popularity means likability—the extent to which a child is sought out by others. Status refers to social standing—the extent to which a child is considered a valued member of a group (Hartup, 1983). Although it may seem obvious that popular children will also be children with high social status, the two factors are not necessarily the same.

Craig Peery (1979) showed preschool children pictures of their classmates and then asked them a series of questions about whom they would like to associate with (positive nominations) and whom they would *not* like to associate with (negative nominations). Based on peer nominations, Peery then assigned each child to one of four categories. **Popular children** were those who had many positive nominations and few negative ones. That is, they were well-liked children who had considerable social impact (that is, they were mentioned frequently). **Amiable children** also had a majority of positive nominations, but they were mentioned less often than the popular children. These children, then, were well liked but had low social impact. **Rejected children** were mentioned frequently, but most nominations were negative; they had high social impact but were not well liked. Finally, the children Peery labeled **isolates** (other researchers have called them **neglected**) were mentioned infrequently (low social impact), and when they were mentioned, the nominations were usually negative. Peery assessed the social skills of children as a function of their sociometric classification and found, not surprisingly, that popular children were the most socially sophisticated and rejected children were the least so.

Characteristics of high- and low-status children

Why are some children popular and others rejected? What are the consequences of a child's social standing for later life, and to what extent can children change their status? Early research examined some physical characteristics of children as they relate to popularity. For example, attractive children are more likely to be popular than less attractive children, whereas children with unusual names and children with physical, behavioral, or mental handicaps are apt to be less popular (see Hartup, 1983). Of more significance to a child's social standing, however, are behavioral or psychological characteristics, and recent research has focused on children's social skills.

If we look at the general characteristics of high- and low-status children, a coherent pattern emerges (Coie, Dodge, & Kupersmidt, 1990). High-status children are described as being considerate and helpful. They follow the rules, particularly rules for social interaction. For school-age children, academic and athletic competence are highly valued, but social competence is increasingly viewed as an important component of popularity. In contrast, low-status or rejected children tend to be aggressive (especially boys), disruptive, and hyperactive, and they don't follow the rules. Rejected girls are often socially withdrawn. John Coie and his colleagues (1990) suggest that social rejection comes *before* social withdrawal. First, children are rebuffed in their attempts to join a group; as a result, they become withdrawn, making few overtures to other children. Similarly, Kenneth Rubin, Lucy LeMare, and Susan Lollis (1990) have proposed that the interaction of temperamental and early environmental conditions may cause some children to behave in aggressive and aversive ways with peers, and that such behavior leads to rejection by their peers and eventual isolation.

There are also differences in how high- and low-status children perceive themselves. Popular children tend to perceive themselves in a relatively positive light, having higher self-esteem than average children. Rejected children, on the other hand, fall into at least two groups. Some rejected children underestimate their competence and have low self-esteem; others have a rather positive view of themselves and try to maintain their self-esteem by refusing to accept their low social status and social competence (Boivin & Bégin, 1989).

What specific social skills do high-status children possess that low-status children do not? Kenneth Dodge and his colleagues have suggested that low-status children process social information ineffectively (Dodge & Feldman, 1990; Dodge, Pettit, McClaskey, & Brown, 1986). Specifically, Dodge proposed that these children misinterpret the social intentions of others and are lacking in three areas of social competence: (a) searching for possible social responses, (b) evaluating a social situation, and (c) enacting a social behavior.

In a review of five decades of research, Martha Putallaz and Aviva Wasserman (1990) noted that ability to enter an ongoing group differentiates high-status from low-status children. High-status children hover strategically, watching the group members "to learn their frame of reference and then applying this knowledge to perform behavior related to the ongoing activity of the group" (pp. 85–86). Low-status children, in contrast, often engage in protracted passive hovering or else disrupt the group with inappropriate behavior. In many ways, low-status children behave much as newcomers do (that is, children who are new to a social group) (Dodge, Schlundt, Schocken, & Delugach, 1983; Gottman, 1977; Putallaz & Wasserman, 1989). Low-status children may also have different motivations than high-status children; they may be more concerned with saving face and not having their social efforts rebuffed, making them more cautious than high-status children.

A number of social skills contribute to peer interaction, including responsiveness (responding to a peer's social gestures) and relevance (making contextually appropriate responses) (Asher, 1983; Putallaz & Gottman, 1981). In a study with preschoolers, Betty Black and Nancy Hazen (1990) found that disliked children, when interacting with children they did not know, were less responsive and more likely to make irrelevant comments than liked children. When interacting with peers they knew, disliked children were not only less responsive and relevant, but also communicated less effectively with the other child.

It seems clear that rejected or unpopular children lack the social skills of their better-liked peers. But do unpopular children appropriately perceive their own situation, or do they lack the social skills necessary to understand the rejection and isolation imposed on them by their peers?

Steven Asher and his colleagues have investigated children's perceptions of their social situations and report that low-status children do indeed feel the sting of peer rejection (Asher, Hymel, & Renshaw, 1984; Asher, Parkhurst, Hymel, & Williams, 1990). Some of the statements used by Asher and his colleagues (1984) are:

> It's easy for me to make new friends at school.
> I have nobody to talk to.
> I'm good at working with other children.
> It's hard for me to make friends.
> I have lots of friends.
> I feel alone.
> I can't find a friend when I need one.
> It's hard to get other kids to like me.
> I don't have anyone to play with.
> I get along with other kids.
> I feel left out of things.
> There's nobody I can go to when I need help.
> I don't get along with other children.
> I'm lonely.
> I am well-liked by the kids in my class.
> I don't have any friends.

Source: Adapted from "Loneliness in Children," by S. R. Asher, S. Hymel, and P. D. Renshaw, *Child Development,* 1984, *55,* 1456–1464. Copyright © The Society for Research in Child Development, Inc. Reprinted by permission.

More than 10% of the third- through sixth-grade children who took the test reported feelings of loneliness and social dissatisfaction. These feelings were related to social status: rejected children reported considerably more loneliness and social dissatisfaction than did their more popular peers. This relationship is shown in Figure 14.2 for third-through fifth-grade children. This pattern of data is robust: it has been found for other samples of

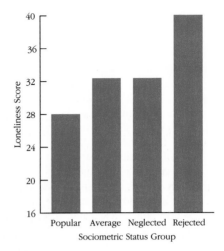

Figure 14.2 Loneliness scores for popular, average, neglected, and rejected third- through fifth-grade children. *Source:* From "Peer Rejection and Loneliness in Childhood," by S. R. Asher, J. T. Parkhurst, S. Hymel, and G. P. Williams. In S. R. Asher and J. D. Coie (eds.), *Peer Rejection in Childhood.* Copyright © 1990 by Cambridge University Press. Reprinted by permission. (Data from Crick & Ladd, 1988.)

school-age children, for preschoolers, and for middle-school children (Asher et al., 1990).

Origins of ineffective social skills What are the origins of the poor social skills of unpopular children? Are some children simply born with personalities that destine them to be popular and well liked, and others with personalities that destine them to be unpopular? Or do parents contribute significantly to children's eventual social status?

Several studies have examined the relationship between parents' social behavior and their children's social standing, and all report differences in how the parents of low- versus high-status children interact with their offspring in social situations (Putallaz & Heflin, 1990). For example, Martha Putallaz (1987) looked at the social interaction of first-grade children and their mothers, comparing it to the children's social status and their interactions with unfamiliar children. In general, mothers who expressed warmth, showed a concern for feelings and open communication, exerted a moderate degree of control but were not demanding had more

Box 14.2

Children without Friends

Through friends children learn about themselves and about society. Friendships provide children with concepts of loyalty, justice, leadership, rule making, and camaraderie. It is through friends that a child learns how to be a kid. Jokes, jump-rope rhymes, secret languages, slang, and games such as jacks and hopscotch are not passed on from adult to child, but from one generation of children to another.

Because friends are so important, children without friends are at a considerable disadvantage. Although estimates vary, research indicates that between 5% and 10% of school-age children are unpopular with their classmates, and approximately 20% report that they feel lonely a lot and wish they had more friends.

What makes a child friendless? Shyness is one obvious reason. For many children (and adults), shyness is a personality trait that has its basis in genetics. However, shy children can make friends and are not necessarily unpopular; they simply may need more time to adjust to new people and new settings than other children and are often content with just a few good friends. We must be careful not to use the gregarious extrovert as our standard for what is expected of children with respect to friendships.

During the school years, conformity to peer stereotypes becomes important, and children who deviate from these standards are more apt to be rejected than more typical kids. The overweight boy, the girl who wears "funny" clothes, the child with

One in five school children report feeling lonely and friendless "a lot."

failing grades, and the kid with the weird first name stand out in a class of fourth-graders and may be targets for rejection. Children who don't do the same things that the others kids do may be in for problems, too. Bobby lives near the school and goes home for lunch while all of his classmates eat in the cafeteria; Jessica is not allowed to play kickball or other running games at recess; Paul hasn't much to say about the latest episode of "The Simpsons" because his parents won't let him watch it. In general, when parents' rules for their children vary substantially from the rules imposed on other kids, children are seen as different and may be excluded from social groups.

Children need opportunities to make friends. School, of course, is a ready-made setting for social interactions, but some classrooms are more conducive to the development of friendships than others. Friendships are more apt to flourish when teachers encourage making friends and provide small-group experiences for different combinations of classmates. After-school activities such as baton twirling, crafts, gymnastics, and soccer provide additional situations for forming friends. Parents can help shy children by becoming involved with families who have children or volunteering to lead a scout troop, coach a Little League team, or drive in a car pool, thus giving the shy child further opportunities to interact with other children.

Shy children don't need to be constantly reminded that they are different. Parents should avoid labeling children or their behavior as inappropriate. They should try not to pressure the reserved child to be more outgoing with adults ("Come on, tell Mrs. Peterson all about your dancing lessons"). Finally, all parents should tell their children—be they shy or bold—about being a friend. They should talk to them about how people's feelings are hurt by being excluded, how kids who are different have feelings too, and that once you get to know them, they may end up being really neat kids. Having a good friend is best accomplished by being a good friend.

Source: Adapted from D. F. Bjorklund and B. R. Bjorklund. (May 1987). Children without Friends. *Parents Magazine,* Vol. 62, No. 5.

socially competent and high-status children than mothers who did not display these characteristics. A similar pattern of results was reported by Kevin Mac-Donald and Ross Parke (1984) for preschool children.

In a related study, Victoria Finnie and Alan Russell (1988) examined the behavior of mothers of high- and low-status preschool children as they attempted to gain entry for their children into an ongoing play group. In one experiment, two children were playing together in a room when a third child and his or her mother entered. The third child, previously identified as having low or high social status, did not know the other two children. The mother was instructed to bring her child over to the two children "and to give as much or as little help as she thought necessary so that the three children might play together as well as possible" (p. 791). Finnie and Russell reported that mothers of high-status children used behaviors that have been identified with high-status children; for example, they encouraged their child to join the group without trying to change the nature of the activity. In contrast, mothers of low-status children behaved in a manner similar to that of low-status children; they were often hostile or intrusive, trying to use their authority to gain entry for their children and frequently disrupting the ongoing play.

Although parental behavior obviously has an impact on children's social behavior, certain characteristics of the children themselves also contribute to their social behavior and, most importantly, interact with how others (including their parents) perceive and treat them. For example, lonely children's reactions to their peers may actually enhance their loneliness. In a study by Ken Rotenberg and Patrick Whitney (in press), lonely sixth- and seventh-grade children were engaged in conversation with other children of the same age. Compared to non-lonely children, lonely boys offered fewer intimate disclosures, whereas lonely girls provided more (at least to other girls). Thus, lonely boys adopted a behaviorally shy disposition, whereas lonely girls tended to be overly eager; neither approach, it would seem, is conducive to making new friends.

In other work, Kenneth Rubin, Lucy LeMare, and Susan Lollis (1990), following the transactional approach discussed in Chapter 1, suggested how infant temperament might interact with environmental conditions to produce children who are rejected by their peers when they reach school age. Infants who are fussy, unpredictable, overactive, and difficult to soothe may be viewed as aversive—especially by parents who have few sources of social support and who are experiencing considerable stress as a result of low income or marital problems. As a result, they may be treated with less nurturance and responsiveness than an "easier" infant would be. This pattern of negative parent-infant interaction can persist into childhood, with children displaying hostile, aggressive behavior toward their peers as a result of the social interaction modeled by their parents. Behavior and reputations tend to remain stable in childhood: other children expect hostility and aggression from these children, leading to rejection and making it difficult to break out of the established pattern. (Compare this to our discussion of child abuse in Chapter 13.)

Rubin and his colleagues suggested an alternative path to rejection for children born with a low threshold for arousal when faced with social stimulation or novelty (Buss & Plomin, 1984). These children are more likely to be shy and may be slow to warm up to other children, but such a temperament in and of itself does not typically lead to rejection. However, when a slow-to-arouse child is born into a family that is experiencing stress, the difference between what parents expect and what infants deliver may result in conflict and a negative parent-infant interaction, similar to that described for the "difficult" child. These children are likely to become anxiously attached (see Chapter 12), which, coupled with their wariness of novelty, results in little exploration and a reluctance to initiate social contact with peers. When these children enter social situations (such as school), they are withdrawn and anxious and, because of their lack of experience, do not have the social skills necessary to form and maintain friendships. Withdrawn children are not sought out as playmates by others, beginning a pattern of isolation and potential rejection that, once again, can be difficult to reverse.

Stability and change of low social status

Rejection and social isolation hurt children. Most of us can remember some times in our childhood when we were rejected or ignored, and we recognize that the pain we felt at that time was real. For most of us, these experiences were short-lived. But for some children, rejection and loneliness are stable over

The inability to make friends as a child is a good predictor of adjustment problems in adulthood.

much of childhood and into their adult years. In one study, children who were described as shy and reserved in late childhood were assessed again 30 years later (Caspi, Elder, & Bem, 1988). Shy boys were more likely to delay marriage, parenthood, and stable careers, and they achieved less in their occupations than their more outgoing peers. Those who did establish a stable career later in life were more likely to experience marital instability. Shy girls were more likely than their peers to follow a conventional pattern of marriage, child rearing, and homemaking. Thus, shyness tends to persist across the life span, with shy, withdrawn children evoking responses (or lack of responses) from others that tend to maintain their withdrawal and social isolation. In research examining early signs of adjustment problems, peer rejection in childhood has consistently emerged as a general predictor of maladjustment in adulthood (Kupersmidt, Coie, & Dodge, 1990).

Because of the long-term effect that peer rejection can have on children's lives, there have been numerous attempts to modify the social behavior of withdrawn or rejected children. In one study, the behavior of socially withdrawn preschool children was modified by having them play with younger children (Furman, Rahe, & Hartup, 1979). Wyndol Furman and his colleagues recorded the number of social contacts children in preschools made, and identified socially withdrawn children, or isolates, who spent relatively little time interacting with

peers. Isolate children were assigned to one of two treatment groups or to a control group. Children in one treatment group participated in ten play sessions with another child the same age (same-age partner). Children in a second treatment group participated in ten play sessions with a child 12 to 20 months younger (younger partner). Isolates in the control group received no treatment. The play sessions were conducted in a room separate from the preschool classroom, with two toys likely to maximize social interaction (for example, puppets and blocks). Following the treatment sessions, these children's peer interaction in preschool was evaluated again and compared to the earlier observations.

The results of this study are shown in Figure 14.3. During the pretreatment observations, isolates spent much less of their time interacting with peers than did nontargeted children. Following treatment, however, the children in both the younger-partner and same-age-partner conditions increased their amount of social interaction, and children in the younger-partner condition interacted with peers as frequently as the general population of preschoolers.

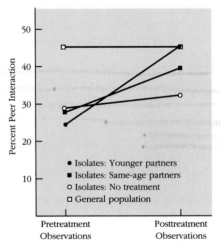

Figure 14.3 Peer interaction rates for socially withdrawn preschoolers, before and after treatment. *Source:* From "Rehabilitation of Socially Withdrawn Preschool Children Through Mixed-Age and Same-Age Socialization," by W. Furman, D. F. Rahe, and W. W. Hartup, *Child Development,* 1979, *50,* 915–922. Copyright © The Society for Research in Child Development, Inc. Reprinted by permission.

Why should playing with another child, particularly a younger child, result in such a dramatic change in peer interaction? Presumably, a socially withdrawn child paired with a younger child had the opportunity to be a leader and to try out different social behaviors in a nonthreatening situation. The social skills of the younger child, because of his or her immaturity, matched those of the older, socially withdrawn child. Such an environment is well suited for the isolate child to develop improved social skills and then to generalize those skills to the preschool environment at large. This is similar to the study of reversing abnormal social behavior in isolation-reared monkeys through the use of younger "therapist" monkeys (Suomi & Harlow, 1972; see Chapter 12).

Despite the success of the Furman study, it applies only to withdrawn children. Children who are rejected by their peers present greater problems than simple shyness; they are often hostile as well as deficient in social skills (Asher & Renshaw, 1981). Thus, simply increasing the frequency of social contacts for rejected children is not likely to result in any positive change. Beginning in the 1970s, researchers have attempted, through various forms of coaching and/or modeling, to train positive social skills in rejected children. Although the findings are not always straightforward, teaching rejected children specific positive social skills has often resulted in improved patterns of social interaction and improvements in social status (Bierman & Furman, 1984; Ladd, 1981).

But rejected children are not simply lacking in positive social skills; often, they are aggressive and disruptive. John Coie and Gina Koeppl (1990) report that about one-third of rejected children in third and fourth grade were rated by their peers as highly aggressive and disruptive, compared to about 10% of nonrejected children. Also, rejected children often lack academic as well as social skills. Thus, the most effective intervention for rejected children must focus not only on social skills, but also on aggression, disruptive behavior, and academic skills.

Coie and Koeppl (1990) point out that rejected children can be trained to reduce their aggression and disruption and to improve their social and academic skills. When such changes are made, there is often a corresponding change in social status (Coie & Krehbiel, 1984). The message here is that children are rejected for different reasons, and that efforts to improve the social standing of rejected children must take into consideration a variety of possibilities. According to Coie and Koeppl (1990), many rejected children "may be deficient in prosocial skills, but . . . they require help beyond that contained in positive play skills training in order to become less aversive to their peers" (p. 329). Moreover, because a child's bad reputation tends to solidify during the school years, making it difficult for rejected children to participate and gain acceptance from their classmates, it is important that intervention for these children begin as early as possible during the preschool years (Mize & Ladd, 1990).

Peer Groups

In reading the previous sections, it would be easy to get the idea that children interact in groups of two or three, usually with other children who can be regarded as friends. They do, of course, but childhood peer interaction often occurs in groups, including both close friends and mere acquaintances. Preschoolers congregate in sandboxes or on the jungle gym, but there is rarely a cohesiveness about the groups they form; tomorrow's group may be very different from today's, and the only purpose or goal they share is "to play." During the school years, however, children begin to see themselves as members of a true **peer group.** According to David Shaffer (1988), a peer group is a confederation that (1) interacts on a regular basis; (2) defines a sense of belonging; (3) shares implicit or explicit norms for the behavior of group members; and (4) develops a hierarchical organization, or **dominance hierarchy.**

Dominance Hierarchies

Dominance hierarchies—"pecking orders" of social influence—can be seen even among preschoolers (Sluckin & Smith, 1977; Strayer & Strayer, 1976). During the first few weeks of preschool, children test one another, and many of these disputes result in fights with clear-cut winners and losers (Strayer & Strayer, 1976). As a result of repeated conflicts, a hierarchy is established, with the top and bottom positions being set first and the middle positions developing later (Sherif, Harvey, White, Hood, & Sherif, 1961).

As children get older, factors other than "who can push around whom" become important in establishing and maintaining group structure, although the factor of literal physical dominance remains important among some groups of children, particularly boys. In a study of 12- to 14-year-old boys and girls at summer camp, Ritch Savin-Williams (1979) noted that boys were more apt to assert themselves physically and to argue with cabinmates than were girls. But dominance hierarchies within a cabin, for both boys and girls, were shaped by factors other than physical assertiveness, including pubertal maturation, athletic ability, and group leadership.

Forming and Maintaining Peer Groups

Dominance hierarchies serve to reduce antagonism within the group, distribute scarce resources, and focus division of labor (Savin-Williams, 1979). The functions of peer-group structure are nicely illustrated in classic studies by Muzafer Sherif and his colleagues (Sherif et al., 1961). In addition, Sherif's studies show how a peer group comes together in the face of conflict with another group, and how between-group conflict can be reduced.

In the Robbers Cave experiment, 22 unacquainted fifth-grade boys attending summer camp were divided into two groups. Over the course of several weeks, each group participated in enjoyable activities such as crafts, building hideouts, and playing organized games. This was done separately in each group, with one group of boys not being aware initially of the other group. Group cohesiveness was emphasized, in part by organizing activities that required cooperation. For example, one evening the staff failed to cook dinner, and the boys had to divide responsibilities and prepare the meal themselves. Over time, clear positions of status emerged, with some children becoming recognized leaders and others followers. Both groups even adopted names: Rattlers and Eagles.

Once group cohesion had been established, the

Box 14.3

All the Other Kids Do

A few weeks before she started third grade, our daughter Heidi announced to us that she wanted to wear low-top, nondesigner sneakers to school. That was the good news. The bad news was that she wanted to wear them without socks and *without shoelaces*! When we told her that it was one of the weirdest ideas we had ever heard, she reacted as generations of third-graders before her: "But all the other kids are wearing them!" And we responded as generations of parents before us: "Well, you're not 'all the other kids.' You can think for yourself and make your own decisions, can't you? If 'all the other kids' jumped in the river, would you do it too?"

If we didn't know better, we would think that parents are programmed to respond reflexively to certain cues from their children, and a mention of "all the other kids" is a prime example. Actually there is merit to our knee-jerk responses, as our experience and common sense tell us. But when it comes to peer-group conformity and school-age children, we should all stop and consider a few arguments on the other side before launching into our pat answers.

"All the other kids" are very important to school-age children School-age children need to be accepted as part of the group. Valuable lessons are learned in these pint-size societies, such as making rules, settling differences, solving problems together, pooling resources, and making the most of each member's talents. Children are often excluded from group activities when they are perceived as "different," such as the boy who must go home immediately after school and do homework instead of meeting "all the other kids" at the park, or the girl who must spend Saturday mornings with her grandmother rather than joining "all the other kids" at the bowling alley.

School-age children spend much

two groups were brought together and a series of "friendly" competitions arranged (for example, baseball, tug-of-war). Although the boys did not know it, the camp counselors arranged the games so that each group won and lost equally. When a group lost a competition, conflict arose, often including threats of physical attack against one another or a change in leadership. As competition continued, however, within-group conflict decreased and group solidarity increased, often expressed by hostility toward the other group. The groups would abuse each other verbally ("You're not Eagles, you're pigeons"); they engaged in raids on the other campsite and theft or destruction of property; and true violence (rock throwing) had to be stopped by counselor intervention. Thus, competition between groups led, after a brief period of disharmony, to greater within-group cohesion and overt hostility toward the other group.

The researchers attempted to reduce the hostility between the groups initially by bringing the Eagles and Rattlers together for some pleasant, noncompetitive activities, such as meals and movies. These attempts were disastrous; if anything, they increased hostility between the groups. The counselors then devised a series of events that required the cooperation of members of both groups. For instance, the water supply "broke down" one hot day, and boys from both groups had to search for the source of the trouble. On another occasion, a truck engine failed, requiring the boys to act cooperatively to get it started. These and other situations that provided a common goal reduced hostility between the two groups and fostered friendship between former "enemies."

Conformity to Peer Pressure

Conformity refers to adjusting one's behavior to that of a group. Conformity has developed a bad reputation, especially among parents whose children claim that "everyone else" is allowed to do whatever the

---

of their time away from home—at school, on playgrounds, and at the homes of friends. If parents' knowledge of "all the other kids" comes solely from their children, they may be making important decisions based on faulty data. Parents should know just who "all the other kids" are and should have firsthand experience of the places their children spend time.

Giving in isn't always giving up   It is important for school-age children's parents to give in to what "all the other kids" are doing when the request is reasonable. It's an age of transition for both parent and child.

Children are forming ideas and opinions that are different from their parents', yet parents still have control over much of their children's lives. Parents still control the checkbook and the car keys. But parents can give their children some freedom when they request it and when it seems appropriate. The end products of parenting are not full-grown children who always do what they are told. The goal is to raise a well-adjusted, happy adult who makes wise, independent decisions.

When it comes to granting requests to do what "all the other kids" are doing, parents have an important responsibility to see that their chil-

dren live according to family values, religious doctrine, school rules, community standards, basic health and safety guidelines, the family budget, and the law. However, there remain some areas that are less critical, and parents of school-age kids need to make that distinction when considering requests from their children to go along with the crowd.

Source: Adapted from D. F. Bjorklund and B. R. Bjorklund. (March 1989). Following the Crowd. *Parents Magazine*, Vol. 64, No. 3.

It is very important to school age children to be part of a group, especially in early adolescence.

parents have just forbidden. However, conformity to group norms is necessary for any society to function.

It is during the school years, when the peer group becomes important for children, that conformity to peer pressure truly begins, generally peaking in early adolescence (Berndt, 1979; Gavin & Furman, 1989). Thomas Berndt (1979) presented children ranging from third to 12th grades with situations in which peers urged them to engage in antisocial, neutral, or prosocial behaviors. Figure 14.4 shows the age trend for antisocial acts. As can be seen, ninth-graders were the most susceptible to peer pressure, with both younger and older children being less influenced by their peers. Despite the beliefs of many parents of adolescents, children of all ages are *less* likely to conform to peer pressure for

antisocial behavior than for more positive behavior (Berndt, 1979; Brown, Clasen, & Eicher, 1986), and teenagers perceive less peer pressure for misconduct (for example, drug/alcohol use, unsafe sex practices, delinquent behavior) than for positive group behaviors, such as socializing with friends (Brown et al., 1986).

Prosocial Behavior

Much of the interaction among peers is positive, or **prosocial,** in that it benefits other people. This should hardly be surprising, since by definition friends are people with whom we share things in common and whose company we enjoy. Acts such as

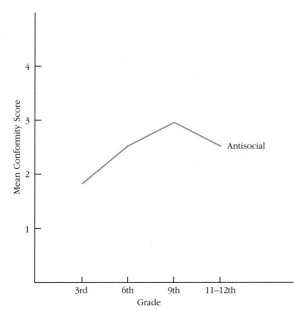

Figure 14.4 Average conformity score for antisocial behavior by age. *Source:* From "Developmental Changes in Conformity to Peers and Parents," by T. J. Berndt, *Developmental Psychology,* 1979, *15,* 608–616. Copyright 1979 by the American Psychological Association. Reprinted by permission.

sharing, helping, and cooperating are expected among friends, and we rarely seek the company of people who fail to behave toward us in prosocial ways.

The Development of Prosocial Behavior

What factors must be present for children to behave in a prosocial way—that is, to behave in a way that helps others even to their own detriment? Martin Hoffman (1981, 1989) postulated that feelings of empathy, or empathic arousal, are necessary before prosocial behavior is possible (see Chapter 15). Children become upset when other people are distressed, says Hoffman, and recognize that their own ill feelings are the result of distress in another person. They then learn that they feel better themselves if they do something to ease the other person's discomfort. Hoffman believes that the ability to feel empathy is rooted in biology, and he has demonstrated empathic crying in neonates (Sagi & Hoffman, 1976).

As children's empathic abilities increase over childhood, so too do their abilities to behave prosocially.

Prosocial behavior comes in many forms, the more frequently studied (at least with children) being comforting, sharing, and helping.

Comforting   Carolyn Zahn-Waxler, Marian Radke-Yarrow, and their colleagues have shown that infants as young as 1 year of age will comfort another person who is distressed, usually by patting, hugging, or offering some valued object (Zahn-Waxler & Radke-Yarrow, 1982). Attempts to comfort a distressed person become more elaborate over the second and third years, including expressing concern, providing suggestions, and giving "gifts" (Zahn-Waxler, Radke-Yarrow, & King, 1979). An example of

Very young children will hug and pat someone who is distressed.

comforting by a 22-month-old is provided by the following excerpt from a mother's observations:

> Today there was a little 4-year-old girl here, Susan. Todd (96 weeks) and Susan were in the bedroom playing and all of a sudden Susan started to cry and ran to her mother. Todd slowly followed after and watched. I said, "What happened?" and she said, "He hit me." I said, "Well, tell him not to hit you," and I said, "Todd!" He didn't seem particularly upset; he was watching her cry. I said, "Did you hit Susan? Why would you hit Susan? You don't want to hurt people." Then they went back in the bedroom and there was a second run-in and she came out. That's when I said sternly, "No, Todd, you mustn't hit people." He just watched her sniffle as she was being stroked by her mom, and her mom was saying, "He's just a little boy and boys do that sometimes." On the table right by us were some fallen petals from a flower and he picked up one little petal and smiled and handed it to her and said, "Here." She kind of reached and took it and then he searched for other petals and gave them to her; so he was trying to either make up or give her something to stop the crying (Zahn-Waxler et al., 1979, p. 322).

Sharing   Sharing can be observed, in small amounts, among toddlers. For example, 12-month-olds will point out objects to other people, "sharing" the sights they see with someone else (Rheingold, Hay, & West, 1976). But sharing sights and sharing toys are different things, and spontaneous sharing of valuable possessions is something that toddlers and 2-year-olds do not do often or easily. Sharing is more common among 3- and 4-year-olds, but many children, well into the early school years, find sharing toys a difficult concept to put into practice (Yarrow & Waxler, 1976). In fact in a study that looked at conflict between pairs of 21-month-olds, 84% of all disputes concerned struggles over toys (Hay & Ross, 1982).

More recent research indicates that toddlers who have had others share with them are more likely to share their own toys when given the opportunity (Levitt, Weber, Clark, & McDonnell, 1985). Pairs of children (ages 29 to 36 months), accompanied by their mothers, were separated by a see-through gate.

Only one child in each pair was given toys to play with. If the child with the toys did not share with the other child within 4 minutes, the child's mother encouraged her child to share. After another minute, all the toys were removed. Following this, another set of toys was introduced, but this time they were given to the child who initially had no toys. Mary Levitt and her colleagues reported that none of the children shared spontaneously, confirming our earlier description of toddlers as nonsharers. This was true even though many of the "toy-deprived" children stood at the gate watching the other child, who were "keenly aware of the other child's presence and actions, even though they often turned their backs to the other child" (p. 123). When asked by their mothers to share, however, 13 of 20 children did so. What is more interesting here is that children who received toys in the second phase of the experiment were more likely to share if they had been shared with first. In fact, in 9 out of 10 cases, when the first child did not share, the second child didn't either. Thus, these young children displayed the principle of reciprocity: "I'll share with you if you shared with me." Yet even children who were shared with earlier only shared after being requested to do so by their mothers.

Sharing is more common in older children. For example, in a study by Francis Green and Frank Schneider (1974), children ranging in age from 5 to 14 years were given the opportunity to share some candy with other children in their school. The children had earned five candy bars by assisting the experimenter on a project to "help poor children." Among 5- and 6-year-olds, 60% shared at least one candy bar; the percentage of children sharing increased to 92% for 7- and 8-year-olds and 100% for 9- and 10-year-olds and 13- and 14-year-olds. Also, the average number of candy bars shared (maximum = 5) increased with age (5/6-year-olds = 1.36; 7/8-year-olds = 1.84; 9/10-year-olds = 2.88; 13/14-year-olds = 4.24). Thus, at least when requested by an adult, children's willingness to share with unspecified peers increases steadily over the school years.

Helping   Anyone who has spent much time with preschoolers knows that they often want to "help"—assisting a parent, for example, in cooking dinner, mowing the lawn, or repairing a leaky faucet. Such "help" often increases the work for the adult per-

Preschoolers enjoy helping and this tendency increases with age. Fortunately, so does their coordination.

forming the task, but young children seem earnest in their attempts to assist. Harriet Rheingold (1982) asked the parents of 18- to 30-month-old children and other adults to perform some common household chores and recorded the children's reactions. Rheingold reported that children spontaneously and promptly assisted the adults in most of the tasks they performed, regardless of whether the adult was the child's parent or an unfamiliar person.

Research with children between the ages of 18 months and 6.5 years found that helping other children made up between 10% and 20% of their total social contacts during free-play activities in preschool, but that this amount did not increase systematically with age (Bar-Tal, Raviv, & Goldberg, 1982). However, the percentage of helping acts that occurred in a "real" as opposed to play situation increased with age: 67% of all helping acts were "real" for children under 2.5 years, compared with 97% for children 5.5 years and older.

Spontaneous helping increases over the school years. In the study by Green and Schneider (1974), children between the ages of 5 and 14 years of age were asked to help an adult put together books for poor children. In the process of working, the adult "accidentally" knocked over some pencils as he walked across the room. The adult made no comment about the pencils, other than to say "uh" and shrug when they fell. The percentage of children who spontaneously picked up the pencils increased with age; about half the 5- and 6-year-olds picked up the pencils, but virtually all of those over 9 did so.

Fostering Prosocial Behavior

The extent to which children act in prosocial ways is related to how their parents act. Children who view their parents as warm and loving are more generous, supportive, comforting, and cooperative than other children (Hoffman, 1975; Hoffman & Saltzstein, 1967). In a study with preschoolers, Carolyn Zahn-Waxler and her associates (1979) found that prosocial young children were apt to have mothers who focused on their children's misdeeds ("Look what you did!") and who made it clear that they expected proper behavior ("Don't you see you hurt Amy? Don't ever pull hair!"). Effective mothers did not calmly reason with their preschool children, but were adamant about their feelings. These same mothers also modeled empathic behavior, comforting their own children when they were hurt.

To what extent can children's prosocial behavior be shaped by rewarding them for good deeds? We discussed in Chapter 8 how children who are rewarded for specific behaviors often lose their motivation for these behaviors when the rewards are removed (Lepper, Greene, & Nisbett, 1973); this generalization seems to hold true for prosocial behavior as well. A recent study has investigated the relationship between experience with instrumental rewards (if you do X, you get Y) and prosocial motivation in elementary school children (Fabes, Fultz, Eisenberg, May-Plumlee, & Christopher, 1989). To assess mothers' attitudes and practices regarding the use of tangible rewards for activities that children did not find attractive, the researchers used items such as:

> The use of rewards to motivate children can be considered a type of bribery.
> The use of rewards to motivate children can help produce desired behavior.
> The use of rewards to motivate children makes them stop working when the rewards are no longer available.
> To what extent do you provide your child with a reward for behaving properly?
> To what extent do you give your child a reward for doing something he or she does not like to do?

Mothers responded to each statement or question on a 5-point scale, depending on how well it described their beliefs or behavior.

The children of these mothers were seen separately and given the opportunity to help make a game for kids in the hospital by arranging pieces of paper according to color. Some of the children were offered a reward for helping (a small toy); other children were not. Later in the session, all children were given a second chance to "help the sick children," but rewards were not offered to anyone (free-choice period). Richard Fabes and his colleagues reported that the offer of rewards increased helping behavior in the first situation. However, during the free-choice period, previously rewarded children were less likely to help, and this effect was greatest for those children whose mothers put a high value on instrumental rewards. Thus, although the use of

Box 14.4

Giving Children the Gift of Giving

D uring the months of November and December, our thoughts turn to helping others who are not as fortunate as we are. Thanksgiving reminds us of our families' good fortune, and the Christmas season, regardless of our religious beliefs, reminds us to share our good fortune with others. Parents get a double benefit from giving: first, they receive the warm feelings that come from making life a little better for a fellow human being, and second, they have the opportunity to teach their children, by their example, an important lesson in caring for others.

Unfortunately, most of our giving is designed to be efficient and cost effective instead of understandable to children. For example, we may have a set amount of money deducted from each paycheck and delivered automatically to a community agency that oversees local charities. While adults may understand the invisible processes and transfers going on and feel the joy of such abstract giving, children have problems connecting all the dots between the check, the

When family charity takes place at a level children can understand, the joy of giving begins early.

rewards may enhance prosocial behavior immediately, "they may also undermine subsequent prosocial motivation in situations where rewards are no longer forthcoming" (Fabes et al., 1989, p. 514).

These results do not mean that children should never be offered a reward for good behavior. They mean that the desired behavior is more likely to occur if rewards for prosocial behavior are used with other techniques, such as modeling prosocial behavior (Moore & Eisenberg, 1984). In fact, modeling has been found to be a very effective technique for inducing prosocial behavior in children, especially when the model is perceived as warm, influential, and powerful (see Perry & Bussey, 1984). Parents, it seems, are the best models for prosocial behavior in their children, and what parents *do* may be far more important than what they *say* (see Box 14.4).

---

agency, and the hungry family at the city shelter. The result is a golden opportunity missed for teaching family values.

This is by no means an argument against contributing to large agencies and institutions. However, it *is* a suggestion that parents make a special effort at holiday time to do some extra giving in ways that will transmit more clearly the message of charity to their children.

Make a family tradition of giving

Kids can best understand the problems of the less fortunate when they can relate them to their own lives. For example, incidents of children staying home from school on cold days because they have no warm clothes is a reality in many northern school districts, and children can easily imagine how it would feel to be in that situation. Families can make an annual autumn practice of sorting out winter clothing and donating items that are outgrown or not needed to the school clothing bank in time for distribution before the cold weather hits. If parents tell their children year after year

how good it makes them feel to know that their efforts are keeping children warm and in school, they will be carving out a family tradition of giving that may well extend into the next generation.

Give to "real" children

Children understand giving best if it's done for a specific individual instead of an abstract group. Some of the best ideas we have seen are the "angel trees" sponsored the past few years by shopping malls and fast-food chains. The sponsors, working with community agencies, decorate a Christmas tree with paper angels containing the first name of a needy child, his or her age, and a short wish list of gifts in a range of prices. Families can select an angel from the tree, shop for whatever gifts they wish to provide, and bring the gifts back to the tree to be displayed until Christmas Eve, when they are distributed by the agency to the children. Christmas morning can be even more meaningful when the family pauses to think of the happiness their gifts have brought their special "angels."

Small things that have no words

All children seem to have a special place in their hearts for animals. Holiday time is a good opportunity to let the kids give something extra to their furry friends. Call ahead to the Humane Society and ask what is needed in the way of food, then make a family trip to buy the cat or dog chow and deliver it to the shelter. Kids will feel like Santa's elves, providing a holiday feast for their animal friends.

In their joy of giving to their children during the holidays, parents often forget that their children might like the opportunity to feel that joy also. It takes a little extra effort, but one of the best things parents can give their children is the gift of giving.

Source: Adapted from D. F. Bjorklund and B. R. Bjorklund. (December 1989). The Art of Giving. *Parents Magazine,* Vol. 64, No. 12.

Aggression

Aggression has been a favorite topic of psychologists throughout this century. Freud and the early behaviorists viewed aggression as a "drive" that children must learn to control or direct into socially appropriate channels. Some researchers have viewed aggression as a behavioral technique for obtaining resources, and thus as a normal and functional aspect of life (Archer, 1989; Wilson, 1978). When social psychologists look at aggression, however, they rarely see it as a positive approach to a problem; rather, contemporary social developmentalists define aggression simply as "behavior aimed at harming another person" (Perry, Perry, & Boldizar, 1990, p. 135). When viewed from this perspective, aggression is seen as generally maladaptive, especially now in our history when the tools of violence are no longer sticks, rocks, and fists but assault rifles, nerve gas, and nuclear missiles.

Aggression is universal, found in varying degrees in all human cultures and within the behavioral repertoire of every healthy individual. Yet aggression is not an inevitable response to any particular stimulus; social pressures determine, to a substantial degree, the conditions under which an aggressive response is appropriate or not. Thus, the question of whether aggression is "innate" or "learned" is not a useful one. As human beings, we are all capable of acting aggressively; but as members of a culture, we are all subject to societal pressures that influence when, how, and to what extent we will behave aggressively.

Some children are prone to behave more aggressively than others. Both biological and environmental factors, and their transaction, influence individual differences in aggression.

The Development of Aggression

Aggression is not limited to any one age group; physical aggression has been observed between toddlers, school-age children, adolescents, and various combinations of these age groups. Moreover, the nature of aggression tends to change with age, making any simple statements such as "aggression decreases with age" overly simplistic. Nor is aggression limited to one sex. However, boys are, on average, more aggressive than girls at every age, beginning in toddlerhood.

Aggression is surprisingly common among young preschoolers, but decreases over the years from 2 to 5 (Cummings, Iannotti, & Zahn-Waxler, 1989; Hartup, 1974). Mark Cummings and his colleagues (1989) observed pairs of 2-year-old children playing at home and recorded the incidence of (a) bodily aggression (hitting, kicking, pushing, or biting the other child), (b) object-related aggression (attempting to take away an object the other child had), (c) initiations of aggression (starting an aggressive bout), and (d) average duration of an aggressive episode. They observed the same children three years later, at age 5, in a similar situation. The results (see Table 14.1) indicated that children at age 5 were less likely to initiate or engage in aggression and that aggressive bouts were of shorter duration, as compared to similar situations that occurred in these same children at age 2.

In a review of age changes in antisocial and delinquent behavior, Rolf Loeber (1982) concluded that the incidence of fighting and physical attacks declines during the years between 6 and 16. The incidence of boys' fighting and physical attacks against people, based on parent and teacher ratings, are shown in Figure 14.5. As can be seen, the trend is generally downward, with a peak at about age 13 but almost no incidents of fighting by age 16. In more recent research, Robert Cairns and his associates (Cairns, Cairns, Neckerman, Ferguson, & Gariépy, 1989) assessed aggression in children over a six-year period (fourth through ninth grades) and reported that both teacher ratings and self-ratings of children's aggression declined with age.

Although the disagreements and quarrels of young children often lead to tears, they don't usually

Table 14.1 Average number of aggressive incidents per hour and average duration of aggressive bouts at ages 2 and 5

Aggressive Measure	Age 2	Age 5
Bodily aggression	3.00	1.74
Object-related aggression	6.02	4.92
Initiation of aggression	6.98	3.78
Duration (in seconds)	14.11	7.60

Source: Adapted from "Aggression Between Peers in Early Childhood: Individual Continuity and Developmental Change," by E. M. Cummings, R. J. Iannotti, and C. Zahn-Waxler, *Child Development,* 1989, *60*, 887–895. Copyright © The Society for Research in Child Development, Inc. Reprinted by permission.

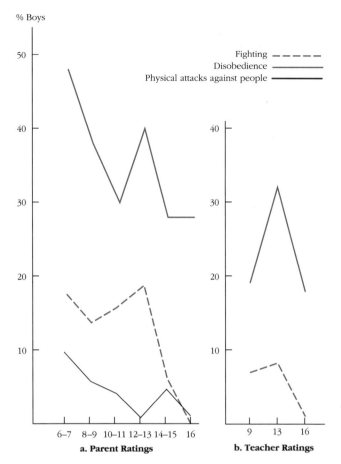

% Boys

Fighting -----
Disobedience ——
Physical attacks against people ——

a. Parent Ratings

b. Teacher Ratings

Figure 14.5 Parent (a) and teacher (b) ratings of fighting, disobedience, and attacks against people for boys of different ages. *Source:* Adapted from "The Stability of Antisocial and Delinquent Child Behavior: A Review," by R. Loeber, *Child Development,* 1982, *53,* 1431–1446. Copyright © The Society for Research in Child Development, Inc. Reprinted by permission. (Data from Achenbach & Edelbrock, 1981; Loeber, Patterson, & Dishion, 1982.)

lead to bodily injury. The same cannot be said for adolescent aggression: arrests for violent crimes and assaults increase sharply between the ages of 10 and 19 years (Cairns & Cairns, 1986). In a study by Tamara Ferguson and Brendan Rule (1980), older children (eighth-graders) judged aggression to be less reprehensible than did younger children (second-graders), implying that aggression becomes more acceptable with age. Although acts of overt aggression decline in adolescence, Loeber (1982) reported that this reduction was accompanied by an increased tendency to engage in covert antisocial acts, such as theft, truancy, and alcohol and drug use. Thus, children don't necessarily become better behaved with age; rather, the nature of their transgressions changes.

There is evidence that individual differences in aggression are relatively stable; that is, children who rate high on aggression relative to their peers at one age are likely to retain their high rank when aggression is measured at a later age. For example, Cummings and his associates (1989) reported substantial stability for aggression between ages 2 and 5, especially for boys. Similarly, Cairns and his colleagues (1989) reported relatively high stability of teacher ratings of aggression for both boys and girls between the fourth and ninth grades, and Dan Olweus (1978) found high stability of aggression for boys between the ages of 13 and 16 (girls were not tested). In a more recent report, Olweus (1987) found that children described as highly aggressive at 13 and 15 years of age were more likely, at age 24, to be involved in criminal and antisocial activities. In general, serious aggression is more likely to be displayed by adults and adolescents who were highly aggressive as children.

Aggressive children at all age levels are not as popular as their less aggressive peers (Coie & Kupersmidt, 1983; Perry, Perry, & Rasmussen, 1986). As we mentioned earlier, many rejected children are also highly aggressive (Coie & Koeppl, 1990); however, not all aggressive children are rejected. In one study, aggressive fourth- and seventh-graders were found to be less popular overall than their peers, but were no more apt to be rejected than nonaggressive children (Cairns, Cairns, Neckerman, Gest, & Gariépy, 1988). Aggressive children were involved in social networks and were often listed by their peers as "best friends." The catch is that aggressive children tended to be friends with other aggressive children, which serves to maintain and possibly even increase their aggressiveness (Patterson, 1986).

Factors That Influence Aggression

The acceptability of aggression varies considerably among cultures. Some groups reward aggressive behavior and encourage children to "stand up for themselves"; others view aggression as a serious transgression, with children being encouraged to cooperate and handle their differences in non-aggressive ways (Eibl-Eibesfeldt, 1989). Childhood aggression is generally frowned upon by most parents in modern societies, in part because it is not viewed as adaptive. Society, in the form of police and the legal system, has gradually taken over the responsibilities of protection that once belonged to individuals and families. Parents thus expect children to suppress their aggressive impulses because, in a system of law and order, other agencies are supposed to act on their behalf (Besag, 1989). Some parents in modern society, however, do not fully share this perspective; these parents actively encourage and reward aggression, even when society punishes people for behaving violently. And of course, some children and adults live in subcultures where law and order do not prevail, making aggression, at least in the short run, an adaptive response to some situations.

Aggression, as any social behavior, is influenced by many factors, including family, peers, and temperament. In addition, in North American society at least, television also plays a role.

Family influences on aggression   Probably the most potent influence on a child's aggressive behavior is the family. Many aggressive children come from homes where parents practice aggression (McCord, 1979; Patterson, 1986). For example, children with physically abusive parents are more aggressive, both at the home and in school (George & Main, 1979; Trickett & Kuczynski, 1986). In a study by Penelope Trickett and Leon Kuczynski (1986), parents from abusive and nonabusive families recorded incidents of their children's misbehavior and their responses to those incidents. Children from abusive homes committed more aggressive acts than did children from nonabusive homes, and their parents' responses generally took the form of physical punishment, regardless of the nature of the misbehavior. Parents from nonabusive families were more likely to use reasoning and simple commands to handle their children's misbehavior. (For a further discussion of parental practices and child abuse, see Chapter 13.)

Parents of aggressive children often do not set clear limits for their children's behavior and are ineffective at stopping their children's aggres-

Parents who are hostile toward their children and use physical means to control them, often find their children using the same tactics with siblings and classmates.

sion when it occurs (Olweus, 1980; Patterson & Stouthamer-Loeber, 1984). These parents may nag, threaten, and scold, but rarely follow through on their ultimatums (Patterson, 1986). Paradoxically, such permissiveness often results in children who are out of control and parents who resort to physical punishment. As David Perry and his colleagues (1990) state: "Parents who are ineffective at nipping deviant behavior in the bud sometimes find themselves becoming more and more exasperated as their child's deviant behavior escalates. They may suddenly explode with anger and assault the child" (p. 139).

G. R. Patterson, who has studied aggressive children and their families for more than 20 years, has proposed a theory of aggressive development centered around family interaction style (Patterson, 1980, 1986; see also Chapter 13). Patterson sees the parents of aggressive children as having many deficiencies in their parenting skills, including feelings of hostility toward their children, permissive and inconsistent discipline, and a failure to monitor the behavior and whereabouts of their children. Patterson proposed that much aggression in children is an attempt to "turn off" the threats and aversive stimulation coming from parents or siblings. Not all of the aversive stimulation is serious. Some of the bothersome irritants include parents' lack of attention, expressions of disapproval, or teasing. All children experience such irritations growing up in families, but when the home atmosphere lacks warmth and security, these minor irritants can be the source of major disruptions. Aggression in these contexts sometimes "works," with aggressive children getting their way, thus reinforcing the use of aggression as a way to solve problems.

Peer influences on aggression Most aggression in childhood is directed at other children. As noted earlier, children often use aggression or the threat of aggression to establish dominance hierarchies. Once a dominance hierarchy is established, there is less aggression among members of the group. When a conflict does occur, children use body and facial gestures as signs of dominance or submission; these gestures serve as signals to let others know what would likely happen if the conflict came to blows, thus settling the conflict without the need for actual fighting (Strayer & Strayer, 1976; Zivin, 1977).

Once children get a reputation for being aggressive, that reputation may serve to maintain their behavior. In an experiment by Kenneth Dodge (1980), boys in grades 2, 4, and 6 were read stories about peers—some of whom were known to be aggressive, and others nonaggressive. In one of the stories, a carton of milk on the peer's lunch tray spilled all over the child's back. There was no clue in the story as to whether the spilling was intentional or accidental. Children were asked to tell how they thought the incident might have happened; then they were asked a series of questions about how they would have behaved and if they thought the milk had been spilled on purpose. When the subject of the story was an aggressive peer, children frequently attributed hostile intentions to him and were more apt to say that they would aggress against him, expect fu-

ture aggression from him, and refuse to trust him. Moreover, this tendency to attribute hostile motives to aggressive children increased with age, suggesting that children's reputations become more entrenched as they get older (see also Hymel, Wagner, & Butler, 1990). This distrust by other children, in turn, may cause aggressive children to expect hostility intents from others. In fact, one study found that aggressive second-grade boys were frequently the targets of aggressive behavior by other children, although not to the extent that they aggressed toward others (Dodge & Frame, 1982). It is thus easy to see a cycle being established: aggressive children are perceived as hostile and treated with distrust and scorn by their peers, which in turn makes aggressive children feel rejected and the object of hostile intentions, which in turn maintains their aggressive behavior.

Temperamental influences on aggression Are some children "naturally" more aggressive than others? Dan Olweus (1980) assessed the effects of early temperament (general activity level, intensity of temperament from calm to hot-tempered), along with environmental factors (mother's negativism, mother's permissiveness, mother's and father's use of punitive discipline methods), on peer ratings of aggressiveness in sixth- and ninth-grade Swedish boys. He found that the best predictors of children's aggression were mother's negativism and permissiveness, although children's temperaments also had a significant, though slightly smaller, direct effect on aggression; of greater significance, however, was the *indirect* effect that early temperament had on aggression. According to Olweus, an impetuous and active boy may tire his mother, causing her to become more permissive, which then leads to increased aggression in the child. Similarly, the punitive and hostile responses of many parents of aggressive children may stem, in part, from the antisocial behavior of their children, particularly in parents who lack coping skills (Patterson, 1986). This is exactly the type of relationship one would expect to find following the transactional model of development (see Chapter 1). Characteristics of the children interact with characteristics of the parents to produce a pattern of development that cannot be explained by looking solely at the child or at the environment, but only by looking at their ongoing transaction.

The influence of television   Perhaps the most prevalent concern about television, from researchers and parents alike, has been the relationship between TV violence and children's aggression. Violence was the main focus of the Surgeon General's Scientific Advisory Committee on Television and Social Behavior appointed in the late 1960s, and private organizations, such as the National Coalition on Television Violence, continue to monitor TV violence and advocate action by government officials, broadcasters, and viewers to reduce the amount of aggression shown on television.

The research questions are basic ones. Will children who watch aggression on TV become more aggressive themselves? Does a constant diet of TV violence desensitize children to real pain and suffering? Or does viewing violence on television have a cathartic, or cleansing, effect, making children *less* likely to aggress in real life? Are the effects of watching aggressive television the same for all children, or are some more susceptible than others?

The results of over 30 years of research are relatively straightforward and can be summarized as follows:

1. *Children can and do learn aggressive behavior from watching it on television.* Children who watch aggressive TV tend to be *more* aggressive (not less) immediately afterward than children who do not watch such programming. For example, in laboratory studies in which preschoolers watched as people displayed novel aggressive behaviors (for instance, kicking and punching an adult-size inflated plastic clown), children imitated the behaviors when given an opportunity (Bandura, Ross, & Ross, 1963; Bandura & Walters, 1963).
2. *Children who watch more aggressive television at home are, on average, more aggressive than children who watch less aggressive television at home* (Hearold, 1986). Moreover, the amount of aggressive television children watch predicts their level of aggression as adults (Huesmann, 1986; Huesmann, Eron, Lefkowitz, & Walder, 1984; Lefkowitz, Eron, Walder, & Huesmann, 1972; Singer & Singer, 1981). For example, in the study by Monroe Lefkowitz and his colleagues (1972), the amount of aggressive TV boys watched in the third grade predicted the amount of aggressive behavior they displayed at age 19. Even more dra-

matic is the follow-up to this study done when the subjects were age 30 (Huesmann, 1986; Huesmann et al., 1984). As can be seen in Figure 14.6, the amount of aggressive TV boys watched at 8 years of age clearly predicted criminal behavior at 30, with children who watched more hours of aggressive television being involved in more serious crimes. These findings led L. Rowell Huesmann (1986) to conclude that "if a child's observation of media violence promotes learning of aggressive habits, it can have harmful lifelong consequences. Consistent with this theory, early television habits are in fact correlated with criminality" (pp. 129–130).

3. *The effects of aggressive television on children are not uniform.* Viewing filmed aggression results in an increase in aggressive behavior only for some children—primarily those who are more aggressive than average to begin with. In a study by Lynette Friedrich and Aletha Stein (1973), previously discussed in Chapter 2, preschool chil-

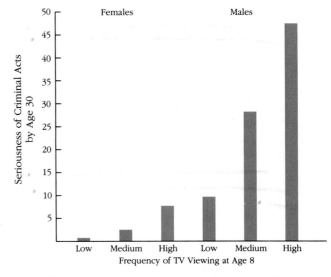

Figure 14.6 Relation between frequency of TV viewing at age 8 and seriousness of criminal convictions at age 30. *Source:* From "Psychological Processes Promoting the Relation between Exposure to Media Violence and Aggressive Behavior by the Viewer," by L. R. Huesmann, *Journal of Social Issues,* 1986, *42,* 125–139. Copyright © 1986 by Plenum Publishing Corporation. Reprinted by permission.

dren who were shown aggressive TV shows (such as "Batman" and "Superman") became more aggressive in the classroom. But the increase in aggression was found only for those children who were rated high in aggression before watching the shows; viewing aggressive TV shows had no noticeable effect on children initially rated low in aggression. Similar findings were reported by Ross Parke and his colleagues (Parke, Berkowitz, Leyens, West, & Sebastian, 1977) for groups of male adolescent delinquents living in minimum security institutions. Boys who viewed aggressive films showed more general and verbal aggression than did those who viewed neutral films; but, again, the effects were most pronounced for those boys who were initially high in aggression (see Figure 14.7).

What can we conclude, then, about the effect of television violence on children's behavior? First,

most researchers would agree there is a causal relationship: aggressive film viewing produces aggressive behavior in children. However, most would also agree that this effect is limited: aggressive television has its greatest influence on children who are highly aggressive to begin with. And even those who believe that aggressive television is generally harmful to children will acknowledge that television is only *one* of the many causes of aggression and not the only one.

Modifying Aggressive Behavior

Highly aggressive children are unpopular, disruptive to schools, families, and other children, and more prone to commit crimes when they become teenagers and adults. Not surprisingly, many programs have been designed to reduce the aggressiveness of children. G. R. Patterson and his colleagues, for example, reported significant, long-lasting reductions in aggressive and antisocial behavior as a result of teaching family-management techniques to the parents of aggressive children (Patterson, 1980; Patterson, Reid, Jones, & Conger, 1975). Parents were trained to use social and nonsocial reinforcers to strengthen prosocial behaviors and to use nonphysical types of punishment (such as loss of privileges), and were also given training in family communication skills.

Other intervention programs have concentrated on providing aggressive children with better social cognitive skills in an attempt to reduce their antisocial behavior (Guerra & Slaby, 1990). Aggressive children have been shown to be deficient in social information-processing skills: they are quicker to attribute hostile motivations to others, they generate fewer appropriate responses to social situations, they evaluate aggressive outcomes more favorably, and they have fewer skills for enacting cooperative or prosocial behaviors than do less aggressive children (Dodge et al., 1986; Slaby & Guerra, 1988; Perry et al., 1990). After demonstrating many of these information-processing deficiencies in a group of male and female incarcerated adolescents (Slaby & Guerra, 1988), Nancy Guerra and Ronald Slaby (1990) developed an intervention program designed to improve the poor social cognitive abilities of these teenagers. Adolescents in the cognitive mediation training group received instruction in (1) attending to relevant and nonhostile social cues,

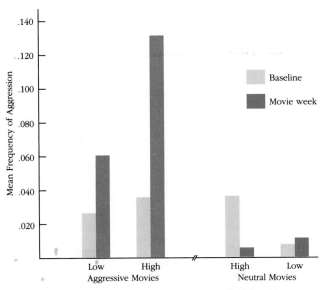

Figure 14.7 Physical aggression as a result of watching aggressive or neutral movies for initially high- and low-aggressive boys. *Source:* Adapted from "Some Effects of Violent and Nonviolent Movies on the Behavior of Juvenile Delinquents," by R. D. Parke, L. Berkowitz, J. P. Leyens, S. G. West, and R. J. Sebastian, *Advances in Experimental Social Psychology,* Vol. 10. Copyright © 1977 by Academic Press. Reprinted by permission.

(2) seeking additional information, (3) generating a variety of responses and consequences, (4) generating priorities for potential responses in terms of their effectiveness in achieving goals in nonviolent ways, (5) giving full consideration to the implications of aggression for themselves and others, and (6) impulse control. Compared to a control group, the adolescents who received the 12-session program showed significant improvements in social problem-solving skills, a decrease in endorsements of beliefs supporting aggression, and a decrease in aggressive, impulsive, and inflexible behaviors as reported by correctional facility staff. A follow-up of some of the adolescents 24 months after release showed that teenagers in the cognitive mediation program had an average parole-violation rate of 34%, compared to a rate of 44% for children in control groups. This difference, though in the desired direction, was not statistically significant. Although cognitive intervention can change adolescent offenders' aggressive beliefs and behavior in the short term, Guerra and Slaby concluded that long-term changes are more problematic: "To the extent that an offender's postrelease environment may lack the social support for maintaining the new pattern of cognitive mediation, the offender may be expected eventually to revert to his or her old patterns of cognitive mediation and social behavior" (1990, p. 276).

State of the Art
Bullies and Their Victims

The schoolyard bully has had a rather colorful image in Anglo-American folklore, probably dating back to Georgie Porgie who harassed his female class-mates until the other boys showed up to chase him away.

Children who are bullies may be viewed by their parents with some pride as being able to "stand up for themselves" and "not let anyone push them around." Children who are victims are often ashamed and afraid to tell their parents. Adults in charge hesitate to intervene when bullies pick on their victims, thinking it's just a stage kids go through or believing their intervention would do more harm than good. And in the absence of adult intervention, the other kids on the playground usually have little sympathy for their hapless playmate, thinking the victim must have done something to deserve his or her plight (Besag, 1989; Olweus, 1987).

Researchers in child development are taking a closer look at schoolyard violence and finding that it is far more serious than previously believed. Serious examination of schoolyard bullying began in Norway in 1982 with the suicides of three 10- to 14-year-old boys, each of whom had been severely bullied by his peers (Olweus, 1987). The Norwegian Ministry of Education established a nationwide campaign against bullying and urged serious study of bully/victim problems. Research and intervention into schoolyard bullying quickly spread to Sweden, and later to Great Britain and Japan (Besag, 1989). Much less research has been done in North America—though this is not because bullying is absent here. In 1987, the National School Safety Center sponsored the Schoolyard Bully Practicum, bringing together for the first time researchers from the fields of psychology, education, law enforcement, and public relations. Their conclusions make it clear that bullying is a serious problem in American schools (Stephens, 1987).

Who Are the Bullies and the Victims?

How prevalent is bullying in schools, and who is involved? Research from Scandinavia indicates that in grades 1 through 9, about 9% of children are chronic victims and about 7% can be labeled as bullies (Olweus, 1978). Research in the United States indicates that about 10% of school-age children can be classified as extremely victimized (Perry, Kusel, & Perry, 1988). Dan Olweus (1978, 1980, 1987), a researcher from the University of Bergen in Norway who has been studying bullying since the early 1970s, states that a "person is being bullied when he or she is exposed, repeatedly and over time, to negative actions on the part of one or more persons" (1987, p. 4). Negative actions include attempts to inflict injury, but also nonphysical aggression, such as verbal abuse.

Our earlier description of highly aggressive children basically describes bullies: they may be active or hot-tempered in disposition, their mothers are often negative and permissive, and both parents may use physical punishment as a means of discipline

When bullies are allowed to victimize their classmates, children learn that violence is acceptable.

(Olweus, 1980). In sharp contrast to the folklore view of the bully as a misunderstood and sensitive fellow under a "tough guy" veneer, bullies, for the most part, are insensitive to their victims, have normal self-esteem, and take a relatively positive view of themselves and their violent ways (Besag, 1989; Olweus, 1987). In a study assessing how aggressive and nonaggressive third- through sixth-grade children view the outcomes of aggression, aggressive children placed a higher value on achieving control of a victim and a lower value on victim suffering. Moreover, they did not fear retaliation from the victim, did not worry about their peers' thinking less of them for acting aggressively, and did not think less of themselves for acting aggressively (Boldizar, Perry, & Perry, 1989). The characteristics of bullies have been summarized by Valerie Besag (1989):

1. Aggressive to parents, teachers, peers, siblings; impulsive

2. Positive attitude to aggression and aggressive means, little anxiety; not a tough surface hiding a deeper anxiety

3. No guilt, shame or embarrassment, little empathy with the victims

4. Strong, tough, powerful, well-coordinated, dominant, confident; peers perhaps confuse this with leadership skills

5. Good communicator, quick-witted, fast verbal responses, able to talk way out of trouble

6. A sense of fun, more popular than victim, popularity decreases with age

7. Bullying may be only one component of a general pattern of antisocial and rule-breaking behavior, a predictor of later antisocial and criminal behavior in adulthood

8. Girls: an exaggerated loudness, shouting, rudeness to staff, domineering to staff and peers [p. 18]

Bullies do not pick on everyone equally. One widely held belief is that victims are often children with "external deviations"; that is, they stand out in a group because of their size (overly fat or thin), speech (stuttering or an unusual dialect), dress, or other nonnormative features. This seems not to be the case, however. Olweus (1978) reports that children with external deviations are no more apt to be victims of bullying than are control ("normal") children. One physical distinction between victims and bullies, however, is strength: victims, especially boys, are physically weaker than children in general, whereas bullies are generally stronger than average.

Although most victims don't differ from normal children in appearance (other than in strength), victims do differ psychologically. The typical characteristics of victims—Olweus (1978) calls them *passive victims* [italics added]—have also been summarized by Besag (1989):

1. Anxious, insecure, cautious, sensitive, quiet, submissive

2. Reacts to attack by crying, yelling, withdrawal, helpless anger, ineffective retaliation, temper outbursts

3. Negative view of self and the situation

4. Feels a failure, stupid, ashamed, unattractive, lonely and abandoned, no single close friend or supporter in the school, not provocative, bewil-

dered and confused, unable to understand why bullied and how to find ways to become accepted

5. Poor communicator, unable to talk way out of trouble

6. Secondary nervous habits, e.g. stammering, biting nails or rocking

7. Physically weaker, poor coordination, frequently younger than the attacker, small stature [p. 18]

Source: Adapted from *Bullies and Victims in Schools,* by V. E. Besag. Copyright © 1989 by Open University Press. Reprinted by permission.

This description of victims as anxious and insecure, shy and quiet, and often friendless, fits our earlier description of rejected children, and rejected children are frequently the targets of bullies (Perry et al., 1988). When attacked by other children, they frequently cry (at least in the lower grades) and withdraw. Victims often think of themselves as failures, feeling ashamed and stupid. In other words, children who are routinely victimized spend their childhoods with anxiety, insecurity, and low self-esteem.

The behavior and negative self-concept of these children seems to signal to other children that they are easy targets for aggression. In a recent study, school-age children were asked how they would feel about aggressing toward victimized versus nonvictimized classmates (Perry, Willard, & Perry, 1990). When children imagined aggressing against a victimized classmate, they said they expected that these children would show signs of suffering and would not be likely to fight back. They also said they could expect some tangible rewards for aggressing against a victimized classmate, and they were less disturbed by the thought of hurting a victimized classmate than a nonvictimized one.

Not all victims fit this general description. Olweus (1978) described some children (about 20% of all victims) as *provocative victims*. Unlike their passive counterparts, these children often provoke the attacks on themselves. They are restless, hot-tempered children whose teasing of other children invites fights. These provocative victims fight back, but usually ineffectively. David Perry and his associates (1988) reported that nearly half their sample of victims were rated as highly aggressive, making them analogous to Olweus's provocative victims. Moreover, these aggressive victims were the most rejected members of the peer group. The many differences between Olweus's and Perry's samples and methodologies make it impossible to state definitively what proportion of victims are the passive or the provocative type. Clearly, victims are not a homogeneous group, although most seem to be rejected. The question of which comes first, rejection or aggression, cannot be answered at this time, although there is evidence that, at least in some cases, being the victim of aggression leads to rejection (Dodge, 1983; Coie & Kupersmidt, 1983).

Stopping Schoolyard Bullying

For some children, attending school is a frightening affair. They are constantly anxious, fearing for their safety and possessions, ashamed of themselves for their victimization, with no one to turn to for help. The school system often makes it easy for bullies to operate, for teachers rarely think that stopping bullies is part of their job. In Scandinavia, before government programs brought attention to the problem, most victimized children reported that teachers rarely if ever tried to put a stop to bullying. Parents, too, are often not informed (or not concerned) about the bullying that goes on in school, and only occasionally talk to their bullying or bullied children about the problem (Olweus, 1987).

Norwegian schools have now instituted programs to bring the issue of schoolyard bullying to the attention of teachers, parents, and schoolchildren and to stamp out schoolyard violence. The program, based on the fundamental right of all children to safety and security at school, requires adults to take a hard-line approach to schoolyard aggression. Its specific goals are (Olweus, 1987):

1. To increase awareness of the problem of bullying and knowledge about it.

2. To achieve active involvement of parents and teachers. This means that adults must realize that bullying is not just "a kid's problem," but a responsibility of adults.

3. To develop clear rules against bullying. Teachers make clear to their students that aggressive behavior at school is not acceptable and will not be tolerated. Students are encouraged to report aggression and threats, and those incidents are dealt with seriously.

4. To provide support and protection for the victims.

Although the findings are still preliminary, after two years, the intervention program has resulted in a 50% decline in bully/victim violence.

In a class where aggression is tolerated, all children lose—bullies, victims, and bystanders, all of whom are taught that violence is acceptable.

Summary

Infants have peer relations only in the loosest sense, and toddlers' peer relations fall short of what most of us think of as friendship. Peer interaction of all types increases over the preschool years. Preschoolers engage in rough-and-tumble play; much of the time, they exhibit parallel as opposed to cooperative play. The preference for same-sex playmates increases in school-age children, and children's ideas of friendship change over time.

Based on peer ratings of popularity and social impact, children can be classified into four groups: popular, amiable, rejected, and isolates (or neglected). High-status children are socially more competent than low-status children, who have poor social information-processing abilities. Children's temperaments and parent characteristics are both related to social status. Research has demonstrated long-term effects of peer rejection, but programs aimed at improving shy or rejected children's social skills have proved successful in some cases.

During the school years, peer groups become increasingly important, and dominance hierarchies are established. Dominance hierarchies serve to reduce antagonisms within a group and to focus division of labor. Children are more apt to conform to group pressure for positive group behavior than for misconduct.

Prosocial behaviors, such as comforting, sharing, and helping, increase with age. Parents can play an important role in fostering prosocial behavior, but the use of rewards seems to reduce prosocial behavior when the rewards are removed.

Aggression is quite common among preschoolers but decreases from the early school years into adolescence. However, the nature of aggressive behavior changes with age. Aggression in children is influenced by parenting style, other children's responses to a child, and the child's temperament. Watching violence on television has been found to increase aggression, but only for children who were highly aggressive to begin with. Programs have been developed to reduce aggressive behavior in children, with varying success.

About 10% of school-age children are victimized by bullies at school, with slightly fewer children being described as bullies. Schoolyard bullying presents a serious problem, and efforts to control it must involve both schools and parents.

Key Terms and Concepts

peer relations
    peer
    reciprocity
    rough-and-tumble play
    parallel play
popularity
social status
social impact
    popular children
    amiable children
    rejected children
    isolates (neglected children)
peer group
    dominance hierarchy
    conformity
prosocial behavior
    comforting
    sharing
    helping
    instrumental rewards
aggression
bullies
victims
    passive victims
    provocative victims

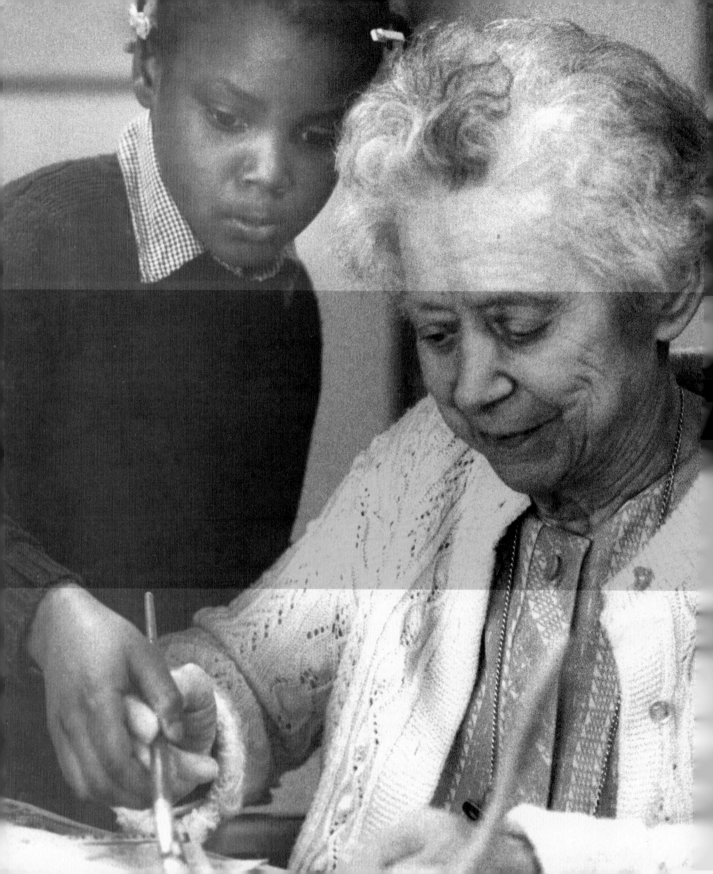

Thinking about the Self and Others

One morning a young mother was doing some housework after her older children had left for school. Her youngest child, 4-year-old Derek, was "helping." She entered her 10-year-old daughter's room and, upon seeing the disorder, sighed aloud and said, "I just don't know what we're going to do about Debbie and this room!" Her young son quickly answered, "Let's just not feed her anymore and maybe she'll go live somewhere else."

The mother was shocked. She had always been a positive, nurturing person and was pleased that her three children had warm, loving relationships with each other and with their parents. Derek had always adored his sister and often watched out the window in the afternoon waiting for her to come home from school. How could he say such a thing? After all, it was only a messy room.

Actually this statement is not so unusual for a child this age; it reflects the moral reasoning typical of 4-year-olds. Their beliefs about good and evil, right and wrong, crime and punishment, are extreme and limited by their ability to understand the consequences of their behavior and the motivations behind the behavior of others. In other words, children's moral reasoning is a function of their cognitive development.

In this chapter, we will focus on how children perceive and act upon their social world. Central to this is the concept of *self*. How do children define who they are as social beings? How does the self develop, and how does it affect other aspects of social behavior? Related to children's sense of self is their knowledge of social roles and their ability to understand the social perspectives of others. Finally, we will examine how children develop a sense of morality and how this development is related to their level of cognitive development. How do children define good and evil? Should moral values be taught in school? And if so, whose moral values should be taught?

The Self

The concept of self is the cornerstone of social development. By **self-concept** we mean an awareness of ourselves as unique, thinking individuals, distinct

"I KNOW WHAT I THINK, BUT WHAT'S IMPORTANT IS WHAT MY MOM THINKS I THINK!"

Knowing that someone else has thoughts and being able to infer those thoughts has important social and intellectual implications. *Source:* DENNIS THE MENACE® used by permission of Hank Ketcham and © by North America Syndicate.

from all other people and objects. Some theorists have speculated that a conscious awareness of one-self greatly influences cognitive development, particularly the use of goal-directed strategies (Bjorklund & Harnishfeger, 1990; Bullock & Lutkenhaus, 1988). Others have stressed the significance of a sense of self for social and emotional development (Brooks-Gunn & Lewis, 1984; Gallup, 1979). Many believe that it is our well-developed sense of self that makes humans unique as a species. In fact, some people have speculated that it was the development of self-awareness that vaulted our hominid ancestors to full human cognition and social organization (Alexander, 1987; Crook, 1980; Gould, 1980). The significance of the concept of self for the developing person and for the species cannot be overstated.

Infants enjoy looking at the baby in the mirror, but only at about 15 months do they begin to recognize it as their own reflection.

The Origins of Self-Concept: Self-Recognition

How can we know if young children have a concept of self? If they are too young to talk, we cannot ask them and must infer self-awareness from their behavior. Jean Piaget (1952), among others, proposed that infants only gradually come to recognize themselves as distinct from the objects around them, with the distinction becoming fully developed sometime around 18 to 24 months of age (see Chapter 7).

Still, the ability to differentiate one's self from the environment is a far cry from what we typically mean by a sense of self. One definition of self that comes closer to our everyday meaning is self-recognition. Children prove that they have a sense of self by recognizing themselves in mirrors. The mirror-recognition technique was developed by Gordon Gallup (1970) while working with chimpanzees, and it has been used by a number of child-development researchers in the past 20 years (Bertenthal & Fischer, 1978; Lewis & Brooks-Gunn, 1979; Lewis, Sullivan, Stanger, & Weiss, 1989). The procedure involves placing a mark on a child's nose or forehead and then seeing the child's reaction to his or her image in the mirror. Children's behavior in the marked condition is then compared to their behavior when there are no marks on their faces or to the behavior of other unmarked children.

Children show the first signs of self-recognition beginning around 15 months by touching the mark on their face rather than touching the mirror (Lewis & Brooks-Gunn, 1979). Not all studies report mark-directed behavior this early (Schulman & Kaplowitz, 1977), but by 18 to 24 months this form of self-recognition is found in about 75% of all children tested. It is also found in the great apes—chimpanzees, orangutans, and gorillas (Gallup, 1979)—but their level of self-awareness does not advance beyond the basic self-recognition shown by 2-year-old children.

The development of a sense of self, as reflected by self-recognition, has important consequences for emotional, social, and cognitive development. Jeanne Brooks-Gunn and Michael Lewis (1984) make this clear: "The acquisition of the self by the end of the second year not only facilitates the acquisition of social knowledge, but underlies social competence, peer relations, gender identity, and empathy" (p. 234). The change from a helpless newborn, who seemingly cannot distinguish where he or she ends and the world begins, to a self-conscious child is a remarkable and important change indeed.

Changes in Self-Concept over Childhood

Mirror recognition is not the only sign of self-awareness that develops late in the second year. In one study, the ability to recognize oneself in a mirror was associated with the tendency to become embarrassed in certain situations, suggesting that both are related to the emergence of a child's concept of self (Lewis et al., 1989). But perhaps the most important indicators of a sense of self can be gleaned from children's use of language. Late in the second year or early in the third, many children begin using the personal pronouns *I, me, my,* and *mine,* thereby indicating a distinction between themselves and others (Lewis & Brooks-Gunn, 1979).

Once children realize they are distinct from other people and objects, how can we determine how they think about themselves? One way of gaining some insight into children's self-concepts is simply to ask them to describe themselves. Preschool children generally describe themselves in terms of physical characteristics ("I'm strong," "I have brown hair," "I have blue eyes"), by their actions ("I run real fast," "I play baseball," "I walk my dog"), where they live, and who's in their family (Keller, Ford, & Meachum, 1978; Livesley & Bromley, 1973; Peevers & Secord, 1973). Rarely do preschool children provide psychological descriptions of themselves (for example, "I'm happy," "I'm smart," "I'm friendly"). This self-definition in terms of physical characteristics is consistent with the Piagetian idea that children's thinking is concrete and tied to specific experiences. This picture does not change substantially over the early school years.

Box 15.1

Erikson's Theory of Psychosocial Development

Erik Erikson (1950, 1968) was a disciple of Freud who postulated a progression of psychosocial development to accompany Freud's theory of psychosexual development (see Chapter 17). Erikson was primarily concerned with how people develop a sense of identity. The answer to the question "Who am I?" depends on which stage of psychosocial development a person is in and how he or she has resolved the conflicts of each previous stage.

Stage 1: Basic trust versus mistrust (birth to 1 year)   Erikson (1968) defined basic trust as "an essential trustfulness of others as well as a fundamental sense of one's own trustworthiness" (p. 96). When infants receive warm maternal care and have their needs met promptly, they come to believe that people are predictable and dependable and that the world is a safe and kind place. When infants are not treated with love and respect and their needs are not met in a timely fashion, mistrust develops. Infants who develop a sense of basic trust during this first year will be better able to face the crises to come than infants who develop mistrust.

Stage 2: Autonomy versus shame and doubt (1 to 3 years)   In the second and third years, children gain increasing mastery over their bodies. They are able to crawl, walk, and climb and have a desire to explore the world around them. However, with these newly developed skills comes conflict. Children may try new skills but fail to achieve their goals. How parents (and other adults who interact with them frequently, such as day-care workers) handle this

Parents who encourage their children's independence and don't ridicule them for their failures are fostering lifelong self-confidence.

time of investigation and independence determines whether children will develop a sense of autonomy or a sense of shame and doubt. When parents recognize children's developing abilities and encourage their independence, they help them develop a

As children approach adolescence, their thinking becomes more abstract, and so does the way they view themselves. Children are now more likely to define themselves in terms of psychological qualities—things they like and personality characteristics. Raymond Montemayor and Marvin Eisen (1977) gave children of different ages a sheet with 20 spaces and asked them to write 20 different answers to the question "Who am I?" Here are some sample responses:

Boy, age 9

My name is Bruce C. I have brown eyes. I have brown hair. I have brown eyebrows. I'm nine years old. I LOVE! Sports. I have seven people in my family. I have great! eye site. I have lots!

sense of mastery over their own bodies and their environment. When parents ridicule children's failures and insist upon doing things for children that they can very well do for themselves, a sense of shame or doubt may develop.

Stage 3: Initiative versus guilt (3 to 6 years)

Children have mastered their bodies to a significant degree and are now ready to initiate motor and social activities. They learn the roles of society through fantasy play, setting goals for themselves and attaining them, and competing with other children.

How parents respond to children's self-initiated activities will determine whether children complete this stage with a sense of initiative or its opposite—a sense of guilt. Children develop ambition and social responsibility when parents support their emerging sense of purpose. Their initiative is reinforced when they are given the freedom to try out new behaviors such as skating, sliding, wrestling, painting, or sculpting. Their intellectual initiative is also reinforced when parents answer children's questions and do not ridicule them for their make-believe play. In contrast, when parents insist on too much self-control and competence, criticize children's attempts at adultlike behavior, make fun of their fantasy play, and treat their questions as a nuisance, a sense of guilt can develop.

Stage 4: Industry versus inferiority (6 years to puberty)

During the early school years, children's intellectual development takes a dramatic leap. Children are now capable of logical thought, and in many ways their thinking is more like that of an adult than a young child. Partly because of their increased cognitive abilities, children are fascinated with how things work and how they are made, from the mechanisms of a clock and a car engine to the changing seasons and a newborn baby. Children who are encouraged to build or make things (birdhouses, cookies, model cars) and who are praised for their accomplishments develop a sense of industry. However, children whose parents see their efforts as imperfect and concentrate on the mess they make rather than the products of their labor may develop a sense of inferiority.

Stage 5: Identity versus identity confusion (12 to 18 years)

Each conflict resolution up to this point has contributed to a child's sense of self—his or her identity. The dramatic changes that occur in adolescence, however, cause children to consider seriously for the first time their eventual adult status. With sexual maturation comes the realization that adult sexual relations and marriage are not too far away. Educational systems are preparing children for occupational roles, and only a handful of adolescents cling to the fantasies that they will become major league baseball players or rock stars. Children's cognitions are changing, and they are now able to think abstractly. They are able to evaluate society and their place in it.

Children's major task during this stage is the integration of various identities brought from childhood into a more complete identity that will provide **(Continued)**

of friends. I live on 1923 Pinecrest Dr. I'm going on 10 in September. I'm a boy. I have a uncle that is almost 7 feet tall. My school is Pinecrest. My teacher is Mrs. V. I play Hockey! I'm almost the smartest boy in the class. I LOVE! food. I love fresh air. I LOVE School.

Girl, age 11½

My name is A. I'm a human being. I'm a girl. I'm a truthful person. I'm not pretty. I do so-so in my studies. I'm a very good cellist. I'm a very good pianist. I'm a little bit tall for my age. I like several boys. I like several girls. I'm old-fashion. I play tennis. I am a *very* good swimmer. I try to be helpful. I'm always ready to be friends with anybody. Mostly I'm good, but I lose my temper. I'm not well-liked by some girls and boys. I don't know if I'm liked by boys or not.

Box 15.1 (Continued)

During middle adulthood one is likely to become concerned for the well-being of the next generation and may serve as a mentor for a young colleague.

continuity with the past and prepare them for the future. Young people get some of their identity from social groups such as church, ethnic background, and school organizations, and through peer groups, including clubs and gangs. This is a period of reorganization. If adolescents cannot come to terms with who they are and who they are to be, the result is identity confusion.

Stage 6: Intimacy versus isolation (young adulthood)   Intimacy is the ability to care about and share with another person without fear of losing one's own identity in the process. In this stage, which covers the period of courtship, marriage, and early family life, intimacy obviously involves sexuality in love relationships, but it also involves close relations among friends. Partners beginning a new business, sorority sisters, or soldiers serving together under dangerous circumstances may experience this sense of intimacy. Failure to establish intimacy can result in isolation—the inability to share life's experiences with anyone.

Stage 7: Generativity versus stagnation (middle adulthood)   Generativity refers to an interest in future generations. During this stage, the individual's interests expand beyond his or her immediate family to include the general well-being of younger colleagues or the future state of society or the world. This is a time in life when a person may serve as a mentor to a younger colleague or devote time to charitable causes. People who do not have a positive view of the future or a belief in humanity may fall into self-absorption or stagnation, stopping psychological growth.

Stage 8: Integrity versus despair (late adulthood)   During the later years, people reflect on their lives and the contributions they have made. When they can look back with satisfaction, they experience a sense of integrity: they see themselves as part of a bigger picture that includes past generations and future generations. Others, who look back and see only missed opportunities and regret for what they have done, experience despair.

Girl, age 17

I am a human being. I am a girl. I am an individual. I don't know who I am. I am a Pisces. I am a moody person. I am an indecisive person. I am an ambitious person. I am a very curious person. I am not an individual. I am a loner. I am an American (God help me). I am a Democrat. I am a liberal person. I am a radical. I am a conservative. I am a pseudoliberal. I am an atheist. I am not a classifiable person (i.e., I don't want to be).

As can be seen, 9- and 10-year-old children used more concrete terms to describe themselves than did 11- and 12-year-olds, who were more concrete than 16- and 17-year-olds.

The Development of Self-Efficacy

As the self develops, children acquire knowledge that influences their thought and behavior. How children think of themselves determines what activities they participate in and how they evaluate their performance. They come to think of themselves as having an effect on people and events in their lives. This sense of **self-efficacy** has been given a central role in Albert Bandura's social cognitive theory.

Self-efficacy develops through experience. By thinking about themselves, "people are able to analyze their own experiences and think about their own thought processes" (Bandura, 1989a, p. 41). Children evaluate the effectiveness of their own actions, compare it to the actions of others, and are told by others how their behavior meets certain stan-

Box 15.2

Young Children's Overestimation of Their Abilities and Perceived Self-Efficacy

As we saw in an earlier chapter, young children frequently overestimate their physical and mental abilities. Preschool children think that they can remember more items, communicate more effectively, and imitate a model more accurately than they actually can (Bjorklund, Gaultney, & Green, 1992; Glucksberg, Krauss, & Weisberg, 1966; Yussen & Levy, 1975). Young children's beliefs that they know more than they actually do and can do more than they actually can provides them with positive perceptions of their own skills. This positive sense of self-efficacy may encourage children to attempt things that they would not try if they had a more realistic idea of their abilities.

This point is made by Deborah Stipek and her colleagues (Stipek, 1984; Stipek & Daniels, 1988), who found that young children can make relatively accurate predictions of how other children are likely to perform on schoollike tasks but are overly optimistic in predicting their own future performance (see also Schneider, 1991). Stipek suggested that this

overoptimistic self-perception is due to "wishful thinking": children *wish* for A's on their report card; therefore, they *expect* A's. By the third or fourth grade, children's assessments of their own abilities move closer to reality, and they are able to tell the difference between what they wish to happen and what they can reasonably expect to happen.

Stipek believes that this tendency to overestimate their own abilities enhances children's self-efficacy and gives them the confidence to attempt things they would not otherwise try. There is some preliminary evidence that brighter 3-year-olds overestimate their abilities (on an imitation task) more than less-bright 3-year-olds, suggesting an adaptive value of overestimation in young children (Bjorklund et al., 1992). Stipek (1984) proposes that rather than trying to make young children's self-assessments more accurate, we should "try harder to design educational environments which maintain their optimism and eagerness."

Parents teach independence by giving children control over such matters as clothing selection.

dards. Children who believe they are competent (even if they are not) develop feelings of positive self-efficacy (see Box 15–2). Conversely, when self-efficacy is poor, people tend to behave ineffectually, regardless of their actual abilities (Bandura, 1982, 1989a). Developing feelings of positive self-efficacy has important consequences for children's social, emotional, and intellectual development.

The development of self-efficacy begins early, as infants learn that they can exert some control over their environment. Beginning around 3 or 4 months, babies learn that their actions have consequences— that if they kick their feet the mobile over the crib will move and if they smile and coo their parents will smile and talk back to them. Infants who have experienced some control over their environment are better able to learn new behaviors (Finkelstein & Ramey, 1977). Mary Ainsworth and her colleagues have proposed that parents' responsiveness to their infants' attempts to communicate their needs, giving the infants some sense of control over their parents, is related to later social and cognitive development (Ainsworth, Blehar, Waters, & Wall, 1978; see also Chapter 12).

With the development of language and other symbols, children are able to reflect upon their new social and intellectual abilities and evaluate what others tell them about their skills. Initially, the family provides children with feedback on their effectiveness. As children approach school age, their peer group becomes a valuable source of information,

and school itself is a potent agent in forming children's self-efficacy. Children learn through daily experience with teachers and peers that they are good at some tasks and not so good at others (Bandura, 1989b).

Carol Dweck and her colleagues (Dweck, 1975, 1986; Dweck & Leggett, 1988; Dweck & Reppucci, 1973) have found in some children a maladaptive pattern of achievement behavior that they describe as *helplessness*. These children avoid challenge, do not persist in the face of difficulty, and tend to attribute their failure on tasks to a lack of ability rather than a lack of effort or an inappropriate strategy. Other children display an adaptive pattern termed *mastery orientation*: they enjoy and seek challenge, persist in the face of obstacles, and tend to view their failings as due to lack of effort or strategy use rather than to a lack of ability. Not surprisingly, mastery-oriented children have a better-developed sense of self-efficacy and are more likely to be successful on a wide range of tasks than children showing the helpless pattern.

With adolescence come new challenges and new opportunities to develop a positive sense of self-efficacy. Adolescents must learn to deal with sexual and romantic relationships as well as becoming independent members of adult society. Adolescence is a time of experimentation as young people learn how to handle difficult situations for which they have little experience. The transition to adulthood, from dependency to independency, is a complicated one, particularly in modern societies where young people must choose among many possible lifestyles

The transition from childhood to adulthood includes mastering new skills and responsibilities.

Box 15.3

Giving Children Control

Most parents would do anything for their children. They work hard to provide a safe and comfortable home and the best in food and medical care. They give their time and love. They are so concerned about doing the right things for their children that they sometimes have a problem recognizing and meeting another important need that children have—the need for control over their own lives.

Giving a child control is a different kind of giving, and it can be a very difficult one for conscientious parents. First, it involves *not* doing things more than doing things. And second, it often involves letting children make mistakes, fail, and suffer—experiences parents want to protect them from. But if parents smooth all the rough edges of life for their children, not only won't they learn how to handle them later when their parents are not around, they won't learn that they *can* handle them—that they are capable, competent, and powerful in their own right. Instead, they will learn the lesson that they can't handle things and, as a result, will stop trying.

This theme has been attributed to Martin E. P. Seligman of the University of Pennsylvania. He believes that if children learn they have an effect on the world, they will tackle problems confidently and rebound from failures with new plans. Children who don't feel they have control may never know the limits of their own talents and abilities and will be reluctant to attempt activities they don't believe they can do.

Although parents have good intentions, it's not always best to make life easy for children. Not everything in life has to be fun. Children should be encouraged to complete tasks that have become frustrating and boring. Parents should stand back when they can and let their children take the consequences of their actions instead of finding ways to remedy situations for them. And parents should teach children to believe in their own abilities. They may not be superheroes, but they are already competent problem solvers whose skills will continue to improve.

Parents need to realize that problem behavior can sometimes reflect a child's need to be in control, especially during stressful times such as moving to a new neighborhood or trying out for the swim team. Children often behave "out of control" because they really are! Giving them some control, even over small details such as their breakfast menu, may improve the situation.

As children's abilities develop, their area of control should expand. Parents' job with school-age children is to define that kingdom and then step back, allowing the child to rule. Sometimes parents can give free reign. For example, they can set aside a section of the closet for school clothes and then let children decide what to wear each day. Or they can allow them to choose what dessert the family will have for a special meal.

Other areas of control can be limited by giving children a multiple-choice option. "Would you like to go out tonight for pizza or fried chicken?" Or "The hedge needs clipping, and the dog needs a bath; you pick one, and I'll do the other." Parents must first make sure they can live with whatever choice the child makes. Then they should go for pizza (or wash the dog) cheerfully.

Some aspects of a child's life are too big for even a multiple-choice option. Decisions such as family vacations, major purchases, and choice of a child's school should be made by the parents. But children can be asked for input on these matters, and parents can let them know that their feelings will be considered.

When children learn to walk, parents move the furniture out of the way and follow close behind to catch them if they topple. Giving control to an older child is similar: you clear the way as much as possible and then hover at a safe distance. You're not abandoning them—only backing away a little.

Source: Adapted from D. F. Bjorklund and B. R. Bjorklund (July 1987). Control. *Parents Magazine,* Vol. 62, No. 7.

and where recognition as an adult is not achieved by means of society-recognized rituals. How successfully that transition is made, states Bandura, depends "on the strength of personal efficacy built up through prior mastery experiences" (1989a, p. 48).

Learning about Others:
Social Perspective Taking

Being social requires interacting with other people, and successful interaction requires understanding other people's perspectives. Piaget proposed that children younger than 7 or 8 years of age are egocentric: they see the world from their own perspective and have a difficult time understanding that other people may have points of view different from their own. According to Piaget, this egocentric attitude permeates children's entire cognitive life, including their understanding of social relations.

Although it is certainly true that young children are more egocentric than older children, it is not an all-or-nothing matter. As we've seen in previous chapters, perspective-taking abilities develop gradually over early childhood. For example, 4-year-olds will modify their speech when talking to a 2-year-old, using a different tone of voice and sentence structure, just as adults do when talking to infants or young children (Shatz & Gelman, 1973). Yet when the tasks get more complex, children's performance deteriorates, reflecting their still egocentric perspective (see Chapter 7). Sometimes the same child will display both egocentric and nonegocentric perspectives in the same behavior.

Selman's Theory of the Development of Role Taking

One neo-Piagetian theory that deals specifically with the development of this ability to take the perspective (or role) of another is that of Robert Selman (1976). Selman presented various dilemmas to children of different ages. For example, one story dealt with a little girl named Holly, who was the best tree climber in the whole neighborhood. Holly's father worried about her safety and made her promise not to climb trees anymore. Later, a friend asked Holly to climb a tree to rescue a kitten that was stuck in the branches. Holly was the only person in the

neighborhood who could climb well enough to save the kitten; yet she had promised her father not to climb trees. After hearing this story, children were asked what Holly should do and why. From children's answers to these and other dilemmas, Selman was able to infer different levels of perspective-taking ability.

Selman proposed five levels of perspective taking in children (see Table 15.1). During the earliest stage, children between the ages of about 3 and 6 know that other people are different from them and that these people have thoughts and feelings; however, they believe that other people's thoughts and feelings are nearly identical to their own. For example, in the story about Holly, a child may say that Holly's dad would be pleased if Holly saved the kitten. Holly sees the importance of it, so surely her father would too. At this stage, children understand the thoughts and emotions of others by projecting their own past experiences onto them. Selman referred to this as stage 0, egocentric role taking.

Stage 1, social-informational role taking, covers children between the ages of about 6 and 8 years. During this stage, children realize that two people can have different perspectives that can lead them to different actions. What motivates one person to one action may not motivate another in the same way. Despite this ability, children have great difficulty keeping both viewpoints in mind at once and are apt to focus on one perspective at the expense of another. For example, in the story about Holly, children may concentrate on her promise to her father or on the importance of saving the kitten. They have the capability to notice the conflict, but it is not obvious to them. Children at this stage begin to think of the intention behind actions and realize that other people also take intent into consideration when behaving or when evaluating someone else's behavior.

In stage 2, self-reflective role taking, children between the ages of about 8 and 10 begin to realize that other people can evaluate *their* actions. They understand that their own perspective is not the only valid one and can begin to evaluate themselves in terms of how others view them. However, children of this age cannot coordinate their own and another's perspective simultaneously. For example, a child in stage 2 may know her own desires (wanting to rescue the kitten) and her father's (wanting to keep his daughter safe) but be unable to coordinate the two to yield a successful compromise.

Table 15.1 Selman's stages of role taking

Stage	Approximate Age	Description
0. Egocentric role taking	3 to 6 years	Children cannot take the perspective of others; can understand their own feelings, but not that others may interpret social actions differently.
1. Social informational role taking	6 to 8 years	Children understand that people can have different views of events and different motivations, but have difficulty keeping both perspectives in mind simultaneously.
2. Self-reflective role taking	8 to 10 years	Children realize that other people evaluate their actions and that others may have legitimate views; can reflect on their own thoughts from another perspective, but cannot reflect on their own perspective and that of another person at the same time.
3. Mutual role taking	10 to 12 years	Children can take two points of view at the same time and realize that other people can do the same.
4. Social and conventional system role taking	12 to 15 years	Adolescents can take a detached view of a relationship and see it from the perspective of a third party; can interpret their behavior and that of others from a societal perspective.

Source: From "Social-Cognitive Understanding: A Guide to Educational and Clinical Practice," by R. L. Selman. In T. Lockona (ed.), *Moral Development and Behavior.* Copyright © 1976 by Holt, Rinehart and Winston. Reprinted by permission of the author.

In stage 3, mutual role taking, 10- to 12-year-olds are able to take two points of view simultaneously. They also realize that other people can take their perspective. In the story about Holly, a stage 3 child would realize that Holly's father might not agree with Holly about her climbing the tree to rescue the kitten; however, they believe that Holly's father would be able to understand why she did what she did. Her motives could be expressed and understood by her father.

In the final stage, social and conventional system role taking, adolescents are able to take a detached view of a relationship and see it from the perspective of a third person. This third person could be a peer, a parent or teacher, or society. Adolescents begin to compare their own views with those of society at large and realize that the social system in which they operate is a product of the shared views of its members.

Selman's theory has generally received support from the research literature (Gove & Keating, 1979; Selman & Byrne, 1974; Selman, Schorin, Stone, & Phelps, 1983). Children's perspective-taking ability improves gradually with age, and children progress through these stages in order (Selman, 1980). The percentage of children between 4 and 10 years of age found to have reached each of Selman's first four

role-taking stages is shown in Table 15.2. As children's perspective-taking skills improve, so too does their ability to interact successfully with others and to take a broader view of the world.

Social Interaction and Role Taking

Obviously, many of the changes that occur in children's role taking are the result of maturation and general experience; one cannot expect a 3-year-old, no matter how socially experienced, to have the role-taking abilities of a 12-year-old. However, as children become less egocentric with age, they do

Table 15.2 Percentage of children achieving a given level of role-taking ability in Selman's theory

Stage	Age 4	Age 6	Age 8	Age 10
0	80%	10%	0%	0%
1	20	90	40	20
2	0	0	50	60
3	0	0	10	20

Source: From "A Structural-Developmental Analysis of Levels of Role Taking in Middle Childhood," by R. L. Selman and D. F. Byrne, *Child Development,* 1974, *45,* 803–806. Copyright © The Society for Research in Child Development, Inc. Reprinted by permission.

not automatically become socially astute. Although a less egocentric attitude may be necessary for improved role-taking abilities, it is not sufficient (Shantz, 1983).

Children's social experiences are also important in the development of role-taking abilities. Playing with others enables children to become increasingly aware of the different perspectives of playmates (Piaget, 1965b). Conflicts arise during play, and when there is no ultimate authority (such as a parent or teacher) to resolve them, children must learn to settle conflicts themselves. This often involves compromise, which requires appreciating the other child's point of view. Piaget emphasized the importance of equal status among peers in resolving conflict: when two children have equal status and abilities, resolution cannot be easily attained by force or deference to the "socially superior" individual; some agreement among equals must be achieved. It is under these conditions that role-taking skills are most likely to develop.

Thus, although cognitive factors such as degree of egocentricity underlie children's social role-taking abilities, these skills develop most readily in social situations, reflecting the complex and continuous interaction between social and cognitive factors in development.

The Development of Empathy

Empathy is a special case of perspective taking: the ability to experience the emotions of others. Martin Hoffman (1981) has proposed that feelings of empathy (or empathic arousal) in children serve as the basis for later prosocial behavior. Children first learn to recognize that distress in someone else is the cause of their own ill feelings and then learn to feel better by doing something to relieve the other person's discomfort.

Hoffman has postulated four levels in the development of empathy. The first level, from birth to about 1 year, he calls global empathy: infants experience distress merely by witnessing distress in others; they cannot distinguish the distress others experience from the distress they feel. At the second level, egocentric empathy, toddlers 1 to 2 years old realize that others experience distress independent of their own feelings; however, they do not understand the internal state of others and assume it is the

Teenagers can understand the emotions of people in situations far different from their own.

same as their own. Thus, for example, a child will give his crying mother his teddy bear because it comforts him when he is sad. Level 3, empathy for another's feelings, characterizes children from about 2 to 11 years of age. These children are aware of other people's feelings and realize that other people have different needs, experiences, and interpretations than they do. Empathic responses improve as children's role-taking abilities increase and as they learn more about emotions. Finally, at around 11 years, children achieve level 4, empathy for another's life condition. Children can now express empathy for a person's larger life experience, not just specific situations, and can begin to feel empathic for groups of people (minorities, victims of child abuse, children in the Third World).

There is some evidence that empathic responses are present early in infancy. In one study (Sagi & Hoffman, 1976), infants less than 3 days old were exposed to the cries of another baby, an artificial simulation of an infant's cry, or nothing. Infants who heard the real baby crying soon began to cry themselves and to show other signs of distress such as grimacing and kicking (see also Martin & Clark, 1982). Such responding, proposes Hoffman (1981, 1989), reflects a specific empathy in newborns to the cries of human infants; other equally loud sounds, even simulated cries, do not have the same effect.

Young children's empathic reactions to other people's emotions develop gradually over infancy and childhood. During the first year, infants may not even be aware that the distress they are feeling is empathic; rather, they feel as if they are personally experiencing the trauma. For example, a 1-year-old will put her thumb in her mouth, whimper, and bury her head in her mother's lap upon seeing another child fall and cry; she responds to the other child's distress as if the event had happened to her. This reaction decreases substantially during the second year (Thompson, 1987).

Moral Development

When do children know right from wrong? When can they be held accountable for their actions? When and how do children acquire the moral standards of their family and community? These are important questions, because any community, be it a small tribe in the Amazon rain forest or a nation the size of China, has a moral code by which it functions, and the success of that community depends on its children to continue that code. Thus, children's moral development becomes an issue of interest not just to parents or developmental psychologists, but to society as a whole.

The study of moral development is complicated for several reasons. What exactly is moral behavior? Is stealing always bad? Is honesty always the best policy? Is there never a situation in which killing another person is morally right? Do intentions count? Is breaking a cup when helping Mom with the dishes the same as breaking a cup while reaching for a forbidden cookie? Are teenagers moral if they refuse to shoplift for fear of getting caught, or only if they refuse to shoplift because they earnestly believe it is wrong?

Some of these problems have been bypassed by studying children's *moral reasoning*—how children at different ages make decisions about moral issues. The primary method of doing research on children's moral reasoning has been to see how they respond to moral dilemmas—stories in which children must make a decision about the appropriateness or morality of some action. Jean Piaget (1965b, originally published in 1932) was the first to investigate moral reasoning in detail; his work has been extended by Lawrence Kohlberg (1969, 1984).

Piaget's Theory of Moral Reasoning

A little boy who is called John is in his room. He is called to dinner. He goes into the dining room. But behind the door there is a chair, and on the chair there was a tray with fifteen cups on it. John couldn't have known that there was all this behind the door. He goes in, the door knocks against the tray, bang go the fifteen cups and they all get broken!

Once there was a little boy whose name was Henry. One day when his mother was out he tried to get some jam out of the cupboard. He climbed up in to a chair and stretched out his arm. But the jam was too high up and he couldn't reach it and have any. But while he was trying to get it he knocked over a cup. The cup fell down and broke.

Piaget (1965b, p. 122) gave these and other stories to children of different ages and asked them who was naughtier—John, who broke 15 cups by accident, or Henry, who broke one cup while sneaking some jam from the cupboard. Not surprisingly, children about 10 years and older said that Henry was naughtier. After all, the only reason the cup broke was that he was doing something he wasn't supposed to be doing. John, on the other hand, was a victim of circumstances. He was doing exactly what his mother told him, and he couldn't have known that the tray of cups was behind the door. But ask a younger child, and the answer is often very different. John is naughtier than Henry because he broke 15 cups and Henry broke only one. Yes, they admit, John didn't know the cups were behind the door, and yes, Henry was doing something that he wasn't supposed to be doing. But these children cannot decenter themselves from the magnitude of the crimes. Fifteen cups are smashed to smithereens because of John's actions. Intention means little to young children; the greater the damage, the naughtier the behavior.

Based on this research, Piaget proposed three basic stages of moral reasoning: the premoral stage (approximate ages, 2 to 5 years), the stage of moral realism (approximate ages, 6 to 10 years), and the stage of moral relativism (approximately 10 to 12 years and beyond).

During the **premoral stage,** children are generally unaware of rules as being cooperative agreements. When playing games, they make up their own rules and think that the point of the game is to play and not necessarily to win. For example, when 5-year-old Mark watched the older children in the family play Monopoly, he thought the aim of the game was to move the pieces around the board and give money and hotels to everyone. Although he could count the spots on the dice and move accordingly, he didn't know the rest of the rules and didn't seem to care when the others tried to teach him.

The stage of **moral realism** begins at about age 5 or 6. Children now understand that there are rules families and societies must live by. To these children, the rules—whether for games of marbles (a favorite topic for Piaget), traffic laws, or classroom behavior—are absolute, passed on by some high authority figure, and *all* violations of them are wrong. Piaget referred to this way of thinking as **moral absolutism.** Speeding, for example, is wrong in all circumstances, even on a trip to the emergency room. As in the story of John and Henry, motivation is not considered. Although these children seem to grasp the idea of doing something "on purpose" versus "by accident," they don't consider intentionality when evaluating right or wrong. Children in this stage also believe in **imminent justice:** good deeds will be rewarded, and misdeeds will be punished. Thus, if something bad happens to a person, that person presumably deserved it. (Many adults in both traditional and technological cultures hang on to this belief.)

In the stage of **moral relativism,** beginning about age 10 or 11, children come to realize that social rules are arbitrary agreements among people that can be modified through social discussion. The

Ten- and eleven-year-olds realize that rules are not 'set in stone,' but can be changed by mutual agreement.

Monopoly rules can be changed if everyone agrees to play by "house rules." Societal laws can be challenged and even modified or overthrown. For children in this stage, rule breakers are not judged solely by their behavior, but also by their motivations. The person who is racing down the road to get his daughter to the emergency room is no longer considered a wrongdoer.

Piaget's theory has been very influential in directing research on children's moral reasoning, and much of it confirms his ideas. However, as with other aspects of Piaget's theory (see Chapter 7), young children are often more competent than Piaget believed them to be. For example, more recent research has shown that children in Piaget's moral realism stage, and even his premoral stage, often do consider intention when judging an action (Nelson-LeGall, 1985; Shultz, Wright, & Schleifer, 1986). And young children don't always view adults—even their parents—as absolute authority figures (Tisak, 1986). Yet Piaget was the first to describe children's

"I'M SORRY I DID IT, AN' I'M REALLY SORRY I GOT CAUGHT!"

Young children judge the goodness or badness of an action by its consequences to them.
Source: DENNIS THE MENACE® used by permission of Hank Ketcham and © by North America Syndicate.

moral reasoning in terms of stages, and this approach was adopted by Lawrence Kohlberg, whose theory of moral development has dominated research in the field for the past 20 years.

Kohlberg's Theory of Moral Development

Kohlberg (1969, 1984) continued Piaget's method of presenting children with moral dilemmas, such as the following:

> In Europe, a woman was near death from cancer. One drug might save her, a form of radium that a druggist in the same town recently discovered. The druggist was charging $2,000, ten times what the drug cost him to make. The sick woman's husband, Heinz, went to everyone he knew to borrow the money, but he could get together only about half of what it cost. He told the druggist that his wife was dying and asked him to sell the drug cheaper or let him pay later. But the druggist said no. The husband got desperate and broke into the man's store to steal the drug for his wife. Should the husband have done that? Why? (Kohlberg, 1969, p. 379)

Kohlberg was not concerned with whether children viewed the action as right or wrong; rather, he was interested in how they reasoned about the action, and the thinking behind their reasoning. Kohlberg developed a theory that sees moral reasoning as progressing through three levels, each containing two stages. It is not a stage theory in the strictest sense because, although people progress from lower to higher stages as a function of cognitive development, once they attain the ability to reason at a higher level they do not always function at that level. Kohlberg's stages of moral reasoning are summarized in Table 15.3.

Preconventional morality Children at the level of **preconventional morality** conform to rules in order to gain rewards and avoid punishment. Moral reasoning is not internalized: "good" actions are those that are rewarded, and "bad" actions are those that are punished. In stage 1, beginning usually during the late preschool years, getting caught doing a misdeed is wrong—not the deed itself. Children at this stage think much like the moral realists of Piaget's theory: the amount of punishment a person receives should be proportional to the amount of harm done; motivation or intention is not important, only the magnitude of the "crime." In the case of Heinz and the drug, a stage 1 child is likely to say that Heinz should not steal the drug because he would be breaking the law and would get caught. The drug is very expensive, making its theft a serious crime.

During stage 2, children act in ways that will satisfy their personal needs; what is good is what brings good things to them. This is the morality of the marketplace: "You scratch my back and I'll scratch yours." Good deeds will likely pay off in the future, and this prospect of rewards justifies following rules or helping other people. During this stage, children

Table 15.3 Kohlberg's stages of moral development

Level/Stage	Description
Level 1 Preconventional morality	Obey rules to get rewards and avoid punishment; no internalized rules or standards, only consequences of one's actions
Stage 1 Orientation toward punishment and unquestioning deference to superior power	Obey rules to avoid punishment; morality defined only by physical consequences
Stage 2 Naive hedonism	Do good deeds for the rewards they bring, immediate or future; fairness, reciprocity, sharing strictly pragmatic
Level 2 Conventional morality	Defer to rules imposed by legitimate authority (parental, religious, legal)
Stage 3 Good-boy/good-girl orientation	Behave to help or please others, win their approval; intention is important; golden rule
Stage 4 Orientation toward authority, fixed rules, and maintenance of the social order	Do one's duty, respect authority, maintain the existing social order; law-and-order stage
Level 3 Postconventional morality	Follow personal, internalized moral principles
Stage 5 Social-contract orientation	Rules and laws must be democratic, based on generally agreed-upon rights, open to challenge and change, morality underlying U.S. Constitution
Stage 6 Morality of individual principles and conscience	Ethical principles are self-chosen, abstract, universal

take the intention of the actor into consideration when judging how right or wrong an action is. Looking again at the story of Heinz, a stage 2 child may say that he shouldn't have stolen the drug because the druggist just wants to make money like everybody else.

Conventional morality   At the second level, **conventional morality,** children (or adults) try to conform to rules imposed by some legitimate authority,

Kohlberg's stage of conventional morality involves obeying rules set by a legitimate authority.

such as parents, school officials, or the legal system. In stage 3, following a parent's wishes or the teacher's rules wins the child approval from these authorities. A stage 3 person strives to be viewed as "nice," seeking approval from significant people in his or her life (including peers). Stage 3 morality is expressed by the golden rule from the Jewish and Christian traditions: do unto others as you would have them do unto you. A stage 3 reason for Heinz's stealing the drug might be that a loving husband can't be blamed for trying to save his wife; in fact, he might be blamed if he didn't try to save her.

In stage 4, people conform to rules and conventions to maintain social order. Social rules, such as "Thou shalt not steal" or "Buckle up for safety," are seen as dictated by legitimate authorities and worth preserving. A stage 4 antitheft argument would hold that one must follow the law, regardless of circumstances.

Postconventional morality It is only at the third level, **postconventional morality,** that individuals develop a set of principles that go beyond any external authority figure. This level is never seen prior to adolescence and rarely used in adulthood. Postconventional morality reflects the internalization of a personal set of moral values. In stage 5, rules must be arrived at through a democratic process, and laws that are restrictive to members of society can be questioned and changed. This stage of moral reasoning is reflected in the United States Constitution. A stage 5 reason for Heinz to steal the drug would be based on the recognition that this is a special condition—that although it is against the law to steal, most people would recognize the uniqueness of the situation and believe that Heinz is justified in stealing the drug.

In stage 6, an individual defines right and wrong on the basis of self-chosen moral principles that are abstract and can be applied universally (for example, universal justice, individual rights). A stage 6 reason for stealing the drug would be that human life is above any law.

Kohlberg's theory is a considerable extension over Piaget's. Piaget's final stage, moral relativism, is achieved by most children around 10 to 12 years of age, implying that an adult's moral reasoning is no more sophisticated than that of a 12-year-old. Kohl-

berg's theory addresses in more detail the moral reasoning of adolescents and adults. According to Kohlberg, most adolescent moral reasoning is at a stage 3 level, and reasoning at stages 5 and 6 is virtually nonexistent until early adulthood, if at all (Colby, Kohlberg, Gibbs, & Lieberman, 1983).

Cultural and sex differences in moral reasoning Who achieves these higher, postconventional levels of moral reasoning as defined by Kohlberg? As it turns out, stages 5 and 6 are typically reached only by educated people in technological societies. In fact, there is a substantial relationship between adults' level of moral reasoning and years of formal education (Colby et al., 1983; Rest & Thoma, 1985). People from small, traditional communities rarely achieve moral reasoning beyond stage 3 (Kohlberg, 1969). What this suggests is that the social and political values of Western civilization play a significant role in determining one's adult level of moral reasoning. Kohlberg proposed that the thinking skills of people from nontechnological societies are limited to concrete operational abilities, and that postconventional reasoning depends upon the formal operations that are achieved through formal education in technological societies. (For a discussion of cultural differences in thinking, see Chapter 11.) Other interpretations are possible, however. For example, the small, tight-knit social groups typical of traditional societies function on the basis of interpersonal relations, making stage 3 reasoning (loyalty to friends, following the golden rule) a highly adaptive form of morality for those societies. It is not that people in traditional societies are any less moral than people in technological societies; it's just that the structure of their culture does not require the more abstract cognitive abilities associated with modern societies.

Some studies have reported sex differences in moral reasoning, with males typically peaking at stage 4 and females at stage 3 (Haan, Langer, & Kohlberg, 1976; Holstein, 1976). In response to these findings, Carol Gilligan (1977, 1982) has suggested that women are reared to be attentive to interpersonal relations and to care for other people, whereas men are brought up to consider moral dilemmas as unavoidable conflicts that social rules and institutions are designed to resolve. As a result, in

Kohlberg's terms, women display more stage 3 reasoning, and men display more stage 4 reasoning. Gilligan argues that moral reasoning follows different criteria for women and men: a morality of caring versus a morality of abstract justice.

Gilligan's theory has received much attention, but as yet has found little research support. Most studies, in fact, show no sex differences in moral reasoning (L. J. Walker, 1986; Walker & de Vries, 1985). In a review of 80 studies of moral development, Lawrence Walker and Brian de Vries (1985) found only 22 with sex differences, and 9 of these showed higher levels of moral reasoning for females. What Gilligan's work has done, however, is redefine what constitutes an adequate description of moral development. According to Mary Brabeck (1983), "When Gilligan's and Kohlberg's theories are taken together, the moral person is seen as one whose moral choices reflect reasoned and deliberate judgments that ensure justice be accorded each person while maintaining a passionate concern for the well-being and care of each individual" (p. 289).

Moral reasoning and moral behavior   Are children generally consistent in their moral behavior? Does moral reasoning relate to moral behavior?

In a classic study by Hugh Hartshorne and Mark May (1928–1930), more than 10,000 children, ages 8 to 16 years, were observed in situations where they were tempted to lie, cheat, and steal. The most remarkable finding of this study was that there seemed to be no general trait for honesty. Children who were honest in one situation would cheat or lie in another. In other words, morality was situationally specific: whether children would lie, cheat, or steal depended on the situation and not on the individual's overall level of moral development.

What about the relationship between level of moral reasoning and moral behavior? In a review of 75 studies, Augusto Blasi (1980) reported that 76% of them found a significant relationship between moral reasoning and behavior. In one interesting seminaturalistic study, researchers evaluated the moral reasoning of college students who joined in a campus free-speech and human-rights demonstration during the 1960s (Haan, Smith, & Block, 1968). They found that protesters showed generally higher levels of moral reasoning on Kohlberg's scale than nonprotesting students.

At first look, these findings would seem to indicate a strong relationship between moral reasoning and moral behavior, but that is not always the case. For example, in most of the studies reviewed by Blasi, the significant relationships between moral reasoning and behavior were only moderate. And the college protesters in the study by Haan et al. did not all display postconventional (stages 5 and 6) moral reasoning; some, in fact, were clearly preconventional (stages 1 and 2), expressing rebellious motivations for protesting rather than the higher moral principles of postconventional students. Thus, it seems, moral reasoning does influence moral behavior, but the relationship is not clear-cut. Many factors determine the moral stance a person will take in any situation, and moral reasoning ability is only one of them.

State of the Art
Moral Education

The buzzword for the late 1980s was "ethics." Our leaders lacked them, our technology demanded them, and our children weren't being taught them. Everyone agreed that something should be done. The question was: who should do the teaching, and exactly what should be taught?

One of the biggest problems in teaching ethics in public school is that the U.S. Constitution requires separation of church and state. Public schools cannot require students to participate in any activity that stresses one particular religious denomination over another, or over none at all. While some groups have sought to change the Constitution, others have tried to design instructional programs acceptable to it.

Beginning in the 1960s, following the lead of Lawrence Kohlberg, some schools began using a program called "values clarification." The idea was simply to present moral dilemmas to kids and encourage discussion, thus allowing them to exercise their moral reasoning abilities. Sample dilemmas (from Castell & Stahl, 1975) were:

1. Should a retarded newborn be given expensive life-saving surgery or left to die peacefully?

2. During a flood, a policeman is putting up a roadblock at a dangerous bridge. Only one vehicle can cross before the bridge is closed. Which would you choose?
   a. Someone taking a warning to other bridges downstream?
   b. Someone transporting a rare type of blood needed for transfusion to an important government official?
   c. A critically injured pregnant woman and her teenage son?
   d. A fire engine on the way to a nursing home fire?
   e. A mailman with social security checks?
3. A wealthy man has died and left his entire estate to his son, but only if his son has a child in the next five years. If not, the money all goes to charity. The son has a genetic defect that has a 50-50 probability of being passed on to his children. Should he have a child to collect the inheritance?
4. A group of workers are striking for higher wages. The court rules their strike illegal. Should they continue to strike?
5. You overhear a group of older kids talking about how they have rigged up fake flying saucers to land near a home for the elderly. Several patients have had heart attacks and everyone is panicked. What should you do?

As it turned out, many parents and other concerned citizens reacted negatively, arguing that values clarification programs were worse than no values instructions at all. If schools weren't going to teach the *right* way to do things, they at least didn't have to encourage kids to think up *wrong* ways. The criticism was so heated that many educators decided to wash their hands of the whole subject and leave the teaching of values solely to the parents.

It has taken two decades for another attempt at values education in the public schools. Responding to cries of help from parents, businesses, colleges, social agencies, and even the police, public schools are again trying to find a way to teach moral values in a way that will please everyone, and this time it look as though they are succeeding.

In 1984, the Baltimore County school system, in response to a mandate from the governor of Maryland, appointed a task force made up of parents, educators, and community leaders to answer the question: what values are necessary for the survival of a free society? By approaching values as essential to democracy rather than as part of religion, the task force was able to agree on a list of 24 common core values (Baltimore County Public Schools, 1988):

Compassion	Objectivity
Courtesy	Order
Critical inquiry	Patriotism
Due process	Rational consent
Equality of	Reasoned argument
opportunity	Respect for others'
Freedom of thought	rights
and action	Responsibility
Honesty	Responsible
Human worth and	citizenship
dignity	Rule of law
Integrity	Self-respect
Justice	Tolerance
Knowledge	Truth
Loyalty	

The next step was to formulate a plan to teach these values at every grade level, embedded in the regular curriculum. For example, responsibility is taught in kindergarten during lessons in fire safety; in fourth grade during lessons in first aid; in seventh-grade science class along with the dangers of tobacco, alcohol, and drugs; and in twelfth-grade home economics class along with other lessons about parenthood.

Other school systems have begun using values education programs, some formulating their own, as Baltimore County did, and others using programs supplied by textbook publishers and research institutes, such as the Thomas Jefferson Research Center, which supplies character-building programs to 25,000 classrooms in the United States. One of these programs, called "How to Be Successful," is aimed at building a sense of personal responsibility and ethical decision making in middle school/junior high school students, based on the following set of values:

Accepting the consequences of one's own actions

Using ethical decision-making and problem-solving techniques

Accepting that attendance, punctuality, and reliability are part of being personally responsible

Developing self-confidence, self-esteem, and positive attitudes

Understanding that success comes from taking initiative and persevering

This program is taught in 5- to 10-minute lessons each day at the beginning of class, supplemented by classroom posters and tapes for parents to listen to at home. The basic program for a school with 30 classroom teachers costs more than $2000; supplementary lessons, posters, and tapes are available at additional charge.

Does it work? It's difficult to measure values directly, but indirect measures are encouraging. After three years of "How to Be Successful," one junior high school in California won the First Place Golden Bell Award from the state school board association for its progress in character building and personal responsibility. The number of straight-A students at San Marcos Junior High School has doubled (from 2.2% to 4.5%), and the proportion of students scoring in the lower fourth of the California Tests of Basic Skills had fallen from 16.4% to 11.7%. Teachers reported that the program had resulted in big changes in students' lifestyles and positive attitudes about themselves and others.

Another program, the Character Education Curriculum developed by educators in San Antonio, Texas, is now used in thousands of classrooms in major school districts including Chicago, St. Louis, and Pasadena (Goble, 1988). The character traits to be used in this program are those shared by major religions around the world:

Honesty	Tolerance
Kindness	Freedom
Courage	Sound use of one's
Justice	talents

Educators using this program have found a dramatic decrease in discipline problems and school vandalism, and a vast improvement in attendance, social relations among students, and positive school spirit.

Although the debate continues about whose job it is to teach values, it seems that most parents welcome help from the schools, now that some universal values have been agreed upon.

Summary

The concept of self changes over childhood and is reflected in how children describe themselves. Self-efficacy refers to the sense of control people have over their lives. Feelings of self-efficacy begin in infancy and develop over childhood.

Children's abilities to take the social perspective of others also develops over childhood. Selman's neo-Piagetian theory of role taking postulates five levels of perspective taking. Children learn social roles through interaction with others, with interactions among friends providing the ideal conditions for changes in social perspective. Empathy is the ability to experience the emotions of others. Hoffman has proposed four developmental levels of empathy, beginning in infancy.

The most frequently studied aspect of children's moral development has been moral reasoning. Piaget proposed three stages of moral reasoning: premoral (2 to 5 years), moral realism (6 to 10 years), and moral relativism (10 years and older). Kohlberg expanded upon Piaget's theory, postulating three levels of moral reasoning—preconventional, conventional, and postconventional—with two stages at each level. The reasoning of most adolescents is at the conventional level, and people in nontechnological cultures rarely reason in postconventional ways. Gilligan proposed that moral reasoning differs in women and men and proposed a theory to capture these differences.

The teaching of ethics and values in public schools has caused concern, partly because of the difficulty of deciding whose values to teach. Values clarification programs, begun in the 1960s, encountered much criticism from parents, and many schools abandoned the teaching of values. More recently, schools have been developing values education programs based on a consensus of values important to a free society, values important for personal success, or values shared by major religions around the world.

Key Terms and Concepts

self-concept
    self-recognition
    mirror recognition
self-efficacy
    helplessness
    mastery orientation
role taking
empathy
moral reasoning

moral dilemmas
premoral stage
moral realism
    moral absolutism
    imminent justice
moral relativism
preconventional morality
conventional morality
postconventional morality
values clarification

Gender Development and Sex Differences

413

Four-year-old Michael was watching his mother bathe and dress his new baby brother. Michael was fascinated with the new baby, but he became upset when the infant's diaper was removed. "Hey," he said to his mother, "I thought you said this was a boy!" His mother answered that it was indeed a boy, and then Michael asked, "Then what's that?" pointing to the baby's genitals. "Why, that's a penis, Mike. All boys have them. You have one, too." At that Michael stretched out the elastic band on the front of his shorts, looked into his pants, and said "Oh yeah, I forgot."

As the story of Michael illustrates, our sense of gender is not innate. Though based in biology, our sense of maleness or femaleness, with all the consequences it entails, develops gradually.

Gender is one of the few characteristics that do not change. We become older, change jobs and marital status, but (with a few notable exceptions) we don't change our sex. Whether we are conscious of it or not, we treat boys (and men) differently than we treat girls (and women), and have different expectations for how males and females are supposed to behave in certain situations. We define who we are in terms of our gender, and children learn very quickly that being a boy or a girl is more than just a label—it is an important part of their personal identity.

The process of identifying oneself as male or female and adopting the roles and values of that sex is referred to as **gender identification.** There is no universal set of roles and behaviors that all boys (and men) or all girls (and women) in the world must learn; culture plays a critical role in shaping gender identification. What *is* universal is the significance that gender has in defining an individual's place in society, and the fact that children around the world strive to acquire an appropriate gender role. The process of gender identification involves biological, social/environmental, and cognitive factors, and we will examine how these various factors interact. We will also look at some differences in behavior and cognition between the sexes, particularly those found in childhood and adolescence.

Gender Identification

Biological Bases of Gender Identification[1]

Gender differentiation There is no debate that there are biological differences between the sexes. Boys and girls, men and women, are physically different, and this difference is obviously rooted in early biology.

At the chromosome level, males and females differ only on the 23rd pair—the sex chromosomes—with females having two Xs and males having an X and a smaller Y (see Chapter 3). Immediately after conception, there are no apparent physical, or morphological, differences between males and females. Differences are developing beneath the surface, however. In girls, genes on the two X chromosomes are directing the construction of ovaries; in boys, genes on the Y chromosome are directing the construction of testes. Once these organs begin functioning, they produce sex hormones—**androgens** in males and **estrogens** in females. The testes also produce **mullerian-inhibiting hormone,** which appears early in prenatal development and has a short life span (Money, 1988). From this point on, it is the hormones—specifically, the presence of male hormones—that determines further sexual differentiation.

In the absence of any prenatal hormones, the embryo develops into a female. In the genetic anomaly of Turner's syndrome, where there is only a single X

[1]By biological factors in gender development, we mean genetic and hormonal factors. We contrast these endogenous, or internal, effects with environmental effects that are exogenous, or external to the child. John Money (1988) believes it is counterproductive to make such a distinction. "The postnatal determinants that enter the brain through the senses by way of social communication and learning also are biological, for there is a biology of learning and remembering. That which is not biological is occult, mystical, or, to coin a term, spookological" (p. 50). We understand Money's point of view and, indeed, agree with it. However, we find it convenient for purposes of communication to differentiate biological and environmental effects, even though we realize that once environmental effects have influenced a person, they become part of that person's biology. We ask students to keep this in mind, and not to think of environmental effects as "spookological" in nature.

chromosome, no functioning ovaries develop, and no estrogen is produced; yet, at birth, the child is easily recognized as a girl. That is, in the absence of any sex hormone or in the presence of estrogen, nature produces a girl. It is the presence of androgen (most particularly **testosterone,** the most potent of the various androgen hormones) that is responsible for maleness, and the presence of mullerian-inhibiting hormone that inhibits feminization. When mullerian-inhibiting hormone is absorbed into the tissues destined to become the sex organs, feminization is halted by stopping the construction of female reproductive organs such as the uterus and fallopian tubes. Testosterone's role is not to defeminize the embryo, but to masculinize it. The presence of testosterone and its derivatives promotes the growth of the male reproductive organs, including penis, prostate, seminal vesicles, and scrotum (see Money, 1988).

Prenatal hormones and behavior   The presence of androgen affects not only the physical structure of the fetus but also its behavior. In nonhuman mammals, females given large doses of androgen prenatally show characteristic male social and sexual behavior, despite the presence of female genitalia. Similarly, nonhuman mammal males who are castrated early in life or given drugs that prevent the further absorption of androgen, display characteristic female behavior, such as nest building and nurturing pups (see Money & Ehrhardt, 1972). At the extreme, a genetic female exposed early to large quantities of androgen will develop the outward appearance of a male. Similarly, if little or no androgen is absorbed into the body of a genetic male fetus (a condition known as **androgen insensitivity**), the outward appearance will be that of a female.

Comparable situations occur in humans. Abnormal hormone exposure during the prenatal period can result in children born with ambiguous genitalia (for example, a structure that is neither a functional penis nor clitoris); at the extreme, a child's morphological sex can be different from his or her genetic sex. More common are situations in which prenatal hormone exposure is not so extreme, as when genetic girls are overexposed to androgen during the fetal period because of malfunctioning adrenocortical glands, which also produce androgen (**adrenogenital syndrome**). These girls are more apt to be classified as "tomboys" during childhood than are nonandrogenized girls. Androgenized girls tend to prefer high-energy activities over more sedentary pursuits; they show little maternalism in the form of doll play or interest in babysitting when older; and their aspirations for the future are more typical of boys their age than of girls (Ehrhardt & Baker, 1974; Ehrhardt & Money, 1967). This was the case even when parents were not aware of their child's hormonal condition or when they encouraged traditional, female behaviors in their daughters. As young adults, a disproportionate number of these women reported having homosexual and/or bisexual imagery, with or without actual experience (Money, Schwartz, & Lewis, 1984). This finding is consistent with other recent research suggesting that adult sexual orientation (that is, homosexuality or heterosexuality) is influenced by prenatal hormone exposure (Ellis & Ames, 1987).

One hypothesis for the origins of these differences is that the presence of androgen during the fetal period "masculinizes" the brain—specifically, the hypothalamus (Ellis, 1986). The hypothalamus plays a critical role in the regulation of behavior, including feeding and sexual behaviors, and may also have a role in information processing (Reinisch, 1974; Reinisch, Gandelman, & Speigel, 1979). In general, the hypothalamus influences the release of sex hormones during all stages of life, which may affect certain aspects of behavior. Male hormones affect the developing brain later in pregnancy than they do the reproductive organs, apparently during the last trimester. There is some suggestion that the effects of hormones on brain development may extend through the first three months after birth, when, in boys, there is a surge of testosterone from the testes (Money, 1988).

Sex hormones, which play such a critical role before birth, are at a low level during childhood but begin to increase again during early adolescence. The changes that occur during puberty in the bodies of both boys and girls are mediated, to a large degree, by the presence of sex hormones (see Chapter 5). Just as sex hormones prior to birth influence the structure of the body and brain of the fetus, hormones circulating through the adolescent bloodstream produce other gender-related changes.

Rate of maturation obviously influences sex-related behavior. Early-maturing children will exhibit interest in sex sooner than late-maturing children. Similarly, children with sex-stereotypic physical characteristics (the athletic teenage boy, the curvaceous teenage girl) may be treated in a more sex-stereotypic fashion than their peers. Children who *look* the role may be expected to *play* the role, with biology indirectly affecting how others treat them and how they perceive themselves (see Nash, 1979; see also Chapter 5).

Unquestionably, biology sets the stage for gender identification and for sex differences in cognition and behavior. But biology is not destiny, and what is judged to be appropriate male and female behavior

in different cultures varies tremendously. Thus, environmental factors contribute significantly to developmental patterns of gender identification. The *process* of gender identification may be based in biology, but the *content* is determined in large part by environment.

Social/Environmental Bases of Gender Identification

Parents' role in gender identification   Parents play an important role in directing children to adopt sex-appropriate behaviors and attitudes. They provide different toys for their daughters than for their sons (Schau, Kahn, Diepold, & Cherry, 1980; Rheingold & Cook, 1975) and profess different expectations about what is important in rearing boys and girls

Box 16.1

Freud on Sex and Gender Development

Gender is determined by one's genitals, and nothing short of surgery will alter what biology pronounced months before we were born. Sigmund Freud proposed that this genital basis of gender has a profound impact on personality: realizing that half the people in the world have penises and half don't, and figuring out which half one belongs to, is of central importance in determining with whom one will identify. According to Freud's theory, boys, realizing they have penises and afraid of losing them (castration anxiety), identify with their fathers, the most likely person to threaten the boys' masculinity should they not identify with them. Girls, envious that they have no penis and apparently never will have one (penis envy), identify with their mothers, whom they blame for their loss and who, anatomically speaking, share their fate.

Although Freud seems to have been on the right track concerning parents' influence on children's personalities, it is questionable that young children's knowledge about the genital basis of sex has as significant an impact on their thinking and personalities as Freud hypothesized. In a study conducted in

Sweden by Maureen McConaghy (1979), preschool children were shown boy and girl dolls dressed in boys' or girls' clothing, and asked what sex the dolls were. Similar studies done in the United States show that preschool children judge the sex of a child on the basis of the type of clothing he or she wears, so that a boy doll wearing girls' clothes is recognized as a girl. One difference between McConaghy's study and those done in the United States is that the dolls' genitals were visible when she asked questions about boy and girl dolls. For example, some children were shown a boy doll with male genitals, and a dress was placed on the doll but in such a way that the doll's genitals were still visible. McConaghy found that knowing the genital basis of sex and even being able to see the genitals made no difference in young children's judgments. Little boy dolls who are dressed as little girls become girls, regardless of whether the doll's genitals can be seen or not. This suggests that the important thing about gender for young children is not biology but behavior: what a person does or wears is central, with the genital basis of sex only an afterthought.

Parents influence children's understanding of what behavior is considered appropriate to their gender and what is not.

(Block, 1979, 1983). For example, in reviewing research on sex differences in child-rearing practices, Jeanne Block (1979) reported that parents emphasized achievement, competition, control of emotions, responsibility for one's actions, and independence more for their sons than for their daughters. Boys were also more apt to be punished and dealt with more strictly than girls. In contrast, parents emphasized trustworthiness, truthfulness, "ladylike behavior," and reflection upon life more for their daughters than for their sons. Girls' relationships with their parents were characterized by greater warmth and physical closeness. From her review of the literature, Block (1983) drew two basic conclusions: "(a) males and females grow up in psychological learning contexts that are importantly different, and (b) these differing contexts have large implications for the subsequent psychological functioning of males and females" (p. 1335).

Unconscious biases   Adults are not always aware that they behave differently toward girls than toward boys. In a study by Beverly Fagot (1978), 24 families, each with a child between 20 and 24 months, were observed in their homes. Fagot reported significant differences in parents' behaviors toward their sons and daughters. Parents reacted favorably when their

children engaged in sex-stereotypic behaviors (for instance, girls playing with dolls) and negatively when children engaged in cross-sex activities (for instance, girls playing with trucks). Girls were given more positive responses than boys when they engaged in adult-oriented, dependent behaviors. Yet when parents were asked to describe their own behavior toward their children, what they said did not correlate highly with what they did.

Adults' unconscious biases regarding the behavior of boys and girls were demonstrated in an experiment by John and Sandra Condry (1976). In their study, college students observed the reactions of a 9-month-old infant to four stimuli: a teddy bear, a jack-in-the-box, a doll, and a buzzer. For each toy, the students were to evaluate the intensity of the infant's emotions. Three emotions were rated: pleasure, anger, and fear. Although all subjects saw the same tape with the same infant, half were led to believe that they were watching a little girl, and the other half that they were watching a little boy.

The college students' ratings varied as a function of which sex they thought the infant was. For example, when they evaluated the infants' obvious distress to the jack-in-the-box, "boy" infants were more likely to be rated high for anger, whereas "girl" infants were more likely to be rated high for fear. John Condry and David Ross (1985) reported similar results of gender labeling in the perception of aggression in children, with "boys" being perceived as more aggressive than "girls," even though the adult subjects all viewed the same child.

Other adults and children as role models   Evidence of adult gender bias might seem to suggest that sex-stereotypic behavior would be eliminated if parents simply treated boys and girls identically; if parents were to expect the same of their sons and daughters and treat them accordingly, sex differences in children's social behavior should disappear. This view, however, ignores the role of the child in his or her own gender development. Once children realize the importance of gender, they work hard at finding out exactly *what* it is they're supposed to be doing. What is it that boys and men versus girls and women do that's so different? Obviously, a child's parents are important role models for sex-appropriate behavior, but they aren't the only ones. David Perry and Kay Bussey (1979) proposed that children observe a wide range of adult behaviors and learn which behaviors are proper for their sex by how often various members of each sex display them. Thus, for example, if a boy's dad does all the housework at home but the son rarely sees other men engaging in such activity, it's unlikely that doing housework will be viewed as part of the male role, even though it does characterize the boy's own father.

It is not only adults who serve as models for children, but also other children. Beginning in the preschool years and continuing until puberty, children around the world tend to segregate themselves into same-sex play groups, with the degree of segregation increasing from early to middle childhood (Whiting & Edwards, 1988; Maccoby & Jacklin, 1987; see Chapter 14). Boys and girls learn important lessons in these groups about what it means to be male and female. Of course, their conceptions of male and female roles will be affected by the values and opportunities that their culture provides them. Yet

"SHE MAKES YOU GLAD YOU'RE A BOY, HUH, JOEY?"

Children identify with members of their own sex, often rejecting characteristics of the opposite sex. *Source:* DENNIS THE MENACE® used by permission of Hank Ketcham and © by North America Syndicate.

within the larger culture, children develop a finer sense of what is appropriate and inappropriate from interacting with their same-sex peers.

Once children start mingling with other children, what other children do will determine to a large extent what is viewed as appropriate male and female behavior. For example, friends of ours refused to buy guns for their 3-year-old son and restricted the amount of aggressive TV the boy watched. Nevertheless, the boy learned from his preschool pals that gun play was a male activity, and the child ran around the house pointing sticks, spoons, or fingers at people and saying "pow," despite constant reprimands from his parents. He had learned from other 3-year-olds one special thing that boys do and, over his parents' objections, was making it something that he, as a boy, did also.

Androgyny   We typically think of masculinity and femininity as opposite ends of a continuum: a person can be highly masculine, highly feminine, or somewhere in between, but cannot be both highly masculine and highly feminine at the same time. Yet that is exactly what Sandra Bem (1974, 1977) suggested many well-adjusted people are. Bem proposed that masculinity and femininity can be viewed as separate dimensions, so that a person can possess many characteristics usually associated with masculinity (assertiveness, competitiveness) and, at the same time, possess many characteristics usually associated with femininity (cooperation, nurturance). This phenomenon is known as **androgyny.** Androgynous people are able to behave in a variety of ways depending on the context; they have available to them a range of characteristics that are stereotypically male (*andro*) and female (*gyno*).

Research in which people complete questionnaires describing their personality characteristics has found that approximately one-third of college-student subjects are androgynous (Bem, 1974; Spence & Helmreich, 1978). Similar findings have been reported for children 8 to 11 years old (Hall & Halberstadt, 1980). Moreover, androgynous adolescents and adults tend to be more flexible and better adjusted overall (Massad, 1981; Spence, 1982). To our knowledge, there is no evidence, one way or the other, linking androgyny to adjustment in childhood.

If being androgynous is adaptive, as Bem and others propose, how does one raise an androgynous person? It has been proposed that androgynous parents would be highly responsive and supportive

Androgyny means having strengths in a range of characteristics, some typically male and some typically female.

of their children's achievements, thus producing highly competent children (Spence & Helmreich, 1978). However, the only published study investigating the relationship between sex-role classification of parents and their children's adjustment found just the opposite: Diana Baumrind (1982) reported that 9-year-old children of androgynous parents were somewhat *less* competent than the children of sex-typed parents.

Does this mean that children of strongly sex-typed parents will grow up to be more competent and better adjusted adults? Not necessarily. It may be that androgynous models do not become important for adjustment until adolescence. Until that time, it may be more important for children to develop a solid sense of themselves as boys or girls, which can be accomplished more easily with sex-typed parents. It is only when children's identities as males or females are well established, presumably in late ado-

lescence or early adulthood, that they can be comfortable displaying some opposite-sex characteristics—that is, behaving androgynously. This interpretation, and all others, are highly speculative, for there is little evidence on "how to raise an androgynous person." Based on Baumrind's findings, however, we cannot assume that androgynous parents necessarily raise androgynous adults. The question is still open.

Cognitive Bases of Gender Identification

Children learn early that gender is important and then work at learning the roles and behaviors that characterize their sex. As we have seen, many factors contribute to children's gender identification. One is their ability to understand gender as a concept; another is the realization that gender is stable over time and consistent over situations.

What children know about gender thus varies as a function of their level of cognitive development. Children cannot be expected to model behavior of their own gender if they are not aware of the differences between males and females or that their own gender is constant. In fact, it's not uncommon to find preschool children who haven't yet made up their minds about their future adult gender. Most little girls want to be women when they grow up, but some prefer to leave the question open.

Kohlberg's theory of gender identification One of the first people to postulate a cognitive basis for gender identification was Lawrence Kohlberg (1966, 1969). Following Piaget's model of cognitive development, Kohlberg proposed that children do not have a mature idea of gender until the beginning of concrete operations, at about 7 years of age.

Kohlberg proposed that, during the preschool years, children must acquire several pieces of knowledge about gender. First, they must discover that the world is made up of males and females, and they must identify themselves as one or the other. Discriminating between males and females is not simply a matter of recognizing genitals; for young children, Kohlberg proposed, it is the differences in outward appearance and activities of men and women (and, to a lesser extent, of boys and girls) that determine gender differentiation. Finally, children must realize that gender is not merely a transitory phenomenon, but is constant over time and situations. **Gender constancy** refers to the belief

Before children begin imitating adults of their own gender, they need to know that their gender is permanent.

that gender remains the same despite changes in physical appearance, time, and behavior.

The development of gender constancy In an early study of the development of gender constancy, Ronald Slaby and Karin Frey (1975) asked preschool children a series of questions concerning their beliefs about gender. The first class of questions dealt with the concept of **gender identity:** could children identify themselves as boys or girls, and could they correctly identify pictures of males and females? The second set of questions concerned the concept of **gender stability:** do children know that gender is stable over time? To test this, for example, a boy would be asked, "When you were a little baby, were you a little girl or a little boy? Were you ever a little girl? When you grow up, will you be a mommy or a daddy? Could you ever be a mommy?" The third set of questions assessed the concept of **gender consistency:** does one's gender remain the same over a variety of situations? For example, a little girl would be asked, "If you wore boys' clothes, would you be a girl or a boy? If you played boys' games, would you be a girl or a boy? Could you be a boy if you wanted to?"

Slaby and Frey found age-related increases in children's abilities to answer these questions. With very few exceptions, they reported that children could correctly answer the gender-identity questions first, followed by the gender-stability questions, and finally the gender-consistency questions: identity → stability → consistency. Most children

could answer all three types of questions correctly by 5 years of age. Other researchers have confirmed this three-stage sequence, with gender identity being achieved, on average, by 2.5 years, gender stability by 4 or 5 years, and gender consistency by 6 or 7 years (Eaton & Von Bargen, 1981; Ruble, Balaban, & Cooper, 1981). This sequence of development is not confined to North America or to industrialized countries, but has also been found in nontechnological communities in Belize, Kenya, Nepal, and American Samoa (Munroe, Shimmin, & Munroe, 1984).

As with many other aspects of cognition in young children, however, performance can be enhanced or hindered by subtle changes in the task. For example, Sally MacKain (1987) asked 3- and 4-year-olds gender-constancy questions about children seen on videotape; counter to other research with children this age, two-thirds of the 3- and 4-year-olds answered all the gender-constancy questions correctly. In other research, preschoolers and second-grade children were asked gender-constancy questions in which a pictured child was referred to by a proper name (John or Jane), a personal pronoun (he or she), or a neutral phrase ("this child"). Children at both grade levels answered most of the constancy questions correctly when a proper name was used. Only the second-grade children continued to show constancy when pronouns were used, and even they failed to show high levels of constancy when the neutral phrase was used (Beal & Lockhart, 1989). Thus, seemingly subtle differences in how the gender-constancy task is administered can result in dramatic changes in children's responses (see also Bem, 1989). These findings suggest that children's beliefs about the constancy of gender are not firmly established until middle childhood. However, they also reflect the fact that even preschoolers sometimes believe that gender is constant over time and situations. The range of situations to which they believe this to apply is, however, limited.

The consequences of gender constancy for behavior Children who understand that gender is stable over time and circumstances are more apt to pick up on sex differences than children who do not. Investigating this relationship, Diane Ruble, Terry Balaban, and Joel Cooper (1981) rated preschool children as high or low in their knowledge of gender constancy, using a procedure similar to that used by Slaby and Frey (1975). These children were then

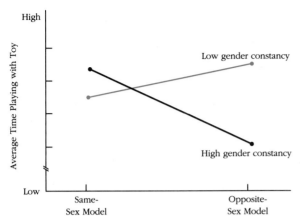

Figure 16.1 Average time spent playing with a toy as a function of gender constancy (high versus low) and sex of model in the commercial (same sex versus opposite sex). *Source:* Adapted from "Gender Constancy and the Effects of Sex-typed Televised Toy Commercials," by D. N. Ruble, T. Balaban, and J. Cooper, *Child Development,* 1981, *52,* 667–673. Copyright © The Society for Research in Child Development, Inc. Reprinted by permission.

shown some cartoons, accompanied by a commercial of a child playing with a new toy. Half of the low-gender group and half of the high-gender group saw a child of their own gender in the commercial; the others saw a child of the opposite gender. Children were later given the chance to play with the advertised toy, among several others. The amount of time each group of children played with the toy is shown in Figure 16.1. Children rated high in gender constancy were influenced by the gender of the child in the commercial: if a same-sex child had been playing with the toy in the commercial, they were more likely to play with it; if an opposite-sex child had been playing with it, they were more likely to stay away. Children who had been rated low in gender constancy showed no such influence: they were about equally likely to play with the toy whether it had been demonstrated by a same-sex or an opposite-sex child. The high-gender children knew which gender they were and that it was permanent; now they were doing their best to behave in a manner consistent with this knowledge.

Findings such as these raise the question of whether there is a relationship between level of cognitive development and sex-stereotypic behavior. If

there is, children who are more advanced with respect to gender constancy (a reflection of cognitive development) should be more aware of the differences between the sexes in behavior, roles, and expectations. This pattern has been found by several researchers: brighter or more cognitively advanced preschoolers have more knowledge of sex stereotypes (Kuhn, Nash, & Brucken, 1978) and behave in a more sex-stereotypic way than average or less-bright preschool children (Connor & Serbin, 1977; Fagot, Leinbach, & Hagan, 1986; Weintraub, Clemens, Sockloff, Ethridge, Gracely, & Myers, 1984). Preschoolers are just learning gender as a concept, and it makes sense that brighter children will acquire this concept (as other concepts) sooner than less-bright children. But once these concepts have been acquired by all children, brighter children are not more sex-stereotyped than less-bright children (Serbin & Sprafkin, 1986).

Children's theories of gender Children continually gain knowledge about what differentiates males and

"How old do babies hafta get to start bein' boys and girls?"

Children formulate theories about the nature of gender. Many of these theories are wrong. *Source:* Reprinted with special permission of King Features Syndicate, Inc.

females in our society, and with this knowledge they continually generate and test theories about sex differences. Early theories are simplistic, based on the coarsest of characteristics. For example, a young boy may notice that his mother and sister play tennis while he and his father enjoy bicycling. His hypothesis might be that tennis is female and bicycling is male. However, much as the scientist delving into a new field of research, rejection of the old theories leads to new ones, and eventually, most children acquire the meaning of gender that is implicitly agreed upon by members of their society.

Box 16.2

Children's Theories of Gender

Five-year-old Bobby didn't have much experience with babies, and so he was fascinated by our 6-month-old daughter, Heidi. "She's a girl, right?" he asked. "That's right," I answered. "And she has brown hair just like me," he said. "So she does," I replied. There was a pause, and his next question caught me by surprise. "Does that mean that she'll be a boy when she grows up?" I told him no, and he quickly said, "Oh, I know that. I was just kidding."

Kidding, indeed. What gender we are is very important to us all; it's one of the few characteristics we possess that doesn't change over time. We define who we are in terms of our gender, and children learn very quickly that being a boy or a girl is more than just a label. They are continually developing and testing theories about gender, then abandoning most of them on their way to an adult understanding of gender.

Our modern, technological society is very permissive in terms of what is appropriate for males and females. Yet each of us could easily list characteristics of dress and behavior that differentiate boys and girls of various ages. Girls are dressed in pink and surrounded by ruffles at an early age, whereas baby boys' clothes are more apt to be blue and functional, lacking the frills that their sisters wear. Dresses are strictly girl stuff, as is makeup. Young children learn these "rules" but, because of the flexibility of dress and behavior our culture allows, they must deal with contradictions. Our daughter Heidi at 3 years didn't quite know what to make of her brother's 15-year-old friend Brett. He certainly looked, talked, and acted like a boy, but that earring he wore confused her. "Is Brett a he or a she?" she asked, and when told, she wondered aloud why he wore an earring. "Is he a girl when he wears it? Does he sleep with it? Maybe he's a boy who really wants to be a girl?" At about the same age, Heidi proclaimed certain rules about dress, declaring that her father could not wear a pink shirt because if he did he'd be a girl, and that the major difference between boys and girls was that girls wear pink and boys don't. Always fashion conscious, she added that both boys and girls could wear blue and yellow. Pink, it seemed, was the critical color.

The significance of dress in determining gender for young children is illustrated in an observation reported by L. Joseph Stone and Joseph Church in their 1973 book, *Childhood and Adolescence: A Psychology of the Growing Person*. A new family had moved into the neighborhood with a baby, and when a 4-year-old girl was asked whether the baby was a boy or a girl she responded, "I don't know. It's so hard to tell at that age, especially with their clothes off."

In our society, the distinctions between appropriate male and female behaviors and roles are difficult ones to make, even for adults. But kids develop their own theories and test them out. They're often wrong. Take for example, the two families that went out to an Italian restaurant for dinner. The 4-year-old son from one of the families showed a marked preference for sharing the pizza that his father and the other gentleman had ordered, rather than his mother's lasagna. On the way home, after some unusually quiet moments, he announced that he'd figured it out. "Men eat pizza and women don't," he proclaimed. Oh, but it should be that easy.

Source: Adapted from D. F. Bjorklund (February 1987). What Are Little Boys (and Girls) Made Of? *Parents Magazine,* Vol. 62, No. 2.

It seems clear that cognitive differences among children contribute substantially to their developing identification with members of their own sex. Questions remain, however, concerning what aspects of cognitive development are most important and how cognitive factors influence children's sex roles and behaviors.

Sex Differences

Physical differences between the sexes are indisputable. Although sex differences in size, strength, and the ability to bear and nurse children may have been critical in determining social roles in primitive hunter/gatherer cultures, they are of less consequence in the technological cultures of today. Our survival depends less on strength and more on intellectual and social skills. Yet sex differences remain of interest to most members of society. Our culture assumes differences in personality, social dispositions, and even intelligence between males and females, and these perceived differences (whether real or not) can influence a child's development and his or her position in society.

The study of sex differences has a long and continuous history in psychology. A highly influential book published in 1974 by Eleanor Maccoby and Carol Jacklin, *The Psychology of Sex Differences,* summarized the existing scientific literature. Some culturally perceived sex differences, they reported, were confirmed by research; others were small in magnitude; still others were not found at all. In general, research since the publication of this book has done little to contradict its basic findings, although new research has caused us to examine some sex differences more closely.

Before looking into sex differences, it is worth mentioning a few areas in which sex differences have *not* been found, despite cultural biases to the contrary. Personality characteristics such as shyness and general sociability do not vary reliably between boys and girls. Boys and girls both form strong attachments to their parents in infancy and are equally apt to be generous or helpful to other children (Maccoby, 1980). Girls are not more suggestible than boys, nor do they have lower self-esteem. Also, boys and girls score similarly on tests of intelligence. Thus, many of the stereotypes people have about sex differences do not hold up under scientific scrutiny.

Sex Differences in Social/Emotional Behavior

One of the areas in which Maccoby and Jacklin (1974) found clear evidence of sex differences was aggression. Males, from the age of about 2 years through young adulthood, are more aggressive than females. However, there is as much difference in aggression from boy to boy (and from girl to girl) as there is between groups of boys and girls; thus, the difference in aggression that can be attributed to sex alone, though real, is relatively small. In a review of 68 studies examining sex differences in aggression, Janet Hyde (1984) determined that approximately 5% of the individual differences could be explained simply by knowing the sex of the child. This means that about 95% of individual differences in aggression are caused by factors other than sex.

One possible reason for boys' greater aggression may be sex differences in activity level. Boys have been found to be more active than girls at birth (Phillips, King, & DuBois, 1978), and this difference increases with age (Eaton & Enns, 1986). As with aggression, when looking at differences in activity level across a large number of studies, approximately 5% of the observed differences can be attributed to sex (Eaton & Enns, 1986). Consistent with this observation, boys are more apt to engage in rough-and-tumble play than girls (DiPietro, 1981; see Chapter 14).

Another area in which boys and girls are believed to differ is risk taking: boys are more willing to take chances than girls. In an interesting study by Harvey Ginsburg and Shirley Miller (1982), children between the ages of 3 and 7 years were observed during a visit to the zoo. The frequency of riding an elephant alone, petting a burro (who sometimes bites), feeding animals in a petting zoo, and playing on a river bank that adjoined the park were noted for both boys and girls. At all ages, about twice as many boys participated in these "risky" behaviors as girls. Again, one reason for this difference may be the greater general activity level of boys; another may be parenting practices that encourage boys to take risks.

Whereas boys are more aggressive, active, and inclined to take risks, girls tend to be more nurturing toward infants and young children. Greater nurturance in girls is reported as young as 3 years of age, and also in different cultures (Whiting & Edwards, 1988; Frodi & Lamb, 1978).

One difference between boys and girls is that boys take more risks.

Parent-child social interactions have also been found to vary between the sexes. Boys are more demanding of their parents' attention (Martin, 1980), are more likely to get into mischief as toddlers (Smith & Daglish, 1977), and are less apt to comply with parents' requests (Whiting & Edwards, 1988). Conversely, girls are more likely than boys to respond positively to their mothers' playful initiatives (Gunnar & Donahu, 1980). Although these differences are often small and found only for children as a group, they do provide some support for the old wives' tale that boys are more difficult to raise than girls.

Boys and girls differ in other ways as well, such as in the games they like and the toys they play with (Connor & Serbin, 1977). Some studies have reported different toy preferences in children as young as 2 years of age (Caldera, Huston, & O'Brien, 1989; Perry, White, & Perry, 1984). Some of these differences, appearing early in life as they do, likely have a basis in biology. However, it has also been found that parents of toddlers encourage their children to play with sex-appropriate toys (Caldera et al., 1989; Fagot & Leinbach, 1989) and that parents of infants and toddlers interact differently with males than with females (Fagot, 1978; Snow, Jacklin, & Maccoby, 1983).

Sex Differences in Cognition

The idea that the sexes differ in intellectual abilities goes back to ancient history. During the 19th and early 20th centuries, scientists looked for differences in overall intelligence and generally found men to be more intelligent than women; their findings, however, were seriously biased by prevailing political and social views (Gould, 1981). More recently, researchers have turned away from investigations of global "intelligence" and have concentrated on examining sex differences in specific cognitive abilities. Reliable sex differences have been found in verbal ability, favoring girls, and in mathematical and spatial abilities, favoring boys.

Sex differences in verbal ability
Sex differences in rate of language acquisition in infancy have been found in some studies (Clarke-Stewart, 1973; T. Moore, 1967), but not in others (McCarthy, 1954). In related research, Michael Lewis and his colleagues reported greater vocalization by infant girls than boys: 3-month-old girls were found to vocalize more than boys in response to their mother's initiation of "talking" (Lewis & Freedle, 1973); infant girls between the ages of 3 and 13 months vocalized more to faces than did boys of the same age (Lewis, 1969). However, a more recent study conducted in Greece, where infant boys are "much more welcomed, valued, and interacted with than female children," found greater vocalization in boys than in girls, suggesting a significant role of environment (Roe, Drivas, Karagellis, & Roe, 1985, p. 373).

Differences in verbal ability past infancy are found primarily in early adolescence and beyond, when "girls begin to come into their own in verbal performance" (Maccoby & Jacklin, 1974, p. 84). As a group, girls this age are apt to be better readers and to solve verbal problems such as anagrams more easily than boys. However, such effects are not robust: more studies have failed to find sex differences in verbal abilities during adolescence and adulthood than have succeeded in finding them (Maccoby & Jacklin, 1974). Taken together, these studies suggest that about 1% of observed differences in verbal ability can be attributed to sex (Hyde, 1981; Plomin & Foch, 1981).

Sex differences in mathematical ability Maccoby and Jacklin reported that most studies examining children's mathematical performance found differences favoring boys, though such differences were not found until adolescence. More recent research has shown that sex differences are most pronounced among children who score in the top 5% of all students in mathematical achievement (Benbow & Stanley, 1980, 1983). Based on the mathematics portion of the Scholastic Aptitude Test (SAT), Camille Benbow and Julian Stanley (1983) found that the higher the score (out of a possible 800 maximum), the higher the ratio of boys to girls. For those scoring 420 or more, the ratio was 1.5 to 1; 500 or higher, 2.1 to 1; 600 or higher, 4.1 to 1; and for those scoring 700 and above, the ratio was 13 to 1.

Other research has found that differences in math performance are diminished and sometimes eliminated when the study considers the number of math and math-related courses children have taken (Fennema & Sherman, 1977). However, not all of the differences found in math achievement can be attributed to class experience; biological factors do contribute, especially among the most mathematically talented students (Raymond & Benbow, 1986). Overall, about 5% of the differences in mathematics ability can be attributed solely to sex (Hyde, 1981).

Sex differences in spatial ability In studies of children's ability to orient themselves with respect to a map of their environment, most researchers report sex differences favoring males, beginning in the preschool years. For example, researchers have investigated sex differences in the formation of "cognitive maps"—mental representations of a spatial layout, such as a college campus, a model town, or a set of connected classrooms. In these studies, children are asked questions about a familiar area (for example, their classroom), or are asked to learn the location of objects in some display (such as their school building or a model town). In experiments with children ranging in age from 3 to 10 years, boys have been found to perform better on such tasks than girls at every age tested (Herman & Siegel, 1978; Herman, Shiraki, & Miller, 1985; Siegel & Schadler, 1977).

Sex differences in spatial cognition have also been reported on tasks such as the Embedded Figures Test (Witkin et al., 1954), in which a subject must find a simple figure embedded in a more complex one (see Chapter 6). Another simple test of spatial ability that has consistently yielded sex differences in performance is Piaget and Inhelder's (1967) water-level problem (see Figure 16.2). In this problem, subjects are shown tilted bottles and asked to judge the position of the water; to answer correctly, subjects must indicate (usually by drawing a line) that the level of the water will be horizontal across the bottle. In Piaget and Inhelder's work, preoperational children had difficulty with the task, often showing the water level parallel to the bottom of the bottle rather than parallel to the horizon. Other researchers have found that many adolescents and young adults also have difficulty with the concept, with a disproportionate number of females experiencing such difficulties (Kalichman, 1988; Liben, 1978; Liben & Golbeck, 1984; Thomas, Jamison, & Hummel, 1973; Willemsen & Reynolds, 1973). Based on all the studies of individual differences in spatial abilities, approximately 5% of those differences can

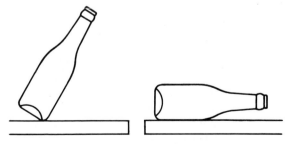

Figure 16.2 Water-level problem. Subjects are asked to draw a line on each bottle showing how it would look if it were half-filled with water.

be attributed solely to sex (Hyde, 1981; Linn & Petersen, 1985).

Despite the research emphasis on the subject, sex differences in behavior and cognition are in fact small. The overall distribution of verbal and of visual/spatial and quantitative abilities for males and females is shown in Figure 16.3. Although there are average differences in ability levels between the sexes, what is more compelling is the substantial overlap. This does not mean that sex differences are uninteresting, because they can shed light on the nature of individual differences in general. However, given the small magnitude of the differences (rarely greater than 5%), we must be cautious about interpretation. For example, knowing only the sex of a child would not help a school counselor decide whether the child should be enrolled in advanced mathematics or computer classes rather than classes in literature or history (see Box 16.3).

The Origins of Sex Differences

Sex differences in behavior and cognition have been found repeatedly. Some of the differences, as in ac-

Box 16.3

Sexism in the Schools

"No Boys Allowed." "Girls Keep Out And This Means YOU!!" These seem to be the battle cries of the elementary-school crowd. Although this is an important stage in gender development, this small-scale war between the sexes can escalate into large-scale problems in the future for both boys and girls, especially if adults are supplying arms to both sides.

One of the biggest problem areas is computer class. Although enrollment may be open to both girls and boys, the computer room often becomes a "Boys Only" territory, with few girls willing to fight the peer pressure for access. The results? Girls don't get the computer time boys do. Girls don't continue with advanced computer classes. And perhaps the biggest tragedy, girls *and* boys learn that computers are "boys' stuff" and that girls aren't as good at computer work.

It's not always the girls that end up on the losing side, either. For example, a school with several state-ranked female tennis players can quickly transmit the message that tennis is "girls' stuff," leaving boys the choice of either playing tennis and risking the taunts of their classmates or taking up a "boys'" sport. The damage is

When the school computer room becomes "boys only" territory, whether by rule or by custom, all children learn distorted lessons about gender.

tivity level and aggression, are relatively robust, whereas others, as in cognition, are small and not reliably found. Given the nature of these differences, the role of biology (genetics and hormones) cannot be ignored; after all, sex is genetically determined, making it a plausible source of differences in behavior and cognition. Yet it is equally clear that all societies have different roles and expectations for males and females, and that differences in the experiences of boys and girls begin in infancy. Thus, environmental differences, too, must be considered as a possible source of variation. It is more likely, of course, that many sex differences are due to the transaction of both nature and nurture.

Hormonal differences between girls and boys produce different brain structures that are hypothesized to be responsible for different patterns of mental abilities (Reinisch et al., 1979). However, it is possible that such direct effects on information processing play only a small role in sex differences in thinking. In fact, nearly all researchers who propose biologically determined sex differences in cognition stress that environment also plays a critical role (Petersen, 1976). Other biologically induced

---

double-deckered: the boy who might have found his life's greatest pleasure on the tennis court will have to settle for something less, and the boys and girls in that school will have been taught that the grown-up world is full of "Keep Out" signs for one gender or the other.

This unintended lesson can be learned in math, language, art, music, or any other class where children segregate themselves by sex. The critical factor is whether the adults in charge (including parents) give tacit approval by turning their backs, or intervene and teach children the lesson that there are other important distinctions in the adult world besides a person's gender.

Do parents' words match their deeds? One study showed that parents often express strong beliefs that computer ability is as vital to girls as it is to boys. In actual practice, however, parents are more apt to buy a home computer for their sons, spend more time working at the computer with their sons, and give their sons more encouragement to enter a computer-related career than their daughters.

What is being taught at school? Other studies have shown that even the most fair-minded, conscientious teachers may be relaying subtle messages to children that sex differences are as big a deal in adult life as they are in third grade.

Do we still believe the old wives' tales that boys are better in math and girls are better in verbal activities such as reading? Although recent studies have found small sex differences in these areas, they don't show up until adolescence. And if anything, those findings should point to the need for *more* math classes for girls and *more* English classes for boys, not the opposite.

Are students divided by sex during activities for which gender is irrelevant, such as lunch or art projects?

What is this teaching children? Can't we be more creative?

And if children are divided by sex, what happens then? It's one thing to have separate P.E. classes for girls and boys, but it's another if the boys get to exercise with the expensive athletic equipment in the gym while the girls sit on the benches outside and talk. Do the female classroom helpers clean up after snack, whereas their male counterparts set up the video equipment? What is this teaching our children?

The job of parents is to open doors to the future and help their sons and daughters choose which ones to pass through. We have problems enough without having to deal with doors someone has designated, like public restrooms, for either "Ladies" or "Gentlemen."

Source: Adapted from D. F. Bjorklund and B. R. Bjorklund (April 1988). Sexism in the Schools. *Parents Magazine*, Vol. 63, No. 4.

a. Verbal Ability

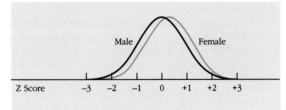

b. Visual/Spatial and Quantitative Abilities

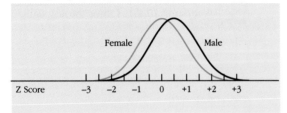

Figure 16.3 Idealized distribution of performance of males and females for (a) verbal and (b) visual/spatial and quantitative abilities, expressed in terms of standard scores. *Source:* From "How Large are Cognitive Gender Differences? A Meta-analysis Using ω^2 and d," by J. S. Hyde, *American Psychologist,* 1981, *36,* 892–901. Copyright 1981 by the American Psychological Association. Reprinted by permission.

characteristics may affect cognition *indirectly* (Newcombe & Bandura, 1983). For example, individual differences in personality traits may cause people to choose activities consistent with those traits, as in Scarr and McCartney's (1983) theory (see Chapter 3). To the extent that personality characteristics are determined by genes (Bouchard, 1985; Plomin, 1986), biology would indirectly influence a child's style of thinking.

Thus, for example, sex differences in activity level found in infancy are apparently biological in nature (Phillips et al., 1978): boys are more active than girls. As a result of this inherent difference, boys and girls, on the average, may explore the environment differently and engage in different types of play activities (DiPietro, 1981; Halverson & Waldrop, 1973). Such a biologically based difference would affect the types of experiences boys and girls have, which, in turn, may affect their patterns of thinking (Connor & Serbin, 1977; Hazen, 1982).

In seeking the origins of sex differences, possible genetic and early hormonal differences cannot be dismissed out of hand—nor can the crucial role of experience. Future research needs to focus on how biology and experience interact to yield various patterns of performance.

State of the Art
Providing Black Male Role Models

Fathers provide far more to their children than food and shelter; they also serve as role models for their children's future adult behavior. Boys watch their fathers and learn about being a man, and girls interact with their fathers and learn about being a woman. Children learn about relationships and marriage by watching their fathers and mothers interacting together.

Our human flexibility allows for substitutes in this important job. If fathers are absent, children can learn these important lessons from grandfathers, stepfathers, and uncles. Older brothers sometimes fill in as male role models, and even teachers or football coaches can do the job. However, when there is a shortage of adult men in a culture, and when many of the adult men who *are* available are not positive role models, children grow up with distorted ideas about adulthood and their roles as men and women. This is the case in many inner-city black communities today. The good news is that groups of black men have banded together as volunteer role models for their brothers' children.

The Problem

The status of young black men has deteriorated in several significant areas. Young black men are missing from their urban communities because an unusually high number of them are dead or in prison. Black males in the United States have a higher rate of death in infancy than any other group. The number-one cause of death among young black men is homicide, and suicide is number three (Gibbs, 1988). The death rates for heart disease, drugs, and AIDS are all higher for black men than for either black women or whites of either gender (Milloy, 1989). And a sobering report in 1990 showed that

Throughout the United States, black men volunteer as role models for young black boys who lack positive images.

23% of black men in their 20s are either in prison, on probation, or on parole (McAllister, 1990).

Black men who are present in the inner-city communities often do not provide positive role models for children because of unemployment, lack of education, or involvement with drugs and alcohol. The unemployment rate for this group is 40% to 60%, in part because of lack of education. Almost half of all black males in inner-city schools drop out before graduation. One-fifth of young black males cannot read at a fourth-grade level, making them ineligible for entry-level jobs, apprenticeship programs, and the military (Gibbs, 1988). And young black males who do graduate from high school do not go on to college. In fact, the number of black men in college has actually decreased over the past decade (Vobejda, 1989).

As a result, young inner-city children have few positive male role models to interact with. They also have few successful adult male-female relationships to observe and to base their adult expectations on. A shortage of men means fewer husbands and fathers, a shortage of employed men means that mothers fare better being single than being married (Meisler & Fulwood, 1990).

A *Few Hundred* Solutions

Fortunately, many people are concerned about this problem, and many solutions are being put into action. Some of the best have come from young black men in inner-city areas who *do* have educations, jobs, good health, and positive attitudes. Many grew up in situations similar to today's children, and they want to show them that success is possible. Others had better childhood experiences and want to share their good fortune. Regardless of their motives, young black men from all over the country have volunteered to work with inner-city children through several hundred programs, a few of which will be described here.

WDCU–*Malcolm* X *mentor program* In 1988, two friends in Washington, D.C., began a program to provide black male mentors for elementary school boys. The two friends were Joe Carter, Jr., assistant principal at Malcolm X Elementary School, and Ernest White, director of community affairs at radio station WDCU-FM. Carter had noticed for a few years that his bright, enthusiastic third-grade boys would return from summer vacation as cynical, unmotivated fourth-graders. He also learned that these were early warning signs for dropping out of school (Milloy, 1988).

Carter discussed the situation with his friend White, and they agreed that black boys needed positive role models to counteract the influence of the streets. White broadcast a call for employed black men to volunteer as mentors. He immediately got offers from 25 men, including a carpenter, a jeweler, a lawyer, a teacher, a bike repairman, and a martial arts instructor. They were checked out by the school security office and received some training on how best to serve as positive role models (Milloy, 1988).

The rules of the program are that each mentor help his "mentee" with schoolwork once a week, do some fun activity with him each month, and be available "just to talk."

The WDCU–Malcolm X mentor program is going strong today and, according to *Washington Post* columnist William Raspberry (1989), is the city's most successful effort at providing role models for troubled boys. (Although the Big Brothers/Big Sisters of America program is bigger and older—founded in 1905—the programs differ in that they provide friendly guidance and advice rather than a surrogate family relationship.) There are now 35 or more volunteers, mostly single black men between 25 and 32. The program has sparked some jealousy among girls and boys who are excluded from it, but Carter and White believe that it is accomplishing what they set out to do—to save high-risk boys from dying on the streets (Raspberry, 1989).

One Hundred Black Men   This group was begun in 1963 in New York City when a group of black men gathered together to offer themselves as positive role models for inner-city children. There were 100 men at the first meeting, so they selected that tally for their group's name. Since that time, One Hundred Black Men groups have been formed in urban areas all over the United States. In Miami, Florida, a newly formed branch has only 25 members, most from working-class backgrounds, but already they have become a significant presence in the community. At the end of the school year, they chose four predominantly black middle schools and presented certificates of achievement to 12 black boys who had made the honor roll. Then they had the names displayed on two community billboards with the slogan "Watch this list grow!" (Hackett, 1990).

One Hundred Black Men of Miami also works with high school students through Project Success, which is aimed at helping young black men develop job-interview skills. They also make it possible for interested young men to visit college campuses to see what university life is like. Most of the funding so far has come from the mentors' pockets, says Albert E. Dotson, Jr., president of the group. "We realize the problem is immense," he says. "We don't have any grandiose plans to be the savior of the black community . . . but we do recognize that we have an obligation to make a difference" (Hackett, 1990).

Project 2000   This mentor project was started in 1988 in Washington, D.C., by a group called Concerned Black Men, and is now present in many urban areas across the country. It is not limited to black men and boys, but includes role models for all mi-

nority children. Project 2000 brings minority professionals from the community into elementary schools to tell about their jobs and education and to counsel students about their futures (Hackett, 1990). Volunteer mentors also include students from Howard University, a prestigious, predominantly black institution in the D.C. area.

Project 2000 began at Stanton Elementary School in the inner-city section of Washington, D.C., and got its name from the year its first group of students will graduate from high school—the class of 2000 (Sanchez, 1990). One thing that makes it different from other mentor programs is that the men come to the school and work half-day shifts as teachers' aides. Founder Spencer Holland, a school psychologist at Stanton Elementary School and a member of Concerned Black Men, cites statistics showing that 80% of the students at his school live in mother-only homes. Many of them don't know their fathers. The school provides little in the way of male role models, having only two male teachers, and as Holland explains, "these boys . . . begin very early to define learning as a very feminine thing to do." A major objective, says Holland, is "just for them to see that it's all right to be a man and like to read" (Sanchez, 1990).

Building Black Men   This program, started in 1981 in Chicago, is a blend of Christianity and black consciousness that stresses decision-making skills, black history, and community service. Black adult males who volunteer from the community serve as role models and lead group activities that help counter the pressures of the street. Group coordinator Richard Simmons says that young people's participation in the Chicago Building Black Men program is directly related to the amount of participation by adult volunteers. He acknowledges the difficulty black men have in finding time for volunteer work, but he also believes they have a "special responsibility to get involved" (Smothers, 1989).

These programs, based on black adults helping black boys grow up, have been successful in part because they don't place blame or wait for government-financed support. If these programs are successful, as *Washington Post* columnist William Raspberry (1989) says, it will be because black leaders "had the guts to go public with an embarrassing problem, put aside the search for scapegoats, and look for workable answers to some fiendishly difficult questions."

Summary

Gender identification refers to the process of identifying oneself as male or female and adopting the roles and values of that sex. Gender differences start with the chromosomes, with the sex chromosomes of all normal males being XY and of all normal females being XX. The chromosomes determine the gonads (testes or ovaries), which produce hormones (androgens and mullerian-inhibiting hormone in males, estrogen in females). Mullerian-inhibiting hormone stops feminization of the fetus, and androgen (specifically, testosterone) directs the construction of male sex organs and affects the developing brain.

Parents behave differently toward male and female children, often unconsciously. Parents and other adults are important role models for children's gender identity, but other children also serve as important models for gender-appropriate behavior.

Masculinity and femininity can be viewed not as a single continuum but as independent dimensions. People who have many characteristics of both males and females are said to be androgynous. Androgynous adults have been shown to behave more flexibly and to be better adjusted than strongly sex-typed people.

Children's knowledge of the constancy of gender has been proposed to be important for gender identification. Research has shown a developmental progression of gender constancy: first, children are able to identify males and females; then they understand that gender is stable over time; finally, they realize that gender remains consistent over situations. Level of gender constancy has been associated with children's attention to same-sex models, knowledge of sex stereotypes, and, for preschool children, intelligence.

Research has found no sex differences in shyness, sociability, strength of infant attachment to parents, suggestibility, self-esteem, or general intelligence. Sex differences have been found in other areas, however. In terms of social and emotional behaviors, boys are more aggressive, active, and prone to take risks than girls, whereas girls are more nurturing and less demanding of parental attention than boys. Boys and girls also differ in their preferences for toys and games, and some of the differences are evident very early in life. Sex differences in cognition have been found in verbal skills, favoring girls, and in mathematical and spatial skills, favoring boys. Although these differences are reliable, they are small in magnitude. Some sex differences appear to be based on genetic or prenatal hormone exposure, whereas others are indirectly related to biological differences.

Because of unemployment, crime, and higher death rates among black men, many black American children are growing up without adult male role models, and this seems to be particularly troublesome for black boys. A number of mentor programs, organized and run by black men, have arisen in urban areas throughout the United States to provide positive role models for black boys.

Key Terms and Concepts

gender identification
gender differentiation
    sex chromosomes
    morphological differences
    androgens
    estrogens
    mullerian-inhibiting hormone
    testosterone
    androgen insensitivity
    adrenogenital syndrome
androgyny
gender constancy
    gender identity
    gender stability
    gender consistency
sex differences
mentor programs

The Development of Sexuality

An elderly woman in our neighborhood provides after-school care for about half a dozen children each afternoon. They call her Granny, and she gives them old-fashioned, no-nonsense discipline. Granny's kids walk from the neighborhood elementary school without dawdling, and they have home-baked cookies and milk before buckling down to homework at the kitchen table. They also get refresher courses on "please" and "thank you," proper grammar, and adding "sir" and "ma'am" onto their answers to adults' questions. Parents pay top dollar for Granny's day care, and there is always a waiting list.

One Saturday afternoon while we were doing yardwork, Granny stopped by on her morning walk. She was having a problem with one of her after-school kids and wanted some advice. This 10-year-old boy seemed to be thinking about sex an awful lot. He had set up situations outdoors where he could look up girls' dresses, and he had drawn genitals on some of the pictures in his science book. His parents had noticed similar behavior at home and asked Granny's advice. Now she wondered what we thought.

We told her that the behavior she described seemed more like normal curiosity than obsession, and suggested that his parents bring up the subject of sex differences and see if he had any questions or comments.

Then Granny chuckled and told us about her own sex education some 60 years earlier. "My mother sat me down one day and told me all the facts—the names for everything and how they worked to make babies. Then she told me, 'OK, now you know it. Now forget it!' And it was never mentioned again."

The boy of Granny's quandary moved away soon after that, so we never will find out if our advice helped or not, but Granny's sex education at her mother's knee has remained a topic of discussion for us ever since—not because it was so old-fashioned and unusual, but because it is not too different from the instruction that young people get today. But unlike Granny, children today grow up in a world saturated with sexuality. They learn fast, regardless of their parents' deficient lectures. But what do they learn? And how do these often-distorted lessons affect their developing sexuality and their thoughts about themselves as sexual beings?

Sexuality refers to an individual's erotic thoughts and activities. While few question the fact that all normal adult humans have erotic thoughts and almost all engage in erotic behavior, little is known about how these important components of our identity develop. We are not naive enough to think that such a complex set of thoughts and behavior appears fully developed on one's wedding night (or, to be more liberal, on one's 18th birthday), but much of the course of the development of sexuality over childhood and adolescence remains a mystery.

John Money (1976) referred to the study of childhood sexuality as "the last frontier in sex research." Volumes have been written about adult sexuality, but scientific inquiry into childhood sexuality is limited, for the most part, to how sexual pathology develops and the effects of sexual child abuse on its victims. We find ourselves in the curious situation of knowing more about the development of sexual deviance than the development of sexual normalcy (Finkelhor, 1979).

Sexuality develops. There is a strong genetic and hormonal basis for our sexuality, but as with all aspects of human development, social and environmental factors also play vital roles. In this chapter, we will examine how these factors influence the development of sexuality, beginning before birth and continuing into early adulthood. We will also discuss some of the reasons for the lack of research on this important topic and take a look at the development of children's thinking about their own sexuality and what happens when adults withhold information. We conclude the chapter with a discussion of the consequences of teenage pregnancy—both for the teenage mothers and for their children.

The Process of Sexual Development

Early Physiological Capabilities

It has been known for some time that during the first 24 hours of life, newborns are capable of the physiological components of sexual arousal: penile erection in males, and clitoral erection and vaginal lubrication in females (Halverson, 1940; Masters & Johnson, 1966; Langfeldt, 1981). In fact, ultrasound pictures of 7-month male fetuses show that penile erection occurs before birth (Calderone, 1983). The debate goes on as to whether or not these behaviors should be considered "sociosexual erotic awakenings" and whether it is necessary to have certain memory and fantasy abilities before this behavior is considered comparable to adult sexuality, but the basic fact remains: newborns are capable of human sexual responses.

Masturbation

Infants before the age of 1 have been observed to masturbate—that is, to stimulate their genitals intentionally, either manually or by rubbing their bodies against some object; in fact, there is one report of an ultrasound video of a male fetus masturbating (Meizner, 1987). Alfred Kinsey and his colleagues (Kinsey, Pomeroy, & Martin, 1953) recorded their observations of such behavior in a 7-month-old infant and in five 12-month-olds. In fact, genital manipulation occurs in infants at the same age that their motor coordination allows them to reach for and intentionally handle other objects in their environment.

Bjorn Gundersen, Per Melas, and Jens Skar (1981) interviewed 60 preschool teachers in Norway about their students' sexual behavior, yielding information on 400 children. When asked about the occurrence of masturbation, 51 of the 60 teachers said that it occurred during the school day. Of these 51, 39 said it occurred "seldom or now and then," and 12 said it occurred "often or very often."

Glenn Ramsey (1943a) summarized six studies regarding onset age of masturbation in boys, with the following results:

Age	Percent who masturbate
8	14%
9	23%
10	29%
11	54%
12	73%
13	85%
14	95%
15	98%

Orgasm

At what age does masturbation lead to orgasm? Kinsey and his colleagues (1953) found that 50% of the 3- and 4-year-old boys they studied could masturbate and achieve orgasm. (Recall from Chapter 5 that the neural connections underlying orgasm are established early in development, but ejaculation does not occur until puberty.) In Gundersen's interviews

of preschool teachers, of the 51 who observed their students engaging in masturbation, 12 said the children experienced orgasm, and 36 did not know. Of 90 subjects in Norway, ages 7 to 67, interviewed by Thore Langfeldt (1981), 18 (20%) reported having orgasms in early childhood.

Popular views hold that "normal" sexuality begins during puberty, when hormones are released and adolescents become capable of reproduction (males by producing sperm and females by releasing ova). However, it is apparent from the research reported here that puberty and its hormones are not necessary for erotic behavior in children (Langfeldt, 1981). By the time puberty arrives, the majority of children are already capable of the physical acts of masturbation and orgasm.

Rene Spitz (1971) suggested a developmental progression of normal sexual development, with emotionally healthy children displaying some genital play by 12 months, masturbation in the preschool years, and intercourse by late adolescence. Spitz believed that these manifestations of childhood sexuality are as much an indicator of good emotional health as adult sexuality is.

Early Peer Influence

Although early sexuality typically involves masturbation and genital self-exploration, they do not seem to be strictly solitary activities. Teachers report that young children seldom let the presence of other children or the teacher interfere with these activities (Gundersen et al., 1981). Preschool children also exhibit interest in other children's genitals. Of the 60 teachers interviewed by Gundersen and his colleagues, 38 said that their students were "sometimes" interested in other students' genitals, and 19 said their students were "often" or "very often" interested in their classmates' genitals. Interest increased with age. Boys showed more interest in the genitals of others than girls did, and both boys and girls were more interested in boys' genitals.

This sex difference has been found in other studies, and some researchers attach importance to the fact that boys' genitals and their arousal are more apparent than those of girls (Langfeldt, 1981). As a result, boys' sexuality is more a focus of social interest than girls', and the word "penis" is learned earlier by both boys and girls than either "clitoris" or "vagina." Boys are more apt to notice the sexual arousal of another boy and to comment on it. Studies also show that boys often practice masturbation together, exchange sexual information, and engage in pretend male-female sexual behavior. Similar behavior is not reported for girls, who tend to practice

private masturbation and exchange less sexual information (Langfeldt, 1981).

Heterosexual sex play has also been observed in preschoolers. Of the 60 preschool teachers interviewed by Gundersen and associates (1981), 39 said

Box 17.1

Freud's Psychosexual Theory of Development

Sigmund Freud developed a theory of psychosexual development that served as the cornerstone of clinical psychology for most of this century. Freud believed that sexually based conflict was the driving force for personality development and that psychological problems in adulthood could often be traced to childhood experiences.

Freud proposed that the sex drive is a primary instinct, expressed at all stages of life, that is centered on various erogenous zones in the body. These zones change during the course of development, shifting from the oral to the anal area over the course of early childhood, and then to the genital area. According to Freud, how parents deal with their children's sexual impulses has significant consequences for their later development. Freud placed great importance on experiences during the first five years of life, which, he believed, to a large extent determine adult personality. He believed that parents had to walk a fine line between permitting their children too much gratification of sexual impulses and too little.

Freud divided development into five stages: the **oral stage** (birth to 1 year); the **anal stage** (1 to 3 years); the **phallic stage** (3 to 5 years); the **latency stage** (5 years to puberty); and the **genital stage,** which is the mature state of psychosexual development. As in any stage theory, the ages are approximate. What distinguishes the various stages is the source of sexual excitation.

The oral stage (birth to 1 year)   During the earliest period of development, sexual excitation is centered around the mouth. Sucking, chewing, eating, and biting produce pleasure for the infant. These early

forms of gratification become associated, of course, with the satisfaction of hunger. In fact, the infant must learn to adapt its oral behavior in order to eat. Thus, the newly developing ego directs oral behavior to the breast or bottle.

The most important accomplishment of the oral period, according to Freud, is the infant's attachment to its mother—the basis for all later intimate relations. Much of children's oral gratification comes from their mothers, and infants invest a significant portion of their sex drive in her, making mother their first love object. A strong, secure attachment serves as the basis for healthy psychosexual development, whereas deficient attachment is at the root of much pathology (Bowlby, 1958; see Chapter 12).

The anal stage (1 to 3 years)   Beginning around the end of the first year, children's focus changes to the anal area. This does not mark a termination of oral needs; rather, the oral needs exist alongside the anal needs, with the latter becoming increasingly important to the child.

Freud proposed that how parents deal with toilet training has important implications for future personality development. If toilet training is attempted too early or is overly harsh, it can become a source of great anxiety to the child, which can generalize to other areas in which children must deal with authority figures.

Phallic stage (3 to 5 years)   During the next period, a child's attention is diverted from the anal area to the genital area. At this time, boys become cognizant

their students engaged in adult role-playing (65%), and of those 39, 19 said the adult role-playing involved some sort of sexual exploration or genital manipulation.

Children are more likely to begin heterosexual sex play during early childhood (5 to 7 years) than during late childhood (7 years to puberty). Alfred Kinsey and his colleagues (1948) interviewed adult men about their memories of childhood sexuality, and 20% to 25% reported that by age 12 they had

that they possess a penis (phallus), and girls become aware that they do not. Stimulation of the genitals now becomes a source of sexual tension and, if gratified, a source of pleasure. However, the main accomplishment of the phallic stage is the resolution of the **Oedipus complex,** when children's sexual focus becomes the parent of the opposite sex. (The Oedipus complex derives its name from the Greek drama in which a young man, Oedipus, unknowingly murders his father and marries his mother.)

Freud proposed that boys have sexual desires for their mothers and see their fathers as competitors. As a result, boys fear their fathers, believing that, as competitors for their mother's love, they will castrate them or remove their penises—a fear known as **castration anxiety.** This conflict between wanting the exclusive love of their mothers and fearing their fathers is resolved by repressing these feelings and identifying with the father—a process Freud referred to as **identification with the aggressor.** By identifying with and emulating his father/competitor, the boy is assuring himself that his father will not castrate him. Boys internalize their fathers' values, which presumably reflect the values of society, contributing substantially to the development of morality and self-control.

A similar process occurs for girls (sometimes referred to as the **Electra complex**). Because girls do not have penises, they believe they have already been castrated and experience **penis envy.** They love their fathers and blame their mothers for their castration. However, Freud believed that the conflict faced by girls was less intense than that faced by boys; as a result, girls' identification with their mothers is weaker.

Latency stage (5 years to the beginning of puberty)

The first three stages in Freud's theory are dynamic indeed, characterized by constant conflicts between children's sexual desires and their parents' wishes to socialize them. Freud proposed that these conflicts are often so painful that people actively repress memories from these early years. This is the reason, Freud believed, for our general inability to remember much before we entered school (see Chapter 8 for a discussion of infantile amnesia).

The conflicts diminish considerably during the latency period. During this time, no area of the body arouses sexual tension, and children seem to forget the sexual urges and conflicts of earlier years. During this time, children begin to disengage from the family and learn the ways of larger social groups, such as school and church. They become social beings, generally playing in same-sex groups and directing sexual energy into nonsexual, mainly social areas.

Genital stage (adolescence and adulthood)

With the onset of puberty, sexual impulses, repressed during the latency period, come to the fore. These new (or more mature) sexual urges are melded with the earlier, less mature sexual impulses, but are now directed toward a same-age member of the opposite sex. Ideas of romantic love and of mature sexuality are seen now, although a person's behavior is still influenced by his or her earlier experiences. For example, a young man may "want a girl just like the girl who married dear old Dad," or look for a woman who is domineering, overly dependent, or masochistic, depending on his experiences during the oral, anal, and phallic stages of development.

attempted intercourse with a female. Glenn Ramsey (1943b) found that 33% of the 10- to 12-year-old boys in his study had attempted intercourse with a female.

The Effect of Parents and Other Adults on Sexuality

Rene Spitz (1971) observed infants with widely varying maternal relationships and concluded that early attachment to one's mother plays an important role in the development of sexuality. Institutionalized infants, with no maternal relationships, showed no genital play or other autoerotic activity during the first year. Home-reared infants with good maternal relationships showed almost universal genital play, and nursery children with a wide range of maternal relationships showed a corresponding range of autoerotic activity (rocking, genital play, fecal play). Infants with the worst maternal relationships showed an absence of autoerotic activity. Spitz concluded that a child's developmental progress is related to his or her maternal relationship and is also related to autoerotic behavior.

Middle childhood is a time of learning about the world and about what's right and wrong according to adult society. Some of these lessons are explicit; others are more subtle. Children first learn that their bodies feel good and then that the bodies of others are interesting. Then they learn how to interpret these feelings by the responses of the adults around them. When adults answer their questions and respond to their developing sexuality in a positive way, they learn to accept these thoughts and feelings as an intrinsic part of their self-concept. But when the adult response is to prohibit, prevent, and punish sexuality, many children learn sexual prudery, and they practice sexuality out of the sight of adults (Money & Tucker, 1975). In fact, the Freudian period of latency (see Box 17.1) has been explained by some as the stage in which children learn that sexuality is forbidden by adults and they take their sexual questions and behavior "underground" (Goldman & Goldman, 1982).

John Money and Patricia Tucker (1975) believe that the development of sexuality should be monitored and cultivated by parents in the same way as the development of walking and talking. This is difficult when there are no guidelines for development of normal sexuality and when children are compelled to keep their erotic thoughts and questions a secret. Money and Tucker compare this dilemma to a hypothetical society that represses the topic of eating. "Consider the pathology you would have to expect in a society that prescribed secret eating, banned cookbooks and pictures of food, and pretended that children didn't eat at all" (p. 142).

Sexual problems in adulthood   The result of driving normal sex play into clandestine activities, according to Money and Tucker (1975), is that it becomes associated with guilt and secrecy. Parents' attitudes often teach the lesson that sex is dirty and disgusting. Ironically, these parents are at the same time teaching that young people should remain pure and

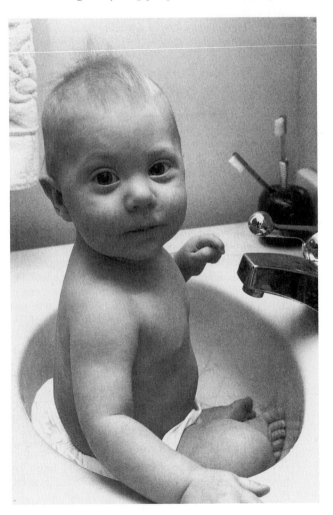

Parents convey positive or negative messages to children about their bodies and their sexuality.

chaste until marriage. The total, twisted message becomes: sex is filthy and disgusting, so you should save it for the one you truly love.

From cross-cultural studies (Ford & Beach, 1951), we know that societies that restrict adolescent and preadolescent sex play and limit girls to modest, retiring, and submissive roles produce adult women who are sexually passive and unresponsive. Richard Currier (1981) concludes that in a society where sex is presented to children as something negative and problematic, and where they are given mixed messages by their parents, it is "probably impossible to have a sexually happy marriage."

Lags in moral thinking Ronald Goldman and Juliette Goldman (1982) stated that when children grow up in a sexually restrictive atmosphere and their questions about sex and reproduction are met with embarrassment and reprimand by the adults around them, they don't develop thinking and problem-solving skills in those areas as quickly as they do in other, more accepted areas. This leads to retarded intellectual development in thinking about sexuality and reproduction. Similar findings come from work in moral development (Gilligan, Kohlberg, Lerner, & Belenky, 1971), in which teenagers show lower levels of cognitive processing in answering moral questions involving sexual dilemmas than questions involving more neutral topics. This is also consistent with research in more conventional areas of cognitive development showing that the sophistication of children's thinking varies as a functioning of their knowledge about the topic in question (Bjorklund, Muir-Broaddus, & Schneider, 1990; see Chapter 8).

Abnormal sexuality The study of **paraphilias** (sexual perversions) has received more attention and has a longer history than the study of normal sexuality. After years of clinical study of patients who practice paraphilias such as masochism and sadism, John Money (1980, 1986a) has hypothesized that the root of abnormal sexuality is in childhood when adults punish children's sexual behavior, causing feelings of sexual arousal to become intermingled with fear, pain, and other nonsexual thoughts and objects.

Adolescent Sexuality

Physical changes during puberty Puberty marks the beginning of the development of adult appearance and functions (see Chapter 5). These changes serve to further differentiate males from females and the immature individual of either gender from the adult. Puberty is set into motion when an individual's biological clock signals the sex glands to begin production of hormones. Secondary sexual characteristics—secondary because they are not vital to reproduction—that develop at this time include pubic and underarm hair in males and females, the Adam's apple and deep voice in males, and breasts and broader hips in females.

Effects on developing sexuality Children who have well-developed secondary sexual characteristics will be perceived by others as being closer to adulthood. They are apt to be given more freedom and privileges than their younger-appearing peers, and are more apt to have older friends who participate in adultlike activities. Because our self-perception is based partially on how others perceive us, a physically mature young person will begin to think of himself or herself as being psychologically and socially mature also (Brooks-Gunn & Furstenberg, 1989; see Chapter 5).

Effects on erotic thinking One effect of sex hormones is the lowering of thresholds for activation of brain pathways dealing with erotic content. These pathways are formed prenatally and, years later, are "turned on" by adult hormones (Money, 1988; Money & Tucker, 1975). In boys, sex hormones directly influence their "wet dreams" (nocturnal emissions) and sexual thoughts. In girls, pubertal hormones pique their sexual interest, but actual sexual behavior is more dependent on social influence than it is for boys (Money & Tucker, 1975).

It is important to state that one's erotic content (for example, being heterosexual) is *not* determined at puberty, but is simply activated at that time. John Money (1986a) has termed this content a **lovemap,** which he defines as a "personalized, developmental representation or template in the mind and in the brain that depicts the idealized lover and the idealized program of sexuoerotic activity with that lover as projected in imagery and ideation, or actually engaged in with that lover" (Money, 1988, p. 127). This lovemap is wired prenatally and extended during childhood. Its content is discovered explicitly by boys during wet dreams and more gradually by girls in romantic fantasies. The content of the lovemap is unavoidable, unchangeable, and probably set for life (Money & Tucker, 1975).

Related to erotic content is the phenomenon of falling in love, which sometimes occurs in puberty independent of the physical/hormonal changes that are taking place. Few scientists study falling in love, but those who do find that it typically happens first in adolescence, can happen over and over again, and

Box 17.2

Children and Sexuality

Lawrence A. Siegel M.A., AASECT
Health and Sexuality Educator
Planned Parenthood of South Palm Beach
and Broward Counties, Florida
How we feel about ourselves, how we feel about our bodies, how we interact with members of the same and opposite sex, and biological processes such as intercourse and childbirth, are all aspects of our sexuality. Because of its very nature, any definition of sexuality must be broad-based and somewhat general. Sexuality is the largest, most integral part of our personalities; it is what makes us human beings.

Sexuality education is a process, one that begins at birth and ends only at death. If we hope to teach children about sex, and to instill healthy attitudes and values, it is important that we understand children's sexuality.

From the very first day of life, a child begins to learn about sexuality, and parents are the primary source of this education. A touch, caress, smile, hug, or coo communicates love, comfort, and security to the infant. The feeling this conveys—that one is lovable and attractive—is the precursor to the development of a healthy ego and normal sexual functioning. Thus, sexuality becomes an integral part of one's capacity for love, warmth, tenderness, and intimate relationships, and can be considered the root of interpersonal behavior.

Through the years, there are countless opportunities for parents to educate and send messages about sex and sexuality. One thing that is certain is that the child will ask questions. At first, a young child may ask "What's this?" All he or she may want to know is a name by which something is called. Later, there will be other questions, and the good answers are the simple ones—the ones that tell only what the child is asking. It is important that the child's questions be answered in a straightforward and concise manner.

Children's sexuality develops in bits and pieces. We, as parents and educators, help them to fit those pieces together into a healthy, well-functioning pattern. Many of the ideas that children have about what's good or bad, comfortable or uncomfortable, come from what they see around them. In other words, children learn from the attitudes, the affection, the caring, *the sexuality* of their parents.

Reprinted by permission.

Although hormones activate erotic thoughts at puberty, the images have been forming throughout childhood.

lasts anywhere from a few hours to two years, when it can be replaced by the more mellow state of "being in love." Falling in love seems to involve more environmental factors than puberty does, because children with precocious puberty do not fall in love until they reach the teenage years, even though they have masturbation fantasies and nocturnal emissions at ages consistent with their physical development. Some people in their 30s and 40s may have developed normally, even had children, but never fallen in love (Money & Tucker, 1975).

Adolescent sexual behavior   Although puberty is not the beginning of sexuality, it does signal a change in the frequency and intensity of sexual thoughts and behaviors. Masturbation is practiced by almost all teenage boys and by many teenage girls, often accompanied by sexual fantasies. One study found that more than 90% of adolescents who reported mastur-

bating also reported fantasizing during masturbation (Sorenson, 1973). According to William Masters, Virginia Johnson, and Robert Kolodny (1985), masturbation with fantasies serves several useful purposes during adolescence: it is a safe substitute for intercourse and also provides a chance to rehearse mentally for later sexual situations and to practice using sexual imagery for future relationships. Regardless of how normal and useful masturbation is during adolescence, more than half the teenagers interviewed in one study reported guilt and other negative feelings about it "sometimes" or "often" (Sorenson, 1973).

In adolescence, erotic activity between males and females is termed "petting," especially if it is centered around the genitals but doesn't result in intercourse. Alfred Kinsey and his team (1948, 1953) found that 39% of the women and 57% of the men in their adult samples reported having engaged in heterosexual petting by the time they were 15 years old. By age 18, 80% of both sexes reported doing so; however, only 20% reported that they had experienced orgasm as a result of heterosexual petting.

What is the difference between childhood sex play and adolescent petting? One difference is in the characteristics of the partners. Younger children seem less selective about their sex-play companions: opportunity seems to be the deciding factor, with most children engaging in sex play with classmates, neighborhood playmates, and siblings regardless of other factors, including gender and number (Langfeldt, 1981). With adolescence, sex play (or petting) becomes more adultlike in form, with partners chosen for gender and desirable physical/social/personality characteristics, in the context of a more romantic partnership (Sorenson, 1973).

The difference between petting and heterosexual intercourse is a slight one, with two exceptions: intercourse can produce pregnancy, and it delineates the virgins from the nonvirgins—a distinction that is important to society and, therefore, important also to adolescents and their developing sense of identity.

Most information we have on adolescent heterosexual intercourse is survey-style, which tells us what adolescents report to the survey team (see Table 17.1). As with child sexuality, some of the surveys consist of what adults recall (or admit) about their childhood sexual behavior. Other information comes from teenage pregnancy and abortion data, which tell us that those teenage girls have definitely

Table 17.1 Percentage of unmarried teenage females who report having coital experience

Age	Study			
	Kinsey et al. (1953)	Sorenson (1973)	Zelnik and Kantner (1980)	
			[1971]	[1979]
13	1	9	—	—
14	2	15	—	—
15	3	26	14	23
16	5	35	21	38
17	9	37	26	49
18	14		40	57
		45		
19	17		46	69

Source: From *Human Sexuality*, 2nd Ed., by W. H. Masters, V. E. Johnson, and R. C. Kolodny. Copyright © 1985 by W. H. Masters and V. E. Johnson. Reprinted by permission.

had intercourse within the past year, but little about how long they had been having intercourse and under what circumstances before they became pregnant. It also tells us nothing about the other adolescent boys and girls who also had intercourse but did not get "caught." And, more important, it tells us little about sexuality. The results of an international survey examining the frequency of births to teenagers are shown in Figure 17.1.

What determines whether a young person has heterosexual intercourse early or late in adolescence? Besides physical maturity, other factors have been found to influence the timing of first intercourse. Those with close ties to their parents and those whose mothers have told them about sex (for both male and female adolescents) tend to have intercourse at a later age than adolescents with distant parents and boys whose fathers have told them about sex (Jessor & Jessor, 1977; Kahn, Smith, & Roberts, 1984). Teens who date early are more apt to have intercourse early, and those who have poor grades and low expectations for their future are apt to have intercourse earlier than better students and those who have higher expectations for the future (Smith & Udry, 1985).

Mature sexuality includes responsibility for one's sexual relations and is often measured by use of contraceptives. When this yardstick is used, North American adolescents rank among the most sexually immature. Although the rate of intercourse during adolescence is equal to that of other countries, the teenage birthrate is higher in the United States than

in almost every other industrialized country (Jones et al., 1985; see Figure 17.1). Only 50% of American teenagers use contraceptives during their first experience of sexual intercourse (Zelnik & Shah, 1983). Not surprisingly, older adolescents are more apt to use contraceptives than younger adolescents. Figures for sexual maturity by sex and race show that about half of white girls and boys and half of black girls use contraceptives at first intercourse, compared to only 25% of black boys. Although these figures are for the first act of intercourse, they are not independent of the teenage pregnancy rate.

Around the world, cultural attitudes toward sexuality range from repressive to supportive.

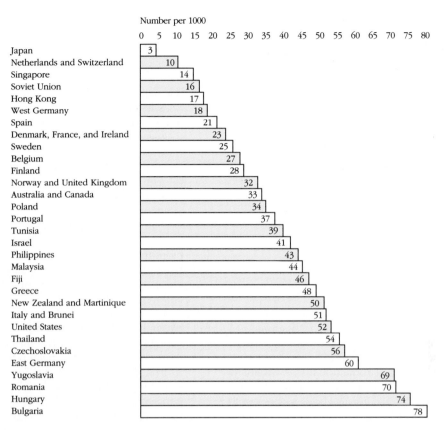

Number per 1000

Figure 17.1 Number of births per 1000 women younger than 20, selected countries, mid- to late 1970s. *Source:* From *Teenage Pregnancy: The Problem Hasn't Gone Away,* by Alan Guttmacher Institute. Copyright © 1981 by Alan Guttmacher Institute. Reprinted by permission.

Studies of teenage pregnancies show that 20% occur in the first month after intercourse begins and 50% occur within six months of first intercourse (Zabin, Kantner, & Zelnik, 1979).

What factors seem to be related to use of contraceptives? Teens are less likely to use contraceptives if they come from low socioeconomic groups, have no steady sexual partner or have infrequent intercourse, have poor communication with parents, low grades and educational aspirations, high anxiety, and low self-esteem, and feel powerless and alienated (Brooks-Gunn & Furstenberg, 1989).

Another measure of mature sexuality is being knowledgeable about sexually transmitted diseases and taking preventive measures not to contract them or, if contracted, not to pass them on. American teenagers do not rank favorably on these measures of

sexual maturity either. After homosexual men and prostitutes, teenage girls have the highest rate of any group in the United States for gonorrhea, cytomegalovirus, chlamydia cervicitis, and pelvic inflammatory disease (Cates & Raugh, 1985; Mosher, 1985). Though the numbers are not high, adolescent cases of AIDS have been doubling each year; 20% of all cases are in 20- to 29-year-olds, who may have contracted it during late adolescence (Curran et al., 1988).

Sex education is important for adolescents. Although they are exposed to adult eroticism in movies and TV programs, teenagers often lack the basic facts of human reproduction. In a 1977 study, for example, only 33% of older teens could tell the phase of a woman's menstrual cycle during which she was most likely to get pregnant—namely, at midcycle, when ovulating (Zelnik & Kantner, 1977). Another study reported on the surprised responses of teenage girls after being informed at a family planning clinic that they were pregnant. Reasons for surprise included thinking that they could not get pregnant at a particular phase of their menstrual cycle, that they had not had sex often enough to get pregnant, that they could not get pregnant unless they had an orgasm, and that they were too young to get pregnant (Shah, Zelnik, & Kantner, 1975).

Dealing with teen sexuality, however, involves more than transmitting facts of reproduction. Parents and other adults need to recognize that adolescents are sexually mature individuals who need to learn about responsible love and relationships.

Why Do We Know So Little about Sexual Development?

The topic of childhood sexuality is not a new one. Sigmund Freud wrote about it at the beginning of the century; and in the 1920s, Jean Piaget speculated on the difficulties of conducting research on children's thinking about reproduction (1969, originally published in 1929). Although many other topics of that era have generated extensive bodies of research findings, the development of sexuality and children's thinking about reproduction have remained largely a mystery.

Our Restrictive/Permissive Society

We may view ourselves and our society as being open-minded and liberal about sexuality, but when the topic becomes children's erotic thoughts and behavior, most adults become closed-minded and ultraconservative. Since the 19th century, children in most technological cultures have been presumed to be asexual and innocent, and society has tried to protect them from the "harsh realities" of adulthood (Gagnon & Simon, 1973). Evidence of child sexuality was viewed as dangerous and confined to a few "evil" children. When Freud made his pronouncement that normal children had erotic thoughts and behavior, it was particularly shocking to think that these occurred in most or almost all normal children.

For example, as recently as 100 years ago, masturbation in children was viewed as a serious problem. Parents tried to discourage masturbation by forcing their children to wear metal mittens or straitjackets to bed, buckling them into "genital cages" that resembled medieval chastity belts, and inserted boys' penises into spikelike tubes designed to inhibit erections (Reinisch, 1990). Children's hands were tied to

Table 17.2 Types of human cultures by attitudes toward sex

Type	Attitude	Locations	Premarital Sex Allowed?	Adolescent Sex Allowed?	Child Sex Play Allowed?
Repressive	Sex is denied; seen as dangerous	Common in Europe, Catholic countries	No	No	No
Restrictive	Sex is limited; seen as problematic	Dominant in other developed countries: parts of U.S. and Canada, non-Catholic countries	For one gender (usually males)	For one gender (usually males)	No
Permissive	Sex is tolerated; rules exist but are not enforced	Parts of U.S. and Canada, non-Catholic Europe	Not allowed, but common	Not allowed, but common	Not allowed, but common
Supportive	Sex is cultivated; seen as indispensable; should begin early	Chewa (Africa); Ifregao (Philippines); Tepcha (India); Maori, Easter Island, Trobriand (Oceania)	Yes	Yes; times, places, and encouragement provided	Yes; times, places, and encouragement provided

Source: Adapted from "Juvenile Sexuality in Global Perspective," by R. L. Currier. In L. L. Constantine and F. M. Martinson (eds.), *Children and Sex: New Findings, New Perspectives.* Copyright © 1981 by Little, Brown, & Co. Reprinted by permission.

bedposts, their legs were tied together, and even surgical procedures (including castration and removal of the clitoris) were prescribed. Special diets were suggested to curb masturbation, and during the 1800s, some foods were developed specifically to reduce sexual arousal. Two of these products failed to prevent masturbation but became popular in their own right and can be found on our grocery shelves today: Graham Crackers and Kellogg's Corn Flakes (Money, 1985).

Clellan Ford and Frank Beach (1951) studied the sexual play of children in many societies around the world and categorized the societies according to adult attitudes toward sexual expression in children—restrictive, semirestrictive, and permissive—with American society at that time being in the restrictive category. Richard Currier (1981), expanding on Ford and Beach's work, postulated four categories: repressive, restrictive, permissive, and suppor-

tive (see Table 17.2). According to Currier, western society from 1900 to 1950 advanced from repressive to restrictive, and people born in the 1960s may raise their children with a permissive attitude. Thus, American society is now in a stage between restrictive and permissive in its attitude toward sexuality.

Freud's Latency Period

One of the reasons psychologists do not study childhood sexuality is, ironically, a portion of Freud's theory of psychosexual development (Janus & Best, 1981; see Box 17.1). Although he had much to say about sexuality at other times of life and was the first to suggest that children were sexual beings, Freud considered the years from 5 to 11 to be the stage of latency, which is widely interpreted as a period during which children are released from sexual thoughts and desires and can concentrate on other

Box 17.3

Memories from Childhood: College Students Recall Asking Adults about Sex and Reproduction

"In first grade, some of us girls were sitting around the playground with our dolls and we started talking about where real babies come from. We decided to ask our teacher. So we ran over to where she was standing on the playground and asked all our questions. She said that recess was over and we had to go inside."

"At 8 I asked my mother where babies came from and she said you have to put in an order and then the stork brings them."

"When I was 9, my mother was pregnant and I asked how the baby got inside her. She said it grew from a seed. Later I asked how the baby got out. She said the doctor took it out."

"When I was 7 and my brother was 5, our mom went to the hospital to have a baby. We stayed with our aunt. We kept asking her questions about where the baby came from and how it was going to get

out of our mother, but she kept sending us outside to play."

"Our parents always told us that the wolves brought us."

"My grandmother said that I was left on the doorstep and my parents decided to keep me."

"When I was 7 or 8, I asked my mother about where babies came from. She said, 'From God. And you have to be married first!'"

"My mother told me she would explain when I was older. I was *10.*"

"My family is East European and they told me they bought me from the gypsies—and if I wasn't good, they would sell me back."

"I never got up the nerve to ask my parents."

interests, such as schoolwork and friendships. When infantile sexuality is explained away as exploration and curiosity, and sexuality during the years of 5 through 11 dismissed as latent, sexuality becomes enmeshed with reproductive ability and is viewed as beginning in adolescence. However, current research on children's thinking about sexuality and reproduction provides strong evidence against a latency period—"so strong as to merit the description of 'the myth of latency'" (Goldman & Goldman, 1982, p. 391).

Age Segregation

Although we give it little thought, age is an important issue in Western society. Sharp distinctions are made between parent and child, teacher and student—between adults and children in general. These distinctions become problematic when they affect the important early relationships children have with parents and other adults close to them. There are some topics—above all, sexuality—that parents do not feel comfortable discussing with children, even children in their own family (see Box 17.3).

The reverse side of this is that children don't like to discuss sexuality with their parents. How many teenagers or preteens have been mortified when their mothers became pregnant? How many adolescents and young adults become embarrassed or break into nervous laughter at the thought of their parents having sexual relations? When sexuality is viewed as the personal property of adults, it is often considered "off limits" to parent-child conversation.

The Role of Research

Parents of young children are not the only ones who feel awkward about childhood sexuality. Scientists, and the people who fund their research, often feel uncomfortable about investigating childhood sexuality, and if they attempt to do so, they run into problems. Children cannot be used in research without the permission of their parents, the school district (if the research is done in schools), and the university ethics board (see Chapter 2). It is difficult enough to study the development of children's mathematical reasoning, much less erotic thinking!

This was the dilemma faced by Ernest Borneman (1983), an Austrian researcher who decided early in his career to study children's sexuality. He first tried to get parental permission to interview children, but most of the parents he approached refused. Then he got permission from several schools, but most of the children would not answer his questions because they thought he was a spy from the school authorities. His next approach was to make a tape of children's "smutty" songs and rhymes and play it in a public park. He found that children were attracted by the songs and rhymes, frequently offered additional verses, and easily discussed their thoughts and questions about sexuality. The only problem was that he and his research assistants were arrested frequently and had to carry proof of their university

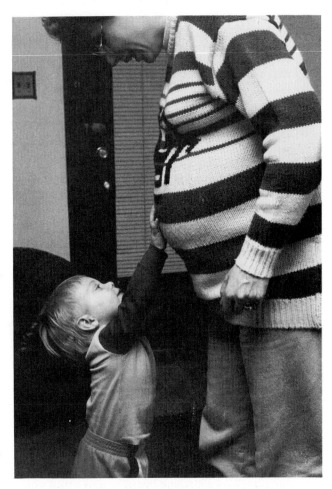

Children absorb information about reproduction and then adapt it to their cognitive structures, often with surprising results.

affiliation and academic credentials. Finally, he trained children to run the tape recorder and interview other children. Over a 30-year period, he managed to gather interviews with 2000 children, but not without a lot of effort.

Many researchers cited previously in this chapter bypassed these problems by studying childhood sexuality without using children as subjects. Alfred Kinsey, Wardell Pomeroy, and Clyde Martin (1948, 1953) interviewed adults about their childhood sexual play with other children, and David Finkelhor (1981) surveyed college students about their sexual play with siblings. Robert Kolodny (1980) interviewed parents of 6- and 7-year-olds about their children's sex play with other children and siblings. Bjorn Gundersen, Per Melas, and Jens Skar (1981) interviewed preschool teachers about their students' sexual behavior and questions about sex. Some (such as Ramsey, 1943b) managed to interview older children (10, 11, and 12) about their erotic thoughts and behavior.

Larry Constantine and Floyd Martinson (1981), in their collection of studies on childhood sexuality, write of the reluctance to investigate this area by giving the ancient mapmakers' caution about uncharted locations of the world: "Here There Be Dragons." By presenting this material, we hope to show future psychologists, teachers, pediatricians, nurses, and parents that, although we may not know exactly what this area of development contains, there certainly are not any dragons.

Children's Thinking about Sexuality and Reproduction

In the 1920s, Jean Piaget was interested in the development of children's thinking about reproduction; however, he limited his research to reviewing what children had told other investigators. He was well aware of the problems of interviewing children directly about these matters. "It would be well to know children's ideas on the birth of babies," he wrote. "But it goes without saying that there are grave moral and pedagogic reasons for not pursuing such an investigation directly" (1969, p. 360). During the next half-century, although morality changed somewhat, few researchers took advantage of the more open atmosphere to pursue this line of inquiry.

The Development of Knowledge about Reproduction

In 1975, Anne Bernstein and Philip Cowan did a study of children's knowledge of the origin of babies. They used 30 boys and 30 girls, ranging in age from 3 to 12 years, to demonstrate that this knowledge develops in stages and that those stages follow the same general blueprint as Piaget's stages of cognitive development (see Table 17.3). The researchers concluded that children actively construct their notions about babies rather than wait to be told. These self-constructed ideas reflect their present cognitive structures and often are based on information they received but were unable to take in (assimilate) until they transformed it in some way to fit their cognitive level. Thus, parents can give the same talk about the origin of babies to their children every few years, and each time their children will learn something different—not just extra bits and pieces of information, but qualitatively different versions of it.

Bernstein and Cowan suggested that parents and educators learn to assess their children's present level of thinking so they can understand what to expect in the way of questions and speculations about the origins of babies. They also commented about research done to determine the best level of information children should be given at different ages (Turiel, 1969) and suggested that parents and educators give children information one level beyond their current understanding.

More recently, Ronald and Juliette Goldman (1982) interviewed 838 children in four countries to investigate not only developmental differences but also cultural differences in children's sexual thinking. Consistent with the findings of Bernstein and Cowan (1975), they reported several well-defined levels of understanding that follow Piaget's stages of cognitive development. They found, however, that Swedish children progressed through these levels of thinking well ahead of Australian and English children, and that North American children were the slowest.

Goldman and Goldman discussed the implications of their study in terms that should be of interest to parents and professionals working with children. First, the finding that American children lagged far behind in their thinking and problem-solving skills pertaining to sexuality suggests that parents and educators should rethink their ideas on sex education and begin it earlier, when children are curious and interested, and present honest information at a level that children can best understand. The Goldmans recommend that, with few exceptions, the basic biology of sexuality and reproduction can be understood by elementary school children. (The two concepts elementary school children have trouble with are why the birth of a baby occurs when it does and how the baby's gender is determined genetically.)

Second, the Goldmans note that much of the confusion children have about sexuality and reproduction can be traced to parents' inhibitions and reluctance to use correct terminology when giving children information about these topics. They recommend that adults take care in their use of analogy to explain reproduction to children. For example, using terms such as "seeds" and "fertilize" is easily accepted by children as a gardening scenario (see also Reinisch, 1990).

Third, the findings of this study suggest that sex education needs to be taught by parents in the preschool years and then offered in the schools as part of a family/school cooperative program.

Children's Views on Sex Education

As part of their research project, Goldman and Goldman also asked children in four cultures about their thoughts on sex education. Should children be taught about sex? Of all the children in the sample, ages 5 to 15, 92% said yes; the dissenters were almost all younger children. Should children learn about sex at school? An overwhelming majority (83%) said yes; again, it was the younger children who said no. Among the older children, ages 9 to 15, 91% favored sex education in school. When they were asked whether they had received such lessons, however, large cultural differences were found: 87%

***Table* 17.3** Development of children's thinking about reproduction

Level	Piagetian Stage	Ages	Name	Description	Example
1	Preoperational	3–7	Geographer	Babies have always existed in completed form; need to be acquired (bought, found, ordered, delivered).	Mommy got me at the hospital.
2	Preoperational	4–8	Manufacturer	Babies haven't always existed in completed form; need to be assembled.	Mommy made me out of blood and bones she had left over from my brother.
3	Transitional	5–10	In-betweens	Babies need two parents in special relationship, sexual intercourse, sperm and egg; process is unclear.	Doctor put a seed in Mommy, and Daddy put some stuff in to make the seed grow.
4	Concrete operations	7–12	Reporters	Know the basic facts but don't speculate on why; only accuracy counts.	Daddy puts sperm in Mommy, and the baby starts growing. (Why?) I guess it loosens up the egg or something.
5	Transitional	10–13	Theoreticians	Know basic facts and basic why's; don't understand that eggs and sperm can join to produce a third entity.	Baby is in the egg, and the sperm makes it start growing.
6	Formal operations	14–adult	Putting it all together	Know that two distinct entities, sperm and ovum, can become one qualitatively different entity, the embryo.	The male injects sperm into the female's womb and fertilizes the egg and it grows into a fetus, and nine months later a baby is born.

Source: Adapted from *The Flight of the Stork,* by A. C. Bernstein. Copyright © 1978 by Anne C. Bernstein. Used by permission of Delacorte Press, a division of Bantam Doubleday Dell Publishing Group, Inc.

Mothers are almost always the source of sex education in the family, for both sons and daughters.

of Swedish youths, 57% of the English, 47% of the Australians, and only 40% of North American children reported actually receiving sex education at school.

When Goldman and Goldman asked children about the source of their knowledge about sex, school was the most prevalent answer (24%), followed closely by mothers (23%) and the media (21%). Other sources of sex information were both parents together (10%), peers (8%), siblings (5%), and fathers (2.5%).

Children and Their Own Sexuality

The research discussed so far involves children's thinking about sexuality in objective terms, or about sexuality in general. To our knowledge, comparable work has not been done on a more subjective level—that is, interviewing children about their own sexuality. Aside from some clinical interviews with children (Martinson, 1973; Langfeldt, 1981), we have very little information on what children think about their own sexuality.

Children's subjective sexual thinking is as difficult to study as children's sexual behavior. However, this much is known. Ramsey (1943b) asked a group of 10-, 11-, and 12-year-old boys to rate a list of items on how sexually arousing they were. The top 13 items were sex conversation, female nudity, obscene

pictures, movies, daydreaming, burlesque or stage shows, nude art, motion when riding, literature, their own body, male nudity, dancing, and music. Half of the subjects reported sexual arousal to "nonerotic" stimuli or stimuli involving fear or other emotions, such as carnival rides, war movies, being late for school, reciting before class, fast rides, playing musical solos, band music, and punishment.

Sexual Orientation

Gender identity consists of at least three factors: **morphological gender,** the body one has; **personal gender,** the concept of oneself as male or female; and **erotic orientation,** which gender one is sexually attracted to. In most individuals, all three components are reasonably consistent. But in some individuals, there is an inconsistency. When morphological gender and personal gender are inconsistent, the result is a transsexual—a person who feels he or she was born with the wrong body. Many transsexuals have undergone sex-reassignment surgery and hormone treatment, often with good results. When eroticorientation is at odds with morphological and personal gender, the result is homosexuality—the person's erotic thoughts and behavior are centered around members of his or her own morphological gender.

We usually think of **sexual orientation**[1] as a dichotomy—heterosexual versus homosexual—or a trichotomy: heterosexual, homosexual, and bisexual (R. Brown, 1987). In actuality, sexual orientation can

---

[1]We use the term *sexual orientation* here and throughout this chapter, rather than the frequently used term *sexual preference,* because "preference" implies a choice. We concur with John Money (1988), who states:

> A heterosexual man or woman does not become heterosexual by preference. There is no option, no plan. Becoming heterosexual is something that happens—an example of the way things are, like being tall or short, left-handed or right-handed, color-blind or color seeing. Being homosexual is no more a preference than being heterosexual. No one, boy or girl, man or woman, prefers to be homosexual instead of heterosexual. Likewise, no one prefers to be bisexual instead of monosexual. One is or is not bisexual, homosexual, or heterosexual. (p. 11)

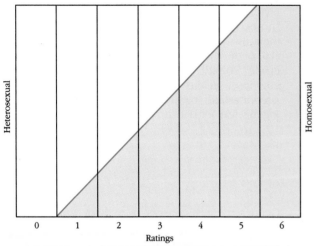

Definitions of the ratings are as follows: 0 = entirely heterosexual. 1 = largely heterosexual, but with incidental homosexual history. 2 = largely heterosexual, but with a distinct homosexual history. 3 = equally heterosexual and homosexual. 4 = largely homosexual, but with distinct heterosexual history. 5 = largely homosexual, but with incidental heterosexual history. 6 = entirely homosexual.

Figure 17.2 Continuum of sexual orientation. *Source:* From *Sexual Behavior in the Human Female,* by A. C. Kinsey, W. B. Pomeroy, and C. E. Martin. Copyright © 1953 by W. B. Saunders & Co. Reprinted by permission of The Kinsey Institute for Research in Sex, Gender, and Reproduction, Inc.

be understood best as a continuum, with heterosexuality at one end, homosexuality at the other, and various degrees of bisexuality in between (Ellis, Burke, & Ames, 1987). Kinsey and his associates (Kinsey, Pomeroy, & Martin, 1953) represented this continuum graphically, as shown in Figure 17.2.

Although, in principle, sexual orientation is a matter of degree, for a majority of people, most erotic thoughts and behaviors are oriented toward members of either the same or the opposite sex (Ellis et al., 1987). In the remainder of this section, therefore, we will use the terms *heterosexual* and *homosexual* to refer to people's primary sexual orientation.

Heterosexuality is the norm in most societies, as it must be in order to procreate the species. However, homosexuality has been found in all cultures throughout history and is condoned by the majority of human societies (Ford & Beach, 1951). In fact, in some societies, it is "normal" for there to be a prolonged period of homosexuality prior to marriage

and the commencement of heterosexual relations. For example, various tribes in the Pacific islands of Melanesia have institutionalized bisexuality, requiring that males between the ages of 9 and 19 leave their families and reside together in a single house. Until the age of 19, which is the prescribed age of marriage, they all participate in homosexual activities. After marriage, homosexual activities cease or are infrequent (Money, 1988).

In modern American culture, homosexuality is not encouraged. Nevertheless, even in societies where homosexuality is discouraged or severely punished, its incidence is substantial. Although it is difficult to get an accurate measure because of many homosexuals' reluctance to make their sexual orientation public, it is estimated that between 4% and 10% of the American population is homosexual (Bell, Weinberg, & Hammersmith, 1981).

There have been many theories about the origins of sexual orientation, particularly male homosexuality. Prior to the 20th century, most explanations of homosexuality were nonscientific, involving the will of God or the devil. (A theory heard more recently is that switching sexes between incarnations causes gender confusion.) Scientific explanations, based on empirical data, however, emphasize either the environmental/learning or the genetic/hormonal basis of sexual orientation (Ellis & Ames, 1987).

Environmental Explanations

One popular theory is that homosexuality is rooted in early experience. This explanation holds that children learn their sexual orientation in childhood, and although society may not approve of or reinforce a homosexual orientation, perhaps a child's parents unwittingly do so. Although these environmental explanations are widely believed, research has generally failed to find strong support for them.

The most influential theorist of this type was Sigmund Freud (1953), who believed that homosexuality in males was caused by problems in a child's psychosexual development. Modern Freudians have popularized the belief that a domineering mother and/or weak father causes a homosexual orientation in boys. Other psychoanalytically oriented psychologists have attributed homosexuality in boys to childhood seduction by the mother or by an older male child or playmate (Cameron, 1963).

Other environmental explanations have tied sexual orientation to the acquisition of sex roles. Children whose mannerisms and interests resemble those of the opposite sex may be responded to by others with reciprocal mannerisms, causing sex-role confusion (East, 1946). According to this explanation, the boy who plays with dolls and acts effeminately will be perceived the way girls are generally perceived and treated accordingly. Because of social reinforcement, children come to see themselves as others see them, making a homosexual orientation part of their self-description (Kagan, 1964; Plummer, 1981).

Environmental explanations are consistent with both psychoanalytic and learning theories of development. However, more recent research has seriously questioned a strong environmental explanation for homosexuality. Perhaps the most compelling data against the environmental explanation come from detailed interviews of more than 1300 men and women, including both homosexuals and heterosexuals, by Alan Bell, Martin Weinberg, and Sue Keifer Hammersmith (1981) of the Kinsey Institute. Examining the hypothesis that male homosexuality is associated with strong mothers and weak fathers, they found no evidence of a connection between male homosexuality and strong mothers, nor was there any evidence that the mothers of homosexual men had acted seductively toward their sons.

Bell and his colleagues concluded that, in most cases, there was nothing that parents "did" to make their children homosexuals. This belief is echoed by Carolyn Griffin, Marian Wirth, and Arthur Wirth (1986). In their book, *Beyond Acceptance,* based in part on interviews with parents of homosexuals, the authors state unequivocally that parents should not feel that their son's or daughter's homosexuality was caused by some failure on their part. Such fears and guilt are not conducive to developing a positive relationship between parents and their homosexual offspring.

Another popular theory holds that young boys are "seduced" into homosexuality by older males. The Kinsey Institute group found no support for this theory. Homosexual men generally recalled their first homosexual experiences as being with males close to their own age. In fact, the childhood sexual experiences reported by homosexual and heterosexual men in the Kinsey study were strikingly similar. Both reported early sexual play with both boys and girls. However, the experience in itself was not as important as the feelings that accompanied it. Significantly more homosexuals than heterosexuals reported feelings of homosexual arousal during late childhood and adolescence—often before experiencing either type of adult sexual relationship.

Evidence that effeminate boys often "turn off" their fathers was reported in a longitudinal study by Richard Green (1987), who followed 44 extremely effeminate boys from preadolescence to adulthood, comparing them to a matched set of noneffeminate boys. Green reported that the "sissy" boys had poorer relations with their fathers, and that the fathers were apt to express displeasure with their effeminate sons. Green believed that the effeminate behavior was the *cause* of the fathers' displeasure rather than the *result* of the fathers' negative attitudes (see also Bell et al., 1981).

Early effeminate behavior was found to be a predictor of later homosexuality in both the Bell and Green studies. Of the 44 effeminate boys in Green's sample, 33 grew up to be homosexual or bisexual. However, as should be obvious, not all homosexual men are effeminate, and not all effeminate men are homosexual. Of the 44 sissy boys in Green's study, 11 grew up to be heterosexuals, and 18% of the homosexual men in the Bell study described themselves as having been "very masculine" as boys. Most of the homosexual men in the Kinsey Institute study did *not* recall having enjoyed girls' games and activities as children, nor did they describe themselves as being feminine.

Parents don't need to worry about the sexual orientation of their children's teachers or coaches. Homosexuality is neither taught nor contagious.

Genetic/Hormonal Explanations

Genetic or hormonal explanations of sexual orientation have an equally impressive history. Early proponents of nonspecific "inborn" causes of homosexuality were Richard von Kraft-Ebbing (1886/1965) and Havelock Ellis (1915). Since that time, much has been learned about the biology of sexuality and gender development (see Chapter 16). To review briefly, prenatal hormones determine whether male or female genitals are constructed, and also influence the developing brain and subsequent sex-related behavior. In nonhuman mammals, variations in prenatal hormone exposure affect adult sexual orientation (Money & Ehrhardt, 1972).

Genetic/hormonal explanations of sexual orientation are appealing for several reasons. One is the lack of evidence for environmental explanations. If it's not experience, then what is it? Second is the clear evidence from experiments done with mammals. Given the many similarities in the reproductive biology of mammals, including humans, it is tempting to conclude that our sexual orientation must be affected by the same biological factors that affect rats, sheep, and monkeys.

Much of the human and animal research was reviewed by Lee Ellis and M. Ashley Ames (1987), who concluded that "complex combinations of genetic, hormonal, and environmental factors operating prior to birth largely determine what an individual's sexual orientation will be, although the orientation itself awaits the onset of puberty to be activated, and may not entirely stabilize until early adulthood" (p. 251; see also Money, 1988).

One genetically caused hormonal imbalance that has been documented for human females is **adrenogenital syndrome,** which occurs when the adrenal glands of females produce too much androgen (comparable to what is typically produced in males). These androgenized females are more masculine in their play activities and attitudes and exhibit more masculine mannerisms (Ehrhardt & Baker, 1974; Money & Ehrhardt, 1972); as adolescents, approximately one-third of them express a homosexual or bisexual orientation (Money, Schwartz, & Lewis, 1984; see Chapter 16).

Other evidence for the biological explanation involves the connection between prenatal experiences and sexual orientation. In several studies, mothers of homosexual men recalled more episodes of extreme stress during their pregnancies than did mothers of heterosexual men; there was no relation between maternal stress and female homosexuality (Ellis, Ames, Peckham, & Burke, 1988). Results of animal research have similarly indicated feminization of male rats as a result of prenatal stress, with the effects on female rats being generally minimal (Beckhardt & Ward, 1982; Politch & Herrenkohl, 1984; Ward, 1972).

Ellis and Ames further suggested that if homosexuality has a biological basis, it may involve a significant degree of heritability and should be difficult to alter. Support for each of the hypotheses has been found. If one identical twin is homosexual, it is highly likely that the other twin will be also; this similarity is not found to the same degree in nonidentical twins (Cooper, 1978). As to modification of a homosexual orientation, psychotherapy of all types has proved only minimally effective, with success limited, for the most part, to self-referred bisexuals. In fact, amount of prior heterosexual experience seems to be the best predictor of success in modifying a homosexual orientation, and some researchers have concluded that homosexuals who have had no pleasurable heterosexual experiences will obtain no benefit from therapy (Acousta, 1975).

Origins of Sexual Orientation

Despite recent research indicating a strong genetic/hormonal basis to sexual orientation, the prevailing view, among behavioral scientists and the public, favors an environmental explanation (Ellis & Ames, 1987). The reluctance of people to accept a biological cause for sexual orientation has many possible explanations. One good reason is the lack of data, given the social significance of the topic.

Even if genetics and prenatal hormones should prove to be the primary cause of homosexuality, this does not mean that learning cannot have an influence. Patterns of sexual practices vary widely around the world, indicating a flexibility of sexual behavior in humans not found in other mammals (Money, 1988; Money & Ehrhardt, 1972). In fact, John Money (1986b, 1988) has proposed two crucial periods in the development of human sexual orientation: one, which occurs during the prenatal period, involves exposure to sex hormones; the other, which occurs during late infancy and early childhood, is a function of juvenile sex play and the health or pathology of the parental sexual relationship.

Money compares the development of gender identity, and thus sexual orientation, to the development of language. Biology dictates that children will learn language in all but a silent environment, but the language they learn depends on what speech they are exposed to. Furthermore, if language is to

Box 17.4

The Difficulties of Growing Up Gay

Although many gays report feeling "different" all through childhood, the realization that one is homosexual typically doesn't hit home until adolescence. The teen years are difficult for most children, but are particularly difficult for gays. While other teens are learning how to date and establish romantic relationships, many gay teenagers learn how to hide their feelings. The period of adolescence is typically one of conformity, and teens are afraid to deviate far from the conventions of the crowd. Being homosexual is viewed as being about as different as an adolescent can be; and heterosexual teenagers are usually sufficiently insecure with their own sexuality that they fear accepting a peer whose sexual orientation is so different. Adolescence can be a very difficult time indeed for young people who first discover their homosexuality.

According to Fort Lauderdale clinical psychologist Dr. Hilda Besner, one of the most difficult things homosexual adolescents and young adults must face is telling their parents about their homosexuality. Dr. Besner points out, however, that difficulty in talking to their parents is often not something new. Children who grow up feeling different usually recognize that their feelings are not socially

The teen years can be especially difficult for a young person who is gay.

"proper" and often have no one to talk to about this. Who can they share their feelings with? Parents are often tacitly aware that something is different about their child, but choose to ignore it or even degrade it ("Why can't you be more like your brother?"). Children feel as if there is something wrong with them, and their parents, often the source of these feelings, are the last people they feel they can tell.

Dr. Besner emphasizes that parents must be approachable by their chil-dren—all of their children. However, she also recognizes that not all parents will be easily able to accept a child's homosexuality. It is important, she says, for parents to get in touch with their own feelings first, even if those feelings are not positive. Parents must then provide an ear for their children. They don't have to be thrilled with what their children tell them, but the message they give should be: "I'm available, and although I may not like everything I **(Continued)**

be learned proficiently, exposure to it must occur early in life (see Chapter 9). Money suggests a similar pattern for sexual behavior—or more specifically, for the formation of lovemaps, discussed earlier, which he believes are learned in childhood through sexual rehearsal play. Because the sex-play hypothesis, by itself, cannot account for the available data (there is no research on the history of juvenile

---

Box 17.4 (Continued)

hear, I want to hear it." Children need to develop a sense of self-worth—a sense that although they may feel different from others, there is nothing *wrong* with them. Parents need to send a message to their children of acceptance and unconditional love. In their book, *Beyond Acceptance,* Carolyn Welch Griffin, Marian J. Wirth, and Arthur G. Wirth note that parental support enriches the lives of homosexual children, leading them to greater self-acceptance and the courage to face an often hostile world.

Can being sensitive, approachable, and unconditionally loving prevent a child from being homosexual? Probably not. But being sensitive approachable, and unconditionally loving *will* foster a strong family relationship, providing a child with feelings of high self-esteem and self-worth. Children who grow up in such families have the greatest chance of becoming well-adjusted, productive members of society, no matter what their erotic orientation.

Our lives may not turn out as we expected, but becoming a parent is not simply claiming a guaranteed prize; it is opening oneself up to the possibilities of life, and having a homosexual child is but one of them. We can't always choose the roles parenthood gives us, but we can choose to perform them well.

Loving parents can help their gay children build a sense of self-worth.

Source: Adapted from B. R. Bjorklund and D. F. Bjorklund. (October 1988). Straight or Gay? *Parents Magazine,* Vol. 63, No. 10.

sexual rehearsal play in people who become homo-sexuals as adults), he finds the prenatal-hormone hypothesis the more appealing one, at least for now (Money, 1986b). However, not all the evidence can be accounted for by prenatal hormones either, suggesting the need for further research into the development of sexual orientation during early childhood.

State of the Art
A New Look at Adolescent Sexuality, Pregnancy, and Parenthood

One of the consequences of heterosexual inter-course is pregnancy, and there has been consider-able concern in the United States over the past decade about the rate at which "children are having children." In the 1980s, about 20% of white females and 40% of black females became pregnant by the age of 18 (Furstenberg, Brooks-Gunn, & Chase-Lansdale, 1989; Hayes, 1987). In contrast to earlier

In the 1980s, the vast majority of teen mothers were unmarried when their babies were born.

Child developmentalists should pay attention to what young people know about sexuality, how they talk to their friends and dates about it, and what their feelings are about this aspect of life.

decades, most pregnant teenagers do not get mar-ried before (or shortly after) becoming pregnant. By the early 1980s, nearly two-thirds of all white teen-age mothers and nearly all black teen mothers (97%) were single at the time their child was born. Not all teen mothers complete their pregnancies, however. It is estimated that 40% of all teenage pregnancies end in abortion, amounting to more than 400,000 in 1984 alone and accounting for 25% of all abortions performed in the United States (Hayes, 1987). Teen-agers who decide to abort tend to be more educa-tionally ambitious, better students, from a higher socioeconomic background, less religious, and to have fewer friends who are single mothers, than teenagers who choose not to abort (see Furstenberg et al., 1989).

Most teenagers do not deliberately intend to be-come pregnant when they do. As Frank Furstenberg, Jeanne Brooks-Gunn, and Lindsay Chase-Lansdale (1989) put it, "if teens had to take the pill to *become* pregnant, relatively few would do so" (p. 314). Most pregnant adolescents have significant misgivings about becoming parents; their attitudes become in-creasingly positive, however, as pregnancy proceeds. Observing a teenager only late in pregnancy, one could get the impression that she was highly moti-vated from the beginning to become a parent, when in fact such an attitude was only belatedly acquired.

What are the consequences of becoming a teenage parent? Most of what we know about the effects of teenage parenthood concerns the mothers. Because unmarried fathers are frequently uninvolved in the upbringing of their children, either as a caregiver or a source of financial support, the main responsibility of caring for the child rests with the mother. Teen mothers are more likely to drop out of school and less likely to find stable, well-paying jobs than women of similar socioeconomic background and age who postpone having children. Teenage mothers are more likely to receive welfare assistance and, in general, are less well off economically than later childbearers (see Furstenberg et al., 1989). Recent findings have shown, however, that over the long run, the effects of teenage motherhood are less severe than previously thought (Furstenberg, Brooks-Gunn, & Morgan, 1987). Many teenage mothers get off public assistance when their youngest children start school, and although they rarely achieve as much economically as women who postpone childbearing, the economic gap diminishes over time.

The consequences of teen parenthood are felt not only by the adolescent parents (mainly the mothers), but also by their offspring. Children of teenage mothers generally fare less well, intellectually and socially, than children of older mothers. Compared to children of older mothers, these children show poorer cognitive functioning, are more aggressive, have less self-control, and have lower school achievement in adolescence. Moreover, these intellectual differences tend to increase as the children get older (Brooks-Gunn & Furstenberg, 1986). Perhaps the primary reason for the poorer developmental outcomes of these children involves the adverse social and economic conditions under which many children of young mothers live. Teenage mothers are generally poor and undereducated, live in disadvantaged neighborhoods, and send their children to poor-quality schools (Furstenberg et al., 1989). Moreover, parents living in poverty and stressful conditions are more likely to use ineffective parenting practices that lead to poor school achievement and social competence in their children (see Chapter 13). This may be especially true for teen mothers, who may be emotionally unprepared for parenthood (Brooks-Gunn & Furstenberg, 1986).

Given the consequences of teenage parenthood for young mothers and their children, much national attention has focused on pregnancy prevention among teenagers (Hayes, 1987). A number of programs have been implemented around the country, attempting either to prevent pregnancy or to improve the welfare of teen mothers and their children. These programs are often difficult to evaluate, and some are too new to determine whether or not they are effective (Furstenberg et al., 1989). According to Frank Furstenberg and his colleagues (1989), contraceptive and family-planning services have the best chance of reducing the rate of early childbearing. Programs providing educational assistance to teenage parents, prenatal medical care, and postnatal parenting education have also produced positive results, but the effectiveness of most of these programs is modest, and not all teenage parents take advantage of or benefit from them.

Most of our early attempts to change these behaviors have been based on denying that sexuality exists among children and adolescents. If we accept sexuality as a lifelong human quality that develops in childhood, however, we can begin to teach and encourage responsible sexuality (Brooks-Gunn & Furstenberg, 1989).

The National Academy of Sciences Panel on Early Childbearing (Hayes, 1987) offered the following suggestions to reduce pregnancy rates among adolescents: enhance life options, delay sexual initiation, encourage contraceptive use once sex begins, teach assertiveness and decision-making skills, reduce the media's glorification of irresponsible sex, increase contraceptive advertising, and provide more school-based medical clinics.

Young people need to be taught about various types of sexual behavior and know the risks associated with each. Educators and parents need more information about the development of sexuality. What is normal, and what needs to be attended to? What do children know about homosexuality? How do they discuss sex with their friends? How do they initiate intimate relations? How do they discuss contraceptive use? How do they *feel* about all these things?

According to educators, as well as surveys of children themselves, education about sexuality is needed at all grade levels (Goldman & Goldman, 1982). Children are curious about more than "where babies come from," and until they have basic information about sexuality as a normal human quality, there is evidence that they will be hampered in their ability to make mature decisions regarding sexual behavior at adolescence (Goldman & Goldman, 1982).

The development of normal sexuality needs to be researched and this information made available both to adults who work with children and to children

Box 17.5

Beyond the Birds and the Bees

By the time children are through the middle years of childhood, most parents have managed to give them basic information about sex and reproduction—some parents doing a better job than others (and, to be fair, some children doing a better job than others of asking the right questions and listening respectfully to their parents' answers). The good news is that Part Two is much easier and can be fun for both parents and children.

Beyond the facts of life is a world of information that schoolchildren find fascinating. It's the world of how babies develop before birth, how different living things reproduce and care for their young, how unusual events happen such as twins and test tube babies, and how certain traits are inherited from parents and grandparents.

If you are lucky enough to have a pregnancy in the family while your children are of school age, it will open up nine months' worth of questions. Our older daughter, Debbie, was pregnant when our younger daughter, Heidi, was 8. Heidi quickly became an expert on fetal development, prenatal care, and Lamaze exercises. Her favorite book was Sheila Kitzinger's *Being Born,* which features Lennart Nilsson's photographs of developing fetuses. Although some adults we know are upset and re-

pulsed by "those creepy pictures," Heidi and her friends were fascinated. And the whole family had to brush up on their science lessons to answer all the questions.

One of our sons became interested in twins when he was 9. A set of identical twins moved into our neighborhood, and he wanted to know all about multiple births. We found a great book written by the National Organization of Mothers of Twins, full of all sorts of pictures and information about twins. He wrote a report on the topic in third grade and revised it every time a research project was assigned for the next several years. His chances of fathering twins are about 15 in 1000, but if he does, he will be well prepared!

A 10-year-old cousin in our family recently found out that he was color-blind and that it had been inherited. He began a small-scale research project, giving color-vision tests to relatives and diagramming the family tree according to who was color-blind, who was a proven carrier, and who was a possible carrier. Some other kids in the family became interested and decided to investigate blood types, which also follow genetic lines. Future scientists? Who knows. But we're sure they will grow up with a little stronger feeling for family bonds than if they had spent the time playing Nintendo.

Animal babies are another great

topic for school-age children (and their parents). For example, did you know that father Emperor penguins sit on their babies' eggs for two cold months without leaving even to eat? When the baby bird hatches, the father regurgitates the one mouthful of food he has saved in his stomach and gives it to the newcomer, then slides off toward the sea to replenish his own body while the mother takes over child rearing for a while.

Experts tell us that our school-age children should be well versed in the topic of human sexuality. For their own protection, they should know about child molesting, sexually transmitted diseases, and unwanted pregnancies. The scientists in us agree 100%, but the parents in us can't help but feel that we are giving our children a peek at adulthood through dingy windows. The compromise in this family is to follow Sex Education 101 with a whole curriculum of advanced courses, giving kids a taste of the miracle of life reproducing itself and caring for its young. These may be fun facts and good stories, but between the lines our children are learning our values—positive lessons about the sanctity of life and the responsibility of parenthood.

Source: Adapted from D. F. Bjorklund and B. R. Bjorklund. (October 1989). Beyond the Birds and the Bees. *Parents Magazine,* Vol. 64, No. 10.

themselves. Knowledge limited only to pathology is bound to cause more wounds than it heals (Money & Tucker, 1975). Children, regardless of sexual orientation, need to know that their sexual thoughts are not unusual; adults need to know the range of normal sexuality during childhood and adolescence, both to confirm their own "normality" and to teach and counsel children.

Summary

The development of sexuality has not received extensive research attention, primarily because of societal attitudes toward children and sex. Infants (even fetuses) are capable of the physiological components of sexual arousal, and genital manipulation is observed in infants. Masturbation is normal behavior for both boys and girls and increases in frequency over childhood. Research has shown that masturbation can lead to orgasm in children as young as 3 and 4 years of age.

Physical changes commencing at puberty cause people to perceive children differently, which in turn affects adolescents' self-image. Puberty also affects erotic thinking. Masturbation usually increases during adolescence, accompanied by erotic fantasies. Most teenagers engage in heterosexual sex play (petting), with many having intercourse. A number of social/environmental factors have been associated with age of first intercourse, teenage pregnancy, and tendency to use contraceptives. Parental attitudes toward sexuality influence children's attitudes about sex and have been associated with adult sexual adjustment and ability to solve sex-related problems.

Children's knowledge about sexuality and reproduction follows a developmental course similar to that suggested by Piaget. Cross-cultural research indicates that North American children lag far behind Swedish children in their knowledge of sexuality and reproduction.

Research on the origins of sexual orientation has typically examined male homosexuality. Although environmental explanations for homosexuality continue to be popular, most recent evidence points to the importance of genetic and hormonal factors. Specifically, prenatal hormonal exposure has been shown to be related to adult homosexuality, at least in males.

Approximately 20% of white females and 40% of black females in the United States become pregnant by the age of 18. Teen mothers are more likely to drop out of school and do poorly economically than older first-time mothers. Children of adolescent parents fare less well intellectually and socially than children of older mothers.

Key Terms and Concepts

sexuality
masturbation
Freud's psychosexual theory
    oral stage
    anal stage
    phallic stage
        Oedipus complex
        castration anxiety
        identification with the aggressor
        Electra complex
        penis envy
    latency stage
    genital stage
paraphilias
lovemap
morphological gender
personal gender
erotic orientation
sexual orientation
    adrenogenital syndrome

References

ABRAMOVITCH, R., & GRUSEC, J. (1978). Peer imitation in a natural setting. *Child Development, 49,* 60–65.

ABRAVANEL, E., & SIGAFOOS, A. D. (1984). Explaining the presence of imitation during early infancy. *Child Development, 55,* 381–392.

ACHENBACH, T. M., & EDELBROCK, C. S. (1981). Behavioral problems and competencies reported by parents of normal and disturbed children aged four through sixteen. *Monographs of the Society for Research in Child Development, 46* (Serial No. 188).

ACOUSTA, F. (1975). Etiology and treatment of homosexuality: A review. *Archives of Sexual Behavior, 4,* 9–29.

ADAMS, R. J., MAURER, D., & DAVIS, M. (1986). Newborns' discrimination of chromatic from achromatic stimuli. *Journal of Experimental Child Psychology, 41,* 262–281.

AINSWORTH, M. D. S. (1979). Infant-mother attachment. *American Psychologist, 34,* 932–937.

AINSWORTH, M. D. S., BELL, S. M., & STAYTON, D. J. (1971). Individual differences in strange situation behavior of one-year-olds. In H. R. Schaffer (Ed.), *The origins of human social relations.* London: Academic Press.

AINSWORTH, M. D. S., BLEHAR, M. C., WATERS, E., & WALL, S. (1978). *Patterns of attachment: A psychological study of the strange situation.* Hillsdale, NJ: Erlbaum.

AINSWORTH, M. D. S., & WITTIG, D. S. (1969). Attachment and exploratory behavior of one-year-olds in a strange situation. In B. M. Foss (Ed.), *Deter-minants of infant behavior* (Vol. 4). London: Methuen.

ALEXANDER, R. D. (1987). *The biology of moral systems.* New York: Hawthorne.

ALEXANDER, R. D. (1989). Evolution of the human psyche. In P. Mellers & C. Stringer (Eds.), *The human revolution: Behavioral and biological perspectives on the origins of modern humans.* Princeton, NJ: Princeton University Press.

ALLEN, G. (1975). *Life science in the twentieth century.* New York: Wiley.

ALLISON, P. D., & FURSTENBERG, F. F., JR. (1989). How marital dissolution affects children: Variations by age and sex. *Developmental Psychology, 25,* 540–549.

ALWITT, L. F., ANDERSON, D. R., LORCH, E. P., & LEVIN, S. R. (1980). Preschool children's visual attention to television. *Human Communication Research, 7,* 52–67.

AMERICAN PSYCHIATRIC ASSOCIATION. (1987). *Diagnostic and statistical manual of mental disorders* (3rd ed. rev.). Washington, DC: Author.

AMNESTY INTERNATIONAL. (1990). *Annual report.* London: Author.

ANDERSON, D. R., ALWITT, L. F., LORCH, E. P., & LEVIN, S. R. (1979). Watching children watch television. In G. A. Hale & M. Lewis (Eds.), *Attention and cognitive development.* New York: Plenum.

ANDERSON, D. R., & COLLINS, P. A. (1988). *The impact on children's education: Television's influence on cognitive development.* Washington, DC: Office of Educational Research and Improvement, U.S. Department of Education.

ANDERSON, R. C., HIEBERT, E. H., SCOTT, J. A., & WILKINSON, I. A. G. (1984). *Becoming a nation of readers: The report of the Commission on Reading.* Washington, DC: U.S. Department of Education.

ANGLIN, J. M. (1977). *Word, object, and conceptual development.* New York: Norton.

ANISFELD, M. (1991). Neonatal imitation: A review. *Developmental Review, 11,* 60–97.

ANNETT, M. (1970). The growth of manual preference and speech. *British Journal of Psychology, 61,* 545–558.

ANNETT, M. (1973). Laterality of childhood hemiplegia and the growth of speech and intelligence. *Cortex, 9,* 4–33.

APA TASK FORCE ON PEDIATRIC AIDS. (1989). Pediatric AIDS and human immunodeficiency virus infection. *American Psychologist, 44,* 258–264.

APGAR, V. (1953). A proposal for a new method of evaluation in the newborn infant. *Current Research in Anesthesia and Analgesia, 32,* 260–267.

ARCHER, J. (1989). *The behavioral biology of aggression.* Cambridge: Cambridge University Press.

AREND, R., GOVE, F., & SROUFE, L. A. (1979). Continuity of individual adaptation from infancy to kindergarten: A predictive study of ego-resiliency and curiosity in preschoolers. *Child Development, 50,* 950–959.

ARLIN, M., & BRODY, R. (1976). Effects of spatial presentation and blocking on organization and verbal recall at three grade levels. *Developmental Psychology, 12,* 113–118.

ASHCRAFT, M. H. (1982). The development of mental arithmetic: A chronometric approach. *Developmental Review, 2,* 213–236.

ASHCRAFT, M. H. (1990). Strategic processing in children's mental arithmetic: A review and proposal. In D. F. Bjorklund (Ed.), *Children's strategies: Contemporary views of cognitive development.* Hillsdale, NJ: Erlbaum.

ASHCRAFT, M. H., & FIERMAN, B. A. (1982). Mental addition in third, fourth, and sixth grades. *Journal of Experimental Child Psychology, 33,* 216–234.

ASHER, S. R. (1983). Social competence and peer status: Recent advances and future directions. *Child Development, 54,* 1427–1434.

ASHER, S. R. (1990). Recent advances in the study of peer rejection. In S. R. Asher & J. D. Coie (Ed.), *Peer rejection in childhood.* Cambridge: Cambridge University Press.

ASHER, S. R., HYMEL, S., & RENSHAW, P. D. (1984). Loneliness in children. *Child Development, 55,* 1456–1464.

ASHER, S. R., PARKHURST, J. T., HYMEL, S., & WILLIAMS, G. A. (1990). Peer rejection and loneliness in childhood. In S. R. Asher and J. D. Coie (Eds.), *Peer rejection in childhood.* Cambridge: Cambridge University Press.

ASHER, S. R., & RENSHAW, P. D. (1981). Children without friends: Social knowledge and social skill training. In S. R. Asher & J. M. Gutterman (Eds.), *The development of children's friendships.* New York: Cambridge University Press.

ASHMEAD, D. H., & PERLMUTTER, M. (1980). Infant memory in everyday life. In M. Perlmutter (Ed.), *New directions for child development: Children's memory.* San Francisco: Jossey-Bass.

ASLIN, R. N., & JACKSON, R. W. (1979). Accommodative-convergence in young infants: Development of a synergistic sensory-motor system. *Canadian Journal of Psychology, 33,* 222–231.

ASLIN, R. N., PISONI, D. B., & JUSCZYK, P. W. (1983). Auditory development and speech perception in infants. In M. M. Haith & J. J. Campos (Eds.), *Infancy and developmental psychobiology,* Vol. 2 of P. H. Mussen (Gen. Ed.), *Handbook of child psychology* (4th ed.). New York: Wiley.

ATKINSON, R. C., & SHIFFRIN, R. M. (1971). The control of short-term memory. *Scientific American, 225,* 82–90.

AULT, R. L., CRAWFORD, D. E., & JEFFREY, W. E. (1972). Visual scanning strategies of reflective, impulsive, fast-accurate, and slow-inaccurate children on the Matching Familiar Figures Test. *Child Development, 43,* 1412–1417.

BAILLARGEON, R. (1987). Object permanence in 3½- and 4½-month-old infants. *Developmental Psychology, 23,* 655–664.

BAKEMAN, R., & BROWNLEE, J. R. (1980). The strategic use of parallel play: A sequential analysis. *Child Development, 51,* 873–878.

BAKER, L. (1985). How do we know when we don't understand? Standards for evaluating text comprehension. In D. L. Forest-Pressley, G. E. MacKinnon, & T. G. Waller (Eds.), *Metacognition, cognition, and human performance* (Vol. 1). Orlando, FL: Academic Press.

BAKER-WARD, L., ORNSTEIN, P. A., & HOLDEN, D. J. (1984). The expression of memorization in early childhood. *Journal of Experimental Child Psychology, 37,* 555–575.

BALL, S. J., & BOGATZ, G. A. (1970). *The first year of Sesame Street: An evaluation.* Princeton, NJ: Educational Testing Service.

BALTIMORE COUNTY PUBLIC SCHOOLS. (1988). *1984 and beyond: A reaffirmation of values.* Baltimore: Author.

BANDURA, A. (1982). Self-efficacy mechanism in human agency. *American Psychologist, 37,* 122–147.

BANDURA, A. (1986). *Social foundations of thought and action: A social cognitive theory.* Englewood Cliffs, NJ: Prentice-Hall.

BANDURA, A. (1989a). Social cognitive theory. In R. Vasta (Ed.), *Annals of child development* (Vol. 6). Greenwich, CT: JAI Press.

BANDURA, A. (1989b). Regulation of cognitive processes through perceived self-efficacy. *Developmental Psychology, 25,* 729–735.

BANDURA, A., ROSS, D., & ROSS, S. A. (1963). Vicarious reinforcement and imitative learning. *Journal of Abnormal and Social Psychology, 67,* 601–607.

BANDURA, A., & WALTERS, R. H. (1963). *Social learning theory and personality development.* New York: Holt, Rinehart & Winston.

BANKS, M. S. (1980). The development of visual accommodation during early infancy. *Child Development, 51,* 646–666.

BARCLAY, L. K. (1985). *Infant development.* New York: Holt, Rinehart & Winston.

BARDEN, R. C., FORD, M. I., JENSEN, A. G., ROGERS-SALYER, M., & SALYER, K. E. (1989). Effects of craniofacial deformity in infancy on the quality of mother-infant interactions. *Child Development, 60,* 819–824.

BARGLO, P., VAUGHN, B. E., & MOLITOR, N. (1987). Effects of maternal absence due to employment on the quality of infant–mother attachment in a low-risk sample. *Child Development, 58,* 945–954.

BARKER, R. G. (1965). Explorations in ecological psychology. *American Psychologist, 20,* 1–14.

BAROODY, A. J., & GINSBURG, H. P. (1986). The relationship between initial meaningful and mechanical knowledge of arithmetic. In J. Hiebert (Ed.), *Conceptual and procedural knowledge: The case of mathematics.* Hillsdale, NJ: Erlbaum.

BARR, H. M., STREISSGUTH, A. P., DARBY, B. L., & SAMPSON, P. D. (1990). Prenatal exposure to alcohol, caffeine, tobacco, and aspirin: Effects on fine and gross motor performance in 4-year-old children. *Developmental Psychology, 26,* 339–348.

BAR-TAL, D., RAVIV, A., & GOLDBERG, M. (1982). Help-ing behavior among preschool children: An observational study. *Child Development, 53,* 396–402.

BATHURST, K., & GOTTFRIED, A. W. (1987). Untestable subjects in child development. *Child Development, 58,* 1135–1144.

BAUMRIND, D. (1967). Child care practices anteceding three patterns of preschool behavior. *Genetic Psychology Monographs, 75,* 43–88.

BAUMRIND, D. (1971). Current patterns of parental authority. *Developmental Psychology Monographs, 4,* (1, Pt. 2).

BAUMRIND, D. (1972). An exploratory study of socialization effects on black children: Some black-white comparisons. *Child Development, 43,* 261–267.

BAUMRIND, D. (1973). The development of instrumental competence through socialization. In A. D. Pick (Ed.), *Minnesota Symposium on Child Psychology* (Vol. 7). Minneapolis: University of Minnesota Press.

BAUMRIND, D. (1982). Are androgynous individuals more effective persons and parents? *Child Development, 53,* 44–75.

BAYLEY, N. (1949). Consistency and variability in the growth of intelligence from birth to eighteen years. *Journal of Genetic Psychology, 75,* 165–196.

BAYLEY, N. (1969). *The Bayley Scales of Infant Development.* New York: Psychological Corporation.

BEAL, C. R., & LOCKHART, M. E. (1989). The effect of proper name and appearance change on children's reasoning about gender constancy. *International Journal of Behavioral Development, 12,* 195–205.

BECKER, J. M. T. (1977). A learning analysis of the development of peer-oriented behavior in nine-month-old infants. *Developmental Psychology, 13,* 481–491.

BECKER, W. C., & GERSTEN, R. (1982). A follow-up of Follow Through: The later effects of the direct instruction model on children in fifth and sixth grades. *American Educational Research Journal, 19,* 75–92.

BECKHARDT, S., & WARD, I. L. (1982). Reproductive functioning in the prenatally stressed female rat. *Developmental Psychobiology, 16,* 111–118.

BEE, H. L., BARNARD, K. E., EYRES, S. J., GRAY, C. A., HAMMOND, M. A., SPIETZ, A. L., SNYDER, C., & CLARK, B. (1982). Prediction of IQ and language skill from prenatal status, child performance, family characteristics, and mother-infant interaction. *Child Development, 53,* 1134–1156.

BELL, A. P., WEINBERG, M. S., & HAMMERSMITH, S. K. (1981). *Sexual preference: Its development in men and women.* Bloomington: Indiana University Press.

BELL, R. Q. (1979). Parent, child and reciprocal influences. *American Psychologist, 34,* 821–826.

BELLUGI, U. (1967). *The acquisition of negation.* Unpublished doctoral dissertation, Harvard University, Cambridge, MA.

BELLUGI, U., & KLIMA, E. S. (1972). The roots of language in the sign talk of the deaf. *Psychology Today, 6.*

BELSKY, J. (1984). The determinants of parenting: A process model. *Child Development, 55,* 83–96.

BELSKY, J. (1986). Infant day care: A cause for concern? *Zero to Three, 6,* 1–9.

BELSKY, J. (1988). The "effects" of infant day care reconsidered. *Early Childhood Research Quarterly, 3,* 235–272.

BELSKY, J., GILSTRAP, B., & ROVINE, M. (1984). The Pennsylvania Infant and Family Development Project: I. Stability and change in mother-infant and father-infant interactions in a family setting at one, three, and nine months. *Child Development, 55,* 692–705.

BELSKY, J., & ROVINE, M. (1988). Nonmaternal care in the first year of life and infant-parent attachment security. *Child Development, 59,* 157–167.

BELSKY, J., ROVINE, M., & TAYLOR, D. (1984). The Pennsylvania Infant and Family Development Project: III. The origin of individual differences in infant-mother attachment: Maternal and infant contributions. *Child Development, 55,* 718–728.

BELSKY, J., & STEINBERG, L. D. (1978). The effects of day care: A critical review. *Child Development, 49,* 929–949.

BEM, S. L. (1974). The measurement of psychological androgyny. *Journal of Consulting and Clinical Psychology, 42,* 155–162.

BEM, S. L. (1977). On the utility of alternative procedures for assessing psychological androgyny. *Journal of Consulting and Clinical Psychology, 45,* 196–205.

BEM, S. L. (1989). Genital knowledge and gender constancy in preschool children. *Child Development, 60,* 649–662.

BENBOW, C. P., & STANLEY, J. C. (1980). Sex differences in mathematical ability: Fact or artifact? *Science, 210,* 1262–1264.

BENBOW, C. P., & STANLEY, J. C. (1983). Sex differences in mathematical reasoning: More facts. *Science, 222,* 1029–1031.

BENDER, B., LINDEN, N., & ROBINSON, A. (in press). Environment and development risk in children with sex chromosome abnormalities. *Journal of the American Academy of Child Psychiatry.*

BENEDICT, H. (1979). Early lexical development: Comprehension and production. *Journal of Child Language, 6,* 183–200.

BERCH, D. B., & BENDER, B. C. (Eds.). (1990). *Sex chromosome abnormalities and human behavior.* Boulder, CO: Waterview Press.

BEREITER, C., & ENGELMANN, S. (1966). *Teaching disadvantaged children in the preschool.* Englewood Cliffs, NJ: Prentice-Hall.

BERGER, K. S. (1983). *The developing person through the life span.* New York: Worth.

BERK, L. E. (1986). Relationship of elementary school children's private speech to behavioral accompaniment to task, attention, and task performance. *Developmental Psychology, 22,* 671–680.

BERK, L. E., & GARVIN, R. A. (1984). Development of private speech among low-income Appalachian children. *Developmental Psychology, 20,* 271–286.

BERKO GLEASON, J. B. (1985). *The development of language.* Columbus, OH: Charles E. Merrill.

BERNDT, T. J. (1979). Developmental changes in conformity to peers and parents. *Developmental Psychology, 15,* 608–616.

BERNSTEIN, A. C., & COWAN, P. A. (1975). Children's concepts of how people get babies. *Child Development, 46,* 77–91.

BERTENTHAL, B. I., CAMPOS, J., & BARRETT, L. (1984). Self-produced locomotion: An organizer of emotional, cognitive, and social development in infancy. In R. Emde & R. Harmon (Eds.), *Continuities and discontinuities in development.* New York: Plenum.

BERTENTHAL, B. I., & FISCHER, K. W. (1978). The development of self-recognition in the infant. *Developmental Psychology, 11,* 44–50.

BESAG, V. E. (1989). *Bullies and victims in schools.* Philadelphia: Open University Press.

BEST, D. L., & ORNSTEIN, P. A. (1986). Children's generation and communication of mnemonic organizational strategies. *Developmental Psychology, 22,* 845–853.

BICKERTON, D. (1990). *Language and species.* Chicago: University of Chicago Press.

BIERMAN, K. L., & FURMAN, W. (1984). The effects of social skills training and peer involvement on the social adjustment of preadolescents. *Child Development, 55,* 155–162.

BIGELOW, B. J. (1977). Children's friendship expectations: A cognitive-developmental study. *Child Development, 48,* 246–253.

BINET, A., & SIMON, T. (1905). Methodes nouvelles pour le diagnostic du niveau intellectuel des anormaux. *L'Année Psychologique, 11,* 245–336.

BINET, A., & SIMON, T. (1908). Le développement de l'intelligence chez les enfants. *L'Année Psychologique, 14,* 1–90. [Reprinted in A. Binet & T. S. Simon, *The development of intelligence in children.* Baltimore: Williams & Wilkins, 1916.]

BIRCH, L. L. (1981). Generalization of a modified food preference. *Child Development, 52,* 755–758.

BISANZ, J., & LeFEVRE, J. (1990). Strategic and non-strategic processing in the development of mathematical cognition. In D. F. Bjorklund (Ed.), *Children's strategies: Contemporary views of cognitive development.* Hillsdale, NJ: Erlbaum.

BJORKLUND, B. R., & BJORKLUND, D. F. (1990). *Parents book of discipline.* New York: Ballantine.

BJORKLUND, D. F. (1985). The role of conceptual knowledge in the development of organization in children's memory. In C. J. Brainerd & M. Pressley (Eds.), *Basic processes in memory development: Progress in cognitive development research.* New York: Springer-Verlag.

BJORKLUND, D. F. (1987a). A note on neonatal imitation. *Developmental Review, 7,* 86–92.

BJORKLUND, D. F. (1987b). How age changes in knowledge base contribute to the development of children's memory: An interpretive review. *Developmental Review, 7,* 93–130.

BJORKLUND, D. F. (1989). *Children's thinking: Developmental function and individual differences.* Pacific Grove, CA: Brooks/Cole.

BJORKLUND, D. F. (Ed.). (1990). *Children's strategies: Contemporary views of cognitive development.* Hillsdale, NJ: Erlbaum.

BJORKLUND, D. F., & BJORKLUND, B. R. (1985). Organization versus item effects of an elaborated knowledge base on children's memory. *Developmental Psychology, 21,* 1120–1131.

BJORKLUND, D. F., GAULTNEY, J. F., & GREEN, B. L. (1992). "I watch, therefore I can do": The development of meta-imitation during the preschool years and the advantage of optimism about one's imitative skills. In M. L. Howe & R. Pasnak (Eds.), *Emerging themes in cognitive development* (Vol. 2). New York: Springer-Verlag.

BJORKLUND, D. F., & GREEN, B. L. (1992). The adaptive nature of cognitive immaturity. *American Psychologist, 47.*

BJORKLUND, D. F., & HARNISHFEGER, K. K. (1987). Developmental differences in the mental effort requirements for the use of an organizational strategy in free recall. *Journal of Experimental Child Psychology, 44,* 109–125.

BJORKLUND, D. F., & HARNISHFEGER, K. K. (1990). Children's strategies: Their definition and origins. In D. F. Bjorklund (Ed.), *Children's strategies: Contemporary views of cognitive development.* Hillsdale, NJ: Erlbaum.

BJORKLUND, D. F., & MUIR, J. E. (1988). Children's development of free recall memory: Remembering on their own. In R. Vasta (Ed.), *Annals of child development* (Vol. 5). Greenwich, CT: JAI Press.

BJORKLUND, D. F., MUIR-BROADDUS, J. E., & SCHNEIDER, W. (1990). The role of knowledge in the development of strategies. In D. F. Bjorklund (Ed.), *Children's strategies: Contemporary views of cognitive development.* Hillsdale, NJ: Erlbaum.

BJORKLUND, D. F., ORNSTEIN, P. A., & HAIG, J. R. (1977). Development of organization and recall: Training in the use of organizational techniques. *Developmental Psychology, 13,* 175–183.

BJORKLUND, D. F., & ZEMAN, B. R. (1982). Children's organization and metamemory awareness in their recall of familiar information. *Child Development, 53,* 799–810.

BLACK, B., & HAZEN, N. L. (1990). Social status and patterns of communication in acquainted and unacquainted preschool children. *Developmental Psychology, 26,* 379–387.

BLASI, A. (1980). Bridging moral cognition and moral action: A critical review of the literature. *Psychological Bulletin, 88,* 593–637.

BLOCK, J. (1979). Another look at sex differentiation in socialization behavior of mothers and fathers. In J. Sherman & F. L. Denmark (Eds.), *Psychology of women: Future directions of research.* New York: Psychological Dimensions.

BLOCK, J. (1983). Differential premises arising from differential socialization of the sexes: Some conjectures. *Child Development, 54,* 1335–1354.

BLOCK, J., BLOCK, J. H., & HARRINGTON, D. M. (1974). Some misgivings about the Matching Familiar Figures Test as a measure of reflection-impulsivity. *Developmental Psychology, 10,* 611–632.

BLOCK, J., BLOCK, J. H., & KEYES, S. (1988). Longitudinally foretelling drug usage in adolescence: Early childhood personality and environmental precursors. *Child Development, 59,* 336–355.

BLOCK, J. H., BLOCK, J., & GJERDE, P. F. (1986). The personality of children prior to divorce: A prospective study. *Child Development, 57,* 827–840.

BLOCK, J. H., BLOCK, J., & MORRISON, A. (1981). Parental agreement-disagreement on child-rearing orientations and gender-related personality correlates in children. *Child Development, 52,* 965–974.

BLOOM, L., & CAPATIDES, J. (1987). Expression of affect and the emergence of language. *Child Development, 58,* 1513–1522.

BLOOM, L., HOOD, L., & LIGHTBOWN, P. (1974). Imitation in language development: If, when and why. *Cognitive Psychology, 6,* 380–420.

BLOOM, L., LIGHTBOWN, P., & HOOD, L. (1975). Structure and variation in child language. *Monographs of the Society for Research in Child Development, 40* (Serial No. 160).

BLOUNT, B. G. (1972). Parental speech and language acquisition: Some Lao and Samoan examples. *Anthropological Linguistics, 14,* 119–130.

BOHLINE, D. S. (1985). Intellectual and affective characteristics of attention deficit disordered children. *Journal of Learning Disabilities, 18,* 604–608.

BOHMAN, M., CLONINGER, R., SIGVARDSSON, S., & VONKNORRING, A. L. (1987). The genetics of alcoholism and related disorders. *Journal of Psychiatric Research, 21,* 447–452.

BOIVIN, M., & BÉGIN, G. (1989). Peer status and self-perception among early elementary school children: The case of the rejected children. *Child Development, 60,* 591–596.

BOLDIZAR, J. P., PERRY, D. G., & PERRY, L. C. (1989). Outcome values and aggression. *Child Development, 60,* 571–579.

BONNICKSON, A. L. (1989). *In vitro fertilization: Building policy from laboratories to legislatures.* New York: Columbia University Press.

BORKE, H. (1975). Piaget's mountains revisited: Changes in the egocentric landscape. *Developmental Psychology, 11,* 240–243.

BORKOWSKI, J. G., PECK, V. A., REID, M. K., & KURTZ, B. (1983). Impulsivity and strategy transfer: Metamemory as mediator. *Child Development, 54,* 459–473.

BORNEMAN, E. (1983). Progress in empirical research on children's sexuality. *SEICUS Report, 12,* 1–5.

BORNSTEIN, M. H. (1989). Stability in early mental development: From attention and information processing in infancy to language and cognition in childhood. In M. H. Bornstein & N. A. Krasnegor (Eds.), *Stability and continuity in mental development: Behavioral and biological perspectives.* Hillsdale, NJ: Erlbaum.

BORNSTEIN, M. H., FERDINANDSEN, K., & GROSS, C. G. (1981). Perception of symmetry in infancy. *Developmental Psychology, 17,* 82–86.

BORNSTEIN, M. H., KESSEN, W., & WEISKOPF, S. (1976). Color vision and hue categorization in young infants. *Journal of Experimental Psychology: Human Perception and Performance, 2,* 115–129.

BORNSTEIN, M. H., & SIGMAN, M. D. (1986). Continuity in mental development from infancy. *Child Development, 57,* 251–274.

BOUCHARD, T. J., JR. (1985). Twins reared together and apart: What they tell us about human diversity. In S. W. Fox (Ed.), *The chemical and biological bases of individuality.* New York: Plenum.

BOUCHARD, T. J., JR., LYKKEN, D. T., MCGUE, M., SEGAL, N. L., & TELLEGEN, A. (1990). Sources of human psychological differences: The Minnesota study of twins reared apart. *Science, 250,* 223–228.

BOUÉ, J. G. (1974). *Chromosomal studies in more than 900 spontaneous abortuses.* Paper presented at the Teratology Society Meeting. Cited in R. Plomin, J. C. DeFries, & G. E. McClearn, 1990.

BOUSFIELD, W. A. (1953). The occurrence of clustering in recall of randomly arranged associates. *Journal of General Psychology, 49,* 229–240.

BOWER, G. H. (1970). Organizational factors in memory. *Cognitive Psychology, 1,* 18–46.

BOWER, T. G. R. (1982). *Development in infancy.* San Francisco: W. H. Freeman.

BOWLBY, J. (1958). The nature of the child's tie to his mother. *International Journal of Psychoanalysis, 39,* 350–373.

BOWLBY, J. (1969). *Attachment and loss: Vol. 1. Attachment.* London: Hogarth.

BOWLBY, J. (1973). *Attachment and loss: Vol. 2. Separation: Anxiety and anger.* London, Hogarth.

BRABECK, M. (1983). Moral judgment: Theory and research on differences between males and females. *Developmental Review, 3,* 274–291.

BRADLEY, R. H. (1989). The use of the HOME inventory in longitudinal studies of child development.

In M. H. Bornstein & N. A. Krasneger (Eds.), *Stability and continuity in mental development: Behavioral and biological perspectives.* Hillsdale, NJ: Erlbaum.

BRADLEY, R. H., & CALDWELL, B. M. (1976). The relation of infants' home environments to mental test performance at fifty-four months: A follow-up study. *Child Development, 47,* 1172–1174.

BRADLEY, R. H., & CALDWELL, B. M. (1980). The relation of home environment, cognitive competence, and IQ among males and females. *Child Development, 51,* 1140–1148.

BRAINERD, C. J. (1974). Training and transfer of transitivity, conservation, and class inclusion of length. *Child Development, 45,* 324–334.

BRAINERD, C. J. (1977). Cognitive development and concept learning: An interpretive review. *Psychological Bulletin, 84,* 919–939.

BRAINERD, C. J. (1978). *Piaget's theory of intelligence.* Englewood Cliffs, NJ: Prentice-Hall.

BRAINERD, C. J., & ALLEN, T. W. (1971). Training and generalization of density conservation: Effects of feedback and consecutive similar stimuli. *Child Development, 42,* 693–704.

BRAINERD, C. J., & ORNSTEIN, P. A. (1991). Children's memory for witnessed events: The developmental backdrop. In J. Doris (Ed.), *The suggestibility of children's memory.* Washington, DC: American Psychological Association.

BRAZELTON, T. B. (1973). Neonatal behavioral assessment scale. *Clinics in Developmental Medicine, No. 50.* Philadelphia: Lippincott.

BRECHER, E. (1990, June 3). The class of 2000: Second grade finds students with a collage of backgrounds working and learning together. *Miami Herald.*

BRENNAN, W. M., AMES, E. W., & MOORE, R. W. (1966). Age differences in infants' attention to patterns of different complexity. *Science, 151,* 354–356.

BRETHERTON, I. (1980). Young children in stressful situations: The supporting role of attachment figures and unfamiliar caregivers. In G. V. Coehlho & P. Ahmed (Eds.), *Uprooting and development.* New York: Plenum.

BRETHERTON, I. (1985). Attachment theory: Retrospect and prospect. In I. Bretherton & E. Waters (Eds.), Growing points of attachment theory and research. *Monographs of the Society for Research in Child Development, 50* (Serial No. 209).

BRETHERTON, I., & RIDGEWAY, D. (1987, April). *3-year-olds' internal working models of attachment.* Paper presented at the meeting of the Society for Research in Child Development, Baltimore.

BRIEN, J. F., LOOMIS, C. W., TRANMER, J., & McGRATH, M. (1983). Disposition of ethanol in human maternal venous blood and amniotic fluid. *American Journal of Obstetrics and Gynecology, 146,* 181–186.

BRIGHAM, C. C. (1923). *A study of American intelligence.* Princeton, NJ: Princeton University Press.

BRONFENBRENNER, U. (1974). *Is early intervention effective? A report on longitudinal evaluations of preschool programs* (Vol. 2). Washington, DC: Department of Health, Education and Welfare, Office of Child Development.

BRONFENBRENNER, U. (1977). Toward an experimental ecology of human development. *American Psychologist, 32,* 513–531.

BRONSON, W. C. (1981). *Toddlers' behaviors with agemates: Issues of interaction, cognition, and affect.* Norwood, NJ: Ablex.

BROOKS-GUNN, J., & FURSTENBERG, F. F., JR. (1986). The children of adolescent mothers: Physical, academic and psychological outcomes. *Developmental Review, 6,* 224–251.

BROOKS-GUNN, J., & FURSTENBERG, F. F. (1989). Adolescent sexual behavior. *American Psychologist, 44,* 249–257.

BROOKS-GUNN, J., & LEWIS, M. (1984). The development of early self-recognition. *Developmental Review, 4,* 215–239.

BROUGHTON, J. M., & FREEMAN-MOIR, D. J. (Eds.). (1982). *The cognitive developmental psychology of James Mark Baldwin.* Norwood, NJ: Ablex.

BROWING, M. (1987, August 16). Pampering parents spoiling kids rotten. *Miami Herald.*

BROWN, A. L. (1978). Knowing when, where, and how to remember: A problem of metacognition. In R. Glasser (Ed.), *Advances in instructional psychology.* New York: Halsted.

BROWN, A. L., & SCOTT, M. S. (1971). Recognition memory for pictures in preschool children. *Journal of Experimental Child Psychology, 11,* 401–412.

BROWN, A. L., & SMILEY, S. S. (1978). The development of strategies for studying texts. *Child Development, 49,* 1076–1088.

BROWN, B. B., CLASEN, D. R., & EICHER, S. A. (1986). Perceptions of peer pressure, peer conformity dispositions, and self-reported behavior among adolescents. *Developmental Psychology, 22,* 521–530.

BROWN J. L., & PIZER, H. F. (1987). *Living hungry in America.* New York: Macmillan.

BROWN, R. (1968). The development of *wh* questions in child speech. *Journal of Verbal Learning and Verbal Behavior, 7,* 279–290.

BROWN, R. (1973). *A first language: The early stages.* Cambridge, MA: Harvard University Press.

BROWN, R. (1987). *Social psychology.* New York: Free Press.

BROWN, R., & HANLON, C. (1970). Derivational complexity and the order of acquisition in child speech. In R. Brown (Ed.), *Psycholinguistics.* New York: Free Press.

BRUNER, J. S. (1966). On cognitive growth. In J. S. Bruner, R. R. Olver, & P. M. Greenfield (Eds.), *Studies in cognitive growth.* New York: Wiley.

BRUNER, J. S. (1972). The nature and uses of immaturity. *American Psychologist, 27,* 687–708.

BRUNER, J. S. (1980). *Under five in Britain.* London: Methuen.

BRUNER, J. S. (1983). *Child's talk: Learning to use language.* New York: Norton.

BRYANT, P. E., & BRADLEY, L. (1985). *Children's reading problems.* Oxford: Blackwell's.

BRYANT, P. E., MACLEAN, M., BRADLEY, L. L., & CROSSLAND, J. (1990). Rhyme and alliteration, phoneme detection, and learning to read. *Developmental Psychology, 26,* 429–438.

BRYANT, P. E., & TRABASSO, T. (1971). Transitive inference and memory in young children. *Nature, 232,* 456–458.

BUGELSKI, B. R., & ALAMPAY, D. A. (1961). The role of frequency in developing perceptual set. *Canadian Journal of Psychology, 15,* 205–211.

BUGENTAL, D. B., BLUE, J., & CRUZCOZA, M. (1989). Perceived control over caregiving outcomes. *Developmental Psychology, 25,* 532–539.

BULLOCK, M., & LUTKENHAUS, P. (1988). The development of volitional behavior in the toddler years. *Child Development, 59,* 664–674.

BURCHINAL, M., LEE, M., & RAMEY, C. (1989). Type of day-care and preschool intellectual development in disadvantaged children. *Child Development, 60,* 128–137.

BUREAR, M. A., SHAPCOTT, D., BERTHIAUMES, Y., MONETTE, J., BLOUIN, D., BLANCHARD, P., & BEGIN, R. (1983). Maternal cigarette smoking and fetal oxygen transport: A study of P50, 2, 3-diphosphogly-cerate, total hemoglobin, hematocrit, and type F hemoglobin in fetal blood. *Pediatrics, 72,* 22–26.

BUSS, A. H., & PLOMIN, R. (1984). *Temperament: Early developing personality traits.* Hillsdale, NJ: Erlbaum.

BUTTER, E. J. (1979). Visual and haptic training and cross-model transfer of reflectivity. *Journal of Educational Psychology, 71,* 212–219.

BUTTER, E. J., KENNEDY, C. B., & SHOEMAKER-KELLY, K. E. (1982). Prediction of third grade reading ability as a function of performance on visual, auditory, and visual-auditory cognitive style tasks. *The Alberta Journal of Educational Research, 28,* 347–359.

BUTTERFIELD, E. C., & SIPERSTEIN, G. N. (1972). Influence of contingent auditory stimulation on nonnutritional suckle. In J. F. Bosma (Ed.), *Third symposium on oral sensation and perceptions: The mouth of the infant.* Springfield, IL: Charles C Thomas.

BYRNE, R., & WHITEN, A. (Eds.). (1988). *Machiavellian intelligence: Social expertise and the evolution of intellect in monkeys, apes, and humans.* Oxford: Clarendon Press.

CAHAN, S., & COHEN, N. (1989). Age versus schooling effects on intelligence development. *Child Development, 60,* 1239–1249.

CAIRNS, R. B. (1983). The emergence of developmental psychology. In W. Kessen (Ed.), *History, theory, and methods,* Vol. 1 of P. H. Mussen (Gen. Ed.), *Handbook of child psychology* (4th ed.). New York: Wiley.

CAIRNS, R. B., & CAIRNS, B. D. (1986). The developmental-interactional view of social behavior: Four issues of adolescent aggression. In D. Olweus, J. Block, & M. Radke-Yarrow (Eds.), *Development of antisocial and prosocial behavior: Research, theories, and issues.* New York: Academic Press.

CAIRNS, R. B., CAIRNS, B. D., NECKERMAN, H. J., FERGUSON, L. L., & GARIÉPY, J. (1989). Growth and aggression: Childhood to early adolescence. *Developmental Psychology, 25,* 320–330.

CAIRNS, R. B., CAIRNS, B. D., NECKERMAN, H. J., GEST, S. D., & GARIÉPY, J. (1988). Social networks and aggressive behavior: Peer support or peer rejection? *Developmental Psychology, 24,* 815–823.

CALDERA, Y. M., HUSTON, A. C., & O'BRIEN, M. (1989). Social interactions and play patterns of parents and toddler with feminine, masculine, and neutral toys. *Child Development, 60,* 70–76.

CALDERONE, M. (1983). Fetal erection and its message to us. *SIECUS Report, 11*(5/6), 9–10.

CALDWELL, B. M., & BRADLEY, R. H. (1978). *Home observation for measurement of the environment.* Little Rock: University of Arkansas at Little Rock.

CAMERON, R. (1984). Problem-solving inefficiency and conceptual tempo: A task analysis of underlying factors. *Child Development, 55,* 2031–2041.

CAMERON, N. (1963). *Development and psychopathology.* Boston: Houghton Mifflin.

CAMPOS, J., HIATT, S., RAMSEY, D., HENDERSON, C., & SVEJDA, M. (1978). The emergence of fear on the visual cliff. In M. Lewis & L. A. Rosenblum (Eds.), *The development of affect.* New York: Plenum.

CAPON, N., & KUHN, D. (1979). Logical reasoning in the supermarket: Adult females' use of a proportional reasoning strategy in an everyday context. *Developmental Psychology, 15,* 450–452.

CAREY, S. (1977). The child as a word learner. In M. Halle, J. Bresnan, & G. A. Miller (Eds.), *Linguistic theory and psychological reality.* Cambridge, MA: MIT Press.

CAREY, S. (1985). *Conceptual changes in childhood.* Cambridge, MA: MIT Press.

CARLSON, V., CICCHETTI, D., BARNETT, D., & BROUNWALD, K. (1989). Disorganized/disoriented attachment relationships in maltreated infants. *Development Psychology, 25,* 525–531.

CARMICHAEL, L. (Ed.). (1946). *Manual of child psychology.* New York: Wiley.

CARMICHAEL, L. (Ed.). (1954). *Manual of child psychology* (2nd ed.). New York: Wiley.

CARMICHAEL, L. (Ed.). (1970). The onset and early development of behavior. In P. H. Mussen (Ed.), *Carmichael's handbook of child psychology* (3rd ed.) (Vol. 1). New York: Wiley.

CARON, A. J., CARON, R. F., & CARLSON, V. R. (1979). Infant perception of the invariant shape of objects varying in slant. *Child Development, 50,* 716–721.

CARPENTER, T. P., & MOSER, J. M. (1982). The development of addition and subtraction problem-solving skills. In T. P. Carpenter, J. M. Moser, & T. A. Romberg (Eds.), *Addition and subtraction: A cognitive perspective.* Hillsdale, NJ: Erlbaum.

CARR, M., KURTZ, B. E., SCHNEIDER, W., TURNER, L. A., & BORKOWSKI, J. G. (1989). Strategy acquisition and transfer among American and German children: Environmental influences on metacognitive development. *Developmental Psychology, 25,* 765–771.

CASE, R. (1974). Mental strategies, mental capacity and instruction: A neo-Piagetian investigation. *Journal of Experimental Child Psychology, 18,* 382–397.

CASE, R. (1985). *Intellectual development: Birth to adulthood.* New York: Academic Press.

CASEY, B. J., & RICHARDS, J. E. (1988). Sustained visual attention in young infants measured with an adapted version of the visual preference paradigm. *Child Development, 59,* 1514–1521.

CASPI, A., ELDER, G. H., JR., & BEM, D. J. (1988). Moving away from the world: Life-course patterns of shy children. *Developmental Psychology, 24,* 824–831.

CASSIDY, J. (1987, April). *An assessment of the working model of the self within the attachment relationship.* Paper presented at the meeting of the Society for Research in Child Development, Baltimore.

CASSIDY, J. (1988). Child-mother attachment and the self in six-year-olds. *Child Development, 59,* 121–134.

CASTELL, J. D., & STAHL, R. J. (1975). *Values clarification in the classroom.* Palisades Park, CA: Goodyear.

CATES, W., JR., & RAUGH, J. L. (1985). Adolescents and sexually transmitted diseases: An expanding problem. *Journal of Adolescent Health Care, 6,* 1–5.

CATTELL, R. B. (1963). Theory of fluid and crystallized intelligence: A critical experiment. *Journal of Educational Psychology, 54,* 1–22.

CATTELL, R. B. (1971). *Abilities: Their structure, growth and action.* Boston: Houghton Mifflin.

CAVANAUGH, J. C., & BORKOWSKI, J. G. (1980). Searching for metamemory-memory connections: A developmental study. *Developmental Psychology, 16,* 441–453.

CECI, S. J. (1990). *On intelligence . . . More or less: A bio-ecological treatise on intellectual development.* Englewood Cliffs, NJ: Prentice Hall.

CECI, S. J. (1991). How much does schooling influence general intelligence and its cognitive components? A reassessment of the evidence. *Developmental Psychology, 27,* 703–722.

CECI, S. J., ROSS, D. F., & TOGLIA, M. D. (1987). Suggestibility of children's memory: Psychological implications. *Journal of Experimental Psychology: General, 116,* 38–49.

CECI, S. J., ROSS, D. F., TOGLIA, T. M. (Eds.). (1989). *Perspectives on children's testimony.* New York: Springer-Verlag.

CHALL, J. S. (1979). The great debate: Ten years later, with a modest proposal for reading stages. In L. B. Resnick & P. A. Weaver (Eds.), *Theory and practice of early reading.* Hillsdale, NJ: Erlbaum.

CHALL, J. S. (1983). *Stages of reading development.* New York: McGraw-Hill.

CHANDLER, M., FRITZ, A. S., & HALA, S. (1989). Small-scale deceit: Deception as a member of two-, three-, and four-year-olds' early theories of mood. *Child Development, 60,* 1263–1277.

CHERRY, S. H. (1987). *Planning ahead for pregnancy.* New York: Viking Press.

CHI, M. T. H. (1978). Knowledge structure and memory development. In R. Siegler (Ed.), *Children's thinking: What develops?* Hillsdale, NJ: Erlbaum.

CHI, M. T. H., & CECI, S. J. (1987). Content knowledge: Its role, representation, and restructuring in memory development. In H. W. Reese (Ed.), *Advances in child development and behavior* (Vol. 20). Orlando, FL: Academic Press.

CHILDREN'S DEFENSE FUND. (1987). *A children's defense budget, FY 1988: An analysis of our nation's investment in children.* Washington, DC: Author.

CHOMSKY, N. (1957). *Syntactic structures.* The Hague: Mouton.

CICCHETTI, D., & RIZLEY, R. (1981). Developmental perspectives on the etiology, intergenerational transmission, and sequelae of child maltreatment. *New Directions for Child Development, 11,* 31–55.

CLARK, E. A., & HANISEE, J. (1982). Intellectual and adaptive performance of Asian children in adoptive American settings. *Developmental Psychology, 18,* 595–599.

CLARK, H. H., & CLARK, E. V. (1977). *Psychology and language: An introduction to psycholinguistics.* New York: Harcourt Brace Jovanovich.

CLARKE, A. D. B., & CLARKE, A. M. (1976). Formerly isolated children. In A. M. Clarke & A. D. B. Clarke (Eds.), *Early experience: Myth and evidence.* London: Open Books.

CLARKE-STEWART, K. A. (1973). Interactions between mothers and their young children: Characteristics and consequences. *Monographs of the Society for Research in Child Development, 38* (Serial No. 153).

CLARKE-STEWART, K. A. (1980). The father's contribution to children's cognitive and social development in early childhood. In F. A. Pedersen (Ed.), *The father-infant relationship: Observational studies in a family setting.* New York: Praeger.

CLARKE-STEWART, K. A. (1989). Infant day care: Maligned or malignant? *American Psychologist, 44,* 266–273.

CLARKE-STEWART, K. A., & FEIN, G. G. (1983). Early childhood programs. In M. M. Haith & J. J. Campos (Eds.), *Infancy and developmental psychobiology,* Vol. 2 of P. H. Mussen (Gen. Ed.), *Handbook of child psychology* (4th ed.). New York: Wiley.

CLARKE-STEWART, A., THOMPSON, W. C., & LEPORE, S. (1989, April). Manipulating children's interpretations through interrogation. In G. S. Goodman (Chair), *Can children provide accurate eyewitness reports?* Symposium conducted at meeting of the Society for Research in Child Development, Kansas City, MO.

COATES, D. L., & LEWIS, M. (1984). Early mother-infant interaction and infant cognitive status as predictors of school performance and cognitive behavior in six-year-olds. *Child Development, 55,* 1219–1230.

COHEN, F. L. (1984). *Clinical genetics in nursing practice.* Philadelphia: Lippincott.

COHEN, L. B., & GELBER, E. R. (1975). Infant visual memory. In L. B. Cohen & P. Salapatek (Eds.), *Infant perception: From sensation to cognition* (Vol. 1). New York: Academic Press.

COHEN, L. B., & STRAUSS, M. S. (1979). Concept acquisition in the human infant. *Child Development, 50,* 419–424.

COHEN, S. E., & BECKWORTH, L. (1979). Preterm infant interaction with the caregiver during the first year of life and competence at age two. *Child Development, 50,* 767–776.

COHN, D. A. (1990). Child-mother attachment of six-year-olds and social competence at school. *Child Development, 61,* 152–162.

COIE, J. D., DODGE, K. A., & KUPERSMIDT, J. B. (1990). Peer group behavior and social status. In S. R. Asher & J. D. Coie (Eds.), *Peer rejection in childhood.* Cambridge: Cambridge University Press.

COIE, J. D., & KOEPPL, G. K. (1990). Adapting intervention to the problems of aggressive and disruptive rejected children. In S. R. Asher & J. D. Coie (Eds.), *Peer rejection in childhood.* Cambridge: Cambridge University Press.

COIE, J. D., & KREHBIEL, G. (1984). Effects of academic tutoring on the social status of low-achieving, socially rejected children. *Child Development, 55,* 1465–1478.

COIE, J. D., & KUPERSMIDT, J. B. (1983). A behavioral analysis of emerging social status in boys' groups. *Child Development, 54,* 1400–1416.

COLBY, A., KOHLBERG, L., GIBBS, J., & LIEBERMAN, M. (1983). A longitudinal study of moral judgment. *Monographs of the Society for Research in Child Development, 48* (Serial No. 200).

CONDON, W., & SANDER, L. (1974). Synchrony demonstrated between movements of the neonate and adult speech. *Child Development, 45,* 456–462.

CONDRY, J. C., & CONDRY, S. (1976). Sex differences: A study of the eye of the beholder. *Child Development, 47,* 812–819.

CONDRY, J. C., & ROSS, D. F. (1985). Sex and aggression: The influence of gender label on the perception of aggression in children. *Child Development, 56,* 225–233.

CONGER, R. D., McCARTY, J. A., YANG, R. K., LAHEY, R. B., & KROOP, J. P. (1984). Perception of child, child-rearing values, and economic distress as mediating links between environmental stressors and observed maternal behavior. *Child Development, 55,* 2234–2247.

CONNOR, J. M., & SERBIN, L. A. (1977). Behaviorally based masculine- and feminine-activity-preference scales for preschoolers: Correlates with other classroom behaviors and cognitive tests. *Child Development, 48,* 1411–1416.

CONSTANTINE, L. L., & MARTINSON, F. M. (Eds.). (1981). *Children and sex: New findings, new perspectives.* Boston: Little, Brown.

COOK, T. D., APPELTON, H., CONNER, R. F., SHAFFER, A., TABKIN, G., & WEBER, J. S. (1975). *Sesame Street revisited.* New York: Russell Sage Foundation.

COOPER, A. J. (1978). Aetiology of homosexuality. In J. A. Loraine (Ed.), *Understanding homosexuality.* New York: Elsevier.

COOPERSMITH, S. (1967). *The antecedents of self-esteem.* New York: W. H. Freeman.

CORBALLIS, M. C., & BEALE, I. L. (1983). *The ambivalent mind: The neuropsychology of left and right.* Chicago: Nelson-Hall.

COREN, S., PORAC, C., & DUNCAN, P. (1981). Lateral preference behaviors in preschool children and young adults. *Child Development, 52,* 443–450.

CORNELL, E. (1974). Infants' discrimination of photographs of faces following redundant presentation. *Journal of Experimental Child Psychology, 18,* 98–106.

CORSALE, K., & ORNSTEIN, P. A. (1980). Developmental changes in children's use of semantic information in recall. *Journal of Experimental Child Psychology, 30,* 231–245.

COWAN, N., & DAVIDSON, G. (1984). Salient childhood memories. *Journal of Genetic Psychology, 145,* 101–107.

COWART, B. J. (1981). Development of taste perception in humans: Sensitivity and preference throughout the life span. *Psychological Bulletin, 90,* 43–73.

COX, D., & WATERS, H. S. (1986). Sex differences in the use of organization strategies: A developmental analysis. *Journal of Experimental Child Psychology, 41,* 18–37.

COZBY, P. C., WORDEN, P. E., & KEE, D. W. (1989). *Research methods in human development.* Mountain View, CA: Mayfield.

CRICK, N. R., & LADD, G. W. (1988, March). *Rejected and neglected children's perceptions of their peer experiences: Loneliness, social anxiety, and social avoidance.* Paper presented at the Conference on Human Development, Charleston, SC.

CRNIC, K. A., & GREENBERG, M. T. (1990). Minor parenting stresses with young children. *Child Development, 61,* 1628–1637.

CROOK, J. H. (1980). *The evolution of human consciousness.* Oxford: Clarendon Press.

CROSS, T. G. (1977). Mother's speech adjustments: The contribution of selected child listener variables. In C. E. Snow & C. A. Ferguson (Eds.), *Talking to children: Language input and acquisition.* Cambridge: Cambridge University Press.

CULBERTSON, J. L., KROUS, H. F., & BENDELL, R. D. (Eds.). (1988). *Sudden infant death syndrome: Medical aspects and psychological management.* Baltimore: Johns Hopkins Press.

CUMMINGS, E. M. (1980). Caregiver stability and day care. *Developmental Psychology, 16,* 31–37.

CUMMINGS, E. M., IANNOTTI, R. J., & ZAHN-WAXLER, C. (1989). Aggression between peers in early childhood: Individual continuity and developmental change. *Child Development, 60,* 887–895.

CURRAN, J. W., JAFFE, H. W., HARDY, A. M., MORGAN, W. M., SELITE, R. M., & DONDERO, T. J. (1988). Epidemiology of HIV infection and AIDS in the United States. *Science, 239,* 610–616.

CURRIER, R. L. (1981). Juvenile sexuality in global perspective. In L. L. Constantine & F. M. Martinson

(Eds.), *Children and sex: New findings, new perspectives.* Boston: Little, Brown.

CURTISS, S. (1977). *Genie: A psycholinguistic study of a modern day "wild child."* New York: Academic Press.

CUVO, A. J. (1975). Developmental differences in rehearsal and free recall. *Journal of Experimental Child Psychology, 19,* 265–270.

DAEHLER, M. W., & BUKATKO, D. (1977). Recognition memory for pictures in very young children: Evidence from attentional preferences using a continuous presentation procedure. *Child Development, 48,* 693–696.

DALE, P. S. (1976). *Language development: Structure and function* (2nd ed.). New York: Holt, Rinehart & Winston.

DANEMAN, M., & BLENNERHASSETT, A. (1984). How to assess the listening comprehension skills of prereaders. *Journal of Educational Psychology, 76,* 1372–1381.

DANEMAN, M., & CARPENTER, P. (1980). Individual differences in working memory and reading. *Journal of Verbal Learning and Verbal Behavior, 19,* 450–466.

DANEMAN, M., & GREEN, I. (1986). Individual differences in comprehending and producing words in context. *Journal of Memory and Language, 25,* 1–18.

DANSKY, J. L. (1980). Make-believe: A mediator of the relationship between play and associative fluency. *Child Development, 51,* 576–579.

DARWIN, C. (1877). A biographical sketch of an infant. *Mind, 2,* 286–294.

DARWIN, C. (1959). *The origin of species.* New York: Modern Library. (Original work published 1859.)

DASEN, P. R. (Ed.). (1977). *Piagetian psychology: Cross-cultural contributions.* New York: Gardner.

DAVIS, K. (1947). Final note on a case of extreme isolation. *American Journal of Sociology, 53,* 432–437.

DAWKINS, R. (1976). *The selfish gene.* New York: Oxford University Press.

DAWKINS, R. (1982). *The blind watchmaker.* Essex, England: Longman.

DEAL, J. E., HALVERSON, C. F., JR., & WAMPLER, K. S. (1989). Parental agreement on child-rearing orientations: Relations to parental, marital, family, and child characteristics. *Child Development, 60,* 1025–1034.

DE BEER, G. (1958). *Embryos and ancestors* (3rd ed.). Oxford: Clarendon Press.

DECASPER, A. J., & FIFER, W. P. (1980). Of human bonding: Newborns prefer their mother's voice. *Science, 208,* 1174–1176.

DECASPER, A. J., & SPENCE, M. J. (1986). Prenatal maternal speech influences newborns' perception of speech sounds. *Infant Behavior and Development, 9,* 133–150.

DEHIRSCH, K., JANSKY, J., & LANGFORD, W. (1966). *Predicting reading failure.* New York: Harper & Row.

DELOACHE, J. S. (1986). Memory in very young children: Exploitation of cues to the location of a hidden object. *Cognitive Development, 1,* 123–138.

DELOACHE, J. S., & BROWN, A. L. (1983). Very young children's memory for the location of objects in a large scale environment. *Child Development, 54,* 888–897.

DELOACHE, J. S., CASSIDY, D. J., & BROWN, A. L. (1985). Precursors of mnemonic strategies in very young children's memory for the location of hidden objects. *Child Development, 56,* 125–137.

DELOACHE, J. S., & TODD, C. M. (1988). Young children's use of spatial categorization as a mnemonic strategy. *Journal of Experimental Child Psychology, 46,* 1–20.

DEMARIE-DREBLOW, D., & MILLER, P. H. (1988). The development of children's strategies for selective attention: Evidence for a transitional period. *Child Development, 59,* 1504–1513.

DE MAUSE, L. (1974). The evolution of childhood. In L. de Mause (Ed.), *The history of childhood.* New York: Psychohistory Press.

DEMPSTER, F. N. (1981). Memory span: Sources of individual and development differences. *Psychological Bulletin, 89,* 63–100.

DEMPSTER, F. N. (1985). Short-term memory development in childhood and adolescence. In C. J. Brainerd & M. Pressley (Eds.), *Basic processes in memory development: Progress in cognitive development research.* New York: Springer.

DENNIS, W. (1973). *Children of the Crèche.* New York: Appleton-Century-Crofts.

DE VILLIERS, J. G., & DE VILLIERS, P. A. (1973). A cross-sectional study of the acquisition of grammatical morphemes in child speech. *Journal of Psycholinguistic Research, 2,* 267–278.

DE VILLIERS, J. G., & DE VILLIERS, P. A. (1978). *Language*

acquisition. Cambridge, MA: Harvard University Press.

DE VILLIERS, P. A., & DE VILLIERS, J. G. (1979). *Early language.* Cambridge, MA: Harvard University Press.

DE VRIES, R. (1969). Constancy of generic identity in the years three to six. *Monographs of the Society for Research in Child Development, 34* (Serial No. 127).

DIAMOND, A. (1985). Development of the ability to use recall to guide action as indicated by infants' performance on AB̄. *Child Development, 56,* 868–883.

DIAMOND, J. (1989). The cruel logic of the genes. *Discover, 10* (10).

DIAMOND, M. C., ROSENZWIEG, M. R., BENNETT, E. L., LINDNER, B., & LYON, L. (1972). Effects of environmental enrichment and impoverishment on rat cerebral cortex. *Journal of Neurobiology, 3,* 47–64.

DICK-READ, G. (1959). *Childbirth without fear: The principles and practices of natural childbirth.* New York: Harper & Brothers. (Original work published 1944)

DIPIETRO, J. A. (1981). Rough and tumble play: A function of gender. *Developmental Psychology, 17,* 50–58.

DISHION, T. J. (1990). The family ecology of boys' peer relations in middle childhood. *Child Development, 61,* 874–892.

DIX, T., RUBLE, D. N., & ZAMBARANO, R. J. (1989). Mothers' implicit theories of discipline: Child effects, parent effects, and the attribution process. *Child Development, 60,* 1373–1391.

DIXON, D. (1981). *After man: A zoology of the future.* New York: St. Martin's Press.

DOBSON, J. (1970). *Dare to discipline.* Toronto: Bantam Books.

DODGE, K. A. (1980). Social cognition and children's aggressive behavior. *Child Development, 51,* 162–170.

DODGE, K. A. (1983). Behavioral antecedents of peer social status. *Child Development, 54,* 1386–1399.

DODGE, K. A. (1990). Developmental psychopathology in children of depressed mothers. *Developmental Psychology, 26,* 3–6.

DODGE, K. A., & FELDMAN, E. (1990). Issues in social cognition and sociometric status. In S. R. Asher and J. D. Coie (Eds.), *Peer rejection in childhood.* Cambridge: Cambridge University Press.

DODGE, K. A., & FRAME, C. L. (1982). Social cognitive biases and deficits in aggressive boys. *Child Development, 53,* 620–635.

DODGE, K. A., PETTIT, G. S., MCCLASKEY, C. L., & BROWN, M. M. (1986). Social competence in children. *Monographs of the Society for Research in Child Development, 51* (Serial No. 213).

DODGE, K. A., SCHLUNDT, D. G., SCHOCKEN, I., & DELUGACH, J. D. (1983). Social competence and children's social status: The role of peer group entry strategies. *Merrill-Palmer Quarterly, 29,* 309–336.

DODSON, F. (1977). *How to discipline with love.* New York: Signet.

DODSON, F. (1981). *Give your child a head start in reading.* New York: Simon & Schuster.

DOLHINOW, P. J., & BISHOP, N. H. (1970). The development of motor skills and social relationships among primates through play. In J. P. Hill (Ed.), *Minnesota Symposia on Child Psychology.* Minneapolis: University of Minnesota Press.

DOLLARD, J., DOOB, L. W., MILLER, N. E., MOWRER, O. H., & SEARS, R. R. (1939). *Frustration and aggression.* New Haven, CT: Yale University Press.

DOMAN, G. (1984). *How to multiply your baby's intelligence.* Garden City, NY: Doubleday.

DOMINICK, J. R., & GREENBERG, B. S. (1972). Attitudes toward violence: The interactions of television exposure, family attitudes and social class. In G. A. Comstock & E. A. Rubinstein (Eds.), *Television and social behavior: Vol. 3. Television and adolescent aggressiveness.* Washington, DC: U.S. Government Printing Office.

DORFMAN, A. (1989, August 28). Alcohol's youngest victims. *Time,* p. 60.

DOUGLAS, V. I., BARR, R. G., O'NEILL, M. E., & BRITTON, B. G. (1986). Short term effects of methylphenidate on the cognitive, learning and academic performance of children with attention deficit disorder in the laboratory and the classroom. *Journal of Child Psychology and Psychiatry, 27,* 191–211.

DOWD, J. M., & TRONICK, E. F. (1986). Temporal coordination of arm movements in early infancy: Do infants move in synchrony with adult speech? *Child Development, 57,* 762–776.

DRACH, K. M. (1969). *The language of the parent: A pilot study.* Working paper no. 14, Berkeley: University of California. Cited in J. G. de Villiers & P. A. de Villiers, 1978.

DRACHMAN, D. B., & COULOMBRE, A. J. (1962). Experimental clubfoot and arthrogryposis multiplex congenita. *Lancet, 523*–526.

DRAEGER, S., PRIOR, M., & SANSON, A. (1986). Visual and auditory attention performance in hyperactive children: Competence or compliance. *Journal of Abnormal Child Psychology, 14,* 411–424.

DUFREE, J. T., & LEE, L. C. (1973, August). *Infant-infant interaction in a daycare setting.* Paper presented at the meeting of the American Psychological Association, Montreal.

DUKE, P. M., CARLSMITH, J. M., JENNINGS, D., MARTIN, J. A., DORNBUSCH, S. M., GROSS, R. T., & SIEGEL-GORELICK, B. (1982). Educational correlates of early and late sexual maturation in adolescence. *Journal of Pediatrics, 100,* 633–637.

DWECK, C. S. (1975). The role of expectations and attributions in the alleviation of learned helplessness. *Journal of Personality and Social Psychology, 31,* 674–685.

DWECK, C. S. (1986). Motivational processes affecting learning. *American Psychologist, 41,* 1040–1048.

DWECK, C. S., & LEGGETT, E. L. (1988). A social-cognitive approach to motivation and personality. *Psychological Review, 95,* 256–273.

DWECK, C. S., & REPPUCCI, N. D. (1973). Learned helplessness and reinforcement responsibility in children. *Journal of Personality and Social Psychology, 25,* 109–116.

EAST, W. N. (1946). Sexual offenders. *Journal of Nervous and Mental Disease, 103,* 626–666.

EATON, W. O., & ENNS, L. R. (1986). Sex differences in human motor activity. *Psychological Bulletin, 100,* 19–28.

EATON, W. O., & VON BARGEN, D. (1981). Asynchronous development of gender understanding in preschool children. *Child Development, 52,* 1020–1027.

ECCLES, J. C. (1989). *Evolution of the brain: Creation of the self.* New York: Routledge.

ECKERMAN, C. O., DAVIS, C. C., & DIDOW, S. M. (1989). Toddlers' emerging ways of achieving social coordinations with a peer. *Child Development, 60,* 440–453.

ECKERMAN, C. O., WHATLEY, J. L., & KUTZ, S. L. (1975). Growth of social play with peers during the second year of life. *Developmental Psychology, 11,* 42–49.

EDEY, M. A., & JOHANSON, D. C. (1989). *Blueprints: Solving the mystery of evolution.* Boston: Little, Brown.

EDWARDS, C. P., & WHITING, B. B. (1988). *Children of different worlds.* Cambridge, MA: Harvard University Press.

EGELAND, B. (1974). Training impulsive children in the use of more efficient scanning techniques. *Child Development, 45,* 165–171.

EGELAND, B., JACOBVITZ, D., & SROUFE, L. A. (1988). Breaking the cycle of abuse. *Child Development, 59,* 1080–1088.

EGELAND, B., & SROUFE, L. A. (1981). Attachment and early maltreatment. *Child Development, 52,* 44–52.

EHRHARDT, A. A., & BAKER, S. W. (1974). Fetal androgens, human central nervous system differentiation, and behavior sex differences. In R. C. Friedman, R. M. Richart, & R. L. Vande Wiele (Eds.), *Sex differences in behavior.* New York: Wiley.

EHRHARDT, A. A., & MONEY, J. (1967). Progestin-induced hermaphroditism: IQ and psychosexual identity in a study of ten girls. *Journal of Sex Research, 3,* 83–100.

EIBL-EIBESFELDT, I. (1989). *Human ethology.* New York: Aldine de Gruyter.

EIMAS, P. D., SIQUELAND, E. R., JUSCZYK, P., & VIGORITO, J. (1971). Speech perception in infants. *Science, 71,* 303–306.

ELARDO, R., BRADLEY, R. H., & CALDWELL, B. M. (1977). A longitudinal study of the relation of infants' home environments to language development at age three. *Child Development, 48,* 595–603.

ELKIND, D. (1967). Egocentrism in adolescence. *Child Development, 38,* 1025–1033.

ELKIND, D. (1978). *The child's reality: Three developmental theories.* Hillsdale, NJ: Erlbaum.

ELKIND, D. (1981). *The hurried child: Growing up too fast too soon.* Reading, MA: Addison-Wesley.

ELKIND, D. (1987). *Miseducation: Preschoolers at risk.* New York: Knopf.

ELKIND, D., & BOWEN, R. (1979). Imaginary audience behavior in children and adolescents. *Developmental Psychology, 15,* 38–44.

ELLIS, H. (1915). *Studies in the psychology of sex: Vol. 2. Sexual inversion.* Philadelphia: Davis.

ELLIS, L. (1986). Evidence of neuroandrogenic etiology of sex roles from a combined analysis of human, nonhuman primate and nonprimate mammalian studies. *Personality and Individual Differences, 7,* 519–552.

ELLIS, L., & AMES, M. A. (1987). Neurohormonal functioning and sexual orientation: A theory of homosexuality-heterosexuality. *Psychological Bulletin, 101,* 233–258.

ELLIS, L., AMES, M. A., PECKHAM, W., & BURKE, D. (1988). Sexual orientation of human offspring may be altered by severe maternal stress during pregnancy. *The Journal of Sex Research, 25,* 152–157.

ELLIS, L., BURKE, D. M., & AMES, M. A. (1987). Sexual orientation measures as a continuous variable. *Archives of Sexual Behavior, 16,* 523–529.

ELMER-DEWITT, P. (1990, November 5). Revolution in making babies. *Time,* pp. 76–77.

ELSON, J. (1989, July 24). The rights of frozen embryos. *Time,* p. 63.

EMERY, R. E. (1982). Interparental conflict and the children of discord and divorce. *Psychological Bulletin, 92,* 310–330.

EMERY, R. E. (1989). Family violence. *American Psychologist, 44,* 321–328.

ENTUS, A. K. (1977). Hemispheric asymmetry in processing of dichotically presented speech and nonspeech stimuli by infants. In S. J. Segalowitz & F. A. Gruber (Eds.), *Language development and neurological theory.* New York: Academic Press.

ERICKSON, L. G., & OTTO, W. R. (1973). Effect of intra-list similarity and impusivity-reflectivity on kindergarten children's word recognition performance. *Journal of Educational Research, 66,* 466–470.

ERICKSON, M. F., SROUFE, L. A., & EGELAND, B. (1985). The relationship between quality of attachment and behavior problems in preschool in a high-risk sample. In I. Bretherton & E. Waters (Eds.), Growing points of attachment theory and research. *Monographs of the Society for Research in Child Development, 50* (Serial No. 209).

ERICKSON, M. T. (1987). *Behavior disorders of children and adolescents.* Englewood Cliffs, NJ: Prentice-Hall.

ERIKSON, E. H. (1950). *Childhood and society.* New York: Norton.

ERIKSON, E. H. (1968). *Identity: Youth and crisis.* New York: Norton.

ETAUGH, C. (1980). Effects of nonmaternal care on children: Research evidence and popular views. *American Psychologist, 35,* 309–319.

EVANS, M. A. (1985). Self-initiated speech repairs: A reflection of communicative monitoring in young children. *Developmental Psychology, 21,* 365–371.

EVELETH, P. B., & TANNER, J. M. (1976). *Worldwide variation in human growth.* Cambridge: Cambridge University Press.

FABES, R. A., FULTZ, J., EISENBERG, N., MAY-PLUMLEE, T., & CHRISTOPHER, F. S. (1989). Effects of rewards on children's prosocial motivation: A socialization study. *Developmental Psychology, 25,* 509–515.

FAGAN, J. F., III. (1973). Infants' delayed recognition memory and forgetting. *Journal of Experimental Child Psychology, 16,* 424–450.

FAGAN, J. F., III. (1974). Infant recognition memory: The effects of length of familiarization and type of discrimination task. *Child Development, 45,* 351–356.

FAGAN, J. F., III. (1984). The intelligent infant: Theoretical implications. *Intelligence, 8,* 1–9.

FAGAN, J. F., III, & SINGER, L. T. (1983). Infant recognition memory as a measure of intelligence. In L. P. Lipsitt & C. K. Rovee-Collier (Eds.), *Advances in infancy research* (Vol. 2). Norwood, NJ: Ablex.

FAGOT, B. I. (1978). The influence of sex of child on parental reactions to a toddler child. *Child Development, 49,* 459–465.

FAGOT, B. I., & LEINBACH, M. D. (1989). The young child's gender schema: Environmental input, internal organization. *Child Development, 60,* 663–672.

FAGOT, B. I., LEINBACH, M. D., & HAGAN, R. (1986). Gender labeling and the adoption of sex-typed behaviors. *Developmental Psychology, 22,* 440–443.

FANTZ, R. L. (1958). Pattern vision in young infants. *Psychological Record, 8,* 43–47.

FANTZ, R. L. (1961). The origin of form perception. *Scientific American, 204,* 66–72.

FANTZ, R. L., & MIRANDA, S. B. (1975). Newborn attention to form of contour. *Child Development, 46,* 224–228.

FAUST, M. S. (1960). Developmental maturity as a determinant of prestige in adolescent girls. *Child Development, 31,* 173–184.

FAY, W. H., & SCHULER, A. L. (1980). *Emerging language in autistic children.* Baltimore: University Park Press.

FENNEMA, E., & SHERMAN, J. (1977). Sex-related differences in mathematics achievement, spatial visualization, and affective factors. *American Educational Research Journal, 4,* 51–71.

FERGUSON, T. J., & RULE, B. C. (1980). Effects of inferential set, outcome severity, and basis for responsibility on children's evaluations of aggressive acts. *Developmental Psychology, 16,* 141–146.

FERNALD, A. (1981, April). *Four-month-olds prefer to listen to "motherese."* Paper presented at the meeting of the Society for Research in Child Development, Boston.

FERNALD, A., & KUHL, P. K. (1981, April). *Fundamental frequency as an acoustic determinant of infant preference for motherese.* Paper presented at the meeting of the Society for Research in Child Development, Boston.

FIELD, D. (1987). A review of preschool conservation training: An analysis of analyses. *Developmental Review, 7,* 210–251.

FIELD, T. (1984). Early interactions between infants and their postpartum depressed mothers. *Infant Behavior and Development, 7,* 517–522.

FIELD, T., HEALY, B., GOLDSTEIN, S., & GUTHERTZ, M. (1990). Behavior-state matching and synchrony in mother-infant interactions of nondepressed versus depressed dyads. *Developmental Psychology, 26,* 7–14.

FIELD, T., & VEGA-LAHR, N. (1984). Early interactions between infants with cranio-facial anomalies and their mothers. *Infant Behavior and Development, 7,* 527–530.

FIELD, T., WOODSON, R., GREENBERG, R., & COHEN, D. (1982). Discrimination and imitation of facial expression by neonates. *Science, 218,* 179–181.

FINKELHOR, D. (1979). *Sexually victimized children.* New York: Free Press.

FINKELHOR, D. (1984). *Child sexual abuse: New theory and research.* New York: Free Press.

FINKELSTEIN, N. W., DENT, C., GALLAGHER, K., & RAMEY, C. T. (1978). Social behavior of infants and toddlers in a daycare environment. *Developmental Psychology, 14,* 257–262.

FINKELSTEIN, N. W., & RAMEY, C. T. (1977). Learning to control the environment in infancy. *Child Development, 48,* 806–819.

FINNIE, V., & RUSSELL, A. (1988). Preschool children's social status and their mothers' behavior and knowledge in the supervisory role. *Developmental Psychology, 24,* 789–801.

FISCHER, K. W. (1980). A theory of cognitive development: The control and construction of hierarchies of skills. *Psychological Review, 87,* 477–531.

FITZGERALD, H. E., & BRACKBILL, Y. (1976). Classical conditioning in infancy: Development and constraints. *Psychological Bulletin, 83,* 353–376.

FLAVELL, J. H. (1963). *The developmental psychology of Jean Piaget.* Princeton, NJ: D. Van Nostrand.

FLAVELL, J. H. (1970). Developmental studies of mediated memory. In H. W. Reese & L. P. Lipsitt (Eds.), *Advances in child development and child behavior* (Vol. 5). New York: Academic Press.

FLAVELL, J. H. (1978). Metacognitive development. In J. M. Scandura & C. J. Brainerd (Eds.), *Structural/process theories of complex human behavior.* Alphen a.d. Rijn, The Netherlands: Sythoff and Noordhoff.

FLAVELL, J. H. (1982). On cognitive development. *Child Development, 53,* 1–10.

FLAVELL, J. H., BEACH, D. R., & CHINSKY, J. H. (1966). Spontaneous verbal rehearsal in a memory task as a function of age. *Child Development, 37,* 283–299.

FLAVELL, J. H., SPEER, J. R., GREEN, F. L., & AUGUST, D. L. (1981). The development of comprehension monitoring and knowledge about communication. *Monographs of the Society for Research in Child Development, 46* (Serial No. 192).

FLAVELL, J. H., & WELLMAN, H. M. (1977). Metamemory. In R. V. Kail, Jr. & J. W. Hagen (Eds.), *Perspectives on the development of memory and cognition.* Hillsdale, NJ: Erlbaum.

FLEMING, A. S., RUBLE, D. N., FLETT, G. L., & VAN WAGNER, V. (1990). Adjustment in first-time mothers: Changes in mood and mood content during the early postpartum months. *Developmental Psychology, 26,* 137–143.

FLORIDA MEDICAL ASSOCIATION. (1989). *Clinical manual on HIV and AIDS.* Jacksonville, FL: Author.

FOLDS, T. H., FOOTO, M. M., GUTTENTAG, R. E., & ORNSTEIN, P. A. (1990). When children mean to remember: Issues of context specificity, strategy effectiveness, and intentionality in the development of memory. In D. F. Bjorklund (Ed.), *Children's strategies: Contemporary views of cognitive development.* Hillsdale, NJ: Erlbaum.

FONTAINE, R. (1984). Imitative skill between birth and six months. *Infant Behavior and Development, 7,* 323–333.

FORD, C. S., & BEACH, F. A. (1951). *Patterns of sexual behavior.* New York: Harper & Row.

FRAIBERG, S. (1971). Intervention in infancy. *Journal of the American Academy of Child Psychiatry, 10,* 381–405.

FRAIBERG, S. (1974). Blind infants and their mothers: An examination of the sign system. In M. Lewis &

L. A. Rosenblum (Eds.), *The effect of the infant on its caregiver.* New York: Wiley.

FRANCKE, L. B. (1983). *Growing up divorced.* New York: Fawcett Crest.

FRANKENBERG, W. K., & DODDS, J. B. (1976). The Denver Developmental Screening Test. *Journal of Pediatrics, 71,* 181–191.

FRAUENGLASS, M. H., & DIAZ, R. M. (1985). Self-regulatory functions of children's private speech: A critical analysis of recent challenges to Vygotsky's theory. *Developmental Psychology, 21,* 357–364.

FREEDLE, R. V., & LEWIS, M. (1977). Prelinguistic conversation. In M. Lewis & L. Rosenblum (Eds.), *Interaction, conversation, and the development of language.* New York: Wiley.

FREUD, A. (1946). *The ego and the mechanisms of defense.* London: Hogarth.

FREUD, S. (1938). *An outline of psychoanalysis.* London: Hogarth.

FREUD, S. (1953). *The standard edition of the complete psychological works of Sigmund Freud* (J. Strachey, Ed. and Trans.). London: Hogarth and the Institute of Psychoanalysis.

FRIEDMAN, S. (1972). Habituation and recovery of visual response in the alert human newborn. *Journal of Experimental Child Psychology, 13,* 339–349.

FRIEDRICH, L. K., & STEIN, A. H. (1973). Aggressive and prosocial television programs and the natural behavior of preschool children. *Monographs of the Society for Research in Child Development, 38* (Serial No. 151).

FRODI, A. M., & LAMB, M. E. (1978). Sex differences in responsiveness to infants: A developmental study of psychophysiological and behavioral responses. *Child Development, 49,* 1182–1188.

FRODI, A. M., & LAMB, M. E. (1980). Child abusers' responses to infant smiles and cries. *Child Development, 51,* 238–241.

FULLER, J. L., & CLARK, L. D. (1966). Genetic and treatment factors modifying the postisolation syndrome in dogs. *Journal of Comparative and Physiological Psychology, 61,* 251–257.

FURMAN, W., RAHE, D. F., & HARTUP, W. W. (1979). Rehabilitation of socially withdrawn preschool children through mixed-age and same-age socialization. *Child Development, 50,* 915–922.

FURSTENBERG, F. F., JR., BROOKS-GUNN, J., & CHASE-LANSDALE, L. (1989). Teenaged pregnancy and childbearing. *American Psychologist, 44,* 313–320.

FURSTENBERG, F. F., JR., BROOKS-GUNN, J., & MORGAN, S. P. (1987). *Adolescent mothers in later life.* New York: Cambridge University Press.

FURTH, H., & MILGRAM, N. (1973). Labeling and grouping effects in the recall of pictures by children. *Child Development, 44,* 511–518.

FUSON, K. C., SECADA, W. G., & HALL, J. T. (1983). Matching, counting, and conservation of numerical equivalence. *Child Development, 54,* 91–97.

GAGNON, J. H., & SIMON, W. (1973). *Sexual conduct: The social sources of human sexuality.* Chicago: Aldine.

GALLUP, G. G., JR. (1970). Chimpanzees: Self recognition. *Science, 167,* 86–87.

GALLUP, G. G., JR. (1979). Self-recognition in chimpanzees and man: A developmental and comparative perspective. In M. Lewis & L. A. Rosenblum (Eds.), *Genesis of behavior: Vol. 2. The child and its family.* New York: Plenum.

GALST, J. P., & WHITE, M. A. (1976). The unhealthy persuader: The reinforcing value of television on children's purchase-influencing attempts at the supermarket. *Child Development, 47,* 1089–1096.

GARBER, H. L. (1988). *The Milwaukee project: Preventing mental retardation in children at risk.* Washington, DC: American Association on Mental Retardation.

GARBER, H. L., & HEBER, R. (1981). The efficacy of early intervention with family rehabilitation. In E. M. Hetherington & R. D. Ross (Eds.), *Contemporary readings in child psychology* (2nd ed.). New York: McGraw-Hill.

GARDNER, H. (1983). *Frames of mind: The theory of multiple intelligences.* New York: Basic Books.

GARDNER, H. (1984a). Human intelligence isn't what we think. *U. S. News and World Report,* March 19, pp. 75–78.

GARDNER, H. (1984b). Assessing intelligence: A comment on "Testing intelligence without IQ tests." *Phi Delta Kappan, 65,* 699–700.

GARDNER, H., & HATCH, T. (1989). Multiple intelligences go to school: Educational implications of the theory of multiple intelligences. *Educational Researcher, 18,* 4–10.

GARDNER, J., & GARDNER, H. (1970). A note on selective imitation by a six-week-old infant. *Child Development, 41,* 1209–1213.

GARNER, R. (1990). Children's use of strategies in reading. In D. F. Bjorklund (Ed.), *Children's strategies: Contemporary views of cognitive development*. Hillsdale, NJ: Erlbaum.

GAVIN, L. A., & FURMAN, W. (1989). Age differences in adolescents' perceptions of their peer groups. *Developmental Psychology, 25,* 827–834.

GAY, J., & COLE, M. (1967). *The new mathematics and an old culture*. New York: Holt, Rinehart & Winston.

GAZZANIGA, M. S. (1985). *The social brain: Discovering the networks of the mind*. New York: Basic Books.

GELMAN, R. (1969). Conservation acquisition: A problem of learning to attend to relevant attributes. *Journal of Experimental Child Psychology, 7,* 167–187.

GELMAN, R., & GALLISTEL, R. (1978). *The child's understanding of number*. Cambridge, MA: Harvard University Press.

GELMAN, R., & SHATZ, M. (1977). Appropriate speech adjustments: The operation of conversational constraints on talk to 2-year-olds. In M. Lewis & L. Rosenblum (Eds.), *Interaction, conversation, and the development of language*. New York: Academic Press.

GEORGE, C., & MAIN, M. (1979). Social interaction of young abused children: Approach, avoidance, and aggression. *Child Development, 50,* 306–318.

GESELL, A., & AMATRUDA, C. (1954). *Developmental diagnosis*. New York: Paul B. Holber.

GHATALA, E. S., LEVIN, J. R., PRESSLEY, M., & GOODWIN, D. (1986). A componential analysis of the effects of derived and supplied strategy-utility information on children's strategy selections. *Journal of Experimental Child Psychology, 41,* 76–92.

GHOLSON, B. (1980). *The cognitive-developmental basis of human learning: Studies in hypothesis testing*. New York: Academic Press.

GHOLSON, B., & DANZINGER, S. (1975). Effects of two levels of stimulus complexity upon hypothesis sampling systems among second and sixth grade children. *Journal of Experimental Child Psychology, 20,* 105–118.

GIBBS, J. T. (1988, May 29). Young, black, in critical condition. *Los Angeles Times*.

GIBSON, E. J. (1969). *Principles of perceptual learning and development*. New York: Appleton-Century-Crofts.

GIBSON, E. J., GIBSON, J. J., PICK, A. D., & OSSER, H. (1962). A developmental study of the discrimination of letter-like forms. *Journal of Comparative and Physiological Psychology, 55,* 897–906.

GIBSON, E. J., & LEVIN, H. (1975). *The psychology of reading*. Cambridge, MA: MIT Press.

GIBSON, E. J., & WALK, R. D. (1960). The "visual cliff." *Scientific American, 202,* 64–71.

GILLIGAN, C. (1977). In a different voice: Women's conceptions of self and morality. *Harvard Educational Review, 47,* 481–517.

GILLIGAN, C. (1982). *In a different voice: Psychological theory and women's development*. Cambridge, MA: Harvard University Press.

GILLIGAN, C., KOHLBERG, L., LERNER, J., & BELENKY, M. (1971). Moral reasoning about sexual dilemmas. *Technical report to the U.S. Commission on Obscenity and Pornography* (Vol. 1, pp. 145–173).

GINSBURG, H. (1977). *Children's arithmetic: The learning process*. New York: D. Van Nostrand.

GINSBURG, H. J., & MILLER, S. M. (1982). Sex differences in children's risk-taking behavior. *Child Development, 53,* 426–428.

GJERDE, P. F., BLOCK, J., & BLOCK, J. N. (1985). Longitudinal consistency of Matching Familiar Figures Test performance from early childhood to preadolescence. *Developmental Psychology, 21,* 262–271.

GLANZER, D., & DODD, D. (1975, April). *Developmental changes in the language spoken to children*. Paper presented at the meeting of the Society for Research in Child Development, Denver.

GLICK, J. A. (1975). Cognitive development in cross-cultural perspective. In T. D. Horowitz (Ed.), *Review of child development research*. Chicago: University of Chicago Press.

GLUCKSBERG, S., KRAUSS, R. M., & WEISBERG, R. (1966). Referential communication in nursery school children: Method and some preliminary findings. *Journal of Experimental Child Psychology, 3,* 333–342.

GOBLE, F. G. (1988, January 8). Building ethics from the classroom up. *Wall Street Journal*.

GOLDBERG, S. (1983). Parent-infant bonding: Another look. *Child Development, 54,* 1355–1382.

GOLDFARB, W. (1945). Effects of psychological deprivation in infancy and subsequent stimulation. *American Journal of Psychiatry, 102,* 18–33.

GOLDFARB, W. (1947). Variations in adolescent adjustment of institutionally reared children. *American Journal of Orthopsychiatry, 17,* 449–457.

GOLDMAN, R., & GOLDMAN, J. (1982). *Children's sexual thinking: A comparative study of children aged 5 to 15 years in Australia, North America, Britain, and Sweden.* London: Routledge & Kegan Paul.

GOODENOUGH, F. L. (1926). *The measurement of intelligence through drawing.* Yonkers-on-the-Hudson, NY: Holt.

GOODENOUGH, W. (1964). Cultural anthropology and linguistics. In D. Hymes (Ed.), *Language in culture and society.* New York: Harper & Row.

GOODMAN, G. S., BOTTOMS, B. L., HERSCOVICI, B. B., & SHAVER, P. (1989). Determinants of the child victim's perceived credibility. In S. J. Ceci, D. F. Ross, & M. P. Toglia (Eds.), *Perspectives on children's testimony.* New York: Springer-Verlag.

GOODMAN, G. S., & CLARKE-STEWART, A. (1991). Suggestibility in children's testimony: Implications for sexual abuse investigations. In J. Doris (Ed.), *The suggestibility of children's recollections.* Washington, D.C.: American Psychological Association.

GOODMAN, G. S., GOLDING, J. M., HEGELSON, V. S., HAITH, M. M., & MICHELLI, J. (1987). When a child takes the stand: Jurors' perceptions of children's eyewitness testimony. *Law and Human Behavior, 11,* 27–40.

GOODMAN, G. S., & REED, R. S. (1986). Age differences in eyewitness testimony. *Law and Human Behavior, 19,* 317–332.

GOODNOW, J. J. (1962). A test of milieu differences with some Piagetian tasks. *Psychological Monographs, 76,* 36.

GOODRICH, F. W., JR. (1950). *Natural childbirth.* New York: Prentice-Hall.

GOODZ, N. S. (1982). Is before really easier to understand than after? *Child Development, 53,* 822–825.

GORTMAKER, S. (1988). TV blamed for "fattening" of young Americans. Interview reported in *The Miami Herald,* October.

GOTTLIEB, G. (1971). Ontogenesis of sensory function in birds and mammals. In E. Tobach, L. R. Aronson, & E. Shaw (Eds.), *The biopsychology of development.* New York: Academic Press.

GOTTMAN, J. M. (1977). Toward a definition of social isolation in children. *Child Development, 48,* 513–517.

GOULD, S. J. (1977). *Ontogeny and phylogeny.* Cambridge, MA: Harvard University Press.

GOULD, S. J. (1980). *The panda's thumb: More reflections in natural history.* New York: Norton.

GOULD, S. J. (1981). *The mismeasure of man.* New York: Norton.

GOVE, F. L., & KEATING, D. P. (1979). Empathic role-taking precursors. *Developmental Psychology, 15,* 594–600.

GREEN, D. (1987). *The "sissy boy syndrome" and the development of homosexuality.* New Haven, CT: Yale University Press.

GREEN, F. P., & SCHNEIDER, F. W. (1974). Age differences in the behavior of boys on three measures of altruism. *Child Development, 45,* 248–251.

GREEN, D. (1987). *The "sissy boy syndrome" and the development of homosexuality.* New Haven, CT: Yale University Press.

GREENBERG, D. J., & O'DONNELL, W. J. (1972). Infancy and the optimal level of stimulation. *Child Development, 43,* 905–918.

GREENFIELD, P. M. (1966). On culture and conservation. In J. S. Bruner, R. P. Olver, & P. M. Greenfield (Eds.), *Studies in cognitive growth.* New York: Wiley.

GREENOUGH, W. T., BLACK, J. E., & WALLACE, C. S. (1987). Experience and brain development. *Child Development, 58,* 539–559.

GREENOUGH, W. T., MCDONALD, J., PARNISARI, R., & CAMEL, J. E. (1986). Environmental conditions modulate degeneration and new dendrite growth in cerebellum of senescent rats. *Brain Research, 380,* 136–143.

GREGG, N. M. (1942). Congenital cataract following German measles in the mother. *Transactions of the Ophthalmological Society of Australia, 3,* 35–46.

GRIBBIN, J., & CHERFAS, J. (1982). *The monkey puzzle tree: Reshaping the evolutionary tree.* New York: Pantheon.

GRIESER, D. L., & KUHL, P. K. (1988). Maternal speech to infants in a tonal language: Support for universal prosodic features in motherese. *Developmental Psychology, 24,* 14–20.

GRIFFIN, C. W., WIRTH, M. J., & WIRTH, A. G. (1986). *Beyond acceptance: Parents of lesbians and gays talk about their experiences.* Englewood Cliffs, NJ: Prentice-Hall.

GROEN, G. J., & PARKMAN, J. M. (1972). A chronometric analysis of simple addition. *Psychological Review, 79,* 329–343.

GROEN, G. J., & RESNICK, L. B. (1977). Can preschool

children invent addition algorithms? *Journal of Educational Psychology, 69,* 645–652.

GRUSEC, J. E., & ABRAMOVITCH, R. (1982). Imitation of peers and adults in a natural setting: A functional analysis. *Child Development, 53,* 233–240.

GUERRA, N. G., & SLABY, R. G. (1990). Cognitive mediators of aggression in adolescent offenders: 2. Intervention. *Developmental Psychology, 26,* 269–277.

GUIDUBALDI, J., & PERRY, J. D. (1985). Divorce and mental health sequelae for children: A two-year follow-up of a nationwide sample. *Journal of the American Academy of Child Psychiatry, 24,* 531–537.

GUILFORD, J. P. (1967). *The nature of human intelligence.* New York: McGraw-Hill.

GUILFORD, J. P. (1988). Some changes in the structure-of-the-intellect model. *Educational and Psychological Measurement, 48,* 1–4.

GUNDERSEN, B. H., MELAS, P. S., & SKAR, J. E. (1981). Sexual behavior of preschool children: Teachers' observations. In L. L. Constantine & F. M. Martinson (Eds.), *Children and sex: New findings, new perspectives.* Boston: Little, Brown.

GUNNAR, M. R., & DONAHUE, M. (1980). Sex differences in social responsiveness between six months and twelve months. *Child Development, 51,* 262–265.

GUNNAR, M. R., MALONE, S., VANCE, G., & FISCH, R. O. (1985). Coping with aversive stimulation in the neonatal period: Quiet sleep and plasma cortisol levels during recovery from circumcision. *Child Development, 56,* 824–834.

GUTTENTAG, R. E. (1984). The mental effort requirement of cumulative rehearsal: A developmental study. *Journal of Experimental Child Psychology, 37,* 92–106.

GUTTMACHER INSTITUTE (1981). *Teenage pregnancy: The problem hasn't gone away.* New York: Author.

GZESH, S. M., & SURBER, C. F. (1985). Visual perspective-taking skills in children. *Child Development, 56,* 1204–1213.

HAAN, N., LANGER, J., & KOHLBERG, L. (1976). Family patterns of moral reasoning. *Child Development, 47,* 1204–1206.

HAAN, N., SMITH, M. B., & BLOCK, J. (1968). Moral reasoning of young adults: Political-social behavior, family background, and personality correlates. *Journal of Personality and Social Psychology, 10,* 183–201.

HACKETT, D. C. (1990, November 11). Volunteers find ways to provide role models. *Miami Herald.*

HAGEN, J. W. (1972). Strategies for remembering. In S. Farnham-Diggory (Ed.), *Information processing in children.* New York: Academic Press.

HAGEN, J. W., & STANOVICH, K. G. (1977). Memory: Strategies of acquisition. In R. V. Kail, Jr., & H. W. Hagen (Eds.), *Perspectives on the development of memory and cognition.* Hillsdale, NJ: Erlbaum.

HAITH, M. M. (1966). The response of the human newborn to visual movement. *Journal of Experimental Child Psychology, 3,* 235–243.

HALL, J. A., & HALBERSTADT, A. G. (1980). Masculinity and femininity in children: Development of the children's attributes questionnaire. *Developmental Psychology, 16,* 270–280.

HALVERSON, C. F., & WALDROP, M. F. (1973). The relations of mechanically recorded activity level to varieties of preschool play behavior. *Child Development, 44,* 678–681.

HALVERSON, H. M. (1940). Genital and sphincter behavior in the male infant. *Pedagogical Seminar and Journal of Genetic Psychology, 53,* 365–430.

HAMANN, M. S., & ASHCRAFT, M. H. (1985). Simple and complex mental addition across development. *Journal of Experimental Child Psychology, 40,* 49–72.

HANSEN, J. (1981). The effects of inference training and practice on young children's reading comprehension. *Reading Research Quarterly, 16,* 391–417.

HANSEN, J., & PEARSON, P. D. (1983). An instructional study: Improving the inferential comprehension of good and poor readers. *Journal of Educational Psychology, 75,* 821–829.

HANSON, J. W., JONES, K. L., & SMITH, D. W. (1976). Fetal alcohol syndrome: Experience with 31 patients. *Journal of the American Medical Association, 235,* 1458–1460.

HARLOW, H. F. (1962). The heterosexual affectional system in monkeys. *American Psychologist, 17,* 1–9.

HARLOW, H. F., DODSWORTH, R. O., & HARLOW, M. K. (1965). Total isolation in monkeys. *Proceedings of the National Academy of Science, 54,* 90–97.

HARLOW, H. F., & HARLOW, M. K. (1977). The young monkeys. In *Readings in developmental psychology today* (2nd ed.). Del Mar, CA: CRM Books.

HARLOW, H. F., HARLOW, M. K., DODSWORTH, R. O., & ARLING, G. L. (1966). Maternal behavior of rhesus monkeys deprived of mothering and peer associations as infants. *Proceedings of the American Philosophical Society, 110,* 88–98.

HARLOW, H. F., & ZIMMERMAN, R. R. (1959). Affectional responses in the infant monkey. *Science, 130,* 421–432.

HARNISHFEGER, K. K., & BJORKLUND, D. F. (1990). Children's strategies: A brief history. In D. F. Bjorklund (Ed.), *Children's strategies: Contemporary views of cognitive development.* Hillsdale, NJ: Erlbaum.

HARNISHFEGER, K. K., & BJORKLUND, D. F. (1992). The ontogeny of inhibition mechanisms: A renewed approach to cognitive development. In M. L. Howe & R. Pasnak (Eds.), *Emerging themes in cognitive development* (Vol. 2). New York: Springer-Verlag.

HART, S. (1991). UN Convention on the Rights of the Child. *American Psychologist, 46,* 50–52.

HARTSHORNE, H., & MAY, M. S. (1928–1930). *Studies in the nature of character: Vol. 1. Studies in deceit; Vol. 2. Studies in self-control; Vol. 3. Studies in the organization of character.* New York: Macmillan.

HARTUP, W. W. (1974). Aggression in childhood: Developmental perspectives. *American Psychologist, 29,* 336–341.

HARTUP, W. W. (1983). Peer relations. In E. M. Hetherington (Ed.), *Socialization, personality, and social development,* Vol. 4 of P. H. Mussen (Gen. Ed.), *Handbook of child psychology* (4th ed.). New York: Wiley.

HARTUP, W. W., & COATES, B. (1967). Imitation of a peer as a function of reinforcement from peer group and rewardingness of the model. *Child Development, 38,* 1003–1016.

HARTUP, W. W., LAURSEN, B., STEWART, M. I., & EASTENSON, A. (1988). Conflict and the friendship relations of young children. *Child Development, 59,* 1590–1600.

HASHER, L., & ZACKS, R. T. (1979). Automatic and effortful processes in memory. *Journal of Experimental Psychology: General, 108,* 356–388.

HASKETT, G. J. (1971). Modification of peer preferences of first-grade children. *Developmental Psychology, 4,* 429–433.

HASKINS, R. (1985). Public school aggression among children with varying day-care experience. *Child Development, 56,* 689–703.

HASKINS, R. (1989). Beyond metaphor: The efficacy of early childhood education. *American Psychologist, 44,* 274–282.

HASKINS, R., & MCKINNEY, J. D. (1976). Relative effects

of response tempo and accuracy on problem solving and academic achievement. *Child Development, 47,* 690–696.

HAY, D. F., & ROSS, H. S. (1982). The social nature of early conflict. *Child Development, 53,* 105–113.

HAYDEN, L., TARULLI, D., & HYMEL, S. (1988, May). *Children talk about loneliness.* Paper presented at the biennial meeting of the University of Waterloo Conference on Child Development, Waterloo, Ontario.

HAYES, C. D. (Ed.). (1987). *Risking the future* (Vol. 1). Washington, DC: National Academy Press.

HAYES, L. A., & WATSON, J. S. (1981). Neonatal imitation: Fact or artifact? *Developmental Psychology, 17,* 655–660.

HAYNES, H., WHITE, B. L., & HELD, R. (1965). Visual accommodation in human infants. *Science, 148,* 528–530.

HAZEN, N. L. (1982). Spatial exploration and spatial knowledge: Individual and developmental differences in very young children. *Child Development, 53,* 826–833.

HAZEN, N. L., & DURRETT, M. E. (1982). Relationship of security of attachment to exploration and cognitive mapping abilities in 2-year-olds. *Developmental Psychology, 18,* 751–759.

HEAROLD, S. (1986). A synthesis of 1043 effects of television on social behavior. In G. Comstock (Ed.), *Public communication and behavior* (Vol. 1). New York: Academic Press.

HEBB, D. O. (1949). *The organization of behavior.* New York: Wiley.

HEIMANN, M. (1989). Neonatal imitation gaze aversion and mother-infant interaction. *Infant Behavior and Development, 12,* 495–505.

HELD, R., & HEIN, A. (1963). Movement-produced stimulation in the development of visually guided behavior. *Journal of Comparative and Physiological Psychology, 56,* 872–876.

HENRY, W. A., III. (1990, April 9). Beyond the melting pot. *Time.*

HERMAN, J. F., SHIRAKI, J. H., & MILLER, B. S. (1985). Young children's ability to infer spatial relationships: Evidence from a large familiar environment. *Child Development, 56,* 1195–1203.

HERMAN, J. F., & SIEGEL, A. W. (1978). The development of cognitive mapping of the large scale environment. *Journal of Experimental Child Psychology, 26,* 389–406.

HETHERINGTON, E. M. (1989). Coping with family transitions: Winners, losers, and survivors. *Child Development, 60,* 1–14.

HETHERINGTON, E. M., COX, M., & COX, R. (1985). Long-term effects of divorce and remarriage on the adjustment of children. *Journal of the American Academy of Child Psychiatry, 24,* 518–530.

HETHERINGTON, E. M., STANLEY-HAGAN, M., & ANDERSON, E. R. (1989). Marital transitions: A child's perspective. *American Psychologist, 44,* 303–312.

HEY, R. P. (1989, August 1). Congress studies aid to black males. *Christian Science Monitor.*

HILGARD, E. R. (1987). *Psychology in America: A historical survey.* San Diego: Harcourt Brace Jovanovich.

HILL, W. C., BOROVSKY, D., & ROVEE-COLLIER, C. (1988). Continuities in infant memory development. *Developmental Psychobiology, 21,* 43–62.

HINDE, R. A. (1979). *Toward understanding relationships.* Ontario/London: Academic Press.

HIRSCH, E. D. (1987). *Cultural literacy: What every American needs to know.* Boston: Houghton Mifflin.

HISCOCK, M., & KINSBOURNE, M. (1980). Asymmetries of selective listening and attention switching in children. *Developmental Psychology, 16,* 70–82.

HOCK, E., & DEMEIS, D. K. (1990). Depression in mothers of infants: The role of maternal employment. *Developmental Psychology, 26,* 285–291.

HOFFER, M. A. (1981). *The roots of behavior.* San Francisco: W. H. Freeman.

HOFFMAN, M. L. (1975). Altruistic behavior and the parent-child relationship. *Journal of Personality and Social Psychology, 31,* 937–943.

HOFFMAN, M. L. (1981). Is altruism part of human nature? *Journal of Personality and Social Psychology, 40,* 121–137.

HOFFMAN, M. L. (1989). Empathy and prosocial activism. In N. Eisenberg, J. Reykowski, & T. E. Stoob (Eds.), *Social and moral values: Individual and societal perspectives.* Hillsdale, NJ: Erlbaum.

HOFFMAN, M. L., & SALTZSTEIN, H. D. (1967). Parent discipline and the child's moral development. *Journal of Personality and Social Psychology, 5,* 45–47.

HOLSTEIN, C. (1976). Irreversible, stepwise sequence in the development of moral judgment: A longitudinal study of males and females. *Child Development, 47,* 51–61.

HONZIK, M. P., MCFARLANE, J. W., & ALLEN, L. (1948). Stability of mental test performance between 2 and 18 years. *Journal of Experimental Education, 17,* 309–324.

HOUSEHOLDER, J., HATCHER, R., BURNS, W., & CHASNOFF, I. (1982). Infants born to narcotic-addicted mothers. *Psychological Bulletin, 92,* 453–468.

HOWE, M. L., & O'SULLIVAN, J. T. (1990). The development of strategic memory: Coordinating knowledge, metamemory, and resources. In D. F. Bjorklund (Ed.), *Children's strategies: Contemporary views of cognitive development.* Hillsdale, NJ: Erlbaum.

HOWES, C. (1988). Relations between early child care and scheduling. *Developmental Psychology, 24,* 53–57.

HOWES, C. (1990). Can age of entry into child care and the quality of child care predict adjustment in kindergarten? *Developmental Psychology, 26,* 292–303.

HOWES, C., & OLENICK, M. (1986). Family and child care influences on toddler compliance. *Child Development, 57,* 202–216.

HOWES, C., & RUBINSTEIN, J. (1985). Determinants of toddlers' experience in daycare: Age of entry and quality of setting. *Child Care Quarterly, 14,* 140–151.

HOWES, C., & STEWART, P. (1987). Child's play with adults, toys, and peers: An examination of family and child-care influence. *Developmental Psychology, 23,* 422–430.

HOWES, P., & MARKMAN, H. J. (1989). Marital quality and child functioning: A longitudinal investigation. *Child Development, 60,* 1044–1051.

HRUBEC, Z., & NEEL, J. V. (1978). The National Academy of Sciences—National Research Council Twin Registry: Ten years of operation. In W. E. Nance (Ed.), *Twin research: Part B. Biology and epidemiology.* New York: Alan R. Liss.

HUDSON, W. (1960). Pictorial depth perception in subcultural Africa. *Journal of Social Psychology, 52,* 183–208.

HUESMANN, L. R. (1986). Psychological processes promoting the relation between exposure to media violence and aggressive behavior by the viewer. *Journal of Social Issues, 42,* 125–139.

HUESMANN, L. R., ERON, L. D., LEFKOWITZ, M. M., & WALDER, L. O. (1984). Stability of aggression over time and generations. *Developmental Psychology, 20,* 746–775.

HUMPHREY, G. K., HUMPHREY, D. E., MUIR, D. W., & DODWELL, P. C. (1986). Pattern perception in infants: Effects of structure and transformation. *Journal of Experimental Child Psychology, 41,* 128–148.

HUMPHREY, N. K. (1976). The social function of intellect. In P. P. G. Bateson & R. A. Hinde (Eds.), *Growing points in ethology.* Cambridge: Cambridge University Press.

HUMPHREYS, A. P., & SMITH, P. K. (1984). Rough and tumble in preschool and playground. In P. K. Smith (Ed.), *Play in animals and humans.* Oxford: Basil Blackwell.

HUMPHREYS, A. P., & SMITH, P. K. (1987). Rough and tumble, friendship, and dominance in schoolchildren: Evidence for continuity and change with age. *Child Development, 58,* 201–212.

HYDE, J. S. (1981). How large are cognitive gender differences? A meta-analysis using ω^2 and *d. American Psychologist, 36,* 892–901.

HYDE, J. S. (1984). How large are gender differences in aggression? A developmental meta-analysis. *Developmental Psychology, 20,* 722–736.

HYMEL, S., WAGNER, E., & BUTLER, L. J. (1990). Reputational bias: View from the peer group. In S. R. Asher & J. D. Coie (Eds.), *Peer rejection in childhood.* Cambridge: Cambridge University Press.

HYMES, D. (1972). On communicative competence. In J. B. Pride & J. Holmes (Eds.), *Sociolinguistics.* Harmondsworth, England: Penguin.

HYMOVITCH, B. (1952). The effects of experimental variations on problem solving in the rat. *Journal of Comparative and Physiological Psychology, 45,* 313–321.

HYSON, M. C., HIRSCH-PASEK, K., & RESCORLA, L. (1989). *Academic environments in early childhood: Challenge or pressure?* Summary report to The Spencer Foundation.

INGRAM, D. (1989). *First language acquisition: Method, description, and explanation.* London: Cambridge University Press.

INHELDER, B., & PIAGET, J. (1958). *The growth of logical thinking from childhood to adolescence.* New York: Basic Books.

INHELDER, B., & PIAGET, J. (1964). *The early growth of logic in the child.* New York: Norton.

IRVINE, J. T. (1978). Wolof "magical thinking": Culture and conservation revisited. *Journal of Cross-Cultural Psychology, 9,* 300–310.

ITARD, J. M. G. (1962). *The wild boy of Aveyron* (G. Humphrey & M. Humphrey, trans.). New York: Appleton-Century-Crofts.

JACOBSON, M. (1969). Development of specific neuronal connections. *Science, 163,* 543–547.

JACOBSON, S. W. (1979). Matching behavior in the young infant. *Child Development, 50,* 425–430.

JAFFE, J., STERN, D. N., & PERRY, J. C. (1973). "Conversational" coupling of gaze behavior in prelinguistic human development. *Journal of Psycholinguistic Research, 2,* 321–330.

JAKOBSON, R. (1968). *Child language, aphasia, and phonological universals.* The Hague: Mouton.

JAMES, W. (1890). *The principles of psychology.* New York: Holt.

JANUS, S. S., & BEST, B. E. (1981). *Latency: Fact or fiction?* In L. L. Constantine & F. M. Martinson (Eds.), *Children and sex: New findings, new perspectives.* Boston: Little, Brown.

JENSEN, A. R. (1969). How much can we boost IQ and scholastic achievement? *Harvard Educational Review, 39,* 1–123.

JENSEN, A. R. (1980). *Bias in mental testing.* New York: Free Press.

JESSOR, R., & JESSOR, S. (1977). *Problem behavior and psychosocial development: A longitudinal study.* New York: Academic Press.

JOHANSON, D., & EDEY, M. (1981). *Lucy: The beginnings of humankind.* New York: Simon & Schuster.

JOHNSON, C. N., & WELLMAN, H. M. (1980). Children's developing understanding of mental verbs: Remember, know, and guess. *Child Development, 51,* 1095–1102.

JOHNSON, J. S., & NEWPORT, E. L. (1989). Critical period effects in second language learning: The influence of maturational state on the acquisition of English as a second language. *Cognitive Psychology, 21,* 60–99.

JOHNSON, L. D., DRISCOLL, S. G., HERTIG, A. T., COLE, P. T., & NICKERSON, R. J. (1979). Vaginal adenosis in stillborns and neonates exposed to diethylstilbestrol and steroidal estrogens and pregestins. *Obstetrics and Gynecology, 53,* 671–679.

JOHNSON, R. C., McCLEARN, G. E., YUEN, S., NAGOSHI, C. T., AHERN, F. M., & COLE, R. E. (1985). Galton's data a century later. *American Psychologist, 40,* 875–892.

JONES, E. F., FORREST, J. D., GOLDMAN, N., HENSHAW, S., LINCOLN, R., ROSOFF, J. I., WESTOFF, C. F., & WULF, D.

(1985). Teenage pregnancies in developed countries: Determinants and policy implications. *Family Planning Perspectives, 17,* 53–63.

JONES, H. E. (1971). Psychological factors related to physical abilities in adolescent boys. In M. C. Jones, N. Bayley, J. W. MacFarlane, & M. P. Honzik (Eds.), *The course of human development.* Waltham, MA: Xerox Publishing.

JONES, K. L., & SMITHE, D. W. (1973). Recognition of the fetal alcohol syndrome in early infancy. *Lancet, 2,* 999–1001.

JONES, M. C. (1965). Psychological correlates of somatic development. *Child Development, 36,* 899–911.

JONES, M. C., & BAYLEY, M. (1950). Physical maturing among boys as related to behavior. *Journal of Educational Psychology, 41,* 129–148.

JUDSON, H. F. (1979). *The eighth day of creation: Makers of the revolution in biology.* New York: Touchstone.

KAGAN, J. (1964). Acquisition and significance of sex typing and sex role identity. In M. L. Hoffman & L. W. Hoffman (Eds.), *Review of child development research* (Vol. 1). New York: Russell Sage Foundation.

KAGAN, J. (1965). Reflection-impulsivity and reading ability in primary grade children. *Child Development, 36,* 609–628.

KAGAN, J. (1969). Inadequate evidence and illogical conclusions: Environment, heredity, and intelligence. *Harvard Educational Review, 39,* 126–129.

KAGAN, J. (1971). *Change and continuity in infancy.* New York: Wiley.

KAGAN, J. (1976). New views on cognitive development. *Journal of Youth and Adolescence, 5,* 113–129.

KAGAN, J. (1984). *The nature of the child.* New York: Basic Books.

KAGAN, J., & KLEIN, R. E. (1973). Cross-cultural perspectives on early development. *American Psychologist, 28,* 947–961.

KAGAN, J., KLEIN, R. E., FINLEY, G. E., ROGOFF, B., & NOLAN, E. (1979). A cross-cultural study of cognitive development. *Monographs of the Society for Research in Child Development, 44* (Serial No. 180).

KAGAN, J., & MOSS, H. A. (1962). *Birth to maturity: A study of psychological development.* New York: Wiley.

KAGAN, J., ROSMAN, B. L., DAY, D., ALBERT, J., & PHILIPS, W. (1964). Information processing in the child: Significance of analytic and reflective attitudes. *Psychological Monographs, 78* (No. 578).

KAHN, J., SMITH, K., & ROBERTS, E. (1984). *Familial communication and adolescent sexual behavior* (Final report to the Office of Adolescent Pregnancy Programs). Cambridge, MA: American Institutes for Research.

KAIL, R. (1988). Developmental functions for speeds of cognitive processes. *Journal of Experimental Child Psychology, 45,* 339–364.

KAITZ, M., MESCHULACH-SARFATY, O., AUERBACH, J., & EIDELMAN, A. (1988). A reexamination of newborns' ability to imitate facial expressions. *Developmental Psychology, 24,* 3–7.

KALICHMAN, S. C. (1988). Individual differences in water-level task performance: A component-skills analysis. *Developmental Review, 8,* 273–295.

KALYAN-MASIH, V. (1985). Cognitive performance and cognitive style. *International Journal of Behavioral Development, 8,* 39–54.

KAMIN, L. J. (1974). *The science and politics of IQ.* Potomac, MD: Erlbaum.

KAPLAN, N. (1987, April). *Internal representations of attachment in 6-year-olds.* Paper presented at the meeting of the Society for Research in Child Development, Baltimore.

KAREN, R. (1990, February). Becoming attached. *Atlantic Monthly,* pp. 35–70.

KARMEL, B. Z., & MAISEL, E. B. (1975). A neuronal activity model for infant visual attention. In L. B. Cohen & P. Salapatek (Eds.), *Infant perception: From sensation to cognition* (Vol. 1). New York: Academic Press.

KARP, S. A., & KONSTADT, N. (1971). *Children's Embedded Figures Test.* Palo Alto, CA: Consulting Psychologists Press.

KATZ, D. L., & POPE, H. G., JR. (1988). Psychiatric effects of anabolic steroids. In W. E. Garrett, Jr. & T. R. Malone (Eds.), *Nutritional alternatives to anabolic steroids* (Report to the Ross Symposium). Columbus, OH: Ross Laboratories.

KATZ, M. B. (1986). *In the shadow of the poor house: A social history of welfare in America.* New York: Basic Books.

KATZ, S., LAUTENSCHLAGER, G. J., BLACKBURN, A. B., & HARRIS, F. H. (1990). Answering reading comprehension questions without passages on the SAT. *Psychological Science, 1,* 122–127.

KAUFMAN, J., & CICCHETTI, D. (1989). Effects of maltreatment on school-age children's socioemotional development: Assessments in a day-care setting. *Developmental Psychology, 25,* 516–524.

KAZDIN, A. E. (1984). *Behavior modification in applied settings* (3rd ed.). Pacific Grove, CA: Brooks/Cole.

KEARSLEY, R. (1973). Newborn's response to auditing stimulation. *Child Development, 44,* 582–590.

KEE, D. W., & DAVIES, L. (1988). Mental effort and elaboration: A developmental analysis. *Contemporary Educational Psychology, 13,* 221–228.

KEE, D. W., & DAVIES, L. (1990). Mental effort and elaboration: Effects of accessibility and construction. *Journal of Experimental Child Psychology, 49,* 264–274.

KEENEY, T. J., CANNIZZO, S. R., & FLAVELL, J. H. (1967). Spontaneous and induced verbal rehearsal in a recall task. *Child Development, 38,* 953–966.

KELLAS, G., MCCAULEY, C., & MCFARLAND, C. E. (1975). Developmental aspects of storage and retrieval. *Journal of Experimental Child Psychology, 19,* 51–62.

KELLER, A., FORD, L. H., JR., & MEACHUM, J. A. (1978). Dimensions of self-concept in preschool children. *Developmental Psychology, 14,* 483–489.

KENDLER, H. H., & KENDLER, T. S. (1962). Vertical and horizontal processes in problem solving. *Psychological Review, 69,* 1–16.

KERMOIAN, R., & CAMPOS, J. J. (1988). Locomotor experience: A facilitator of spatial cognitive development. *Child Development, 59,* 908–917.

KESSEN, W. (1965). *The child.* New York: Wiley.

KINGSLEY, P. R., & HAGEN, J. W. (1969). Induced versus spontaneous rehearsal in short-term memory in nursery school children. *Developmental Psychology, 1,* 40–46.

KINSEY, A. C., POMEROY, W. B., & MARTIN, C. E. (1948). *Sexual behavior in the human male.* Philadelphia: Saunders.

KINSEY, A. C., POMEROY, W. B., & MARTIN, C. E. (1953). *Sexual behavior in the human female.* Philadelphia: Saunders.

KLAUS, M. H., & KENNELL, J. H. (1976). *Maternal-infant bonding.* St. Louis: C. V. Mosby.

KLAUS, M. H., & KENNELL, J. H. (1982). *Parent-infant bonding.* St. Louis: C. V. Mosby.

KLAUS, R. A., & GRAY, S. (1968). The early training project for disadvantaged children: A report after five years. *Monographs of the Society for Research in Child Development, 33* (Serial No. 120).

KOBAK, R. R. (1987, April). *Attachment in late adolescence: Working models affect regulation and representation of self and others.* Paper presented at the meeting of the Society for Research in Child Development, Baltimore.

KOBASIGAWA, A. (1974). Utilization of retrieval cues by children in recall. *Child Development, 45,* 127–134.

KOEPKE, J. E., HAMM, M., LEGERSTEE, M., & RUSSELL, M. (1983). Neonatal imitation: Two failures to replicate. *Infant Behavior and Development, 6,* 97–102.

KOHLBERG, L. (1966). A cognitive-developmental analysis of children's sex-role concepts and attitudes. In E. E. Maccoby (Ed.), *The development of sex differences.* Stanford, CA: Stanford University Press.

KOHLBERG, L. (1969). Stage and sequence: The cognitive-developmental approach to socialization. In D. A. Goslin (Ed.), *Handbook of socialization theory and research.* Chicago: Rand McNally.

KOHLBERG, L. (1984). *Essays on moral development: Vol. 2. The psychology of moral development.* San Francisco: Harper & Row.

KOHLBERG, L., YAEGER, J., & HJERTHOLM, E. (1968). Private speech: Four studies and a review of theories. *Child Development, 39,* 691–736.

KOLATA, G. B. (1986). Obese children: A growing problem. *Science, 225,* 302–303.

KOLB, B., & WHISHAW, I. Q. (1981). Neonatal frontal lesions in the rat: Sparing of learned but not species typical behavior in the presence of reduced brain weight and critical thickness. *Journal of Comparative and Physiological Psychology, 95,* 235–276.

KOLB, B., & WHISHAW, I. Q. (1989). Plasticity in the neocortex: Mechanisms underlying recovery from early brain damage. *Progress in Neurobiology, 32,* 863–879.

KOLB, B., & WHISHAW, I. Q. (1990). *Fundamentals of human neuropsychology* (3rd ed.). New York: W. H. Freeman.

KOLODNY, R. C. (1980, November). *Adolescent sexuality.* Paper presented at the Michigan Personnel and Guidance Association Annual Convention, Detroit.

KOLUCHOVA, J. (1972). Severe deprivation in twins: A case study. *Journal of Child Psychology and Psychiatry, 13,* 107–114.

KOLUCHOVA J. (1976). A report on the further development of twins after severe and prolonged deprivation. In A. M. Clarke & A. D. B. Clarke (Eds.),

Early experience: Myth and evidence. London: Open Books.

KONNER, M. (1991). Universals of behavioral development in relation to brain myelinization. In K. R. Gibson & A. C. Petersen (Eds.), *Brain maturation and cognitive development: Comparative and cross-cultural perspectives.* New York: Aldine de Gruyte.

KOPP, C. B., & McCALL, R. B. (1982). Predicting later mental performance for normal, at-risk, and handicapped infants. In P. B. Baltes & O. G. Brim (Eds.), *Life-span development and behavior* (Vol. 4). New York: Academic Press.

KORNER, A. F., & THOMAN, E. B. (1972). The relative efficacy of contact and vestibular-proprioceptive stimulation in soothing neonates. *Child Development, 43,* 433–454.

KORNHUBER, H. H., BECHINGER, D., JUNG, H., & SAUER, E. (1985). A quantitative relationship between the extent of localized cerebral lesions and the intellectual and behavioral deficiency in children. *European Archives of Psychiatry and Neurological Science, 235,* 125–133.

KOTELCHUK, M. (1976). The infant's relationship to the father: Experimental evidence. In M. E. Lamb (Ed.), *The role of the father in child development.* New York: Wiley.

KOZOL, J. (1985). *Illiterate America.* New York: New American Library.

KOZOL, J. (1988). *Rachel and her children: Homeless families in America.* New York: Crown Publishers.

KRAFT-EBBING, R. (1965). *Psychopathia sexualis* (Franklin S. Klaf, Trans.). New York: Stein & Day. (Original work published 1886)

KRAMER, J. A., HILL, K. T., & COHEN, L. B. (1975). Infants' development of object permanence: A refined methodology and new evidence for Piaget's hypothesized ordinality. *Child Development, 46,* 149–155.

KRESS, G. (1982). *Learning to write.* Boston: Routledge & Kegan Paul.

KREUTZER, M. A., LEONARD, C., & FLAVELL, J. H. (1975). An interview study of children's knowledge about memory. *Monographs of the Society for Research in Child Development, 40* (Serial No. 159).

KROLL, B. M. (1981). Developmental relationships between speaking and writing. In B. M. Kroll & R. J. Vann (Eds.), *Exploring speaking-writing relationships: Connections and contrasts.* Urbana, IL: National Council of Teachers of English.

KRUMHANSL, C. L., & JUSCZYK, P. W. (1990). Infants' perception of phrase structure in music. *Psychological Science, 1,* 70–73.

KUHN, D., LANGER, J. KOHLBERG, L., & HAAN, N. S. (1977). The development of formal operations in logical and moral judgment. *Genetic Psychology Monographs, 95,* 97–188.

KUHN, D., NASH, S. C., & BRUCKEN, L. (1978). Sex role concepts of two- and three-year-olds. *Child Development, 49,* 445–451.

KUPERSMIDT, J. B., COIE, J. D., & DODGE, K. A. (1990). The role of poor peer relationships in the development of disaster. In S. R. Asher & J. D. Coie (Eds.), *Peer rejection in childhood.* Cambridge: Cambridge University Press.

KURTZ, B. E. (1990). Cultural differences in children's cognitive and metacognitive development. In W. Schneider & F. E. Weinert (Eds.), *Interactions among aptitudes, strategies, and knowledge in cognitive performance.* New York: Springer-Verlag.

KURTZ, B. E., & BORKOWSKI, J. G. (1987). Development of strategic skills in impulsive and reflective children: A longitudinal study of metacognition. *Journal of Experimental Child Psychology, 43,* 129–146.

KURTZ, B. E., SCHNEIDER, W., CARR, M., BORKOWSKI, J. G., & RELLINGER, E. (1990). Strategy instruction and attributional beliefs in West Germany and the United States: Do teachers foster metacognitive development? *Contemporary Educational Psychology, 15,* 268–283.

LABORATORY OF COMPARATIVE HUMAN COGNITION. (1983). Culture and cognitive development. In W. Kessen (Ed.), *History, theory, and methods,* Vol. 1 of P. H. Mussen (Gen. Ed.), *Handbook of child psychology,* (4th ed.). New York: Wiley.

LADD, G. W. (1981). Effectiveness of social learning method for enhancing children's social interactions and peer acceptance. *Child Development, 52,* 171–178.

LAFRENIERE, P. J., & SROUFE, L. A. (1985). Profiles of peer competence in the preschool: Interrelations between measures, influence of social ecology, and relation to attachment history. *Developmental Psychology, 21,* 56–69.

LAMB, M. E. (1975). Fathers: Forgotten contributors to child development. *Human Development, 18,* 245–266.

LAMB, M. E. (1981). The development of father-infant

relationships. In M. E. Lamb (Ed.), *The role of the father in child development*. New York: Wiley.

LAMB, M. E. (1981). Early contact and maternal-infant bonding: One decade later. *Pediatrics, 70,* 763–768.

LAMB, M. E., CAMPOS, J. J., HWANG, C.-P., LEIDERMAN, P. H., SAGI, A., & SVEJDA, M. (1983). Joint reply to 'maternal infant bonding': A joint rebuttal. *Pediatrics, 72,* 574–576.

LANE, D. M., & PEARSON, D. A. (1982). The development of selective attention. *Merrill-Palmer Quarterly, 28,* 317–337.

LANGE, G. W., & JACKSON, P. (1974). Personal organization in children's free recall. *Child Development, 45,* 1060–1067.

LANGFELDT, T. (1981). Childhood masturbation: Individual and social organization. In L. L. Constantine & F. M. Martinson (Eds.), *Children and sex: New findings, new perspectives*. Boston: Little, Brown.

LANGINVAINIO, H., KOSKENVUO, M., KAPRIO, J., & SISTONEN, P. (1984). Finnish twins reared apart: II. Validation of zygosity, environmental dissimilarity and weight and height. *Acta Geneticae Medicinae et Gemellologiae, 33,* 251–258.

LANGLOIS, J. H., & ROGGMAN, L. A. (1990). Attractive faces are only average. *Psychological Science, 1,* 115–121.

LANGLOIS, J. H., ROGGMAN, L. A., CASEY, R. J., RITTER, J. M., RIESER-DANNER, L. A., & JENKINS, V. Y. (1987). Infant preferences for attractive faces: Rudiments of a stereotype? *Developmental Psychology, 23,* 363–369.

LANGLOIS, J. H., ROGGMAN, L. A., & RIESER-DANNER, L. A. (1990). Infants' differential social responses to attractive and unattractive faces. *Developmental Psychology, 26,* 153–159.

LANGSTON, E. L. (1990). Statement of the American Medical Association to the Senate Committee on the Judiciary, RE: Scheduling of anabolic steroids, April 3, 1989. In Committee on the Judiciary, U. S. Senate, *Steroids in amateur and professional sports: The medical and social costs of steroid abuse*. Washington, DC: U.S. Government Printing Office.

LAURENDEAU-BENDAVID, M. (1977). Culture, schooling, and cognitive development: A comparative study of children in French Canada and Rwanda. In P. R. Dasen (Ed.), *Piagetian psychology: Cross-cultural contributions*. New York: Gardner.

LAZAR, I., DARLINGTON, R., MURRAY, H., ROYCE, J., & SNIPPER, A. (1982). Lasting effects of early education: A report from the Consortium for Longitudinal Studies. *Monographs of the Society for Research in Child Development, 47,* (Serial No. 195).

LEAL, L., CRAYS, N., & MOELY, B. E. (1985). Training children to use a self-monitoring study strategy in preparation for recall: Maintenance and generalization effects. *Child Development, 56,* 643–653.

LECOURS, A. R. (1975). Myelogenetic correlates of the development of speech and language. In E. H. Lenneberg & E. Lenneberg (Eds.), *Foundations of language development: A multidisciplinary approach*. New York: Academic Press.

LEFKOWITZ, M. M., ERON, L. D., WALDER, L. O., & HUESMANN, L. R. (1972). Television violence and child aggression: A follow-up study. In G. A. Comstock & E. A. Rubinstein (Eds.), *Television and social behavior: Vol. 3. Television and adolescent aggressiveness*. Washington, DC: U. S. Government Printing Office.

LEIPPE, M. R., & ROMANCZYK, A. (1987). Children on the witness stand: A communication/persuasion analysis of jurors' reactions to child witnesses. In S. J. Ceci, M. P. Toglia, & D. F. Ross (Eds.), *Children's eyewitness memory*. New York: Springer-Verlag.

LEMPERS, J. D., CLARK-LEMPERS, D., & SIMONS, R. L. (1989). Economic hardship, parenting and distress in adolescence. *Child Development, 60,* 25–39.

LENNEBERG, E. H. (1967). *Biological foundations of language*. New York: Wiley.

LENZ, W., & KNAPP, K. (1962). Foetal malformations due to thalidomide. *German Medical Monthly, 7,* 253–258.

LEPPER, M. R., GREENE, D., & NISBETT, R. E. (1973). Undermining children's intrinsic interest with extrinsic rewards: A test of the overjustification hypothesis. *Journal of Personality and Social Psychology, 28,* 129–137.

LERNER, R. M. (1984). *On the nature of human plasticity*. New York: Cambridge University Press.

LESSER, H. (1977). *Television and the preschool child*. New York: Academic Press.

LEVER, J. (1976). Sex differences in the games children play. *Social Problems, 23,* 470–487.

LEVIN, S. R., PETROS, T. V., & PETRELLA, F. W. (1982). Preschoolers' awareness of television advertising. *Child Development, 53,* 933–937.

LEVITT, M. J., WEBER, R. A., CLARK, M. C., & MCDONNELL, P. (1985). Reciprocity of exchange in toddler sharing behavior. *Developmental Psychology, 21,* 122–123.

LEWAK, N., ZEBAL, B. H., & FRIEDMAN, S. B. (1984). Management of infants with apnea and potential apnea: A survey of pediatric opinion [Special issue: Pulmonary disease]. *Clinical Pediatrics, 23,* 369–373.

LEWIN, R. (1988). *In the age of mankind.* Washington, DC: Smithsonian Books.

LEWIS, M. (1969). Infants' responses to facial stimuli during the first year of life. *Developmental Psychology, 1,* 75–86.

LEWIS, M., & BROOKS-GUNN, J. (1979). *Social cognition and the acquisition of self.* New York: Plenum.

LEWIS, M., & FEIRING, C. (1989). Infant, mother, and mother-infant interaction behavior and subsequent attachment. *Child Development, 60,* 831–837.

LEWIS, M., FEIRING, C., MCGUFFOG, C., & JASKIR, J. (1984). Predicting psychopathology in six-year-olds from early social relations. *Child Development, 55,* 123–136.

LEWIS, M., & FREEDLE, R. (1973). Mother-infant dyad: The cradle of meaning. In P. Pilner, L. Krames, & T. Alloway (Eds.), *Communication and affect: Language and thought.* New York: Academic Press.

LEWIS, M., & SULLIVAN, M. W. (1985). Imitation in the first month of life. *Merrill-Palmer Quarterly, 31,* 315–333.

LEWIS, M., SULLIVAN, M. W., STANGER, C., & WEISS, M. (1989). Self development and self-conscious emotions. *Child Development, 60,* 146–156.

LEWIS, M., YOUNG, G., BROOKS, J., & MICHALSON, L. (1975). The beginning of friendship. In M. Lewis & L. A. Rosenblum (Eds.), *Friendship and peer relations.* New York: Wiley.

LIBEN, L. S. (1978). Performance in Piagetian spatial tasks as a function of sex, field dependence, and training. *Merrill-Palmer Quarterly, 24,* 97–110.

LIBEN, L. S., & GOLDBECK, S. L. (1980). Sex differences in performance on Piagetian spatial tasks: Differences in competence or performance? *Child Development, 51,* 594–597.

LIBEN, L. S., & GOLDBECK, S. L. (1984). Performance on Piagetian horizontality and verticality tasks: Sex-related differences in knowledge of relevant physical phenomena. *Developmental Psychology, 20,* 595–606.

LIBERMAN, I. Y., & SHANKWEILER, D. (1977). Speech, the alphabet, and teaching to read. In L. B. Resnick & P. A. Weaver (Eds.), *Theory and practice of early reading.* Hillsdale, NJ: Erlbaum.

LIBERMAN, I. Y., SHANKWEILER, D., FISCHER, R. N., & CARTER, B. (1974). Explicit syllable and phoneme segmentation in the young child. *Journal of Experimental Child Psychology, 18,* 201–212.

LIEBERMAN, P. (1967). *Intonations, perception, and language.* Cambridge, MA: MIT Press.

LIEBERT, R. M., & SPRAFKIN, J. (1988). *The early window: Effects of television on children and youth* (3rd ed.). New York: Pergamon Press.

LIN, C.-Y. C., & FU, V. R. (1990). A comparison of child-rearing practices among Chinese, immigrant Chinese, and Caucasian-American parents. *Child Development, 61,* 429–433.

LINN, M. C. (1978). Influence of cognitive style and training on tasks requiring the separation of variables schema. *Child Development, 49,* 874–877.

LINN, M. C., & PETERSON, A. C. (1985). Emergence and characterization of sex differences in spatial ability: A meta-analysis. *Child Development, 56,* 1479–1498.

LINTZ, L. M., FITZGERALD, H. E., & BRACKBILL, Y. (1967). Conditioning the eyeblink response to sound in infants. *Psychonomic Science, 7,* 405–406.

LIPSITT, L. P. (1979). Infants at risk: Perinatal and neonatal factors. *International Journal of Behavioral Development, 2,* 23–42.

LIPSITT, L. P. (1982). Infant learning. In T. M. Field et al. (Eds.), *Review of human development.* New York: Wiley.

LIPSITT, L. P. (1990). Review of "Sudden infant death syndrome: Medical aspects and psychological management." *Child Development Abstracts and Bibliography, 64,* 91–93.

LIPSITT, L. P., STURNER, W. Q., & BURKE, P. (1979). Perinatal indicators and subsequent crib death. *Infant Behavior and Development, 2,* 325–328.

LITTLE, A. H., LIPSITT, L. P., & ROVEE-COLLIER, C. (1984). Classical conditioning and retention of the infant's eyelid response: Effects of age and interstimulus interval. *Journal of Experimental Child Psychology, 37,* 512–524.

LIVESLEY, W., & BROMLEY, D. (1973). *Person perception in childhood and adolescence.* New York: Wiley.

LJUNG, B. O., BERGSTEN-BRUCEFORS, A., & LINDGREN, G. (1974). The secular trend in physical growth in Sweden. *Annals of Human Biology, 1,* 245–256.

LODICO, M. G., GHATALA, E. S., LEVIN, J. R., PRESSLEY, M., & BELL, J. A. (1983). The effects of strategy-monitoring on children's selection of effective memory strategies. *Journal of Experimental Child Psychology, 35,* 263–277.

LOEBER, R. (1982). The stability of antisocial and delinquent child behavior: A review. *Child Development, 53,* 1431–1446.

LOEBER, R., PATTERSON, G. R., & DISHION, T. J. (1982). *Boys who fight: Familiar and antisocial correlates.* Unpublished manuscript, Oregon Social Learning Center, Eugene. Cited in Loeber, R. (1982). The stability of antisocial and delinquent child behavior: A review. *Child Development, 53,* 1431–1446.

LORENZ, K. (1943). Die angeborenen Formen möglicher Erfahrung. *Zeitschrift fur Tierpsychologie, 5,* 235–409.

LORENZ, K. (1971). *Studies in animal and human behavior.* Cambridge, MA: Harvard University Press.

LURIA, A. R. (1976). *Cognitive development: Its cultural and social foundations.* Cambridge, MA: Harvard University Press.

LUSH, J. L. (1951). Genetics and animal breeding. In L. C. Dunn (Ed.), *Genetics in the twentieth century.* New York: Macmillan.

LYONS-RUTH, K., CONNELL, D. B., GRUNEBAUM, H. U., & BOTEIN, S. (1990). Infants at social risk: Maternal depression and support services as mediators of infant development and security of attachment. *Child Development, 61,* 85–98.

MACCOBY, E. E. (1980). *Social development.* San Diego: Harcourt Brace Jovanovich.

MACCOBY, E. E. (1988). Gender as a social category. *Developmental Psychology, 24,* 755–756.

MACCOBY, E. E., & HAGEN, J. W. (1965). Effects of distraction upon central versus incidental recall: Developmental trends. *Journal of Experimental Child Psychology, 2,* 280–289.

MACCOBY, E. E., & JACKLIN, C. N. (1974). *The psychology of sex differences.* Stanford, CA: Stanford University Press.

MACCOBY, E. E., & JACKLIN, C. N. (1987). Gender segregation in childhood. In H. W. Rose (Ed.), *Advances in child development and behavior* (Vol. 20). New York: Academic Press.

MACDONALD, K. & PARKE, R. D. (1984). Bridging the gap: Parent-child play interaction and peer interactive competence. *Child Development, 55,* 1265–1277.

MACFARLANE, A. (1975). Olfaction in the development of social preferences in the human neonate. *CIBA Foundation Symposium 33: Parent-infant interaction.* Amsterdam: Elsevier.

MACKAIN, S. (1987, April). *Gender constancy: A realistic approach.* Paper presented at the meeting of the Society for Research in Child Development, Baltimore.

MACKINNON, C. E. (1989). An observational investigation of sibling interactions in married and divorced families. *Developmental Psychology, 25,* 36–44.

MAGENIS, R. W., & CHAMBERLIN, J. (1981). Parental origin of nondisjunction. In F. F. de la Cruz & P. S. Gerald (Eds.), *Trisomy 21 (Down syndrome): Research perspectives.* Baltimore: University Park Press.

MAIN, M. (1981). Avoidance in the service of attachment: A working paper. In K. Immelmann, G. Barlow, L. Petrinovich, & M. Main (Eds.), *Behavioral development: The Bielefeld interdisciplinary project.* New York: Cambridge University Press.

MAIN, M. (1987, April). *States of mind with respect to attachment in adulthood: Why the relationship to infant attachment classification?* Paper presented at the meeting of the Society for Research in Child Development, Baltimore.

MAIN, M., & CASSIDY, J. (1988). Categories of response to reunion with the parent at age 6: Predictable from infant attachment classification and stable over a 1-month period. *Developmental Psychology, 24,* 415–426.

MAIN, M., & GEORGE, C. (1985). Responses of abused and disadvantaged toddlers to distress in agemates: A study in the day care setting. *Developmental Psychology, 21,* 407–412.

MAIN, M., & HESSE, E. (in press). The parents of insecure–disorganized/disoriented infants: Observations and speculations. In M. Greenberg, D. Cicchetti, & M. Cummings (Eds.), *Attachment in the preschool years.* Chicago: University of Chicago Press.

MAIN, M., KAPLAN, N., & CASSIDY, J. (1985). Security in infancy, childhood, and adulthood: A move to the level of representation. In I. Bretherton & E. Waters (Eds.), Growing points of attachment theory and research. *Monographs of the Society for Research in Child Development, 50* (Serial No. 209).

MAIN, M., & SOLOMON, J. (1986). Discovery of an insecure disorganized/disoriented attachment pattern. In T. B. Brazelton & M. W. Yogman (Eds.), *Affective development in infancy.* Norwood, NJ: Ablex.

MAIN, M., & WESTON, D. R. (1981). The quality of the toddler's relationship to mother and to father: Related to conflict and the readiness to establish new relationships. *Child Development, 52,* 932–940.

MAKIN, J. W., & PORTER, R. H. (1989). Attractiveness of lactating females' breast odors to neonates. *Child Development, 60,* 803–810.

MANDLER, G. (1967). Organization and memory. In K. W. Spence & J. T. Spence (Eds.), *The psychology of learning and motivation* (Vol. 1). New York: Academic Press.

MANDLER, J. M., SCRIBNER, S., COLE, M., & DeFOREST, M. (1980). Cross-cultural invariance in story recall. *Child Development, 51,* 19–26.

MARATSOS, M. (1983). Some current issues in the study of the acquisition of grammar. In J. H. Flavell & E. M. Markman (Eds.), *Cognitive development,* Vol. 3 of P. H. Mussen (Gen. Ed.), *Handbook of child psychology* (4th ed.). New York: Wiley.

MARCH OF DIMES BIRTH DEFECTS FOUNDATION. (1989a). *Chicken pox during pregnancy.* White Plains, NY: Author.

MARCH OF DIMES BIRTH DEFECTS FOUNDATION. (1989b). *Cocaine use during pregnancy.* White Plains, NY: Author.

MARKMAN, E. M. (1977). Realizing that you don't understand: A preliminary investigation. *Child Development, 48,* 986–992.

MARKMAN, E. M., & SEIBERT, J. (1976). Classes and collections: Internal organization and resulting holistic properties. *Cognitive Psychology, 8,* 561–577.

MARSHALL, W. A., & TANNER, J. M. (1970). Variations in the pattern of pubertal changes in boys. *Archives of the Diseases in Childhood, 45,* 13–23.

MARTIN, G. B., & CLARK, R. D., III. (1982). Distress crying in neonates: Species and peer specificity. *Developmental Psychology, 18,* 3–9.

MARTIN, H., BREEZLEY, P., CONWAY, E., & KEMPE, H. (1974). The development of abused children: A review of the literature. *Advances in Pediatrics, 21,* 119–134.

MARTIN, J. A. (1980). A longitudinal study of the consequences of early mother-infant interaction: A microanalytic approach. *Monographs of the Society for Research in Child Development, 45* (Serial No. 190).

MARTINSON, F. M. (1981). Eroticism in infancy and childhood. In L. L. Constantine & F. M. Martinson (Eds.), *Children and sex: New findings, new perspectives.* Boston: Little, Brown.

MARTINSON, R. (1973). *Infant and child sexuality: A sociological perspective.* St. Peter, MN: Gustavus Adolphus College.

MASON, M. K. (1942). Learning to speak after six and one-half years of silence. *Journal of Speech Disorders, 7,* 295–304.

MASSAD, C. M. (1981). Sex-role identity and adjustment during adolescence. *Child Development, 52,* 1290–1298.

MASTERS, W. H., & JOHNSON, V. E. (1966). *Human sexual response.* Boston: Little, Brown.

MASTERS, W. H., JOHNSON, V. E., & KOLODNY, R. C. (1985). *Human sexuality* (2nd ed.). Boston: Little, Brown.

MATAS, L., AREND, R. A., & SROUFE, L. A. (1978). Continuity of adaptation in the second year: The relationship between quality of attachment and later competence. *Child Development, 49,* 547–556.

MAYR, E. (1982). *The growth of biological thought: Diversity, evolution, and inheritance.* Cambridge, MA: Belknap Press.

McALLISTER, B. (1990, February 27). Study: 1 in 4 young black men is in jail or court-supervision. *Washington Post.*

McBRIDGE, S., & BELSKY, J. (1988). Characteristics, determinants, and consequences of maternal separation anxiety. *Developmental Psychology, 24,* 407–414.

McCABE, A. E., SIEGEL, L. S., SPENCE, I., & WILKINSON, A. (1982). Class-inclusion reasoning: Patterns of performance from three to eight years. *Child Development, 53,* 780–785.

McCALL, R. B. (1977). Challenges to a science of developmental psychology. *Child Development, 48,* 333–344.

McCALL, R. B. (1981). Nature-nurture and the two realms of development: A proposed integration with respect to mental development. *Child Development, 52,* 1–12.

McCALL, R. B., APPELBAUM, M. I., & HOGARTY, P. S. (1973). Developmental changes in mental performance. *Monographs of the Society for Research in Child Development, 38* (Serial No. 150).

McCALL, R. B., EICHORN, D. H., & HOGARTY, P. S. (1977).

Transitions in early mental development. *Monographs of the Society for Research in Child Development, 42* (Serial No. 171).

McCall, R. B., Kennedy, C. B. (1980). Subjective uncertainty, variability of experience, and the infant's response to discrepancies. *Child Development, 51,* 285–287.

McCall, R. B., Kennedy, C. B., & Appelbaum, M. I. (1977). Magnitude of discrepancy and the distribution of attention in infants. *Child Development, 48,* 772–785.

McCarthy, D. (1954). Language development in children. In L. Carmichael (Ed.), *A manual of child psychology* (2nd ed.). New York: Wiley.

McCartney, K., Harris, M. J., & Bernieri, F. (1990). Growing up and growing apart: A development meta-analysis of twin studies. *Psychological Bulletin, 97,* 226–237.

McConaghy, M. J. (1979). Gender permanence and the genital basis of gender: Stages in the development of constancy of gender identity. *Child Development, 50,* 1223–1226.

McCord, J. (1979). Some child-rearing antecedents of criminal behavior in adult men. *Journal of Personality and Social Psychology, 37,* 1477–1486.

McGhee, P. E. (1974). Cognitive mastery and children's humor. *Psychological Bulletin, 81,* 721–730.

McGhee, P. E. (1976). Children's appreciation of humor: A test of the cognitive congruency principle. *Child Development, 47,* 420–426.

McGhee, P. E. (1979). *Humor: Its origins and development.* San Francisco: W. H. Freeman.

McKenzie, B., & Over, R. (1983). Young infants fail to imitate facial and manual gestures. *Infant Behavior and Development, 6,* 85–96.

McKusick, V. A. (1986). The gene map of Homo sapiens: Status and prospectus. *Cold Spring Harbor Symposium on Quantitative Biology, 51,* 15–27.

McLoyd, V. C. (1990). The impact of economic hardship on black families and children: Psychological distress, parenting, and socioemotional development. *Child Development, 61,* 311–346.

McNeill, D. (1970). *The acquisition of language: The study of developmental psycholinguistics.* New York: Harper & Row.

Meents, C. K. (1989). Attention deficit disorder: A review of the literature. *Psychology in the Schools, 26,* 168–178.

Meichenbaum, D. H., & Goodman, J. (1971). Training impulsive children to talk to themselves: A means of developing self-control. *Journal of Abnormal Psychology, 77,* 115–126.

Meisler, S., & Fulwood, S., III. (1990, July 7). Number of inner-city single parents on rise. *New York Times.*

Meizner, I. (1987). Sonographic observation of in utero fetal "masturbation." *Journal of Ultrasound in Medicine, 6,* 11.

Meltzoff, A. N. (1988). Infant imitation after a 1-week delay: Long-term memory for novel acts and multiple stimuli. *Developmental Psychology, 24,* 470–476.

Meltzoff, A. N., & Moore, M. K. (1977). Imitation of facial and manual gestures by human neonates. *Science, 198,* 75–78.

Meltzoff, A. N., & Moore, M. K. (1983). Newborns imitate adult facial gestures. *Child Development, 54,* 702–709.

Menning, B. E. (1988). *Infertility: A guide for childless couples* (2nd ed.). Englewood Cliffs, NJ: Prentice-Hall.

Merola, J. L., & Liederman, J. (1985). Developmental changes in hemispheric independence. *Child Development, 56,* 1184–1194.

Miller, L. B., & Bizzell, R. P. (1984). Long-term effects of four preschool programs: Ninth- and tenth-grade results. *Child Development, 55,* 1570–1587.

Miller, L. C., Lechner, R. E., & Rugs, D. (1985). Development of conversational responsiveness: Preschoolers' use of responsive listener cues and relevant comments. *Developmental Psychology, 21,* 473–480.

Miller, P. H. (1985). Metacognition and attention. In D. L. Forrest-Pressley, G. E. MacKinnon, & T. G. Waller (Eds.), *Metacognition, cognition, and human performance* (Vol. 2). New York: Academic Press.

Miller, P. H. (1990). The development of strategies of selective attention. In D. F. Bjorklund (Ed.), *Children's strategies: Contemporary views of cognitive development.* Hillsdale, NJ: Erlbaum.

Miller, P. H., Haynes, V. F., DeMarie-Dreblow, D., & Woody-Ramsey, J. (1986). Children's strategies for gathering information in three tasks. *Child Development, 57,* 1429–1439.

Miller, P. H., & Weiss, M. G. (1981). Children's attention allocation, understanding of attention, and performance on the incidental learning task. *Child Development, 52,* 1183–1190.

Miller, R. W. (1979). Radiation injury. In V. C. Vaughan, R. J. McKau, & R. E. Behrman (Eds.),

Nelson's textbook of pediatrics (11th ed.). Philadelphia: Saunders.

MILLER-JONES, D. (1989). Culture and testing. *American Psychologist, 44,* 360–366.

MILLOY, C. (1988, September 11). A volunteer squad of role models. *Washington Post.*

MILLOY, C. (1989, February 2). For whom the bell tolls. *Washington Post.*

MITCHELL, C., & AULT, R. L. (1979). Reflection-impulsivity and the evaluation process. *Child Development, 50,* 1043–1049.

MIZE, J., & LADD, G. W. (1990). Toward the development of successful social skills training for preschool children. In S. R. Asher & J. D. Coie (Eds.), *Peer rejection in childhood.* Cambridge: Cambridge University Press.

MOERK, E. L. (1986). Environmental factors in early language acquisition. In G. J. Whitehurst (Ed.), *Annals of child development* (Vol. 3). Greenwich, CT: JAI Press.

MOLFESE, D. L., & MOLFESE, V. J. (1980). Cortical responses of preterm infants to phonetic and nonphonetic speech stimuli. *Developmental Psychology, 16,* 574–581.

MOLFESE, D. L., & MOLFESE, V. J. (1985). Electrophysiological indices of auditory discrimination in newborn infants: The bases for predicting later language development? *Infant Behavior and Development, 8,* 197–211.

MONEY, J. (1976). Childhood: The last frontier in sex research. *The Sciences, 16,* 12–27.

MONEY, J. (1980). *Love and love sickness.* Baltimore: Johns Hopkins University Press.

MONEY, J. (1985). *The destroying angel: Sex, fitness, and food in the legacy of degeneracy theory, Graham Crackers, Kellogg's Corn Flakes, and American health history.* Buffalo: Prometheus Books.

MONEY, J. (1986a). *Lovemaps: Clinical concepts of sexual/erotic health and pathology, paraphilias, and gender transposition in childhood, adolescence, and maturity.* New York: Irvington.

MONEY, J. (1986b). Homosexual genesis, outcome studies, and a nature/nurture paradigm shift. *The American Journal of Social Psychiatry, 6,* 95–98.

MONEY, J. (1988). *Gay, straight, and in-between: The sexology of erotic orientation.* New York: Oxford University Press.

MONEY, J., ALEXANDER, D., & WALKER, H. T., JR. (1965). *A standardized road-map test of direction sense.* Baltimore: Johns Hopkins University Press.

MONEY, J., & EHRHARDT, A. A. (1972). *Man & woman, boy & girl.* Baltimore: Johns Hopkins University Press.

MONEY, J., SCHWARTZ, M., & LEWIS, V. G. (1984). Adult erotosexual status and fetal hormonal masculinization and demasculinization: 46, XX congenital virilizing adrenal hyperplasia and 46, XY androgen-insensitivity syndrome compared. *Psychoneuroendocrinology, 9,* 405–414.

MONEY, J., & TUCKER, P. (1975). *Sexual signatures: On being a man or a woman.* Boston: Little, Brown.

MONTEMAYOR, R., & EISEN, M. (1977). The development of self-conceptions from childhood to adolescence. *Developmental Psychology, 13,* 314–319.

MOORE, B. S., & EISENBERG, N. (1984). The development of altruism. In G. J. Whitehurst (Ed.), *Annals of Child Development,* (Vol. 1), 107–174.

MOORE, L. K. (1977). *The developing human* (2nd ed.). Philadelphia: Saunders.

MOORE, T. (1967). Language and intelligence: A longitudinal study of the first eight years: Part I. Patterns of development in boys and girls. *Human Development, 10,* 88–106.

MOORES, D. F. (1974). Nonvocal systems of verbal behavior. In R. L. Schiefelbusch & L. L. Lloyd (Eds.), *Language perspectives: Acquisition, retardation, and intervention.* Baltimore: University Park Press.

MORRISON, F. J. (1991, April). *Making the cut: Early schooling and cognitive growth.* Paper presented at the meeting of the Society for Research in Child Development, Seattle.

MOSHER, W. D. (1985). Reproductive impairments in the United States, 1965–1982. *Demography, 22,* 415–430.

MOWRER, O. (1960). *Learning theory and symbolic processes.* New York: Wiley.

MUELLER, E., & BRENNER, J. (1977). The origins of social skills and interaction among playgroup toddlers. *Child Development, 48,* 854–861.

MUNROE, R. H., MUNROE, R. L., & WHITING, B. B. (Eds.). (1981). *Handbook of cross-cultural human development.* New York: Garland STPM Press.

MUNROE, R. H., SHIMMIN, H. S., & MUNROE, R. L. (1984). Gender understanding and sex role preference in four cultures. *Developmental Psychology, 20,* 673–682.

MURCHISON, C. (Ed.). (1931). *A handbook of child psychology.* Worcester, MA: Clark University Press.

MURCHISON, C. (Ed.). (1933). *A handbook of child*

psychology (2nd ed.). Worcester, MA: Clark University Press.

MUSSEN, P. H. (Ed.). (1970). *Carmichael's manual of child development.* New York: Wiley.

MUSSEN, P. H. (1983). *Handbook of child psychology.* New York: Wiley.

NAISBITT, J., & ABURDENE, P. (1990). *Megatrends 2000.* New York: Morrow.

NASH, S. C. (1979). Sex roles as a mediator of intellectual functioning. In M. A. Wittig & A. C. Petersen (Eds.), *Sex-related differences in cognitive functioning.* New York: Academic Press.

NAZARIO, T. A. (1988). *In defense of children: Understanding the rights, needs, and interests of the child.* New York: Scribner's.

NEISSER, U. (Ed.). (1982). *Memory observed: Remembering in natural contexts.* San Francisco: W. H. Freeman.

NELSON, J., & ABOUD, F. E. (1985). The resolution of social conflict between friends. *Child Development, 56,* 1009–1017.

NELSON, K. (1974). Concept, word, and sentence: Interrelations in acquisition and development. *Psychological Review, 81,* 267–285.

NELSON-LEGALL, S. A. (1985). Motive-outcome matching and outcome foreseeability: Effects on attribution of intentionality and moral judgments. *Developmental Psychology, 21,* 332–337.

NETLEY, C. (1986). Summary overview of behavioral development in individuals with neonatally identified X and Y aneurploidy. *Birth defects: Original article series, 22,* 293–306.

NEWCOMBE, N., & BANDURA, M. M. (1983). Effects of age at puberty on spatial ability in girls: A question of mechanism. *Developmental Psychology, 19,* 215–244.

NEWPORT, E. L. (1975). *Motherese: The speech of mothers to young children* (Tech. Rep. No. 52). San Diego: University of California, Center for Human Information Processing.

NEWPORT, E. L. (1990). Maturational constraints on language learning. *Cognitive Science, 14,* 11–28.

NEW TURN IN A COUPLE'S FIGHT OVER EMBRYOS. (1990, May 27). *New York Times.*

NICHAMIN, S. J., & WINDELL, J. (1984). *A new look at attention deficit disorder: A problem not outgrown but treatable.* Waterford, MI: Minerva Press.

NIGRO, G. N., BUCKLEY, M. A., HILL, D. E., & NELSON, J. (1989). When juries "hear" children testify: The effects of eyewitness age and speech style on jurors' perception of testimony. In S. J. Ceci, D. F. Ross, & M. P. Toglia (Eds.), *Perspectives on children's testimony.* New York: Springer-Verlag.

NOVAK, M. A. (1979). Social recovery of monkeys isolated for the first year of life: II. Long-term assessment. *Developmental Psychology, 15,* 50–61.

NOWAKOWSKI, R. S. (1987). Basic concepts of CNS development. *Child Development, 58,* 568–595.

NYITI, R. M. (1982). The validity of "cultural differences explanation" in the rate of Piagetian cognitive development. In D. A. Wagner & H. W. Stevenson (Eds.), *Cultural perspectives on child development.* San Francisco: W. H. Freeman.

O'CONNOR, M. J., SIGMAN, M., & BRILL, N. (1987). Disorganization of attachment in relation to maternal alcohol consumption. *Journal of Consulting and Clinical Psychology, 55,* 831–836.

O'CONNOR, S., VIETZE, P. M., SHERROD, K. B., SANDLER, H. M., & ALTEMEIER, W. A. (1980). Reduced incidence of parenting inadequacy following rooming-in. *Pediatrics, 66,* 176–183.

OKONJI, O., OGBOLU, O., & OLAGBAIYE, O. O. (1975). Field dependence and the coordination of perspectives. *Developmental Psychology, 11,* 520.

OLLER, D. K. (1980). The emergence of the sounds of speech in infancy. In G. Yeni-Komshian, J. F. Kavanaugh, & C. A. Ferguson (Eds.), *Child phonology: Vol. 1. Productions.* New York: Academic Press.

OLSEN, L. (1988, November). Crossing the school bus border: Immigrant children in California. *Phi Delta Kappan,* pp. 211–218.

OLSON, S. L., BATES, J. E., & BAYLES, K. (1984). Mother-infant interaction and the development of individual differences in children's cognitive performance. *Developmental Psychology, 20,* 166–179.

OLWEUS, D. (1978). *Aggression in schools: Bullies and whipping boys.* Washington, DC: Hemisphere.

OLWEUS, D. (1980). Familial and temperamental determinants of aggressive behavior in adolescent boys: A causal analysis. *Developmental Psychology, 16,* 644–660.

OLWEUS, D. (1987, Fall). Schoolyard bullying: Grounds for intervention. *School Safety,* pp. 4–11.

OMANSON, R. C., BECK, I. L., VOSS, J. F., & McKEOWN, M. G. (1984). The effects of reading lessons on comprehension: A processing description. *Cognition and Instruction, 1,* 45–67.

OPPENHEIM, R. W. (1981). Ontogenetic adaptations and retrogressive processes in the development of the nervous system and behavior. In K. J. Connolly & H. F. R. Prechtl (Eds.), *Maturation and development: Biological and psychological perspectives.* Philadelphia: International Medical Publications.

ORENBERG, C. L. (1981). *DES: The complete story.* New York: St. Martin's Press.

ORNSTEIN, P. A., BAKER-WARD, L., & NAUS, M. J. (1988). The development of mnemonic skill. In M. Weinert & M. Perlmutter (Eds.), *Memory development.* Hillsdale, NJ: Erlbaum.

ORNSTEIN, P. A., GORDON, B. N., & LARUS, D. M. (in press). Children's memory for a personally experienced event: Implications for testimony. *Applied Developmental Psychology.*

ORNSTEIN, P. A., LARUS, D. M. & CLUBB, P. A. (in press). Understanding children's testimony: Implications on research on the development of memory. In R. Vasta (Ed.), *Annals of Child Development* (Vol. 7). London: Jessica Kingsley.

ORNSTEIN, P. A., & NAUS, M. J. (1978). Rehearsal processes in children's memory. In P. A. Ornstein (Ed.), *Memory development in children.* Hillsdale, NJ: Erlbaum.

ORNSTEIN, P. A., NAUS, M. J., & LIBERTY, C. (1975). Rehearsal and organizational processes in children's memory. *Child Development, 46,* 818–830.

ORNSTEIN, P. A., NAUS, M. J., & STONE, B. P. (1977). Rehearsal training and developmental differences in memory. *Developmental Psychology, 13,* 15–24.

ORNSTEIN, R., & EHRLICH, P. (1989). *New world, new mind.* New York: Simon & Schuster.

OSOFSKY, H. J. (1975). Relationships between nutrition during pregnancy and subsequent infant and child development. *Obstetrical and Gynecological Survey, 30,* 227–241.

OWEN, M. T., EASTERBROOKS, M. A., CHASE-LANSDALE, L., & GOLDBERG, W. A. (1984). The relation between maternal employment status and stability of attachments to mother and to father. *Child Development, 55,* 1894–1901.

PALINCSAR, A. S., & BROWN, A. L. (1984). Reciprocal teaching of comprehension-monitoring activities. *Cognition and Instruction, 1,* 117–175.

PARIS, S. G., NEWMAN, R. S., & MCVEY, K. A. (1982). Learning the functional significance of mnemonic actions: A microgenetic study of strategy acquisition. *Journal of Experimental Child Psychology, 34,* 490–509.

PARIS, S. G., & OKA, E. R. (1986). Children's reading strategies, metacognition, and motivation. *Developmental Review, 6,* 25–56.

PARK, K. A., & WATERS, E. (1989). Security of attachment and preschool friendships. *Child Development, 60,* 1079–1081.

PARKE, R. D., BERKOWITZ, L., LEYENS, J. P., WEST, S. G., & SEBASTIAN, R. J. (1977). Some effects of violent and non-violent movies on the behavior of juvenile delinquents. In L. Berkowitz (Ed.), *Advances in experimental social psychology* (Vol. 10). New York: Academic Press.

PARKE, R. D., & SAWIN, D. B. (1976). The father's role in infancy. *Family Coordinator, 25,* 265–271.

PARKINSON, J. S. (1977). Behavioral genetics in bacteria. *Annual Review of Genetics, 11,* 397–414.

PARTEN, M. (1932). Social participation among preschool children. *Journal of Abnormal and Social Psychology, 27,* 243–269.

PASTOR, D. (1981). The quality of mother-infant attachment and its relationship to toddler's initial sociability with peers. *Developmental Psychology, 17,* 326–335.

PATTERSON, G. R. (1980). Mothers: The unacknowledged victims. *Monographs of the Society for Research in Child Development, 45* (Serial No. 186).

PATTERSON, G. R. (1986). Performance models for antisocial boys. *American Psychologist, 41,* 432–444.

PATTERSON, G. R., DEBARSHYSHE, B. D., & RAMSEY, E. (1989). A developmental perspective on antisocial behavior. *American Psychologist, 44,* 329–335.

PATTERSON, G. R., REID, J. B., JONES, R. R., & CONGER, R. E. (1975). *A social learning approach to family intervention: Vol. 1. Families with aggressive children.* Eugene, OR: Castalia.

PATTERSON, G. R., & STOUTHAMER-LOEBER, M. (1984). The correlation of family management practices and delinquency. *Child Development, 55,* 1299–1307.

PEARSON, K. (1924). *The life, letters, and labours of Francis Galton* (Vol. 1). London: Cambridge University Press.

PEARSON, P. D., HANSEN, J., & GORDON, C. (1979). The effect of background knowledge on young children's comprehension of explicit and implicit information. *Journal of Reading Behavior,* 201–209.

PEDERSEN, N. L., FRIBERG, L., FLODERUS-MYRHED, B., MCCLEARN, G. E., & PLOMIN, R. (1984). Swedish early separated twins: Identification and characterization. *Acta Geneticae Medicinae et Gemellologiae, 33,* 243–250.

PEDERSON, D. R., MORAN, G., SITKO, C., CAMPBELL, K., GHESQUIRE, K., & ACTON, H. (1990). Maternal sensitivity and the security of infant-mother attachment: A Q-sort study. *Child Development, 61,* 1974–1983.

PEERY, J. C. (1979). Popular, amiable, isolated, rejected: A reconceptualization of sociometric status in preschool children. *Child Development, 50,* 1231–1234.

PEEVERS, B. H., & SECORD, P. F. (1973). Developmental changes in attribution of descriptive concepts to persons. *Journal of Personality and Social Psychology, 27,* 120–128.

PELLEGRINI, A. D. (1988). Elementary-school children's rough-and-tumble play and social competence. *Developmental Psychology, 24,* 802–806.

PERERA, K. (1986). Language acquisition and writing. In P. Fletcher & M. Garman (Eds.), *Language acquisition: Studies in first language development.* Cambridge: Cambridge University Press.

PERRY, D. G. (1989, April). *Social learning theory.* Paper presented at the meeting of the Society for Research in Child Development, Kansas City, MO.

PERRY, D. G., & BUSSEY, K. (1979). A social learning theory of sex differences: Imitation is alive and well. *Journal of Personality and Social Psychology, 37,* 1699–1712.

PERRY, D. G., & BUSSEY, K. (1984). *Social development.* Englewood Cliffs, NJ: Prentice-Hall.

PERRY, D. G., KUSEL, S. J., & PERRY, L. C. (1988). Victims of peer aggression. *Developmental Psychology, 24,* 807–814.

PERRY, D. G., PERRY, L. C., & BOLDIZAR, J. P. (1990). Learning of aggression. In M. Lewis & S. Miller (Eds.), *Handbook of developmental psychopathology.* New York: Plenum.

PERRY, D. G., PERRY, L. C., & RASMUSSEN, P. (1986). Cognitive learning mediators of aggression. *Child Development, 57,* 700–711.

PERRY, D. G., WHITE, A. J., & PERRY, L. C. (1984). Does early sex typing result from children's attempts to match their behavior to sex role stereotypes? *Child Development, 55,* 2114–2121.

PERRY, D. G., WILLARD, J. C., & PERRY, L. C. (1990). Peers' perceptions of the consequences that victimized children provide aggressors. *Child Development, 61,* 1310–1325.

PETERSEN, A. C. (1976). Physical androgyny and cognitive functioning in adolescence. *Developmental Psychology, 12,* 524–533.

PETTIT, G. S., DODGE, K. A., & BROWN, M. M. (1988). Early family experience, social problem solving patterns, and children's social competence. *Child Development, 59,* 107–120.

PHILLIPS, S., KING, S., & DUBOIS, L. (1978). Spontaneous activities of female versus male newborns. *Child Development, 49,* 590–597.

PIAGET, J. (1952). *The origins of intelligence in children.* New York: Norton.

PIAGET, J. (1954). *The construction of reality in the child.* New York: Basic Books.

PIAGET, J. (1955). *The language and thought of the child.* New York: World Publishing.

PIAGET, J. (1962). *Play, dreams, and imitation in childhood.* New York: Norton.

PIAGET, J. (1965a). *The child's conception of number.* New York: Norton.

PIAGET, J. (1965b). *The moral judgment of the child.* New York: Free Press.

PIAGET, J. (1967). Genesis and structure in the psychology of intelligence. In J. Piaget, *Six psychological studies.* New York: Vintage.

PIAGET, J. (1968). *On the development of memory and identity.* Worcester, MA: Clark University Press.

PIAGET, J. (1969). *The child's conception of the world.* Totowa, NJ: Littlefield & Adams.

PIAGET, J. (1972). Intellectual evolutions from adolescence to adulthood. *Human Development, 15,* 1–12.

PIAGET, J. (1983). Piaget's theory. In J. H. Flavell & E. M. Markman (Ed.), *Cognitive development,* Vol. 3 of P. H. Mussen (Gen. Ed.), *Handbook of child psychology* (4th ed.). New York: Wiley.

PIAGET, J., & INHELDER, B. (1964). *The early growth of logic in the child.* New York: Norton.

PIAGET, J., & INHELDER, B. (1967). *The child's conception of space.* New York: Norton.

PIAGET, J., & INHELDER, B. (1969). *The psychology of the child.* New York: Basic Books.

PIEN, D., & ROTHBART, M. K. (1980). Incongruity, humor, play, and self-regulation of arousal in young children. In P. E. McGhee & A. J. Chapman (Eds.), *Children's humor.* New York: Wiley.

PIERCE, B. A. (1990). *Family genetic sourcebook.* New York: Wiley.

PLOMIN, R. (1986). Behavioral genetic methods. *Journal of Personality, 54,* 15–24.

PLOMIN, R. (1989). Environment and genes: Determinants of behavior. *American Psychologist, 44,* 105–111.

PLOMIN, R., CORLEY, R., DeFRIES, J. C., & FULKER, D. E. (1990). Individual differences in television viewing in early childhood: Nature as well as nurture. *Psychological Science, 1,* 371–377.

PLOMIN, R., & DANIELS, D. 1987. Why are children in the same family so different from each other? *Behavioral and Brain Sciences, 10,* 1–16.

PLOMIN, R., DeFRIES, J. C., & McCLEARN, G. E. (1990). *Behavioral genetics: A primer* (2nd ed.). New York; W. H. Freeman.

PLOMIN, R., & FOCH, T. T. (1981). Sex differences and individual differences. *Child Development, 52,* 383–385.

PLUMMER, K. (1981). Pedophilia: Constructing a sociological baseline. In M. Cook & K. Howells (Eds.), *Adult sexual interest in children.* New York: Academic Press.

POIRIER, F. E., & SMITH, E. O. (1974). Socializing functions of primate play. *American Zoologist, 14,* 275–287.

POLITICH, J. A., & HERRENKOHL, L. R. (1984). Effects of prenatal stress on reproduction in male and female mice. *Physiology and Behavior, 32,* 95–99.

PRESSLEY, M. (1982). Elaboration and memory development. *Child Development, 53,* 296–309.

PRESSLEY, M., & LEVIN, J. R. (1977). Task parameters affecting the efficacy of a visual imagery learning strategy in younger and older children. *Journal of Experimental Child Psychology, 24,* 53–59.

PREYER, W. (1882). *Die Serle des Kindes.* Leipzig: Fernan. [*The mind of the child* (2 vols.). New York: Appleton, 1888–1889.]

PREYER, W. (1885). *Specialle Physiologie des Embryo: Untersuchungen über die Lebenserscheinwagen vol der Geburt.* Leipzig: Grieben.

PRIOR, M. (1984). Developing concepts of childhood autism: The influence of experimental cognitive research. *Journal of Consulting and Clinical Psychology, 52,* 4–16.

PROVENCE, S., & LIPTON, R. C. (1962). *Infants in institutions: A comparison of their development with family-reared infants during the first year of life.* New York: International Universities Press.

PROVINE, R. R., & WESTERMAN, J. A. (1979). Cross the midline: Limits of early eye-hand behavior. *Child Development, 50,* 437–441.

PUTALLAZ, M. (1987). Maternal behavior and children's sociometric status. *Child Development, 58,* 324–340.

PUTALLAZ, M., & GOTTMAN, J. M. (1981). An interactional model of children's entry into peer groups. *Child Development, 52,* 402–408.

PUTALLAZ, M., & HEFLIN, A. H. (1990). Parent-child interaction. In S. R. Asher & J. D. Coie (Eds.), *Peer rejection in childhood.* Cambridge: Cambridge University Press.

PUTALLAZ, M., & WASSERMAN, A. (1989). Children's naturalistic entry behavior and sociometric status: A developmental perspective. *Developmental Psychology, 25,* 297–305.

PUTALLAZ, M., & WASSERMAN, A. (1990). Children's entry behavior. In S. R. Asher & J. D. Coie (Eds.), *Peer rejection in childhood.* Cambridge: Cambridge University Press.

RABINOWITZ, M., & McAULEY, R. (1990). Conceptual knowledge processing: An oxymoron? In W. Schneider & F. E. Weinert (Eds.), *Interactions among aptitudes, strategies and knowledge in cognitive performance.* New York: Springer-Verlag.

RAMEY, C. T., CAMPBELL, F. A., & FINKELSTEIN, N. W. (1984). Course and structure of intellectual development in children at risk for developmental retardation. In P. H. Brooks, R. Sperber, & C. McCauley (Eds.), *Learning and cognition in the mentally retarded.* Hillsdale, NJ: Erlbaum.

RAMEY, C. T., LEE, M. W., & BURCHINAL, M. R. (1989). Developmental plasticity and predictability: Consequences of ecological change. In M. H. Bornstein & N. A. Krasnegor (Eds.), *Stability and continuity in mental development: Behavioral and biological perspectives.* Hillsdale, NJ: Erlbaum.

RAMSAY, D. S., & WEBER, S. L. (1986). Infants' hand preference in a task involving complementary roles for the two hands. *Child Development, 57,* 300–307.

RAMSEY, G. V. (1943a). The sexual development of boys. *American Journal of Psychology, 56,* 217–234.

RAMSEY, G. V. (1943b). The sex information of

younger boys. *American Journal of Orthopsychiatry, 13,* 347–352.

Raspberry, W. (1989, October 11). Mentors in the city. *Washington Post.*

Raven, J. C., Court, J. H., & Raven, J. (1975). *Manual for Raven's Progressive Matrices and Vocabulary Scales.* London: Lewis.

Raymond, C. L., & Benbow, C. P. (1986). Gender differences in mathematics: A function of parental support and student sex typing? *Developmental Psychology, 22,* 808–819.

Recht, D. R., & Leslie, L. (1988). Effect of prior knowledge on good and poor reader's memory for text. *Journal of Educational Psychology, 80,* 16–20.

Reeder, K. (1981). How young children learn to do things with words. In P. S. Dale & D. Ingram (Eds.), *Child language: An international perspective.* Baltimore: University Park Press.

Reese, H. W. (1962). Verbal mediation as a function of age level. *Psychological Bulletin, 59,* 502–509.

Reinisch, J. M. (1974). Fetal hormones, the brain and human sex differences: A heuristic, integrative review of the recent literature. *Archives of Sexual Behavior, 3,* 51–90.

Reinisch, J. M. (1990). *The Kinsey Institute new report on sex: What you must know to be sexually literate.* New York: St. Martin's Press.

Reinisch, J. M., Gandelman, R., & Speigel, F. S. (1979). Prenatal influence on cognitive abilities: Data from experimental animals and human genetic and endocrine syndromes. In M. A. Wittig & A. C. Petersen (Eds.), *Sex-related differences in cognitive functioning.* New York: Academic Press.

Reissland, N. (1988). Neonatal imitation in the first hour of life: Observations in rural Nepal. *Developmental Psychology, 24,* 464–469.

Rest, J. R., & Thoma, S. J. (1985). Relation of moral judgment development to formal education. *Developmental Psychology, 21,* 709–714.

Reynolds, G. S. (1968). *A primer of operant conditioning.* Glenview, IL: Scott, Foresman.

Rheingold, H. L. (1982). Little children's participation in the work of adults: A nascent prosocial behavior. *Child Development, 53,* 114–125.

Rheingold, H. L. (1985). Development as the acquisition of familiarity. *Annual Review of Psychology, 36,* 1–17.

Rheingold, H. L, & Cook, K. V. (1975). The content of boys' and girls' rooms as an index of parents' behavior. *Child Development, 46,* 459–463.

Rheingold, H. L., & Eckerman, C. D. (1970). The infant separates himself from his mother. *Science, 168,* 78–83.

Rheingold, H. L., Hay, D. F., & West, M. J. (1976). Sharing in the second year of life. *Child Development, 47,* 1148–1158.

Rice, M. L. (1989). Children's language acquisition. *American Psychologist, 44,* 149–156.

Rice, M. L., Huston, A. C., Truglio, R., & Wright, J. (1990). Words from "Sesame Street": Learning vocabulary while viewing. *Developmental Psychology, 26,* 421–428.

Ringel, B. A., & Springer, C. J. (1980). On knowing how well one is remembering: The persistence of strategy use during transfer. *Journal of Experimental Child Psychology, 29,* 322–333.

Riva, D., & Cazzaniga, L. (1986). Late effects of unilateral brain lesions sustained before and after age one. *Neuropsychology, 24,* 423–428.

Roberts, K. (1988). Retrieval of a basic-level category in prelinguistic children. *Developmental Psychology, 24,* 21–27.

Roberts, K., & Horowitz, F. D. (1986). Basic level categorization in seven- and nine-month-old infants. *Journal of Child Language, 13,* 191–206.

Robson, K. (1967). The role of eye-to-eye contact in maternal-infant attachment. *Journal of Child Psychology and Psychiatry, 8,* 13–25.

Rode, S. S., Chang, P.-N., Fisch, R. O., & Sroufe, L. A. (1981). Attachment patterns of infants separated at birth. *Developmental Psychology, 17,* 188–191.

Roe, K. V., Drivas, A., Karagellis, A., & Roe, A. (1985). Sex differences in vocal interaction with mother and stranger in Greek infants: Some cognitive implications. *Developmental Psychology, 21,* 372–377.

Rogoff, B. (1990). *Apprenticeship in thinking: Cognitive development in social context.* New York: Oxford University Press.

Rogoff, B., & Mistry, J. J. (1985). Memory development in cultural context. In M. Pressley & C. Brainerd (Eds.), *Progress in cognitive development.* New York: Springer-Verlag.

Rogoff, B., & Morelli, G. (1989). Perspectives on children's development from cultural psychology. *American Psychologist, 44,* 343–348.

Rogoff, B. & Waddell, K. J. (1982). Memory for information organized in a scene by children from two cultures. *Child Development, 53,* 1224–1228.

Rohwer, W. D., Jr., Raines, J. M., Eoff, J., & Wagner, M. (1977). The development of elaborative propensity during adolescence. *Journal of Experimental Child Psychology, 23,* 472–492.

Rose, S. A., Feldman, J. F., & Wallace, I. F. (1988). Individual differences in infant information processing: Reliability, stability, and prediction. *Child Development, 59,* 589–603.

Rose, S. A., Feldman, J. F., & Wallace, I. F., & McCarton, C. (1989). Infant visual attention: Relation to birth status and developmental outcome during the first 5 years. *Developmental Psychology, 25,* 560–576.

Rosemond, J. K. (1981). *Parent power.* New York: Pocket Books.

Rosenstein, D., & Oster, H. (1988). Differential facial responses to four basic tastes in newborns. *Child Development, 59,* 1555–1568.

Ross, D. (1972). *G. Stanley Hall: The psychologist as prophet.* Chicago: University of Chicago Press.

Ross, D. F., Miller, B. S., & Moran, P. (1987). The child in the eyes of the jury: Assessing mock jurors' perceptions of child witness. In S. J. Ceci, M. P. Toglia, & D. F. Ross (Eds.), *Children's eyewitness memory.* New York: Springer-Verlag.

Ross, D. F., Dunning, D., Toglia, M. P., & Ceci, S. J. (1989). Age stereotypes, communication modality, and mock jurors' perceptions of the child witnesses. In S. J. Ceci, D. F. Ross, & M. P. Toglia (Eds.), *Perspectives on children's testimony.* New York: Springer-Verlag.

Ross, H. S., & Lollis, S. P. (1989). A social relations analysis of the peer relationships. *Child Development, 60,* 1082–1091.

Rotenberg, K. J., & Whitney, P. (in press). Loneliness and disclosure process in preadolescence. *Merrill-Palmer Quarterly.*

Rovee-Collier, C. K., & Fagen, J. W. (1981). The retrieval of memory in early infancy. In L. P. Lipsitt & C. K. Rovee-Collier (Eds.), *Advances in infancy research* (Vol. 1). Norwood, NJ: Ablex.

Rubinstein, J., & Howes, C. (1976). The effects of peers on toddler interaction with mothers and toys. *Child Development, 47,* 597–605.

Rubin, K. H., LeMare, L. J., & Lollis, S. (1990). Social withdrawal in childhood: Developmental pathways to peer rejection. In S. R. Asher & J. D. Coie (Eds.), *Peer rejection in childhood.* Cambridge: Cambridge University Press.

Rubin, K. H., Watson, K. S., & Jambor, T. W. (1978). Free-play behaviors in preschool and kindergarten children. *Child Development, 49,* 534–536.

Ruble, D. N., Balaban, T., & Cooper, J. (1981). Gender constancy and the effects of sex-typed televised toy commercials. *Child Development, 52,* 667–673.

Ruff, H. A., & Birch, H. G. (1974). Infant visual fixation: The effect of concentricity, curvilinearity, and number of directions. *Journal of Experimental Child Psychology, 17,* 460–473.

Rutter, M. (1979). Protective factors in children's responses to stress and disadvantage. In M. W. Kent & J. E. Rolfe (Eds.), *Primary prevention of psychopathology: 3. Social competence in children.* Hanover, NH: University Press of New England.

Rutter, M. (1987). Psychosocial resilience and protective mechanisms. *American Journal of Orthopsychiatry, 57,* 316–331.

Rutter, M. (1990). Commentary: Some focus and process considerations regarding effects of parental depression on children. *Developmental Psychology, 26,* 60–67.

Sachs, J. (1977). The adaptive significance of linguistic input to prelinguistic infants. In C. E. Snow & C. A. Ferguson (Eds.), *Talking to children: Language input and acquisition.* Cambridge: Cambridge University Press.

Sacks, O. (1990). *Seeing voices: A journey into the world of the deaf.* New York: HarperPerennial.

Sagi, A., & Hoffman, M. L. (1976). Empathic distress in newborns. *Developmental Psychology, 12,* 175–176.

Salapatek, P. & Kessen, W. (1966). Visual scanning of triangles by the human newborn. *Journal of Experimental Child Psychology, 3,* 155–167.

Salatas, H., & Flavell, J. H. (1976). Behavioral and metamnemonic indicators of strategic behavior under remember instructions in first grade. *Child Development, 47,* 81–89.

Salkind, N. J., & Nelson, C. F. (1980). A note on the developmental nature of reflection-impulsivity. *Developmental Psychology, 16,* 237–238.

Samalin, N. (1987). *Loving your child is not enough: Positive discipline that works.* New York: Viking Press.

Sameroff, A. J. (1975). Early influences on development: Fact or fancy? *Merrill-Palmer Quarterly, 21,* 267–294.

Sameroff, A. J., & Chandler, M. J. (1975). Reproductive risk and the continuum of caretaking causality. In F. D. Horowitz (Ed.), *Review of child development research* (Vol. 4). Chicago: University of Chicago Press.

SANCHEZ, R. (1990, February 28). Adding gentle but firm persuasion. *Washington Post.*

SANDELOWSKI, M. (1984). *Pain, pleasure, and American children: From the Twilight Sleep to the Read Method, 1914–1916.* Westport, CT: Greenwood Press.

SATTLER, J. M. (1988). *Assessment of children.* San Diego: Jerome M. Sattler.

SAUER, M. V., PAULSON, R. J., & LOBO, R. A. (1990). A preliminary report on oocyte donation extending reproductive potential to women over 40. *New England Journal of Medicine, 323,* 1157–1160.

SAVIN-WILLIAMS, R. C. (1979). Dominance hierarchies in groups of early adolescents. *Child Development, 50,* 923–935.

SAXE, G. B. (1979). Developmental relations between notational counting and number conservation. *Child Development, 50,* 180–187.

SAXE, G. B., GUBERMAN, S. R., & GEARHART, M. (1987). Social processes in early number development. *Monographs of the Society for Research in Child Development, 52* (Serial No. 216).

SCAMMON, R. E. (1930). The measurement of the body in childhood. In J. A. Harris, C. M. Jackson, D. G. Paterson, & R. E. Scammon (Eds.), *The measurement of man.* Minneapolis: University of Minnesota Press.

SCARR, S., & McCARTNEY, K. (1983). How people make their own environments: A theory of genotype → environment effects. *Child Development, 54,* 424–435.

SCARR, S., PHILLIPS, D., & McCARTNEY, K. (1990). Facts, fantasies and the future of child care in the United States. *Psychological Science 1,* 26–35.

SCARR-SALAPATEK, S., & WILLIAMS, M. L. (1973). The effects of early stimulation on low-birth-weight infants. *Child Development, 44,* 94–101.

SCHAFFER, H. R., & EMERSON, P. E. (1964). The development of social attachments in infancy. *Monographs of the Society for Research in Child Development, 29* (Serial No. 94).

SCHAU, C. G., KAHN, L., DIEPOLD, J. H., & CHERRY, F. (1980). The relationship of parental expectations and preschool children's verbal sex typing to their sex-typed toy play behavior. *Child Development, 51,* 266–271.

SCHEIBE, C., & CONDRY, J. (1987, April). *Learning to distinguish fantasy from reality: Children's beliefs about Santa Claus and other fantasy characters.* Paper presented at the meeting of the Society for Research in Child Development, Baltimore.

SCHIFF, A. R., & KNOPF, I. J. (1985). The effect of task demands on attention allocation in children of different ages. *Child Development, 56,* 621–630.

SCHNEIDER, W. (1985). Developmental trends in the metamemory-memory behavior relationship: An integrated review. In D. L. Forrest-Pressley, G. E. MacKinnon, & T.- G. Waller (Eds.), *Cognition, metacognition, and human performance* (Vol. 1). New York: Academic Press.

SCHNEIDER, W. (1991, April). *Performance prediction in young children: Effects of skill, metacognition, and wishful thinking.* Paper presented at the meeting of the Society for Research in Child Development, Seattle.

SCHNEIDER, W., BORKOWSKI, J. G., KURTZ, B. E., & KERWIN, K. (1986). Metamemory and motivation: A comparison of strategy use and performance in German and American children. *Journal of Cross-Cultural Psychology, 17,* 315–336.

SCHNEIDER, W., KÖRKEL, J., & WEINERT, F. E. (1989). Domain-specific knowledge and memory performance: A comparison of high- and low-aptitude children. *Journal of Educational Psychology, 81,* 306–312.

SCHNEIDER, W., KÖRKEL, J., & WEINERT, F. E. (1990). Expert knowledge, general abilities, and text processing. In W. Schneider & F. E. Weinert (Eds.), *Interactions among aptitude, strategies, and knowledge in cognitive performance.* New York: Springer-Verlag.

SCHNEIDER, W., & PRESSLEY, M. (1989). *Memory development between 2 and 20.* New York: Springer-Verlag.

SCHNEIDER-ROSEN, K. BRAUNWALD, K., CARLSON, V., & CICCHETTI, D. (1985). Current perspectives in attachment theory: Illustration from the study of maltreated infants. In I. Bretherton & E. Waters (Eds.), *Monographs of the Society for Research in Child Development, 50* (Serial No. 209).

SCHULMAN, A. H., & KAPLOWITZ, C. (1977). Mirror-image response during the first two years of life. *Developmental Psychobiology, 10,* 133–142.

SCHWARTZ, M., & DAY, R. H. (1979). Visual shape perception in early infancy. *Monographs of the Society for Research in Child Development, 44* (Serial No. 182).

SCHWARZ, J. C., KROLICK, G., & STRICKLAND, G. (1973).

Effects of early day care experience on adjustment to a new environment. *American Journal of Orthopsychiatry, 43,* 340–346.

Science 84. (1984, September). 20 discoveries that changed our lives: Century of the sciences. Washington, DC: American Association for the Advancement of Science.

SEABROOK, C. (1987, February 19). Children: "Third wave" of AIDS victims. *Atlanta Journal.*

SEARS, R. R. (1975). Your ancients revisited: A history of child development. In E. M. Hetherington (Ed.), *Review of child development research* (Vol. 5). Chicago: University of Chicago Press.

SELMAN, R. L. (1976). Social-cognitive understanding: A guide to educational and clinical practice. In T. Lickona (Ed.), *Moral development and behavior.* New York: Holt, Rinehart & Winston.

SELMAN, R. L. (1980). *The growth of interpersonal understanding.* New York: Academic Press.

SELMAN, R. L., & BYRNE, D. F. (1974). A structural-developmental analysis of levels of role taking in middle childhood. *Child Development, 45,* 803–806.

SELMAN, R. L., SCHORIN, M. Z., STONE, C. R., & PHELPS, E. (1983). A naturalistic study of children's social understanding. *Developmental Psychology, 19,* 82–102.

SERBANESCU-GRIGORDIU, M., CHRISTODOVESCU, D., JIPESCU, I., TOTOESCU, A., MARINESCU, E., & ARDELEAN, V. (1989). Psychopathology in children aged 10–17 of bipolar parents: Psychopathology rates and correlation of the severity of the psychopathology. *Journal of Affective Disorders, 16,* 167–179.

SERBIN, L. A., & SPRAFKIN, C. (1986). The saliency of gender and the process of sex typing in three- to seven-year-old children. *Child Development, 57,* 1188–1199.

SHAFFER, D. R. (1988). *Social and personality development* (2nd ed.). Pacific Grove, CA: Brooks/Cole.

SHAH, F., ZELNIK, M., & KANTNER, J. (1975). Unprotected intercourse among unwed teenagers. *Family Planning Perspectives, 7,* 39–44.

SHANTZ, C. U. (1983). Social cognition. In J. H. Flavell & E. M. Markman (Eds.), *Cognitive development,* Vol. 3 of P. H. Mussen (Gen. Ed.), *Handbook of child psychology* (4th ed.). New York: Wiley.

SHARP, D., COLE, M., & LAVE, C. (1979). Education and cognitive development: The evidence from experimental research. *Monographs of the Society for Research in Child Development, 44* (Serial No. 170).

SHATZ, M. (1983). Communication. In J. H. Flavell & E. M. Markman (Eds.), *Cognitive development,* Vol. 3 of P. H. Mussen (Gen. Ed.), *Handbook of child psychology* (4th ed.). New York: Wiley.

SHATZ, M., & GELMAN, R. (1973). The development of communication skills. *Monographs of the Society for Research in Child Development, 38* (Serial No. 152).

SHEINGOLD, K., & TENNEY, Y. (1982). Memory for a salient childhood event. In U. Neisser (Ed.), *Memory observed: Remembering in natural contexts.* San Francisco: W. H. Freeman.

SHER, G. & MARRIAGE, V. A. (1988). *From infertility to in vitro fertilization.* New York: McGraw-Hill.

SHERIF, M., HARVEY, O. J., WHITE, B. J., HOOD, W. R., & SHERIF, C. W. (1961). *Inter-group conflict and cooperation: The Robbers Cave experiment.* Norman: University of Oklahoma Press.

SHERROD, K. B., O'CONNOR, S., VIETZE, P. M., & ALTEMEIER, W. A. (1984). Child health and maltreatment. *Child Development, 55,* 1174–1183.

SHIFFRIN, R. M., & SCHNEIDER, W. (1977). Controlled and automatic human information processing: II. Perceptual learning, automatic attending, and a general theory. *Psychological Review, 84,* 129–190.

SHIPLEY, E., SMITH, C., & GLEITMAN, L. (1969). A study in the acquisition of language: Free responses to commands. *Language, 45,* 322–342.

SHORTER, E. (1982). *History of women's bodies.* New York: Basic Books.

SHULTZ, T. R. (1972). Role of incongruity and resolution in children's appreciation of cartoon humor. *Journal of Experimental Child Psychology, 13,* 456–477.

SHULTZ, T. R., & HORIBE, F. (1974). Development of the appreciation of verbal jokes. *Developmental Psychology, 10,* 13–20.

SHULTZ, T. R., & PILON, R. (1973). Development of the ability to detect linguistic ambiguity. *Child Development, 44,* 728–733.

SHULTZ, T. R., & ROBILLARD, J. (1980). The development of linguistic humor in children: Incongruity through rule violation. In P. E. McGhee & A. J. Chapman (Eds.), *Children's humor.* New York: Wiley.

SHULTZ, T. R., WRIGHT, K., & SCHLEIFER, M. (1986). Assignment of moral responsibility and punishment. *Child Development, 57,* 177–184.

SIEGAL, M. WATERS, L. J., & DINWIDDY, L. S. (1988). Misleading children: Causal attributions for inconsistency under repeated questioning. *Journal of Experimental Child Psychology, 45,* 438–456.

SIEGEL, A. W., & SCHADLER, M. (1977). The development of young children's spatial representations of their classrooms. *Child Development, 48,* 388–394.

SIEGEL, L. S. (1989). A reconceptualization of prediction from infant test scores. In M. H. Bornstein & N. A. Krasnegor (Ed.), *Stability and continuity in mental development: Behavioral and biological perspectives.* Hillsdale, NJ: Erlbaum.

SIEGEL, L. S., McCABE, A. E., BRAND, A. E., & MATTHEWS, J. (1978). Evidence for the understanding of class inclusion in preschool children: Linguistic factors and training effects. *Child Development, 49,* 688–693.

SIEGLER, R. S. (1987). The perils of averaging data over strategies: An example from children's addition. *Journal of Experimental Psychology: General, 116,* 250–264.

SIEGLER, R. S. (1988). Individual differences in strategy choices: Good students, not-so-good students, and perfectionists. *Child Development, 59,* 833–851.

SIEGLER, R. S. (1990). How content knowledge, strategies, and individual differences interact to produce strategy choice. In W. Schneider & F. E. Weinert (Eds.), *Interactions among aptitudes, strategies, and knowledge in cognitive performance.* New York: Springer-Verlag.

SIEGLER, R. S., & JENKINS, E. (1989). *How children discover strategies.* Hillsdale, NJ: Erlbaum.

SIEGLER, R. S., & ROBINSON, M. (1982). The development of numerical understanding. In H. Reese & L. Lipsitt (Eds.), *Advances in child development and behavior* (Vol. 16). New York: Academic Press.

SIEGLER, R. S., ROBINSON, M., LIEBERT, D. E., & LIEBERT, R. M. (1973). Inhelder and Piaget's pendulum problem: Teaching preadolescents to act as scientists. *Developmental Psychology, 9,* 97–101.

SIEGLER, R. S., & SHRAGER, J. (1984). Strategy choices in addition and subtraction: How do children know what to do? In C. Sophian (Ed.), *Origins of cognitive skills.* Hillsdale, NJ: Erlbaum.

SILBER, S. J. (1991). *How to get pregnant with the new technology.* New York: Warner Books.

SINGER, J. L. (1980). The power and limitations of television: A cognitive affective analysis. In P. H. Tannenbaum & R. Abeles (Eds.), *The entertain-*

ment functions of television. London: Academic Press.

SINGER, J. L., & SINGER, D. G. (1981). *Television, imagination, and aggression: A study of preschoolers.* Hillsdale, NJ: Erlbaum.

SKEELS, H. M. (1966). Adult status of children with contrasting early life experiences. *Monographs of the Society for Research in Child Development, 31* (Serial No. 105).

SKEELS, H. M., & DYE, H. B. (1939). A study of the effects of differential stimulation on mentally retarded children. *Program of the American Association of Mental Deficiency, 44,* 114–136.

SKINNER, B. F. (1957). *Verbal behavior.* New York: Appleton-Century-Crofts.

SLABY, R. G., & FREY, K. S. (1975). Development of gender constancy and selective attention to same-sex models. *Child Development, 46,* 849–856.

SLABY, R. G., & GUERRA, N. G. (1988). Cognitive mediators of aggression in adolescent offenders: 1. Assessment. *Developmental Psychology, 24,* 580–588.

SLATER, A., COOPER, R., ROSE, D., & MORISON, V. (1989). Prediction of cognitive performance from infancy to early childhood. *Human Development, 32,* 137–147.

SLATER, A., EARLE, D. C., MORISON, V., & ROSE, D. (1985). Pattern preferences at birth and their interaction with habituation-induced novelty preferences. *Journal of Experimental Child Psychology, 39,* 37–54.

SLOBIN, D. I. (1970). Universals of grammatical development in children. In G. B. Flores, J. Arcais, & W. J. M. Levelt (Eds.), *Advances in psycholinguistics.* Amsterdam: North-Holland Publishing.

SLUCKIN, A. M., & SMITH, P. K. (1977). Two approaches to the concept of dominance in preschool children. *Child Development, 48,* 917–923.

SMITH, C. L. (1979). Children's understanding of natural language categories. *Journal of Experimental Child Psychology, 30,* 191–205.

SMITH, E. A., & UDRY, J. R. (1985). Coital and noncoital sexual behavior of white and black adolescents. *American Journal of Public Health, 75,* 1200–1203.

SMITH, M. (1926). An investigation of the development of the sentence and the extent of vocabulary in young children. *University of Iowa Studies in Child Welfare, 3* (5).

SMITH, P. K., & DAGLISH, L. (1977). Sex differences in

parent and infant behavior. *Child Development, 48,* 1250–1254.

SMOTHERS, R. (1989, May 4). Parley aims at nurturing black youths. *New York Times.*

SMUTS, A. B. (1985). The National Research Council Committee on Child Development and the founding of the Society for Research in Child Development, 1925–1933. In A. B. Smuts & J. W. Hagen (Eds.), History and research in child development. *Monographs of the Society for Research in Child Development, 50* (Serial No. 211).

SNOW, C. E. (1977). Mothers' speech research: From input to interaction. In C. E. Snow & C. A. Ferguson (Eds.), *Talking to children: Language input and acquisition.* Cambridge: Cambridge University Press.

SNOW, C. E. (1986). Conversations with children. In P. Fletcher & M. Garman (Eds.), *Language acquisition: Studies in first language development.* Cambridge: Cambridge University Press.

SNOW, C. E., & FERGUSON, C. A. (Eds.). (1977). *Talking to children: Language input and acquisition.* Cambridge: Cambridge University Press.

SNOW, M. E., JACKLIN, C. N., & MACCOBY, E. E. (1983). Sex-of-child differences in father-child interaction at one year of age. *Child Development, 54,* 227–232.

SNYDERMAN, M., & ROTHMAN, S. (1987). Survey of expert opinion on intelligence and aptitude testing. *American Psychologist, 42,* 137–144.

SODIAN, B., SCHNEIDER, W., & PERLMUTTER, M. (1986). Recall, clustering, and metamemory in young children. *Journal of Experimental Child Psychology, 41,* 395–410.

SOLKOFF, N., YAFFEE, S., WEINTRAUB, D., & BLASE, B. (1969). Effects of handling on the subsequent development of preterm infants. *Developmental Psychology, 1,* 765–768.

SOMMERVILLE, C. J. (1982). *The rise and fall of childhood.* Beverly Hills, CA: Sage.

SORENSON, R. C. (1973). *Adolescent sexuality in contemporary America.* New York: World.

SPEAR, N. E. (1984). Ecologically determined dispositions control the ontogeny of learning and memory. In R. V. Kail, Jr., & N. E. Spear (Eds.), *Comparative perspectives on the development of memory.* Hillsdale, NJ: Erlbaum.

SPEARMAN, C. (1927). *The abilities of man.* New York: Macmillan.

SPELKE, E. S. (1985). Perception of unity, persistence, and identity: Thoughts on infants' conception of objects. In J. Mehler & R. Fox (Eds.), *Neonate cognition.* Hillsdale, NJ: Erlbaum.

SPENCE, J. T. (1982). Comment on Baumrind's "Are androgynous individuals more effective persons and parents?" *Child Development, 53,* 76–80.

SPENCE, J. T., & HELMREICH, R. L. (1978). *Masculinity and femininity: Their psychological dimensions, correlates, and antecedents.* Austin: University of Texas Press.

SPITZ, R. (1945). Hospitalism: An inquiry into the genesis of psychiatric conditions in early childhood. *Psychoanalytic Study of the Child, 1,* 53–74.

SPITZ, R. (1971). Autoerotism re-examined: The role of early sexual behavior patterns in personality formation. In Children's Medical Center (Ed.), *Sex in childhood.* Tulsa, OK: Children's Medical Center.

SPREEN, O., TUPPER, D., RISSER, A., TUOKKO, H., & EDGELL, D. (1984). *Human developmental neuropsychology.* New York: Oxford University Press.

SPRINGER, S. P., & DEUTSCH, G. (1985). *Left brain, right brain* (2nd ed.). New York: W. H. Freeman.

STAATS, A. (1971). Linguistic-mentalistic theory versus an explanatory S-R learning theory of language development. In D. Slobin, (Ed.), *The ontogenesis of grammar.* New York: Academic Press.

STAFFORD, I. P. (1984). Relation of attitudes toward women's self-esteem. *Journal of Counseling Psychology, 31,* 332–334.

STANLEY, A. (1990, June 18). Child warriors. *Time.*

STANOVICH, K. E., CUMMINGHAM, A. E., & CRAMER, B. R. (1984). Assessing phonological awareness in kindergarten children: Issues of task compatibility. *Journal of Experimental Child Psychology, 38,* 175–190.

STARK, R. (1979). Prespeech segmental feature development. In P. Fletcher & M. Garman (Eds.), *Language acquisition.* New York: Cambridge University Press.

STEINBERG, E. R., & ANDERSON, R. C. (1975). Hierarchical semantic organization in 6-year-olds. *Journal of Experimental Child Psychology, 19,* 544–553.

STEINBERG, L. (1987). Single parents, stepparents, and the susceptibility of adolescents to antisocial peer pressure. *Child Development, 58,* 269–275.

STEINBERG, L., ELMEN, J. D., & MOUNTS, N. J. (1989). Authoritative parenting, psychosocial maturity and academic success in adolescents. *Child Development, 60,* 1424–1436.

STEINER, J. E. (1979). Human facial expressions in response to taste and smell stimulation. In H. W. Reese & L. P. Lipsitt (Eds.), *Advances in child development and behavior* (Vol. 13). New York: Academic Press.

STEPHENS, R. D. (1987, Fall). NSSC Report: Educating the public about bullies. *School Safety,* p. 2.

STERN, D. N., SPIEKER, S., & MACKAIN, K. (1982). Intonation contours as signals in maternal speech to prelinguistic infants. *Developmental Psychology, 18,* 727–735.

STERNBERG, R. J. (1984). Fighting butter battles: A reply. *Phi Delta Kappan, 65,* 700.

STERNBERG, R. J. (1985). *Beyond IQ: A triarchic theory of human intelligence.* Cambridge: Cambridge University Press.

STERNBERG, R. J., CONWAY, B. E., KETRON, J. L., & BERNSTEIN, M. (1981). People's conceptions of intelligence. *Journal of Personality and Social Psychology, 41,* 37–55.

STERNBERG, R. J., & SLATER, W. (1982). Conceptions of intelligence. In R. J. Sternberg (Ed.), *Handbook of human intelligence.* Cambridge: Cambridge University Press.

STEVENS, J. H., JR. (1988). Social support, locus of control, and parenting in three low-income groups of mothers: Black teenagers, black adults, and white adults. *Child Development, 59,* 635–642.

STEVENSON, H. W., & LEE, S.-Y. (1990). Context of achievement. *Monographs of the Society for Research in Child Development, 55* (Serial No. 221).

STEVENSON, H. W., LEE, S.-Y., STIGLER, J. W. (1986). Mathematics achievement of Chinese, Japanese, and American children. *Science, 231,* 693–699.

STEVENSON, H. W., STIGLER, J. W., LEE, S.-Y., LUCKER, W., KITAMURA, S., & HSU, C. (1985). Cognitive performance and academic achievement of Japanese, Chinese, and American children. *Child Development, 56,* 718–734.

STIGLER, J. W., LEE, S.-Y., & STEVENSON, H. W. (1987). Mathematics classrooms in Japan, Taiwan, and the United States. *Child Development, 58,* 1272–1285.

STILLMAN, R. J. (1982). In utero experience to diethylstilbestrol: Adverse effects on the reproductive tract and reproductive performance in male and female offspring. *American Journal of Obstetrics and Gynecology, 142,* 905–921.

STIPEK, D. (1984). Young children's performance expectations: Logical analysis or wishful thinking? In J. G. Nicholls (Ed.), *Advances in motivation and achievement: Vol. 3. The development of achievement motivation.* Greenwich, CT: JAI Press.

STIPEK, D., & DANIELS, D. (1988). Declining perceptions of competence: A consequence of changes in the child or the educational environment? *Journal of Educational Psychology, 80,* 352–356.

STONE, C. A., & DAY, M. C. (1978). Levels of availability of a formal operational strategy. *Child Development, 49,* 1054–1065.

STONE, L. J., & CHURCH, J. (1973). *Childhood and adolescence: A psychology of the growing person.* New York: Random House.

STONE, L. J., SMITH, H. T., & MURPHY, L. B. (Eds.). (1973). *The competent infant: Research and commentary.* New York: Basic Books.

STORFER, M. D. (1990). *Intelligence and giftedness: The contributions of heredity and early environment.* San Francisco: Jossey-Bass.

STRAYER, F. F., & STRAYER, J. (1976). An ethological analysis of social agonism and dominance relations among preschool children. *Child Development, 47,* 980–989.

STRAYER, F. F., WAREING, S., & RUSHTON, J. P. (1979). Social constraints on naturally occurring preschool altruism. *Ethology and Sociobiology, 1,* 3–11.

SULLIVAN, M. W., ROVEE-COLLIER, C. K., & TYNES, D. M. (1979). A conditioning analysis of infant long-term memory. *Child Development, 50,* 152–162.

SUOMI, S., & HARLOW, H. (1972). Social rehabilitation of isolate-reared monkeys. *Developmental Psychology, 6,* 487–496.

SUPER, C. M. (1981). Behavioral development in infancy. In R. H. Munroe, R. L. Munroe, & B. B. Whiting (Eds.), *Handbook of cross-cultural human development.* New York: Garland.

SURGEON GENERAL'S ADVISORY ON ALCOHOL AND PREGNANCY. (1981). *FDA Drug Bulletin, 11,* 9–10.

SVEJDA, M., CAMPOS, J. J., & EMDE, R. N. (1980). Mother-infant "bonding": Failure to generalize. *Child Development, 51,* 775–779.

TAMIS-LEMONDA, C. S., & BORNSTEIN, M. H. (1989). Habituation and maternal encouragement of attention in infancy as predictors of toddler language, play, and representational competence. *Child Development, 60,* 738–751.

TANNER, J. M. (1978). *Fetus into man: Physical growth from conception to maturity.* Cambridge, MA: Harvard University Press.

TANNER, J. M. (1962). *Growth at adolescence.* Oxford: Blackwell Scientific.

TARRANT, B. (1989, July 15). Child slavery pervades south Asia. *Miami Herald.*

TAUSSIG, H. B. (1962). A study of the German outbreak of phocomelia. *Journal of the American Medical Association, 180,* 1106–1114.

TELLEGEN, A., LYKKEN, D. T., BOUCHARD, T. J., JR., WILCOX, K., SEGAL, N., & RICH, S. (1988). Personality similarity in twins reared apart and together. *Journal of Social and Personality Psychology, 54,* 1031–1039.

THELEN, E. (1983). Learning to walk is still an "old" problem: A reply to Zelazo. *Journal of Motor Behavior, 15,* 139–161.

THELEN, E., FISHER, D. M., & RIDLEY-JOHNSON, R. (1984). The relationship between physical growth and a newborn reflex. *Infant Behavior and Development, 7,* 479–493.

THOMAS, H., JAMISON, W., & HUMMEL, D. D. (1973). Observation is insufficient for discovering that the surface of still water is invariantly horizontal. *Science, 101,* 173–174.

THOMPSON, J. R., & CHAPMAN, R. S. (1977). Who is "Daddy" revisited? The status of two-year-olds' overextended words in use and comprehension. *Journal of Child Language, 4,* 359–375.

THOMPSON, R. A. (1987). Development of children's inferences of the emotions of others. *Developmental Psychology, 23,* 124–131.

THORNDIKE, R. L., HAGEN, E. P., & SATTLER, J. M. (1986). *The Stanford-Binet Intelligence Scale* (4th ed.): *Guide for administering and scoring.* Chicago: Riverside.

TIFFT, S. (1990a, August 6). Diamonds in the rough. *Time.*

TIFFT, S. (1990b, November 5). It's all in the (parental) genes. *Time.*

TIJO, J. H., & LEVAN, A. (1956). The chromosome number of man. *Hereditas, 42,* 1–6.

TISAK, M. S. (1986). Children's conceptions of parental authority. *Child Development, 57,* 166–176.

TONKOVA-YAMPOL'SKAYA, R. V. (1969). Development of speech intonation in infants during the first two years of life. *Soviet Psychology, 7,* 48–54.

TREHUB, S. E., SCHNEIDER, B. A., & ENDMAN, M. (1980). Developmental changes in infants' sensitivity to octave-band noises. *Journal of Experimental Child Psychology, 29,* 282–293.

TRICKETT, P. K., & KUCZYNSKI, L. (1986). Children's misbehaviors and parental discipline strategies in abusive and nonabusive families. *Developmental Psychology, 22,* 115–223.

TULKIN, S. R., & KAGAN, J. (1972). Mother-child interaction in the first year of life. *Child Development, 43,* 31–41.

TURIEL, E. (1969). Developmental processes in the child's moral thinking. In P. Mussen, J. Langer, & M. Covington (Eds.), *New directions in psychology.* New York: Holt, Rinehart & Winston.

TURNBULL, C. M. (1961). *The forest people.* New York: Simon & Schuster.

TURNER, A. M., & GREENOUGH, W. T. (1985). Differential rearing effects on rat visual cortex synapses: I. Synaptic and neuronal density and synapses per neuron. *Brain Research, 329,* 195–203.

U. S. HOUSE OF REPRESENTATIVES, WAYS AND MEANS COMMITTEE, SUBCOMMITTEE ON HUMAN RESOURCES. (1990, June 12). *The enemy within: Crack-cocaine and America's families.* Washington, DC: U. S. Government Printing Office.

UZGIRIS, I. C., & HUNT, J. McV. (1975). *Assessment in infancy: Original scales of psychological development.* Urbana: University of Illinois Press.

VANDELL, D. L., HENDERSON, V. K., & WILSON, K. S. (1988). A longitudinal study of children with daycare experiences of varying quality. *Child Development, 59,* 1286–1292.

VANDELL, D. L., & MUELLER, E. C. (1980). Peer play and friendships during the first two years. In H. C. Foot, A. J. Chapman, & J. R. Smith (Eds.), *Friendship and social relations in children.* New York: Wiley.

VANDER LINDE, E., MORRONGIELLO, B. A., & ROVEE-COLLIER, C. (1985). Determinants of retention in 8-week-old infants. *Developmental Psychology, 21,* 601–613.

VANIJZENDOORN, M. H., & KROONENBERG, P. M. (1988). Cross-cultural patterns of attachment: A meta-analysis of the strange situation. *Child Development, 59,* 147–156.

VAUGHN, B. E., BLOCK, J. H., & BLOCK, J. (1988). Parental agreement on child rearing during early childhood and the psychological characteristics of adolescents. *Child Development, 59,* 1020–1033.

VAUGHN, B. E., EGELAND, B. R., SROUFE, L. A., & WATERS, E. (1979). Individual differences in infant-mother attachment at twelve and eighteen months: Stability and change in families under stress. *Child Development, 50,* 971–975.

Vaughn, B. E., Lefever, B. G., Seifer, R., & Barglow, P. (1989). Attachment behavior, attachment security, and temperament during infancy. *Child Development, 60,* 728–737.

Vinter, A. (1986). The role of movement in eliciting early imitations. *Child Development, 57,* 66–71.

Visintine, A. M., Nahmais, A. J., & Josey, W. E. (1978). Genital herpes. *Perinatal Care, 2,* 32–41.

Vobejda, B. (1989, January 6). Black males increasingly rare in college. *Washington Post.*

Volpe, E. P. (1971). *Human heredity and birth defects.* Indianapolis: Bobbs-Merrill.

Vurpillot, E. (1968). The development of scanning strategies and their relation to visual differentiation. *Journal of Experimental Child Psychology, 6,* 632–650.

Vygotsky, L. S. (1962). *Thought and language.* Cambridge, MA: MIT Press. (Original work published 1934)

Vygotsky, L. S. (1978). *Mind in society: The development of higher psychological processes.* Cambridge, MA: Harvard University Press.

Waggener, T. B., Southall, D. P., & Scott, L. A. (1990). Analysis of breathing in a prospective population of term infants does not predict susceptibility to sudden infant death syndrome. *Pediatric Research, 7,* 113–117.

Wagner, D. A. (1981). Culture and memory development. In H. Triandis & A. Heron (Eds.), *Handbook of cross-cultural psychology* (Vol. 4). Boston: Allyn & Bacon.

Wagner, R., & Torgesen, J. (1987). The nature of phonological processing and its causal role in the acquisition of reading skills. *Psychological Bulletin, 101,* 192–212.

Walk, R. D. (1981). *Perceptual development.* Pacific Grove, CA: Brooks/Cole.

Walk, R. D., & Gibson, E. J. (1961). A comparative and analytical study of visual depth perception. *Psychological Monographs, 75* (15, Whole No. 519).

Walker, C. H. (1987). Relative importance of domain knowledge and overall aptitude in acquisition of domain-related information. *Cognition and Instruction, 4,* 25–42.

Walker, L. J. (1986). Sex differences in the development of moral reasoning: A rejoinder to Baumrind. *Child Development, 57,* 522–526.

Walker, L. J. (1989). A longitudinal study of moral reasoning. *Child Development, 60,* 157–166.

Walker, L. J., & de Vries, B. (1985). *Moral stages/moral orientations: Do the sexes really differ?* Paper presented at the meeting of the American Psychological Association, Los Angeles.

Walker, L. J., de Vries, B., & Trevethan, S. D. (1987). Moral stages and moral orientations in real-life and hypothetical dilemmas. *Child Development, 58,* 842–858.

Waller, N. G., Kojetin, B. A., Bouchard, T. J., Jr., Lykken, D. T., & Tellegen, A. (1990). Genetic and environmental influences on religious interests, attitudes, and values: A study of twins reared apart and together. *Psychological Science, 1,* 138–142.

Wallerstein, J. S., Corbin, S. B., & Lewis, J. M. (1988). Children of divorce: A ten-year study. In E. M. Hetherington & J. Arastem (Eds.), *Impact of divorce, single-parenting and stepparenting on children.* Hillsdale, NJ: Erlbaum.

Wallerstein, J. S., & Kelly, J. B. (1980). *Surviving the breakup.* New York: Basic Books.

Ward, I. L. (1972). Prenatal stress feminizes and demasculinizes the behavior of males. *Science, 175,* 82–84.

Ward, S., Reale, G., & Levinson, D. (1972). Children's perceptions, explanations, and judgments of television advertising: A further exploration. In E. A. Rubinstein, G. A. Comstock, & J. P. Murray (Eds.), *Television and social behavior: Vol. 4. Television in day-to-day life: Patterns of use.* Washington, DC: U. S. Government Printing Office.

Waters, E. (1978). The reliability and stability of individual differences in infant-mother attachment. *Child Development, 49,* 483–494.

Waters, E., Vaughn, B. E., & Egeland, B. R. (1980). Individual differences in mother-infant attachment relationships at age one: Antecedents in neonatal behavior in an urban, economically disadvantaged sample. *Child Development, 51,* 208–216.

Waters, E. Wippman, J., & Sroufe, L. A. (1979). Attachment, positive affect, and competence in the peer group: Two studies in construct validation. *Child Development, 50,* 821–829.

Watson, J. B. (1928). *Psychological care of infant and child.* New York: Norton.

Watson, J. S. (1973). Smiling, cooing, and "the game." *Merrill-Palmer Quarterly, 18,* 323–339.

Watson, J. B., & Morgan, J. J. B. (1917). Emotional reactions and psychological experimentation. *American Journal of Psychology, 28,* 163–174.

Watson, J. B., & Raynor, R. A. (1920). Conditional

emotional reactions. *Journal of Experimental Psychology, 3,* 1–14.

WAXMAN, S., & GELMAN, R. (1986). Preschoolers' use of superordinate relations in classification and language. *Cognitive Development, 1,* 139–156.

WEBER, R. A., LEVITT, M. J., & CLARK, M. C. (1986). Individual variation in attachment security and strange situation behavior: The role of maternal and infant temperament. *Child Development, 57,* 56–65.

WECHSLER, D. (1974). *Manual for the Wechsler Intelligence Scale for Children–Revised.* New York: Psychological Corporation.

WEINERT, F. E., & SCHNEIDER, W. (1987). *The Munich Longitudinal Study on the Genesis of Individual Competencies (LOGIC).* Munich: Max Planck Institute for Psychological Research.

WEINERT, F. E., & SCHNEIDER, W. (Eds.). (1989). *The Munich Longitudinal Study on the Genesis of Individual Competencies (LOGIC): Report No. 5. Results of wave three.* Munich: Max Planck Institute for Psychological Research.

WEINTRAUB, M., CLEMENS, L. P., SOCKLOFF, A., ETHRIDGE, T., GRACELY, E., & MYERS, B. (1984). The development of sex role stereotypes in the third year: Relationships to gender labeling, gender identity, sex-typed toy preference, and family characteristics. *Child Development, 55,* 1493–1503.

WELLMAN, H. M. (1977). Tip of the tongue and feeling of knowing experiences: A developmental study of memory monitoring. *Child Development, 48,* 13–21.

WELLMAN, H. M. (1988). The early development of memory strategies. In F. Weinert & M. Perlmutter (Eds.), *Memory development: Universal changes and individual differences.* Hillsdale, NJ: Erlbaum.

WELLMAN, H. M. (1990). *The child's theory of mind.* Cambridge, MA: MIT Press.

WELLMAN, H. M., COLLINS, J., & GLIEBERMAN, J. (1981). Understanding the combination of memory variables: Developing conceptions of memory limitations. *Child Development, 52,* 1313–1317.

WELLMAN, H. M., & ESTES, D. (1986). Early understanding of mental entities: A reexamination of childhood realism. *Child Development, 57,* 910–923.

WELLMAN, H. M., FABRICIUS, W. V., & SOPHIAN, C. (1985). The early development of planning. In H. M. Wellman (Ed.), *Children's searching: The development of search skills and spatial representation.* Hillsdale, NJ: Erlbaum.

WELLMAN, H. M., & JOHNSON, C. N. (1979). Understanding mental processes: A developmental study of *remember* and *forget. Child Development, 50,* 79–88.

WELLMAN, H. M., & LEMPERS, J. D. (1977). The naturalistic communicative and organismic point of view. In D. B. Harris (Ed.), *The concept of development.* Minneapolis: University of Minnesota Press.

WELLMAN, H. M., RITTER, K., & FLAVELL, J. H. (1975). Deliberate memory behavior in the delayed reactions of very young children. *Developmental Psychology, 11,* 780–787.

WERTSCH, J. V. (1985). *Vygotsky and the social formation of mind.* Cambridge, MA: Harvard University Press.

WEXLER-SHERMAN, C., GARDNER, H., & FELDMAN, D. H. (1988). A pluralistic view of early assessment: The project spectrum approach. *Theory into Practice, 27,* 77–83.

WHITE, B. L. (1978). *Experience and environment: Major influences on the development of the young child* (Vol. 2). Englewood Cliffs, NJ: Prentice-Hall.

WHITE, B. L., CAREW-WATTS, J., BARNETT, I C., KABAN, B., MARMOR, J., & SHAPIRO B. (1973). *Experience and environment: Major influences on the development of the young child* (Vol. 1). Englewood Cliffs, NJ: Prentice-Hall.

WHITE, B. L., & HELD, R. (1966). Plasticity of sensorimotor development. In J. F. Rosenblith & W. Allinsmith (Eds.), *The causes of behavior* (2nd ed.). Boston: Allyn & Bacon.

WHITE, J. L., & LaBARBA, R. C. (1976). The effects of tactile and kinesthetic stimulation on neonatal development in the preterm infant. *Developmental Psychobiology, 9,* 569–577.

WHITE, L. R., & SEVER, J. Y. (1967). Etiological agents: I. Infectious agents. In A. Rubin (Ed.), *Handbook of congenital malformations.* Philadelphia: Saunders.

WHITE, S. H., & PILLEMER, D. B. (1979). Childhood amnesia and the development of a socially accessible memory system. In J. F. Kihlstrom & F. J. Evans (Eds.), *Functional disorders of memory.* Hillsdale, NJ: Erlbaum.

WHITEHURST, G. J., & SONNENSCHEIN, S. (1985). The development of communication: A functional analysis. In G. J. Whitehurst (Ed.), *Annals of child development* (Vol. 2). Greenwich, CT: JAI Press.

WHITING, B. B., & EDWARDS, C. P. (1988). *Children of*

different worlds: The formation of social behavior. Cambridge, MA: Harvard University Press.

WICKELGREN, L. (1967). Convergence in the human newborn. *Journal of Experimental Child Psychology, 5,* 74–85.

WILCOX, J., & WEBSTER, E. (1980). Early discourse behavior: An analysis of children's responses to listener feedback. *Child Development, 51,* 1120–1125.

WILLATTS, P. (1990). Development of problem-solving strategies in infancy. In D. F. Bjorklund (Ed.), *Children's strategies: Contemporary views of cognitive development.* Hillsdale, NJ: Erlbaum.

WILLEMSEN, E., & REYNOLDS, B. (1973). Sex differences in adults' judgment of the horizontal. *Developmental Psychology, 8,* 309.

WILLIAMS, H. G. (1983). *Perceptual and motor development.* Englewood Cliffs, NJ: Prentice-Hall.

WILSON, E. O. (1975). *Sociobiology: The new synthesis.* Cambridge, MA: Harvard University Press.

WILSON, E. O. (1978). *On human nature.* Cambridge, MA: Harvard University Press.

WILSON, J. Q., & HERRNSTEIN, R. J. (1985). *Crime and human nature.* New York: Simon & Schuster.

WILSON, M., DUE, T., & HACKETT, D. C. (1990, November 18). Crisis of the black male: Promises broken, promise unfulfilled. *Miami Herald.*

WINER, G. A. (1980). Class-inclusion reasoning in children: A review of the empirical literature. *Child Development, 51,* 309–328.

WINGERSON, L. (1990). *Mapping our genes: The Genome Project and the future of medicine.* New York: Dutton.

WINICK, M. (1976). *Malnutrition and brain development.* New York: Oxford University Press.

WINICK, M., MEYER, K. K., & HARRIS, R. C. (1975). Malnutrition and environmental enrichment by early adoption. *Science, 190,* 1173–1175.

WITELSON, S. F. (1985). On hemisphere specialization and cerebral plasticity from birth: Mark II. In C. Best (Ed.), *Hemisphere function and collaboration in the child.* New York: Academic Press.

WITELSON, S. F. (1987). Neurobiological aspects of language in children. *Child Development, 58,* 653–688.

WITKIN, H. A., DYK, R. B., FATERSON, H. F., GOODENOUGH, D. R., & KARP, S. A. (1962). *Psychological differentiation.* New York: Wiley.

WITKIN, H. A., GOODENOUGH, D. R., & KARP, S. A. (1967). Stability of cognitive style from childhood to young adulthood. *Journal of Personality and Social Psychology, 7,* 291–300.

WITKIN, H. A., LEWIS, H. B., HERTZMAN, M., MACHOVER, K., MEISSNER, P., & WAPNER, S. (1954). *Personality through perception.* New York: Harper.

WITTER, F., & KING, T. M. (1980). Cigarettes and pregnancy. *Progress in Clinical and Biological Research, 36,* 83–92.

WOLF, T. H. (1973). *Alfred Binet.* Chicago: University of Chicago Press.

WOODS, B. T., & CAREY, S. (1979). Language deficits after apparent clinical recovery from childhood aphasia. *Annals of Neurology, 6,* 405–409.

WOODY-RAMSEY, J., & MILLER, P. H. (1988). The facilitation of selective attention in preschoolers. *Child Development, 59,* 1497–1503.

YAKOVLEV, P. I., & LECOURS, A. R. (1967). The myelinogenetic cycles of regional maturation of the brain. In A. Minkowski (Ed.), *Regional development of the brain in early life.* Oxford: Blackwell.

YARROW, M. R., SCOTT, P., deLEEUW, L., & HEINIG, C. (1962). Child-rearing in families of working and nonworking mothers. *Sociometry, 25,* 122–140.

YARROW, M. R., & WAXLER, C. Z. (1976). Dimensions and correlates of prosocial behavior in young children. *Child Development, 47,* 118–125.

YESALIS, C. E. (1990). Testimony before the Senate Committee on the Judiciary, April 3, 1989. In Committee on the Judiciary, U. S. Senate, *Steroids in amateur and professional sports: The medical and social costs of steroid abuse.* Washington, DC: U. S. Government Printing Office.

YOUNGER, B. A., & COHEN, L. B. (1983). Infant perception of correlates among attributes. *Child Development, 54,* 858–867.

YUSSEN, S. R. (1974). Determinants of visual attention and recall in observational learning by preschoolers and second graders. *Developmental Psychology, 10,* 93–100.

YUSSEN, S. R., & LEVY, V. M., JR. (1975). Developmental changes in predicting one's own span of short-term memory. *Journal of Experimental Child Psychology, 19,* 502–508.

ZABIN, L. S., KANTNER, J. F., & ZELNIK, M. (1979). The risk of adolescent pregnancy in the first months of intercourse. *Family Planning Perspectives, 11,* 215–222.

ZAHN-WAXLER, C., CUMMINGS, E. M., McKNEW, D. H., & RADKE-YARROW, M. (1984). Altruism, aggression, and social interactions in young children with a manic-depressive parent. *Child Development, 55,* 112–122.

ZAHN-WAXLER, C., RADKE-YARROW, M., & KING, R. M. (1979). Childrearing and children's prosocial initiations toward victims of distress. *Child Development, 50,* 319–330.

ZELAZO, P. R., ZELAZO, N. A., & KOLB, S. (1972). "Walking" in the newborn. *Science, 176,* 14–15.

ZELNIK, M., & KANTNER, J. F. (1977). Sexual and contraceptive experience of young unmarried women in the United States, 1976 and 1971. *Family Planning Perspectives, 9,* 55–71.

ZELNIK, M., & SHAH, F. K. (1983). First intercourse among young Americans. *Family Planning Perspectives, 15,* 64–70.

ZELNIKER, T., & JEFFREY, W. E. (1976). Reflective and impulsive children: Strategies of information processing underlying differences in problem solving. *Monographs of the Society for Research in Child Development, 41* (Serial No. 168).

ZELNIKER, T., JEFFREY, W. E., AULT, R., & PARSONS, J. (1972). Analysis and modification of search strategies of impulsive and reflective children on the Matching Familiar Figures test. *Child Development, 43,* 321–335.

ZEMBAR, M. I., & NAUS, M. J. (1985, April). *The combined effects of knowledge base and mnemonic strategies on children's memory.* Paper presented at the meeting of the Society for Research in Child Development, Toronto.

ZESKIND, P. S. (1986, April). *Infant crying: A biobehavioral synchrony between infants and caregivers.* Paper presented at the Conference on Human Development, Nashville.

ZESKIND, P. S., & RAMEY, C. T. (1978). Fetal malnutrition: An experimental study of its consequences on infant development in two caregiver environments. *Child Development, 49,* 1155–1162.

ZESKIND, P. S., & RAMEY, C. T. (1981). Sequelae of fetal malnutrition: A longitudinal, transactional, and synergistic approach. *Child Development, 52,* 213–218.

ZIVIN, G. (1977). On becoming subtle: Age and social rank in the use of a facial gesture. *Child Development, 48,* 1314–1321.

Glossary

Accommodation: In Piaget's theory, the process of changing a mental structure in order to incorporate new information; compare with *assimilation* (Chapter 7); in vision, the process of adjusting the lens of the eye to focus on objects at different distances (Chapter 4).

Adaptation: In Piaget's theory, the process of adjusting one's cognitive structures to meet environmental demands; includes the complementary processes of *assimilation* and *accommodation* (Chapter 7).

Adoption studies: Studies that compare the similarities of biological parent/child pairs with the similarities of adoptive parent/child pairs in order to compare the roles of genetic and environmental effects (Chapter 3).

Adrenal glands: Glands located one above each kidney that secrete androgens (Chapter 5).

Adrenogenital syndrome: A disorder caused by malfunctioning of the adrenal glands. In genetic females, the results can be masculinized genitalia at birth and tomboyish behavior during childhood (Chapters 16, 17).

Afterbirth: The third and final stage of birth, involving expulsion of the placenta and other membranes from the uterus (Chapter 4).

Alpha-fetoprotein test (AFP): A prenatal diagnostic tool in which a sample of blood is drawn from a pregnant woman and analyzed for the presence of alpha-fetoprotein, which would suggest an abnormality in the fetus (Chapter 4).

Ambiguous figures: Drawings or pictures that can be interpreted in several different ways (Chapter 6).

American Sign Language (ASL): The language of sign that is used by most deaf people in the United States (Chapter 9).

Amiable children: In sociometric measures, children who are well liked but who have low social impact (Chapter 14).

Amniocentesis: A prenatal diagnostic tool in which a sample of amniotic fluid is withdrawn from the woman's uterus and the fetal cells it contains are analyzed for chromosome abnormalities (Chapter 4).

Amniotic sac: The fluid-filled membrane that encases and protects the embryo and fetus (Chapter 4).

Anal stage: In Freud's theory, the second stage of psychosexual development (1 to 3 years), with the focus on anal gratification (Chapter 17).

Androgen insensitivity: Genetic disorder in which androgen cannot be absorbed by the body. In genetic males, the results are feminized genitalia at birth and further feminization at puberty (Chapter 16).

Androgens: A class of hormones, including testosterone, that are found at higher levels in males than females and that influence physical growth and sexual development (Chapters 5, 16, 17).

Androgyny: A range of personality characteristics in one person that includes both stereotypically male and female traits (Chapter 16).

Anorexia nervosa: An eating disorder characterized by excessive dieting and weight loss that affects adolescents and young adults, especially girls (Chapter 5).

Anxious/avoidant attachment: In Ainsworth's Strange Situation, a form of insecure attachment in which an infant explores only minimally and tends to avoid the mother or treat her with indifference (Chapter 12).

Anxious/resistant attachment: In Ainsworth's Strange Situation, a form of insecure attachment in which an infant appears anxious even in the presence of the mother, displaying distress when she leaves and anger when she returns and often resisting contact with her (Chapter 12).

Apgar test: A test that quickly evaluates a baby's biological fitness immediately after birth (Chapter 4).

Assimilation: In Piaget's theory, the process of incorporating information into already existing cognitive structures; compare with *accommodation* (Chapter 7).

Attachment: Close emotional bond between parent and child (Chapter 12).

Attention-Deficit Hyperactivity Disorder (ADHD): A condition characterized by developmentally inappropriate degrees of inattention, impulsiveness, and hyperactivity, observed more frequently in boys (Chapter 6).

Authoritarian parenting style: A style of parenting in which parents expect absolute obedience and frequently enforce rules with physical punishment and withdrawal of love (Chapter 13).

Authoritative parenting style: Style of parenting in which parents set clear standards and enforce the rules with warmth and explanations (Chapter 13).

Autosomes: In humans, the 45 chromosome pairs excluding the sex chromosomes (Chapter 3).

Axon: The long fiber of a neuron that carries messages from that cell to another (Chapter 5).

Basic reflexes (stage of): In Piaget's theory, the first substage of sensorimotor development, in which infants know the world only in terms of their inherited action patterns (Chapter 7).

Behavior modification: Application of the principles of operant conditioning to control or change behavior (Chapter 8).

Behavioral genetics: The study of genetic effects on behavior and on complex psychological characteristics such as intelligence and personality (Chapter 3).

Behaviorism: Theory popular in the United States through the middle of this century, holding that behavior and development are shaped by environmental influences (Chapter 8).

Bidirectionality of structure and function: The interaction of structure and function to produce a pattern of development (Chapter 1).

Blastocyst: A hollow sphere formed by cells as they divide at different rates and into different structures during the period of the zygote (Chapter 4).

Bonding: In attachment theory, the process of a mother's "falling in love" with her infant shortly after birth (Chapter 12).

Caesarean section (C-section): Delivery of a baby through a surgical incision in the abdomen (Chapter 4).

Case study: Detailed descriptions of a single individual made by an expert observer (Chapter 2).

Castration anxiety: In Freud's theory, a boy's belief that his penis will be taken away by his father because of competition for his mother's love (Chapter 17).

Centration: In Piaget's theory, the tendency of preoperational children to attend to one aspect of a situation to the exclusion of others (Chapter 7).

Cephalocaudal development: The head-to-foot sequence of physical growth (Chapter 5).

Cerebral cortex: The outer layer of the brain that gives humans their highly developed intelligence (Chapter 5).

Cerebral lateralization: Functional specialization of the two hemispheres of the brain (Chapter 5).

Child-directed speech: The specialized register of speech adults and older children use when talking to infants and young children (Chapter 9).

Child study movement: The application of science to the study of children, which began in the United States around 1900 (Chapter 1).

Chorionic sac: A membrane that protects the embryo and fetus (Chapter 4).

Chorionic villous sampling (CVS): A prenatal diagnostic tool in which fetal cells are collected and tested for chromosome abnormalities; can be used as early as the 9th to 12th week of pregnancy (Chapter 4).

Chromosomes: The rod-shaped strands of DNA found in the nucleus of cells that contain genetic information (Chapter 3).

Class inclusion: In Piaget's theory, the knowledge that a subordinate class (for example, dogs) must always be smaller than the superordinate class in which it is contained (for example, animals) (Chapter 7).

Classical conditioning: A type of learning in which a previously neutral stimulus is paired with another stimulus that elicits some response (Chapter 8).

Clinical interviews: Interviews, used extensively by Piaget, in which the examiner probes a child's knowledge about a given topic (Chapter 2).

Clustering (in memory tasks): The degree to which items from the same category are recalled together (Chapter 8).

Cognitive self-guidance system: In Vygotsky's theory, the use of private speech to guide problem-solving behavior (Chapter 9).

Collective monologues: A form of egocentric speech in which two or more children talk about some common activity but not in conversation with one another (Chapter 9).

Communicative competence: Mastery of five aspects of language: semantics, syntax, morphology, phonology, and pragmatics (Chapter 9).

Componential subtheory: In Sternberg's triarchic theory, an information-processing model of intelligence (Chapter 10).

Conceptual tempo: The relative speed with which an individual makes decisions on complex tasks (Chapter 6).

Concordance rate: In behavioral genetics, the probability that one member of a pair (identical or fraternal twins, for example) will display a trait possessed by the other member (Chapter 3).

Concrete operations: In Piaget's theory, the third major stage of cognitive development, in which children can decenter their perception, are less egocentric, and can think logically about concrete objects (Chapter 7).

Conservation: In Piaget's theory, the knowledge that a substance remains the same despite changes in its form (Chapter 7).

Contextual subtheory: In Sternberg's triarchic theory, the idea that intelligence must be viewed in terms of the context in which it occurs (Chapter 10).

Continuity versus discontinuity of development: The scientific debate over whether developmental change is gradual (continuity) or relatively abrupt (discontinuity) (Chapter 1).

Conventional morality: In Kohlberg's theory, the second level of moral reasoning, in which individuals conform to rules imposed by some legitimate authority (Chapter 15).

Coordination of secondary circular reactions: In Piaget's theory, the stage of sensorimotor development in which infants are able to coordinate two or more behavior patterns to achieve a goal (Chapter 7).

Corpus callosum: A thick mass of nerves that connects the right and left hemispheres of the cerebral cortex (Chapter 5).

Correlational studies: Research method that examines two or more factors to determine if changes in one are associated with changes in another (Chapter 2).

Cross-sectional studies: Developmental research method that compares different individuals of different ages at the same point in time; compare with *longitudinal studies* (Chapter 2).

Crossing-over: A process of genetic exchange that occurs during meiosis when two corresponding chromosomes exchange pieces of DNA (Chapter 3).

Crystallized abilities (crystallized intelligence): Intellectual abilities that develop from cultural context and learning experience; compare with *fluid abilities* (Chapter 10).

Cued recall: In memory research, a task in which a subject recalls information after being given prompts or cues (Chapter 8).

Cultural relativism: The idea that intellectual skills critical for survival in one culture may not be important in another (Chapter 10).

DES (diethylstilbestrol): A drug once prescribed for pregnant women to prevent miscarriage that was later found to affect the reproductive systems of the offspring (Chapter 4).

DNA (deoxyribonucleic acid): The chains of nucleotide pairs that make up chromosomes, segments of which are genes (Chapter 3).

DQ test (development quotient test): A test of infant abilities, such as the Bayley Scales of Infant Development (Chapter 10).

Decentration: In Piaget's theory, the ability of concrete operational children to consider multiple aspects of a stimulus or situation (Chapter 7).

Deep structure: The grammatical organization and meaning that underlies all language (Chapter 9).

Delivery: The second stage of childbirth, during which the infant travels through the birth canal (Chapter 4).

Dendrites: The numerous fibers of a neuron that receive messages from other neurons (Chapter 5).

Development: Predictable changes that occur in structure or function over the life span (Chapter 1).

Deviation IQ: Method of constructing IQ scores that compares a child's performance to that of other children the same age; compare with *mental age* (Chapter 10).

Differentiation (of neurons): The final stage of neuronal development, in which neurons gain in size, produce more dendrites, and extend their axons further away from the cell body (Chapter 5).

Discontinuity of development: See *Continuity versus discontinuity of development.*

Discrepancy principle: The idea that infants are most attentive to slightly novel stimuli (Chapter 6).

Dishabituation: The tendency to show renewed interest in a stimulus when some features of it have been changed (Chapter 6).

Disorganized/disoriented attachment: In Ainsworth's Strange Situation, a form of insecure attachment in which infants show no coherent strategy for dealing with stress during separation and reunion (Chapter 12).

Dominance hierarchy (social hierarchy): The relatively stable organization of a group in which some members are seen as leaders and others as followers (Chapter 14).

Dominant gene: A gene that is expressed as a trait regardless of the corresponding gene of the pair; compare with *recessive gene* (Chapter 3).

Down syndrome (trisomy 21): Hereditary disorder that involves physical abnormalities and intellectual deficits and is caused by an extra 21st chromosome (Chapter 3).

Egocentric speech (private speech): Children's speech apparently for self and not directed to others (Chapter 9).

Egocentricity: In Piaget's theory, the tendency to interpret objects and events from one's own perspective (Chapter 7).

Elaboration: A memory strategy that involves creating associations between two or more unrelated items (Chapter 8).

Electra complex: In Freud's theory, alternate term for the Oedipus complex in girls (Chapter 17).

Embedded Figures Test: Test used to assess field dependence/field independence (Chapter 6).

Embryo (period of): The prenatal period from approximately 2 to 8 weeks after conception, during which organs are formed and begin to function (Chapter 4).

Embryo freezing: The process of freezing an embryo for purposes of later fertilization (Chapter 4).

Embryo transfer: Process in which a woman donates an ovum (egg) to be fertilized and later transferred into the uterus of another woman (Chapter 4).

Empathy: The ability to experience vicariously the emotions of others (Chapter 15).

Endocrine system: A system of glands that produces hormones, many of which are responsible for directing growth (Chapter 5).

Equilibration: In Piaget's theory, the process by which balance is restored to the cognitive structures through assimilation and accommodation (Chapter 7).

Erotic orientation: The gender to which one is sexually attracted (Chapter 17).

Estrogen: Hormone produced primarily by the ovaries that regulates female sexual development during puberty (Chapters 5, 16).

Experiential subtheory: In Sternberg's triarchic theory, the subtheory concerned with how prior knowledge influences performance—with the individual's ability to deal with novelty and the degree to which processing is automatized (Chapter 10).

Experimental studies: Research method in which a researcher manipulates one or more factors, then observes how these manipulations change the behavior under investigation (Chapter 2).

Factors: In psychometric approaches to intelligence, a set of related mental skills (such as a verbal or spatial factor), that underlie intellectual functioning (Chapter 10).

Factor analysis: A statistical technique used to define mental *factors* by analyzing results from intelligence tests (Chapter 10).

Fact retrieval: In information processing, the retrieval of a fact directly from long-term memory without using effortful procedures (Chapter 8).

Fallopian tubes: In the female reproductive system, the tubes through which mature ova travel from the ovaries to the uterus, and where conception actually takes place (Chapter 4).

Family pedigree charts: Charts using standardized symbols to show biological relationships within a family and the incidence of certain inherited traits (Chapter 3).

Fetal alcohol syndrome (FAS): Set of symptoms, including physical abnormalities and intellectual deficits, that occur in children as a result of alcohol consumption by the mother during pregnancy (Chapter 4).

Fetal monitoring: The assessment of the physiological characteristics, such as heart rate, of the fetus (Chapter 4).

Fetoscopy: Technique of passing a viewing instrument through a pregnant woman's abdomen and into the amniotic sac that has been used experimentally for fetal surgery (Chapter 4).

Fetus (period of): The prenatal period from approximately 8 weeks after conception to birth (Chapter 4).

Field dependence/field independence (FD/FI): Thinking styles defined by the ability to perceive parts of a visual field separately from the whole (Chapter 6).

Fluid abilities (fluid intelligence): Intellectual abilities that are biologically determined and reflected in tests of memory span and spatial thinking; compare with *crystallized abilities* (Chapter 10).

Fontanels: Soft gaps that separate the bones of the skull in infants (Chapter 5).

Forebrain: The area of the brain that contains the cerebral cortex, responsible for higher sensory, motor, and intellectual functioning (Chapter 5).

Formal operations: In Piaget's theory, the final stage of cognitive development, in which children are able to apply abstract logical rules (Chapter 7).

Free recall: In memory research, a task in which a subject recalls information without cues or prompts (Chapter 8).

Function: In developmental psychology, action related to a structure, such as movement of a muscle, nerve firing, or the activation of a mental representation (contrast with *structure; see bidirectionality of structure and function*). (Chapter 1).

Functional invariants: In Piaget's theory, the processes of organization and adaptation that characterize all biological systems and operate throughout the life span (Chapter 7).

g (Spearman's g, general intelligence): In psychometric theory, the idea that intelligence can be expressed in terms of a single factor, first formulated by Spearman in the 1920s (Chapter 10).

Gamete intrafallopian transfer (GIFT): Alternative to in vitro fertilization in which ova and sperm are introduced directly into the fallopian tubes (Chapter 4).

Gender consistency: The concept that gender remains the same despite changes in behavior (Chapter 16).

Gender constancy: The concept that gender remains the same despite changes in physical appearance, time, and behavior; includes *gender identity, gender stability,* and *gender consistency* (Chapter 16).

Gender identification: Process of identifying oneself as male or female and adopting the roles and values of that gender (Chapter 16).

Gender identity: The ability of children to identify themselves as either boys or girls (Chapter 16).

Gender stability: The concept that gender remains the same over time (Chapter 16).

Gene: The basic unit of heredity; segment of DNA that codes for a particular protein (Chapter 3).

Gene mapping: The process of determining the order of DNA segments on a chromosome (Chapter 3).

Genetic linkage: The tendency of genes that are located close to each other on a chromosome to be inherited together more often than genes located farther apart (Chapter 3).

Genetic mosaic: An individual who has normal genes in some cells and altered genes in others, caused by mutation early in the prenatal period (Chapter 3).

Genital stage: In Freud's theory, the fifth stage of psychosexual development (adolescence and adulthood), reflecting mature expression of sexual impulses (Chapter 17).

Genotype: An individual's entire genetic endowment; compare with *phenotype* (Chapter 3).

Gestational surrogate: A woman who is implanted with an embryo produced in vitro using the ova and sperm of another couple (Chapter 4).

Guilford's structure of the intellect: A theory of intelligence derived from factor analysis, postulating 180 factors (Chapter 10).

Habituation: The tendency to decrease responding to a stimulus that has been presented repeatedly (Chapter 6).

Hemispheres: The two approximately equal halves of the cerebral cortex (Chapter 5).

Heritability: The extent to which differences in any trait within a population can be attributed to inheritance (Chapter 3).

Hindbrain: The area of the brain critical to motor coordination and maintaining balance (Chapter 5).

Hormones: Chemical substances produced by glands and sent through the bloodstream transporting instructions from one part of the body to another (Chapter 5).

Hospitalism: Term used to describe the deteriorating effects on infants of long-term confinement to hospitals or similar institutions (Chapter 12).

Human growth hormone: Pituitary hormone that stimulates duplication of most body cells, affecting growth (Chapter 5).

Huntington's disease: A neurological disorder, caused by a dominant gene, which is not usually expressed until adulthood (Chapter 3).

Hypothetico-deductive reasoning: In Piaget's theory, a formal operational ability to think hypothetically (Chapter 7).

IQ tests (intelligence tests): Aptitude tests, such as Stanford-Binet and Wechsler scales, that are intended to measure aspects of intellectual functioning (Chapter 10).

Identification with the aggressor: In Freud's theory, the idea that a boy comes to identify with his father, whom he sees as a competitor for his mother's love; see *Oedipus complex* and *castration anxiety* (Chapter 17).

Imminent justice: The belief that good deeds will be rewarded and misdeeds will be punished (Chapter 15).

Impulsives: Individuals who make quick decisions about complex problems and make many errors in the process; compare with *Reflectives* (Chapter 6).

In vitro fertilization (IVF): Fertilization of ova by sperm outside a woman's body, usually in a laboratory container (Chapter 4).

Incidental learning: Acquiring knowledge about noncentral aspects of a task or situation (Chapter 6).

Inductive reasoning: The type of thinking that goes from specific observations to broad generalizations and, in Piaget's theory, is characteristic of formal operational thought (Chapter 7).

Infantile amnesia: The inability to remember events from infancy and early childhood (Chapter 8).

Inner speech: In Vygotsky's theory, the covert language used to guide thought (Chapter 9).

Institutionalization studies: Studies of the effects of minimal human contact on children reared in institutions (Chapters 10, 12).

Interobserver reliability: The extent to which behavior seen by one observer is agreed upon by a second observer (Chapter 2).

Intrinsic activity: In Piaget's theory, the assumption that babies are born ready to make contact with their environment and that cognitive structures, by their very nature, seek to be active (Chapter 7).

Invention of new means through mental combinations: In Piaget's theory, the final stage of sensorimotor development, a transition between the action-oriented world of the infant and the symbol-oriented world of the child (Chapter 7).

Isolates (neglected children): In sociometric measures, children who have low social impact and are usually referred to negatively by other children (Chapter 14).

Labor: The first stage of childbirth, from the dilation of the cervix until the infant's head begins to emerge into the birth canal (Chapter 4).

Language acquisition device (LAD): In Chomsky's theory, the hypothetical construct possessed by all humans at birth enabling them to acquire language (Chapter 9).

Language acquisition support system (LASS): According to Bruner, the idea that adults and older children have learning devices that interact with children's language acquisition devices (LAD) (Chapter 9).

Latency stage: In Freud's theory, the fourth stage of psychosexual development (5 years to the beginning of puberty), during which time there is no area of the body that arouses sexual tension (Chapter 17).

Lateralization: See *cerebral lateralization.*

Law of independent assortment: Mendel's law stating that different traits are inherited independently (Chapter 3).

Law of segregation: Mendel's law stating that for each inherited trait there are two elements of heredity (Chapter 3).

Longitudinal studies: Research method that assesses developmental change by following a person or group of people over an extended period of time; compare with *Cross-sectional studies* (Chapter 2).

Lovemap: According to Money, a personalized representation of the idealized lover and idealized sexuoerotic activity (Chapter 17).

Matching Familiar Figures Test (MFFT): A visual match-to-sample test used to measure conceptual tempo (Chapter 6).

Mean length of utterance (MLU): A measure of language development defined by the average number of meaningful language units (root words and endings) a child uses at any one time (Chapter 9).

Mediation deficiency: The inability of children to use a strategy even if it is taught to them (Chapter 8).

Meiosis: The type of cell division that occurs when sperm and ova are being formed (Chapter 3).

Memory strategies: See *Mnemonics.*

Menarche: A woman's first menstrual period (Chapter 5).

Mental age: Level of mental functioning (in years) as measured by the number of items passed on an intelligence test, formerly used in determining IQ scores; compare with *deviation IQ* (Chapter 10).

Metacognition: Knowledge about one's own thoughts and the factors that influence thinking (Chapter 8).

Metacommunication: Children's knowledge about the adequacy of their own communication abilities (Chapter 9).

Metamemory: Knowledge of one's own memory abilities and the factors that influence memory (Chapter 8).

Midbrain: The top of the brain stem, which serves as a relay system between various parts of the brain (Chapter 5).

Migration (of neurons): The movement of neurons to their permanent positions in the brain, most of which is completed during the prenatal period (Chapter 5).

Min strategy: An arithmetic strategy in which children faced with an addition problem start with the largest addend and count up from there (Chapter 8).

Mitosis: The process of cell division for growth and development (Chapter 3).

Mnemonics (memory strategies): Effortful techniques used to improve memory, including rehearsal, organization, and elaboration (Chapter 8).

Molecular genetics: Field of science that is concerned with the structure and function of DNA and its role in inheritance (Chapter 3).

Moral absolutism: In Piaget's theory of moral development, the tendency of children in the stage of moral realism to interpret laws and rules as absolute (Chapter 15).

Moral realism: In Piaget's theory of moral development, the stage in which children understand that there are rules society must live by and perceive these rules as absolute (Chapter 15).

Moral relativism: In Piaget's theory of moral development, children's realization that social rules are arbitrary agreements among people that can be modified through social discussion (Chapter 15).

Morphemes: Meaningful language units (Chapter 9).

Morphology: In the study of language development, the knowledge of word formation (Chapter 9).

Mullerian-inhibiting hormone: A hormone produced by the testes early in prenatal development that inhibits feminization of the fetus (Chapter 16).

Multiple classification: The ability to classify items in terms of more than one dimension simultaneously, such as shape and color (Chapter 7).

Multiple intelligences: See *Gardner's theory of multiple intelligences*.

Mutations: Irregularities in the DNA duplication process that result in an altered genetic message (Chapter 3).

Myelin: A sheet of fatty substance that develops around the neurons to promote faster transmission of electrical signals through the nervous system (Chapter 5).

Myelinization: The development of myelin around neurons, which proceeds at different rates in different areas of the brain (Chapter 5).

Naturalistic studies: Studies in which the researcher observes individuals in their own environments, intervening as little as possible (Chapter 2).

Neglected children: See *isolates*.

Neonatal imitation: The ability of newborns to reproduce some behavior, such as a facial expression, that they have seen in others (Chapter 4).

Neonate: An infant from birth through the first month of life (Chapter 4).

Neoteny: Retention of the infantile characteristics of an evolutionary ancestor (Chapter 5).

Neurons: The cells of the nervous system through which electrical and chemical signals are transmitted (Chapter 5).

Obesity: A body weight that is 20% or more higher than normal for the person's height, age, sex, and stature (Chapter 5).

Objectivity: In scientific description, a behavior that is clearly observable, irrespective of the observer's emotion, prior expectation, or personal belief (Chapter 2).

Object permanence: The knowledge that objects have an existence in time and space independent of one's own perception or action on those objects (Chapter 7).

Observational learning: The ability to learn about the world simply by watching (Chapter 8).

Oedipus complex: In Freud's theory, children's sexual focus on the opposite-sex parent during the phallic stage of psychosexual development; also called *Electra complex* in girls (Chapter 17).

Operant conditioning: Changing behavior through rewards and punishment (Chapter 8).

Oral stage: In Freud's theory, the first stage of psychosexual development (birth to 1 year), when sexual excitation is centered around the mouth (Chapter 17).

Organization: In Piaget's theory, the idea that every intellectual operation is related to all other acts of intelligence (Chapter 7); in memory research, the structure discovered or imposed upon a set of items that is used to guide memory performance (Chapter 8).

Ossification: The gradual replacement of cartilage by bone tissue, beginning during the fetal period (Chapter 5).

Overextensions: In the study of language development, the stretching of a familiar word beyond its correct meaning—for example, calling all four-legged mammals "doggie" (Chapter 9).

Overregularization: In the study of language development, the tendency to apply rules to words when they are not appropriate—for example, "runned," "foots," "mices" (Chapter 9).

Parallel play: The play of two or more children close together, possibly involved in similar activities, but not engaged in social interaction (Chapter 14).

Paraphilias: Sexual perversions (Chapter 17).

Parenting styles: The general way parents interact with their children (Chapter 13).

Peer group: A group that interacts on a regular basis, defines a sense of belonging, shares implicit or explicit norms for the behavior of group members, and develops a hierarchical organization (Chapter 14).

Peer review: The evaluation of a scientist's research by other scientists in the same field, usually with recommendations to a journal editor regarding publication (Chapter 2).

Penis envy: In Freud's theory, a girl's belief that she once possessed a penis and that it was taken away by her mother (Chapter 17).

Permissive parenting style: A style of parenting in which parents exert little control over their children (Chapter 13).

Personal gender: The concept of oneself as male or female (Chapter 17).

Phallic stage: In Freud's theory, the third stage of psychosexual development (3 to 5 years), when a child's sexual excitement is centered on the genitals (Chapter 17).

Phenotype: The actual expression of a genetic trait; compare with *genotype* (Chapter 3).

Phonological recoding: Reading skills used to translate written symbols into sounds and words (Chapter 9).

Phonology: The knowledge of how words are pronounced (Chapter 9).

Pituitary gland: The master gland that produces hormones that influence growth (Chapter 5).

Placenta: The organ along the uterine wall of a pregnant woman that serves as the transport system between mother and fetus (Chapter 4).

Plasticity (of behavior): The degree to which behavior can be changed (Chapter 1).

Polygenic inheritance: Inherited traits that are determined by multiple genes (Chapter 3).

Popular children: In sociometric measures, children who are well liked and have high social impact (Chapter 14).

Postconventional morality: In Kohlberg's theory, the third level of moral development, in which individuals develop a set of principles that go beyond any authority figure (Chapter 15).

Pragmatics: In the study of language development, knowledge about how language can be adjusted to fit different circumstances (Chapter 9).

Preconventional morality: In Kohlberg's theory, the first level of moral development, in which children conform to rules to gain rewards and avoid punishment (Chapter 15).

Prenatal diagnostic testing: Techniques used to evaluate the health of a fetus. See *alphafetoprotein testing, amniocentesis, chorionic villus sampling, fetal monitoring, fetoscopy,* and *ultrasound* (Chapter 4).

Preoperational period: In Piaget's theory, the second major stage of cognitive development (approximately ages 2 to 7), characterized by prelogical, intuitive thought (Chapter 7).

Premoral stage: In Piaget's theory of moral development, the stage at which children are unaware of rules as cooperative agreements (Chapter 15).

Primary circular reactions: In Piaget's theory, the stage of sensorimotor development in which infants extend their reflexes to acquire new patterns of behavior that were not present at birth (Chapter 7).

Production deficiency: Children's tendency not to use spontaneously a strategy that they are capable of using when instructed (Chapter 8).

Productive language: The language a child can actually produce, or speak; contrast with *receptive language* (Chapter 9).

Progesterone: A hormone produced by the ovaries that promotes sexual development (Chapter 5).

Proliferation (of neurons): The process of nerve-cell division by mitosis (Chapter 5).

Prosocial behavior: Behavior that benefits other people (Chapter 14).

Psychometric approach: The theory that intelligence can be described in terms of mental factors and that tests can be constructed that reveal individual differences in the factors underlying mental performance (Chapter 10).

Puberty: The period during which the testes, prostate gland, and seminal vesicle (in boys) or the uterus and vagina (in girls) enlarge (Chapter 5).

Quickening: The time that a mother first feels her baby move (Chapter 4).

Receptive language: The language that a child can understand; contrast with *productive language* (Chapter 9).

Recessive gene: A gene that is expressed only when matched with another recessive gene; compare with *dominant gene* (Chapter 3).

Reciprocal determinism: In Bandura's theory, the belief that children have as much of an effect on their environment as the environment has on them (Chapter 8).

Reciprocity: In peer interactions, changing one's behavior to match that of another (Chapter 14).

Recombinant DNA: The technique of "snipping out" pieces of DNA and transplanting them into simple organisms, where they will be duplicated; also called gene cloning and genetic engineering (Chapter 3).

Reflectives: Individuals who make decisions about complex problems slowly and deliberately and usually arrive at correct solutions; compare *impulsives* (Chapter 6).

Rehearsal: A memory strategy in which target information is repeated (Chapter 8).

Rejected children: In sociometric measures, children who are mentioned frequently and negatively by their peers (Chapter 14).

Reliability: The trustworthiness of a research finding; includes *interobserver reliability* and *replicability* (Chapter 2).

Replicability: The extent to which a research finding can be repeated (Chapter 2).

Reversibility: In Piaget's theory, the knowledge that an operation can be reversed; characteristic of the concrete operational period (Chapter 7).

Schemas: Abstract representations of objects and events (Chapter 6).

Scheme: See structures (in Piaget's theory).

Secondary circular reactions: In Piaget's theory, the stage of sensorimotor development in which infants first learn to control events in the external world (Chapter 7).

Secure attachment: In Ainsworth's Strange Situation, the positive parent-child relationship in which the child displays confidence when the parent is present, shows mild distress when the parent leaves, and quickly reestablishes contact when the parent returns (Chapter 12).

Selective attention: Concentration on chosen stimuli without distraction by nontarget stimuli (Chapter 6).

Selective cell death: Early developmental process in which neurons that are not activated by sensory and motor experience die (Chapter 5).

Self-concept: The way a person defines himself or herself (Chapter 15).

Self-efficacy: The belief that one can influence one's own thoughts and behavior (Chapter 15).

Semantics: In language acquisition, knowledge of the meaning of words and sentences (Chapter 9).

Sensorimotor period: In Piaget's theory, the first major stage of cognitive development (birth to approximately 2 years), in which children understand their world through sensory and motor experiences (Chapter 7).

Sex chromosomes: In humans, the 23rd chromosome pair that determines gender (Chapters 3, 4, 16).

Sex-linked inheritance: Recessive traits that are inherited by way of a single gene on the sex chromosomes, usually the X chromosome; also called *X-linked inheritance* (Chapter 3).

Sexual orientation: A continuum with heterosexuality at one end, homosexuality at the other, and various degrees of bisexuality in between (Chapter 17).

Sexuality: An individual's erotic thoughts and activities (Chapter 17).

Social cognitive theory: Bandura's theory of how individuals operate cognitively on their social experiences and how these cognitive operations influence their behavior and development (Chapter 8).

Social hierarchy: See *Dominance hierarchy.*

Society for Research in Child Development (SRCD): An international society with more than 4000 members, involved in child-development research (Chapter 1).

Spearman's g: See *g (general intelligence).*

Stability: In developmental psychology, the degree to which a characteristic remains constant over time, or the extent to which a person maintains the same rank order for a particular characteristic (Chapters 1, 10).

Stages: Relatively discrete periods of time in which functioning is qualitatively different from functioning at other periods (Chapters 1, 7).

Stanford-Binet: An individually administered IQ test (Chapter 10).

Strange Situation: A technique developed by Ainsworth and her colleagues to assess quality of attachment in young children (Chapter 12).

Strategies: Goal-directed and deliberately implemented mental operations used to facilitate task performance (Chapter 8).

Structure: In developmental psychology, a substrate of the organism that develops, such as muscle, nervous tissue, or mental knowledge (contrast with *function;* see *bidirectionality of structure and function).* (Chapter 1).

Structure of the intellect: See *Guilford's structure of the intellect.*

Structures (schemes): In Piaget's theory, the enduring knowledge base by which children interpret their world (Chapter 7).

Sudden infant death syndrome (SIDS): The death of a seemingly healthy infant during sleep for no apparent reason (Chapter 4).

Sum strategy: A simple addition strategy used by young children that involves counting together the two addends of a problem (Chapter 8).

Surrogate motherhood: The practice in which a woman bears a child for adoption by another couple, often conceived through artificial insemination with the adoptive father's sperm (Chapter 4).

Synapse: The tiny space between the dendrite of one neuron and the axon of another through which chemical messages are passed (Chapter 5).

Syntax: In language acquisition, the knowledge of sentence formation (Chapter 9).

Tay Sachs disease: A recessive genetic disorder resulting in early death (Chapter 3).

Teratogens: External agents, such as drugs and radiation, that can have harmful effects on a developing embryo or fetus (Chapter 4).

Tertiary circular reactions: In Piaget's theory, the stage of sensorimotor development in which infants invent slightly new behaviors to achieve their goals (Chapter 7).

Testis determining factor gene: Gene on the Y chromosome that is responsible for the development of testes in males (Chapter 3).

Testosterone: A form of androgen or male hormone, produced primarily by the testes, that promotes sexual maturation (Chapters 5, 16).

Theory: A scientific explanation that organizes facts and provides the framework for understanding behavior (Chapter 2).

Theory of mind: The way in which children conceptualize mental activity (Chapter 8).

Theory of multiple intelligences (Gardner's): Theory postulating seven components, or modules, of intelligences: (1) linguistic, (2) logical/mathematical, (3) musical, (4) spatial, (5) bodily/kinesthetic, (6) interpersonal, and (7) intrapersonal (Chapter 10).

Thyroxine: A hormone produced by the thyroid gland that influences growth and prenatal brain development (Chapter 5).

Transactional model: A framework that views development as the continuous and bidirectional interchange between an active organism, with a unique biological constitution, and a changing environment (Chapter 1).

Triarchic theory (Sternberg's): Theory that describes intelligence in terms of three subtheories—contextual, experiential, and componential (Chapter 10).

Turner syndrome: A chromosomal disorder in females in which one X chromosome is missing, resulting in a total complement of only 45 chromosomes (Chapter 3).

Twin study method: In behavioral genetics, a technique that measures the concordance of certain traits in twins and in pairs of individuals with varying degrees of relatedness (Chapter 3).

Ultrasound: A diagnostic tool that uses high-frequency sound waves to generate an image of the fetus (Chapter 4).

Umbilical cord: The cord connecting the embryo/fetus to the placenta, transferring waste products and nutrients (Chapter 4).

Utilization deficiency: The inability of children to benefit from strategies they are able to implement (Chapters 6, 8).

Visual cliff: An apparatus designed to test infants for depth perception (Chapter 6).

Visually guided reaching: In infant development, the ability to accurately reach for and grasp a viewed object (Chapter 5).

Wechsler scales: Individually administered IQ tests, including the WPPSI-R, the WISC-R, the WISC-III, and the WAIS-R (Chapter 10).

X-linked inheritance: See *Sex-linked inheritance.*

Y-linked inheritance: Form of sex-linked inheritance in which a recessive trait is inherited by way of a single gene on the Y chromosome (Chapter 3).

Yolk sac: The structure that produces blood cells during the early days of the embryonic period (Chapter 4).

Zone of proximal development: In Vygotsky's theory, the difference between a child's actual level of ability and the level of ability that he or she can achieve when working under the guidance of an instructor (Chapter 11).

Zygote (period of): The first stage of prenatal development, beginning with conception and ending with implantation of the embryo in the uterine wall at about 2 weeks after conception (Chapter 4).

Zygote intrafallopian transfer (ZIFT): A form of in vitro fertilization in which ova and sperm are joined in a laboratory container and the fertilized eggs are implanted into the fallopian tubes (Chapter 4).

Author Index

Subject Index

TO THE OWNER OF THIS BOOK:

We hope that you have found *Looking at Children: An Introduction to Child Development* useful. So that this book can be improved in a future edition, would you take the time to complete this sheet and return it? Thank you.

Instructor's name: _____

Department: _____

School and address: _____

_____

1. The name of the course in which I used this book is: _____

_____

2. My general reaction to this book is: _____

_____

_____

3. What I like most about this book is: _____

_____

_____

4. What I like least about this book is: _____

_____

_____

5. Were all of the chapters of the book assigned for you to read?   Yes   No

    If not, which ones weren't? _____

6. Do you plan to keep this book after you finish the course?   Yes   No

    Why or why not? _____

_____

7. On a separate sheet of paper, please write specific suggestions for improving this book and anything else you'd care to share about your experience in using the book.

Optional:

Your name: _____ Date: _____

May Brooks/Cole quote you, either in promotion for *Looking at Children* or in future publishing ventures?

Yes: _____ No: _____

Sincerely,

David F. Bjorklund
Barbara R. Bjorklund

- -
FOLD HERE

|||||

BUSINESS REPLY MAIL
FIRST CLASS   PERMIT NO. 358   PACIFIC GROVE, CA

POSTAGE WILL BE PAID BY ADDRESSEE

ATT: *David F. Bjorklund and Barbara R. Bjorklund*

Brooks/Cole Publishing Company
511 Forest Lodge Road
Pacific Grove, California 93950-9968

- -
FOLD HERE